Commerce, Culture, and Liberty

Commerce, Culture, *and* Liberty

*Readings on Capitalism
Before Adam Smith*

Edited by Henry C. Clark

Liberty Fund

Indianapolis

This book is published by Liberty Fund, Inc., a foundation established to encourage study of the ideal of a society of free and responsible individuals.

𒀫𒄄

The cuneiform inscription that serves as our logo and as the design motif for our endpapers is the earliest-known written appearance of the word "freedom" (*amagi*), or "liberty." It is taken from a clay document written about 2300 B.C. in the Sumerian city-state of Lagash.

© 2003 by Liberty Fund, Inc.

Cover illustration is from the frontispiece to *Le Parfait négociant* by Jacques Savary, 6th ed. (Lyon: J. Lyons, 1711–12), 4 vols. in 1, and is reproduced by permission of McMaster University Library.

Printed in the United States of America

07 06 05 04 03 C 5 4 3 2 1
07 06 05 04 03 P 5 4 3 2 1

Library of Congress Cataloging-in-Publication Data
Commerce, culture, and liberty : readings on capitalism
before Adam Smith / edited by Henry R. Clark
p.   cm.
Includes bibliographical references and index.
ISBN 0-86597-378-4 (alk. paper)
ISBN 0-86597-379-2 (pbk : alk. paper)
1. Economics—History—17th century.
2. Economics—History—18th century.
3. Economics—Political aspects—History.
4. Economics—Sociological aspects—History.
5. Economics—Moral and ethical aspects—History.
I. Clark, Henry C.
HB81.C66 2003   33.12′2—dc21   2002043439

Liberty Fund, Inc.
8335 Allison Pointe Trail, Suite 300
Indianapolis, Indiana 46250-1684

Contents

Foreword

Although the modern world has been increasingly characterized by commercial culture, the interpretation of the scope, nature, and effects of exchange relations is as controversial today as it was when observers first described commercial society more than two centuries ago. The purpose of this anthology is to contribute to an understanding of the complexity of modern economic life by bringing together some of the most significant writing on its social, cultural, and political dimensions in the era when such writing first began.

In the seventeenth and eighteenth centuries, even the most sophisticated students of economic life combined their analyses with moral and cultural considerations more often than is usually the case in today's specialized intellectual environment. Among the topics discussed then, but in ways that have since often been forgotten, are the nature of exchange relations and their effects on a traditional and hierarchical social order, the role of commerce in fostering civility and sociability, the effects of commerce on the fabric of community life, the dangers to moral virtue posed by increasing prosperity, the impact of commerce on sex roles and the condition of women, and the complex interplay between commerce and civil or political liberty.

This anthology evokes the breadth and depth of consideration of these issues in the early modern period in two ways: first, by bringing together writings by well-known authors from a variety of historical sources and literary genres that are scattered and sometimes difficult to access; second, by bringing to light materials from less well-known sources that were influential at the time or significantly reflective of contemporary opinion in the several generations before the effect of Adam Smith's *Wealth of Nations* (1776) began to be felt.

The terms in the title and subtitle should be explained. The word "commerce" had a resonance in the eighteenth century, and especially the seventeenth century, somewhat different from what it has today. There was a sense in which its primary usage concerned social relations—as, for example, in common phrases such as the "commerce of the sexes" and the "commerce of self-love." The economic dimension often appeared as a metaphor for, or as a part of, the larger whole. (It was partly to illustrate this feature that the Nicole reading was chosen.) In the eighteenth century, on the other hand, a quite different linguistic transfer begins to emerge. As commerce comes to assume a larger place both in the reality of European life and in the imaginations of its best-informed observers, commerce becomes something of a synecdoche for the economy as a whole—a tendency that is especially clear in the Vincent de Gournay reading and to a lesser extent in Abbé Saint-Pierre. In the Scottish tradition of the four-stages theory of historical evolution, represented here by John Millar of Glasgow and by William Robertson, "commerce" comes almost to stand for the modern era in all its facets.

As to "culture," what is meant is evidently not the formal works of art or music often associated with that term, but rather the anthropologist's wider notion of a system of symbols embodying the shared or contested values of any society—the full range of resources a society draws on to lift itself above the status of mere nature. The question arose of how to fit a growing commitment to commerce as a public good into a social order that continued to be largely defined by other values. Some of the most contentious arguments over commerce concerned apprehensions about the broader culture that have simply disappeared from our view. Coyer's *La Noblesse commerçante* (1756), translated and excerpted in this volume for the first time, had an immediacy and a resonance for his contemporaries far beyond the level of sophistication contained in the purely economic analysis that underlay it. Similar points could be made about the readings from other authors such as Pluche, Galiani (especially his analysis of value in *Della moneta*) and the entries in the *Spectator*. Comments about the correlation between religion and economic life are interspersed throughout the writings of many of our authors.

Finally, we come to "liberty." The close connection between the growth of commerce in the seventeenth and eighteenth centuries and the spread of liberty, as an idea and as a reality, has often been observed. Adam Smith, after all, frequently called his ideal economic arrangement a "natural system of liberty." Other writers in the "liberal" tradition, such as Benjamin Constant, detected a "modern" species of liberty appropriate to commercial society and clearly distinct from an "ancient" version that was not. A central purpose of this anthology, therefore, is to flesh out some of the specific ways in which this association between economic liberty and liberty in general came into being.

But again, the theme of liberty was a multifaceted one in the writings of the period. While many authors saw a mutually supportive relationship between the growth of commerce and the spread of liberty (de la Court, Trenchard and Gordon in their *Cato's Letters,* and Hazeland make the connection explicit even in their titles), there were various ways of construing "liberty" in its relation to commercial society. Andrew Fletcher of Saltoun, Jean-Jacques Rousseau, and John Brown (and perhaps the later Galiani) were among many late seventeenth- and eighteenth-century observers who saw the spread of commerce as contributing to a loss of a certain kind of liberty, and their perspective is deliberately well represented in this volume. In addition, there is the question whether an absolute monarchy was less conducive to commercial liberty than a republic. De la Court, Trenchard, and Gordon were among those who certainly thought so, but Law makes an important and not unrepresentative case that the French monarchy, at least, was more likely to guarantee the conditions of flourishing commerce than its competitors. It was the arch-mercantilist Colbert, after all, who famously asserted that "liberty is the soul of commerce." The question, then, was problematic in ways that may surprise some twenty-first-century readers.

If some of the readings contained in this anthology evoke an alien thought world, there are many others likely to bring the reader a shock of recognition. The eighteenth-century complaints about a new philosophy of "self-interest" associated with Mandeville, Hume, and others are redolent of more recent debates about the role of private good in contributing to (or detracting from) the public good. The century-long debate over luxury (see Melon, Voltaire, Brown, and Saint-Lambert for examples) evokes, and puts in perspective, later arguments over every-thing from the redistributive effects of a market economy to the cor-rupting influence of a supposed "decade of greed." Does market moral-ity have a liberating or a dehumanizing effect on the condition of women? *The Spectator,* Hume, Galiani (*On Money*), Gournay, Turgot (*Reflections*), and Millar are among those who already had things to say about the question. Is the spread of capitalism conducive to political lib-erty, as observers of South Korea, the Philippines, and (most important) China have claimed or hoped? De la Court, Hazeland, and *Cato's Letters* have been there before us—in ways similar enough to be revealing and different enough to be intriguing.

The collection is also notable for the textured continuity that emerges in the passage through the texts. So diffuse and open-ended are the au-thorial references one to another, and so little are they dominated by a single voice, a single doctrine, or a single tendency of thought, that it is no exaggeration to call their authors participants in a conversation—an extended and continuing one that picks up intensity as the eighteenth century unfolds. Sometimes the exchanges could be pointed and focused: Mandeville was directly and immediately rebutted by Blewhitt (although not definitively, as Mandeville remained a general presence in the con-versation for the remainder of the century). Voltaire seems to have been inspired to intervene on commercial topics only somewhat less directly by his reading of Melon's essay (Melon in turn was a protégé of John Law, who learned much of what he knew about finance by studying the Dutch scene). Rousseau's critique of Hume is thinly veiled, Saint-Lambert's embrace of Hume lightly wrought. Montesquieu, though not normally viewed as an economist, had a huge impact. His distinction between an "economy of necessity" and an "economy of luxury" was picked up by many writers (cf. Hazeland, ch. 26, and Coyer, ch. 27), and a single com-ment of his on the propriety of noble commerce (bk. 20; see ch. 20) un-leashed a flood of pamphlets (see Brown, ch. 28, and Coyer, ch. 27). The eighteenth-century Frenchman Gournay translated the seventeenth-century Englishman Josiah Child; his protégé Turgot then cited Child and the Dutchman de la Court as the two founding fathers of modern economic theory. In 1768, the Physiocrats were at the height of their in-fluence, and Du Pont de Nemours proudly summarized their achievement. By 1769, Galiani could strike a responsive chord with a hilarious attack upon them. There is no orchestrated or preordained end to such a polyphonic colloquy. No End of History was sensed or articulated by the authors who were grappling with these novel, confusing, indisputably significant matters during the period covered in this volume.

To my knowledge, there is no remotely comparable precedent to what has been attempted here. In the nineteenth century, there were both French and English (and perhaps other) collections of early works on political economy. These anthologies consisted of small numbers of sometimes lengthy and unabridged works deemed to be forerunners of the science of political economy. J. R. McCullough, for example, produced an anthology of eight seventeenth-century tracts—all of them English, and all complete texts—for the Political Economy Club of London (of which he was a member) in 1856. His chief criterion for selection, aside from the work's rarity, was a frankly teleological search for anticipations of "those liberal commercial principles now so generally diffused."[1] Similar observations could be made about other works, such as Eugène Daire's collection, *Economistes financiers du XVIIIe siècle* (Paris: Guillaumin, 1843), which was part of the *Collection des principaux économistes* series by the same publisher. The present volume, however, is less about disciplines than about discourses; the purpose is to convey some of the ways in which contemporaries proceeded to think and write about the "new economy" they were observing.

The present anthology cannot, of course, pretend to be comprehensive. Although there were significant discussions of commercial society by Italian, German, and Dutch writers, among others, this anthology contains almost exclusively works written in English or French. In addition, although there were many interesting discussions of trade and the tradesman in Renaissance Italy and in the sixteenth century, the present work focuses on the seventeenth and eighteenth centuries. Within such limits, however, this volume aims to provide a broadly representative sample of what informed and articulate Europeans were thinking about commerce and commercial society in the century and a half before Adam Smith.

1. J. R. McCulloch, ed., *Early English Tracts on Commerce* (London: Political Economy Club, 1856; reprint, Cambridge, 1952), iii.

The anthology consists of writings by thirty-three authors. Of these, ten were English, thirteen French, five Scottish, two Dutch, and one each were Swiss, Irish, and Italian. As to family background, seven of the authors were born into nobility (North, Fletcher, Saint-Pierre, Hume, Montesquieu, Turgot, and Saint-Lambert), fifteen into what might be described as professional families (de la Court, Nicole, Steele, Law, Trenchard, Mandeville, Melon, Voltaire, Fielding, Brown, Robertson, Galiani, Millar, and Condillac), and seven into the trades (Walwyn, Child, Defoe, Barbon, Gournay, Rousseau, and Du Pont de Nemours). These categories are of course fluid and more than a little arbitrary. Under "professions," for example, I count clerical positions and government officials as well as traditional fields such as law and medicine. "Nobility" includes the meager landed estates of Hume and Saint-Lambert, as well as the august titles of Turgot. By "trades," I mean to include well-to-do exporters such as the Gournay and Child families, as well as the more artisanal backgrounds of Walwyn or Barbon. In addition, it has not proved possible to know with certainty the family backgrounds of all the authors represented here. What binds all our writers together, not surprisingly, is that they hail from the reading classes; there are no sons of illiterate peasants to be found here.

As to the occupations pursued by our thirty-three writers, what is noteworthy is that in the age before the academic discipline of economics developed, significant contributions could be made by persons from a wide variety of careers, mostly of a nonacademic nature. Here, the trades, including commerce and finance, count seven authors (Walwyn, Child, de la Court, North, Law, Gournay, and Barbon after he discontinued his medical practice). The professions account for six more (Mandeville, Montesquieu, Hazeland, Brown, Robertson, and Millar). What might be called the life of private or public service, mainly for noble families or governments, is mostly responsible for six others (Saint-Pierre, Melon, Pluche, Galiani, Turgot, and Condillac). Recognizably noble lives were led by two others (Fletcher and Saint-Lambert), and ten authors are probably best described as men of letters (Steele, Trenchard, Defoe, Voltaire, Hume, Fielding, Coyer, Rousseau, Du Pont de Nemours, and Raynal), with all the uncertainties, anxieties, and ambiguities that that designation often entailed. These categories are even more overlapping and inconclusive than those for family background. Saint-Lambert, for example, abandoned his military career at age forty-two and spent the remainder of his days as a man of letters. Montesquieu began his career in the law but ended it as a writer. Fielding followed something of the opposite trajectory, beginning as a playwright and becoming a magistrate. Several authors straddled the fence between a life of letters and government connections (Du Pont de Nemours and Raynal, among others). Only a very few of our authors were primarily academics, and they tended to be the Scots (Millar and Robertson), a useful reminder of the importance of the university in the Scottish Enlightenment.

There was no necessary connection, of course, between the background or occupation of an author and the content of his writing. The nobleman Fletcher attacked the modern system of commercial liberty; the nobleman Saint-Lambert defended it. The artisan Walwyn promoted free trade; the financial wizard John Law praised absolute monarchy. The young Galiani seemed in *On Money* to be friendly to an extended marketplace; the older Galiani of the *Dialogues* attacked at least the Physiocrats' version of free trade in grain. (Is there a Galiani Problem, then, to go along with the Adam Smith Problem?) The complex and vigorous play of ideas transcended, then as now, the bare biographies of those who fashioned them.

The principles of selection for this volume have proven to be multiple, overlapping, and difficult to harmonize. First, because of the thematic considerations cited above, technical works of economic analysis have for the most part been avoided. Thus, treatises that might be of great interest to twenty-first-century historians of economic thought—such as Quesnay's *Tableau économique* (1759) and other works by the Physiocrats—have not been well represented in this collection. Second, there is the obscurity factor: A principal purpose of the volume has been to bring to light works that were better known in their time than they have since become. Partly, this decision has arisen from the general conviction that a familiarity with more than merely a few enduringly famous authors was in the interests of both historical and philosophical understanding. Partly, it derives from the more specific judgment that there were many writings from the period before Adam Smith that have noteworthy things to say about commercial society and economic life, and that readers who are interested in Adam Smith or his successors might well be interested in some of his predecessors. But third, an effort was also made to choose works that either were influential and well regarded in their own time or are meaningfully illustrative of contemporary opinion. Brown's *Estimate* and Coyer's *La Noblesse commerçante* (both published in 1756) caused quite a stir in their own time, no matter how thoroughly they may have been forgotten since then.

Within these thematic constraints, there are other principles of selection. A concerted effort has been made to minimize editorial intrusion so as to permit readers to judge for themselves the significance of the texts. This was done, in the first instance, by reproducing complete texts wherever possible. Fifteen of the readings offered here are full and unabridged texts: Walwyn, Barbon, North, Fletcher, Law, Voltaire (three separate pieces, each complete), Hume, Gournay, Hazeland, Rousseau, Turgot ("In Praise of Gournay"), Saint-Lambert, and Du Pont de Nemours. Another four are integral and free-standing texts within larger works: Child, Mandeville, the *Spectator* entries, and the *Cato's Letters* entry. Nine other readings are complete chapters or divisions, single or multiple, within larger works: de la Court, Blewhitt, Defoe, Melon, Pluche, Montesquieu, Galiani (*On Money*), Brown, and Raynal. The chief cost of cleaving so closely to a full-text bias in editorial selection is that readers will occasionally find that a text runs on beyond useful or interesting limits, or that it buries its jewels of novelty and insight inconspicuously in the middle or at the end. This was thought to be a cost worth paying in the interest of retaining maximum textual fidelity.

There were, however, some texts and/or authors that seemed so important to the purposes of the collection as to merit risking the charge of editorial intrusiveness in including them, even though it was not possible to present either full texts or clearly defined portions of text. These were Nicole, Saint-Pierre, Fielding, Coyer, Robertson, Turgot (*Reflections*), Galiani (*Dialogues*), Millar, and Condillac. While a good-faith effort has been made to avoid taking these texts out of context, and while some effort has been made to situate the excerpt within its larger work, the only way to be fair to any of these authors, it goes without saying, is to read them whole.

The Adam Smith reference point in the subtitle does not, of course, escape the charge of arbitrariness. There were many obscure and interesting writings after 1776 just as there were before. Nor is there anything overtly teleological about the selections contained here. An author was neither more nor less likely to be included by virtue of having exerted an influence on *The Wealth of Nations*. It simply seemed that 1776 was a convenient terminal point because of the significant ways in which political economy, and the broader discussion of commercial society, evolved after the publication of that sprawling masterwork, and because of how much better known its story is after 1776 than before.

Henry C. Clark
Canisius College

Editor's Note

Some of the following readings are borrowed from modern scholarly editions. These include the works by Walwyn, Fletcher, Mandeville, the *Spectator, Cato's Letters,* Hume, Montesquieu, Fielding, Gournay, Rousseau, Turgot, Robertson, Galiani, Millar, and Condillac. In these cases, most of the scholarly apparatus of the respective editors has been retained, widely variable though they are. In a few cases, I have been obliged to use earlier editions that contain less full editorial apparatus. These include the works of Barbon, North, Law, and Voltaire. For the most part, I have maintained those editions intact with minimal changes, though with occasional explanatory notes and glossary help indicated by the use of brackets. Finally, there are some works reproduced here that come directly from original or near-original editions and that are virtually lacking in editorial apparatus. De la Court, Child, Nicole, Defoe, Saint-Pierre, Pluche, Melon, Hazeland, Coyer, Brown, Saint-Lambert, Du Pont de Nemours, and Raynal fall in this category. Here, though I have refrained from attempting the full-scale historical-critical apparatus one will find, for example, in the Fielding excerpt below, I offer at least some basic identifications and annotations to assist in understanding the authors' arguments.

Unless otherwise indicated, the footnotes are by the original author and this editor's notes will appear in brackets. Where convenient, archaic or foreign terms are clarified in brackets within the text or in footnotes; when they appear more than once, they are usually relegated to the Glossary and indicated by a degree sign. For linguistic help, I have drawn mainly on Samuel Johnson, *A Dictionary of the English Language,* 4 vols. (Philadelphia, 1818–19); Antoine Furetière, *Dictionnaire universel,* 2nd ed. (Rotterdam, 1702; orig. pub. 1690); and *Dictionnaire de l'Académie Française* (Paris: Coignard, 1694).

Translator's Note

About a quarter of the texts contained herein consist of original translations from the French. These include Pierre Nicole, *Essais de morale;* John Law, "Idée générale du nouveau système des finances"; Abbé de Saint-Pierre, *Projet pour perfectionner le Comerse;* Noël-Antoine Pluche, *Spectacle de la nature;* Vincent de Gournay, "Mémoire"; Jean-Jacques Rousseau, "Le Luxe, le commerce et les arts"; Gabriel François Coyer, *La noblesse commerçante;* Jean-François Saint-Lambert, "Luxe," in *Encyclopédie;* Pierre Samuel Du Pont de Nemours, *De l'Origine et progrès d'une science nouvelle;* and Ferdinando Galiani, *Dialogues sur le commerce des bleds.* These translations are the joint effort of the editor and of Pauline Collombier of the Ecole des Hautes Etudes in Paris. Although different texts posed different problems—the government memorandum of a Law or a Gournay is obviously a very different literary production from the dialogues of Galiani—our general aim has been to render the substance of the author's meaning as faithfully as possible, with a minimum of interpretive interjection. Where terms proved difficult to translate into English, we have usually supplied the original in brackets and sometimes provided a glossary entry at the back of the volume, especially if the term was used frequently.

Acknowledgments

Many scholars from diverse fields have responded to my inquiries over the years, among whom I am pleased to thank Garry Apgar, Karen Bloom, Grant Campbell, Noel Chevalier, John Dussinger, Hans Eicholz, David R. Evans, Peter Galie, James E. Gill, Daniel Gordon, M. M. Goldsmith, Thomas Kaiser, Cynthia J. Koepp, Dorothy M. Medlin, Benoit Melancon, George Mosley, Jerry Z. Muller, Hans Rudolf Nollert, Irwin Primer, Salim Rashid, Jane Rendall, Elaine Riehm, and Silvia Sebastiani. They, of course, bear no responsibility for the use I have made of their advice.

Closer to home, David Coffta and Thomas M. Banchich of the Classics Department of Canisius College helped with some of the Latin and Greek translations, Dena Bowman of the History Department office performed innumerable copying and collating tasks, and my research assistant Robert Martin did yeoman service in the compiling of the seed list for the index. The staffs of many libraries offered courteous and efficient service; in particular, the reference staffs and interlibrary loan services at Canisius College and Dartmouth College were both very helpful over a long span of years. Any blunders and deficiencies that remain are entirely my own.

Commerce, Culture, and Liberty

1

Conceptions for a Free Trade
1652

WILLIAM WALWYN was born in 1600, the son of a Worcestershire gentleman and the maternal grandson of the Bishop of Hereford. Walwyn began as an apprentice in the silk industry before setting up his own trade, becoming a member of the Merchant Adventurers guild. A free-thinking Puritan, he had become a separatist Congregationalist by 1641 or 1642, developing a doctrine he called "free justification," by which he seems to have meant the belief that salvation awaited anyone who was genuinely open to divine saving grace. He used to travel around his locale comparing lectures and sermons for doctrinal consistency and for the charitable treatment meted out by the speakers to one another. At home and at London gatherings he sponsored a sort of Socratic method of group discussion, in which the doctrinal claims of competing schools would be pushed to the limits. During the Civil War, he allied himself with the Levellers in 1647, urging his soldiers to revolt against army officers. He was arrested and, in March 1649, committed to the Tower of London, where he spent eight months. Most of his writings concern the Leveller program, including the second "Agreement of the People." Being a member of a privileged trading company did not prevent him from writing strongly worded pieces on behalf of free trade, and those writings may have led to his separation from the Merchant Adventurers guild. At all events, after the Civil War he became an unlicensed practitioner and writer on medicine, which he is said to have taken up partly from compassion for the poor. He remained involved in medicine to the end of his life, and he died in 1680.

The work included here was written in 1652 and presented to the Committee of the Council of State for Trade and Foreign Affairs. It is taken from *The Writings of William Walwyn*, ed. Jack R. McMichael and Barbara Taft (© 1989 by the University of Georgia Press), pp. 447–52, and is reprinted with permission. Unbracketed notes are taken from the Georgia edition; notes in brackets are by the present editor.

Conceptions for a Free Trade

To the Honble Committe for Forraine Affaires Sitting at Whitehall

The humble conceptions of Wm Walwin referring to this Quere vizt whether the restriction and Government of Forraine Trade by Companyes: Or leaving the same equally free to all Englishmen would bee most profitable for the Comon wealth[1]

Humbly sheweth

That seing those who desire a continuance of forraine trade under Companies, and those that propose an absolute freedome therein, doe both hold forth the publike good, as[2] that which ought to be submitted unto: The first thing necessary towards a resolution, seemeth to be a discovery of the true way of discerning what is to be deemed a publique good in England:

And that (if the voyce of experience have any Credit) is to find out

---

1. W. Walwins Conceptions; For a free Trade
2. Comon Rights

what is Common Right in England; Those things which are of Common concernment alwaies adiuged and claimed as native right both before and after alterations (such are common Rights) having ever proved to include what hath been most proper and commodious for the Commonwealth and best for every particular person whose Interest hath not been opposite to that of the publique:

The which Rule of Discovery proving sound and good in this quere of Forraine Trade, the ancient and continuall Claime of Right unto a generall freedome of Trade by Parliaments and the most industrious people at all times, both before and since the alterations and obstructions made therein by prerogative,° would necessarily conclude that for forraine Trade to be universally free to all English men alike, would be most advantagious to the Common wealth; Scarce any the most noted and knowne Right of the Nation (if Parliaments themselves) having been more constantly claimed as Right.

And though this way of discovery of what is to be deemed a publike good and best for the Commonwealth of England may at first appeare not so pertinent to the solution of the question before you; yet be pleased to favor it so farr, as to admitt a serious consideration whether in this and all other queries touching publique good, it be not the safest and speediest way affording and contenting it selfe with a moderate generall experienced good, such as at best men or Nations are capable of, avoyding that uncertainty innovation and a possibility of ever changing for the worse, which either vaine hopes of perfection or pretences of greater good to the publique (the originall of most if not all Companyes) might strongly but pernitiously perswade unto.

For if it be thoroughly considered, it will (as is humbly conceived) apeare that the waveing of this Rule of Discovery of what is most good, by what is most antient certaine and continuall claimed Right, (Except in cases of iminent & extreme danger) for any other way of Discovery, hath generally (if not ever) proved of sad consequence to the Comon wealth and hath been so apprehended in most of former ages; Motions or pleas against comon & knowne Right, though upon never so specious pretences, being hardly admitted, ever suspected, and sometimes deeply censured.

And seemeth to have been soe upon good and sollid grounds; for

waive but this Rule, and admit but pleas and motions against knowne
Right, upon pretences of better and more profittable things, and an entrance is thereby given and roome made for Art, Sophistry, and corrupt
policy to practise upon and against any or all the ancient liberties of
the Nation, to baffle Reason, hold Argument for ever, untill at length it
hath prevailed (as in times foregoing this Parliam^t:) but never without
glorious colour and glosses of publique good, to a Totall subvertion of
Publique Right and an inundation of oppressions & grevances; amongst
which the restriction of Forraine Trade by Companyes (in the beginning
of this Parliament) was not esteemed the least.

So as the premises seriously considered, with what farther may arise
in your grate wisdomes, possibly this breife way of discovering will conduce most to the good of the Common wealth in this case may appeare
most proper and effectuall, and of it selfe so sufficient to prove this so
antient a continuall claymed Right, as freedome to all English men in all
Forraine Trade is knowne to be, as needs no other argument to prove it
more profitable for the Commonwealth, then any way of a restriction on
Companies whatsoever.

But least this way of proving should seeme too strictly & precisely fixt
upon the poynt of Right (which yet is humbly conceived to be the best)
to make it manifest that (as all other the knowne Rights of England) so
this of freedome of Trade doth comprize that wealth & essentiall publique good which in reason can justly be expected, and far beyond what
possibly can be attained by restriction or the Government of Companies:

It is farther humblie offered That if the good of the Commonwealth
accruing by forraine Trade consisteth as surely it doth,

1. In the improvement of Land by the buying & transporting of Native Comodities
2. In occasioning profitable Labour for all industrious people, in buying and transporting all sort of Manufactures, and bringing of all
   sorts of unwrought samples & materialls of Gold & Silver:
3. In keeping other Nations from making the like unto our home
   Manufacture
4. In the increase of Shipping:

5. In the increase of Marriners:

6. In being more secure from advantages of Forraine States:

7. In the increase of Wealth and plenty:

All these are (as is humbly conceived) manifestly to be proved be effected most certainly & substantially, by admitting an universall freedome in all forraine trades; and that by this undeniable production thereof, The increase of Merchants.

1. For as to Merchants increasing (as increase they must in few yeares) they will not continue plodding to one or two townes in a Nation or Province, Trading in a stately manner upon set Dayes, with Grossiers, in great quantityes, making up their gaines in the grosse; but will be dispersed in every Haven and Towne, furnishing (not Grossiers that gain great estates out of our Native Comodities, and soe render them deare to the last user) but the last sellers, and so will be able to give at home the better Rates, which in conclusion redounds to workemen of all sorts, to Farmers, Owners & Land.

2. The numerousness of Merchants will occasion a strife & emulation among them, who shall produce the best ordered goods; and so will be more exquisite in the workmanship of dyings and dressings & the like, and give greater prices for worke; whereas Merchants in Companyes have noe need of such diligence, none being at the places of their sale, but themselves, or very few others: what they have must be taken, there being no other to be sold and workmen must worke at what Rates they please, worke being generally scarce through the scarcity of Merchants: and by setting their owne time of shippings, they make their own Markets for any their Commodities which impoverisheth the maker, worker, grower, growth & Land. The more buyers, the more is bought & sould, all corners of the world would be found out; noe good towne in any province, but where English Merchants would be resident; whence they would returne the Comodities of their respective places from the first hand, and so upon cheaper Rates then to be brought from all parts to one or two Townes in a Nation through divers getting hands, and at great charges; and if any Money of Gold Silver or Bullion be in any place, it could not but find the way to England.

3. They being numerous, and so dispersed into every town & with their fresh goods upon a neat Charge, exempt from Companyes impositions, could be able to sell upon reasonable Termes, & to supply all occasions, as would necessarily beat downe the making of any goods like unto Our Native Manufactures, and by their residence in all Creekes & haven Townes, their own Interest would bind them to watch against the bringing into any forraine parts either Wools or Fullers Earth, more carefully and certainely than any Officers can doe; the want whereof, and the Residence of Merchants in one or two set places, giving advantage & opportunity thereunto; they growing Rich notwithstanding; which hath been of infinite prejudice to this Nation.

4. The numerousness of Merchants would necessarily increase the number of Shipping; as may be seen amongst our diligent neighbours, and good & large & usefull Ships too; although hardly any Merchants ships are soe serviceable or to be trusted to, for Warr or for defence and protection, as those that are built purposely for these uses by the State.

5. Mariners would be exceedingly increased (a thing of very great moment) inriched and incouraged thereby; being free to make the best use of their longe, dangerous voyages to the East & West Indies, to Turky, Spaine, France, & all places; & to Trade and buy & sell with their small stocks, & to make their returne in jewells or any Commodities without that feare & danger incurred from Companyes: every ten shillings, as in some Countries, would be improveable; even servants would adventure their wages with them, and they would in shorter time become able & profitable members of the Commonwealth.

6. The numerousness of Merchants would occasion that as to long voyages and far distant places (as to East & West Indies & the like) many would joyne together for one place, & others for another, in waies forseen to be as secure as Companyes, whether to sea or Land dangers: but being in small inconsiderable bodies, States would have noe such temptations to worke upon them, they being of noe considerable capacity to afford them much at any time, unto which Companyes have been ever liable.

7. And although possibly for some few yeares this inlarging of Trade might not produce so many wealthy men, as have been in the same time by Companies, most of them being borne Rich & adding wealth to

wealth by trading in a beaten Rode to wealth, wherein noe other had liberty to set his foote, yet it will produce Thousands more of able men to beare publique Charges or what other Publique occasions they may be called unto.

All which, & probably much more may (as is humbly conceived) be justly said in behalfe of an absolute & universall freedome in forraine Trade. And where it is said on the other side, that Companyes merit much for finding out of Trades;[3] it is very doubtfull who were the first finders, commonly the first are after a time forgotten, and Companyes grow up after the Trade hath been Ripened and is worth the gathering; then upon Pretence of Reformation (the true ground being to hinder the increase of Traders that for their particular gaine might not be abated) they combine togeather into Companyes; this usually hath been their Originall; however the Law gives noe priviledge to inventions that are once discovered, and only fourteene yeares particular use for incouragement beyond discovery; soe as that in this Case is noe plea.

And for their being at great charges;[4] it being upon a Purchase from prerogative, and against common Right and Common good, the former rule being good is soe farr from deserving Encouragement, that it should not be so much as mentioned; & for having the benefit of mutuall Councells one with another, it is knowne that there is not that Union that is pretended, but that strife & contentions & circumventions doe abound amongst them, the greater lying more heavy upon the more moderate Traders, and the less heavyly complayning of their manifold burthens, by their many unreasonable Orders, Oathes, fines, Censures: soe that however through Custome & Tradition they are wedded ever superstitiously to continue in this way of a perplexed Society, pleasing themselves in spending very much of their time in Courts & meetings about others affaires, doubtless their Lives would be much more Comfortable, and their Trades as gainefull upon the score of Generall & equall freedome, had they hearts & Courages to prove[5] it; Especially considering that their Consciences would not be

---

3. Objections answd: Comp's discovery of Trade
4. Their Charges therein
5. [To try, bring to the test.]

burthened with taking away others Rights for their owne advantage, nor ly under so much hatred for the same as now for many yeares they have done; very many beleiving they have been much injured by them, and some undone.

But all being said that can be, there will not faile multiplicity of words to the contrary, and although the Right & the publique good both are conceived to be undeniably with generall Freedome of Trade; yet the Companyes have at present the advantage of possession, which (all things considered) is very hard on the other side; especially in that the one hath its foundation in Common Right, the other in prerogative, the Common Enemy; so as possibly it were but equall (prerogative being a kind of Forcecible entry) first to put the people into possession of this their Native Right; and then let Companyes or those who have a minde to be such, offer their merits & reasons for their Incorporations, as they shall see cause, if they can justly doe it.

And truly it can hardly be discerned how this Controversy can ever come to a right & good end, so as the Parliam^t shall receive full satisfaction therein, except either they be pleased to proceed to judgm^t upon the ground of knowne Right, & thereupon resolve that Right shall take place as not counting but the yssue must be good: Or else that they will be pleased for Rights sake, to make an experiment of a free Trade for halfe the number of yeares that hath been made proofe of by Companyes; affording only attention thereunto, which is the only thing requisite from Authority. In which time, God preserving the Nation from the banefull interposition of prerogative & its money taking faculty, possibly so great an increase of wealth & strength & prosperity would be seen in short space of time, compared to the long continuance of the contrary Course, as would give a finall & happy solution to this Quere to the contentfull satisfaction even of those that have most contended for the continuance of Companies, & have most opposed Trades freedome; & to the universall good of all well minded people: which is the harty desire of the Author of these weake conceptions, & which with what also is in him, he humbly tenders to the service of your Honours, beseeching your favourable construction of all & every part

As (in duty bound) &c.

2

Political Maxims of the State
of Holland
1662

PIETER DE LA COURT came from a family that was close to republican
circles in Holland. A cloth manufacturer himself, Pieter's grandfather
Jacques had a medallion struck with the insignia "Long live liberty!"
upon the death of the *stadholder* William II in 1650, though Pieter's own
writings on the subject are somewhat more complex and nuanced in their
orientation. His *Interest van Holland* (*The Interests of Holland*) was mostly
completed by 1661. After consulting with Jan de Witt, who suggested a
few changes, de la Court brought the book out in Dutch in 1662. It was
an immediate bestseller, widely read and discussed, but also highly controversial. For the better part of a decade, the author and his book were
subject to disciplinary procedures by church and state. De la Court attempted to balance his political interests with his writer's interest until
1672, at which point the return of the Princes of Orange to power made
his republican political ambitions moot. De la Court died in 1685.

The excerpts presented here are from *Political Maxims of the State of
Holland*, translated by John Campbell (Nourse, 1743), part I, chapters I,
9, 14, 15, and 16, and are derived from the revised and expanded 1669
edition of the *Interest van Holland*, which bore the title *Aanwysing
der heilsame politike gronden en maximen van de republike van Holland*,
from which the English title is taken. This selection is meant to provide
a cross-section of the ways in which the author connected commercial

considerations with political and religious ones. Unbracketed notes are adapted from the English edition; material in brackets is by the current editor.

━━━━━━━━━

The TRUE INTEREST, *and* POLITICAL MAXIMS *of* the *Republick of* Holland *and* West-Friesland.

Chapter I

Wherein are laid down the general political maxims which tend to the prosperity of all countries: and some reasons to make it evident, that the same do aptly agree to Holland *and* West-Friesland.

That we may not abruptly speak of the true interest and political maxims of *Holland* and *West-Friesland,* nor yet surprize the reader with unknown matters, I judge it necessary to begin with a general discourse of the universal and true political maxims of all countries: that the reader being enlightned by such reasoning, may the better comprehend the true political maxims of *Holland* and *West-Friesland.* And seeing that almost all the people in *Europe,* as the *Spaniards, Italians, French,* &c. do express the same by the word *interest,* I shall often have occasion to use the same likewise here for brevity sake, in the same sense that they do; *viz.* seeing the true interest of all countries consists in the joint welfare of the governors and governed; and the same is known to depend on a good government, that being the true foundation whereon all the prosperity of any country is built; we are therefore to know, that a good government is not that where the well or ill-being of the subjects depends on the virtues or vices of the rulers; but (which is worthy of observation) where the well or ill-being of the rulers necessarily follows or depends on the well or ill-being of the subjects. For seeing we must believe that in all societies or assemblies of men, self is always preferred; so all sovereigns or supreme powers will in the first place seek their own advantage in all things, tho' to the prejudice of the subject. But seeing on the other hand true interest cannot be compassed by a government, unless the generality of the people partake thereof; therefore the publick welfare will ever be aimed at by good rulers. All which very aptly agrees with our *Latin* and *Dutch* proverb, that, *Tantum de publicis malis sentimus, quantum ad privatas res pertinet;* i. e. We are only sensible of publick afflictions, in so far as they touch our private affairs; for no body halts of another man's sore.

Whereby it clearly follows, that all wise men, whether monarchs, princes, sovereign lords, or rulers of republicks, are always inclined so to strengthen their country, kingdom, or city, that they may defend themselves against the power of any stronger neighbour. The rulers welfare therefore does so far necessarily depend on the welfare of the subject; else they would soon be conquer'd by stronger neighbouring princes, and be turn'd out of their government. Those monarchs and supreme powers, who by bad education, and great prosperity, follow their pleasures, suffer their government to fall into the hands of favourites and courtiers, and do commonly neglect this first duty; the said favourites in the mean time finding themselves vested with such sovereign power, do for the most part rule to the benefit of themselves, and to the prejudice, not only of such voluptuous and unwary chief magistrates, but also of their subjects; and by consequence to the weaking of the political state; so that we have often seen revolutions of such monarchies by the ill government of favourites. But such princes as are wise, and do not entrust their power in other mens hands, will not omit to strengthen their dominions against their neighbours as much as possible. But when monarchies, or republicks are able enough to do this, and have nothing to fear from their neighbouring states or potentates, then they do usually, according to the opportunity put into their hands by the form of their government, take courses quite contrary to the welfare of the subject.

For then it follows as truly from the said general maxims of all rulers, that the next duty of monarchs, and supreme magistrates, is to take special care that their subjects may not be like generous and metalsome[1] horses, which, when they cannot be commanded by the rider, but are too headstrong, wanton, and powerful for their master, they reduce and keep so tame and manageable, as not to refuse the bit and bridle, I mean taxes and obedience.[2] For which end it is highly necessary to prevent the greatness and power of their cities, that they may not out of their own wealth be able to raise and maintain an army in the field, not only to repel all foreign power, but also to make head against their own lord, or expel him. And as little, yea much less may prudent sovereign lords or monarchs permit that their cities, by their strong fortifications, and training their inhabitants to arms, should have an opportunity easily, if they pleas'd, to discharge and turn off their sovereign. Bot if herein a sovereign had neglected his duty, there's no way left for him, but to wait an opportunity to command such populous cities and strongholds by citadels, and to render them weak and defenceless. And tho' *Aristotle* says, that it very well suits an oligarchical state to have their cities under command of a castle, yet this is only true of a great and populous city, that hath a prince over it, and not of a city that governs itself, or hath a share in the supreme government; for in such a republick, the governor of that citadel would certainly be able to make himself master of that city, and to subjugate or overtop his rulers.[3] And we see that this reason is so strong and clear, and confirm'd by experience, that the history of all former ages, as well as the age we live in, teach us, that the rulers of republicks, whatever they are, have wisely forborn erecting citadels, and do still continue to do so. So that it appears that the said maxim tending to the overthrow of great and populous cities, may be attributed to monarchs and princes at all times, but never to republicks, unless when they have inconsiderately subdued great cities; and tho' not willing to demolish them, yet are willing to keep them distinct from the sovereign government. But if the inconsiderate reader be so far prepossess'd in favour of monarchy and against common freedom, that he neither can nor will submit himself to this way of reasoning, nor to the venerable and antient lessons of old and renowned philosophers, then let him

1. [Mettlesome; spirited, courageous.]
2. Arist[otle], *Polit[ics]* l. 5, c. 11.
3. Ibid., l. 7, c. 11.

know, that the christian and invincible monarch *Justinian* has for ever established the said monarchical maxim by form of law in the *corpus juris,* now become the common law-book of all civiliz'd people, and especially of Christians.[4]

For the said emperor having by his captain general of the east, *Belisarius,* reconquer'd from the *Goths* that part of *Africa* which he had formerly lost, and brought it under his subjection, gave him no order that the inhabitants of great cities should be better disciplin'd and provided with arms, or strengthned by good walls, that they might jointly with ease defend themselves, and their great and populous cities, against the assaults of those barbarous people: but on the contrary, he commands the said captain general *Belisarius* (and consequently, according to the *Roman* laws, all his other governors of provinces) to make such provision, that no city or strong hold lying on the frontiers be so great as it could not be well kept; but in such cases so to order them to be built, that they may be well defended with few soldiers, and particularly such as were in pay, and depended only on the emperor of *Rome.*

And tho' weak, voluptuous, dull and sluggish monarchs neglect all these things, yet will not the courtiers who govern in their stead, neglect to seek themselves, and to fill their coffers whether in war or in peace: and thus the subjects estates being exhausted by rapine, those great and flourishing cities become poor and weak. And to the end that the subject should not be able to hinder or prevent such rapine, or revenge themselves, those favourites omit no opportunities to divest those populous cities of all fortifications, provision, ammunition of war, and to hinder the exercising of the commonalty in the use of arms. Since it appears from the said maxims, that the publick is not regarded but for the sake of private interest; and consequently, that is the best government, where the chief rulers may obtain their own welfare by that of the people. It follows then to be the duty of the governours of republicks to seek for great cities, and to make them as populous and strong as possible, that so all

---

4. Belisario magistro militum per orientem, &c. Interea vero si aliquas civitates seu Castella per limites constituta providerit tua magnitudo nimiae esse magnitudinis, & propter hoc non posse bene custodiri ad talem modum ea construi disponat, ut possint per paucos bene servari, &c. Cod. l. 1. Tit. 27. par. 14.

rulers and magistrates, and likewise all others that serve the publick either in country or city, may thereby gain the more power, honour and benefit, and more safely possess it, whether in peace or war:[5] and this is the reason why commonly we see that all republicks thrive and flourish far more in arts, manufacture, traffick, populousness and strength, than the dominions and cities of monarchs:[6] for where there is liberty, there will be riches and people.

To bring all this home, and make it suit with our state, we ought to consider that *Holland* may easily be defended against her neighbours; and that the flourishing of manufactures, fishing, navigation, and traffick, whereby that province subsists, and (its natural necessities or wants being well considered) depends perpetually on them, else would be uninhabited: I say, the flourishing of those things will infallibly produce great, strong, populous and wealthy cities, which by reason of their convenient situation, may be impregnably fortified: all which to a monarch, or one supreme head, is altogether intolerable. And therefore I conclude, that the inhabitants of *Holland,* whether rulers or subjects, can receive no greater mischief in their polity, than to be governed by a monarch, or supreme lord: and that on the other side, God can give no greater temporal blessing to a country in our condition, than to introduce and preserve a free commonwealth government.

But seeing this conclusion opposeth the general and long-continued prejudices of all ignorant persons, and consequently of most of the inhabitants of these *United Provinces,* and that some of my readers might distaste this treatise upon what I have already said, unless somewhat were spoken to obviate their mistakes, I shall therefore offer them these reasons.

Altho' by what hath been already said, it appears, That the inhabitants of a republick are infinitely more happy than subjects of a land governed by one supreme head; yet the contrary is always thought in a country where a prince is already reigning, or in republicks, where one supreme head is ready to be accepted.

For not only officers, courtiers, idle gentry, and soldiery, but also all those that would be such, knowing, that under the worst government

---

5. Arist[otle], *Pol[itics],* l. 7, c. 11, l. 5, c. 11.
6. *Quippe ubi libertas, ibi & populus & divitiae.*

they use to fare best, because they hope that with impunity they may plunder and rifle the citizens and country people, and so by the corruption of the government enrich themselves, or attain to grandeur, they cry up monarchical government for their private interest to the very heavens: altho God did at first mercifully institute no other but a commonwealth government, and afterwards in his wrath appointed one sovereign over them.[7] Yet for all this, those blood-suckers of the state, and, indeed of mankind, dare to speak of republicks with the utmost contempt, make a mountain of every molehill, discourse of the defects of them at large, and conceal all that is good in them, because they know none will punish them for what they say: wherefore all the rabble (according to the old [8]*Latin* verse) being void of knowledge and judgment, and therefore inclining to the weather or safer side, and mightily valuing the vain and empty pomp of kings and princes, say *amen* to it; especially when kept in ignorance, and irritated against the lawful government by preachers, who aim at dominion, or would introduce an independent and arbitrary power of church-government; and such (God amend it) are found in *Holland*, and the other *United Provinces*, insomuch, that all vertuous and intelligent people have been necessitated to keep silence, and to beware of disclosing the vices of their princes, or of such as would willingly be their governors, or of courtiers and rude military men, and such ambitious and ungovernable preachers as despise God, and their native country.[9]

Nay there are few inhabitants of a perfect free state to be found, that are inclinable to instruct and teach others, how much better a republick is than a monarchy, or one supreme head, because they know no body will reward them for it; and that on the other side,[10] kings, princes, and great men are so dangerous to be conversed with, that even their friends can scarcely talk with them of the wind and weather, but at the hazard of

---

7. 1 Sam[uel] 1:8, 12.

8. ⸺ *Sed quid? / Turba Remi sequitur fortunam, ut semper, & odit damnatos.* Juven. [And what does the mob of Remus say? It follows fortune, as it always does, and rails against the condemned. *Juvenal and Perseus*, trans. G. G. Ramsay (Harvard University Press: Loeb Library, 1918), Satire 10. 73–74.]

9. [Since the death of Stadholder William II in 1650, the Dutch states had been left without a Stadholder and had been dominated by Holland and its councilor pensionary, Jan de Witt, who was thought to have collaborated with de la Court on the present work.]

10. ⸺ *Sed quid violentius aure tyranni, / Cum quo de pluviis aut aestibus aut nimboso / Vere locuturi fatum pendebat amici?* Juven. [Satire 4. 86–88]

their lives; and kings with their long arms can give heavy blows. And al-tho' all intelligent and ingenuous subjects of monarchs, who have not, with lying sycophantical courtiers, cast off all shame, are generally by these reasons, and daily experience, fully convinced of the excellency of a republick above a monarchical government; yet nevertheless, many vertuous persons, lovers of monarchy, do plausibly maintain, that several nations are of that temper and disposition, that they cannot be happily governed but by a single person, and quote for this the examples of all the people in *Asia* and *Africa,* as well as *Europe,* that lie southerly. They do also alledge, that all the people who lie more northerly, are more fit to be governed by a single person, and with more freedom; as from *France* to the northward, all absolute monarchical government ceaseth; and there-fore maintain or assert, with such ignorant persons as I mentioned be-fore, that the *Hollanders* in particular are so turbulent, factious, and disingenuous, that they cannot be kept in awe, and happily governed, but by a single person; and that the histories of the former reigns or govern-ment by earls, will sufficiently confirm it.

But on the other side, the patriots, and lovers of a free-state will say, that the foregoing government by earls is well know[n] to have been very wretched and horrid, their reigns filling history with continual wars, tu-mults, and detestable actions, occasioned by that single person. And that on the contrary, the *Hollanders,* subsisting by manufactures, fishing, nav-igation, and commerce, are naturally very peaceable, if by such a supreme head they were not excited to tumults. Whether this be so or not, may be learned and confirmed too in part from those histories.[11]

But here it may be said, that things are much altered within these 100 years last; for *Holland* then subsisted mostly by agriculture, and there were then no soldiery, treasure, or fortified places to be at the earl's disposal. But when he had wars, it was with the help of his homagers and tenants, only subsidies or money being given him at his request by the states of the country: And moreover, the cities of *Holland,* and castles of the nobility were (according to the then method of war) so strong, that they could not be taken by the said earls, without great forces imployed against them; so

---

11. *Deduct[ie oft declaratie van de staaten van Holland . . .* ('s Gravenhage, 1654)] Part 2, ch. 3, 4, 7, 13.

that the states of *Holland* in their assemblies, have boldly contended for their rights against the earl's encroachments. Therefore these earls, on the other side, by reason of their dignity, had many adherents that depended on them, which must needs make that government by earls every way unsteady, weak and tumultuous.

To this an approver of monarchical government may further add, that *Holland* now wholly subsists by traffick, and that one supreme head, captain-general, or stadtholder, would have his own life-guards at the *Hague,* the place of assembly, and likewise the assistance of a great and well-paid army, and of all the preachers, and by them the love of the whole populace; and that at his pleasure he may dispose of all the impregnable frontier towns of those provinces that have no suffrages or voices in the state, tho' he should not increase his strength by any foreign alliances, or by collusion and flattery with the deputies of the other provinces of the generality; insomuch that the states of *Holland* would not dare, no not in their assemblies, to open their mouths against the interest of such a supreme head, or if they did, he would order his souldiers to take them by the collar, and might easily overpower most of the cities of *Holland,* the people being unaccustomed to arms, and moreover divided, fortifications but slight and mean in comparison of the present way of fortifying: so that one may truly say, that the *Hollanders* by setting up one supreme head over themselves, may now with ease, and without tumult, be govern'd like sheep, by an irresistible sovereign, against whom they durst not speak one word, when he should think fit to sheer, flea [i.e., flay], or devour them.

Now what there is in this, and whether the *Hollanders* would be happy in such a condition, I shall at large hereafter give you my judgment.

But as to the stupidity of the *Hollanders,* whether that be so great, as that they have not wit enough to form a free commonwealth; and having found that precious jewel of freedom, would, with *Esop*'s cocks, prefer a grain of corn before it: This is what hath not been judged so hitherto, but on the contrary. Which that it may be evident to the reader, he may be pleas'd to observe the prudent conduct of the states of *Holland,* at their great assembly in the years 1650 and 1651, as also seriously to ponder and weigh the manifold reasons and examples produced to this end in their *deduction* of the year 1654. All this is yet further confirmed by that magnanimous resolution of the 23*d* of *January* 1657, wherein the states of *Holland* unanimously declared, after consulting the general assemblies, or common-halls of the respective cities in that province, to hold for a fundamental and certain maxim, "That to place a perpetual head, chieftain, or general over the army, is not only needless, but likewise exceeding prejudicial, and that accordingly in this province all things shall be thus directed; that whenever in a time of war, and pressing necessity, the states of *Holland,* with the other provinces, shall think fit to proceed to elect a general for the army, or that upon any other occasion a captain-general should be chosen, then not to chuse such a chieftain as shall have a perpetual commission, but for such an expedition, campaign, or occasion only as may happen, &c." And moreover, you may there see, that these, and other vigorous resolutions of the like nature, were taken with this special proviso, "that the said resolution shall not be dispensed with, but by the unanimous consent of all the members of the said assembly."

By this you may perceive, that the supposition of the *Hollanders* being phlegmatick and dull, and of a slavish nature, is altogether groundless; for seeing they became not free but by the death of the last stadtholder and captain general,[12] and that it was unseasonable and imprudent before that time, for them to shew their commendable zeal for their freedom, and their skill in point of government: and seeing it is evident, that a generation of men that are in freedom, must be overcome, before we can pass a right judgment thereof, and stop the mouths of opposers; we must therefore, leave it to God and time: and if such as like monarchical government, and those base and slavish opposers of liberty survive those times, they will then be able to discern which of the two governments is founded on best reason.

It shall not satisfy me to have said thus much in general; for seeing the states of *Holland* in their deduction, *Chap.* 6. *Art.* 29. declare, that they will not lose their freedom, but with their lives; I shall therefore presume to give my opinion of the political maxims of *Holland,* hoping that my sincere zeal and uprightness to express the same for the benefit of the publick, will be so acceptable to our lawful rulers, that tho' I may have

12. [I.e., William II.]

failed in some things, and by stating the true interest of my country, have been necessitated to reflect on persons, who seek their advantage to the prejudice of *Holland,* as it is now governed; the said rulers, and true lovers of their native country, will so favour this work, and its author, against the said malevolent persons, that it shall never repent him to have been the first generous and bold undertaker of so commendable a work. But howsoever things happen, or times oppose it, *recte fecisse merces est,* & *ipsa sui pretium virtus;* (*i. e.* to do good is a reward of it self, and virtue carries its own recompence along with it) I shall then, having done my duty as an honest man, good citizen, and upright christian, that may not bury his talent, be able to take comfort in my sincere endeavours: and posterity, into whose hands these writings may fall, will, in spite of all the present powers that oppose it, be able to judge impartially, and that with a sound judgment; because by that time they will have learned, by joyful or sad experience, whether *Holland*'s interest can be settled upon any other foundation or maxims than those herein exprest; and whether these reasons of mine will not be confirmed by the experience of following ages.

Chapter IX

That the inhabitants of Holland, *being in a state of freedom, are by a common interest wonderfully linked together; which is also shew'd by a rough calculation of the number of inhabitants, and by what means they subsist.*

We are moreover well to consider, that fishing is not the sole cause of traffick, nor fishing and traffick the cause of manufactury; as also that these three together do not always give occasion for the shipping that is to let out to freight, which is meant by navigation: but that fishing flourishes much more in those parts, because traffick, navigation and manufactures are settled among us, whereby the fish and oil taken may be transported and consumed. Likewise that more than the one half of our trading would decay, in case the trade of fish were destroyed, as well as all other sorts of commodities about which people are imployed in *Holland;* besides that, by consequence the *inland consumption* of all foreign goods being more than one half diminished, the traffick in those parts would fall proportionably.

It is also certain, that of necessity all sorts of manufactures would be lessened more than a moiety,[13] if not annihilated, as soon as this country should come to be bereft of fishing, and of trading in those commodities which are spent abroad. And concerning owners of ships let out to freight, it is evident that they wholly depend on the prosperity or success of fishing, manufactury, and traffick: for seeing our country yields almost nothing out of its own bowels; therefore the ships that lie for freight, can lade nothing but what the merchants or traders put on board them of fish, manufactury, or merchandize. And as little would foreign ships carry goods to *Holland*, in case no fishermen, merchants, or traders dealing in manufactury dwelt there. And contrariwise it is certain, that our fishers, manufacturers and traders, find a mighty conveniency and benefit in our great number of freight-ships, which continually lie for freight in all parts of the world, and are ready to carry the same at an easy rate to any place desired. So that the *English* and *Flemish* merchants, &c. do ofttimes know no better way to transport their goods to such foreign parts as they design, than to carry them first to *Amsterdam*, and from thence to other places, especially when our admiralties, according to their duty, take care to convoy and defend our merchant ships, with men of war, against all pirates, or sea-robbers whatsoever. It is also evident, that the husbandmen, or boors[14] of *Holland*, can very well sell all the product or profit of their land, cattle, firing, &c. to the inhabitants that are fishers, manufacturers, traders, navigators, and those that depend on them; which is a great advantage beyond what all other boors have, who for the most part have their commodities spent abroad, and consequently must bear the charges of freight, and the duties outwards and inwards, and must also allow a double gain to the merchants and buyers. So that this great number of people, that are not husbandmen, are I think the only cause that those country boors, tho' heavily taxed, are able to subsist. And seeing all the said inhabitants have need of meat, drink, cloathing, housing, and of the gain gotten by foreign consumption that

13. [Half.]
14. [Plowmen.]

is needful to support it; it is evident, that all the other inhabitants depend and live upon the aforesaid fishers, traders and navigators.

And how remarkable it is, that all rulers and others, who for any service depend on them, have a benefit by their great numbers, is so clear, that there needs no more to be said for proof: for when there were but few inhabitants in this country, within less than 100 years, the most eminent offices of burgomaster, and *schepens* or sheriffs, were even in the principal cities so great a burden as not to be born without much charge; whereas it is now become profitable to be but a city messenger, or undertaker to freight ships, seeing men are thereby enabled to maintain their families.

Furthermore, having a mind to convince the reader, not only by my reasoning, but by his own experience, that the prosperity of *Holland* is built upon the foresaid means of subsistence, and on no other; I find myself obliged to make a calculation of the number of people in *Holland* that are fixed inhabitants, or depend upon them; and at the same time, as far as I am able, to reckon in what proportion those people are maintain'd by the means of subsistence before mentioned. In order to this I shall on the one hand consider, that Sir *Walter Raleigh,* endeavouring to move king *James* of *England* to advance the fishing trade, manufactures, and traffick by sea, hath possibly exceeded in his account of the profits arising from it, and augmented the number of the people that live upon it somewhat above the truth.

And on the other hand I shall consider what *Gerard Malines* saith, in his *Lex Mercatoria, Ann.* 1622.[15] that in *Flanders* there were then counted one hundred and forty thousand families; which being reckoned, one with another, at five persons each, they would amount to seven hundred thousand people. I shall likewise consider that in *Holland* that same year, the states laid a poll-tax upon all inhabitants, none excepted save strangers, prisoners, and vagrants, and those that were on the other side the line; yet were there found in all *South-Holland* that same wise no more than four hundred eighty one thousand nine hundred thirty and four: altho' the commissioners instructions for that end were very strict

---

15. [Gerard Malynes (1586–1641), *Consuetudo, vel Lex mercatoria, or, The ancient law-merchant* (London: Islip, 1622; repr. Goldbach, 1997).]

and severe, to prevent all fraud and deceit. However that we may make the better guess whether this was a faithful account, I shall give you the particulars of it as registred in the chamber of Accounts.

Dort with its villages,	40523
Haerlem with its villages,	69648
Delft with its villages,	41744
Leyden and *Rynland,*	94285
Amsterdam and its villages,	115022
Goude and its villages,	24662
Rotterdam with its villages,	28339
Gornichem with its villages,	7585
Schiedam with its villages,	10393
Schoonhoven with its villages,	10703
Briel with its villages,	20156
The *Hague,*	17430
Heusden.	1444
	481934

And supposing that *West-Friesland* might yield the fourth part of the inhabitants of *South Holland,* it would amount to   120483

In all 602417

But because possibly none but intelligent readers, and such as have travelled, will believe, what we see is customary in all places, that the number of people in all populous countries is excessively magnified, and that the common readers will think, that since many would be willing to evade the poll-tax, there was an extraordinary fraud in the number given in: I shall therefore follow the common opinion, and conclude, that the number of people was indeed much greater, and that these countries are since that time much improved in the number of inhabitants; and accordingly I shall give a guess as by vulgar report, that the whole number, without excluding any inhabitants whatsoever, may amount to two millions and four hundred thousand people, and that they maintain themselves as followeth, *viz.*

By the fisheries at sea, and setting them out with ships, rigging, cask,

salt, and other materials, or instruments, and the traffick that depends
thereon,   450000.
By agriculture, inland-fishing, herding, hay-making, turf-making,
and by furnishing those people with all sorts of materials as they are
boors, or husbandmen,   200000.
By making all manner of manufactures, shipping, works of art, mechanick or handicraft works, which are consumed abroad; as likewise by
trade relating to the said manufactures,   650000.
By navigation or sailing for freight and trade jointly, by which I mean
carriage into foreign parts for selling and buying; as also carrying to and
from *Holland* all such wares and merchandise as relate not to our fishing
and manufactury, nor depend thereon: and lastly, I include herein also all
inhabitants that are any ways serviceable to such traders, and ships let out
to freight, amounting in all to.   250000.
By all these inhabitants, as being men, women, and children, that
must be provided, and by working about what is spent in this country, as
food, drink, cloathing, housing, and by making or selling houshould
stuff, and all other things for art, ease, pleasure, or ornament.   650000.
By the labour and care of all the above-mentioned persons, being gentry without employment or calling, civil magistrates and officers, those
that live upon their estates or money, soldiers, the poor in hospitals, beggars, &c.   200000.
                                                     In all 2400000.

And tho' this calculation, whether considered as to the number of the
inhabitants, or their proportionable means of subsistence, is very rough
and uncertain; yet I suppose it to be evident, that the eighth part of the
inhabitants of *Holland* could not be supplied with necessaries out of its
own product, if their gain otherwise did not afford them all other necessaries: so that *homo homini deus in statu politico*, one man being a god to
another under a good government, it is an unspeakable blessing for this
land, that there are so many people in it, who according to the nature of
the country are honestly maintain'd by such suitable or proportionable
means, and especially that the welfare of all the inhabitants (the idle gentry, and foreign soldiers in pay excepted) from the least to the greatest,

does so necessarily depend on one another: and above all, it is chiefly considerable, that there are none more really interested in the prosperity of this country than the rulers of this aristocratical government, and the persons that live on their estates.

For fishers, boors, or country people, owners of ships let to freight, merchants and manufacturers, in a general destruction of a country, could easily transport themselves into foreign parts, and there set up their fishing, agriculture, or husbandry, shipping, merchandize and manufactures: But such as have lands, or immovable estates cannot do this; and supposing they could, and should sell their estates and remove into other countries, yet would they there have no calling to subsist by, much less can they expect to be made use of in the government, or procure any office or advantage depending upon it.

However, this excellent and laudable harmony and union may be violated, even to the ruin of all the inhabitants, none excepted but courtiers and soldiers, and that by one sole mistake in government, which is the electing one supreme head over all these inhabitants, or over their armies. For seeing such a single person for the increase of his grandeur, may curb and obstruct *Holland*'s greatness and power, by the deputies of the lesser provinces of the generality, who also may in their course check the great and flourishing cities in their own provincial assemblies, by the suffrages or votes of the envious gentry. And the lesser cities, and the great persons, courtiers and soldiers being all of his party, and depending on him, must needs prey upon the industrious or working inhabitants, and so will make use of all their power for their own benefit, and to the detriment of the commonalty. And to the end they may receive no let from the great and strong cities of *Holland*, it follows that they would either weaken or lessen all such cities, and impoverish the inhabitants, to make them obedient without controul. Which if so, we have just cause continually to pray, *A furore monarcharum libera nos Domine;* God preserve *Holland* from the fury of a monarch, prince, or one supreme head. But what there is of reality in this, shall be handled hereafter in a chapter apart.

Chapter XIV

That freedom or toleration in, and about the service or worship of God, is a powerful means to preserve many inhabitants in Holland, *and allure foreigners to dwell amongst us.*

In the first place it is certain, that not only those that deal in manufactures, fishing, traffick, shipping, and those that depend on them, but also all civilized people must be supposed to pitch upon some outward service of God as the best, and to be averse from all other forms; and that such persons do abhor to travel, and much more to go and dwell in a country, where they are not permitted to serve and worship God outwardly, after such a manner as they think fit. And also that as to freedom about the outward service of God, during the troubles, and shortly after; when the manufactures, trading, and navigation for freight began to settle in *Holland,* the magistrate was so tender and indulgent, that there were very few useful inhabitants driven thence by any rigour or hardship, much less any foreigners: so that it brings that maxim into my mind, that [16]the surest way to keep any thing, is to make use of the same means whereby it was at first acquired.

And among those means, comes first into consideration the freedom of all sorts of religion differing from the Reformed. For in regard all our neighbours (except *Great Britain* and the *United Provinces*) and for the most part all far remote lands, are not of the reformed religion; and that the clergy under the papacy have their own jurisdiction: and seeing, if not all those that are called *spiritual,* yet the clergy at least that differ from us, have in all countries a settled livelihood, which depends not on the political welfare of the land: we see that through human frailty, they do in all these countries think fit to teach and preach up all that can have a tendency to their own credit, profit, and ease, yea, tho' it be to the ruin of the whole country; and moreover, when the doctrine, counsel, and admonition of these men is not received by any of their auditors, these clergymen do then very unmercifully use to prosecute them *odio theologico.*[17]

16. Res facile iisdem artibus retinentur quibus initio partae sunt.
17. [Out of doctrinal hatred.]

Whereas nevertheless all christian clergymen ought to rest satisfied, according to their master's doctrine, to enlighten the minds of men with the truth, and to shew them the way to eternal life, and afterwards to endeavour to perswade, and turn such enlightned persons in all humility and meekness into the path that leads to salvation. It is evident that all people, especially Christians, and more particularly their publick teachers, ought to be far from compelling, either by spiritual or bodily punishment, those that for want of light and persuasion are not inclined to go to the publick church, to do any outward act, or to speak any words contrary to their judgment; for *potestas coercendi,* the coercive power is given only to the civil magistrate; all the power and right which the ecclesiasticks have, if they have any, must be derived from them, as the same is excellently and unanswerably shewn by *Lucius Antistius Constans,* in his book *de Jure Ecclesiasticorum* lately printed.[18]

Indeed the essential and only difference between the civil and ecclesiastical power is this, that the civil doth not teach and advise as the other doth, but commands and compels the inhabitants to perform or omit such outward actions, or to suffer some certain punishment for their disobedience; so that they have dominion over the subject, *sive volentes, sive nolentes,* whether they will or no. Whereas on the other side, the duty of christian teachers is to instruct and advise men to all christian virtues, as trusting in God our Saviour, the hope of possessing a future eternal blessed life, and the love of God and our neighbour.[19] Which virtues consisting only in the inward thoughts of our minds, cannot be put into us by any outward violence or compulsion, but only by the inlightning and convincing reasons of ministers, who to effect this, must on all occasions comply with the state and condition of their hearers, and be the least amongst them: and thus making themselves the least, and thereby converting most, and bringing forth most good fruits, they shall be the first in the kingdom of heaven. *Whosoever will be chief among you, let him be your servant.*[20] And besides, it is well known that our Lord Christ pretended to no other kingdom or dominion on earth (*his kingdom not being*

18. [Lucii Antistii Constantis (i.e., Benedict de Spinoza), *De Jure Ecclesiasticorum* (Amsterdam, 1665).]
19. I Cor. 13.
20. Matt. 20:27.

of this world[21]) than that every one being convinced of this his true doctrine, and wholesome advice, and of his holy sufferings for us, should freely be subject to him, not with the outward man only, to do or omit any action, to speak or be silent, but with the inward man *in spirit and truth,* to love God, himself, and his neighbour; to trust in that God and Saviour in all the occurrences of our lives, and by his infinite wisdom, mercy and power, to hope for a blessed and everlasting state for our souls.[22] So that it became not his disciples, or followers, and apostles, much less our present publick preachers, to set themselves above their spiritual lord and master, to lord it over others. *The kings of the Gentiles exercise lordship over them; but ye shall not be so.*[23] The gospel also teacheth us, that they should not lord it over the people, but ought to be their servants, and ministers of the word of God. But notwithstanding all this, we see, that by these evil ambitious maxims of the clergy, almost in all countries, the dissenters, or such as own not the opinion of the publick preachers, are turned out of the civil state and persecuted; for they are not only excluded from all government, magistracies, offices and benefices (which is in some measure tolerable for the secluded inhabitants, and agrees very well with the maxims of polity, in regard it is well known by experience in all countries to be necessary, as tending to the common peace, that one religion should prevail and be supported above all others, and accordingly is by all means authorized, favoured, and protected by the state, yet not so, but that the exercise of other religions at the same time be in some measure publickly tolerated, at least not persecuted) but are so persecuted, that many honest and useful inhabitants, to escape those fines, banishments, or corporal punishments, to which by adhering to the prohibited service of God they are subject, abandon their own sweet native country, and, to obtain their liberty, chuse to come and sit down in our barren and heavy tax'd country.

Yea, and which is more, in some countries these churchmen will go so far, as by an inquisition to inquire who they are that differ from the opinion of the authorized preachers; and first by admonition and excommunication, bereave them of their credit, and afterwards of their liberty,

21. John 18:36.
22. John 4.
23. Luke 22:25, 26.

estate or life. And as heretofore the *Romish* clergy were not satisfied with obstructing the divine service of those that dissented from them, but laboured to bring the inquisition into all places; so would it be a great wonder if the ecclesiasticks in *Holland* should not follow the same worldly course, to the ruin of the country, if they conceiv'd it tended to the increase of their own profit, honour, power and grandeur. At least we see it in almost all countries, where the best and most moderate, yea even where the reformed clergy bear sway, that dissenting assemblies are prohibited. And seeing that the publick divine worship is so necessary for mankind, that without it they would fall into great ignorance about the service of God, and consequently into a very bad life; and since man's life is subject to many miseries, therefore every one is inclined in this wretched state to nourish or comfort his soul with the hope of a better: and as men hope very easily to obtain the same by a free and willing attention to a doctrine they think to be built on a good foundation; so every one may easily perceive how impossible it is to make any man by compulsion to hope for such advantage, in that which he cannot apprehend to be well grounded; and accordingly the dissenting party clearly discover[24] the vanity of all manner of force in matters of religion.

Moreover, seeing all matters of fact, and likewise of faith, must in some measure be proved by testimony of good credit, such as is irreproachable, or beyond exception; and that all that are thus persecuted, whether by excommunication, fines, banishment or corporal punishments, reproach and hate their persecutors, to wit, the publick authorised preachers, as their enemies; it is evident that those persecutors lose all their weight to persuade people in matters of faith by means of their publick authority, which otherwise would be great among the common people. And besides, we see, that all persecuted people continually exercise their thoughts upon any thing that seems to confirm their own judgment, and oft-times out of mere stomachfulness[25] and animosity will not ponder and sedately consider their enemies reasons: so that the persecuted people being wholly turn'd aside from the truth of God's worship by such violence and compulsion, become hardned in their error. By this

24. [I.e., reveal.]
25. [Stubbornness, obstinacy.]

means manifold wars, miseries and removals of habitations have been occasioned since the reformation: and the like actions will still have the like effects. How prejudicial such coercive practices are, especially in rich trafficking cities, *Lubeck, Collen,* and *Aix la Chapelle* may instruct us, where both the rulers and subjects of those lately so famous cities have since the reformation lost most of their wealth, and chiefly by such compulsion in religion; many of the inhabitants being thereby driven out of their respective cities, and strangers discouraged from coming to reside in them. And tho' according to clear reason, and holy writ, the true glory and fame of all rulers consists in the multitude of their subjects, yet do these churchmen (forgetting their credit, their country, and their God, which is a threefold impiety) continue to teach, that it is better to have a city of an orthodox or sound faith, ill stocked with people, than a very populous, and godly city, but tainted with heresy. Thus it is evident that to allow all men the exercise of their religion with more freedom than in other nations, would be a very effectual means for *Holland* to allure people out of other countries, and to fix them, that are there already; provided such freedom be not prejudicial to our civil state and free government.[26] For, as on the one side those of the *Romish* religion have their spiritual heads, and the K. of *Spain* (heretofore Earl of *Holland*) for their neighbour, who may help the *Romanists* in the time of intestine division; so on the other side it is manifest, that our own government by length of time is enlarged, and the *Spanish Netherlands* become weak; and that notwithstanding the renunciation of the said superiority over *Holland* we are in peace with them, it is also certain that by persecuting the *Romanists* we should drive most of the strangers out of our country; and the greatest number of the dissenting old inhabitants, *viz.* the gentry, monied-men and boors, who continue to dwell amongst us, would become so averse to the government, that in time it would be either a means to bring this country into the hands of our enemy, or else drive those people out of the country: which cruelty would not only be pernicious, but altogether unreasonable in the rulers and reformed subjects, who always us'd to boast that they fought for their liberty, and constantly

26. [Johan de la Court,] *Pol*[*itike*] *Disc*[*oursen* (Leiden: Hackius, 1662),] lib. 4. Disc. 6[7?]. p. 320.

maintain'd, that several publick religions may be peaceably tolerated and practised in one and the same country; that true religion hath advantage enough when it's allowed to speak, *errantis poena doceri*,[27] and that there is no greater sign of a false religion (or at least of one to the truth of which men dare not trust) than to persecute the dissenters from it. So that it appears that toleration and freedom of religion is not only exceeding beneficial for our country in general, but particularly for the reformed religion, which may and ought to depend upon its own evidence and veracity.

Chapter XV

A second means to keep Holland *populous, is a plenary freedom for all people that will cohabit with us, to follow any occupation for a livelihood.*

Next to a liberty of serving God, follows the liberty of gaining a livelihood without any dear-bought city-freedom, but only by virtue of a fixed habitation to have the common right of other inhabitants: which is here very necessary for keeping the people we have, and inviting strangers to come among us. For it is self-evident that landed-men, or others that are wealthy, being forced by any accident to leave their country or habitation, will never chuse *Holland* to dwell in, being so chargeable a place, and where they have so little interest for their mony. And for those who are less wealthy, it is well known, that no man from abroad will come to dwell or continue in a country where he shall not be permitted to get an honest maintenance. And it may be easily considered how great an inconveniency it would be in this country, for the inhabitants, especially strangers, if they should have no freedom of chusing and practising such honest means of livelihood as they think best for their subsistence; or if, when they had chosen a trade, and could not live by it, they might not chuse another. This then being evident, that strangers without freedom of earning their bread, and seeking a livelihood, cannot live amongst us: and as it is certain, that our manufactures, fisheries, traffick and naviga-

27. [That punishments be taught to the wayward.]

tion, with those that depend upon them, cannot without continual supplies of foreign inhabitants be preserved here, and much less augmented or improved; it is likewise certain, that among the endless advantages which accrue to *Holland* by strangers, and which might accrue more, our boors may be likewise profited. For we see that for want of strangers in the country, the boors must give such great yearly and day-wages to their servants, that they can scarcely live but with great toil themselves, and their servants live rather in too great plenty. The same inconveniencies we are likewise sensible of in cities amongst tradesmen and servants, who are here more chargeable and burdensome, and yet less serviceable than in any other countries.

It is certain, that in all cities, tho' they invite strangers to cohabit with them, the ancient inhabitants have advantage enough by the government and its dependencies. And it is evident, that the old inhabitants, who live by their occupations, have a great advantage over the new comers, by their many relations, customers and acquaintance, most of the old manufactures, and great inland consumption: all which particulars yield the old inhabitants certain gain. But new comers leaving their own country upon any accident, and besides their moveable goods, bringing with them the knowledge of what is abounding, or wanting in their native country, and of all sorts of manufactures; they cannot live in *Holland* upon the interest of their money, nor on their real estates: so that they are compelled to lay out all their skill and estate in devising and forming of new fisheries, manufactures, traffick and navigation, with the danger of losing all they have. For he that sits idle in *Holland,* must expect to get nothing but certain and speedy poverty; but he that ventures may gain, and sometimes find out and meet with a good fishery, manufacture, merchandize or traffick: and then the other inhabitants may come in for a share in that new occupation, which is also very needful, because the old handicraft works being beaten down lower and lower in price, yield less profit. And therefore it is necessary that all strangers that are masters, journey-men, consumptioners, merchants, traders, &c. should live peaceably amongst us, without any disturbance, let, or molestation whatever, and use their own estates and trades as they shall judge best.

And tho' this will be ever detrimental to some old inhabitants, who would have all the profit, and bereave others of it, and under one pretext

or other exclude them from their trade; and therefore will alledge, that a
citizen ought to have more privilege than a stranger; yet all inhabitants
who have here a certain place of abode, or desire to have it as they are
then no strangers, but inhabitants, so ought they to be permitted, as well
as the burghers, to earn their necessary food, seeing they are in greater
want than their opposers. And it is notorious, that all people, who to the
prejudice of the common good would exclude others, that are likewise
inhabitants of this land, from the common means of subsistence, or out
of the respective cities, and for that end would have some speculiar[28]
favour from the rulers beyond the rest, are very pernicious and mischievous inhabitants: it is also certain, that a state which cannot subsist of itself, ought not to deny that strangers should live amongst them with
equal freedom with themselves, under pretence of privilege and right of
cities; nor should they exclude any strangers, but endeavour continually
to allure in new inhabitants; else such a state will fall to ruin. For the
great dangers of carrying on new designs, of being robb'd at sea, of selling their goods by factors to unknown people, on twelve months credit,
and at the same time running the hazard of all revolutions by wars and
monarchical governments against this state, and of losses among one another, are so important (yet all to be expected) that many inhabitants
concerned in the fisheries, traffick, manufactury, and consequently in
ships set out to freight, will give over their trade, and depart the country
when they have been so fortunate as to have gained any considerable estate, to seek a securer way of living elsewhere. On the other hand, we are
to consider, that there will ever be many bankrupts and forsaken trades,
both by reason of the dangers of foreign trade, and intolerable domestick
taxes, which cannot be denied by any that knows that in *Amsterdam* alone
there are yearly about three hundred abandoned or insufficient estates
registred in the chamber of accompts of that city; and therefore there are
continually many inhabitants, who finding the gain uncertain, and the
charge great, are apt to relinquish it. So that it is ever necessary that we
leave all ways open for people to subsist by, and a full liberty, as aforesaid,
to allure foreigners to dwell among us. Moreover, tho' it be not convenient in general for strangers (*i.e.* such who, tho' they dwell in *Holland,*

28. [Improper; or perhaps peculiar, i.e., exclusive.]

and have continued there some considerable time, are not natives) to partake of the government, yet is it very necessary, in order to fix them here, that we do not exclude them by laws.

Chapter XVI

That monopolizing companies and guilds, excluding all other persons from their societies, are very prejudicial to Holland.

Much less ought we to curb or restrain our citizens and natives, any more than strangers, from their natural liberty of seeking their livelihoods in their native country, by select and authoriz'd companies and guilds: for when we consider, that all the trade of our common inhabitants is circumscribed or bounded well nigh within *Europe,* and that in very many parts of the same, as *France, England, Sweden,* &c. our greatest trade and navigation thither is crampt by the high duties, or by patent companies, like those of our *Indian* societies; as also how small a part of the world *Europe* is, and how many merchants dwell in *Holland,* and must dwell there to support it; we shall have no reason to wonder, if all the beneficial traffick in these small adjacent countries be either worn out, or in a short time be glutted with an over-trade. But we may much rather wonder, why the greatest part of the world should seem unfit for our common inhabitants to trade in, and that they should continue to be debarred from it, to the end that some few persons only may have the sole benefit of it. It is certainly known that this country cannot prosper, but by means of those that are most industrious and ingenious, and that such patents or grants do not produce the ablest merchants. But on the other hand, because the grantees, whether by burghership, select companies, or guilds, think they need not fear that others, who are much more ingenious and industrious than themselves, and are not of the burghership, companies and guilds, shall lessen their profits; therefore the certain gains they reap make them dull, slow, unactive, and less inquisitive. Whereas on the other side, we say that necessity makes the old wife trot, hunger makes raw beans sweet, and poverty begets ingenuity. And besides, it is well known, now especially when *Holland* is so heavily taxed, that other less burdened people, who have no fisheries, manufactures, traffick and freight ships, cannot long subsist but by their industry, subtilty, courage, and frugality. In a word, these patent companies and guilds do certainly exclude many useful inhabitants from that trade and traffick. But those that possess those privileges with sufficient knowledge and fitness, need not fear that others that are more industrious and ingenious than themselves, shall prevent them of their profit by the exercise of the like abilities and parts; neither can it be so fully carried on and improved for the common benefit of the country, by a small number of people, as by many: so that in the mean time other people that we cannot exclude from that traffick or manufacture by means of our grants and guilds, have a great opportunity of profitably improving that which so foolishly, and with so much churlishness is prohibited to our common inhabitants. Whereas otherwise, the provident and industrious *Hollanders* would easily draw to them all foreign trade, and the making of incredibly more manufactures than we now work on. That which is objected against this is, that the *Hollanders* are a people of such a nature, that if the trade were open into *Asia, Africa,* and *America,* they would overstock all those countries with goods, and so destroy that trade to the prejudice of *Holland;* which is so far from the truth, and all appearance thereof, that it is hardly worth answering. For first, so great and mighty a trade by the *Hollanders,* in those vast and trafficking countries, would be the greatest blessing to them that could be wished for upon earth; would to God any of us could ever see *Holland* so happy. And next it cannot be denied, that even in this small *Europe,* the overstocking of countries with goods may indeed lessen the gains of some particular merchants; but yet after such a manner that the said overstocking with the said goods really is, and can be no other than an effect or fruit of a present overgrown trade of this country, in proportion to the smallness of those countries with which we are permitted to traffick. And thirdly, it is evident, that the *Hollanders* by such overstocking have never yet lost any trade in any country or place of *Europe,* nor can they lose it so long as that trade remains open, because that superfluity of goods transported is soon spent, and that same trade is by the same or some other of our merchants immediately reassumed and taken up, so soon as by a following scarcity in those countries there is any appearance of making more profit by those, or other commodities.

But supposing it to be true, that the *Dutch* merchants by overstocking those trading countries should run a risque of losing that trade in some parts; yet considering the smallness of those lands, it would then be doubly necessary to prevent the same by setting open the trade to *Asia, Africa* and *America,* for all the merchants of *Holland.* But on the other side, it is certain that the licensed monopolizing companies, by the unfaithfulness, negligence, and chargeableness of their servants, and by their vast, and consequently unmanageable designs, who are not willing to drive any trade longer than it yields excessive profit, must needs gain considerably in all their trade, or otherwise relinquish and forsake all countries that yield it not, which nevertheless would by our common inhabitants be very plentifully carried on.

In this respect it is worthy observation, that the authorized *Greenland* company made heretofore little profit by their fishing, because of the great charge of setting out their ships, and that the train-oil, blubber and whale-fins were not well made, handled, or cured; and being brought hither and put into warehouses, were not sold soon enough, nor to the company's best advantage. Whereas now that every one equips their vessels at the cheapest rate, follow their fishing diligently, and manage all carefully, the blubber, train-oil, and whale-fins are imployed for so many uses in several countries, that they can sell them with that conveniency, that tho' there are now fifteen ships for one which formerly sailed out of *Holland* on that account, and consequently each of them could not take so many whales as heretofore; and notwithstanding the new prohibition of *France,* and other countries, to import those commodities; and tho' there is greater plenty of it imported by our fishers, yet those commodities are so much raised in the value above what they were whilst there was a company, that the common inhabitants do exercise that fishery with profit to the much greater benefit of our country, than when it was (under the management of a company) carried on but by a few. It is besides very considerable, that for the most part all trades and manufactures managed by guilds in *Holland,* do sell all their goods within this country to other inhabitants who live immediately by the fisheries, manufacturies, freight ships, and traffick: so that no members of those guilds, under what pretext soever, can be countenanced or indulged in their monopoly, or charter, but by the excluding of all other inhabitants, and consequently to the hindrance of their country's prosperity. For how much soever those members sell their pains or commodities dearer than if that trade or occupation was open or free, all the other better inhabitants that gain their subsistance immediately, or by consequence by a foreign consumption, must bear that loss. And indeed our fishermen, dealers in manufactures, owners of freight-ships, and traders, being so burdened with all manner of imposts, to oppress them yet more in their necessity by these monopolies of guilds, and yet to believe that it redounds to the good of the land, because it tends to the benefit of such companies, is to me incomprehensible. These guilds are said indeed to be a useful sort of people; but next to those we call idle drones, they are the most unprofitable inhabitants of the country, because they bring in no profit from foreign lands for the welfare of the inhabitants of *Holland*. Esop hath well illustrated this folly by a cat, who first lick'd off the oil from an oiled file, and continued licking, not observing that she had by little and little lick'd her tongue thorough which was given her to sustain her life, and carry nourishment into her body, nor that she fed not on a file which did not consume, but on her own blood before her tongue was totally consumed.

On the contrary, I can see no good, nor appearance of good, which the guilds in *Holland* do produce, but only that foreign masters and journeymen artificers, having made their works abroad, and endeavouring to sell them to our inhabitants, thereby to carry the profit out of our country into their own, are herein check'd and opposed by our masters of guilds or corporations. But besides that this is more to the prejudice than advantage of the country, since by consequence our fishers, manufacturers, traders, and owners of ships let to freight, are thereby bereft of the freedom of buying their necessaries at the cheapest rate they can; it is also evident, that this feeding of foreigners upon the *Hollander* would be more strenuously and profitably opposed and prevented, in case all handicraft work and occupations were permitted to be made, sold and practised by all, and no other people, except such as have their settled habitations in this country.

3

A New Discourse of Trade
1668

JOSIAH CHILD (1630–99) was born in Lincoln, the second son of the
merchant Richard Child. Beginning as a merchant-apprentice, he was by
1655 furnishing stores for the Navy in Portsmouth, where he remained for
many years. He also became a Member of Parliament for various elec-
tion districts in 1659, from 1673 to 1678, and from 1685 to 1687. He received
a baronetcy in 1678. His association with the East India Company was
long and profitable. He became a director in 1677, was deputy-governor
from 1684 to 1686 and again from 1688 to 1690, and was governor from
1681 to 1683 and 1686 to 1688. By 1683, his fortune was said to be in the
vicinity of 200,000 pounds. He attempted to imitate the Dutch in en-
hancing the political power of the Company, collaborating with his
brother, the military governor of Britain's Indian settlements, toward
this end. When his brother's successor talked of governing by strict rule
of law, Child is reported to have said that English laws were "a heap of
nonsense, compiled by a few ignorant country gentlemen, who hardly
knew how to make laws for the good government of their own families,
much less for the regulation of companies and foreign commerce." His
enemies accused him of bribery both at Court and at Westminster Hall.
A New Discourse of Trade, whose introduction is reproduced here, was
written in 1665 and first published in 1668. It is notable for its discussion
of money and interest rates, and for its enumeration of the keys to Dutch
commercial success, among other things. Its argument for a low statu-
tory interest rate was attacked by John Locke in his 1692 tract "Some

Considerations of the Consequences of the Lowering of Interest." Some
of its specific recommendations—on poor relief, for example—were
adopted. It had a deep influence on eighteenth-century writers such as
Vincent de Gournay and Turgot (see chapter 29 in this volume).

The edition used here is *A New Discourse of Trade* (1690; reprint,
Foulis, 1751). The Introduction, a free-standing essay, is reproduced in its
entirety. All notes are by the present editor.

A New Discourse of Trade

The prodigious increase of the Netherlanders in their domestic and foreign trade, riches, and multitude of shipping, is the envy of the present,
and may be the wonder of future generations: and yet the means whereby
they have thus advanced themselves, are sufficiently obvious, and in a
great measure imitable by most other nations, but more easily by us of
this kingdom of England, which I shall endeavour to demonstrate in the
following discourse.

Some of the said means by which they have advanced their trade, and
thereby improved their estates, are these following,

First, They have in their greatest councils of state and war, trading-
merchants that have lived abroad in most parts of the world; who have
not only the theoretical knowledge, but the practical experience of trade;
by whom laws and orders are contrived, and peaces with foreign princes
projected, to the great advantage of their trade.

Secondly, Their law of gavel-kind,[1] whereby all their children possess
an equal share of their fathers estates after their decease, and so are not

---

1. [Johnson's Dictionary reports that the custom is in force in various parts of England, but especially in Kent. See Silas Taylor, *The History of Gavel-kind* (London: John
Starkey, 1663; repr. 1970).]

left to wrestle with the world in their youth, with inconsiderable assistance of fortune, as most of our youngest sons of gentlemen in England are, who are bound apprentices to merchants.

Thirdly, Their exact making of all their native commodities, and packing of their herring, codfish, and all other commodities, which they send abroad in great quantities; the consequence of which is, that the repute of their said commodities abroad, continues always good, and the buyers will accept of them by the marks, without opening; whereas the fish which our English make in Newfoundland and New-England, and herrings at Yarmouth, often prove false and deceitfully made; and our pilchards[2] from the west-country false packed seldom contain the quantity for which the hogsheads are marked in which they are packed.

And in England the attempts which our forefathers made for regulating of manufactures, when left to the execution of some particular person, in a short time resolved but into a tax upon the commodity, without respect to the goodness of it; as most notoriously appears in the business of the AULNAGE,[3] which doubtless our predecessors intended for a scrutiny into the goodness of the commodity; and to that purpose a seal was invented, as a signal that the commodity was made according to the statutes, which seals, it is said, may now be bought by thousands, and put upon what the buyers please.

Fourthly, Their giving great encouragement and immunities to the inventors of new manufactures, and the discoverers of any new mysteries in trade, and to those that shall bring the commodities of other nations first in use and practice amongst them; for which the author never goes without his due reward allowed him at the public charge.

Fifthly, Their contriving and building of great ships to sail with small charge, not above one third of what we are at, for ships of the same burthen in England; and compelling their said ships, being of small force to sail always in fleets, to which in all time of danger they allow convoy.

Sixthly, Their parsimonious and thrifty living, which is so extraordinary,

2. [Also pilcher; a herring-like fish caught in Cornwall.]
3. [See also Edward Misselden, *Free Trade, or The Meanes to Make Trade Florish* (London: Legatt, 1622).]

that a merchant of one hundred thousand pounds estate with them, will scarce expend so much per cent. as one of fifteen hundred pounds estate in London.

Seventhly, The education of their children, as well daughters as sons; all which, be they of never so great quality or estate, they always take care to bring up to write perfect good hands, and to have the full knowledge and use of arithmetic and merchants accounts; the well understanding and practice of which, does strangely infuse into most that are the owners of that quality, of either sex, not only an ability for commerce of all kinds, but a strong aptitude, love, and delight in it; and in regard the women are as knowing therein as the men, it does encourage their husbands to hold on their trades to their dying days, knowing the capacity of their wives to get in their estates, and carry on their trades after their deaths: whereas if a merchant in England arrive at any considerable estate, he commonly withdraws his estate from trade, before he comes near the confines of old age; reckoning that if God should call him out of the world, while the main of his estate is engaged abroad in trade, he must lose one third of it, through the unexperience and unaptness of his wife to such affairs; and so it usually falls out.

Besides, it has been observed in the nature of arithmetic, that like other parts of the mathematics, it does not only improve the rational faculties, but inclines those that are expert in it to thriftiness and good husbandry, and prevents both husbands and wives in some measure in running out of their estates, when they have it always in their heads what their expences do amount to, and how soon by that course their ruin must overtake them.

Eightly, The lowness of their customs, and the height of their excise, which is certainly the most equal and indifferent tax in the world, and least prejudicial to any people, as might be made appear, were it the subject of this discourse.

Ninthly, The careful providing for, and employment of their poor, which it is easy to demonstrate can never be done in England comparatively to what it is with them, while it is left to the care of every parish to look after their own only.

Tenthly, Their use of banks, which are of so immense advantage to them, that some not without good grounds have estimated the profit of them to the public, to amount to at least one million of pounds sterling per annum.

Eleventhly, Their toleration of different opinions in matters of religion: by reason of which many industrious people of other countries, that dissent from the established government of their churches, resort to them with their families and estates, and after a few years co-habitation with them, become of the same common interest.

Twelfthly, Their law-merchant, by which all controversies between merchants and tradesmen are decided in three or four days time, and that not at the fortieth part, I might say in many cases not the hundredth part, of the charge they are with us.

Thirteenthly, The law that is in use among them for transferring of bills for debt from one man to another: this is of extraordinary advantage to them in their commerce; by means of which, they can turn their stocks twice or thrice in trade, for once that we can in England; because having sold our foreign goods here, we cannot buy again to advantage, till we are possest of our money; which perhaps, we shall be six, nine, or twelve months in recovering: and if what we sell be considerable, it is a good man's work all the year to be following vintners and shopkeepers for money, whereas, were the law for transferring bills in practice with us, we could presently after sale of our goods, dispose of our bills, and close up our accounts, to do which, the advantage, ease, and accommodations it would be to trade, is so great, that none but merchants who have lived where that custom is in use, can value to its due proportion.

Fourteenthly, Their keeping up public registers of all lands and houses, sold or mortgaged, whereby many chargeable law-suits are prevented, and the securities of lands and houses rendred indeed, such as we commonly call, real securities.

Lastly, The lowness of interest of money, with them, which in peaceable times exceeds not three per cent. per annum; and is now during this war with England,[4] not above four per cent. at most.

Some more particulars might be added, and those aforesaid further improved, were it my purpose to discourse at large of trade, but most of the former particulars are observed and granted by all men that make it

4. [I.e., the Second Anglo-Dutch War, 1665–67.]

any part of their business to inspect the true nature and principles of trade; but the last is not so much as taken notice of by the most ingenious, to be any cause of the great increase of the riches and commerce of that people.

I shall therefore in this paper confine myself to write principally my observations touching that, viz.

The profit that people have received, and any other may receive, by reducing the interest of money to a very low rate.

This, in my poor opinion, is the CAUSA CAUSANS of all the other causes of the riches of that people; and that if interest of money were with us reduced to the same rate it is with them, it would in a short time render us as rich and considerable in trade as they now are, and consequently be of greater damage to them, and advantage to us, than can happen by the issue of this present war, though the success of it should be as good as we could wish, except it end in their total ruin and extirpation.

To illustrate this, let us impartially search our books, and enquire in what the state and condition of this kingdom was, as to trade and riches, before any law concerning the interest of money was made: the first of which that I can find, was anno 1545. and we shall be informed that the trade in England then was inconsiderable, and the merchants very mean and few: and that afterwards, viz. anno 1635. within ten years after interest was brought down to eight per cent. there were more merchants to be found upon the exchange worth each one thousand pounds and upward, than were in the formers days, viz. before the year 1600. to be found worth one hundred pounds each.

And now since interest has been for about twenty years at six per cent. notwithstanding our long civil wars, and the great complaints of the deadness of trade, there are more men to be found upon the exchange now worth ten thousand pounds estates, than were then of one thousand pounds.

And if this be doubted, let us ask the aged, whether five hundred pounds portion with a daughter sixty years ago, were not esteemed a larger portion than two thousand pounds now: and whether gentlewomen in those days would not esteem themselves well cloathed in a serge gown, which a chamber-maid now will be ashamed to be seen in:

whether our citizens and middle sort of gentry now are not more rich in cloaths, plate, jewels, and houshold goods, &c. than the best sort of knights and gentry were in those days. And whether our best sort of knights and gentry now do not exceed by much in those things the nobility of England sixty years past: many of whom then would not go to the price of a whole satten doublet; the embroiderer being yet living, who has assured me he has made many hundreds of them for the nobility with canvas backs.

Which way ever we take our measures, to me it seems evident, that since our first abatement of interest, the riches and splendor of this kingdom is increased to above four, I might say above six, times so much as it was.

We have now almost one hundred coaches for one we had formerly, we with ease can pay a greater tax now in one year, than our fore-fathers could in twenty.

Our customs are very much improved, I believe above the proportion aforesaid, of six to one; which is not so much in advance of the rates of goods, as by increase of the bulk of trade; for though some foreign commodities are advanced, others of our native commodities and manufactures are considerably abated, by the last book of rates.

I can myself remember since there were not in London used so many wharfs or keys for the landing of merchants goods, by at least one third part as now there are; and those that were then, could scarce have employment for half what they could do; and now notwithstanding one third more used to the same purpose, they are all too little in a time of peace, to land the goods at, which come to London.

If we look into the country, we shall find lands as much improved since the abatement of interest, as trade, &c. in cities; that now yielding twenty years purchase, which then would not have sold for above eight or ten at most.

Besides, the rent of farms have been for these last thirty years much advanced; and altho' they have for these three or four last years fallen, that has no respect at all to the lowness of interest at present, nor to the other mistaken reasons which are commonly assigned for it.

But principally to the vast improvement of Ireland, since a great part of it was lately possessed by the industrious English, who were soldiers in the late army, and the late great land taxes.

More might be said, but the premises being considered, I judge will sufficiently demonstrate how greatly this kingdom of England has been advanced in all respects for these last fifty years: and that the abatement of interest has been the cause of it, to me seems most probable; because as it appears, it has been in England, so I find it is at this day in all Europe and other parts of the world; insomuch that to know whether any country be rich or poor, or in what proportion it is so, no other question needs to be resolved, but this, viz. what interest do they pay for money?

Near home we see it evidently, in Scotland and Ireland, where ten and twelve per cent. is paid for interest; the people are poor and despicable, their persons ill clothed, their houses worse provided, and money intolerable scarce, notwithstanding they have great plenty of all provisions, nor will their land yield above eight or ten years purchase at most.

In France where money is at seven per cent. their lands will yield about eighteen years purchase; and the gentry who possess lands, live in good condition, tho' the peasants are little better than slaves, because they can possess nothing but at the will of others.

In Italy money will not yield above three per cent. to be let out upon real security; there the people are rich, full of trade, well attired, and their lands will sell at thirty five to forty years purchase; and that it is so, or better with them in Holland, is too manifest.

In Spain the usual interest is ten and twelve per cent. and there, notwithstanding they have the only trade in the world for gold and silver, money is no where more scarce; the people poor, despicable, and void of commerce, other than such as the English, Dutch, Italians, Jews, and other foreigners bring to them; who are to them in effect, but as leeches, who suck their blood and vital spirits from them.

I might urge many other instances of this nature, not only out of Christendom, but from under the Turks dominions, East-India and America: but every man by his experience in foreign countries, may easily inform himself, whether this rule does universally hold true or not: for my part, to satisfy my own curiosity, I have for some years, as occasion offered, diligently enquired of all my acquaintance that had knowledge of foreign countries, and I can truly say that I never found it to fail in any particular instance.

Now if upon what has been said, it be granted that de facto, this kingdom is richer at least four-fold, I might say eight fold, than it was before any law for interest was made, and that all countries are at this day richer or poorer in an exact proportion to what they pay, and have usually paid for the interest of money; it remains that we enquire carefully, whether the abatement of interest be in truth the cause of the riches of any country, or only the concomitant or effect of the riches of a country; in which seems to lie the intricacy of this question.

To satisfy myself in which, I have taken all opportunities to discourse this point with the most ingenious men I had the honour to be known to, and have searched for, and read all the books that I could ever hear were printed against the abatement of interest, and seriously considered all the arguments and objections used by them against it; all which have tended to confirm me in this opinion, which I humbly offer to the consideration of wiser heads, viz. that the abatement of interest is the cause of the prosperity and riches of any nation, and that the bringing down of interest in this kingdom from 6 to 4, or 3 per cent. will necessarily, in less than twenty years time, double the capital stock of the nation.

The most material objections I have met with against it are as follows:

Object. 1. To abate interest, will cause the Dutch and other people that have money put out at interest in England, by their friends and factors, to call home their estates, and consequently will occasion a great scarcity and want of money amongst us.

To this I answer, that if interest be brought to 4 per cent. no Dutchman will call in his money that is out upon good security in England, because he cannot make above 3 per cent. of it upon interest at home. But if they should call home all the money they have with us at interest, it would be better for us than if they did it not; for the borrower is always a slave to the lender, and shall be sure to be always kept poor, while the other is fat and full: he that uses a stock that is none of his own, being forced for the upholding his reputation to live to the full, if not above the proportion of what he does so use, while the lender possessing much, and using little or none, lives only at the charge of what he uses, and not of what he has.

Besides, if with this law for abatement of interest, a law for transferring bills of debt should pass, we should not miss the Dutch money, were it ten times as much as it is amongst us; for such a law will certainly supply the defect of at least one half of all the ready money we have in use in the nation.

Object. 2. If interest be abated, land must rise in purchase, and consequently rents; and if rents, then the fruits of the land; and so all things will be dear, and how shall the poor live? &c.

Ans. To this I say, if it follow that the fruits of our land, in consequence of such a law for abatement of interest, grow generally dear, it is an evident demonstration that our people grow richer; for generally, wherever provisions are for continuance of years dear in any country, the people are rich; and where they are most cheap throughout the world, for the most part the people are very poor.

And for our own poor in England, it is observed, that they live better in the dearest countries for provisions, than in the cheapest, and better in a dear year than in a cheap, especially in relation to the public good, for in a cheap year they will not work above two days in a week; their humour being such, that they will not provide for a hard time, but just work so much and no more, as may maintain them in that mean condition to which they have been accustomed.

Object. 3. If interest be abated, usurers will call in their money; so what shall gentlemen do, whose estates are mortgaged? &c.

Answ. I answer, that when they know they can make no more of their money by taking out of one, and putting it into another hand, they will not be so forward as they threaten, to alter that security they know is good, for another that may be bad: or if they should do it, our laws are not so severe, but that gentlemen may take time to dispose of part of their land, which immediately after such a law will yield them thirty years purchase at least; and much better it is for them so to do, than to abide longer under that consuming plague of usury, which has insensibly destroyed very many of the best families in England, as well of our nobility as gentry.

Object. 4. As interest is now at 6 per cent. the king's majesty upon any emergency can hardly be supplied; and if it should be reduced to 4 per cent. how shall the king find a considerable sum of money to be lent him by his people?

Answ. I answer, the abatement of interest to the people, is the abatement of interest to the king, when he has occasion to take up money; for what is borrowed of the city of London, or other bodies politic, nothing can be demanded but the legal interest; and if the king have occasion to take up money of private persons, seeing his majesty, according to good right, is above the common course of law, the king must, and always has given more than the legal rate. As for instance; the legal rate is now 6 per cent. but his majesty, or such as have disposed of his majesty's exchequer-tallies, have been said to give ten and twelve in some cases; and if the legal rate were 10, his majesty might probably give 13 or 14; so if interest be brought to 4 per cent. his majesty in such cases as he now gives 10, must give but 6 or 7; by which his majesty would have a clear advantage.

Object. 5. If interest be abated, it will be a great prejudice to widows and orphans, who have not knowledge and abilities to improve their estates otherwise.

Answ. I answer, that by our law now, heirs and orphans can recover no interest from their parents executors, except it be left fully and absolutely to the executors to dispose and put out money at the discretion of the executors, for the profit and loss of the heirs and orphans; and if it be so left to the executors discretion, they may improve the monies left them in trade, or purchase of lands and leases, as well as by interest; or when not, the damage such heirs and orphans will sustain in their minority, being but two per cent. is inconsiderable, in respect of the great advantage that will accrue to the nation in general, by such abatement of interest.

Besides, when such a law is made, and in use, all men will so take care in their life to provide for and educate their children, and instruct their wives, as that no prejudice can happen thereby, as we see there does not in Holland and Italy, and other places where interest is so low.

Having now offered my thoughts in answer to the aforesaid objections, it will not be amiss that we enquire who will be advantaged, and who will receive prejudice, in case such a law be made.

First, his majesty, as has been said in answer to that objection, will, when he has occasion, take up money on better terms. Besides which, he will receive a great augmentation to his revenue thereby, all his lands being immediately worth, after the making such a law, double to what they were before; his customs will be much increased by the increase of trade, which must necessarily ensue from the making such a law.

The nobility and gentry, whose estates lie mostly in land, may presently upon all they have, instead of fifty write one hundred.

The merchants and tradesmen, who bear the heat and burthen of the day, (most of our trade being carried on by young men that take up money at interest) will find their yoke sit lighter upon their shoulders, and be encouraged to go on with greater alacrity in their business.

Our mariners, shipwrights, porters, clothiers, packers, and all sorts of labouring people that depend on trade, will be more constantly and fully employed.

Our farmers will sell the product of their lands at better rates. And whereas our neighbours, the Netherlanders (who in regard of the largeness of their stocks and experiences, the sons continually succeeding the fathers in trade to many generations, we may not unfitly in this case term sons of Anach, and men of renown)[5] against whom we fight dwarfs and pigmies in stocks and experience, being younger brothers of gentlemen that seldom have above one thousand pounds, sometimes not two hundred to begin the world with: instead, I say, of such young men and small stocks, if this law pass, we shall bring forth our Sampsons and Goliaths in stocks, subtilty, and experience in trade to cope with our potent adversaries on the other side, there being to every man's knowledge that understands the exchange of London, divers English merchants of large estates, who have not much past their middle age, and yet have wholly left off their trades, having found the sweetness of interest, which if that should abate, must again set their hands to the plough, which they are as able to hold and govern now as ever, and also will engage them to train up their sons in the same way, because it will not be so easy to make them country gentlemen as now it is, when lands sell at thirty or forty years purchase.

For the sufferers by such a law, I know none but idle persons that live at as little expence as labour, neither scattering by their expences, so as the poor may glean any thing after them, nor working with their hands or heads to bring either wax or honey to the common hive of the kingdom; but swelling their own purses by the sweat of other mens brows, and the contrivances of other mens brains. And how unprofitable it is for any nation to suffer idleness to suck the breast of industry, needs no demonstration. And if it be granted me, that these will be the effects of

5. [I.e., giants; cf. Numbers 13:33.]

an abatement of interest, then I think it is out of doubt, that the abatement of interest does tend to the enriching of a nation, and consequently has been one great cause of the riches of the Dutch and Italians, and the increase of the riches of our own kingdom in these last fifty years.

Another argument to prove which, we may draw from the nature of interest itself, which is of so prodigious a multiplying nature, that it must of necessity make the lenders monstrous rich, if they live at any moderate expence, and the borrowers extream poor; a memorable instance of which we have in old Audley deceased, who did wisely observe, that one hundred pounds only, put out at interest at 10 per cent. does in seventy years, which is but the age of a man, increase to above one hundred thousand pounds; and if the advantage be so great to the lender, the loss must be greater to the borrower, who, as has been said, lives at a much larger expence. And as it is between private persons, so between nation and nation, that have communication one with another. For whether the subjects of one nation lend money to subjects of another, or trade with them for goods, the effect is the same. As for example, a Dutch merchant that has but four or five thousand pounds clear stock of his own, can easily borrow and have credit for fifteen thousand pounds more at 3 per cent. at home; with which, whether he trade or put it to use in England, or any country where interest of money is high, he must necessarily, without very evil accidents attend him, in a very few years treble his own capital.

This discovers the true cause, why the sugar-bakers of Holland can afford to give a greater price for Barbadoes sugars in London, besides the second freight and charges upon them between England and Holland, and yet grow exceeding rich upon their trade; whereas our sugar-bakers in London, that buy sugars here at their own doors, before such additional freight and charges come upon them, can scarce live upon their callings; ours here paying for a good share of their stocks 6 per cent. and few of them employ in their sugar works above six to ten thousand pounds at most; whereas in Holland they employ twenty, thirty, to forty thousand pounds stock in a sugar-house, paying but 3 per cent. at most for what they take up at interest, to fill up their said stocks, which is sometimes half, sometimes three quarters of their whole stocks. And as it is with this trade, the same rule holds throughout all other trades whatsoever. And for us to say, if the Dutch put their money to interest among us, we shall have the advantage, by being full and flush of coin at home, it is a mere chimera, and so far from an advantage, that it is an extream loss, rendring us only in the condition of a young gallant, that has newly mortgaged his land, and with the money thereby raised, stuffs his pockets, and looks big for a time, not considering that the draught of cordial he hath received, though it be at present grateful to his palate, does indeed prey upon his vital spirits, and will in a short time render the whole body of his estate in a deep consumption, if not wholly consumed. Besides, whatever money the Dutch lend us, they always keep one end of the chain at home in their own hands, by which they can pull back when they please their lean kine,[6] which they send hither to be fatted.

This makes me conclude that Moses, that wise legislator, in his forbidding the Jews to lend money at use one to another, and permitting them to lend their money to strangers, ordained that law as much to a political as a religious intent, knowing that by the latter they should enrich their own nation, and by the former no public good could ensue. The consequence being only to impoverish one Jew to make another rich.

This likewise takes off the wonder how the people of Israel, out of so small a territory as they possessed, could upon all occasions set forth such vast and numerous armies, almost incredible, as all histories, sacred and prophane, report they did; which is neither impossible nor strange to any that have well considered the effects of their laws concerning usury, which were sufficient to make any barren land fruitful, and a fruitful land an entire garden, which by consequence would maintain ten times the number of inhabitants that the same tract of land would do where no such laws were.

To conclude, it is, I think, agreed on by all, that merchants, artificers, farmers of land, and such as depend on them, which for brevity-sake we may here include under one of these general terms, viz. seamen, fishermen, breeders of cattle, gardiners, &c. are the three sorts of people who by their study and labour do principally, if not only, bring in wealth to a nation from abroad; other kinds of people, viz. nobility, gentry, lawyers, physicians, scholars of all sorts, and shopkeepers, do only hand it from one to another at home. And if abatement of interest, besides the general

6. [Cows.]

benefit it brings to all, except the griping dronish usurer, will add new life and motion to those most profitable engines of the kingdom, as I humbly suppose, will be manifest upon serious consideration of what has been said; then I think it will be out of doubt, that the abatement of interest is the cause of the increase of the trade and riches of any kingdom.

Supplement

The foregoing discourse I wrote in the sickness-summer at my country habitation, not then intending to publish it, but only to communicate it to some honourable and ingenious friends of the present parliament, who were pleased to take copies of it for their own deliberate consideration, and digestion of the principles therein asserted; which at first were strange to them, as I expect they will be to most others, till they have spent some time in thinking on them; after which, I doubt not but that all men will be convinced of the truth of them, that have not some private interest of their own against them, external to the general good of the kingdom. For sure I am they have a foundation in nature, and that according to the excellent Sir William Petty's observation in his last discourse, concerning taxes, "res nolent male administrare:" nature must and will have its course, the matter in England is prepared for an abatement of interest, and it cannot long be obstructed; and after the next abatement, whoever lives forty years longer, shall see a second abatement; for we shall never stand on even ground in trade with the Dutch, till interest be the same with us as it is with them.

His majesty was graciously pleased at the opening of the last session of this parliament, to propose to the consideration of both houses, the ballancing of the trade of the nation; to effect which, in my opinion, the abatement of interest is the first and principal engine which ought to be set on work, which notwithstanding, I should not have presumed to expose to public censure, on my own single opinion, if I had not had the concurrences of much better judgments than my own; having never seen any thing in print for it, though much against it, until the latter end of January last; at which time, a friend whom I had often discoursed with upon this subject, met with by accident a small tract to the same purpose, wrote near fifty years ago, which he gave me, and I have, for the public good, thought fit to annex it hereunto verbatim.

The author of the said tract, by its stile, seems to have been a country gentleman, and my education has mostly been that of a merchant, so I hope, that going together, they may in some measure, supply the defect of each other.

Another reason that induced me to the printing of them together, is, because what he wrote then, would be the consequence of the abatement of interest from 10 to 6 per cent. I have, I think, fully proved to the conviction of all men not wilfully blind, they have been the real effects of it, and that to a greater proportion than he did promise; every paragraph of which is written by me, and copies of it delivered to several worthy members of this parliament, many months before ever I saw or heard of this, or any thing else written or printed to the like purpose.

What I have aimed at in the whole, is the good of my native country, otherwise I had not busied my self about it; for I want not employment sufficient of my own, nor have reason to be out of love with that I have.

The several particulars in the beginning of this treatise, relating to trade, I have only hinted in general terms; hoping that some abler pen will hereafter be incited for the service of his king and country, to enlarge more particularly upon them.

Before I conclude, though I have studied brevity in the whole, I cannot omit the inserting of one objection more, which I have lately met with, to the main design of this treatise, viz.

Object. It is said that the lowness of interest of money in Holland, is not the effect of the laws, but proceeds only from their abundance of coin; for that in Holland, there is no law limiting the rate of usury.

Answ. I answer, that it may be true, that in Holland there has not lately been any law, to limit usury to the present rate it is now at, i.e. 3 or 4 per cent. Altho' most certain it is, that many years since, there was a law that did limit it to 5 or 6 at most: and by consequence, there would be a renewing of that law to a lesser rate, were it necessary at this time; it having always been the policy of that people to keep down the interest of their money, 3 or 4 per cent. under the rate of what is usually paid in their neighbouring countries, which, being now naturally done, it is needless to use the artificial stratagem of a law to establish.

Answ. 2. Although they have no law expresly limiting interest at present, yet they have other laws which we cannot yet arrive to, and those do effect the same thing among them, and would do the like among us, if we could have them: one of which, is their ascertaining real securities by their public registers: for we see evidently, money is not so much wanting in England as securities, which men account infallible; a remarkable instance of which is, the east-India company, who can and do take up what money they please, for 4 per cent. at any time.

Another law is, their constitutions of Banks and Lumbards, whereby private persons that have but tolerable credit may be supplied at easy rates from the state.

A third, and very considerable one, is, their law for transferring bills of debt, mentioned in the beginning of this discourse.

A fourth, which is a custom, and in effect may be here to our purpose accounted as a law, is the extraordinary frugality used in all their public affairs, which in their greatest extremities have been such, as not to compel them to give above four per cent for the loan of money. Whereas it is said, his majesty in some cases of exigency, when the national supplies have not come in to answer the present emergencies of affairs, has been enforced to give above the usual rates to goldsmiths; and that encouraged them to take up great sums from private persons at the full rate of 6 per cent. whereas formerly they usually gave but 4 per cent. Otherwise, in human probability money would have fallen of itself to 4 per cent.

But again, to conclude, every nation does proceed according to the peculiar methods of their own in the transactions of their public affairs and law-making: and in this kingdom it has always been the custom to reduce the rate of interest by a law, when nature had prepared the matter fit for such an alteration, as now I say it has. By a law it was reduced from an unlimited rate, to 10; and afterwards from 10 to 8; and after that from 8 to 6. And through the blessing of almighty God, this kingdom has found, as I think I have fully proved, and every man's experience will witness, prodigious success and advantage thereby. And I doubt not, through the like blessing of God almighty, but this generation will find the like great and good effects, by the reduction of it from 6 to 4, which is now at the birth. And that the next generation will yet see far greater advantages by bringing it from 4 to 3 per cent.

4

Moral Essays
1671

PIERRE NICOLE (1625–95) was born into a respectable family of the legal *bourgeoisie* in Chartres. Moving to Paris for his studies, he entered the Jansenist (Augustinian) religious community of Port-Royal, where he was made an instructor. He became a tonsured cleric, stopping short of a full theology degree upon the outbreak of polemic over the Five Propositions of the Jansenists in 1649. He collaborated with the Jansenist Antoine Arnauld and with Pascal in the 1650s, and he aided the latter in composing his *Lettres provinciales*. A strong defender of the Jansenists in public, he tried to temper and moderate their views in private. After the death of the important Jansenist patroness the Duchess of Longueville in 1677, Nicole traveled abroad to Brussels, Liège, and elsewhere for some time, employing many pseudonyms along the way. Spurning Arnauld's invitation to join him in Holland, Nicole—ill and tired in 1679—approached the Archbishop of Paris about returning to France, which he did, to the consternation of the Jansenists, in May 1683. It was then that he turned his attention to the multivolume *Essais de morale*, his most important work, from which the accompanying excerpts are taken. The *Essais de morale* is a polyglot series of reflections on a whole range of moral, social, psychological, and political subjects that have increasingly attracted the favorable attention of modern scholars. His innumerable other works include mainly polemics and works of theology.

The excerpts here are taken from *Essais de morale* (Paris: Desprez, 1733–71; reprint, Geneva: Slatkine, 1971), vol. 1, pp. 193–96 and 261–63;

and vol. 2, pp. 116–18, 36–44, and 55–58. They have been chosen to illustrate both a metaphorical use of the language of "commerce" in a work of moral theory, and a Jansenist view of modern trends in technology and global trade. The unbracketed note is by Nicole; material in brackets is by the editor.

Moral Essays

Vol. 1: On Ways to Keep the Peace with Men

First part

Querite pacem civitatis ad quam transmigrare vos feci: & orate pro ea ad Dominum, quia in pace illius erit pax vobis.

"And seek the peace of the city whither I have caused you to be carried away captives, and pray unto the Lord for it, for in the peace thereof shall ye have peace." (Jer. 29, v. 7)

Chapter I

On men who are citizens of several cities: how they must bring peace to all of them, and strive in particular to live in peace with the society to which they belong and in which they spend their lives.

All the societies we belong to—all the things we have some relation or commerce° with, upon which we act, or which act upon us, and whose varying states are capable of altering the disposition of our souls—are the cities where we spend the time of our pilgrimage; for our souls find both occupation and peace there.

Hence the whole world is our city, since as inhabitants of the world, we have relations with every man; sometimes we benefit from it, and sometimes we suffer harm from it. The Dutch have commerce with the Japanese. We have commerce with the Dutch. So we have commerce with these peoples who live at the very ends of the world; for the advantages the Dutch draw from this enable them either to be useful to us, or to do us harm. One can say as much of any other people. They are all attached to us at some point, and they are all part of the chain linking together all men with the mutual needs they have of one another.

But we are even more especially the citizens of the kingdom where we were born, and where we live; of the city we inhabit; of the society we belong to. And finally, we may say of ourselves, as it were, that we are the citizens of ourselves and of our own hearts. For our various passions and our various thoughts are like a people with which we have to live; and it is often easier to live with the whole external world than with this inner people we carry within ourselves.

The Scripture which obliges us to seek the peace of the city where God has caused us to live, refers also to all those different cities. In other words, it obliges us to seek and desire the peace and tranquillity of the whole world, our kingdom, our city, our society, and ourselves. But since we are more capable of bringing peace to some of these cities than to others, we must strive for that in diverse ways.

Indeed there is scarcely anyone that could bring peace either to the world, or to kingdoms, or to cities, other than by their prayers. Hence our duty in this matter merely consists in sincerely asking [peace] from God, and in believing that we have to do so. And we have to do so indeed, because the external upheavals dividing kingdoms are often due to the carelessness with which those belonging to them ask peace from God—as well as to the fact that they show little gratitude when God has granted it to them.

Worldly wars have such strange sequels and such disastrous effects upon the soul itself, that they could never be feared enough. That is why Saint Paul, as he urges us to pray for the kings of the world, clearly states as a principle of that obligation the need we ourselves have of external tranquillity: *ut quietam & tranquillam vitam agamus.* (1 Tim. 2:1–2)

One brings peace to oneself thanks to the ordering of one's thoughts and passions. And with this internal peace, one contributes much to the peace of the society in which one lives; for hardly anything but passions disrupt it. But because this peace we keep with those bound to us through closer ties and through a more frequent commerce° is extremely important to have us keep the peace within ourselves; and because this peace can be disrupted by nothing but the discord opposed to it, it has to be the one mainly referred to in the prophet's precept: *Quaerite pacem civitatis ad quam transmigrare vos feci.* Seek the peace of the city which is the place of your exile. (Jer. 29:7)

Chapter XV

On the fundamental reasons why civility is a duty.

Men believe that civility is due them, and indeed it is due them the way it is practiced in the world; but they do not know the reason why. If they had no other right to require it than that given by custom, they would not be entitled to it; for it is not enough to bind others to perform certain tedious tasks. One must go further back to the source, as is the case when gratitude is concerned. And if it is true, as a man of God puts it, that there is no one as civil as a good Christian, there must be some divine reasons for it, and what we are about to say may help to uncover them.

Let us therefore consider that men are bound together by an infinity of needs, which oblige them to live in society by necessity—no one being able to do without others. And this society is in accordance with the order of God, because it allows such needs to [fulfill] this end. So everything that is necessary to preserve this society belongs to that order, which is, as it were, under God's command, thanks to this natural law compelling each part to preserve its whole. Now, in order for the society of men to survive, it is absolutely necessary that they love and respect one another; for contempt and hatred are sure causes of disunity. There are an infinity of small things which are extremely necessary for us to live, and can be given for free; and which cannot be traded so that they can be purchased only by love. Besides, this society is composed of men who love themselves, and who are full of self-complacency, so that, if they are not careful to please and treat one another gently, they will end up forming a bunch of people who will be discontented with one another, and who will not be able to remain united. But since the love and esteem we have for one another cannot be seen, men have taken it into their heads to establish between them certain duties, which would testify to their respect and affection. And it necessarily arises from this that to neglect these duties is to express a disposition opposed to love and respect. Therefore, we owe those external actions to the people to whom we owe the disposition they express. And we offend them when we neglect them, for this omission expresses feelings we should not be having towards them.

So one can and one even must be punctilious in performing the duties of civility men have established. And the reasons for that are not only just, but they are also founded on the law of God. One must do so in order to avoid giving the impression that one feels contempt or indifference towards those for whom one will not perform these duties; to preserve human society, to which it is only fair that everyone contributes, since everyone draws considerable advantages from it; and finally, to avoid the internal or external rebukes of those towards whom one would not perform these duties, for those rebukes are the sources of the divisions disrupting the tranquillity of life and the Christian peace dealt with in this discourse.

Vol. 2: On Christian Civility

Chapter I

How self-love produces civility.

There is nothing more natural for men than the desire to be loved by others, because there is nothing more natural than to love oneself. Now one always wants what one loves to be loved. Charity, which loves God, wishes God to be loved by all creatures; and cupidity, which loves itself, would wish us to be loved by all men.

We wish to be loved in order to love ourselves even more. The love others feel towards us leads us to regard ourselves as worthier of love, and the mental picture we have of ourselves presents itself to us in a more agreeable way. We are most pleased that they judge us as we judge our-selves, because our judgement, which is weak and timid when it stands by itself, becomes more assured when it is supported by that of others; and thus one attaches it to oneself with all the more delight as it is less troubled by the fear of being mistaken.

But the love others feel for us is not only the object of our vanity and the nourishment of our self-esteem; it is also where our weakness lies. Our soul is so languid and weak that it could not possibly remain strong, if it were not, as it were, supported by the approval and love of men. And this may be easily acknowledged when one imagines a situation in which everyone would condemn us, in which no one would consider us except with hatred and contempt, in which all men in general were to forget about us. For who could bear this sight without feeling horror, despon-dency, and despair? Now if this sight is a cause of despondency for us, it must be that the opposite sight is of some support to us—without our even thinking about it.

Since the love of men is so necessary to support us, we are naturally drawn to seek it and obtain it. And because we know by experience that we love those who love us, either we love or we pretend to love others in order to attract their affection in return. It is the foundation of human civility, which is only a sort of commerce° of self-love, in which one en-deavours to arouse the love of others by displaying some affection to-wards them.

Those displays of affection are usually false and excessive; in other words, one displays more affection than one feels, because the self-love which attaches us to ourselves, quite diverts us from the love of others; instead of true affection, one uses a substitute—a language of affection, which is always well-received, because one is always well-disposed to lis-ten to everything that is said in our favor with a kindly ear. And there-fore, one may say of all those speeches of civility—which are so com-monly delivered by the worldly types, but are so far removed from the feelings of their hearts—that: *Vana locuti sunt unusquisque ad proximum suum: Labia dolosa in corde & corde locuti sunt;* Everyone speaks and con-verses with his fellow men only about vain subjects: their lips are full of deceit, and they speak with a double heart. (Ps. 11.3)

Discourse Containing a Digest of Natural Proofs of the Existence of God and the Immortality of the Soul

But it is at least certain that a spirit could never appear, as we have shown, and that matter, since it is deprived of thought, will never recognize itself as being differently organized. So one must necessarily confess both that men are new, and that—because all bodily nature is incapable of creating a man—he, as a mortal, could only be created by a more powerful being than nature.

Hence all the inventions of men have a touch of novelty about them, and disavow eternity. We see nothing in the world that looks more ancient than is claimed by the Holy Scriptures. There is no historian earlier than four thousand years ago. Since that time, one has witnessed a perpetual progress in the world, similar to the progress made by a man coming out of childhood and going through all the other ages of life.

Varro[1] testifies to the fact that, among the arts that existed in the world when he was writing, none was more than a thousand years old. Men have always moved forward to find new ways of relieving themselves from necessity; and as we go further back, we always find inventions more imperfect, and men more deprived. We know the origins of almost all the arts, the sciences, the cities, empires and administrations [*polices*°].

I know that an author has just put together the new inventions of recent centuries with several lost inventions from antiquity in a book he entitled: *Vetera deperdita, Nova reperta.*[2] But one can note in this book that those ancient inventions were not very useful, and that they are made good by new inventions which are even nicer and easier, whereas those which have been found recently are, on the one hand, so convenient that it is impossible for them to disappear; and on the other hand, they are so easy that it is strange how long it took to discover them.

For instance, what is more convenient for man's life than the art of us-

---

1. [Marcus Terentius Varro (116–27 B.C.), Roman scholar and encyclopedist.]

2. [The reference may be to Guido Panciroli (1523–99), *Raccolta di alcune cose più segnalate* (Venice, 1612); tr. into Latin as *Nova reperta, sive Rerum memorabilium recens inventarum* by H. Salmuth (1599–1602; 1660 ed.).]

ing these two great elements of nature for his work—wind and water? Most things can only be done nowadays thanks to the forces we borrow from those two bodies. The slightest knowledge of mechanics seems to lead us naturally to draw from them the uses we actually draw from them, since we only search for the forces, the application never being difficult.

One may say with certainty that men will never be so foolish as to be reduced to using only the strength of their arms to do what they can do so conveniently thanks to water and wind. Thus, the invention of windmills can never perish. And yet this invention, which is so useful, is not very ancient, as it appears that before Pliny's time, one had no other means to grind grain than to turn a millstone by the strength of one's arms or with animals.[3] And even though it seems that, according to this author, there were in his time certain water-powered millstones, the way he speaks of it nevertheless shows that this invention was then far from perfect and far from widespread, since he only mentions it as the least ordinary means to grind grain; whereas whenever it has been well known, it has abolished all other means.

There is also nothing simpler and more natural than printing; and there is no point in fearing that this art which makes all things eternal might ever perish. But one may truly admire how we have been so long without finding it. The ancients used to engrave copper. Hence it was easy for them to imagine that if they printed on paper what they had engraved, they could write in an instant what had taken so long to engrave. If they had been struck by this idea and had followed it, they would not have remained long without perfecting it and without finding the blend of ink necessary for printing. And yet it has only been two hundred years since we became aware of this invention, which was destined to become eternal [even] if the world were to last forever.

And cannot the same be said of cannon powder? Can we not claim how useful it is for hunting and war, and how a gun is more convenient to shoot a bird than bows and crossbows? And how many inconvenient and quite inefficient machines have we been ridden of thanks to our cannons and our mines? In the past, one had almost no other means to take towns fortified with good walls than to raise heaps of earth in order to

---

3. Pliny [the Elder], *Natural History*, bk. 18, ch. 10.

fight hand to hand. The smallest places used to stop a victorious army for six months; and Caesar and Alexander, despite all their valor, could never have taken one of the fortified towns of the Netherlands within a year. Men are too mean ever to forget an invention which backs up their passions so well. Its substance has always been exposed to their sight. Its preparation is not difficult. Experimenting with it was easy; and yet it has not been in the world for long.

The compass has such strange uses that it alone has given us the knowledge of a new world, and now links all the peoples on earth through trade. It is so simple that one can really marvel at the fact that men were able to go so long without finding it. For since the magnet's property of attracting iron has always existed—which has often led us to have magnets touch iron—it is difficult to understand how it is that men never, either by accident or on purpose, observed some needle (either loose or dangling) as it is touched by the magnet. For they would have then recognized that it always turns towards the same side. The same thing would have happened if they had hung the magnet to a thread; for they would have also seen that it always turns one of its sides towards one pole, and the other side towards the other pole.

All those inventions and many others are so simple that it is impossible that the world could have lived so long without finding them, and they are so convenient that it is even more impossible they will ever perish once found. Therefore it is obvious that, being new, they are palpable proofs of the fact that men are new, since men would never have failed to discover them sooner if there had always been men, and since men would have never let them disappear once they had been found.

So everything we can see in the world leads us to believe that it has not always existed, and that there has been a being above the world who has created all other beings. And it is in vain that atheists object that this being is incomprehensible, and that we are admitting what we cannot conceive of; for since [this being] is infinite, it is not surprising that it should supersede the capacity of our finite and limited minds. Our reason can go so far as to understand that there are things that are, even though they are incomprehensible. But as soon as this one incomprehensible being is acknowledged, all nature becomes in some sense comprehensible. And there are no more difficulties accounting through reason for an infinity of things which are unexplainable without that. Matter is, because God created it. Movement is, because God has produced it and preserves it. This body is in this place because—since God created it in a certain place—it has come to this one through a series of changes which are not infinite. There are thinking beings because God creates them when he sees bodies prepared to receive them. Mountains are not levelled down, because the world has not lasted long enough yet since its creation to produce that effect. There are men because they were born of a man and a woman whom God created six thousand years ago. There are animals, because God also fashioned those animated machines when he created the world, and provided them with the means to multiply themselves and preserve their species by begetting new generations. There are no histories going back beyond four thousand years ago, for since the world just began six thousand years ago or so, it is not surprising that men first focused on arts that were useful to the preservation of their lives, rather than on writing and making out stories. All that is in perfect accord with what the Scriptures teach us about the Deity and the creation of the world.

But those who, wishing to confine all things within the narrow limits of their minds, refuse to acknowledge this incomprehensible being because they do not understand it, do not for all that avoid the disadvantage they object to in us without any reason; on the contrary, they heighten it. Without an incomprehensible being, which they reject, the world and all its parts become incomprehensible to them. They are obliged to admit that, for everything, there is an infinite succession of causes dependent on one another, without ever finding a first and independent cause, even though there is nothing more incomprehensible and contrary to reason. Why is this man here? It is because he was born of a father, and this father was born of another, and so on ad infinitum. Why is this lion on earth? It is because it was born of that other lion, and so on ad infinitum. Why is this part of matter in this place? It is because it has been pushed out of that other place, and so on ad infinitum. Infinity is everywhere, and thus incomprehensibility is everywhere. Hence their minds are obliged to yield to the slightest thing, as they refuse to bow to the one to whom it is just and glorious to yield.

Discourse, Where It Is Made Clear
How the Conversations of Men Are Dangerous

Chapter III

How common language is the language of concupiscence.

The corruption which arises from language is all the greater in that the wicked are infinitely more numerous than the good. In addition, because the good have not always been so, and are not perfectly so, since they have within them the remains of natural corruption, common language is well and truly the language of concupiscence, which predominates in it and rules it. It always connects the ideas of greatness or pettiness, contempt or esteem to objects just as concupiscence represents them. Thus, it is not surprising that, since it makes us see things as concupiscence does, it triggers and nurtures within us all the movements that arise from those false ideas formed by concupiscence.

Therefore, there is no one who could find a reason for moaning about those wounds men's words have inflicted on his mind, and who could not truly say to God that *the words of the wicked have prevailed over him.* They have prevailed over us when we were young and unable to resist, and they constantly prevail over us through the intelligence they can find in our minds, as they have us see things differently from what they really are— either bigger or smaller than they are.

For one must not imagine that wishing to belong to God, and even actually converting oneself, can entirely reform this corruption of the mind and enable us to appraise each thing for what it is really worth. It is true that, by devoting oneself to God, one prefers him to all other creatures, but this preference is still very small, and does not correspond at all to the disproportion between God and creation, between eternal and worldly things. God often barely gets the better of objects of concupiscence. We continue to prize the advantages of the world infinitely more than they deserve. We are still close to the perfect balance, and if we put a little more weight on the scales—that is to say, if we slightly increased the impression the things of the world have upon our minds—these would easily regain their influence and get the better of God.

Now nothing is more capable of producing that disastrous effect than the speeches delivered by the men of the world [*les hommes du monde*], because they constantly revive those false ideas we have about earthly things; because they always present godly things with this obscurantist pettiness which leads them to be despised by so many people; and because they thus constantly reopen our wounds. That is why no precept is more important than that given by the Sage in the following words: *Watch out for yourself, and pay attention to what you hear for your fate depends on it: Cave tibi, & attende diligenter auditui tuo, quoniam cum subversione tua ambulas.* (Eccli. 13.16) Our falls usually come from our false judgements, our false judgements come from our false impressions, and those false impressions come from the commerce° we have with one another through language. It is the ill-fated chain which plunges us into hell.

5

A Discourse of Trade
1690

Nɪᴄʜᴏʟᴀꜱ Bᴀʀʙᴏɴ was born in London in 1623. He studied medicine at the University of Leiden in 1661, receiving his M.D. at Utrecht and becoming an honorary fellow of the College of Physicians in 1664. He then became a real estate developer, and after the fire of London in 1666, he is said to have introduced fire insurance to England. Barbon developed whole sections of London in both commercial and residential real estate. He was elected a member of Parliament in 1690 and in 1695. He also took part in the land-bank speculations of the time, founding his own land-bank. He died in 1698, after directing in his will that none of his debts be paid.

In addition to the work included here, he wrote an essay on money in response to Locke in 1696, arguing for devaluing the silver currency. He was known also for arguing against the "balance" of trade. The edition used here is Nicholas Barbon, *A Discourse of Trade,* edited by Jacob H. Hollander (1690; repr. Baltimore: Johns Hopkins University Press, 1905), and is reprinted in its entirety. One of the best-known early tracts for freedom of trade, it also discusses topics as varied as the nature of value, the role of fashion in economic life, the importance of moral dispositions such as emulation and vanity, industry and liberality in commerce, and the political effects and implications of commerce. Unbracketed notes are by Hollander; bracketed material is by the present editor.

A Discourse of Trade

The Preface

The Greatness and Riches of the UNITED PROVINCES, and STATES OF VENICE, Consider'd, with the little Tract of Ground that belongs to either of their TERRITORIES, sufficiently Demonstrate the great Advantage and Profit that Trade brings to a Nation.

And since the Old Ammunition and Artillery of the GRECIANS and ROMANS are grown out of Use; such as Stones, Bows, Arrows, and battering Rams, with other Wooden Engines, which were in all Places easily procured or made: And the Invention of Gunpowder hath introduced another sort of Ammunition and Artillery, whose Materials are made of Minerals, that are not to be found in all Countries; such as Iron, Brass, Lead, Salt-petre, and Brimstone; and therefore where they are wanting, must be procured by Traffick. TRADE is now become as necessary to Preserve Governments, as it is useful to make them Rich.

And notwithstanding the great Influence, that TRADE now hath in the Support and Welfare of States and Kingdoms, yet there is nothing more unknown, or that Men differ more in their Sentiments, than about the True Causes that raise and promote TRADE.

LIVY, and those Antient Writers, whose elevated GENIUS set them upon the Inquiries into the Causes of the Rise and Fall of Governments, have been very exact in describing the several Forms of Military Discipline, but take no Notice of TRADE; and MACHIAVEL a Modern Writer, and the best, though he lived in a Government, where the Family of MEDICIS had advanced themselves to the Soveraignty by their Riches, acquired by Merchandizing, doth not mention TRADE, as any way interested in the Affairs of State; for until TRADE became necessary to provide Weapons of War, it was always thought Prejudicial to the Growth of Empire, as too much softening the People by Ease and Luxury, which made their Bodies unfit to Endure the Labour and Hardships of War. And therefore the ROMANS who made War, (the only Way to Raise & Enlarge their Dominion) did in the almost Infancy of their

State, Conquer that Rich and TRADING City of CARTHAGE, though
Defended by HANIBAL their General, one of the greatest Captains in
the World: so that, since TRADE was not in those days useful to provide
Magazines for Wars, an Account of it is not to be expected from those
Writers. The Merchant, and other Traders who should understand the
true Interest of TRADE, do either not understand it, or else, lest it might
hinder their private Gain, will not Discover[1] it. Mr. MUNN a Merchant,
in his Treatise of TRADE,[2] doth better set forth the Rule to make an Accomplished Merchant, than how it may be most Profitable to the Nation; and those Arguments every day met with from the Traders, seem
byassed with Private Interest, and run contrary to one another, as their
Interest are opposite.

The TURKEY-Merchants Argue against the EAST-INDIA-
COMPANY, the WOOLLEN-DRAPER against the MERCERS, and the
UPHOLSTER against the CAIN-CHAIR-MAKER; some think there are
too many TRADERS, and Complain against the Number of BUILDERS;
others against the Number of ALE-HOUSES; some use Argumen's for
the Sole making of particular Commodities, others Plead for the Sole
Trading to particular Countries: So that, if these Gentlemens Reasons
might prevail in getting those Laws they so much solicite, (which all of
them Affirm, would be for the Advance of TRADE, and Publick Good
of the Nation) there would be but a few TRADES left for the next Generation of Men to be Employ'd in, a much fewer sorts of Goods to make,
and not a Corner of the World to Trade to, unless they purchase a License from them.

And how fair and convincing soever their Premises may appear for the
Inlarging and Advancement of TRADE, the Conclusions of their Arguments, which are for Limiting and Confining of it to Number, Persons
and Places, are directly opposite to the Inlarging of it.

The Reasons why many Men have not a true IDEA of TRADE, is, Be-

---

1. [Reveal.]
2. "England's Treasure by Forraign Trade. Or, The Balance of our Forraign Trade is
The Rule of our Treasure" (London, 1664); see chapter I ('The knowledge and qualities,
which are required to be in a perfect Merchant of forraign trade').

cause they Apply their Thoughts to particular Parts of TRADE, wherein they are chiefly concerned in Interest; and having found out the best Rules and Laws for forming that particular Part, they govern their Thoughts by the same Notions in forming the Great Body of TRADE, and not Reflecting on the different Rules of Proportions betwixt the Body and Parts, have a very disagreeable Conception; and like those, who having learnt to Draw well an Eye, Ear, Hand, and other Parts of the Body, (being Unskilful in the Laws of Symmetry) when they joyn them together, make a very Deformed Body.

Therefore, whoever will make a true Representation of TRADE, must Draw a rough Sketch of the Body and Parts together, which though it will not entertain with so much Pleasure as a well-finish't Piece, yet the Agreeableness of the Parts may be as well discern'd, and thereby such Measures taken, as may best suit the Shape of the Body.

Of *Trade* and the *Stock,* or Wares of *Trade.*

Trade is the Making, and Selling of one sort of Goods for another; The making is called Handy-Craft Trade, and the maker an Artificer; The Selling is called Merchandizing, and the Seller a Merchant: The Artificer is called by several Names from the sort of Goods he makes. As a Clothier, Silk-weaver, Shoo-maker, or Hatter, &c. from Making of Cloth, Silk, Shooes, or Hats; And the Merchant is distinguished by the Names of the Countrey he deals to, and is called, *Dutch, French, Spanish* or *Turkey* Merchant.

The chief End or Business of Trade, is to make a profitable Bargain: In making of a Bargain there are these things to be considered; The Wares to be Sold, the Quantity and Quality of those Wares, the Value or Price of them, the Money or Credit, by which the Wares are bought, the Interest that relates to the time of performing the Bargain.

The Stock and Wares of all *Trade* are the Animals, Vegitables, and Minerals of the whole Universe, whatsoever the Land or Sea produceth. These Wares may be divided into Natural and Artificial; Natural Wares are those which are sold as Nature Produceth them; As Flesh, Fish, and

Fruits, &c. Artificial Wares are those which by Art are Changed into another Form than Nature gave them; As Cloth, Calicoes, and wrought Silks, &c. which are made of Wool, Flax, Cotten, and Raw Silks.

Both these Sorts of Wares are called the Staple Commoditys of those Countreys where they chiefly abound, or are made. There are Different Climates of the Heavens, some very Hot, some very Cold, others Temperate; these Different Climates produce Different Animals, Vegitables, & Minerals. The Staples of the hot Country are Spices; the Staples of the Cold, Furrs; but the more Temperate Climates produce much the same sorts of Commoditys; but by difference of the Quality or Conveniency of place where they abound, they become the Staple of each Country, where they are either best or easier acquired or exchanged: Thus, *Herrings*, and other Fish are the Staples of *Holland;* the *Dutch* living amongst the Water, are most naturally inclined to Fishing: *English* Wool being the best in the World, is the Staple of *England*, for the same reason. Oyles of *Italy*, Fruits of *Spain*, Wine of *France*, with several other sorts of Commoditys, are the Staples of their several Countrys.

Staple Commodities may be divided into Native or Forreign; the Native Staple is what Each Country doth Naturally and best produce; Forreign Staple, is any Forreign Commodity, which a Country acquires by the sole *Trade* to a Forreign Place, or sole possession of a particular Art; as Spices are the Staple of *Holland;* and the making of Glass and Paper, were the Staple of *Venice*.

From the Stock, or Wares of *Trade*, these Three Things are Observable: 1. The Native Staple of each Country is the Riches of the Country, and is perpetual, and never to be consumed; Beasts of the Earth, Fowls of the Air, and Fishes of the Sea, Naturally Increase: There is Every Year a New Spring and Autumn, which produceth a New Stock of Plants and Fruits. And the Minerals of the Earth are Unexhaustable; and if the Natural Stock be Infinite, the Artificial Stock that is made of the Natural, must be Infinite, as Woollen and Linnen Cloth, Calicoes, and wrought Silk, which are made of Flax, Wool, Cotton, and Raw Silks.

This sheweth a Mistake of Mr. *Munn*, in his Discourse of *Trade*,[3] who commends Parsimony, Frugality, and Sumptuary Laws, as the means to

3. [London, 1621; repr. New York, 1930.]

make a Nation Rich; and uses an Argument, from a *Simile,* supposing a Man to have 1000 *l.* per *Annum,* and 2000 *l.* in a Chest, and spends Yearly 1500 *l.* per *Annum,* he will in four Years time Waste his 2000 *l.*[4] This is true, of a Person, but not of a Nation; because his Estate is Finite, but the Stock of a Nation Infinite, and can never be consumed; For what is Infinite, can neither receive Addition by Parsimony, nor suffer Diminution, by Prodigality.

2. The Native Staple of Each Country, is the Foundation of it's Forreign *Trade:* And no Nation have any Forreign Commodities, but what are at first brought in by the Exchange of the Native; for at the first beginning of Forreign *Trade,* a Nation hath nothing else to Exchange; The Silver & Gold from *Spain;* the Silks from *Turkey,* Oyls from *Italy,* Wine from *France,* and all other Forreign Goods are brought into *England,* by the Exchange of the *English* Cloth, or some other Staple of *England.*

3. That Forreign Staples are uncertain Wealth: Some Countries by the Sole *Trade* to another Country, or by the Sole Possession of some Arts, gain a Staple of Forreign Commodities, which may be as profitable as the Native, so long as they enjoy the Sole possession of that *Trade* or Art. But that is uncertain; for other Nations find out the way of Trading to the same place: The Artists for Advantage, Travel into other Countries, and the Arts are discover'd. Thus *Portugal* had the Sole *Trade* of *India;* afterwards the *Venetians* got a great Share of the *Trade,* and now the *Dutch* and *English,* have a greater share than both: The Arts of making several sorts of Silks, were chiefly confined to *Genoa,* & *Naples;* afterward Travelled into *France,* since into *England* and *Holland,* and are now Practised there in as great perfection as they were in *Italy;* So have other Arts wander'd, as the making of Looking-Glasses from *Venice* into *England,* the making of Paper from *Venice* into *France* and *Holland.*

Of the Quantity and Quality of Wares.

The Quantity of all Wares are known by Weight or Measure. The Reason of Gravity is not understood, neither is it Material to this Purpose;

---

4. [*England's Treasure*] chap. II ('The means to enrich the Kingdom, and to encrease our Treasure').

Whether it proceeds from the Elastisity of the Air, or Weight of the ut-
most Spheer, or from what other Causes, its sufficient, that the ways of
Trying the Weights of Bodies are perfectly discover'd by the Ballance.
There are Two Sorts of Weights in Common Use, the *Troy*, and
Averdupois.[5]

The First are used to Weigh Goods of most Value, as Gold, Silver and
Silk, &c. The Latter for Coarser, and more Bulky Goods, as Lead,
Iron, &c.

There are Two Sorts of Measures, the one for Fluid Bodies, as the
Bushel, Gallon and Quart, for Measuring Corn, Wine and Oyl; the other
for the Measuring the Dimensions of Solid Bodies, as a Yard, Ell, &c. to
Measure Cloth, Silk. &c.

The Weights and Measures of all Countries differs, but that is no
Prejudice to *Trade;* they are all made certain by the Custom or Laws of
the Place, and the Trader knows the Weight or Measure in Use, in the
Place he Deals to. It is the Care of the Government, to prevent and punish the Fraud of False Weights and Measures, and in most Trading-
Cities, there are Publick Weigh-Houses, and Measurers: The Fraud of
the Ballance, which is from the unequal Length of the end of the Beam,
is least perceivable; and therefore in Weighing Goods of Value, they usually Weigh them in both Scales.

The Qualities of Wares are known by their Colour, Sound, Smell,
Taste, Make, or Shape.

The Difference in the Qualities of Wares are very difficultly distinguished; those Organs that are the proper Judges of those Differencies,
do very much disagree; some Men have clearer Eyes, some more distinguishing Ears, and other nicer Noses and Tastes; and every Man having
a good Opinion of his own Faculties, it is hard to find a Judge to determine which is best: Besides, those Qualities that belong to Artificial
Wares, such as depend upon the Mixture, Make or Shape of them, are
more difficultly discover'd: Those Wares, whose Quality are produced by
the just Mixture of different Bodies, such as Knives and Razors, whose
sharpness arise from the Good Temperament and Mixture of the Steel

---

5. [In Troy weight, a pound is 12 ounces, an ounce is 20 pennyweights, and a penny-
weight is 24 grains. In Averdupois, a pound is 16 ounces.]

& Iron, are not to be found out, but by the Use of them: And so doth the Mixture, and well making of Hats, Cloth, and many other things.

Because the Difference in the Qualities of Wares, are so difficultly understood, it is that the Trader serves an Apprenticeship to learn them; and the Knowledge of them is called the Mystery of Trade; and in common Dealing, the Buyer is forced to rely on the Skill and Honesty of the Seller, to deliver Wares with such Qualities as he affirms them to have: It is the Sellers Interest, from the Expectation of further Dealing, not to deceive; because his Shop, the Place of Dealing, is known: Therefore, those Persons that buy of Pedlars, and Wandering People, run Great Hazard of being Cheated.

Those Wares, whose Chief Qualities consist in Shape, such as all Wearing Apparel, do not so much depend upon the Honesty of the Seller; for tho' the Trader or Maker, is the Inventor of the Shape, yet it is the Fancy and Approbation of the Buyer, that brings it into Use, and makes it pass for a Fashion.

Of the Value and Price of Wares.

The Value of all Wares arise from their Use; Things of no Use, have no Value, as the *English* Phrase is, *They are good for nothing.*

The Use of Things, are to supply the Wants and Necessities of Man: There are Two General Wants that Mankind is born with; the Wants of the Body, and the Wants of the Mind; To supply these two Necessities, all things under the Sun become useful, and therefore have a Value.

Wares, useful to supply the Wants of the Body, are all things necessary to support Life, such are in Common Estimation; all those Goods which are useful to supply the Three General Necessities of Man, Food, Clothes and Lodging; But if strictly Examined, nothing is absolutely necessary to support Life, but Food; for a great Part of Mankind go Naked, and lye in Huts and Caves; so that there are but few things that are absolutely necessary to supply the Wants of the Body.

Wares, that have their Value from supplying the Wants of the Mind, are all such things that can satisfie Desire; Desire implys Want: It is the Appetite of the Soul, and is as natural to the Soul, as Hunger to the Body.

The Wants of the Mind are infinite, Man naturally Aspires, and as his Mind is elevated, his Senses grow more refined, and more capable of Delight; his Desires are inlarged, and his Wants increase with his Wishes, which is for every thing that is rare, can gratifie his Senses, adorn his Body, and promote the Ease, Pleasure, and Pomp of Life.

Amongst the great Variety of things to satisfie the Wants of the Mind, those that adorn Mans Body, and advance the Pomp of Life, have the most general Use, and in all Ages, and amongst all sorts of Mankind, have been of Value.

The first Effects that the Fruit of the Tree of Knowledge wrought upon the Parents of Mankind, was to make them cloath themselves, and it has made the most Visible Distinction of his Race, from the rest of the Creation: It is that by which his Posterity may write Man, for no Creatures adorn the Body but Man: Beside, the decking of the Body, doth not onely distinguish Man from Beast, but is the Mark of Difference and Superiority betwixt Man and Man.

There was never any part of Mankind so wild and barbarous, but they had Difference and Degree of Men amongst them, and invented some things to shew that Distinction.

Those that Cloathed with Skins, wore the Skins of those Beasts that are most difficultly taken; thus *Hercules* wore a Lyons Skin; and the Ermins and Sable, are still Badges of Honour. The Degree of Quality amongst the *Affricans,* is known by the waste Cloth, and amongst those that go naked, by adorning their Bodies with Colours, most rare amongst them, as the Red was the Colour most in Esteem amongst the Ancient *Britains.*

And the most Ancient and best of Histories, the Bible, shews, That amongst the Civilized People of the World, Ear-Rings, Bracelets, Hoods and Vails, with Changeable Suits of Apparel, were then worn: And the same Ornaments for the Body are still, and ever since have been Worn, only differing in Shapes and Fashions, according to the Custom of the Country.

The Shapes of Habits are much in use, to denote the Qualities of several men; but things rare and difficult to be obtained, are General Badges of Honour: From this Use, Pearls, Diamonds, and Precious Stones, have their Value: Things Rare are proper Ensigns of Honour, because it is Honourable to acquire Things Difficult.

The Price of Wares is the present Value; And ariseth by Computing the occasions or use for them, with the Quantity to serve that Occasion; for the Value of things depending on the use of them, the *Over-pluss* of Those Wares, which are more than can be used, become worth nothing; So that Plenty, in respect of the occasion, makes things cheap; and Scarcity, dear.

There is no fixt Price or Value of any thing for the Wares of *Trades;* The Animals, and Vegetables of the Earth, depend on the Influence of Heaven, which sometimes causes Murrains,[6] Dearth, Famine, and sometimes Years of great Plenty; therefore, the Value of things must accordingly Alter. Besides, the Use of most things being to supply the Wants of the Mind, and not the Necessitys of the Body; and those Wants, most of them proceeding from imagination, the Mind Changeth; the things grow out of Use, and so lose their Value.

There are two ways by which the value of things are a little guessed at; by the Price of the Merchant, and the Price of the Artificer: The Price that the Merchant sets upon his Wares, is by reckoning Prime Cost, Charges and Interest.

The Price of the Artificer, is by reckoning the Cost of the Materials, with the time of working them; The Price of Time is according to the Value of the Art, and the Skill of the Artist. Some Artificers Reckon Twelve, others Fifteen, and some Twenty, and Thirty Shillings *per* Week.

Interest is the Rule that the Merchant Trades by; And Time, the Artificer, By which they cast up Profit, and Loss; for if the Price of their Wares, so alter either by Plenty, or by Change of the Use, that they do not pay the Merchant Interest, nor the Artificer for his Time, they both reckon they lose by their Trade.

But the Market is the best Judge of Value; for by the Concourse of Buyers and Sellers, the Quantity of Wares, and the Occasion for them are Best known: Things are just worth so much, as they can be sold for, according to the Old Rule, *Valet Quantum Vendi potest.*

6. [Plague in cattle.]

Of Mony, Credit and Interest.

Mony is a Value made by a Law; And the Difference of its Value is known by the Stamp, and Size of the Piece.

One Use of Mony is, It is the Measure of Value, By which the Value of all other things are reckoned; as when the Value of any thing is expressed, its said, It's worth so many shillings, or so many Pounds: Another Use of Mony is; It is a Change or Pawn for the Value of all other Things: For this Reason, the Value of Mony must be made certain by Law, or else it could not be made a certain Measure, nor an Exchange for the Value of all things.

It is not absolutely necessary, Mony should be made of Gold or Silver; for having its sole Value from the Law, it is not Material upon what Metal the Stamp be set. Money hath the same Value, and performs the same Uses, if it be made of Brass, Copper, Tin, or any thing else. The Brass Mony of *Spain,* the Copper Mony of *Sweeden,* and Tin Farthings of *England,* have the same Value in Exchange, according to the Rate they are set at and perform the same Uses, to Cast up the Value of things, as the Gold and Silver Mony does; Six Pence in Farthings will buy the same thing as Six Pence in Silver; and the Value of a thing is well understood by saying, It is worth Eight Farthings, as that it is worth Two Pence: Gold and Silver, as well as Brass, Copper and Tin Mony, change their Value in those Countries, where the Law has no Force, and yield no more than the Price of the Metal that bears the Stamp: Therefore, all Foreign Coins go by Weight, and are of no certain Value, but rise and fall with the Price of the Metal. Pieces of Eight, yield sometimes 4 *sh.* 6 *d.* 4 *sh.* 7 *d.* and 4 *sh.* 8 *d.* as the Value of Silver is higher or lower: And so doth Dollars, and all Forreign Coin, change their Value; and were it not for the Law that fixeth the Value, an *English* Crown Piece would now yield Five Shillings and Two Pence, for so much is the Value of it, if it were melted, or in a Foreign Country. But the chief Advantage of making Mony of Silver and Gold, is to prevent Counterfeiting; for Silver and Gold, being Metals of great Value, those who design Profit by Counterfeiting the Coin, must Counterfeit the Metals, as well as the Stamp, which is more difficult than the Stamp. There's another Benefit to the Merchant, by such Mony; for Gold and Silver being Commodities for other Uses, than to make Mony; to make Plate, Gold & Silver Lace, Silks, &c. And Coins of little Bulk, in respect of their Value, the Merchant transmits such Mony from Place to Place, in *Specie,* according as he finds his Advantage, by the Rise of Bullion; though this may be a Conveniency to the Merchant, it often proves a Prejudice to the State, by making Mony scarce: Therefore, there are Laws in most Countries, that Prohibit the Transportation of Mony, yet it cannot be prevented; for in *Spain,* though it be Capital, yet in Two Months after the Gallions are come home, there is scarce any Silver Mony to be seen in the Country.

Some Men have so great an Esteem for Gold and Silver, that they believe they have an intrinsick Value in themselves, and cast up the value of every thing by them: The Reason of the Mistake, is, Because Mony being made of Gold and Silver, they do not distinguish betwixt Mony, and Gold and Silver. Mony hath a certain Value, because of the Law; but the Value of Gold and Silver are uncertain, & varies their Price, as much as Copper, Lead, or other Metals: And in the Places where they are dug, considering the smalness of their Veins, with the Charges of getting them, they do not yield much more Profit than other Minerals, nor pay the Miners better Wages for digging them.

And were it not for the Waste, made of Gold and Silver, by Plate, Lace, Silks, and Guilding, and the Custom of the *Eastern* Princes, to lay them up and bury them, that Half which is dug in the *West,* is buried in the *East.* The great Quantities dug out of the Earth, since the Discovery of the *West-Indies,* would have so much lessened the Value, that by this time, they would not have much exceeded the Value of Tin, or Copper: Therefore, How greatly would those Gentlemen be disappointed, that are searching after the *Philosopher's Stone,*[7] if they should at last happen to find it? For, if they should make but so great a Quantity of Gold and Silver, as they, and their Predecessors have spent in search after it, it would so alter, and bring down the Price of those Metals, that it might be a Question, whether they would get so much *Over-plus* by it, as would pay for the Metal they change into Gold and Silver. It is only the Scarcity that keeps up the Value, and not any Intrinsick Vertue or Quality in the Metals; For if the Vertue were to be considered, the *Affrican* that gives

7. [Alchemist's stone thought to convert base metals into gold.]

Gold for Knives, and Things made of Iron, would have the Odds in the
Exchange; Iron being a much more Useful Metal, than either Gold or
Silver. To Conclude this Objection, Nothing in it self hath a certain
Value; One thing is as much worth as another: And it is time, and place,
that give a difference to the Value of all things.

Credit is a Value raised by Opinion, it buys Goods as Mony doe's; and
in all Trading Citys, there's more Wares sold upon Credit, then for present Mony.

There are Two Sorts of Credit; the one, is Grounded upon the Ability of the Buyer; the other, upon the Honesty: The first is called a Good
Man, which implys an Able Man; he generally buys upon short Time;
to pay in a Month, which is accounted as ready Mony, and the Price is
made accordingly. The other is accounted an Honest Man; He may be
poor; he Generally buys for three and Six Months or longer, so as to pay
the Merchant by the Return of his own Goods; and therefore, the Seller
relys more upon the Honesty of the Buyer, than his Ability: Most of the
Retail Traders buy upon this Sort of Credit, and are usually Trusted for
more than double they are worth.

In Citys of great Trade, there are publick Banks of Credit, as at *Amsterdam* and *Venice:* They are of great Advantage to Trade, for they make
Payments easie, by preventing the Continual Trouble of telling[8] over
Mony, and cause a great Dispatch in Business: Publick Banks are of so
great a Concern in Trade, that the Merchants of *London,* for want of such
a Bank, have been forced to Carry their Cash to Gold-Smiths, and have
thereby Raised such a Credit upon Gold-Smiths Notes, that they pass in
Payments from one to another like Notes upon the Bank; And although
by this way of Credit, there hath been very Vast Sums of Mony lost, not
less then too Millions within five and Twenty Years, yet the Dispatch
and Ease in Trade is so great by such Notes, that the Credit is still in
some Measure kept up.

Therefore, it is much to be wondered at, that since the City of *London*
is the Largest, Richest, and Chiefest City in the World, for Trade; Since
there is so much Ease, Dispatch, and Safety in a Publick Bank; and since
such vast Losses has Happened for want of it; That the Merchant and

8. [Counting or numbering.]

Traders of *London* have not long before this time Addressed themselves, to the Government, for the Establishing of a Publick Bank.

The Common Objection, that a Publick Bank cannot be safe in a Monarchy, is not worth the Answering; As if Princes were not Governed by the same Rules of Policy, as States are, To do all things for the Well-fair of the Subjects, wherein their own Interest is concerned.

It is True, in a Government wholly Dispotical, whose Support is alto-gether in it's Millitary Forces; where Trade hath no Concern in the Affaires of the State; Brings no Revenue, There might be a Jealousy, That such a Bank might tempt a Prince to Seize it; when by doing it, he doth not Prejudice the Affaires of his Government: But in *England*, where the Government is not Dispotical; But the People Free; and have as great a Share in the Soveraign Legislative Power, as the Subjects of any States have, or ever had; where the Customs makes great Figures, in the Kings Exchequer; where Ships are the Bullworks of the Kingdom; and where the Flourish of Trade is as much the Interest of the King as of the People, There can be no such Cause of Fear: For, What Objections can any Man make, that his Mony in the Bank, may not be as well secured by a Law, as his Property is? Or; Why he should be more afraid of Los-ing his Mony, than his Land or Goods?

Interest is the Rent of Stock, and is the same as the Rent of Land: The First, is the Rent of the Wrought or Artificial Stock; the Latter, of the Unwrought, or Natural Stock.

Interest is commonly reckoned for Mony; because the Mony Bor-rowed at Interest, is to be repayed in Mony; but this is a mistake; For the Interest is paid for Stock: for the Mony borrowed, is laid out to buy Goods, or pay for them before bought: No Man takes up Mony at In-terest, to lay it by him, and lose the Interest of it.

One use of Interest: It is the Rule by which the Trader makes up the Account of Profit and Loss; The Merchant expects by Dealing, to get more then Interest by his Goods; because of bad Debts, and other Haz-ards which he runs; and therefore, reckons all he gets above Interest, is Gain; all under, Loss; but if no more than Interest, neither Profit, nor Loss.

Another use of Interest, is, It is the measure of the Value of the Rent of Land; it sets the Price in Buying and Selling of Land: For, by adding three Years Interest more than is in the Principle, Makes the usual Value of the Land of the Country; The difference of three Year is allowed; Because Land is more certain than Mony or Stock. Thus in *Holland,* where Mony is at three *per. Cent.* by reckoning how many times three is in a Hundred Pounds, which is Thirty Three; and Adding three Years more; makes Thirty Six Years Purchase; the Value of the Land in *Holland:* And by the same Rule, interest being at six *per Cent.* in *England,* Land is worth but Twenty Years Purchase; and in *Ireland,* but Thirteen; Interest being there at Ten *per Cent:* so that, according to the Rate of Interest, is that Value of the Land in the Country.

Therefore, Interest in all Countrys is setled by a Law, to make it certain; or else it could not be a Rule for the Merchant to make up his Account, nor the Gentleman, to Sell his Land By.

Of the Use and Benefit of *Trade.*

The Use of *Trade* is to make, and provide things Necessary: Or useful for the Support, Defence, Ease, Pleasure, and Pomp of Life: Thus the Brewers, Bakers, Butchers, Poulterers, and Cooks, with the Apothecaries, Surgeons, and their Dependencies provide Food, and Medicine for the support of Life: The Cutlers, Gun-smiths, Powder-makers, with their Company of *Traders,* make things for Defence; The Shoo-makers, Sadlers, Couch, and Chair-makers, with abundance more for the Ease of Life: The Perfumers, Fidlers, Painters, and Booksellers, and all those Trades that make things to gratifie the Sense, or delight the Mind, promote Pleasure: But those Trades that are imploy'd to express the Pomp of Life, are Infinite; for, besides those that adorn Mans Body, as the Glover, Hosier, Hatter, Semstriss, Taylor, and many more, with those that make the Materials to Deck it; as Clothier, Silk-Weaver, Lace-Maker, Ribbon-Weaver, with their Assistance of Drapers, Mercers, and Milliners, and a Thousand more: Those Trades that make the Equipage for Servants, Trappings for Horses; and those that Build, Furnish, and Adorn Houses, are innumerable.

Thus Busie Man is implo2ed, and it is for his own Benefit; For by *Trade,* the Natural Stock of the Country is improved, the Wool and Flax, are made into Cloth; the Skins, into Leather; and the Wood, Lead, Iron and Tin, wrought into Thousand useful Things: The *Over-plus* of these Wares not useful, are transported by the Merchants, and Exchanged for the Wines, Oyls, Spices, and every Thing that is good of Forreign Countries: The Trader hath One Share for his Pains, and the Land-Lord the Other for his Rent: So, that by *Trade,* the Inhabitants in general, are not only well Fed, Clothed and Lodged; but the Richer sort are Furnished with all things to promote the Ease, Pleasure, & Pomp of Life: Whereas, in the same Country, where there's no Trade, the Land-Lords would have but Coarse Diet, Coarser Clothes, and worse Lodgings; and nothing for the Rent of their Lands, but the Homage and Attendance of their Poor Bare-footed Tenants, for they have nothing else to give.

Trade Raiseth the Rent of the Land, for by the Use of several sorts of Improvements, the Land Yieldeth a greater Natural Stock; by which, the Land-lord's Share is the greater: And it is the same thing, whether his Share be paid in Mony, or Goods; for the Mony must be laid out to Buy such Good's: Mony is an Immaginary Value made by a Law, for the Conveniency of Exchange: It is the Natural Stock that is the Real Value, and Rent of the Land.

Another Benefit of *Trade,* is, That, it doth not only bring Plenty, but hath occasioned Peace: For the Northern Nations, as they increased, were forced from the Necessities of their Climates, to Remove; and used to Destroy, and Conquer the Inhabitants of the Warmer Climates to make Room for themselves; thence was a Proverb, *Omne Malum ab Aquilone:*[9] But those Northern People being settled in *Trade,* the Land by their Industry, is made more Fertile; and by the Exchange of the Nations Stock, for Wines and Spices, of Hotter Climates, those Countries become most Habitable; and the Inhabitants having Warmer Food, Clothes, and Lodgings, are better able to endure the Extreamitys of their Cold Seasons: This seems to be the Reason, That for these Seven or Eight Hundred Years last past, there has been no such Invasions from the Northern part of the World, as used to destroy the Inhabitants of the Warmer Countries: Besides, *Trade* Allows a better Price for Labourers,

---

9. [Everything bad comes from the North.]

than is paid for Fighting: So it is become more the Interest of Mankind to live at home in Peace, than to seek their fortunes abroad by Wars.

These are the Benefits of *Trade*, as they Relate to Mankind; those that Relate to Government, are many.

Trade Increaseth the Revenue of the Government, by providing an Imploy for the People: For every Man that Works, pay by those things which he Eats and Wears, somthing to the Government. Thus the Excise and Custom's are Raised, and the more every Man Earns, the more he Consumes, and the King's Revenue is the more Increased.

This shews the way of Determining those Controversies, about which sort of Goods are most beneficial to the Government, by their Making, or Importing: The sole difference is from the Number of hands imploy'd in making them; Hence the Importation of Raw Silk, is more Profitable to the Government than Gold, or Silver; Because there are more Hands imployd in the Throwing, and Weaving of the First; than there can be in working the Latter.

Another Benefit of *Trade* is, It is Useful for the Defence of the Government; It Provides the Magazines of Warr. The Guns, Powder, and Bullets, are all made of Minerals, and are wrought by *Traders;* Besides, those Minerals are not to be had in all Countries; The great Stock of Saltpeter is brought from the *East Indies,* and therefore must be Imported by the Merchant, for the Exchange of the Natives Stock.

The last Benefit is, That *Trade* may be Assistant to the Inlarging of Empire; and if an Universal Empire, or Dominion of very Large Extent, can again be raised in the World, It seems more probable to be done by the Help of *Trade;* By the Increase of Ships at Sea, than by Arms at Land: This is too large a Subject to be here Treated of; but the *French* King's seeming Attempt to Raise Empire in Europe, being that Common Theam of Mens Discourse, has caused some short Reflections, which will appear by Comparing the Difficulty of the one, with the Probability of the other.

The Difficulties of Raising a Dominion of very Large Extent; especially in *Europe,* are Many.

First, *Europe* is grown more Populous than formerly, and there are more Fortified Towns and Cities, than were in the time of the *Roman* Empire, which was the last extended Dominion; and therefore, not easily Subjected to the Power of any one Prince.

Whether *Europe* be grown more Populous, Solely by the Natural Increase of Mankind; There being more Born than Dye, which first Peopled the World?

Or, Whether, since the Inhabitants of *Europe* being Addicted° to *Trade*, the ground is made more Fertile, and yields greater Plenty of Food; which hath prevented famine, that formerly destroy'd great Numbers of Mankind: So that no great Famines, has been taken Notice of by Historians, in these Last Three Hundred Years?

Whether by Dreining Great Bogs, Lakes, and Fens, and Cutting down vast Woods, to make Room for the Increase of Mankind, the Air is Grown more Healthy; So that Plagues, and other Epidemical Diseases, are not so destructive as formerly? none so violent, as *Procopius*[10] and *Wallsingham*[11] Report, which destroyed such Vast Numbers in *Italy*, that there were not left Ten in a Thousand; and in other Parts of *Europe*, not enough alive to Bury the Dead. Whereas, the Plague in (1665) the Greatest since, did not take away the Hundredth Person in *England*, *Holland*, and other Countries, where it Raged?

Whether, since the Invention of Guns and Gun-Powder, so many Men are not slain in the Wars as formerly? *Xerxes* lost 260000 in one Battle against the *Grecians;* Alexander, destroyed 110000 of *Darius's* Army; *Marius*, slew 120000 of the *Cimbri;* and in great Battles, seldome less than 100000 fell: But now 20000 Men are accounted very great Slaughter.

Whether, since the *Northern* People have fallen on *Trade*, such vast Numbers, are not destroyed by Invasions?

Whether, by all those Ways, or by which of them most, *Europe* is grown Populous, is not Material to this Discourse: It is sufficient to shew, That the Matter of Fact is so, which does appear by comparing the Antient Histories of Countries with the Modern?

---

10. "Corpus scriptorum historiae Byzantinae. Edito emendatior et copiosior, consilio B. G. Niebuhrii C. F. instituta auctoritate Academiae Litterarum Regiae Borussicae Continuata, Pars II: Procopius" (Bonnae, 1883); see I, 249–255 (De Bello Persico) and II, 162 (De Bello Gotthico).

11. "Ypodigma Neustriae" (ed. by Henry Thomas Riley in Gt. Brit. Rolls Chron., London, 1876); cf. p. 292 (A. D. 1349). The work was first published in 1574, and again appeared, as part of the "Anglica, Normannica, Hibernica, Cambrica, a Veteribus scripta," of William Camden, published at Frankfort in 1603.

In the Antient Descriptions, the Countries are full of Vast Woods, wild Beasts; the Inhabitants barbarous, and as wild, without Arts, and the Governments are like Colonies, or Herds of People: But in the Modern, the Woods are cut down, and the Lyons, Bears, and wild Beasts destroyed; no Flesh-Eaters are left to inhabit with Man, but those Dogs and Cats that he tames for his Use: Corn grows where the Woods did, and with the Timber are built Cities, Towns and Villages; the People are Cloathed, and have all Arts among them; and those little Colonies and Families, are increased into Great States and Kingdoms; and the most undeniable Proof of the Increase of Mankind in *England*, is the Doom-Day-Book, which was a Survey taken of all the Inhabitants of *England*, in the Reign of *William* the Conquerour; by which it appears, that the People of *England* are increased more than double since that time: But since the *Mosaical Hypothesis* of the Increase of the World, is generally believed amongst the Christians. And the late Lord Chief Justice *Hales*, in his Book of the Origination of Mankind,[12] hath endeavoured to satisfie all the rest of the World. It would be misspending of Time, to use any other Topick for the further Proof thereof, than what naturally follows in this Discourse, which is from the Different Success of Arms, in the Latter and Former Ages.

In the Infancy of the World, Governments began with little Families and Colonies of Men; so that, when ever any Government arrived to greater Heighth than the rest, either by the great Wisdom or Courage of the Governor, they afterwards grew a pace: It was no Difficulty for *Ninus*, that was the oldest Government, and consequently, the most Populous, to begin the *Assyrian* Empire; nor for his Successors to continue and inlarge it: Such Vast Armies of *Cyrus, Darius, Hystospis* and *Xerxes*, the least of their Forces amounting to above 500000, could not be Resisted, when the World was but thin Peopled.

These great Armies might at first sight, seem to infer, That the World was more Populous than now; because the Armies of the greatest Princes, seldom now exceed the Number of Fifty, or Sixty Thousand Men; But the Reason of those great Numbers, was, They were not so

12. Sir Matthew Hale (1609–76) "The Primitive Origination of Mankind, considered and examined according to the Light of Nature." [London: W. Godbid, 1677.]

well Skilled in Military Arts, and shew that the World was in the Infancy of its Knowledge, rather than Populous; for all that were able to bear Arms, went to the Wars: And if that were now the Custom, there might be an Army in *England* of above Three Million, allowing the Inhabitants to be Seven Millions; and by the same Proportion, the King of *France's* Country, (being four Times bigger) might raise Twelve Millions; such a Number was never heard of in this World.

The next Difficulty against the inlarging of Empire by Arms, is, That since Printing, and the Use of the Needle hath been discovered, Navigation is better known, and thence is a Greater Commerce amongst Men, the Countries and Languages are more understood, Knowledge more dispersed, and the Arts of War in all Places known; so that, Men fight more upon equal Terms than formerly; and like two Skilful Fencers, fight a long Time, before either gets Advantage.

The *Assyrians* & *Persians* Conquered more by the Number of Souldiers, than Discipline; the *Grecians* and *Romans,* more by Discipline than Number; as the World grew older, it grew wiser: Learning first flourished among the *Grecians,* afterwards among the *Romans;* and as the Latter succeeded in Learning, so they did in Empire. But now both Parties are Equally Disciplin'd and Arm'd; and the Successes of War are not so great; Victory is seldom gained without some Considerable Loss to the Conquerour.

Another Difficulty to the inlarging of Dominion by Arms, is, That the *Goths* Overcoming the greatest Part of *Europe,* did by their Form of Government, so settle Liberty, and Property of Land, that it is difficult for any Prince to Change that Form.

Whether the *Goths* were Part of the Ten Tribes, as some are of Opinion, and to Countenance their Conjectures, have Compared the Languages of the Inhabitants, *Wales, Finland* and *Orchadis,* and other *Northern* Parts (little frequented by Strangers, which might alter their Language) and find them to agree with the *Hebrew* in many Words and Sound, all their Speech being Guttural. This is certain, their Form of Government seems framed after the Examples of *Moses's* Government in the Land of *Canaan,* by dividing the Legislative Power, according to the Property of Land, according to that Antient Maxim, That Dominion is founded upon Property of Land. There Monarchy seems to be made by an easie Division of Land into Thirds, by a Conquering Army, setting down in Peace; the General being King, has one Third; the Colonels being the Lords, another Third; and the Captains, and other Inferiour Officers being Gentlemen, another; the Common Souldiers are the Farmers, and the Conquered are the Villains: The Legislative Power is divided amongst them, according to their Share in the Land; it being necessary that those that have Property of Land, should have Power to make Laws to Preserve it.

There seems to be but two settled Forms of Government; The *Turkish*, and *Gothick*, or *English* Monarchy: They are both founded upon Property of Land; in the First, the Property and Legislative Power is solely in the Prince; In the Latter, they are in both the Prince and People: The one is best fitted to raise Dominion by Armies; for the Prince must be Absolute to give Command, according to the Various Fortunes of Warr: The other is Best for *Trade;* for men are most industrious, where they are most free, and secure to injoy the Effects of their Labours.

All other Sorts of Government, either *Aristocracy,* or *Democracy,* where the Supream Magistrate is Elective, are Imperfect, Tumultuous, and Unsettled: For Man is Naturally Ambitious; he inherits the same Ruling Spirit that God gave to *Adam,* to Govern the Creation with: And the oftner that the Throne is Empty, the oftner will Contentions and Struggles Happen to get into it: Where *deter digniori* is the Rule, Warr always Ensues for the Golden Prize. Such Governments will never be without such Men as *Marius* and *Scilla,* to disturb them; nor without such a Man as *Caesar* to Usurp them; notwithstanding all the Contrivance for their Defence by those Polititians who seems fond of such Formes of Government.

The *Gothick* Government being a well fixed Form, and the People so free under it, is great hindedrance to the Enlarging of Dominion; for a People under a good Government do more Vigorously Defend it: A free People have more to lose than Slaves, and their Success is better Rewarded than by any Mercenary Pay, and therefore, make a better Resistance: It was the Freedom of the *Grecians* and *Romans* that raised their Courage, and had an equal Share in raising their Empires, with their Millitary Discipline: The free City of *Tyre* put *Alexander* to more Trouble to Conquer, than all the Citys of *Asia.*

The People of *Asia*, living under a Dispotick Power, made little Resistance; *Alexander* subdued *Libia, Phoenicia, Pamphilia,* without much
Opposition in his Journey to meet *Darius; Egypt* came under Subjection
without Fighting, and so did many Countries, being willing to Change
the *Persian* Yoak: Besides, he Fought but two Battles for the whole *Persian Empire;* and the Resistance of those slavish People was so weak, that
he did not lose 500 *Grecians* in either of the Battles, tho' *Darius* Number
far exceeded his; the one being above 260000, and the other not Forty;
And there was as great Disproportion in the Slaughter; for at the Battle
in *Cilicia* he slew 110000, and that at *Arbela* 40000; whereas, the *Spartan,* a Free People, about the same time, fought with *Antipater* his Vice-
Roy of *Macedon;* and in a Fight, where neither Army exceeded 60000,
slew 1012 of the *Macedonians,* which was more than *Alexander* lost in
both his Battles: So great is the Difference of fighting against a Free, and
a Slavish Effeminate People.

For the same Reasons, That the World is grown more Populous, That
the Arts of War are more known. That the People of *Europe* live under a
Free Government. It is as difficult to keep a Country in Subjection, as to
Conquer it. The People are too Numerous to be kept in Obedience: To
destroy the greatest Part, were too Bloody, and Inhuman; To Burn the
Towns, and Villages, and so force the People to remove, Is to lose the
greatest share in Conquest; for the People are the Riches and the Strength
of the Country, And it is not much more Advantage to a Prince, to have
a Title to Lands, in *Terra Incognita,* As to Countries without People.

Besides, Countries and Languages being more known; And Mankind
more acquainted than formerly: The Oppressed People remove into the
next Country they can find Shelter in, & become the Subjects of other
Governments. By such Addition of Subjects, those Governments growing stronger, are better able to Resist the Incroaches of Empire: So that,
every Conquest makes the next more difficult, from the Assistance of
those People before Conquered; To Transplant the Conquered into a
Remote Country, as formerly, Is not to be Practised; There is now no
Room, the World is so full of People.

To Conquer, and leave them Free, only paying Tribute and Homage, Is the same as not to Conquer them: For there is no Reason to expect their Submission longer, than till they are able to Resist; which will

not be long before they make the same Opposition, if they continue in the same Possession; and therefore, though the *Romans* in the Infancy of their Government, did leave several Countries Free, as an Assistance to other Conquest; yet, when they grew stronger, they turned all their Conquest into Provinces, being the surest way to keep them from Revolting.

These are the Difficulties of inlarging Dominion at Land, but are not Impediments to its Rise at Sea: For those Things that Obstruct the Growth of Empire at Land, do rather Promote its Growth at Sea. That the World is more Populous, is no Prejudice, there is Room enough upon the Sea; the many Fortified Towns may hinder the March of an Army, but not the Sailing of Ships: The Arts of Navigation being discover'd, hath added an Unlimited Compass to the Naval Power. There needs no Change of the *Gothick* Government; for that best Agrees with such an Empire.

The Ways of preserving Conquests gain'd by Sea, are different from those at Land. By the one, the Cities, Towns and Villages are burnt, to thin the People, that they may be the easier Governed, and kept into Subjection; by the other, the Cities must be inlarged, and New ones built: Instead of Banishing the People, they must be continued, in their Possession, or invited to the Seat of Empire; by the one, the Inhabitants are inslaved, by the other, they are made Free: The Seat of such an Empire, must be in an Island, that their Defence may be solely in Shipping; the same way to defend their Dominion, as to inlarge it.

To Conclude, there needs no other Argument, That Empire may be raised sooner at Sea, than at Land; than by observing the Growth of the *United Provinces,* within One Hundred Years last past, who have Changed their Style, from *Poor Distressed,* into that of *High and Mighty States of the United Provinces:* And *Amsterdam,* that was not long since, a poor Fisher-Town, is now one of the Chief Cities in *Europe;* and within the same Compass of Time, that the *Spaniard* & *French* have been endeavouring to Raise an Universal Empire upon the Land; they have risen to that Heighth, as to be an equal Match for either of them at Sea; and were their Government fitted for a Dominion of large Extent, and their Country separated from their Troublesome Neighbour the Continent, which would Free them from that Military Charge in defending themselves, they might, in a short Time, Contend for the Soveraignity of the Seats.

But *England* seems the Properer Seat for such an Empire: It is an Island, therefore requires no Military Force to defend it. Besides, Merchants and Souldiers never thrive in the same Place; It hath many large Harbours fitting for a large Dominion: The Inhabitants are naturally Couragious, as appears from the Effects of the Climate, in the Game Cocks, and Mastiff Dogs, being no where else so stout: The Monarchy is both fitted for Trade and Empire. And were there an Act for a General Naturalization, that all Forreigners, purchasing Land in *England,* might Enjoy the Freedom of *Englishmen,* It might within much less Compass of Time, than any Government by Arms at Land, arrive to such a Dominion: For since, in some Parts of *Europe,* Mankind is harrassed and disturbed with Wars; Since, some Governours have incroached upon the Rights of their Subjects, and inslaved them; Since the People of *England* enjoy the Largest Freedoms, and Best Government in the World; and since by Navigation and Letters, there is a great Commerce, and a General Acquaintance among Mankind, by which the Laws and the Liberties of all Nations, are known; those that are oppressed and inslaved, may probably Remove, and become the Subjects of *England:* And if the Subjects increase, the Ships, Excise and Customs, which are the Strength and Revenue of the Kingdom, will in Proportion increase, which may be so Great in a short Time, not only to preserve its Antient Soveraignty over the Narrow Seas, but to extend its Dominion over all the Great Ocean: An Empire, not less Glorious, & of a much larger Extent, than either *Alexander's* or *Ceasar's.*

Of the Chief Causes that Promote Trade.

The Chief Causes that Promote *Trade,* (not to mention Good Government, Peace, and Scituation,[13] with other Advantages) are Industry in the Poor, and Liberality in the Rich: Liberality, is the free Usage of all those things that are made by the Industry of the Poor, for the Use of the

13. [Local respect.]

Body and Mind; It Relates chiefly to Man's self, but doth not hinder him from being Liberal to others.

The Two Extreams to this Vertue, are Prodigality and Covetousness: Prodigality is a Vice that is prejudicial to the Man, but not to *Trade;* It is living a pace, and spending that in a Year, that should last all his Life: Covetousness is a Vice, prejudicial both to Man & *Trade;* It starves the Man, and breaks the Trader; and by the same way the Covetous Man thinks he grows rich, he grows poor; for by not consuming the Goods that are provided for Man's Use, there ariseth a dead Stock, called Plenty, and the Value of those Goods fall, and the Covetous Man's Estates, whether in Land, or Mony, become less worth: And a Conspiracy of the Rich Men to be Covetous, and not spend, would be as dangerous to a Trading State, as a Forreign War; for though they themselves get nothing by their Covetousness, nor grow the Richer, yet they would make the Nation poor, and the Government great Losers in the Customs and Excises that ariseth from Expence.

Liberality ought Chiefly to be Exercised in an equal Division of the Expence amongst those things that relate to Food, Cloaths, and Lodging; according to the Portion, or Station, that is allotted to every Man, with some allowance for the more refined Pleasures of the Mind; with such Distributions, as may please both sect of Philosophers, *Platonist* and *Epicureans:* The Belly must not be starved to cloath the Back-Part.

Those Expences that most Promote *Trade,* are in Cloaths and Lodging: In Adorning the Body and the House, There are a Thousand Traders Imploy'd in Cloathing and Decking the Body, and Building, and Furnishing of Houses, for one that is Imploy'd in providing Food. Belonging to Cloaths, is Fashion; which is the Shape or Form of Apparel.

In some places, it is fixt and certain; as all over *Asia,* and in *Spain;* but in *France, England,* and other places, the Dress alters; Fashion or the alteration of Dress, is a great Promoter of *Trade,* because it occasions the Expence of Cloaths, before the Old ones are worn out: It is the Spirit and Life of *Trade;* It makes a Circulation, and gives a Value by Turns, to all sorts of Commodities; keeps the great Body of *Trade* in Motion; it is an Invention to Dress a Man, as if he Lived in a perpetual Spring; he never sees the Autum of his Cloaths: The following of the Fashion, Is a Respect paid to the Prince and his Court, by approving his Choice in the shape of the Dress. It lyes under an ill Name amongst many Grave and

Sober People, but without any Just Cause; for those that Exclaim against the Vanity of the New Fashion, and at the same time, commend the Decency of the Old one, forget that every Old Fashion was once New, and then the same Argument might have been used against it. And if an *Indian,* or Stranger, that never saw any person Cloathed before, were to be Judge of the Controversy, and were to Determin upon seeing at the same time a well Drest-Courtier in the New Fashion, and another in the Old, which is accounted Decent; and a third in the Robes of an Officer, which by common Esteem, had a Reverence: It will be Two to One, against any One of the Grave Fashions; for it's only Use and Custom by which Habits become Grave and Decent, and not any particular Conveniency in the shape; for if Conveniency were the Rule of Commendation, there would arise a Question not Easily to be Determined, Whether the *Spanish* Garb made strait to the Body, or the loose Habit of the *Turks,* were to be Chosen? And therefore since all Habits are equally handsome, and hard to know which is most Convenient: The Promoting of New Fashions, ought to be Encouraged, because it provides a Livelihood for a great Part of Mankind.

The next Expence that chiefly promotes *Trade,* is Building, which is natural to Mankind, being the making of a Nest or Place for his Birth, it is the most proper and vible Distinction of Riches, and Greatness; because the Expences are too Great for Mean Persons to follow. It is a Pleasure fit to entertain Princes; for a Magnificent Structure doth best represent the Majesty of the Person that lives in it, and is the most lasting and truest History of the Greatness of his Person.

Building is the chiefest Promoter of *Trade;* it Imploys a greater Number of Trades and People, than Feeding or Cloathing: The Artificers that belong to Building, such as *Bricklayers, Carpenters, Plaisterers,* &c. imploy many Hands; Those that make the Materials for Building, such as *Bricks, Lyme, Tyle,* &c. imploy more; and with those that Furnish the Houses, such as *Upholsterers, Pewterers,* &c. they are almost Innumerable.

In *Holland,* where *Trade* hath made the Inhabitants very Rich, It is the Care of the Government, to Incourage the Builder, and at the Charge of the *State,* the Grafts[14] and Streets are made. And at *Amsterdam,* they have three Times, at great Expence, Thrown down the Walls of their

---

14. [Ditches, moats.]

City, and Dreined the Boggs, to make Room for the Builder: For Houses
are the Places where the Artificers make their Goods, and Merchants
Sell them; and without New Houses, the Trades and Inhabitants could
not Increase.

Beside, There is another great Advantage to *Trade*, by Enlarging of
Cities; the Two Beneficial Expences of Cloathing and Lodging, are
Increased; Man being Naturally Ambitious, the Living together, occa-
sion Emulation, which is seen by Out-Vying one another in Apparel,
Equipage, and Furniture of the House; whereas, if a Man lived Solitary
alone, his chiefest Expence, would be Food. It is from this very Custom;
If the Gentry of *France* Living in Cities, with the Invention of Fashion;
That *France*, tho' a Country no way fitted for *Trade*, has so great a share
of it: It is from Fashion in Cloaths, and Living in Cities, That the King
of *France's* Revenues is so great, by which he is become troublesome to
his Neighbours, and will always be so, while he can preserve Peace within
his own Country; by which, those Fountains of Riches, may run Interrupted into his *Exchequer.*

Of the Chief Causes of the Decay of TRADE in *England,* and Fall of the RENTS of LAND.

The Two Chief Causes of the Decay of *Trade*, are the many Prohibitions
and high Interest.

The Prohibition of *Trade*, is the Cause of its Decay; for all Forreign
Wares are brought in by the Exchange of the Native: So that the Prohibiting of any Foreign Commodity, doth hinder the Making and Exportation of so much of the Native, as used to be Made and Exchanged
for it. The Artificers and Merchants, that Dealt in such Goods, lose their
Trades; and the Profit that was gained by such Trades, and laid out
amongst other Traders, is Lost. The Native Stock for want of such Exportation, Falls in Value, and the Rent of the Land must Fall with the
Value of the Stock.

The common Argument for the Prohibiting Foreign Commodities,
is, That the Bringing in, and Consuming such Foreign Wares, hinders

the Making and Consuming the like sort of Goods of our own Native Make and Growth; therefore *Flanders*-Lace, *French*-Hats, Gloves, Silks, *Westphalia*-Bacon, &c. are Prohibited, because it is supposed, they hinder the Consumption of *English*-Lace, Gloves, Hats, Silk, Bacon, &c. But this is a mistaken Reason, and ariseth by not considering what it is that Occasions *Trade.* It is not Necessity that causeth the Consumption, Nature may be Satisfied with little; but it is the wants of the Mind, Fashion, and desire of Novelties, and Things scarce, that causeth *Trade.* A Person may have *English*-Lace, Gloves, or Silk, as much as he wants, and will Buy no more such; and yet, lay out his Mony on a Point of *Venice, Jessimine*-Gloves, or *French*-Silks; he may desire to Eat *Westphalia*-Bacon, when he will not *English;* so that, the Prohibition of Forreign Wares, does not necessarily cause a greater Consumption of the like sort of *English.*

Besides, There is the same wants of the Mind in Foreigners, as in the *English;* they desire Novelties; they Value *English*-Cloth, Hats, and Gloves, and Foreign Goods, more than their Native make; so that, tho' the Wearing or Consuming of Forreign Things, might lessen the Consuming of the same sort in *England;* yet there may not be a lesser Quantity made; and if the same Quantity be made, it will be a greater Advantage to the Nation, if they are Consumed in Foreign Countries, than at Home; because the Charge, and Imploy of the Freight, is Gained by it, which in bulky Goods, may be a Fourth Part of the whole Value.

The particular *Trades* that expect an Advantage by such Prohibition, are often mistaken; For if the Use of most Commodities depending upon Fashion, which often alters; The Use of those Goods cease. As to Instance, Suppose a Law to Prohibit Cane-Chairs; It would not necessarily follow, That those that make *Turkey*-Work Chairs, would have a better *Trade.* For the Fashion may Introduce, Wooden, Leather, or Silk Chairs, (which are already in Use amongst the Gentry, The Cane-Chairs being grown too Cheap and Common) or else, they may lay aside the Use of all Chairs, Introducing the Custom of Lying upon Carpets; the Ancient *Roman* Fashion; still in Use amongst the *Turks, Persians,* and all the *Eastern* Princes.

Lastly, If the Suppressing or Prohibiting of some sorts of Goods, should prove an Advantage to the *Trader,* and Increase the Consumption

of the same sort of our Native Commodity: Yet it may prove a Loss to
the Nation. For the Advantage to the Nation from *Trade,* is, from the
Customs, and from those Goods that Imploys most Hands. So that, tho'
the Prohibition may Increase, as the Consumption of the like sort of the
Native; yet if it should Obstruct the Transporting of other Goods which
were Exchanged for them, that Paid more Custom, Freight, or Imployed
more Hands in making; The Nation will be a loser by the Prohibition:
As to Instance, If Tobacco or Woollen-Cloth were used to Exchange for
Westphaly-Bacon, The Nation loseth by the Prohibition, tho' it should
Increase the Consumption of *English*-Bacon; because the First, Pays
more Freight, and Custom; and the Latter, Imploys more Hands. By this
Rule it appears, That the Prohibiting of all unwrought Goods, such as
raw Silk, Cotton, Flax, &c. and all Bulky Goods; such as Wines, Oyls,
Fruits, &c. would be a Loss to the Nation; because nothing can be sent
in Exchange that Imploys fewer Hands than the First, or Pays greater
Freight than the Latter.

It doth not alter the Case, If the Ballance of the Account, or all the
Foreign Goods, were bought by Silver or Gold; For Silver and Gold, are
Foreign Commodities; Pay but little Freight, and Imploy but few Hands
in the Working; And are at First brought into *England,* by the Exchange
of some Native Goods, and having Paid for their coming hither, must
Pay for the Carriage out. It is true, That if our Serge, Stuffs, or Cloth,
are Exchanged for Unmanufactured Goods, it would be a greater Advantage to the Nation, because of the difference in Number of Hands in
the making of the First, and the Later.

But all Trading Countries Study their Advantage of *Trade,* and Know
the difference of the Profit by the Exchange of wrought Goods, for unwrought: And therefore, for any Nation to make a Law to Prohibit all
Foreign Goods, but such only as are most Advantageous; Is to put other
Nations upon making the same Laws; and the Consequence will be to
Ruine all Foreign *Trade.* For the Foundation of all Foreign *Trade,* is,
from the Exchange of the Native Commodities of each Country, for one
another.

To Conclude, If the bringing in of Foreign Goods, should hinder the
making and consuming of the Native, which will very seldom happen;
this disadvantage is not to be Remedied by a Prohibition of those Goods;

but by Laying so great Duties upon them, that they may be always Dearer than those of our Country make: The Dearness will hinder the common Consumption of them, and preserve them for the Use of the Gentry, who may Esteem them, because they are Dear; and perhaps, might not Consume more of the *English* Growth, were the other not Imported. By such Duties, the Revenue of the Crown, will be Increased; And no Exceptions can be taken by any Foreign Prince, or Government; Since it is in the Liberty of every Government, To Lay what Duty or Imposition they please. *Trade* will continue Open, and Free; and the *Traders,* Enjoy the Profit of their *Trade:* The Dead Stock of the Nation, that is more than can be Used, will be Carried off, which will keep up the *Price* of the Native Stock, and the *Rent* of the *Land.*

The next Cause of the Decay of Trade in *England,* and the Fall of *Rents,* is, That Interest is higher in *England,* than in *Holland,* and other places of great *Trade:* It is at Six *per Cent.* in *England,* and at Three in *Holland;* For all Merchants that *Trade* in the same sort of Goods, to the same Ports, should *Trade* by the same Interest.

Interest is the Rule of Buying and Selling: And being higher in *England,* than in *Holland;* The *English* Merchant Trades with a Disadvantage, because he cannot Sell the same sort of Goods in the same Port, for the same Value as the *Dutch* Merchant. The *Dutch* Merchant can Sell 100 *l.* worth of Goods, for 103 *l.* And the *English* Merchant must Sell the same sort, for 106 *l.* to make the same Account of Principal and Interest.

When Sir *Thomas Gresham* had almost the sole *Trade* of *Spain,* and the *Turky*-Company the sole Selling of Cloth into *Turky,* and several other places; The Difference of Interest was then, no prejudice to *Trade,* tho' Interest was then in *England,* at Eight *per Cent.* Because, whoe're has the sole *Trade* to a place, may set what Price he pleaseth upon his Goods: But now, *Trade* is dispersed, the same sort of Manufacture, is made in several Countries. The *Dutch* and *English* Merchants, *Trade* in the same sort of Goods, to the same Forreign Parts, and therefore they ought to Deal by the same Interest, which is the Measure of *Trade.*

Besides, And the *English* Merchant hath the same Disadvantage in the Return of the Goods he Buys; for the *Dutch* Merchant making his Return in the same sort of Goods, can under-Sell him.

By this Difference of Interest, *Holland* is become to be the great

Magazine, and Store-House of this Part of *Europe*, for all sorts of Goods: For they may be laid up Cheaper in *Holland*, than in *England*.

It is impossible for the Merchant when he has Bought his Goods, To know what he shall Sell them for: The Value of them, depends upon the Difference betwixt the Occasion and the Quantity; tho' that be the Chiefest of the Merchants Care to observe, yet it Depends upon so many Circumstances, that it's impossible to know it. Therefore if the plenty of the Goods, has brought down the Price; the Merchant layeth them up, till the Quantity is consumed, and the Price riseth. But the *English* Merchant, cannot lay up his, but with Disadvantage; for by that time, the Price is risen so as to pay Charges and Interest at Six *per Cent.* the same Goods are sent for from *Holland*, and bring down the Price: For they are laid up there, at Three *per Cent*, and can therefore be Sold Cheaper.

For want of Considering this, in *England*, many an *English* Merchant has been undone; for, though by observing the Bill of Lading, he was able to make some Guess of the Stock that was Imported here; and therefore, hath kept his Goods by him for a Rise: But not knowing what Stock there was in *Holland*, hath not been able to sell his Goods to Profit, the same Goods being brought from thence before the Price riseth high enough to pay Ware-House-Room, and Interest.

So that, now the great part of the *English* Trade is driven by a quick Return, every Day Buying and Selling, according to a Bill of Rate every day Printed. By this Means, the *English* Trade is narrowed and confined, and the King loseth the Revenue of Importation, which he would have, if *England* were the Magazine of *Europe;* and the Nation loseth the Profit, which would arise from the Hands imploy'd in Freight and Shipping.

Interest being so high in *England*, is the Cause of the Fall of Rents; for *Trade* being confined to a Quick Return: And the Merchant being not able to lay up Foreign Goods, at the same Interest as in *Holland*, he Exports less of the Native; and the Plenty of the Native Stock Brings down the Rent of Land; for the rest of the Land that produceth the Stock, must fall, as the Price of the Stock doth.

Whereas, if Interest were at the same Rates as in *Holland*, at Three *per Cent.* it would make the Rent more certain, and raise the Value of the Land.

This Difference of Three *per Cent.* is so Considerable, that many

Dutch Merchants Living in *Holland*, having Sold their Goods in *England*; give Order, to put out their Stock to Interest in *England*; thinking That a better Advantage than they can make by *Trade*.

It will raise the *Rent* of some Estates, and preserve the *Rent* of others: For the Farmer must make up his Account, as the Merchant doth; the Interest of the Stock, must be reckoned, as well as the Rent of Land: Now if the Farmer hath 300 *l.* Stock, upon his Farm, that is so easily Rented, that he Lives well upon it; he may add 9 *l. per Annum* more to the *Rent*, when the Interest is at Three *per Cent.* and make the same Account of Profit from the Farm: As he doth now Interest, is at Six *per Cent.* And those Farmers that are hard Rented, having the same Stock, will have 9 *l. per Annum* Advance in the Account, towards the Easing the *Rent:* For altho' the Farmer gets nothing more at the Years end, yet in making up of Account, there must 9 *l.* add to the Value of Land, and taken from the Account of the Stock. If Interest were at Three *per Cent.* there would always be a Magazine of Corn and Wooll in *England*, which would be a great Advantage to the Farmer, and make his *Rent* more certain; for there are Years of Plenty, and Scarcity; and there are more Farmers undone by Years of great Plenty, than Recover themselves in Years of Scarcity; for when the Price is very low, the Crop doth not pay the Charge of Sowing, Farming, and Carrying to Market; and when it is Dear, It doth not fall to all Mens Fortune that were losers by Plenty, to have a Crop: Now if Interest were at Three *per Cent.* Corn and Wooll in Years of great Plenty, would be Bought and Laid up to be Sold in Years of Scarcity. The Buying in Years of Plenty, would keep the Price from Falling too Low; and the Selling in Years of Scarcity, would prevent it from Rising too High; by this means, a moderate Price, being best upon Corn and Wooll; the Farmers Stock and Rent of the Land, would be more certain.

But now *Holland* being the great Magazine of Corn, Man will Lay up any considerable Quantity in *England* at Six *per Cent.* when he may always Buy as much as he wants, that was Laid up at Three *per Cent.* and may bring it from thence, as Soon, and as Cheap, into any Parts of *England*, as if it were Laid up here.

Thirdly, If Interest were at Three *per Cent.* the Land of *England*, would be worth from Thirty Six, to Forty Years Purchase; for Interest, sets the Price in the Buying and Selling of Land.

The bringing down of Interest, will not alter the Value of other Wares; for the Value of all Wares, arriveth from their Use; and the Dearness and Cheapness of them, from their Plenty and Scarcity: Nor will it make Mony more Scarce. For if the Law allow no more Interest, than Three *per Cent.* they that Live upon it, must Lend at that rate, or have no Interest; for they cannot put it forth any where else to better Advantage. But if it be supposed, That it may make Mony scarce, and that it may be a Prejudice to the Government, who want the Advance of the Mony; It may be provided for, by a Clause, that all that Lend Mony to the King, shall have 6 *l. per Cent.;* such Advantage would make all Men Lend to the Government: And the King will save two *per Cent.* by such a Law.

The seeming Prejudice from such a Law, is, It will lessen the Revenue of those who live upon Interest: But this will not be a General Prejudice; for many of those Persons have Land as well as Mony, and will get as much by the Rise of one, as by the Fall of the other. Besides, many of them, are Persons that live Thriftily, and much within the Compass of their Estates; and therefore, will not want it, but in Opinion. They have had a long Time, the Advantage of the Borrower; for the Land yielding but 4 *l. per Cent.* and the Interest being at 6 *l. per Cent.* a new Debt is every Year contracted of 2 *l. per Cent.* more than the Value of the Debt in Land will pay, which hath Devoured many a good Farm; and eat up the Estates of many of the Ancient Gentry of *England.*

Moses, that Wise Law-Giver, who designed, that the Land, divided amongst the *Jews,* should continue in their Families; forbid the *Jews* to pay Interest, well knowing that the Merchants of *Tyre,* who were to be their near Neighbours, would, by Lending Mony at Interest, at last get their Lands: And that this seems to be the Reason, is plain; For the *Jews* might take Interest of Strangers, but not pay; for by taking Interest, they could not lose their Estates.

The Lawyers have invented Intails, to preserve Estates in Families; and the bringing down of Interest to Three *per Cent.* will much help to continue it; because the Estates being raised to double the Value, will require double the Time, after the same Proportion of Expence to Consume it in.

The raising the Value of Land, at this Time, seems most necessary, when the Nation is Engaged in such a Chargeable War: For the Land is the Fund that must support and preserve the Government; and the Taxes will be lesser and easier payd; for they will not be so great: For 3 *sh.* in the *Pound,* is now 133½ Part of every Mans Estate in Land, reckoning at Twenty Years Purchase. But if the Value of the Land be doubled, it will be the 226 Part of the Land, which may be much easier born.

Campinella, who Wrote an 100 years since, upon considering of the great Tract of the Land of *France;* says, That if ever it were United under one Prince, it would produce so great a Revenue; It might give Law to all *Europe.*[15]

The Effect of this Calculation, Is since, seen by the Attempts of this present King of *France:* And therefore, since *England* is an Island, and the Number of Acres cannot be Increased; It seems absolutely necessary, That the Value of them, should be raised to Defend the Nation against such a Powerful Force: It will be some Recompence to the Gentry, whose Lands must bear the Burthen of the War, to have the Value of their Estates Raised; which is the Fund and Support of the Government; Is a great Advantage to the whole Nation; and it's the greater, because it doth not Disturb, Lessen, nor Alter the Value of any Thing else.

15. "Th. Campenella de Monarchia Hispania." Editio novissima, aucta et emendata ut praefatio ad lectorem indicat (Amsterodami, 1653); see chap. XXIV (De Gallia), p. 187.

6

Discourses upon Trade
1691

DUDLEY NORTH was born the son of the fourth Baron North in 1641. It is said that he was stolen by a beggar-woman for his clothes as a child but was soon recovered. He showed no taste for book learning early in life and was apprenticed to an English merchant named Davis, who made him agent to the Turkish trade at Smyrna in 1661 and Constantinople in 1662. By all accounts, he was a vigorous and successful factor, giving life to what had been a rather sluggish trade there. He was made treasurer of the Turkey Company, and there was apparently some talk of his becoming ambassador of England to Constantinople. Having made a fortune, he returned to London in 1680, a respected man of the world, fluent in Turkish and some of the dialects of the Levant. In 1682, he was named sheriff of London, to the great dismay of the Whigs. Afterward, he became a commissioner for the customs and an agent in the treasury as well as a Tory member of Parliament from Banbury during the reign of James II. After the accession of William of Orange in 1689, he remained in London and was the subject of an inconclusive inquiry for his role in packing the juries that condemned Algernon Sidney and others in 1682. Thereafter, he was active mainly in commercial ventures until his death on the last day of 1691.

The work reprinted here is *Discourses upon Trade* (1691; repr. Baltimore: Johns Hopkins University Press, 1907, ed. Jacob H. Hollander), and is one of the earliest attempts to theorize as a whole the workings of a market economy in England. The unbracketed notes are by Hollander; the bracketed ones are by the present editor.

———

Discourses upon Trade

THE PREFACE

These Papers came directed to me, in order, as I suppose, to be made Publick: And having transmitted them to the Press, which is the only means whereby the University of Mankind is to be inform'd, I am absolv'd of that Trust.

The Author is pleas'd to conceal himself; which after perusal of his Papers, I do not ascribe to any Diffidence of his Reasons, the Disgusts of Great Men, nor overmuch Modesty, which are the ordinary Inducements for lying hid; but rather to avoid the Fatigue of digesting, and polishing his Sentiments into such accurate Method, and clean Style, as the World commonly expects from Authors: I am confident he seeks only the Publick Good, and little regards Censure for the want of Neatness, and Dress, whereof he seems to make a slight account, and to rely wholly upon the Truth, and Justice of his Matter; yet he may reasonably decline the being noted, for either a careless, or an illiterate Person.

The Publick is an acute, as well as merciless Beast, which neither oversees[1] a Failing, nor forgives it; but stamps Judgment and Execution immediately, thô upon a Member of itself; and is no less Ingrateful than common Beggars, who affront their Benefactors, without whose Charity their Understandings would starve.

Wherefore I cannot but excuse our Friend's Retiredment, and shall

———

1. [Overlooks.]

take advantage of his absence so far, as to speak of his Discourses with more freedom, then I verily believe his Presence would bear.

As for the Style, you will find it *English,* such as Men speaks, which, according to *Horace,* is the Law and Rule of Language.[2] Nor do I perceive that the Gentleman intended more than his Title holds forth; common Discourses, which possibly were taken by an *Amanuensis,* and dispatcht without much Correction. Surely no Man would refuse the Conversation of an ingenious Friend, because he doth not speak like *Tully;*[3] And if the Conversation be so desirable, why should we quarrel with the same thing in Writing? Nay, it is very impolitick, by such Exactions of Labour and Pains, to discourage all Ingenious Persons from medling in Print, whereby we lose the benefit of their Judgment, in matters of common concern.

Words are indeed a Felicity, which some have in great perfection; but many times, like a fair Face, prove Temptations to Vice; for I have known very good Sence neglected, and post-poned to an Elegance of Expression; whereas if Words are wanted, the whole Effort is made by pure strength of Reason, and that only is relied on.

The Lawyers in their Deeds, wave all the Decorums of Language, and regard only incontrovertible Expressions. The Merchants in their Policies and Exchanges, use no one Word but what is necessary to their Point, because the Matter and Substance only is intended, and not the Dress; Why then should Reasoners be incumbred, beyond what is necessary to make their Reason understood?

To speak very short, and yet clear, is a Vertue to be envyed; and if directed to Persons, or Assemblies whose business is great, or made so by many Mens interposing in it, it is absolutely necessary; for your Discourse, if it be tedious, is better spared than the time; but it is not so in dealing with lazy Ignorance of any sort, or an Ear-itching Rabble, who are actually impertinent (as well as impetuous) and not sensible of cheat. And I may add, That in Writing, unless in the Epistolary way, (which being supposed hasty, ought to be short and figurative) an abundance of

2. *De Arte Poetica,* 70.
3. [I.e., Cicero.]

Words is more pardonable than obscurity, or want of Sence, because we take our own time, and have leisure to peruse it.

I will grant that amongst opulent and idle Persons, as well as Schollars, whose business lies in Words, the bare polishing of Language, is one of the most commendable Entertainments; and to them we resign it; for to Men of business, it is the most hateful thing, I mean, meer Idleness.

I grant also, that delicacy of Words, now most used in Poetry, is useful for disposing way-ward People to learn, or make them endure to read. But the World is not at such low ebb of Curiosity in this Age. Men are forward enough to run their Noses into Books, especially such as deal in Faction and Controversie: And it were well if they were either Wrote or Read with as much Integrity as Industry; we have no need of Sugarplum devices to wheedle Men into Reading, they are Inquisitive enough; and if the Subject be their own Interest, I am of Opinion, if you can make 'em understand it, you may trust them.

As for the Method used in these Papers, there is so little of it affected, that I am afraid some will say there is none at all: I never thought that true Method consisted in affected Divisions, and Sub-divisions, Firsts, Seconds, Sub-firsts, &c. tho' all that is very useful in Works intended to be consulted as Repertories; but where the Understanding is to be informed, it is meer trash, and the business is often lost in it.

And in such Designs it is enough, if Things lie in the Order of Nature, and the Conclusion is not put before the Premisses, so that the course of the Argument is limpid, and intelligible: A Friend of mine used to say, That if the First Chapter were before the Second, it was all the Method he cared for, meaning only what I have observed, which I suppose you will find here.

This drudgery of Digesting, is another Excise upon Sence, which keeps back a great deal of it from coming forth; and without a singular tallent, and much exercise, it makes composing extreamly difficult. I do not understand why other Men, as well as *Mountaigne*,[4] may not be indulged to ramble in Essays, provided the Sence fails not.

---

4. The first two books of Montaigne's "Essays" were published in 1580, the third in 1588.

The *Scalligerana*,[5] *Pirroana*,[6] *Pensees*,[7] and *Mr. Selden's Table-talk*,[8] are all heaps of incoherent scraps; yet for the wit and spirit esteemed; therefore let that which is most valuable, Reason and Truth be encouraged to come abroad, without imposing such chargeable Equipages upon it, whereby Writers are made to resemble Brewers Horses, very useful Animals, but arrant Drudges.

Methinks when I meet with a great deal of Firsting, and Seconding, I smell one who conceits himself an Author, a Creature as fulsome as any other sort of Impertinents. If there be Reason, and that understood, what could the formal Methodist add? Let me have the Cockle, and who will take the gay shell.

Now after all this it will be injust, not to say somewhat of the Subject-matter of these Discourses, which is Commerce and Trade; and the Author's manner of Treating it.

He seems to be of a Temper different from most, who have medled with this Subject in Publick; for it is manifest, his Knowledge and Experience of Trade is considerable, which could not be attained, unless he were a Trader himself; and yet it is not to be collected from anything he says, of what Nature his dealing hath been; for he speaks impartially of Trade in general, without warping to the Favour of any particular Interest. It hath been observed formerly, when Merchants have been consulted, and the Questions concerned only Trade in general, they agreed in Opinion; but when opposite Interests were concerned, they differed

5. "Scaligeriana, sive Excerpta ex ore Josephi Scaligeri"—a collection of the familiar conversations of Joseph Scaliger (1540–1609), the classicist and scholar—was first printed at The Hague in 1666, and in various editions thereafter. Des Maizeaux, a later editor and the literary historian of the work, characterizes it as "le pere de tous les livres qu' on a publiez sous le titre d' ANA" (cf. "Scaligerana, Thuana, Perroniana, Pithoeana, et Colomesiana . . . avec les notes de plusiers savans." 2 vol. 12°. Amsterdam, 1740).

6. Probably "Perroniana," a collection of the epigrams and observations—critical, historical, and moral—of Cardinal du Perron, made by Christophe Dupuy and first published in 1669 (cf. Des Maizeaux, note 3, above).

7. Pascal's "Pensées" first appeared in 1670, eight years after the author's death, in garbled and fragmentary form.

8. Selden's "Table Talk" was edited by his secretary, Richard Milward, and printed in 1689.

toto caelo.[9] As for his Opinion touching Interest of Money, wherein he is clear, that it should be left freely to the Market, and not be restrained by Law, he is lyable to the same suspicion, which attends those of a different Judgment; that is, partiality to his own Interest; the difference is only in the supposed Cause, which in the one, is Wealth, and in the other Want. He hath given his Judgment with his Reasons, which every one is free to canvas; and there is no other means whereby a wise and honest Person can justifie his Opinions in Publick Concerns.

In the next place, I find Trade here Treated at another rate, than usually hath been; I mean Philosophically: for the ordinary and vulgar conceits, being meer Husk and Rubbish, are waved; and he begins at the quick, from Principles indisputably true; and so proceeding with like care, comes to a Judgment of the nicest Disputes and Questions concerning Trade. And this with clearness enough, for he reduceth things to their Extreams, wherein all discriminations are most gross and sensible, and then shows them; and not in the state of ordinary concerns, whereof the terms are scarce distinguishable.

This Method of Reasoning hath been introduc'd with the new Philosophy, the old dealt in Abstracts more than Truths; and was employed about forming Hypotheses, to fit abundance of precarious and insensible Principles; such as the direct or oblique course of the Atomes in *vacuo,*[10] Matter and Form, Privation, solid Orbs, *fuga vacui,*[11] and many others of like nature; whereby they made sure of nothing; but upon the appearance of *Des Carte's* excellent dissertation *de Methodo,*[12] so much approved and accepted in our Ages, all those Chymera's soon dissolved and vanisht.

And hence it is, that Knowledge in great measure is become Mechanical; which word I need not interpret farther, than by noting, it here means, built upon clear and evident Truths. But yet this great Improvement of Reason which the World hath lately obtained, is not diffus'd

9. [By 180 degrees.]
10. [A vacuum.]
11. [(Nature) abhors a vacuum.]
12. [I.e., René Descartes (1596–1650), *Discourse on Method* (1637).]

enough, and resides chiefly with the studious and learned, the common People having but a small share; for they cannot abstract, so as to have a true and just thought of the most ordinary things, but are possest and full of the vulgar Errors of sense: Except in some few things that fall within the compass of their day-labour, and so gives them an Experience; As when a Common-Seaman, with all his Ignorance, proves a better Mechanick, for actual Service, than the Professor himself, with all his Learning.

The case of Trade is the same; for although to buy and sell, be the Employment of every man, more or less; and the Common People, for the most part, depend upon it for their daily subsistence; yet there are very few who consider Trade in general upon true Principles, but are satisfied to understand their own particular Trades, and which way to let themselves into immediate gain. And out of this active Sphere nothing is so fallacious, and full of Error, as mens Notions of Trade. And there is another Reason, why this matter seems less understood, than in truth it is. For whenever Men consult for the Publick Good, as for the advancement of Trade, wherein all are concerned, they usually esteem the immediate Interest of their own to be the common Measure of Good and Evil. And there are many, who to gain a little in their own Trades, care not how much others suffer; and each Man strives, that all others may be forc'd, in their dealings, to act subserviently for his Profit, but under the covert of the Publick.

So Clothiers would have men be forc'd to buy their Manufacture; and I may mention such as sell Wool, they would have men forc'd to buy of them at an high Price, though the Clothier loseth. The Tinners would have their Tin dear, though the Merchant profits little: And in general all those who are lazy, and do not, or are not active enough, and cannot look out, to vent the Product of their Estates, or to Trade with it themselves, would have all Traders forc'd by Laws, to bring home to them sufficient Prizes, whether they gain or lose by it. And all the while, not one of them will endure to be under a force, to Sell, or Let their own Estates at lower rates, than the free Market of things will produce.

Now it is no wonder, that out of these Ingredients a strange Medley of Error should result, whereby seldom any Publick Order, which hath been establisht, and intended, or at least pretended for the good of Trade in general, hath had a suitable Effect; but on the contrary, hath for the most part proved prejudicial, and thereupon, by common consent, been discontinued. But this is too copious Matter for a Preface, and tho' many Instances occur, I leave all, and return to the matter of Vulgar Errors in Trade.

It is not long since there was a great noise with Inquiries into the Balance of Exportation and Importation; and so into the Balance of Trade, as they called it. For it was fancyed that if we brought more Commodities in, than we carried out, we were in the High-way to Ruin. In like manner have we heard much said against the *East-India* Trade, against the *French* Trade, with many other like politick conceits in Trade; most of which, Time and better Judgment hath disbanded; but others succeed in their room, according as new Persons find Encouragement to invent, and inspire, for promoting their private Interest, by imposing on those, who desire to be cunning. And now we complain for want of Money in specie, that Bullion is Exported or mis-employed to other uses, than making Money; and ascribe the deadness of Trade, especially of Corn, and Cattel in the Country, to this; and hope by a Regulation of the Bullion-Trade, and stinting the Price, except it be in Money, to make a thorough Reformation, and give new Life to all things, with much more, *ejusdem farina,*[13] which I do not particularize, this being enough for a taste.

Now it may appear strange to hear it said,

That the whole World as to Trade, is but as one Nation or People, and therein Nations are as Persons.

That the loss of a Trade with one Nation, is not that only, separately considered, but so much of the Trade of the World rescinded and lost, for all is combined together.

That there can be no Trade unprofitable to the Publick; for if any prove so, men leave it off; and wherever the Traders thrive, the Publick, of which they are a part, thrives also.

That to force Men to deal in any prescrib'd manner, may profit such as happen to serve them; but the Publick gains not, because it is taking from one Subject, to give to another.

---

13. [Of the same grain, the same nature.]

That no Laws can set Prizes[14] in Trade, the Rates of which, must and will make themselves: But when such Laws do happen to lay any hold, it is so much Impediment to Trade, and therefore prejudicial.

That Money is a Merchandize, whereof there may be a glut, as well as a scarcity, and that even to an Inconvenience.

That a People cannot want Money to serve the ordinary dealing, and more than enough they will not have.

That no Man shall be the richer for the making much Money, nor have any part of it, but as he buys it for an equivalent price.

That the free Coynage is a perpetual Motion found out, whereby to Melt and Coyn without ceasing, and so to feed Goldsmiths and Coyners at the Publick Charge.

That debasing the Coyn is defrauding one another, and to the Publick there is no sort of Advantage from it; for that admits no Character, or Value, but Intrinsick.

That the sinking Money by Allay or Weight is all one.

That Exchange and ready Money, are the same, nothing but Carriage and re-carriage being saved.

That Money Exported in Trade is an increase to the Wealth of the Nation; but spent in War, and Payments abroad, is so much Impoverishment.

In short, That all favour to one Trade or Interest against another, is an Abuse, and cuts so much of Profit from the Publick. With many other like Paradoxes, no less strange to most men, than true in themselves; but in my Opinion, clearly flowing from the Principles, and Discourses that follow, which you may freely peruse and censure, for now I have done.

Perhaps my unknown Confident[15] may think me too sawcy, for putting my Oar into his Boat, and I will not excuse my self to him, otherwise than by demanding the same Liberty he hath taken; that is, to have a fling at the World; and as yet the Advantage is his, for he hath two, and better, for my one. And so Farewel.

14. [Prices.]
15. [Confidant.]

A Discourse Concerning the Abatement of Interest

Arguments for Abatement of Interest are many, *viz.*

I. When Interest is less, Trade is incourag'd, and the Merchant can be a Gainer; whereas, when it is great, the Usurer, or Money-owner takes all.

II. The *Dutch*, with whom Interest is low, Trade cheaper, and under-sell us.

III. Land falls in value, as Interest riseth.

With divers others, whereof the Facts may be true, but proceed from another Cause, and conduce nothing to the purpose for which they are alledg'd.

I shall not formally apply myself to answer all the Arguments and Discourses, that commonly are found in Pamphlets, and Conversation upon this Subject; as if I were to Advocate the Cause of Interest: But give my thoughts impartially in the whole matter, with regard to the Profit of the whole Nation, and to no particular Persons project: Wherein I hope to propose, that which may resolve any doubt that can be raised, and leave every one to apply it, as they think fit.

The Question to be considered is, Whether the Government have reason by a Law, to prohibit the taking more than 4 *l. per Cent.* Interest for Money lent, or to leave the Borrower and Lender to make their own Bargains.

In the Disquisition of this, many things are to be considered, and particularly such as relate to Trade, of which a true Notion will set right a World of Mistakes, wherefore that now shall be chiefly treated of.

Trade is nothing else but a Commutation of Superfluities; for instance: I give of mine, what I can spare, for somewhat of yours, which I want, and you can spare.

Thus Trade, whilst it is restrained within the limits of a Town, Country, or Nation, signifieth only the Peoples supplying each other with Conveniences, out of what that Town, Country, or Nation affords.

And in this, he who is most diligent, and raiseth most Fruits, or

maketh most of Manufactory, will abound most in what others make, or
raise; and consequently be free from Want, and enjoy most Conveniences, which is truly to be Rich, altho' there were no such thing as
Gold, Silver, or the like amongst them.

Mettals are very necessary for many Uses, and are to be reckon'd
among the Fruits and Manufactories of the World. And of these, Gold
and Silver being by nature very fine, and more scarce than others, are
higher prized; and a little of them is very reasonably esteem'd equal in
value with a great quantity of other Mettals, &c. For which reason, and
moreover that they are imperishable, as well as convenient for easie
stowage and removal, and not from any Laws, they are made a Standard,
or common Measure to deal with; and all Mankind concur in it, as every
one knows, therefore I need not inlarge further in this matter.

Now it is to be consider'd, that Mankind being fallen into a way of
commuting in this manner, to serve their occasions, some are more provident, others more profuse; some by their Industry and Judgment raise
more Fruits from the Earth, than they consume in supplying their
own occasions; and then the surplus remains with them, and is Property
or Riches.

And Wealth thus contracted, is either commuted for other Mens
Land (supposing all Men to have had some) or massed up in heaps of
Goods; be the same of Mettals, or anything valuable. And those are the
Rich, who transmit what they have to their Posterity; whereby particu-
lar Families become rich; and of such are compounded Cities, Countries,
Nations, &c.

And it will be found, that as some particular Men in a Town grow
richer, and thrive better than others; so also do Nations, who by Trade
serving the occasions of their Neighbours, supply themselves with what
they have occasion for from abroad; which done, the rest is laid up, and
is Silver, Gold, &c. for as I said, these being commutable for everything,
and of small bulk, are still preferr'd to be laid up, till occasion shall call
them out to supply other Necessaries wanted.

Now Industry and Ingenuity having thus distinguisht Men into Rich
and Poor; What is the consequence? One rich Man hath Lands, not only
more than he can manage, but so much, that letting them out to others,
he is supplied with a large over-plus, so needs no farther care.

Another rich Man hath Goods; that is, Mettals, Manufactures, &c. in great quantity, with these he serves his own occasions, and then commutes the rest in Trade; that is, supplies others with what they want, and takes in exchange what they had of, beyond their own occasions, whereby managing cunningly, he must always advance.

Now as there are more Men to Till the Ground than have Land to Till, so also there will be many who want Stock to manage; and also (when a Nation is grown rich) there will be Stock for Trade in many hands, who either have not the skill, or care not for the trouble of managing it in Trade.

But as the Landed Man letts his Land, so these still lett their Stock; this latter is call'd Interest, but is only Rent for Stock, as the other is for Land. And in several Languages, hiring of Money, and Lands, are Terms of common use; and it is so also in some Countries[16] in *England.*

Thus to be a Landlord, or a Stock-lord is the same thing; the Landlord hath the advantage only in this: That his Tenant cannot carry away the Land, as the Tenant of the other may the Stock; and therefore Land ought to yield less profit than Stock, which is let out at the greater hazard.

These things consider'd, it will be found, that as plenty makes cheapness in other things, as Corn, Wool, &c. when they come to Market in greater Quantities than there are Buyers to deal for, the Price will fall; so if there be more Lenders than Borrowers, Interest will also fall; wherefore it is not low Interest makes Trade, but Trade increasing, the Stock of the Nation makes Interest low.

It is said, that in *Holland* Interest is lower than in *England.* I answer, It is; because their Stock is greater than ours. I cannot hear that they ever made a Law to restrain Interest, but am certainly informed, that at this day, the Currant Interest between Merchant and Merchant, when they disburse Money for each others Account, is 6 *per Cent.* and the Law justifies it.

I allow Money is many times lent at 3, and 4 *per Cent.* but it is upon Mortgages, out of which the State hath a Duty, and by the course of Titles there, such dealing is perfectly safe; and this is still by private consent and agreement, and not by co-ersion and order of Law. The like

16. [Regions.]

often happens here, when poor Widows and Orphans purchase the Security of their Livelihoods, and punctual Payment, by lending at small Interest, to such as need not the Money.

It might not be amiss in this place, to say somewhat of the Publick Banks that are in Forreign Parts, as *Amsterdam, Venice,* &c. but that is a Subject I have not time to dilate upon: I shall only say, that it is a cunning way of supplying the Government once with a great Sum; and as long as the Government stands, it is no loss to them that have the Credit, nor no great Inconveniency; for all Bills of Exchange are made by Law payable in Bank, and not otherwise; for Dealers in Exchanges it is best that way, and such as want their Money, find no difficulty in selling their Credits, the price of which riseth and falleth according to Demanders, as of other things.

I do not understand that true, two[17] Banks pay any Interest; it is true there are several Funds, *viz.* The Mint in *Venice,* and the Chamber in *Amsterdam,* with several others in those and other Cities, where Money is put out at Interest for Lives, and several other ways, and at different Rates, more or less, according to the Credit these Funds have, which are the Security; and these may, by mistake, be called the Banks, which they are not, being only such as the Chamber of *London, East-India-House,* &c. were.

I do not believe, but the Usurer, according to the saying, will take half a Loaf, rather than no bread: But I averr, that high Interest will bring Money out from Hoards, Plate, &c. into Trade, when low Interest will keep it back.

Many Men of great Estates, keep by them for State[18] and Honour, great Quantities of Plate, Jewels, &c. which certainly they will be more inclin'd to do, when Interest is very low, than when it is high.

Such as have nothing to subsist by, but the Interest of Money, must either let it out, or Trade with it themselves, and be contented with what they can get; but that hinders not, but very many other Men, who are rich, and not so prest, may, if Interest be very low, choose to make use of their Stocks in Jewels, Plate, &c. rather than run the hazards, and be at

17. *sic.*
18. [Status or dignity.]

the trouble of dealing with necessitous and knavish Men, such as many Borrowers are, for inconsiderable gains.

So that it cannot be denied, but the lowering of Interest may, and probably will keep some Money from coming abroad into Trade; whereas on the contrary, high Interest certainly brings it out.

Next is to be considered, that Dealings between Borrowers and Lenders are of two kinds: 1. Upon Mortgage, or Pawn. 2. Upon Personal Security, and that either by single Bond, or with Sureties; all which, as they differ in goodness, so ought in reason to bear different Prizes. Shall any Man be bound to lend a single Person, upon the same Terms, as others lend upon Mortgages, or Joynt Obligations?

Then again it is to be considered, that the Moneys imployed at Interest in this Nation, are not near the Tenth part, disposed to Trading People, wherewith to manage their Trades; but are for the most part lent for the supplying of Luxury, and to support the Expence of Persons, who though great Owners of Lands, yet spend faster than their Lands bring in; and being loath to sell, choose rather to mortgage their Estates.

So that in truth an Ease to Interest, will rather be a Support to Luxury, than to Trade; the poor Trading Man, who hath but a narrow Stock, or none at all, supplies himself by buying Goods of rich Men at time, and thereby pays Interest, not at the rate of 5, 6, or 8, but 10, 12, and more *per Cent.* And this is not in the Power of any Legislature to prevent, or remedy.

It may be said, let him take Money at Interest, and not buy at Time. But then Men must be found, that will lend; the Legislative must provide a Fund to borrow upon.

The Trade of setting out Ships, runs very much upon this course, wherein it is usual to Bum'em (as they call it) at 36 *per Cent.* And this cannot be remedied; and if it were, it would be a stop, as well to the Building, as the setting out of many Ships; whereby, after all, not only the publick, but the private Persons concern'd are Gainers for the most part.

Thus when all things are considered, it will be found best for the Nation to leave the Borrowers and the Lender to make their own Bargains, according to the Circumstances they lie under; and in so doing you will follow the course of the wise *Hollanders,* so often quoted on this account: and the consequences will be, that when the Nation thrives, and grows rich, Money will be to be had upon good terms, but the clean contrary will fall out, when the Nation grows poorer and poorer.

Let any one Answer me, why do not the Legislators in those poor Countries, where Interest is at 10, & 12 *per Cent*, make such Laws to restrain Interest, and reduce it for the good of the People? If they should attempt it, it wou'd soon appear, that such Laws would not be effectual to do it. For when there are more Borrowers than Lenders, as in poor Countries, where if a rich Man hath 100 *l.* to dispose, and there are four, five or more Men striving for it; the Law would be evaded by underhand Bargains, making Loans in Goods, drawing Bills, and a thousand Ways beside; which cannot be prevented.

It is probable that when Laws restrain Interest of Money, below the Price, which the Reason of Trade settles, and Traders cannot (as we will suppose) evade the Law, or not without great difficulty, or hazard, and have not Credit to borrow at Legal Interest, to make, or increase their Stock; so much of Trade is lopt off; and there cannot be well a greater obstruction to diminish Trade then that would be. The consideration of all these Matters, makes out an universal Maxime, That as more Buyers than Sellers raiseth the price of a Commodity, so more Borrowers than Lenders, will raise Interest.

And the State may with as much Justice make a Law that Lands which heretofore have been Lett for 10 s. *per* Acre, shall not now be Lett for above 8 s. *per* Acre, as that Money, or Stock, from 5 *per Cent*, shall be Lett for 4 *per Cent*, the Property being as good, and as much the Substance of the Kingdom in the one, as in the other.

I will not say any thing to the Theological Arguments against Interest of Moneys; by those 3 *per Cent* is no more lawful, than 4, or 12. But this I shall maintain Politically, that if you take away Interest, you take away Borrowing and Lending. And in consequence the Gentry, who are behind hand,[19] be it for what cause soever, must sell, and cannot Mortgage; which will bring down the Price of Land. And the Trader whatever his skill is, if he hath no Stock, must either sit still, or buy at Time, which is Interest under another Name. And they who are poor, will al-

---

19. [I.e., late, in arrears.]

ways be so, and we should soon relapse into the state of One Thousand Years ago.

And whereas the Stock of the Nation is now reckon'd great, let it be fairly valued, and it will be found much less than it seems to be; for all the Monies that are owing upon Land Securities, must be struck off, and not estimated; or else you will have a wrong Account; for if a Gentleman of 500 *l. per Annum,* owes 8000 *l.* and you value[20] his Land, and the Lender's Stock both, you make an account of the same things twice.

And whereas we make great Accounts of Money'd Men in the Nation, in truth there are but few; for suppose all that have lent upon Mortgage, had Land for their Moneys, as indeed in strictness of Law they have, there wou'd be but few Money'd Men in the Nation left. The borrowing of Money of one, to pay another, call'd, Robbing of *Peter* to pay *Paul,* so much practis'd now-a-days, makes us think the Nation far richer than it is.

A Discourse of Coyned Money

In the former Discourse, it hath been already made appear, that Gold and Silver for their scarcity, have obtained in small quantities, to equal in value far greater quantities of other Metals, &c. And farther, from their easie Removal, and convenient Custody, have also obtained to be the common Measure in the World between Man and Man in their dealings, as well for Land, Houses, &c., as for Goods and other Necessaries.

For the greater Improvement of this Convenience, and to remove some Difficulties, which would be very troublesome, about knowing quantities and qualities in common and ordinary dealing: Princes and States have made it a matter of Publick concern, to ascertain the Allay,[21] and to determine the Weights, *viz.* the quantities of certain Pieces, which we call Coyn, or Money; and such being distinguish'd by Stamps, and Inscriptions, it is made difficult, and highly Penal to Counterfeit them.

20. [Appraise.]
21. [Alloy.]

By this means the Trade of the World is made easie, and all the numerous species of several Commodities have a common Measure. Besides the Gold and Silver being thus coyned into Money, and so become more useful for Commerce than in the Log or Block, hath in all places, except in *England* since the free Coynage, reasonably obtained a greater value than it had before: And that not only above the real charge of making it so, but is become a State-Revenue (except as before) tho' not very great. Whereas if Silver coyned and uncoyned bore the same rate, as it doth with us in *England,* where it is coyned at the Charge of the Publick, it will be lyable frequently to be melted down, as I shall shew anon.

Money being thus the Common Measure of Buying and Selling, every body who hath any thing to sell, and cannot procure Chapmen for it, is presently apt to think, that want of Money in the Kingdom, or Country is the cause why his Goods do not go off; and so, want of Money, is the common Cry; which is a great mistake, as shall be shewn. I grant all stop in Trade proceeds from some cause; but it is not from the want of specifick Money, there being other Reasons for it; as will appear by the following Discourse.

No Man is richer for having his Estate all in Money, Plate, &c. lying by him, but on the contrary, he is for that reason the poorer. That man is richest, whose Estate is in a growing condition, either in Land at Farm, Money at Interest, or Goods in Trade: If any man, out of an humour, should turn all his Estate into Money, and keep it dead, he would soon be sensible of Poverty growing upon him, whilst he is eating out of the quick stock.

But to examine the matter closer, what do these People want, who cry out for Money? I will begin with the Beggar; he wants, and importunes for Money: What would he do with it if he had it? buy Bread, &c. Then in truth it is not Money, but Bread, and other Necessaries for Life that he wants. Well then; the Farmer complains, for the want of Money; surely it is not for the Beggar's Reason, to sustain Life, or pay Debts; but he thinks that were more Money in the Country, he should have a Price for his Goods. Then it seems Money is not his want, but a Price for his Corn, and Cattel, which he would sell, but cannot. If it be askt, if the want of Money be not, what then is the reason, why he cannot get a price? I answer, it must proceed from one of these three Causes.

1. Either there is too much Corn and Cattel in the Country, so that most who come to Market have need of selling, as he hath, and few of buying: Or, 2. There wants the usual vent abroad, by Transportation, as in time of War, when Trade is unsafe, or not permitted. Or, 3. The Consumption fails, as when men by reason of Poverty, do not spend so much in their Houses as formerly they did; wherefore it is not the increase of specifick Money, which would at all advance the Farmers Goods, but the removal of any of these three Causes, which do truly keep down the Market.

The Merchant and Shop-keeper want Money in the same manner, that is, they want a Vent for the Goods they deal in, by reason that the Markets fail, as they will always upon any cause, like what I have hinted. Now to consider what is the true source of Riches, or in the common Phrase, plenty of Money, we must look a little back, into the nature and steps of Trade.

Commerce and Trade, as hath been said, first springs from the Labour of Man, but as the Stock increases, it dilates more and more. If you suppose a Country to have nothing in it but the Land it self, and the Inhabitants; it is plain that at first, the People have only the Fruits of the Earth, and Metals raised from the Bowels of it, to Trade withal, either by carrying out into Foreign Parts, or by selling to such as will come to buy of them, whereby they may be supplyed with the Goods of other Countries wanted there.

In process of time, if the People apply themselves industriously, they will not only be supplied, but advance to a great overplus of Forreign Goods, which improv'd, will enlarge their Trade. Thus the *English* Nation will sell unto the *French, Spaniards, Turk,* &c. not only the product of their own Country, as Cloath, Tin, Lead, &c. but also what they purchase of others, as Sugar, Pepper, Callicoes, &c. still buying where Goods are produc'd, and cheap, and transporting them to Places where they are wanted, making great advantage thereby.

In this course of Trade, Gold and Silver are in no sort different from other Commodities, but are taken from them who have Plenty, and carried to them who want, or desire them, with as good profit as other Merchandizes. So that an active prudent Nation groweth rich, and the sluggish Drones grow poor; and there cannot be any Policy other than this, which being introduc'd and practis'd, shall avail to increase Trade and Riches.

But this Proposition, as single[22] and plain as it is, is seldom so well understood, as to pass with the generality of Mankind; but they think by force of Laws, to retain in their Country all the Gold and Silver which Trade brings in; and thereby expect to grow rich immediately: All which is a profound Fallacy, and hath been a Remora,[23] whereby the growing Wealth of many Countries have been obstructed.

The Case will more plainly appear, if it be put of a single Merchant, or if you please to come nearer the point, of a City or County only.

Let a Law be made, and what is more, be observ'd, that no Man whatsoever shall carry any Money out of a particular Town, County, or Division, with liberty to carry Goods of any sort: so that all the Money which every one brings with him, must be left behind, and none be carried out.

The consequence of this would be, that such Town, or County were cut off from the rest of the Nation; and no Man would dare to come to Market with his Money there; because he must buy, whether he likes, or not: and on the other side, the People of that place could not go to other Markets as Buyers, but only as Sellers, being not permitted to carry any Money out with them.

Now would not such a Constitution as this, soon bring a Town or County to a miserable Condition, with respect to their Neighbours, who have free Commerce, whereby the Industrious gain from the slothful and luxurious part of Mankind? The Case is the same, if you extend your thought from a particular Nation, and the several Divisions, and Cities, with the Inhabitants in them, to the whole World, and the several Nations, and Governments in it. And a Nation restrained in its Trade, of which Gold and Silver is a principal, if not an essential Branch, would suffer, and grow poor, as a particular place within a Country, as I have discoursed. A Nation in the World, as to Trade, is in all respects like a City in a Kingdom, or Family in a City.

Now since the Increase of Trade is to be esteem'd the only cause that Wealth and Money increase, I will add some farther Considerations upon that subject.

22. [Particular.]
23. [A let, or obstacle.]

The main spur to Trade, or rather to Industry and Ingenuity, is the exorbitant Appetites of Men, which they will take pains to gratifie, and so be disposed to work, when nothing else will incline them to it; for did Men content themselves with bare Necessaries, we should have a poor World.

The Glutton works hard to purchase Delicacies, wherewith to gorge himself; the Gamester, for Money to venture at Play; the Miser, to hoard; and so others. Now in their pursuit of those Appetites, other Men less exorbitant are benefitted; and tho' it may be thought few profit by the Miser, yet it will be found otherwise, if we consider, that besides the humour of every Generation, to dissipate what another had collected, there is benefit from the very Person of a covetous Man; for if he labours with his own hands, his Labour is very beneficial to them who imploy him; if he doth not work, but profit by the Work of others, then those he sets on work have benefit by their being employed.

Countries which have sumptuary Laws, are generally poor; for when Men by those Laws are confin'd to narrower Expence than otherwise they would be, they are at the same time discouraged from the Industry and Ingenuity which they would have imployed in obtaining wherewithal to support them, in the full latitude of Expence they desire.

It is possible Families may be supported by such means, but then the growth of Wealth in the Nation is hindered; for that never thrives better, then when Riches are tost from hand to hand.

The meaner sort seeing their Fellows become rich, and great, are spurr'd up to imitate their Industry. A Tradesman sees his Neighbour keep a Coach, presently all his Endeavors is at work to do the like, and many times is beggered by it; however the extraordinary Application he made, to support his Vanity, was beneficial to the Publick, tho' not enough to answer his false Measures as to himself.

It will be objected, That the Home Trade signifies nothing to the enriching a Nation, and that the increase of Wealth comes out of Forreign Trade.

I answer, That what is commonly understood by Wealth, *viz.* Plenty, Bravery, Gallantry, &c. cannot be maintained without Forreign Trade. Nor in truth, can Forreign Trade subsist without the Home Trade, both being connected together.

I have toucht upon these matters concerning Trade, and Riches in general, because I conceive a true Notion of them, will correct many common Errors, and more especially conduce to the Proposition I chiefly aim to prove; which is, that Gold and Silver, and, out of them, Money are nothing but the Weights and Measures, by which Traffick is more conveniently carried on, then could be done without them: and also a proper Fund for a surplusage of Stock to be deposited in.

In confirmation of this, we may take Notice, That Nations which are very poor, have scarce any Money, and in the beginnings of Trade have often made use of something else; as *Sueden* hath used Copper, and the *Plantations,* Sugar and Tobacco, but not without great Inconveniences; and still[24] as Wealth hath increas'd, Gold and Silver hath been introduc'd, and drove out the others, as now almost in the Plantations it hath done.

It is not necessary absolutely to have a Mint for the making Money plenty, tho' it be very expedient; and a just benefit is lost by the want of it, where there is none; for it hath been observed, that where no Mints were, Trade hath not wanted a full supply of Money; because if it be wanted, the Coyn of other Princes will become currant, as in *Ireland,* and the *Plantations;* so also in *Turky,* where the Money of the Country is so minute, that it is inconvenient for great Payments; and therefore the Turkish Dominions are supplied by almost all the Coyns of Christendom, the same being currant there.

But a Country which useth Forreign Coyns, hath great disadvantage from it; because they pay strangers, for what, had they a Mint of their own, they might make themselves. For Coyned Money, as was said, is more worth than Uncoyned Silver of the same weight and allay; that is, you may buy more Uncoyned Silver, of the same fineness with the Money, than the Money weighs; which advantage the Stranger hath for the Coynage.

If it be said, That the contrary sometimes happens, and coyned Money shall be current for less than Bullion shall sell for. I answer, That whereever this happens, the Coyned Money being undervalued, shall be melted down into Bullion, for the immediate Gain that is had from it.

Thus it appears, that if you have no Mint whereby to increase your

24. [To this time, till now.]

Money, yet if you are a rich People, and have Trade, you cannot want Specifick Coyn, to serve your occasions in dealing.

The next thing to be shewed is, That if your Trade pours in never so much Money upon you, you have no more advantage by the being of it Money, then you should have were it in Logs, or Blocks; save only that Money is much better for Transportation than Logs are.

For when Money grows up to a greater quantity than Commerce requires, it comes to be of no greater value, than uncoyned Silver, and will occasionally be melted down again.

Then let not the care of Specifick Money torment us so much; for a People that are rich cannot want it, and if they make none, they will be supplied with the Coyn of other Nations; and if never so much be brought from abroad, or never so much coyned at home, all that is more than what the Commerce of the Nation requires, is but Bullion, and will be treated as such; and coyned Money, like wrought Plate at Second hand, shall sell but for the Intrinsick.

I call to witness the vast Sums that have been coyned in *England*, since the free Coynage was set up; What is become of it all? no body believes it to be in the Nation, and it cannot well be all transported, the Penalties for so doing being so great. The case is plain, it being exported, as I verily believe little of it is, the Melting-Pot devours all.

The rather, because that Practice is so easie, profitable, and safe from all possibility of being detected, as every one knows it is. And I know no intelligent Man who doubts, but the New Money goes this way.

Silver and Gold, like other Commodities, have their ebbings and flowings: Upon the arrival of Quantities from *Spain*, the Mint commonly gives the best price; that is, coyned Silver, for uncoyned Silver, weight for weight. Wherefore is it carried into the *Tower*, and coyned? not long after there will come a demand for Bullion, to be Exported again: If there is none, but all happens to be in Coyn, What then? Melt it down again; there's no loss in it, for the Coyning cost the Owners nothing.

Thus the Nation hath been abused, and made to pay for the twisting of straw, for Asses to eat. If the Merchant were made to pay the price of the Coynage, he would not have sent his Silver to the *Tower* without Consideration; and coyned Money would always keep a value above uncoyned Silver: which is now so far from being the case, that many times it is considerably under, and generally the King of *Spain's* Coyn here is worth One penny *per* Ounce more than our New Money.

This Nation, for many Years last past, hath groaned, and still groans under the abuse of clipt Money, which with respect to their Wisdom, is a great mistake; and the *Irish* whom we ridicule so much, when in Peace, would not be so gulled, but weighed their (Pieces of Eight) Cobbs, as they call them, Piece by Piece; this Errour springs from the same Source with the rest, and needs no other Cure then will soon result from Non-currency. Whereof I shall set down my thoughts.

There is great fear, that if clipt Money be not taken, there will be no Money at all. I am certain, that so long as clipt Money is taken, there will be little other: And is it not strange, that scarce any Nation, or People in the whole World, take diminisht Money by Tale;[25] but the *English?*

What is the reason that a New Half-crown-piece, if it hath the least snip taken from the edge, will not pass; whereas an Old Half-crown clipt to the very quick, and not intrinsically worth Eighteen Pence, shall be currant?

I know no reason, why a Man should take the one, more than the other; I am sure, that if New Money should pass clipt, there would soon be enough served so. And I do not in the least doubt, unless the currency of clipt Money be stopt, it will not be very long before every individual piece of the Old Coynes be clipt.

And if this be not remedied, for fear of the Evil now, how will it be born hereafter, when it will be worse? surely at length it will become insupportable, and remedy itself as Groats[26] have done; but let them look out, in whose time it shall happen; we are all shoving the Evil-Day as far off as may be, but it will certainly come at last.

I do not think the great Evil is so hard to be remedied, nor so chargeable as some have judged; but if rightly managed, it may be done with no intolerable loss, some there will be, and considerable; but when I reflect where it will fall, I cannot think it grievous.

The general Opinion is, That it cannot be done otherwise, then by

25. [Reckoning, numerical account.]
26. [Pieces valued at 4 pence.]

calling in of all the Old Money, and changing of it, for doing which the whole Nation must contribute by a general Tax; but I do not approve of this way, for several Reasons.

For it will be a matter of great trouble, and will require many hands to execute, who will expect, and deserve good pay; which will add to the Evil, and increase the Charge of the Work; and the Trust of it, is also very great, and may be vastly abused.

Now before I give any Opinion for the doing this thing, let some estimate be made of the loss, wherein I will not undertake to compute the Total, but only how the same may fall out in One Hundred Pound: There may be found in it Ten Pound of good New Money, then rests Ninety Pound; and of that I will suppose half to be clipt Money, and half good; so there will be but Five and Forty, in One Hundred Pounds, whereupon there will be any loss; and that will not surely be above a Third part: so I allow 15 *l. per Cent.* for the loss by clipt Money, which is with the most, and in such Computes, it is safest to err on that side.

Now in case it should be thought fit, that the King should in all the Receipts of the Publick Revenue, forbid the taking of clipt Coyn, unless the Subject were content to pay it by weight at 5 *s.* 2 *d. per* Ounce, every Piece being cut in Two, (which must be especially and effectually secured to be done) I grant it would be a great surprize, but no great cause of Complaint when nothing is required, but that the Publick Revenue may be paid in lawful *English* Money.

And those who are to make Payments, must either find good Money, or clip in two their cropt Money, and part with it on such terms; by this Example it would likewise be found, that in a short time, all Men would refuse clipt Money in common Payment.

Now let us consider, where the loss would light, which I have estimated to be about 15 *per Cent.*

We are apt to make Over-estimates of the Quantities of current Money; for we see it often, and know it not again; and are not willing to consider how very a little time it stays in a place; and altho' every one desires to have it, yet none, or very few care for keeping it, but they are forthwith contriving to dispose it; knowing that from all the Money that lies dead, no benefit is to be expected, but it is a certain loss.

The Merchant and Gentleman keep their Money for the most part, with Goldsmiths, and Scriveners; and they, instead of having Ten Thousand Pounds in Cash by them, as their Accounts shew they should have, of other Mens ready Money, to be paid at sight, have seldom One Thousand in Specie; but depend upon a course of Trade, whereby Money comes in as fast as it is taken out: Wherefore I conclude, that the Specifick Money of this Nation is far less than the common Opinion makes.

Now suppose all the loss by clipt Money should happen and fall where the Cash is, it would be severe in very few Places. It could do no great harm to Hoards of Money; because those who intend to keep Money, will be sure to lay up that which is good. It would not signifie much to the poor Man, for he many times hath none; and for the most part, if he hath any, it is very little, seldome Five Shillings at a time. The Farmer is supposed to pay his Landlord, as fast as he gets Money; so it is not likely he should be catcht with much: Wherefore it will light chiefly upon Trading Men, who may sometimes be found with Hundreds by them; and frequently not with many Pounds. Those who happen to have such great Cashes at such time would sustain loss.

In short, clipt Money is an Evil, that the longer it is born with, the harder will the Cure be. And if the Loss therein be lain on the Publick, (as the Common Project is) the Inconveniences are (as hath been shewed) very great; but in the other way of Cure it is not such a terrible Grievance, as most Men have imagined it would be.

So to conclude, when these Reasons, which have been hastily and confusedly set down, are duly considered, I doubt not but we shall joyn in one uniform Sentiment: That Laws to hamper Trade, whether Forreign, or Domestick, relating to Money, or other Merchandizes, are not Ingredients to make a People Rich, and abounding in Money, and Stock. But if Peace be procured, easie Justice maintained, the Navigation not clogg'd, the Industrious encouraged, by indulging them in the participation of Honours, and Imployments in the Government, according to their Wealth and Characters, the Stock of the Nation will increase, and consequently Gold and Silver abound, Interest be easie, and Money cannot be wanting.

Postscript

Upon farther Consideration of the Foregoing Matters, I think fit to add the following Notes.

When a Nation is grown Rich, Gold, Silver, Jewels, and every thing useful, or desirable, (as I have already said) will be plentiful; and the Fruits of the Earth will purchase more of them, than before, when People were poorer: As a fat Oxe in former Ages, was not sold for more Shillings, than now Pounds. The like takes place in Labourers Wages, and every thing whatever; which confirms the Universal Maxim I have built upon, *viz.* That Plenty of any thing makes it cheap.

Therefore Gold and Silver being now plentiful, a Man hath much more of it for his labour, for his Corn, for his Cattle, &c. then could be had Five Hundred Years ago, when, as must be owned, there was not near so much by many parts as now.

Notwithstanding this, I find many, who seem willing to allow, that this Nation at present, abounds with Gold and Silver, in Plate and Bullion; but are yet of Opinion, That coyned Money is wanted to carry on the Trade, and that were there more Specifick Money, Trade would increase, and we should have better Markets for every thing.

That this is a great Error, I think the foregoing Papers makes out: but to clear it a little farther, let it be considered, that Money is a Manufacture of Bullion wrought in the Mint. Now if the Materials are ready, and the Workmen also, 'tis absurd to say, the Manufacture is wanted.

For instance: Have you Corn, and do you want Meal? Carry the Corn to the Mill, and grind it. Yes; but I want Meal, because others will not carry their Corn; and I have none: say you so; then buy Corn of them, and carry it to the Mill your self. This is exactly the Case of Money. A very rich Man hath much Plate, for Honour and Show; whereupon a poorer Man thinks, if it were coyned into Money, the Publick, and his self among the rest, would be the better for it; but he is utterly mistaken; unless at the same time you oblige the rich Man to squander his new coyn'd Money away.

For if he lays it up, I am sure the matter is not mended: if he commutes it for Diamonds, Pearl, &c. the Case is still the same; it is but changed from one hand to another: and it may be the Money is dispatcht to the *Indies* to pay for those Jewels: then if he buys Land, it is no more than changing the hand, and regarding all Persons, except the Dealers only, the Case is still the same. Money will always have an Owner, and never goeth a Beggar for Entertainment, but must be purchast for valuable consideration in *solido.*

If the use of Plate were prohibited, then it were a sumptuary Law, and, as such, would be a vast hindrance to the Riches and Trade of the Nation: for now seeing every Man hath Plate in his House, the Nation is possest of a solid Fund, consisting in those Mettals, which all the World desire, and would willingly draw from us; and this in far greater measure than would be, if Men were not allowed that liberty. For the poor Tradesman, out of an ambition to have a Piece of Plate upon his Cupboard, works harder to purchase it, than he would do if that humour were restrain'd as I have said elsewhere.

There is required for carrying on the Trade of the Nation, a determinate Sum of Specifick Money, which varies, and is sometimes more, sometimes less, as the Circumstances we are in requires. War time calls for more Money than time of Peace, because every one desires to keep some by him, to use upon Emergiences; not thinking it prudent to rely upon Moneys currant in dealing, as they do in times of Peace, when Payments are more certain.

This ebbing and flowing of Money, supplies and accommodates itself, without any aid of Politicians. For when Money grows scarce, and begins to be hoarded, then forthwith the Mint works, till the occasion be filled up again. And on the other side, when Peace brings out the Hoards, and Money abounds, the Mint not only ceaseth, but the overplus of Money will be presently melted down, either to supply the Home Trade, or for Transportation.

Thus the Buckets work alternately, when Money is scarce, Bullion is coyn'd; when Bullion is scarce, Money is melted. I do not allow that both should be scarce at one and the same time; for that is a state of Poverty, and will not be, till we are exhausted, which is besides my subject.

Some have fancied, that if by a Law the Ounce of Silver were restrained to 5 *s.* value, in all dealings, and at the *Tower* the same were coyned into 5 *s.* 4 *d.* or 5 *s.* 6 *d. per* Ounce, all the Plate in *England* would soon be coyned. The answer to this, in short, is: That the Principle they build upon is impossible. How can any Law hinder me from giving another Man, what I please for his Goods? The Law may be evaded a thousand ways. As be it so: I must not give, nor he receive above 5 *s. per* Ounce for Silver; I may pay him 5 *s.* and present him with 4 *d.* or 6 *d.* more; I may give him Goods in barter, at such, or greater profit; and so by other contrivances, *ad Infinitum.*

But put case it took effect, and by that means all the Silver in *England* were coyned into Money; What then? would any one spend more in Cloaths, Equipages, Housekeeping, &c. then is done? I believe not; but rather the contrary: For the Gentry and Commonalty being nipt in their delight of seeing Plate, &c. in their Houses, would in all probability be dampt in all other Expences: Wherefore if this could be done, as I affirm it cannot, yet instead of procuring the desired effect, it would bring on all the Mischiefs of a sumptuary Law.

Whenever the Money is made lighter, or baser in allay, (which is the same thing) the effect is, that immediately the price of Bullion answers. So that in reality you change the Name, but not the thing: and whatever the difference is, the Tenant and Debtor hath it in his favor; for Rent and Debts will be paid less, by just so much as the intrinsick value is less, then what was to be paid before.

For example: One who before received for Rent or Debt, 3 *l.* 2 *s.* could with it buy twelve Ounces, or a Pound of Sterling Silver; but if the Crown-piece be worse in value than now it is, by 3 *d.* I do averr, you shall not be able to buy a Pound of such Silver under 3 *l.* 5 *s.* but either directly, or indirectly it shall cost so much.

But then it is said, we will buy an Ounce for 5 *s.* because 'tis the Price set by the Parliament, and no body shall dare to sell for more. I answer, If they cannot sell it for more, they may coyn it; And then what Fool will sell an Ounce of Silver for 5 *s.* when he may coyn it into 5 *s.* 5 *d.*?

Thus we may labour to hedge in the Cuckow, but in vain; for no People ever yet grew rich by Policies; but it is Peace, Industry, and Freedom that brings Trade and Wealth, and nothing else.

7

Second Discourse on the Affairs of Scotland
1697

ANDREW FLETCHER was born in 1653 to the laird of Saltoun, Sir Robert Fletcher. In his youth, he traveled much and conceived a great interest in books, old buildings, and the great cities of northern Europe (London, Paris, Amsterdam). He early plunged into a political career, becoming commissioner for his county in 1678 and again in 1681. It was then that he first took a position against a standing army. During Monmouth's rebellion, which he supported, he shot dead a man named Dare over his use of Dare's horse in an expedition. After being estranged from Monmouth, he was arrested and imprisoned in Bilbao on orders of the English government in 1686 and sentenced to death for treason. After escaping prison, he next fought with the Hungarians against the Turks (whom he is said to have called the "common enemy of mankind"). By now of marked republican leanings, he refused an amnesty because it emanated from the King and not the legislature. He was with William of Orange in 1688 and returned to Scotland at that time; his lands were restored to him by special act of Parliament in 1690.

In the tumultuous debates of the 1700s, he led the national party against the court party on the Union question. He proposed home rule, a national militia, and annual Scottish Parliaments. As a majority drifted toward the Union position (1704–7), he had to be restrained more than once from the threat of a duel with Lord Stair and the Duke of Hamilton during sessions of Parliament. He was accused of fomenting a French invasion of Scotland for the Pretender in 1708. Acquitted, he left public life. He oversaw the construction (1710) of an innovative barley mill modeled on one he had seen in his travels to Amsterdam. He died a lifelong bachelor in September 1716. The Jacobite Lockhart said of Fletcher that he was "so steadfast to what he thought right that no hazard nor advantage, no, not the universal empire, nor the gold of America, could tempt him to yield or desert it."

The present work was written in 1698 and published as part of a somewhat larger work, *Two Discourses Concerning the Affairs of Scotland* (Edinburgh, 1698). I use the edition of the *Political Works* edited by John Robertson (© in the introduction, index and editorial matter Cambridge University Press 1997. Reprinted with the permission of Cambridge University Press). With one brief bracketed exception, the notes are by the Cambridge editor.

━━━━━━━━━━

Second Discourse on the Affairs of Scotland

The affairs of which I have spoken in the preceding discourse, are such as the present conjuncture makes a proper subject for the approaching session of parliament: but there are many other things which require no less their care, if the urgent and pressing distresses of the nation be considered. I shall therefore with all due respect to the parliament offer my opinion concerning two, which I presume to be of that nature.

The first thing which I humbly and earnestly propose to that honourable court is, that they would take into their consideration the condition of so many thousands of our people who are at this day dying for want of bread. And to persuade them seriously to apply themselves to so indispensable a duty, they have all the inducements which those most powerful emotions of the soul, terror and compassion, can produce. Because from unwholesome food diseases are so multiplied among the poor people, that if some course be not taken, this famine may very probably be followed by a plague; and then what man is there even of those who sit in parliament that can be sure he shall escape? And what man is there in this nation, if he have any compassion, who must not grudge himself every nice bit and every delicate morsel he puts in his mouth, when he considers that so many are already dead, and so many at that minute struggling with death, not for want of bread but of grains, which I am credibly informed have been eaten by some families, even during the preceding years of scarcity. And must not every unnecessary branch of our expence, or the least finery in our houses, clothes or equipage, reproach us with our barbarity, so long as people born with natural endowments, perhaps not inferior to our own, and fellow citizens, perish for want of things absolutely necessary to life?

But not to insist any more upon the representation of so great a calamity, which if drawn in proper colours, and only according to the precise truth of things, must cast the minds of all honest men into those convulsions which ought necessarily to be composed before they can calmly consider of a remedy; and because the particulars of this great distress are sufficiently known to all, I shall proceed to say, that though perhaps upon the great want of bread, occasioned by the continued bad seasons of this and the three preceding years, the evil be greater and more pressing than at any time in our days, yet there have always been in Scotland such numbers of poor, as by no regulations could ever be orderly provided for; and this country has always swarmed with such numbers of idle vagabonds, as no laws could ever restrain. And indeed when I considered the many excellent laws enacted by former parliaments for setting the poor to work, particularly those in the time of King James the sixth, with the clauses for putting them in execution, which to me seemed such as could not miss of the end, and yet that nothing was obtained by them,[1] I was amazed, and began to think upon the case of other

1. The first Scottish Poor Law was the temporary Act of 1574, made permanent in 1579. It was modelled closely on the English Statutes of 1572 and 1575, with the result that the machinery for administering the Act was hardly adapted to Scottish circumstances. A

nations in this particular, persuaded that there was some strange hidden root of this evil which could not be well discovered, unless by observing the conduct of other governments. But upon reflection I found them all subject to the same inconveniencies, and that in all the countries of Europe there were great numbers of poor, except in Holland, which I knew to proceed from their having the greatest share in the trade of the world. But this not being a remedy for every country, since all cannot pretend to so great a part in trade, and that two or three nations are able to manage the whole commerce of Europe; yet there being a necessity that the poor should every where be provided for, unless we will acknowledge the deficiency of all government in that particular, and finding no remedy in the laws or customs of any of the present governments, I began to consider what might be the conduct of the wise antients in that affair. And my curiosity was increased, when upon reflection I could not call to mind that any antient author had so much as mentioned such a thing, as great numbers of poor in any country.

At length I found the original of that multitude of beggars which now oppress the world, to have proceeded from churchmen, who (never failing to confound things spiritual with temporal, and consequently all good order and good government, either through mistake or design) upon the first publick establishment of the christian religion, recommended nothing more to masters, in order to the salvation of their souls, than the setting such of their slaves at liberty as would embrace the christian faith, though our Saviour and his apostles had been so far from making use of any temporal advantages to persuade eternal truths, and so far from invading any man's property, by promising him heaven for it, that the apostle Paul says expressly,

> In whatever condition of life every one is called to the Christian faith, in
> that let him remain. Art thou called being a slave? Be not concerned for
> thy condition; but even though thou mightest be free, chuse to continue

---

further Act in 1592 identified Kirk Sessions as appropriate agents, while justices of the peace, named in the 1579 Act, were finally instituted in Scotland in 1609, and instructed to control vagrants and administer apprenticeships in an Act of 1617. If Fletcher exaggerated the efficacy of the clauses for executing the Acts, he was none the less right to suppose that little or nothing was achieved. See Rosalind Mitchison, "North and South: the development of the gulf in Poor Law practice," in R. A. Houston and I. D. Whyte (eds.), *Scottish Society 1500–1800* (Cambridge, 1989), pp. 200–205.

in it. For he who is called whilst a slave, becomes the freeman of the Lord; and likewise he that is called whilst a free-man, becomes the slave of Christ, who has paid a price for you, that you might not be the slaves of men. Let every one therefore, brethren, in whatever condition he is called, in that remain, in the fear of God.[2]

That the interpretation I put upon this passage, different from our translation, is the true meaning of the apostle, not only the authority of the Greek fathers, and genuine signification of the Greek particles, but the whole context, chiefly the first and last words (which seem to be repeated to inforce and determine such a meaning) clearly demonstrate. And the reason why he recommends to them rather to continue slaves (if they have embraced the christian faith in that condition) seems to be that it might appear they did not embrace it for any worldly advantage, as well as to destroy a doctrine which even in his days began to be preached, that slavery was inconsistent with the christian religion; since such a doctrine would have been a great stop to the progress of it. What the apostle means by saying, we ought not to be the slaves of men, I shall shew hereafter.[3]

This disorder of giving liberty to great numbers of slaves upon their profession of Christianity, grew to such a height, even in the time of Constantine the great, that the cities of the empire found themselves burdened with an infinite number of men, who had no other estate but their liberty, of whom the greatest part would not work, and the rest had been bred to no profession. This obliged Constantine to make edicts in favour of beggars; and from that time at the request of the bishops, hospitals and alms-houses, not formerly known in the world, began to be

2. First Epistle to the Corinthians, 7:20–24.

3. Compared with that of the Authorised Version (probably what Fletcher had in mind by "our translation"), Fletcher's rendering of the passage differed crucially in verse 21. He has: "Art thou called being a slave? Be not concerned for thy condition; but even though thou mightest be free, chuse to continue in it." The Authorised Version reads: "Art thou called being a servant? Care not for it: but if thou mayest be made free, use it rather." The earlier Coverdale and Geneva translations are very similar to those of the Authorised Version. These renderings have been supported by the New English Bible: "Were you a slave when called? Do not let that trouble you; but if a chance of liberty shall come, take it." However, this version also gives a variant reading which is in line with Fletcher's: "but even if a chance of liberty should come, choose rather to make good use of your servitude."

established. But upon the rise of the Mahometan religion, which was chiefly advanced by giving liberty to all their slaves, the Christians were so molested by the continual rebellion of theirs, that they were at length forced to give liberty to them all; which it seems the churchmen then looked upon as a thing necessary to preserve the christian religion, since in many of the writings, by which masters gave freedom to their slaves, 'tis expressly said, they did so, to save their own souls.

This is the rise of that great mischief, under which, to the undoing of the poor, all the nations of Europe have ever since groaned. Because in antient times, so long as a man was the riches and part of the possession of another, every man was provided for in meat, clothes and lodging; and not only he, but (in order to increase that riches) his wife and children also: whereas provisions by hospitals, alms-houses, and the contributions of churches or parishes, have by experience been found to increase the numbers of those that live by them. And the liberty every idle and lazy person has of burdening the society in which he lives, with his mainte-nance, has increased their numbers to the weakening and impoverishing of it: for he needs only to say, that he cannot get work, and then he must be maintained by charity. And as I have shewn before, no nation except one only (which is in extraordinary circumstances) does provide by pub-lick work-houses for their poor: the reason of which seems to be, that publick work-houses for such vast numbers of people, are impracticable except in those places where (besides a vast trade to vend the manufac-tured goods) there is an extraordinary police°, and that though the Hol-landers by reason of the steddiness of their temper, as well as of their gov-ernment (being a commonwealth) may be constant to their methods of providing for the poor; yet in a nation, and under a government like that of France, though vast publick work-houses may be for a while kept in order, 'twill not be long before they fall into confusion and ruin. And in-deed (next to Plato's republick, which chiefly consists in making the whole society live in common)[4] there is nothing more impracticable than

---

4. Plato, *The Republic* (*c.* 380 BC), esp. Books III–V, presented arguments for a polit-ical society ruled by Guardians and their auxiliaries, who would have neither private property nor families, but would be provided for out of common property and a pool of wives, and would thus be free to devote themselves to the life of the community. Fletcher owned more than one edition of *The Republic*.

to provide for so great a part of every nation by publick work-houses. Whereas when such an oeconomy comes under the inspection of every master of a family, and that he himself is to reap the profit of the right management; the thing not only turns to a far better account, but by reason of his power to sell those workmen to others who may have use for them, when he himself has a mind to alter his course of life, the profit is permanent to the society; nor can such an oeconomy, or any such management ever fall into confusion.

I doubt not, that what I have said will meet, not only with all the misconstruction and obloquy, but all the disdain, fury and out-cries, of which either ignorant magistrates, or proud, lazy and miserable people are capable. Would I bring back slavery into the world? Shall men of immortal souls, and by nature equal to any, be sold as beasts? Shall they and their posterity be for ever subjected to the most miserable of all conditions; the inhuman barbarity of masters, who may beat, mutilate, torture, starve, or kill so great a number of mankind at pleasure? Shall the far greater part of the commonwealth be slaves, not that the rest may be free, but tyrants over them? With what face can we oppose the tyranny of princes, and recommend such opposition as the highest virtue, if we make ourselves tyrants over the greatest part of mankind? Can any man, from whom such a thing has once escaped, ever offer to speak for liberty? But they must pardon me if I tell them, that I regard not names, but things; and that the misapplication of names has confounded every thing. We are told there is not a slave in France; that when a slave sets his foot upon French ground, he becomes immediately free: and I say, that there is not a freeman in France, because the king takes away any part of any man's property at his pleasure; and that, let him do what he will to any man, there is no remedy. The Turks tell us, there are no slaves among them, except Jews, Moors, or Christians; and who is there that knows not, they are all slaves to the grand Seignior, and have no remedy against his will? A slave properly is one, who is absolutely subjected to the will of another man without any remedy: and not one that is only subjected under certain limitations, and upon certain accounts necessary for the good of the commonwealth, though such an one may go under that name. And the confounding these two conditions of men by a name common to both, has in my opinion been none of the least hardships put upon those who ought to be named servants. We are all subjected to the laws; and the easier or harder conditions imposed by them upon the several ranks of men in any society, make not the distinction that is between a freeman and a slave.

So that the condition of slaves among the antients, will upon serious consideration appear to be only a better provision in their governments than any we have, that no man might want the necessities of life, nor any person able to work be burdensome to the commonwealth. And they wisely judged of the inconveniences that befal the most part of poor people, when they are all abandoned to their own conduct. I know that these two conditions of men were confounded under the same name, as well by the antients as they are by us; but the reason was, that having often taken in war the subjects of absolute monarchs, they thought they did them no wrong if they did not better their condition: and as in some of their governments the condition of slaves was under a worse regulation than in others, so in some of them it differ'd very little, if at all, from the condition of such a slave as I have defined. But I do not approve, and therefore will not go about to defend any of those bad and cruel regulations about slaves. And because it would be tedious and needless to pursue the various conditions of them in several ages and governments, it shall be enough for me to explain under what conditions they might be both good and useful, as well as I think they are necessary in a well-regulated government.

First then, their masters should not have power over their lives, but the life of the master should go for the life of the servant. The master should have no power to mutilate or torture him; that in such cases the servant should not only have his freedom (which alone would make him burdensome to the publick) but a sufficient yearly pension so long as he should live from his said master. That he, his wife and children, should be provided for in clothes, diet, and lodging. That they should be taught the principles of morality and religion; to read, and be allowed the use of certain books: that they should not work upon sundays, and be allowed to go to church: that in every thing, except their duty as servants, they should not be under the will of their masters, but the protection of the law: that when these servants grow old, and are no more useful to their masters, (lest upon that account they should be ill-used) hospitals should be provided for them by the publick: that if for their good and faithful service, any master give them their freedom, he should be obliged to give them likewise wherewithal to subsist, or put them in a way of living without being troublesome to the commonwealth: that they should wear no habit or mark to distinguish them from hired servants: that any man should be punished who gives them the opprobrious name of slave. So, except it were that they could possess nothing, and might be sold, which really would be but an alienation of their service without their consent, they would live in a much more comfortable condition (wanting nothing necessary for life) than those who having a power to possess all things, are very often in want of every thing, to such a degree, that many thousands of them come to starve for hunger.

It will be said, that notwithstanding all these regulations, they may be most barbarously used by their masters, either by beating them outragiously, making them work beyond measure, suffer cold or hunger, or neglecting them in their sickness. I answer, that as long as the servant is of an age not unfit for work, all these things are against the interest of the master: that the most brutal man will not use his beast ill only out of a humour; and that if such inconveniences do sometimes fall out, it proceeds, for the most part, from the perverseness of the servant: that all inconveniences cannot be obviated by any government; that we must chuse the least; and that to prevent them in the best manner possible, a particular magistrate might be instituted for that end.

The condition of such a servant is to be esteemed free; because in the most essential things he is only subject to the laws, and not to the will of his master, who can neither take away his life, mutilate, torture, or restrain him from the comforts of wife and children: but on the other hand, for the service he does, is obliged to ease him of the inconveniences of marriage, by providing for him, his wife, and children, clothes, food, and lodging: and the condition of a bashaw, or great lord, under arbitrary government (who for the sake, and from a necessity of what they call government, has joined to the quality of a slave the office of a tyrant, and imagines himself a man of quality, if not a little prince, by such preeminence) is altogether slavish; since he is under the protection of no law, no not so much as to his life, or the honour of his wife and children; and is subjected to stronger temptations than any man, of being a slave to men in St. Paul's sense, which is a worse sort of slavery than any I have yet mentioned. That is of being subservient to, and an instrument of the lusts of his master the tyrant: since if he refuse slavishly to obey, he must lose his office, and perhaps his life. And indeed men of all ranks living under arbitrary government (so much preached and recommended by the far greater part of churchmen) being really under the protection of no law, (whatever may be pretended) are not only slaves, as I have defined before, but by having no other certain remedy in any thing against the lust and passions of their superiors, except suffering or compliance, lie under the most violent temptations of being slaves in the worse sense, and of the only sort that is inconsistent with the christian religion. A condition (whatever men may imagine) so much more miserable than that of servants protected by the laws in all things necessary for the subsistence of them and their posterity, that there is no comparison.[5]

I shall now proceed to the great advantages the antients received from this sort of servants. By thus providing for their poor, and making every man useful to the commonwealth, they were not only able to perform those great and stupendous publick works, highways, aqueducts,

---

5. Fletcher provides one of the clearest and most systematic accounts in the classical republican canon of the difference between personal and political slavery, and of why only the latter was to be regarded as true slavery. Political slavery was subjection to the arbitrary, unchecked power of a ruler, who was thereby a tyrant or despot. Contemporaries' use of the concept of political slavery was often much more rhetorical than this: many examples are to be found in the anti–standing army writings of the English radical whig John Trenchard, *An Argument shewing that a Standing Army is inconsistent with a Free Government, and absolutely destructive to the Constitution of the British Monarchy* (London, 1697), and *A Short History of Standing Armies* (London, 1698). David Hume may have had Fletcher in mind when he wrote in a footnote to the essay "Of the Populousness of Ancient Nations" (1752):

> Some passionate admirers of the ancients, and zealous partisans of civil liberty, (for these sentiments, as they are, both of them, in the main, extremely just, are found to be almost inseparable) cannot forbear regretting the loss of this institution; and whilst they brand all submission to the government of a single person with the harsh denomination of slavery, they would gladly reduce the greater part of mankind to real slavery and subjection.(*The Philosophical Works of David Hume*, eds. T. H. Green and T. H. Grose (London 1874–5), III, p. 385; this essay is not included in the Cambridge Texts edition of *David Hume: Political Essays*, ed. K. Haakonssen.) [See David Hume, *Essays moral, political, and literary*, ed. Eugene F. Miller (Indianapolis: Liberty Fund, 1987), p. 383.]

common-shores, walls of cities, sea-ports, bridges, monuments for the
dead, temples, amphitheatres, theatres, places for all manner of exercises
and education, baths, courts of justice, market-places, publick walks, and
other magnificent works for the use and conveniency of the publick, with
which Egypt, Asia, Greece, Italy, and other countries were filled; and to
adorn them with stately pillars and obelisks, curious statues, most exquisite sculpture and painting: but every particular man might indulge himself in any kind of finery and magnificence; not only because he had
slaves to perform it according to his fancy, but because all the poor being
provided for, there could be no crime in making unnecessary expences,
which are always contrary, not only to christian charity, but common humanity, as long as any poor man wants bread. For though we think that
in making those expences, we employ the poor; and that in building
costly houses, and furnishing them, making fine gardens, rich stuffs,
laces and embroideries for apparel, the poor are set to work; yet so long
as all the poor are not provided for, (though a man cannot reproach himself in particular why it is not done) and that there is any poor family in
a starving condition, 'tis against common humanity (and no doubt would
have been judged to be so by the antients) for any man to indulge himself in things unnecessary, when others want what is absolutely necessary
for life, especially since the furnishing of those things to them, does employ workmen as well as our unnecessary expences. So that the antients,
without giving the least check to a tender compassion for the necessities
of others (a virtue so natural to great minds, so nicely to be preserved and
cherished) might not only adorn their publick buildings with all the
refinements of art, but likewise beautify their private houses, villas and
gardens with the greatest curiosity. But we by persisting in the like, and
other unnecessary expences, while all the poor are not provided for (example, vanity, and the love of pleasure, being predominant in us) have
not only effaced all the vestiges of christian charity, but banished natural
compassion from amongst us, that without remorse we might continue
in them.

    This explains to us by what means so much virtue and simplicity of
manners could subsist in the cities of Greece, and the lesser Asia, in the
midst of so great curiosity and refinement in the arts of magnificence and
ornament. For in antient times great riches, and consequently bad arts to

acquire them, were not necessary for those things; because if a man possessed a moderate number of slaves, he might chuse to employ them in any sort of magnificence, either private or publick, for use or ornament, as he thought fit, whilst he himself lived in the greatest simplicity, having neither coaches nor horses to carry him, as in triumph, through the city; nor a family in most things composed like that of a prince, and a multitude of idle servants to consume his estate. Women were not then intolerably expensive, but wholly imployed in the care of domestick affairs. Neither did the furniture of their houses amount to such vast sums as with us, but was for the most part wrought by their slaves.

Another advantage which the antients had by this sort of servants, was, that they were not under that uneasiness, and unspeakable vexation which we suffer by our hired servants, who are never bred to be good for any thing, though most of the slaves amongst the antients were. And though we bestow the greatest pains or cost to educate one of them from his youth, upon the least cross word he leaves us. So that 'tis more than probable this sort of servants growing every day worse, the unspeakable trouble arising from them, without any other consideration, will force the world to return to the former.

Among the antients, any master who had the least judgment or discretion, was served with emulation by all his slaves, that those who best performed their duty, might obtain their liberty from him. A slave, though furnished with every thing necessary, yet possessing nothing, had no temptation to cheat his master; whereas a hired servant, whilst he remains unmarried, will cheat his master of what may be a stock to him when married; and if after his marriage he continue to serve his master, he will be sure to cheat him much more. When the antients gave freedom to a slave, they were obliged to give him wherewithal to subsist, or to put him into a way of living. And how well and faithfully they were served by those they had made free, (whom from a long experience of their probity and capacity, they often made stewards of their estates) all antient history does testify. Now, we having no regular way to enable a servant to provide sufficient maintenance for his family, when he becomes independent on his master, his bare wages (out of which he is for the most part to provide himself with many necessaries for daily use) not being enough for that purpose, and no way left but to cheat his master, we ought not to expect any probity or fidelity in our servants, because, for want of order in this point, we subject them to such strong temptation.

I might insist upon many other advantages the antients had in the way they were served, if to persuade the expedient I propose, I were not to make use of stronger arguments than such as can be drawn from any advantages; I mean those of necessity.

There are at this day in Scotland (besides a great many poor families very meanly provided for by the church-boxes, with others, who by living upon bad food fall into various diseases) two hundred thousand people begging from door to door. These are not only no way advantageous, but a very grievous burden to so poor a country. And though the number of them be perhaps double to what it was formerly, by reason of this present great distress, yet in all times there have been about one hundred thousand of those vagabonds, who have lived without any regard or subjection either to the laws of the land, or even those of God and nature; fathers incestuously accompanying with their own daughters, the son with the mother, and the brother with the sister. No magistrate could ever discover, or be informed which way one in a hundred of these wretches died, or that ever they were baptized. Many murders have been discovered among them; and they are not only a most unspeakable oppression to poor tenants, (who if they give not bread, or some kind of provision to perhaps forty such villains in one day, are sure to be insulted by them) but they rob many poor people who live in houses distant from any neighbourhood. In years of plenty many thousands of them meet together in the mountains, where they feast and riot for many days; and at country weddings, markets, burials, and other the like publick occasions, they are to be seen both men and women perpetually drunk, cursing, blaspheming, and fighting together.[6]

These are such outrageous disorders, that it were better for the nation they were sold to the gallies or West Indies, than that they should continue any longer to be a burden and curse upon us. But numbers of people being great riches, every government is to blame that makes not a right

---

6. No modern historian would venture such estimates of vagabondage—or such a characterisation of lifestyle; the *Scottish Population History*, p. 170, judges Fletcher's estimates "worthless."

use of them. The wholsomeness of our air, and healthfulness of our climate, affords us great numbers of people, which in so poor a country can never be all maintained by manufactures, or publick work-houses, or any other way, but that which I have mentioned.

And to shew that former parliaments struggling with this, otherwise insuperable, difficulty, have by the nature of the thing been as it were forced upon remedies tending towards what I have proposed: by an act of parliament in the year 1579, any subject of sufficient estate is allowed to take the child of any beggar, and educate him for his service, which child is obliged to serve such a master for a certain term of years; and that term of years extended by another act made in the year 1597, for life.[7] So that here is a great advance towards my proposition; but either from some mistake about christian or civil liberty, they did not proceed to consider the necessity of continuing that service in the children of such servants, and giving their masters a power of alienating that service to whom they should think fit. The reason for the first of these is, that being married in that sort of service, their masters must of necessity maintain their wife and children, and so ought to have the same right to the service of the children as of the father. And the reason for the power of alienation is, that no man is sure of continuing always in one sort of employment; and having educated a great many such children when he was in an employment that required many servants, if afterwards he should be obliged to quit it for one that required few or none, he could not without great injustice be deprived of the power of alienating their service to any other man, in order to reimburse to himself the money he had bestowed upon them; especially since the setting them at liberty would only bring a great burden on the publick.

Now what I would propose upon the whole matter is, that for some present remedy of so great a mischief, every man of a certain estate in this nation should be obliged to take a proportionable number of those vagabonds, and either employ them in hedging and ditching his grounds,

---

7. "Act for the punishment of strong and idle beggars and the relief of the poor and impotent" (1579), *The Acts of the Parliaments of Scotland, III: 1567–92* (1814), pp. 139–41; "Strong beggars, vagabonds and Egyptians should be punished" (1597), *Acts of the Parliaments of Scotland, IV: 1593–1625* (1816), p. 140.

or any other sort of work in town and country; or if they happen to be children and young, that he should educate them in the knowledge of some mechanical art, that so every man of estate might have a little manufacture at home which might maintain those servants, and bring great profit to the master, as they did to the antients, whose revenue by the manufactures of such servants was much more considerable than that of their lands. Hospitals and alms-houses ought to be provided for the sick, lame and decrepit, either by rectifying old foundations or instituting new. And for example and terror three or four hundred of the most notorious of those villains which we call jockys,[8] might be presented by the government to the state of Venice, to serve in their gallies against the common enemy of Christendom.

But these things, when once resolved, must be executed with great address, diligence, and severity; for that sort of people is so desperately wicked, such enemies of all work and labour, and, which is yet more amazing, so proud, in esteeming their own condition above that which they will be sure to call slavery; that unless prevented by the utmost industry and diligence, upon the first publication of any orders necessary for putting in execution such a design, they will rather die with hunger in caves and dens, and murder their young children, than appear abroad to have them and themselves taken into such a kind of service. And the Highlands are such a vast and unsearchable retreat for them, that if strict and severe order be not taken to prevent it, upon such an occasion these vagabonds will only rob as much food as they can out of the low-country, and retire to live upon it in those mountains, or run into England till they think the storm of our resolutions is over, which in all former times they have seen to be vain.

Nor indeed can there be a thorough reformation in this affair, so long as the one half of our country, in extent of ground, is possessed by a people who are all gentlemen only because they will not work; and who in every thing are more contemptible than the vilest slaves, except that they always carry arms, because for the most part they live upon robbery. This part of the country being an inexhaustible source of beggars, has always broke all our measures relating to them. And it were to be wished that the

8. Jockie: a Scots' term for a vagrant or gypsy.

government would think fit to transplant that handful of people, and their masters (who have always disturbed our peace) into the low-country, and people the Highlands from hence, rather than they should continue to be a perpetual occasion of mischief to us. 'Tis in vain to say, that whatever people are planted in those mountains, they will quickly turn as savage, and as great beggars as the present inhabitants; for the mountains of the Alps are greater, more desert, and more condemned to snows that those of the Highlands of Scotland, which are everywhere cut by friths and lakes, the richest in fishing of any in the world, affording great conveniences for transportation of timber and any other goods; and yet the Alps which have no such advantages are inhabited every where by a civilized, industrious, honest, and peaceable people: but they had no lords to hinder them from being civilized, to discourage industry, incourage thieving, and to keep them beggars that they might be the more dependent; or when they had any that oppressed them, as in that part of the mountains that belongs to the Swiss, they knocked them on the head.

Let us now compare the condition of our present vagabonds with that of servants under the conditions which I have proposed, and we shall see the one living under no law of God, man or nature, polluted with all manner of abominations; and though in so little expectation of the good things of another life, yet in the worst condition of this, and sometimes starved to death in time of extraordinary want. The other, though sometimes they may fall under a severe master (who nevertheless may neither kill, mutilate, nor torture them, and may be likewise restrained from using them very ill by the magistrate I mentioned) are always sure to have food, clothes and lodging; and have this advantage above other men, that without any care or pains taken by them, these necessaries are likewise secured to their wives and children. They are provided for in sickness, their children are educated, and all of them under all the inducements, encouragements and obligations possible to live quiet, innocent and virtuous lives. They may also hope, if they shew an extraordinary affection, care and fidelity, in the service of their master, that not only they and their families shall have their intire freedom, but a competency to live, and perhaps the estate of the master intrusted to their care. Now if we will consider the advantages to the nation by the one, and the disadvantages arising from the other sort of men, we shall evidently see, that as the one is an excessive burden, curse and reproach to us, so the other may inrich the nation, and adorn this country with publick works beyond any in Europe, which shall not take the like methods of providing for their poor.[9]

This proposal I hope may be a remedy, not only to that intolerable plague of idle vagabonds who infest the nation; but by providing a more regular maintenance for them, go a great way towards the present relief of other poor people who have been oppressed by them. That which follows is calculated to remove the principal and original cause of the poverty which all the commons of this nation lie under, as well as those straitning difficulties in which men of estates are by our present method of husbandry inevitably involved.

The causes of the present poverty and misery in which the commonalty of Scotland live, are many, yet they are all to be imputed to our own bad conduct and mismanagement of our affairs. 'Tis true, trade being of late years vastly increased in Europe, the poverty of any nation is always imputed to their want of that advantage. And though our soil be barren, yet our seas being the richest of any in the world, it may be thought that the cause of all our poverty has been the neglect of trade, and chiefly of our own fishing: nevertheless were I to assign the principal and original source of our poverty, I should place it in the letting of our lands at so excessive a rate as makes the tenant poorer even than his servant whose wages he cannot pay; and involves in the same misery day-labourers, tradesmen, and the lesser merchants who live in the country villages and towns; and thereby influences no less the great towns and wholesale merchants, makes the master have a troublesome and ill-paid rent, his lands not improved by inclosure or otherwise, but for want of horses and oxen fit for labour, everywhere run out and abused.

9. Fletcher's draconian solutions to the problems of poverty and vagrancy were not taken too seriously by contemporaries, and secured nothing like the support he received for his proposals for constitutional change five years later. What he advocated did, as he pointed out, build on the coercive aspects of earlier Scottish legislation for poor relief, but the tendency of subsequent discussion was against anything which smacked of a return to slavery. One of the fullest later eighteenth-century discussions of slavery and its decline since the ancient world was that by John Millar, in *The Origin of the Distinction of Ranks* (1770, 3rd edn 1779), ed. W. C. Lehman, in *John Millar of Glasgow* (Cambridge, 1960). See pp. 318–19 for two paragraphs added to the second edition of the work, which may have been written with Fletcher's scheme in mind.

The condition of the lesser freeholders or heritors (as we call them) is not much better than that of our tenants; for they have no stocks to improve their lands, and living not as husbandmen but as gentlemen, they are never able to attain any: besides this, the unskilfulness of their wretched and half-starved servants is such, that their lands are no better cultivated than those laboured by beggarly tenants.[10] And though a gentleman of estate take a farm into his own hands, yet servants are so unfaithful or lazy, and the country people such enemies of all manner of inclosure, that after having struggled with innumerable difficulties, he at last finds it impossible for him to alter the ordinary bad methods, whilst the rest of the country continues in them.

The places in this country which produce sheep and black cattle, have no provision for them in winter during the snows, having neither hay nor straw, nor any inclosure to shelter them or the grass from the cold easterly winds in the spring; so that the beasts are in a dying condition, and the grass consumed by those destructive winds, till the warm weather, about the middle of June, come to the relief of both. To all this may be added the letting of farms in most part of those grazing countries every year by roop or auction. But our management in the countries cultivated by tillage is much worse, because the tenant pays his rent in grain, wheat, barley or oats: which is attended with many inconveniences, and much greater disadvantages than a rent paid in money.[11]

Money rent has a yearly balance in it; for if the year be scarce, all sorts of grain yield the greater price; and if the year be plentiful, there is the

10. Freeholders or heritors were landowners whose land was held in direct "fee" of the Crown; in feudal terms, they were tenants-in-chief of the Crown. Their land passed by inheritance to their heirs. Only freeholders were entitled to vote in the Scottish counties. Given this restricted definition, the number of "freeholders" was proportionately much smaller in Scotland than in England; and larger estates were the norm in Scotland. Here, however, Fletcher comments on the position of lesser freeholders.

11. Fletcher's critique of the state of Scottish agriculture starts with the methods of letting lands to tenants. He distinguishes between grazing or upland areas, in which farms are let by an annual auction (roup), and arable areas, in which longer leases (tacks) might be available, but where rent was paid in kind, and in particular in grain. His observation seems to have been broadly accurate. Longer, written leases were being introduced into the arable lowlands at the end of the seventeenth century, while annual, verbal leases by auction persisted (into the nineteenth century) on upland estates in the Borders. See Ian Whyte, *Agriculture and Society in Seventeenth-Century Scotland* (Edinburgh, 1979), pp. 152–62.

greater quantity of them to make money. Now a rent paid in corn has neither a yearly, nor any balance at all; for if a plentiful year afford a superplus, the tenant can make but little of it; but if the year be scarce, he falls short in the payment of his corn, and by reason of the price it bears, can never clear that debt by the rates of a plentiful year, by which means he breaks, and contributes to ruin his master. The rent being altogether in corn, the grounds must be altogether in tillage; which has been the ruin of all the best countries in Scotland. The carriage of corn paid for rent, to which many tenants are obliged, being often to remote places, and at unseasonable times, destroys their horses, and hinders their labour. And the hazard of sending the corn by sea to the great towns, endangers the loss of the whole. The master runs a double risque for his rent, from the merchant as well as the tenant; and the merchant making a thousand difficulties at the delivering of the corn if the price be fallen, the bargain sometimes ends in a suit at law. The selling of corn is become a thing so difficult, that besides the cheats used in that sort of commerce, sufficient to disgust any honest man, the brewers, bakers, and sometimes the merchants who send it abroad, do so combine together, that the gentleman is obliged to lay it up, of which the trouble as well as loss is great. This causes him to borrow money for the supply of his present occasions, and is the beginning of most men's debts. We may add to this, that by a rent in corn, a man comes to have one year a thousand pound rent, and the next perhaps but six hundred, so that he never can make any certain account for his expence or way of living; that having one year a thousand pound to spend, he cannot easily restrain himself to six hundred the next; that he spends the same quantity of corn (and in some places where such things are delivered instead of rent), hay, straw, poultry, sheep and oxen, in a dear, as in a plentiful year, which he would not do if he was obliged to buy them. Now the tenant in a plentiful year wastes, and in a scarce year starves: so that no man of any substance will take a farm in Scotland; but every beggar, if he have got half a dozen wretched horses, and as many oxen, and can borrow corn to sow, pretends to be a tenant in places where they pay no other rent than corn.

I know there are many objections made to what has been said concerning the advantages which a rent paid in money has above one paid in corn; but certainly they are all so frivolous, that every man upon a little reflection may answer them to himself. For the chief of them are, either that the tenant will squander away money when he gets it into his hands; or that the master can get a better price for the corn by selling it in gross to merchants in the adjacent towns, or else by sending it to be sold at a great distance. To the first I answer, that no substantial man will squander away money because he has got it into his hands, though such beggars as we now have for tenants might be apt to do so. And to the second, that the hazard of sending corn from one place of the kingdom to another by sea, and the prejudice the tenants suffer from long carriages by land, do in part balance the supposed advantage; besides, if those wholesale bargains were not so frequently made, nor the corn so often carried to be sold at the great towns, the merchants would be obliged to send to the country markets to buy, and the prices in them would rise. In short, the changing of money-rent into corn, has been the chief cause of racking all the rents to that excessive rate they are now advanced. And upon reflection it will soon appear, that the turning of money-rents into rents of corn, has been the invention of some covetous wretches, who have been the occasion that all masters now live under the same uneasiness, and constant care, which they at first out of covetousness created to themselves; and all to get as much as was possible from poor tenants, who by such means are made miserable, and are so far from improving, that they only run out and spoil the ground, ruin their neighbours by borrowing, and at length break for considerable sums, though at first they were no better than beggars.[12]

The method of most other countries is; that all rents are paid in money; that masters receiving a fine, grant long leases of their grounds at easy rents: but this supposes the tenant a man of considerable substance, who cannot only give a fine, but has wherewithal to stock, and also to improve his farm. But in Scotland no such men are willing to take

---

12. The payment of rent in kind (ferme) was traditional throughout Scottish agriculture, Lowland as well as Highland, and was still prevalent at the end of the seventeenth century. (It was not a recent innovation, as Fletcher seems to suggest.) Commutation into money rent had begun by the end of the seventeenth century, but only became widespread in the first half of the eighteenth century: Whyte, *Agriculture and Society*, pp. 192–94; and T. M. Devine, *The Transformation of Rural Scotland. Social Change and the Agrarian Economy 1660–1815* (Edinburgh, 1994), pp. 8–9, 23–25.

farms; nor in truth are the masters willing to let them, as they do in other countries.[13] And though the masters may pretend, that if they could find substantial tenants, they would let their grounds as they do in other places; and men of substance, that if they could have farms upon such conditions, they would turn tenants; yet we see evident marks of the little probability there is that any such thing can be brought about without a general regulation. For in the west and north countries where they let land in feu (or fee) the superiors are so hard, that besides the yearly feu-duty, they make the feuer pay at his first entrance the whole intrinsick value of the land; and the people, though substantial men, are fools and slaves enough to make such bargains.[14] And in the same countries, when they let a small parcel of land to a tradesman, they let it not for what the land is worth, but what both the land and his trade is worth. And indeed 'tis next to an impossibility to alter a general bad custom in any nation, without a general regulation, because of inveterate bad dispositions and discouragements, with which the first beginnings of reformations are always attended. Besides, alterations that are not countenanced by the publick authority, proceed slowly; and if they chance to meet with any check, men soon return to their former bad methods.

The condition then of this nation, chiefly by this abuse of racking the lands, is brought to such extremity, as makes all the commonalty miserable, and the landlords, if possible, the greater slaves, before they can get their rents and reduce them into money. And because this evil is arrived to a greater height with us, than I believe was ever known in any other place; and that, as I have said, we are in no disposition to practise the

13. A "fine" was a fee payable on entering or taking up a tenancy: as Fletcher observes, a high entry fine was often accompanied by a moderate annual rental. The advantage to the landowner lay in the receipt of a cash sum on effecting the lease; as long as they were not fixed by custom, both fine and rent could be adjusted upwards when the lease was determined. The system was characteristic of—though by no means universal in—English agriculture. The emergence in Scotland of a class of substantial tenants had to wait until the second half of the eighteenth century.

14. "Superior" was a feudal term denoting a freehold landowner who held the "superiority" over his lands. If these were let in "feu," the tenant, or "feuar," would pay a substantial cash sum on entry, and a fixed annual "feu-duty," set initially at the level of an economic rent. Provided that he and his heirs could pay the entry-fine, the tenant or feuar enjoyed security of possession in perpetuity.

methods of most other countries, I think we ought to find out some new one which may surmount all difficulties, since in things of this nature divers methods may be proposed very practicable, and much better than any that hitherto have been in use.

I know that if to a law prohibiting all interest for money, another were joined, that no man should possess more land than so much as he should cultivate by servants, the whole money, as well as people of this nation, would be presently employed, either in cultivating lands, or in trade and manufactures; that the country would be quickly improved to the greatest height of which the soil is capable, since it would be cultivated by all the rich men of the nation; and that there would still be vast stocks remaining to be employed in trade and manufactures. But to oblige a man of a great estate in land to sell all, except perhaps two hundred pounds sterling a year (which he might cultivate by his servants) and to employ the whole money produced by the sale of the rest, in a thing so uncertain as he would judge trade to be, and for which 'tis like he might have no disposition or genius, being a thing impracticable: and also to employ the small stocks of minors, widows, and other women unmarried, in trade or husbandry, a thing of too great hazard for them; I would propose a method for our relief, by joining to the law prohibiting all interest of money, and to the other, that no man should possess more land than so much as he cultivates by his servants, a third law, obliging all men that possess lands under the value of two hundred pounds sterling clear profits yearly, to cultivate them by servants, and pay yearly the half of the clear profits to such persons as cultivating land worth two hundred pounds sterling a year, or above, shall buy such rents of them at twenty years purchase. The project in its full extent may be comprehended in these following articles.

All interest of money to be forbidden.

No man to possess more land than he cultivates by servants.

Every man cultivating land under the value of two hundred pounds sterling clear profits a year, to pay yearly the half of the clear profits to some other man who shall buy that rent at twenty years purchase; and for his security shall be preferred to all other creditors.

No man to buy or possess those rents, unless he cultivate land to the value at least of two hundred pounds sterling clear profits yearly.

Minors, women unmarried, and persons absent upon a publick account, may buy or possess such rents, though they cultivate no lands.[15]

By the first article, discharging all interest of money, most men who have small sums at interest, will be obliged to employ it in trade, or the improvement of land.

By the second, that no man is to possess more land, than so much as he cultivates by his servants, the whole land of the kingdom will come into the hands of the richest men; at least there will be no land cultivated by any man who is not the possessor of it. And if he have a greater estate than what he cultivates, he may lay out money upon improvements; or if he have bought a small possession, though he may have no more money left, he may, by selling one half of the rent, procure a sum considerable enough, both to stock and improve it. So that in a few years the country will be every where inclosed and improved to the greatest height, the plough being every where in the hand of the possessor. Then servants, day-labourers, tradesmen, and all sorts of merchants, will be well paid, and the whole commons live plentifully, because they will all be employed by men of substance: the ground by inclosure, and other improvements, will produce the double of what it now does; and the race of horses and black cattel will be much mended.

By the other articles; that no man cultivating land under the value of two hundred pounds sterling clear profits yearly, can purchase rents upon land from any other man; but is obliged to pay yearly the half of the clear profits, to such persons as shall buy them at twenty years purchase; and that only those who cultivate land worth at least two hundred pounds sterling a year, can buy such rents; the men of great land estates having sold all their lands, except so much as may yield two hundred pounds

15. This and the preceding paragraph (i.e., the fourth and fifth "articles" of Fletcher's proposals) were marked to be deleted in the mss emendations to David Fletcher's copy of the *Second Discourse:* see the List of Variants. A number of such changes are indicated on this copy: their concern with detail makes it unlikely that anyone other than Andrew Fletcher himself was responsible for them. The changes are all in the direction of simplifying the proposals and the accompanying explanations. Although they probably date from late in Fletcher's life, they almost certainly indicate his concern lest these proposals in particular be misunderstood. For doubts as to the success of the effort, see below, note 17.

sterling yearly, or so much above that value as they shall think fit to cultivate, may secure, if they please, the whole money they receive for their lands, upon those rents which the lesser possessors are obliged to sell. And so those who had formerly their estates in lands ill cultivated, and corn-rents ill paid, as well as the other three sorts of persons excepted from the general rule, and mentioned in the last article, will have a clear rent in money coming in without trouble, for payment of which they are to be secured in the lands of the said lesser possessors before all creditors. The reason of excepting three sorts of persons before-mentioned from the general rule, is evident; because (as has been said) it were unreasonable to oblige minors, or women unmarried, to venture their small stocks in trade or husbandry: and much more that those who are absent upon a publick account, should be obliged to have any stock employed that way, since they cannot inspect either.

The small possessors by this project are not wronged in any thing; for if they are obliged to pay a rent to others, they receive the value of it. And this rent will put them in mind, not to live after the manner of men of great estates, but as husbandmen, which will be no way derogatory to their quality, however antient their family may be.

The method to put this project in execution is, first to enact; that interest for money should fall next year from six per cent. to five, and so on, falling every year one per cent. till it cease: and to make a law, that all those who at present possess lands under the value of two hundred pounds sterling clear profits yearly, should cultivate them by servants, and sell the half of the clear profits at twenty years purchase to the first minor, woman unmarried, or person absent upon a publick account, who should offer money for them; and in default of such persons presenting themselves to buy, they should be obliged to sell such rents to any other persons qualified as above: and likewise to make another law, that whoever possesses lands at present to the value of two hundred pounds sterling clear profits yearly, or more, should at least take so much of them as may amount to that value, into their own hands. This being done, the yearly falling of the interest of money would force some of those who might have money at interest, to take land for it: others calling for their money, would buy estates of the landed men, who are to sell all except so much as they cultivate themselves: and the prohibition of interest producing many small possessors, would afford abundance of rents upon land to be bought by rich men; of which many might probably be paid out of those very lands they themselves formerly possessed. So that all sorts of men would in a little time fall into that easy method for their affairs, which is proposed by the project.

What the half of the yearly clear profits of any small possessors may be, the usual valuation of lands, in order to publick taxes, which because of improvements must be frequently made, will ascertain.

But it will be said, that before any such thing can every where take place in this nation, all teinds (or tithes) and all sorts of superiorities, must be transacted for, and sold; that the tenures of all lands must be made allodial, to the end that every man may be upon an equal foot with another; that this project, in order to its execution, does suppose things, which though perhaps they would be great blessings to the nation upon many accounts, and in particular by taking away the seeds of most law-suits, and the obstructions to all sorts of improvements; yet are in themselves as great and considerable as the project itself.[16]

Indeed I must acknowledge, that any thing calculated for a good end is (since we must express it so) almost always clogged with things of the same nature: for as all bad, so all good things are chained together, and do support one another. But that there is any difficulty, to a legislative power (that is willing to do good) of putting either this project, or the things last named in execution, I believe no man can shew. Sure I am, that it never was nor can be the interest of any prince or commonwealth, that any subject should in any manner depend upon another subject: and that it is the interest of all good governments at least to encourage a good sort of husbandry.[17]

16. "Teinds" were tithes, payable to the parish ministers; "allodial" land was land wholly owned by its proprietor, with no feudal obligations. Fletcher would appear to be conceding that his proposals required the abolition of all feudal tenures.

17. As the mss emendations to David Fletcher's copy of the *Second Discourse* confirm (see fn 15 above), Fletcher thought carefully about his proposals for agrarian reform, and was anxious to ensure that they were coherent in detail. In this he had limited success. In his hostility to great landowners, whom Fletcher charged with neglecting to improve their lands, he set the tone for much of the subsequent literature of agrarian improvement; but his specific prescriptions were never followed up. Despite the care Fletcher took in setting them out, their likely outcome was by no means clear, even supposing that

I know these proposals, by some men who aim at nothing but private interest, will be looked upon as visionary: it is enough for me, that in themselves, and with regard to the nature of the things, they are practicable; but if on account of the indisposition of such men to receive them, they be thought impracticable, it is not to be accounted strange; since if that indisposition ought only to be considered, every thing directed to a good end is such.

Many other proposals might be made to the parliament for the good of this nation, where every thing is so much amiss, and the publick good so little regarded. Amongst other things, to remove the present seat of the government, might deserve their consideration: for as the happy situation of London has been the principal cause of the glory and riches of England, so the bad situation of Edinburgh has been one great occasion of the poverty and uncleanliness in which the greater part of the people of Scotland live.

A proposal likewise for the better education of our youth would be very necessary: and I must confess I know no part of the world where education is upon any tolerable foot.[18] But perhaps I have presumed too

------

a Scottish parliament had possessed the authority and the administrative powers to implement them.

Fletcher evidently wanted to keep estates to a moderate size, by requiring that they be directly farmed, while those with an income lower than the threshold of £200 sterling a year would be obliged to sell the rent of a part of their lands in order to secure capital for their improvement. By these means great landowners would gradually become wealthy owner-farmers, whose income would be directed away from interest-bearing funds by an enforced reduction in the rate of interest, and into the purchase of rents from lesser landholders, or into investments in manufactures and trade. Poorer freeholders, by contrast, would become rent-paying tenants on at least part of their lands, but by gaining capital to improve their holdings they could expect to become substantial tenant farmers. Obvious difficulties, however, arise from Fletcher's failure to make provision either for increases in productivity or for inflation. He may have hoped that these would enable the lesser landholders to pass the £200 rental qualification, and to buy out those who owned their rents, creating an ever-larger class of owner-farmers. But the greater resources available to wealthy landowners are likely to have given them a continuing competitive advantage, leading to a renewed concentration of land-ownership.

18. A later pamphlet containing such a proposal has been attributed to Fletcher: *Proposals for the Reformation of Schools and Universities, in order to the better education of youth, humbly offered to the serious consideration of the High Court of Parliament*, (1704); but the evidence for the attribution is inconclusive. See also fn 7 to the *Account of a Conversation*.

much in offering my opinion upon such considerable matters as those
which I have treated.

Since I finished the preceding discourses I am informed, that if the present parliament will not comply with the design of continuing the army,
they shall immediately be dissolved, and a new one called. At least those
of the presbyterian persuasion, who expect no good from a new parliament, are to be frighted with the dissolution of the present (which has
established their church-government) and by that means induced to use
their utmost endeavours with the members for keeping up the army, and
promoting the designs of ill men:[19] but I hope no presbyterian will ever
be for evil things that good may come of them; since thereby they may
draw a curse upon themselves instead of a blessing. They will certainly
consider that the interest which they ought to embrace, as well upon the
account of prudence, as of justice and duty, is that of their country; and
will not hearken to the insinuations of ill men who may abuse them, and
when they have obtained the continuation of the army, endeavour to persuade his majesty and the parliament, to alter the present government of
the church, by telling them, that presbyterian government is in its nature
opposite to monarchy, that they maintain a rebellious principle of defen-
sive arms, and that a church government more suitable and subservient
to monarchy ought to be established.

Now if at this time the presbyterians be true to the interest of their
country, all those who love their country, though they be not of that persuasion, will stand by them in future parliaments, when they shall see
that they oppose all things tending to arbitrary power: but if they abandon and betray their country, they will fall unpitied. They must not tell
me, that their church can never fall, since it is the true church of God. If
it be the true church of God, it needs no crooked arts to support it. But
I hope they will not deny that it may fall under persecution; which they
will deserve, if they go along with the least ill thing to maintain it.

19. Immediately after the Revolution, the first session of William's parliament abolished episcopacy in July 1689; an Act establishing Presbyterian government followed in
the second session, in June 1690: *Source Book of Scottish History*, III, pp. 213–15.

8

The Spectator
(nos. 155, 174, 218, 232, 450)
1711–12

RICHARD STEELE was born in Dublin in 1672, the son of a well-off attorney. His friendship with Joseph Addison began in 1684 when they were at Charterhouse school and continued afterward at Oxford. He then spent several years in the Army and fought a duel in June 1700. Briefly thereafter, he composed "The Christian Hero," followed by two plays along the same lines, "The Funeral" and "The Lying Lover" (1701, 1704). He established *The Tatler* in April 1709. About two-thirds of the nearly three hundred numbers were by Steele. The publication ceased to appear in January 1711, perhaps for political reasons; Robert Harley, who had been satirized in some numbers, became head of government in August 1710. *The Spectator* was established just two months later, however, and the more than five hundred numbers of that journal were divided about equally between Addison and Steele (though No. 232 may have been by an occasional contributor such as John Hughes or Henry Martyn). Steele became active in party strife, taking the Whig side, and was at one point expelled from the House of Commons, where he had just taken a seat (March 1714). He died in 1729.

The excerpts here are reprinted from *The Spectator*, edited by Donald F.

[© Oxford University Press 1965. Reprinted from *The Spectator*, Volumes II and IV, edited by Donald F. Bond (1965), by permission of Oxford University Press.]

Bond, 2:107–10, 185–89, 348–51, 401–6, and 4:81–86, by permission of Oxford University Press. They were chosen to illustrate how this important early journalistic arbiter of taste and manners viewed the role of trade in modern social life. Bracketed material is by the present editor; all other notes are by Bond.

═══════════════════

The Spectator

No. 155
Tuesday, August 28, 1711[1]

> . . . Hae nugae seria ducunt
> In mala . . .
>
> Hor.

I have more than once taken Notice of an indecent License taken in Discourse, wherein the Conversation on one Part is involuntary, and the Effect of some necessary Circumstance. This happens in travelling together in the same hired Coach, sitting near each other in any publick Assembly, or the like. I have upon making Observations of this sort received innumerable Messages, from that Part of the fair Sex, whose Lot in Life it is to be of any Trade or publick Way of Life. They are all to a Woman urgent with me to lay before the World the unhappy Circumstances they are under, from the unreasonable Liberty which is taken in their Presence, to talk on what Subject it is thought fit by every Coxcomb who wants Understanding or Breeding. One or two of these Complaints I shall set down.

---

1. *Motto.* Horace, *Arts poetica,* 451 (altered; used also as motto for *Tatlers* 103 and 269):
   These things which now seem frivolous and slight,
   Will prove of serious consequence. ROSCOMMON
[Horace, *Of the art of poetry: a poem,* trans. Wentworth Dillon Roscommon (London: H. Hills, 1709).]

Mr. Spectator,

I keep a Coffee-house, and am one of those whom you have thought fit to mention as an Idol[2] some Time ago: I suffered a good deal of Raillery upon that Occasion; but shall heartily forgive you, who were the Cause of it, if you will do me Justice in another Point. What I ask of you, is to acquaint my Customers (who are otherwise very good ones) that I am unavoidably hasped[3] in my Bar, and cannot help hearing the improper Discourses they are pleased to entertain me with. They strive who shall say the most immodest things in my Hearing: At the same time half a dozen of them loll at the Bar staring just in my Face, ready to interpret my Looks and Gestures, according to their own Imaginations. In this passive Condition I know not where to cast my Eyes, place my Hands, or what to employ my self in: But this Confusion is to be a Jest, and I hear them say in the End, with an insipid Air of Mirth and Subtlety, Let her alone, she knows as well as we for all she looks so. Good Mr. Specta-tor, perswade Gentlemen that this is out of all Decency. Say it is pos-sible a Woman may be modest, and yet keep a publick House. Be pleas'd to argue, that in Truth the Affront is the more unpardonable because I am obliged to suffer it, and cannot fly from it. I do assure you, Sir, the Chearfulness of Life which would arise from the honest Gain I have, is utterly lost to me from the endless, flat, impertinent Pleasantries which I hear from Morning to Night. In a Word, it is too much for me to bear, and I desire you to acquaint them, that I will keep Pen and Ink at the Bar and write down all they say to me, and send it to you for the Press. It is possible when they see how empty what they speak, without the Advan-tage of an impudent Countenance and Gesture, will appear, they may come to some Sense of themselves, and the Insults they are guilty of to-wards me. I am,

Sir,

Your most humble Servant,

The Idol.

This Representation is so just, that it is hard to speak of it without an Indignation which perhaps would appear too elevated to such as can be

---

2. Nos. 73 and 87 (vol. i).
3. No. 132. ["Hasped" means enclosed, shut up.]

guilty of this inhumane Treatment, where they see they affront a modest, plain, and ingenuous Behaviour. This Correspondent is not the only Sufferer in this Kind, for I have long Letters both from the *Royal* and *New Exchange* on the same Subject. They tell me that a young Fop cannot buy a Pair of Gloves, but he is at the same Time straining for some ingenious Ribaldry to say to the young Woman who helps them on. It is no small Addition to the Calamity, that the Rogues buy as hard[4] as the plainest and modestest Customers they have; besides which they loll upon their Counters half an Hour longer than they need, to drive away other Customers, who are to share their Impertinencies with the Milliner, or go to another Shop. Letters from *'Change Alley*[5] are full of the same Evil, and the Girls tell me except I can chace some eminent Merchants from their Shops they shall in a short Time fail. It is very unaccountable, that Men can have so little Deference to all Mankind who pass by them, as to bear being seen toying by two's and three's at a Time, with no other Purpose but to appear gay enough to keep up a light Conversation of common-place Jests, to the Injury of her whose Credit is certainly hurt by it, tho' their own may be strong enough to bear it. When we come to have exact Accounts of these Conversations, it is not to be doubted but that their Discourses will raise the usual Stile of buying and selling: Instead of the plain down-right lying, and asking and bidding so unequally to what they will really give and take, we may hope to have from these fine Folks an Exchange of Complements. There must certainly be a great deal of pleasant Difference between the Commerce° of Lovers, and that of all other Dealers, who are, in a Kind, Adversaries. A sealed Bond or a Bank Note, would be a pretty Gallantry to convey unseen into the Hands of one whom a Director is charmed with; otherwise the City Loiterers are still more unreasonable than those at the other End of the Town: At the *New Exchange* they are eloquent for want of Cash, but in the City they ought with Cash to supply their want of Eloquence.

If one might be serious on this prevailing Folly, one might observe,

---

4. *OED* defines as "parsimoniously"; this is the only quotation given.

5. A short but important street running south from Cornhill to Lombard Street, almost directly in front of the Royal Exchange. Jonathan's and Garraway's coffeehouses were here, and it was a favourite resort of merchants and traders.

that it is a melancholy thing, when the World is mercenary even to the buying and selling our very Persons, that young Women, tho' they have never so great Attractions from Nature, are never the nearer being happily disposed of in Marriage; I say it is very hard under this Necessity, it shall not be possible for them to go into a Way of Trade for their Maintenance, but their very Excellences and personal Perfections shall be a Disadvantage to them, and subject them to be treated as if they stood there to sell their Persons to Prostitution. There cannot be a more melancholy Circumstance to one who has made any Observation in the World, than one of these erring Creatures exposed to Bankruptcy. When that happens, none of these toying Fools will do any more than any other Man they meet to preserve her from Infamy, Insult, and Distemper. A Woman is naturally more helpless than the other Sex; and a Man of Honour and Sense should have this in his View in all Manner of Commerce° with her. Were this well weighed, Inconsideration, Ribaldry, and Nonsense would not be more natural to entertain Women with than Men; and it would be as much Impertinence to go into a Shop of one of these young Women without buying, as into that of any other Trader. I shall end this Speculation with a Letter I have received from a pretty Milliner in the City.

Mr. SPECTATOR,
I have read your Account of Beauties,[6] and was not a little surprized to find no Character of my self in it. I do assure you I have little else to do but to give Audience as I am such. Here are Merchants of no small Consideration, who call in as certainly as they go to *'Change* to say something of my Roguish Eye: And here is one who makes me once or twice a Week tumble over all my Goods, and then owns it was only a Gallantry to see me act with these pretty Hands; then lays out three Pence in a little Ribband for his Wristbands, and thinks he is a Man of great Vivacity. There is an ugly Thing not far off me whose Shop is frequented only by People of Business, that is all Day long as busy as possible. Must I that am a Beauty be treated with for nothing but my Beauty? Be pleased to assign Rates to my kind Glances, or make all pay who come to see me, or I shall be undone by my Admirers for want of Customers. *Albacinda, Eudosia,*

6. No. 144.

and all the rest[7] would be used just as we are, if they were in our Condition; therefore pray consider the Distress of us the lower Order of Beauties, and I shall be

Your oblig'd humble Servant.

T

No. 174
Wednesday, September 19, 1711[8]

Haec memini & victum frustra contendere Thyrsin.
Virg.

There is scarce any thing more common than Animosities between Parties that cannot subsist but by their Agreement: This was well represented in the Sedition of the Members of the human Body in the old *Roman* Fable.[9] It is often the Case of lesser confederate States against a superiour Power, which are hardly held together though their Unanimity is necessary for their common Safety: And this is always the Case of the landed and trading Interest of *Great Britain;* the Trader is fed by the Product of the Land, and the landed Man cannot be cloathed but by the Skill of the Trader; and yet those Interests are ever jarring.

7. See No. 144.
8. *Motto.* Virgil, *Eclogues,* 7. 69:
These rhymes I did to memory commend,
When vanquish'd Thyrsis did in vain contend. DRYDEN
[*Miscellany Poems,* trans. John Dryden (London: Tonson, 1684).]
The motto in the original folio sheets was "Metiri se quemque suo modulo ac pede verum est" ("It is right that each should measure himself by his own rule and standard"), Horace, *Epistles,* 1. 7. 98 (which Steele had used as motto for *Tatler* 206).
9. The fable of the interdependence of the parts of the body (Livy, *History,* 2. 32, and elsewhere) had been used recently by Defoe in the *Review* (1 May 1711) to illustrate the same point: "Your Land might go a begging but for Trade; and for the Landed Men to rail at Trade, is like the Members Mutinying against the Belly." *The Medley* for 12 May 1712 (J. Baker issue) also applies it to show how the landed and trading interests "are equally obliged to each other." In L'Estrange's *Fables of Aesop* (1692) it is Fable No. 50. For the popularity of the story see Heinrich Gombel, *Die Fabel "Vom Magen und den Gliedern" in der Weltliteratur* (Halle, 1934).

We had last Winter an Instance of this at our Club, in Sir ROGER DE COVERLY and Sir ANDREW FREEPORT, between whom there is generally a constant, though friendly, Opposition of Opinions. It happened that one of the Company, in an historical Discourse, was observing, that *Carthaginian* Faith was a proverbial Phrase to intimate Breach of Leagues.[10] Sir ROGER said it could hardly be otherwise: That the *Carthaginians* were the greatest Traders in the World; and as Gain is the chief End of such a People, they never pursue any other: The Means to it are never regarded; they will, if it comes easily, get Money honestly; but if not, they will not scruple to attain it by Fraud or Cosenage: And indeed what is the whole Business of the Trader's Accompt, but to overreach him who trusts to his Memory? But were that not so, what can there great and noble be expected from him whose Attention is for ever fixed upon ballancing his Books, and watching over his Expences? And at best, let Frugality and Parsimony be the Virtues of the Merchant, how much is his punctual Dealing below a Gentleman's Charity to the Poor, or Hospitality among his Neighbours?

Captain SENTRY observed Sir ANDREW very diligent in hearing Sir ROGER, and had a Mind to turn the Discourse, by taking Notice in general from the highest to the lowest Parts of human Society, there was a secret, tho' unjust Way among Men, of indulging the Seeds of ill Nature and Envy, by comparing their own State of Life to that of another, and grudging the Approach of their Neighbour to their own Happiness; and on the other Side, he who is the less at his Ease repines[11] at the other who, he thinks, has unjustly the Advantage over him. Thus the civil and military List look upon each other with much ill Nature; the Soldier repines at the Courtier's Power, and the Courtier rallies the Soldier's Honour; or to come to lower Instances, the private Men in the Horse and Foot of an Army, the Carmen and Coachmen in the City-streets, mutually look upon each other with ill Will, when they are in Competition for Quarters or the Way in their respective Motions.

It is very well, good Captain, interrupted Sir ANDREW: You may

---

10. The Carthaginians "are accounted a sort of faithless People in the World, to whom no Credit is to be given; from whence came the Proverb, *Punica fides, Punick Faith,* to signifie *Knavery,* or *a deceitful Promise*" (Danet). "Punic faith" seems to be the common English form; this quotation is the only example given in *OED* of "Carthaginian faith."

11. [Complains or murmurs.]

attempt to turn the Discourse, if you think fit, but I must however have a
Word or two with Sir ROGER; who, I see, thinks he has paid me off, and
been very severe upon the Merchant. I shall not, continued he, at this
Time remind Sir ROGER of the great and noble Monuments of Charity
and publick Spirit which have been erected by Merchants since the Reformation, but at present content my self with what he allows us, Parsimony and Frugality. If it were consistent with the Quality of so antient
a Baronet as Sir ROGER, to keep an Accompt or measure things by the
most infallible Way, that of Numbers, he would prefer our Parsimony to
his Hospitality. If to drink so many Hogsheads is to be hospitable, we do
not contend for the Fame of that Virtue; but it would be worth while to
consider, whether so many Artificers at work ten Days together by my
Appointment, or so many Peasants made merry on Sir ROGER's Charge,
are the Men more obliged: I believe the Families of the Artificers will
thank me, more than the Housholds of the Peasants shall Sir ROGER. Sir
ROGER gives to his Men, but I place mine above the Necessity or Obligation of my Bounty. I am in very little Pain for the *Roman* Proverb upon
the *Carthaginian* Traders; the *Romans* were their professed Enemies: I
am only sorry no *Carthaginian* Histories have come to our Hands; we
might have been taught perhaps by them some Proverbs against the *Roman* Generosity, in fighting for and bestowing other People's Goods.
But since Sir ROGER has taken Occasion from an old Proverb to be out
of Humour with Merchants, it should be no Offence to offer one not
quite so old in their Defence. When a Man happens to break[12] in *Holland,* they say of him that *he has not kept true Accompts.* This Phrase, perhaps, among us would appear a soft or humorous way of speaking, but
with that exact Nation it bears the highest Reproach; for a Man to be
mistaken in the Calculation of his Expence, in his Ability to answer future Demands, or to be impertinently sanguine in putting his Credit to
too great Adventure, are all Instances of as much Infamy, as with gayer
Nations to be failing in Courage or common Honesty.

Numbers are so much the Measure of every thing that is valuable, that
it is not possible to demonstrate the Success of any Action or the Prudence of any Undertaking without them. I say this in Answer to what Sir

12. [Go bankrupt.]

ROGER is pleased to say, That little that is truly noble can be expected from one who is ever poring on his Cash-book or ballancing his Accompts. When I have my Returns from abroad, I can tell to a Shilling by the Help of Numbers the Profit or Loss by my Adventure; but I ought also to be able to shew that I had Reason for making it, either from my own Experience or that of other People, or from a reasonable Presumption that my Returns will be sufficient to answer my Expence and Hazard; and this is never to be done without the Skill of Numbers. For Instance, if I am to trade to *Turkey*, I ought before-hand to know the Demand of our Manufactures there as well as of their Silks in *England*, and the customary Prices that are given for both in each Country. I ought to have a clear Knowledge of these Matters before-hand, that I may presume upon sufficient Returns to answer the Charge of the Cargo I have fitted out, the Freight and Assurance out and home, the Customs to the Queen, and the Interest of my own Money, and besides all these Expences a reasonable Profit to my self. Now what is there of Scandal in this Skill? What has the Merchant done that he should be so little in the good Graces of Sir ROGER? he throws down no Man's Enclosures, and tramples upon no Man's Corn; he takes nothing from the industrious Labourer; he pays the poor Man for his Work; he communicates his Profit with Mankind; by the Preparation of his Cargo and the Manufacture of his Returns, he furnishes Employment and Subsistance to greater Numbers than the richest Nobleman; and even the Nobleman is oblig'd to him for finding out foreign Markets for the Produce of his Estate, and for making a great Addition to his Rents; and yet 'tis certain that none of all these things could be done by him without the Exercise of his Skill in Numbers.

This is the Oeconomy of the Merchant, and the Conduct of the Gentleman must be the same, unless by scorning to be the Steward, he resolves the Steward shall be the Gentleman. The Gentleman no more than the Merchant is able without the Help of Numbers to account for the Success of any Action or the Prudence of any Adventure. If, for Instance, the Chace is his whole Adventure, his only Returns must be the Stag's Horns in the great Hall, and the Fox's Nose upon the Stable Door. Without Doubt Sir ROGER knows the full Value of these Returns; and if before-hand he had computed the Charges of the Chace, a Gentleman of his Discretion would certainly have hang'd up all his Dogs, he would never have brought back so many fine Horses to the Kennel, he would never have gone so often like a Blast over Fields of Corn. If such too had been the Conduct of all his Ancestors, he might truly have boasted at this Day that the Antiquity of his Family had never been sullied by a Trade; a Merchant had never been permitted with his whole Estate to purchase a Room for his Picture in the Gallery of the COVERLYS, or to claim his Descent from the Maid of Honour.[13] But 'tis very happy for Sir ROGER that the Merchant paid so dear for his Ambition. 'Tis the Misfortune of many other Gentlemen to turn out of the Seats of their Ancestors, to make Way for such new Masters as have been more exact in their Accompts than themselves; and certainly he deserves the Estate a great deal better who has got it by his Industry, than he who has lost it by his Negligence.

T

No. 218
Friday, November 9, 1711[14]

Quid de quoque viro & cui dicas saepe caveto.
Hor.

I happened the other Day, as my Way is, to strole into a little Coffeehouse beyond *Aldgate;*[15] and as I sat there, two or three very plain sensible Men were talking of the SPECTATOR. One said, he had that Morning drawn the great Benefit Ticket;[16] another wished he had; but a third shaked his Head and said, it was pity that the Writer of that Paper was

---

13. See No. 109 (vol. i). Sir Andrew Freeport's defence of the trading interests may be compared with that of Mr. Sealand in Steele's *Conscious Lovers* (IV. i).

14. *Motto.* Horace, *Epistles,* i. 18. 68 ("saepe videto"):
> Take heed of whom you speak, and what it is,
> Take heed to whom. . . . CREECH.

[*The odes, satyrs, and epistles of Horace: done into English,* trans. Thomas Creech (London: Tonson, 1684).]

15. The easternmost part of the city, north of the Tower.

16. See No. 191.

such a sort of Man, that it was no great Matter whether he had it or no. He is, it seems, said the good Man, the most extravagant Creature in the World; has run through vast Sums, and yet been in continual Want; a Man, for all he talks so well of Oeconomy, unfit for any of the Offices of Life, by reason of his Profuseness.[17] It would be an unhappy thing to be his Wife, his Child, or his Friend; and yet he talks as well of those Duties of Life as any one. Much Reflection has brought me to so easy a Contempt for every thing which is false, that this heavy Accusation gave me no Manner of Uneasiness; but at the same Time it threw me into deep Thought upon the Subject of Fame in general; and I could not but pity such as were so weak, as to value what the common People say out of their own talkative Temper, to the Advantage or Diminution of those whom they mention, without being moved either by Malice or Goodwill. It would be too long to expatiate upon the Sense all Mankind have of Fame, and the inexpressible Pleasure which there is in the Approbation of worthy Men, to all who are capable of worthy Actions; but methinks one may divide the general Word Fame into three different Species, as it regards the different Orders of Mankind who have any thing to do with it. Fame therefore may be divided into Glory, which respects the Hero; Reputation, which is preserved by every Gentleman; and Credit, which must be supported by every Tradesman. These Possessions in Fame are dearer than Life to those Characters of Men, or rather are the Life of these Characters. Glory, while the Hero pursues great and noble Enterprizes, is impregnable; and all the Assailants of his Renown do but shew their Pain and Impatience of its Brightness, without throwing the least Shade upon it. If the Foundation of an high Name be Virtue and Service, all that is offered against it is but Rumour, which is too short-lived to stand up in Competition with Glory, which is everlasting.

Reputation, which is the Portion of every Man who would live with the elegant and knowing Part of Mankind, is as stable as Glory if it be as well founded; and the common Cause of humane Society is thought concerned when we hear a Man of good Behaviour calumniated: Besides

17. "These are just such thoughtless exaggerations as were no doubt sometimes expressed by persons discussing Steele's weaknesses; it is curious to find him recording them here so frankly" (Aitken).

which, according to a prevailing Custom amongst us, every Man has his Defence in his own Arm; and Reproach is soon checked, put out of Countenance, and overtaken by Disgrace.

The most unhappy of all Men, and the most exposed to the Malignity or Wantonness of the common Voice, is the Trader. Credit is undone in Whispers: The Tradesman's Wound is received from one who is more private and more cruel than the Ruffian with the Lanthorn and Dagger. The Manner of repeating a Man's Name, As *Mr.* Cash, *Oh! do you leave your Money at his Shop? Why do you know Mr.* Searoom? *He is indeed a general Merchant.* I say, I have seen, from the Iteration of a Man's Name, hiding one Thought of him, and explaining what you hide by saying something to his Advantage when you speak, a Merchant hurt in his Credit; and him who every Day he lived litterally added to the Value of his native Country, undone by one who was only a Burthen and a Blemish to it. Since every Body who knows the World is sensible of this great Evil, how careful ought a Man to be in his Language of a Merchant. It may possibly be in the Power of a very shallow Creature to lay the Ruine of the best Family in the most opulent City; and the more so, the more highly he deserves of his Country; that is to say, the farther he places his Wealth out of his Hands, to draw home that of another Climate.

In this Case an ill Word may change Plenty into Want, and by a rash Sentence a free and generous Fortune may in a few Days be reduced to Beggary. How little does a giddy Prater imagine, that an idle Phrase to the Disfavour of a Merchant may be as pernicious in the Consequence, as the Forgery of a Deed to bar an Inheritance would be to a Gentleman? Land stands where it did before a Gentleman was calumniated, and the State of a great Action is just as it was before Calumny was offered to diminish it, and there is Time, Place, and Occasion expected to unravel all that is contrived against those Characters; but the Trader who is ready only for probable Demands upon him, can have no Armour against the Inquisitive, the Malicious, and the Envious, who are prepared to fill the Cry to his Dishonour. Fire and Sword are slow Engines of Destruction, in Comparison of the Babbler in the Case of the Merchant.

For this Reason I thought it an imitable Piece of Humanity of a Gentleman of my Acquaintance, who had great Variety of Affairs, and used to talk with Warmth enough against Gentlemen by whom he thought himself ill dealt with; that he would never let any thing be urged against a Merchant (with whom he had any Difference) except in a Court of Justice. He used to say, that to speak ill of a Merchant was to begin his Suit with Judgment and Execution. One cannot, I think, say more on this Occasion, than to repeat, That the Merit of the Merchant is above that of all other Subjects; for while he is untouched in his Credit, his Hand-writing is a more portable Coin for the Service of his Fellow-Citizens, and his Word the Gold of *Ophir*[18] in the Country wherein he resides.

T

No. 232
Monday, November 26, 1711[19]

Nihil largiundo gloriam adeptus est.
Sallust.

My wise and good Friend Sir *Andrew Freeport* divides himself almost equally between the Town and the Country: His Time in Town is given up to the Publick and the Management of his private Fortune; and after every three or four Days spent in this Manner, he retires for as many to his Seat within a few Miles of the Town, to the Enjoyment of himself, his Family, and his Friend. Thus Business and Pleasure, or rather, in Sir *Andrew*, Labour and Rest, recommend each other: They take their Turns with so quick a Vicisitude, that neither becomes a Habit, or takes Possession of the whole Man; nor is it possible he should be surfeited with either. I often see him at our Club in good Humour, and yet sometimes too with an Air of Care in his Looks: But in his Country Retreat he is always unbent, and such a Companion as I could desire; and therefore I seldom fail to make one with him when he is pleased to invite me.

18. A place frequently mentioned in the Old Testament for its fine gold. Its position is uncertain.

19. *Motto*. Sallust, *Bellum Catilinae*, 54. 3: Not by distributing largesse did he attain glory.

The other Day, as soon as we were got into his Chariot, two or three Beggars on each Side hung upon the Doors, and sollicited our Charity with the usual Rhetoric of a sick Wife or Husband at Home, three or four helpless little Children all starving with Cold and Hunger. We were forc'd to part with some Money to get rid of their Importunity; and then we proceeded on our Journey with the Blessings and Acclamations of these People.[20]

"Well then, says Sir *Andrew*, we go off with the Prayers and good Wishes of the Beggars, and perhaps too our Healths will be drunk at the next Ale-House: So all we shall be able to value our selves upon, is, that we have promoted the Trade of the Victualler, and the Excises of the Government. But how few Ounces of Wooll do we see upon the Backs of those poor Creatures? And when they shall next fall in our Way, they will hardly be better drest; they must always live in Rags to look like Objects of Compassion. If their Families too are such as they are represented, 'tis certain they cannot be better cloathed, and must be a great deal worse fed: One would think Potatoes should be all their Bread, and their Drink the pure Element; and then what goodly Customers are the Farmers like to have for their Wooll, Corn and Cattle? Such Customers and such a Consumption cannot but advance the landed Interest, and hold up the Rents of the Gentlemen.

"But of all Men living, we Merchants, who live by Buying and Selling, ought never to encourage Beggars. The Goods which we export are indeed the Product of the Lands, but much the greatest Part of their Value is the Labour of the People: But how much of these Peoples Labour shall we export, whilst we hire them to sit still? The very Alms they receive from us, are the Wages of Idleness. I have often thought that no Man should be permitted to take Relief from the Parish, or to ask it in the Street, till he has first purchas'd as much as possible of his own Livelihood by the Labour of his own Hands; and then the Publick ought only to be tax'd to make good the Deficiency. If this Rule was strictly ob-

20. Misson describes London as a city extremely rich, but "crouded with Beggars. Among other Customs of those Gentlemen, it is one with them to knock at Peoples Doors, as boldly as if they were the Masters of the House, when they beg Alms" (p. 221). Miege cites among the inconveniences of London "the importunate *Clamours* of *Street Beggars*, especially within the City and Liberties of *Westminster*" (p. 143).

served, we should see every where such a Multitude of new Labourers, as would in all Probability reduce the Prices of all our Manufactures. It is the very Life of Merchandise to buy cheap and sell dear. The Merchant ought to make his Out-set[21] as cheap as possible, that he may find the greater Profit upon his Returns; and nothing will enable him to do this like the Reduction of the Price of Labour upon all our Manufactures. This too would be the ready Way to increase the Number of our foreign Markets: The Abatement of the Price of the Manufacture would pay for the Carriage of it to more distant Countries; and this Consequence would be equally beneficial both to the landed and trading Interests. As so great an Addition of labouring Hands would produce this happy Consequence both to the Merchant and the Gentleman; our Liberality to common Beggars, and every other Obstruction to the Increase of Labourers, must be equally pernicious to both."[22]

Sir *Andrew* then went on to affirm, That the Reduction of the Prices of our Manufactures by the Addition of so many new Hands, would be no Inconvenience to any Man: But observing I was something startled at the Assertion, he made a short Pause, and then resum'd the Discourse. "It may seem, says he, a Paradox, that the Price of Labour should be re-duc'd without an Abatement of Wages, or that Wages can be abated without any Inconvenience to the Labourer; and yet nothing is more certain than that both these things may happen. The Wages of the Labourers make the greatest Part of the Price of every thing that is useful; and if in Proportion with the Wages the Prices of all other things shall be abated, every Labourer with less Wages would be still able to purchase as many Necessaries of Life, where then would be the Inconvenience? But the Price of Labour may be reduc'd by the Addition of more Hands to a Manufacture, and yet the Wages of Persons remain as high as ever. The admirable Sir *William Petty* has given Examples of this in some of his

21. i.e. primary outlay. The earliest example of this meaning in *OED* is dated 1719.

22. Sir Andrew, of course, is stating the orthodox Whig view of the relationship of labour to national wealth, in opposition to the increasing pressure of Tory propagandists, who continued to insist on land as the real source of the nation's riches. In the first of his *Examiners* Swift had complained that "the Wealth of the Nation, that used to be reckoned by the Value of Land, is now computed by the Rise and Fall of Stocks . . ." (*Examiner* 13, 2 Nov. 1710; *Prose Works*, ed. Herbert Davis, iii. 6).

Writings: One of them, as I remember, is that of a Watch, which I shall endeavour to explain so as shall suit my present Purpose.[23] It is certain that a single Watch could not be made so cheap in Proportion by one only Man, as a hundred Watches by a hundred; for as there is vast Variety in the Work, no one Person could equally suit himself to all the Parts of it; the Manufacture would be tedious, and at last but clumsily performed: But if an hundred Watches were to be made by a hundred Men, the Cases may be assigned to one, the Dials to another, the Wheels to another, the Springs to another, and every other Part to a proper Artist; as there would be no need of perplexing any one Person with too much Variety, every one would be able to perform his single Part with greater Skill and Expedition; and the hundred Watches would be finished in one-fourth Part of the Time of the first one, and every one of them at one-fourth Part of the Cost, though the Wages of every Man were equal. The Reduction of the Price of the Manufacture would increase the Demand of it, all the same Hands would be still employed and as well paid. The same Rule will hold in the Cloathing, the Shipping, and all the other Trades whatsoever. And thus an Addition of Hands to our Manufactures will only reduce the Price of them; the Labourer will still have as much Wages, and will consequently be enabled to purchase more Conveniencies of Life; so that every Interest in the Nation would receive a Benefit from an Increase of our working People.

"Besides, I see no Occasion for this Charity to common Beggars, since every Beggar is an Inhabitant of a Parish, and every Parish is tax'd to the Maintenance of their own Poor.[24] For my own Part, I cannot be mightily pleas'd with the Laws which have done this, which have provided better to feed than employ the Poor. We have a Tradition from our Forefathers, that after the first of those Laws was made, they were insulted with that famous Song,

23. From his essay "Concerning the Growth of the City of London" (1683), one of the *Essays in Political Arithmetick.* See *The Economic Writings of Sir William Petty,* ed. C. H. Hull (Cambridge, 1899), ii. 473.

24. The Act of Settlement of the Poor (1662) provided that a parish in which a labourer settled could send him back to the parish of which he was native, since each parish was responsible only for its own poor. At this period nearly a quarter of the population was occasionally in receipt of parochial relief (Trevelyan, i. 20).

Hang Sorrow, cast away Care,
The Parish is bound to find us, &c.[25]

And if we will be so good-natur'd as to maintain them without Work,
they can do no less in Return than sing us *The merry Beggars.*
"What then? am I against all Acts of Charity? God forbid! I know of
no Virtue in the Gospel that is in more pathetical Expressions recommended to our Practice. *I was hungry and ye gave me no Meat, thirsty and
ye gave me no Drink; naked and ye cloathed me not, a Stranger and ye took me
not in; sick and in Prison and ye visited me not.*[26] Our blessed Saviour treats
the Exercise or Neglect of Charity towards a poor Man, as the Performance or Breach of this Duty towards himself. I shall endeavour to obey
the Will of my Lord and Master: And therefore if an industrious Man
shall submit to the hardest Labour and coarsest Fare, rather than endure
the Shame of taking Relief from the Parish or asking it in the Street, this
is the Hungry, the Thirsty, the Naked; and I ought to believe if any Man
is come hither for Shelter against Persecution or Oppression, this is the
Stranger, and I ought to take him in. If any Countryman of our own is
fallen into the Hands of Infidels, and lives in a State of miserable Cap-
tivity, this is the Man in Prison, and I should contribute to his Ransom.
I ought to give to an Hospital of Invalids, to recover as many useful Subjects as I can; but I shall bestow none of my Bounties upon an Almshouse
of idle People; and for the same Reason I should not think it a Reproach
to me if I had withheld my Charity from those common Beggars. But we
prescribe better Rules than we are able to practise; we are asham'd not to
give into the mistaken Customs of our Country: But at the same Time I
cannot but think it a Reproach worse than that of common Swearing,
that the Idle and the Abandoned are suffered in the Name of Heaven and
all that is sacred, to extort from christian and tender Minds a Supply to
a profligate Way of Life, that is always to be supported but never relieved."[27]

25. See Chappell, *Popular Music of the Olden Time,* p. 777.
26. Matt. xxv. 42–43.
27. The signatures for this number (X in the folio sheets, Z in the 8vo, and unsigned
in 12mo) leave the authorship uncertain. Since Z is used as the signature for some of

No. 450
Wednesday, August 6, 1712[28]

. . . Quaerenda pecunia primum
Virtus post nummos.

Mr. Spectator,[29]

"All Men, through different Paths, make at the same common thing, *Money;* and it is to her we owe the Politician, the Merchant, and the Lawyer; nay, to be free with you, I believe to that also we are beholden for our *Spectator.* I am apt to think, that could we look into our own Hearts, we should see Money ingraved in them in more lively and moving Characters than Self-Preservation; for who can reflect upon the Merchant hoisting Sail in a doubtful Pursuit of her, and all Mankind sacrificing their Quiet to her, but must perceive that the Characters of Self-Preservation (which were doubtless originally the brightest) are sullied, if not wholly defaced; and that those of Money (which at first was only valuable as a Mean to Security) are of late so brightened, that the Characters of Self-Preservation, like a less Light set by a greater, are become almost imperceptible? Thus has Money got the upper Hand of what all Mankind formerly thought most dear, *viz.* Security; and I wish I could say she had here put a Stop to her Victories; but, alass! common Honesty fell a Sacrifice to her. This is the Way Scholastick Men talk of the greatest Good in the World; but I, a Tradesman, shall give you another Account of this Matter in the plain Narrative of my own Life. I think it

---

Hughes's contributions, Nichols and other editors have suggested Hughes as the author. Nichols, however, thought it "more probable" that Henry Martyn wrote the paper, doubtless because of the subject-matter. Morley assigns it to "Hughes? or Henry Martyn?" Gregory Smith thought it "probably" by Henry Martyn. Aitken's note reads: "Though generally attributed to Hughes, this paper may be by Henry Martyn." It is not in Duncombe's list of Hughes's contributions. On the basis of subject-matter the paper may be by Martyn, but there is no external evidence as to authorship.

28. *Motto.* Horace, *Epistles,* I. I. 53–54 (altered):
Gold must first be sought,
Then Virtue. CREECH.

29. The letter, whether contributed, or written by Steele, is designed as an answer to the request made in No. 442.

proper, in the first Place, to acquaint my Readers, that since my setting out in the World, which was in the Year 1660, I never wanted Money; having begun with an indifferent good Stock in the Tobacco Trade, to which I was bred; and by the continual Successes it has pleased Providence to bless my Endeavours with, am at last arrived at what they call a *Plumb.*[30] To uphold my Discourse in the Manner of your Wits or Philosophers, by speaking fine things, or drawing Inferences, as they pretend, from the Nature of the Subject, I account it vain; having never found any thing in the Writings of such Men, that did not savour more of the Invention of the Brain, or what is stiled Speculation, than of sound Judgment or profitable Observation. I will readily grant indeed, that there is what the Wits call Natural in their Talk; which is the utmost those curious Authors can assume to themselves, and is indeed all they endeavour at, for they are but lamentable Teachers. And what, I pray, is Natural? That which is Pleasing and Easy: And what are Pleasing and Easy? Forsooth, a new Thought or Conceit dressed up in smooth quaint Language, to make you smile and wag your Head, as being what you never imagined before, and yet wonder why you had not; meer frothy Amusements! fit only for Boys or silly Women to be caught with.

"It is not my present Intention to instruct my Readers in the Methods of acquiring Riches, that may be the Work of another Essay; but to exhibit the real and solid Advantages I have found by them in my long and manifold Experience: nor yet all the Advantages of so worthy and valuable a Blessing, (for who does not know or imagine the Comforts of being warm[31] or living at Ease? and that Power and Preheminence are their inseparable Attendants?) but only to instance the great Supports they afford us under the severest Calamities and Misfortunes; to shew that the Love of them is a special Antidote against Immorality and Vice, and that the same does likewise naturally dispose Men to Actions of Piety and Devotion: All which I can make out by my own Experience, who think my self no ways particular from the rest of Mankind, nor better nor worse by Nature than generally other Men are.

---

30. A plum is defined in the 1789 edition as "a cant word used by commercial people, to signify an £100,000." The earliest quotation in *OED* is dated 1689–1702.
31. See No. 242 (vol. ii).

"In the Year 1665, when the Sickness was, I lost by it my Wife and two Children, which were all my Stock. Probably I might have had more, considering I was married between 4 and 5 Years; but finding her to be a teeming Woman, I was careful, as having then little above a Brace of thousand Pounds to carry on my Trade and maintain a Family with. I loved them as usually Men do their Wives and Children, and therefore could not resist the first Impulses of Nature on so wounding a Loss; but I quickly rouzed my self, and found Means to alleviate, and at last conquer my Affliction, by reflecting how that she and her Children having been no great Expence to me, the best Part of her Fortune was still left; that my Charge being reduced to my self, a Journeyman, and a Maid, I might live far cheaper than before; and that being now a childless Widower, I might perhaps marry a no less deserving Woman, and with a much better Fortune than she brought, which was but 800 *l*. And to convince my Readers that such Considerations as these were proper and apt to produce such an Effect, I remember it was the constant Observation at that deplorable Time, when so many Hundreds were swept away daily, that the Rich ever bore the Loss of their Families and Relations far better than the Poor; the latter having little or nothing before-hand, and living from Hand to Mouth, placed the whole Comfort and Satisfaction of their Lives in their Wives and Children, and were therefore inconsolable.

"The following Year happened the Fire; at which Time, by good Providence, it was my Fortune to have converted the greatest Part of my Effects into ready Money, on the Prospect of an extraordinary Advantage which I was preparing to lay Hold on. This Calamity was very terrible and astonishing, the Fury of the Flames being such, that whole Streets, at several distant Places, were destroyed at one and the same Time, so that (as it is well known) almost all our Citizens were burnt out of what they had. But what did I then do? I did not stand gazing on the Ruins of our noble Metropolis; I did not shake my Head, wring my Hands, sigh, and shed Tears; I considered with my self what cou'd this avail; I fell a plodding[32] what Advantages might be made of the ready

32. [Studying closely.]

Cash I had, and immediately bethought my self that wonderful Penny-worths[33] might be bought of the Goods that were saved out of the Fire. In short, with about 2000 *l.* and a little Credit, I bought as much Tobacco as raised my Estate to the Value of 10000 *l.* I then *looked on the Ashes of our City, and the Misery of its late Inhabitants, as an Effect of the just Wrath and Indignation of Heaven towards a sinful and perverse People.*

"After this I married again, and that Wife dying, I took another; but both proved to be idle Baggages; the first gave me a great deal of Plague and Vexation by her Extravagancies, and I became one of the By-words of the City. I knew it would be to no manner of Purpose to go about to curb the Fancies and Inclinations of Women, which fly out the more for being restrain'd; but what I cou'd I did. I watch'd her narrowly, and by good Luck found her in the Embraces (for which I had two Witnesses with me) of a wealthy Spark[34] of the Court-end of the Town; of whom I recover'd 15000 Pounds, which made me Amends for what she had idly squander'd, and put a Silence to all my Neighbours, taking off my Re-proach by the Gain they saw I had by it. The last died about two Years after I marry'd her, in Labour of three Children. I conjecture they were begotten by a Country Kinsman of hers, whom, at her Recommenda-tion, I took into my Family, and gave Wages to as a Journey-man. What this Creature expended in Delicacies and high Diet with her Kinsman (as well as I could compute by the Poulterers, Fishmongers, and Grocers Bills) amounted in the said two Years to One hundred eighty six Pounds, four Shillings, and five Pence Half-penny. The fine Apparel, Bracelets, Lockets, and Treats, *&c.* of the other, according to the best Calculation, came in three Years and about three Quarters to Seven hundred forty four Pounds, seven Shillings and nine Pence. After this I resolved never to marry more, and found I had been a Gainer by my Marriages, and the Damages granted me for the Abuses of my Bed, (all Charges deducted) Eight thousand three hundred Pounds within a Trifle.

"I come now to shew the good Effects of the Love of Money on the Lives of Men towards rendring them honest, sober, and religious. When

33. [Things worth a penny.]
34. [A lively, gay, and showy man.]

I was a young Man, I had a Mind to make the best of my Wits, and overreach'd[35] a Country Chap[36] in a Parcel of unsound Goods; to whom,
upon his upbraiding, and threatning to expose me for it, I return'd the
Equivalent of his Loss; and upon his good Advice, wherein he clearly
demonstrated the Folly of such Artifices, which can never end but in
Shame, and the Ruin of all Correspondence, I never after transgress'd.
Can your Courtiers, who take Bribes, or your Lawyers or Physicians in
their Practice, or even the Divines who intermeddle in worldly Affairs,
boast of making but one Slip in their Lives, and of such a thorough and
lasting Reformation? Since my coming into the World I do not remember I was ever overtaken in Drink, save nine times, one at the Christen-
ing of my first Child, thrice at our City Feasts, and five times at driving
of Bargains. My Reformation I can attribute to nothing so much as the
Love and Esteem of Money; for I found my self to be extravagant in my
Drink, and apt to turn Projector, and make rash Bargains. As for
Women, I never knew any, except my Wives: For my Reader must know,
and it is what he may confide in as an excellent Recipe, That the Love of
Business and Money is the greatest Mortifier of inordinate Desires
imaginable, as employing the Mind continually in the careful Oversight
of what one has, in the eager Quest after more, in looking after the Neg-
ligences and Deceits of Servants, in the due Entring and Stating of Accounts, in hunting after Chaps, and in the exact Knowledge of the State
of Markets; which Things whoever thoroughly attends, will find enough
and enough to employ his Thoughts on every Moment of the Day: So
that I cannot call to Mind, that in all the Time I was a Husband, which,
off and on, was about twelve Years, I ever once thought of my Wives but
in Bed. And, lastly, for Religion, I have ever been a constant Church-
man, both Forenoons and Afternoons on *Sundays,* never forgetting to be
thankful for any Gain or Advantage I had had that Day; and on *Satur-
day* Nights, upon casting up my Accounts, I always was grateful for the
Sum of my Week's Profits, and at *Christmas* for that of the whole Year.

---

35. [Deceived.]
    36. i.e. chapman, purchaser, customer. According to *OED* the word came into vulgar
use in the end of the sixteenth century, but it is rare in books, even in the dramatists, before 1700. It is not recognized by Johnson, but is in Bailey's Dictionary (1731).

It is true perhaps, that my Devotion has not been the most fervent; which, I think, ought to be imputed to the Evenness and Sedateness of my Temper, which never would admit of any Impetuosities of any Sort: And I can remember, that in my Youth and Prime of Manhood, when my Blood ran brisker, I took greater Pleasure in Religious Exercises than at present, or many Years past, and that my Devotion sensibly declined as Age, which is dull and unweildy, came upon me.

"I have, I hope, here proved, that the Love of Money prevents all Immorality and Vice; which if you will not allow, you must, that the Pursuit of it obliges Men to the same Kind of Life as they would follow if they were really virtuous: Which is all I have to say at present, only recommending to you, that you would think of it, and turn ready Wit into ready Money as fast as you can. I conclude,

Your Servant,
Ephraim Weed"
T

9

"General Idea of the
New System of Finances"
1720

John Law was born in Scotland in 1671, the son of a prosperous gold-smith and banker. A gambler in his youth, he killed one Edward Wilson in a duel in 1694 and was sentenced to death. While an appeal was under way, he escaped from prison and fled to the Continent. After spending several years there, during which time he familiarized himself with the Dutch financial scene, he returned to Scotland in 1700. Over the next decade, he drafted proposals for paper money (1709) and a state bank, though these were rejected. There followed seven years of travel throughout Europe, with much gambling (successful, for the most part) and more financial schemes, mainly for the financially troubled French government. Though rejected, he made a good impression on the Duke of Orléans, regent after 1715, and was permitted in 1716 to establish his own bank in Paris on his paper money, low-interest principles.

That bank was a great success, and soon the government decreed that tax payments made with his paper notes were to be accepted as legal tender. At his urging, however, banking privileges and territory in the French colonies were signed over to him and his associates, and the Mississippi scheme based on his principles was duly established in 1717. The project expanded to embrace the East India and China companies and the companies of Senegal and of Africa (1719). Soon it became virtually the sole creditor of the state, as he announced plans to pay off the entire royal debt. Taxes and prices thus came down through his efficiencies, and after his conversion from Protestantism, Law was made controller-general of France in January 1720. But when hoarding and exporting of specie became widespread during the speculative bubble of early 1720, Law resorted to highly authoritarian measures to maintain adequate specie in the treasury. Wild inflation crippled trade and industry, and in May 1720 the government repudiated its debt. Law became vilified, his house in Paris was attacked, and he fled the country. In Brussels, he declined an offer to manage Czar Peter's finances in Russia. After much traveling, he was invited back to England in October 1721, though he still wished to return to France. Instead, he spent several years in England before traveling to Italy, where he died in 1729. Voltaire's judgment was not atypical: "A system altogether chimerical produced a commerce that was genuine."

The work included here is a justification of his French system written as a government memorandum, no doubt intended for public consumption. It contains an important discussion of the political implications of new financial and commercial realities, written from a monarchist perspective. It comes from John Law, "Idée générale du nouveau système des finances (1720)," in *Oeuvres complètes*, 3 vols., ed. Paul Harsin (Paris: Sirey, 1934), 3:77–97, and is based on two manuscripts, one of which contains lengthy additions not present in the other. I have preserved some of those additions and have placed them, as well as notes, in brackets.

General Idea of the
New System of Finances

First Part—Description of the System

It is an undeniable principle that the true wealth of a State consists in the productions of nature improved by art, and that, if agriculture and manufactures are encouraged in a large, fertile and populated Kingdom, its inhabitants are not only provided with all their needs and conveniences, but also with superfluities that can be shared with other peoples.

France—thanks to its fertility, its extensive territory, and its large population—has immense resources which it can only consume by exchanging its surplus commodities with those it needs to buy from other peoples, and as the goods it gets from them are inferior to its own, they become its debtors. Therefore, since the balance of trade is favorable to France, foreign countries must bring it their specie to make payment, without France being obliged to give them its own. But to increase this balance of trade through agriculture and the arts, no one may remain idle, everyone must contribute to the public interest with their work and their goods.

The first expedient is a royal bank which increases the monetary wealth of the nation. There are 18 million people in France. To have such a numerous people act, one needs enormous sums of money for daily expenses as well as a constant circulation of a great quantity of currency.

Perennial experience shows clearly that this deficiency in circulation, when it takes place in a State, leads the arts, agriculture, and trade to languish, and even destroys the value of lands and houses, as soon as one lacks a sufficient quantity of men and money to hire craftsmen and workers and to meet the true value of the landed capital.

[In order to make up for this lack of specie, a new currency—as useful, convenient and secure as metallic currencies—had to be created. This is what we are going to see. The origin and foundation of any trade is the exchange between commodities of a certain kind and commodities of another kind. This is how the first men used to trade, using neither gold nor silver, even in countries where those metals were the most abundant. This is how, in the past, Egyptians used to trade with Eastern Indians from the time of Queen Sesostris to that of Alexander the Great and even Emperor Augustus. This is how trade was done in the vast empire of Peru during the reign of the Incas, which lasted several centuries. This is also how the use of gold and silver money was forbidden in Lacedemonia for more than 400 years, when that Republic was the most prosperous, possessing more resources than Greece as a whole. But this exchange of commodities is not convenient, especially when considering all the minute details of domestic trade. Goods cannot be transported without expense, they cannot be distributed without work; they cannot be kept without being spoiled. They increase, decrease and change their value according to time and place. Therefore, there must be a common measure for the value of commodities, susceptible of a fixed denomination, incorruptible, portable, and divisible into several small sums to fulfill all the needs of any citizen. This common measure is what we call money. Up to now, metal appeared to be the most appropriate substance for a currency because it has the properties I just mentioned, but it also has the great drawback of lacking a fixed value. The value of each thing is proportional to the demand for it and to its quantity. Precious stones have a high price, because the quantities found are far less than the demand for it. On the contrary, water has no price because its quantity is greatly superior to the need we have of it. When the demand for specie is greater than the quantity, they become rare and, as a result, expensive. Because they are rare and expensive, everything is cheap, the products of art and nature become degraded, industry is discouraged, the circulation of traded goods stops, and the State languishes. On the other hand, when the quantity of gold and silver is greater than necessary, those metals are cheapened and everything becomes expensive. Debtors pay back their creditors with sums of lesser value than those they had borrowed, and the funds of creditors gradually decrease. Before the Spaniards discovered the mines in Peru, an ounce of gold was worth as much as ten ounces today, so that those who had properties purchasable with money lost nine tenths of their capital solely because of the decrease in the value of metals—not to mention the weakening currency, which also lost three quarters of its value. These variations disturbed not only families, but whole States. Those who had most profited from the Spanish trade had plenty of specie, whereas the other nations had barely enough for the circulation of the products of nature and art.] Credit is resorted to in order to make up for this lack of specie, to remedy the drawbacks of metallic money as well as to facilitate domestic and foreign trade.

Credit in general refers to the written or non-written promise made by one or several people, and which serves as money. [That is an imitation of pure and primitive nature, which leads people to give and receive mutually all the needs and conveniences of life on good faith.] That is how in the whole world, the bulk of commerce is done every day solely through the use of paper.

That way, traders [*négociants*°] do not have to send couriers and ships to carry specie wherever they have credit; their notes [*billets*] are enough—not only within a nation but in all countries—for them to be loaned all the sums they need, and even to have ships loaded with what they want. That is how all the resources of nature are easily and expeditiously put into circulation anywhere, solely by using paper, without being exposed to the dangers, expenses and losses which would be caused by the transport of specie.

The use of paper that is established in France only confirms through public credit what individual Bankers used to do before with private credit—which was nevertheless variable, uncertain, and exposed to a thousand unfortunate accidents.

Thanks to public credit, the republics of Holland, Venice, Genoa, the Kingdom of England and all other trading States have made up for their lack of specie for more than a century.

Thanks to that credit, they maintained their trade and sustained the wars which would have ruined them if cash had been their only resource to put in circulation.

In France, "credit" is authorized by the King, who guarantees the paper, commits his entire State—movable as well as immovable goods—to meet the value of that paper.

The credit of the French nation, concentrated in the person of its King, is infinitely superior to that of all other States which are weaker and governed by the multitude. [The unity of the supreme power is also necessary to exercise all the rights of sovereignty, whether it concerns the troops, laws or finances. In credit, as in military or legislative powers, the supreme power must belong to one person only, and all inferior powers must be united under it, because secrecy, obedience, dispatch, order and union—so necessary for the administration of a state—depend upon such unity of will. The credit of all the members of that state united in the sole person of the prince is infinitely stronger and more secure than that which depends on innumerable diverse individuals. Their conflicting interests may divide them, and therefore diminish public credit. But] when there is one interest, one credit, one power in a large, fertile, well-placed and well-populated Kingdom, everything moves along in rhythm: the common interest becomes the interest of each person in particular; the interest of the leader cannot be considered apart from the interest of each member and one cannot survive without the other.

One must not consider Bank notes as a mere promise to provide the required sums in gold and silver, but as a mutual agreement between the King and his subjects to receive and give back, through the circulation of paper, not only specie, but also its true value.

All the resources of the whole kingdom correspond to the value of this new currency. Everything will be given for it, it will be given for everything. By this means, the King has a resource that is always available for the circulation of everything that can be bought and sold, whatever its nature, anywhere and at any time.

The paper currency that the new System establishes [has therefore all the advantages of metallic money, without its drawbacks. I confess that gold and silver have a real value as metals because they can be employed usefully; thus they can be not only the common measure of the values of goods, but also the legal guarantee for the verification of those goods. Paper does not have that real value, and neither the order of the prince nor the consent of the people could give it to it. But by their credit, that paper becomes a currency more precious than metals; like gold and silver, paper is susceptible of a transferable value, divisible and easily renewed, and therefore it is incorruptible. But it has] even had this advantage over metals: its quantity can always be equal to the demand that is made of it, and it is not subject to the variations of metallic currency.

The second means provided by the new system to enrich nature is the creation of a Company through which the wealthy can lend their money to have it employed in commerce. Nothing was more ruinous than the annuities [*contrats de constitution°*]: in the lifetime of a man, the person borrowing at 5% and for twenty years would pay back the principal three times and his descendants would be forever under its burden.

Therefore it was right to suppress the annuities [*contrats de constitution de rente°*], and to decrease interest rates to combine everything in a Company of traders [*négociants°*] authorized by the State. One day it will be able to give more dividends to shareholders than the yearly interest income on money lent at five per cent, and neither private individuals nor the State will be harmed by that, [since that increase can only come from the increase in agriculture, manufactures, and commerce. The wealth of the State will make that of the subjects. The new System does nothing to increase the wealth of the French people; it only does what the first legislators did in establishing civil societies. By the union of everything in a single body, every member of that body has all the others as protectors or servants. Every individual benefits from all the advantages of government: soldiers to protect him, magistrates to dispense justice, peasants, craftsmen and traders [*négociants°*] to provide for his needs, as if all were made or established for him alone. Likewise, through the same reunion of all opposing interests, individual credits and separate funds, the new System enriches the French nation. It is this unity which makes the wealth as well as the power and strength of States. They all support one another, they all conspire toward the same end; each serves all, and all serve each. Through that mutual union, the common wealth and power increase.

That is why the creation of a Company] had to precede the establishment of foreign trade and domestic manufactures. The whole nation had to have a stake in it by freeing the King and his subjects from their debts. All the members of the State had to be given an interest in a Company that needed immense funds to overcome all the obstacles that may be raised by the jealousy of neighboring nations, and to provide for the extraordinary expenses required by the establishment of commerce in a country as large as France.

There are three businesses [*fonds*] which will always increase dividends: finances, Banks and commerce—not to mention the King's revenues, shrewdly managed, which amount to great sums of money. The latter is necessary only to start the operation of the System.

As for viewing sensibly the annual profits the Banks can legitimately make, it is enough to observe that in all trading nations, private bankers earn 10, 15 and 20 times more with their credit than they would if they simply used their cash; for the constant circulation of their credit makes them earn as much by money-changing as they would if they had their funds in all the countries where they have correspondents.

It is certain that the balance of trade already favors France against other nations, and that it will increase much by encouraging agriculture and the arts, since that way the exchange rate may lead up to 30, 40, 50, 60 and 100 per cent gains.

Is a System based on such principles fanciful?

The successful examples of the Dutch, the English, the Portuguese, and several other nations less rich and powerful than the French nation, do they not provide a sure proof of its soundness and reality? And can there be any doubt that, as it cultivates its own resources, it will be able one day to give its shareholders returns much greater than the interest income yielded by the money lent at five per cent?

Second Part—Answers to Objections

However talented the French nation may be in everything that concerns the mind, one must acknowledge that it has ignored up to now the secrets of a grand commerce. Here is the source of almost all the objections made against this System, as will be proved.

First objection—The paper created recently is a form of State debt.

Answer—Bank paper is a true currency, it fulfills the same intentions. It is in use throughout the whole nation, the King himself receives it in payment of his revenues, just as he gives it to pay the State's expenses. It is a credit which will be accepted in foreign countries in proportion to the increase in the balance of trade for France.

Stocks are of a different nature. They are a promise made by the Company of the Indies to share each year among its shareholders the gains it makes through trade. Those stocks are real and fruitful effects since they provide a sure income which henceforward surpasses that of lands and other real property.

One must therefore reject common prejudices; one must stop considering this paper as a mere equivalent of monetized metal, and thinking that it is an imaginary good because there is more of it in the kingdom than gold or silver. The immense profits of domestic and foreign trade constitute the value of this paper, just as annual interest income made the value of the annuities [*contrats de constitution*°].

Second objection—The new System is incompatible with a monarchy.

Answer—Since the form of the French government contributes more than any other to the establishment of the new system, it is likewise the most appropriate to preserve it. Up to now men have striven in vain to balance the authority of the sovereign by Estates, Parliaments or laws; but it ignores human nature and history to pretend to moderate supreme power by such feeble means. There is only one motive force that actuates virtually all men—interest. In the new System, the sovereign finds a unique interest: here is how.

All the specie in the kingdom was collected in a public Treasury, not to remain dead and useless, but to be diffused throughout the provinces at all times by a circulation that will extend to all the members of the body politic, and that will animate and motivate them all to use their forces and their goods for the arts and commerce. [It is thus that money will constantly return to the Treasury of the Prince, who can neither keep it nor increase its bulk without distributing it to his subjects; so that through this circulation, the life of the body politic should be always characterized by reciprocity between head and members.]

Thus the king will remain depository of the money, and he can increase it with paper credit. Thanks to it, he makes up for the lack of specie necessary to favor agriculture and the arts, and as a result, foreign trade. That trade brings specie back into the bosom of France because it turns other peoples into debtors of France. If the King destroyed such an establishment, he would dry up an inexhaustible source of wealth, and would ruin a credit that is supported only by the natural productions of the country—a credit that makes them circulate not only throughout the whole kingdom, but also in all the other countries of the world, a credit that renders the King master of the specie, and that increases them every year, by adding foreign money to its treasures. If the assets of the miners were put in the stockmarket, they would be infinitely more secure than in city hall.

Contracts were shares on the King or on private individuals, and ruined them. Stocks are on a company of traders [*négociants°*] who share with their stockholders the gains they have made by using their funds for arts useful to the Republic. The minutes of the contracts were deposited with the notaries public. Would it be less safe to have the stocks deposited in the hands of a Company authorized by the State?

Third objection—Commerce is harmful to great States and sooner or later destroys the military virtues so necessary in a monarchy.

Answer—History teaches us that the most bellicose peoples have always favored commerce. That is what M. Huet very well showed in his learned history of the trade and navigation of the ancients, which was written by order of M. Colbert, then controller-general of finances.[1] In great monarchies, one abides by the fundamental rule that military virtues are favored only to defend the country and not at all to make conquests. [The title of unjust conqueror is not only odious in itself, but ruinous for a State. This inhuman ambition renders other peoples jealous; all conspire for the ruin of a prince who wants to extend his kingdom against the rights of men and nations. While he sends his subjects to war, agriculture, the arts, and commerce are neglected; a nation's men and riches are exhausted, and thus it runs the risk of collapse because of the jealousy of foreign countries, and domestic divisions.]

A large, fertile, populous and well-situated kingdom has more secure ways to increase its power by cultivating the arts, lands and commerce; by this multiplication of riches, it finds an increase in power which will ensure that its neighbors will not dare to attack.

A hard-working and well-nourished people, living in neither misery nor abundance, are more fit to bear arms in time of need than a lazy, starving people. [It will always be the arbiter of war and peace; it will command to other nations without dominating them, and will give them

---

1. [Pierre-Daniel Huet (1630–1721), *Histoire du commerce, et de la navigation des anciens* (Paris, 1716; Eng. tr. 1717).]

laws without usurping any of their rights. These qualities are much more glorious than the vain title of universal monarchy, which, extended beyond just limits, finally collapses of its own weight. I confess that it would be dangerous if trade were the only purpose of the nation. But when the bulk of trade [*négoce*] is made by one company only, authorized and supported by the sovereign, it can only be a very useful way to trade.] The people who cannot take part in the slightest details of trade without violating civil or canon laws have the opportunity to lend their funds to the Company and to benefit from its gains without dishonoring their rank and without abandoning their positions in the army, the Church or the magistracy. [That way, the arts, agriculture and commerce will be honored, because the great will no longer despise peasants [*paysans*], craftsmen, and traders [*négociants*°] who, by their industry, increase the income of a company of which they are shareholders.]

This is how the new System makes the interests of the Prince depend upon those of his subjects, without diminishing royal authority, [and, without confusing ranks, it obliges the great to protect the weak. That way, all members of the State are gathered together as if they were one person—France—with all the advantages which come from the unity of the supreme power, and without the drawbacks caused by the absolute authority of the monarch and the great elevation of the lords. It is an expedient which the most skilled legislators searched for in Carthage, Sparta, Rome, England, where the mixed government, dividing the sovereign authority, caused a perpetual combat between opposite forces, and under a false pretence of liberty, consigned the citizens to popular seditions and civil disorders, the greatest of all evils.]

Fourth objection—The jealousy of neighboring countries may destroy this system, and prevent its implementation.

Answer—The English and Dutch, who are the only rivals of French commerce, are in no position to oppose it, and if they were bold enough to do so, France could destroy their credit.

It is known that England and Holland have far fewer resources than France; they cannot implement the exclusive use of paper without specie: first, because the nature of their governments does not allow them to gather all the various interests into one credit under one power; second, because France is the only nation in Europe which can turn others into its debtors merely through the exchange of its commodities. When the balance of trade increases, other nations will have to receive the paper money from France, whereas France will not be obliged to receive theirs—here is the great principle which makes it impractical for other countries in Europe to imitate this System.

Fifth objection—There have been frequent variations in this System, and the means used to have specie brought to banks have been violent.

Answer—The essential basis of the System has always been the same. The plan of a royal Bank to make up for the lack of specie with the credit of a Company which replaces the annuities [*contrats de constitution°*] by commerce has never been modified; these grand designs have never been changed, but different means have been used to reach these goals, and these expedients have seemed to the uninformed like the product of a faltering mind. Since mistrust increased, it was necessary to resort to authority to lead the people to contribute to their own happiness, [and prevent them from rejecting the State's use of specie. Money was nothing but an order of the sovereign to regulate value, and to facilitate the circulation of currency. Its usage belongs to the State. Everything that corresponds to the true value of money, i.e. lands, merchandise, commodities, all those real goods surely belong to individuals, and sovereigns would not] make them feel that, if lands, merchandise and commodities belong to them, so that sovereigns cannot appropriate them without committing an injustice which would sooner or later ruin their power, the money which makes real property circulate and transmits it successively to all the members of the State belongs to the King, and never to a citizen or private individual who merely uses it. That use is made through circulation, and since that circulation makes up the life of the body politic, anybody who arrests it is a parricide. [Lands are only useful through cultivation; specie are only useful through circulation. Untilled lands remain barren; hoarded specie produces nothing. Any man who tills just enough to answer his needs and prevents others from working it is an enemy of the homeland [*patrie°*].] Any man who keeps specie without using it and therefore prevents gains that would result from its circulation is a bad citizen, and in that case, a sovereign is entitled to oblige him to give over his use of it to the State, [as he can oblige them to till the lands when they neglect them through indolence]. Thus one can see that this authority, which inconveniences only the ill-intentioned, is useful to the state and as a result does not deserve the name of violent.

Sixth objection—The sudden decrease in individual annuities [*rentes*°] and the excessive price of everything has ruined an extraordinary number of families.

Answer—The decrease in the annuities was absolutely necessary for the good of the State. We have already shown that the annuities [*contrats de constitution*°] were ruinous, because they overburdened debtors, and favored the idleness of creditors. It is a well-known fact that the decrease in interest rates leads the people into labor and commerce by the establishment of a credit [system] which enables France to do without metals. A very secure means to multiply specie has been found. Therefore, to complain about the decrease in pension incomes is to complain that specie has become too common, and that the nation has enriched itself by the discovery of an inexhaustible treasure. When the late King borrowed at a rate of 10, 20, 30, 40, 50 and even a hundred per cent, it was the people, all overburdened with taxes though they were, who paid that interest to a small number of rich people who lived on usury with impunity.

There are more than 18 million people in France; was it fair that they suffered for a very small number of fellow-citizens who were idle and useless to the Republic because of contracts that were onerous and ruinous to the State?

As for the high cost of everything that people complain so much about, one will note that high prices are either necessary or inevitable or advantageous, according to the 3 reasons which caused them—1st the high cost of specie; 2nd the sterility of the previous year; 3rd the high level of consumption.

The high cost of specie was necessary because otherwise foreigners would have obtained French merchandise too cheaply, and the French would have sold at too low a price the goods they had to buy at high prices in foreign countries.

The sterility of the previous year was inevitable, and was only very partly responsible for high prices.

And one may say that, even if high consumption contributed more to it, it compensated that harm with the abundant circulation of specie, which always has a good effect, because it creates this consumption which in turn leads all members of the State to be employed usefully.

The unprejudiced will find an extreme difference between the current situation of France and the one it was in not so long ago. Everybody knows that the King's debts amounted to more than 2 billion livres, that he often borrowed at the rate of 40, 50 and even a hundred per cent, and that his only resource was the creation of positions that were costly for the State, as well as new taxes which did not by themselves enable him to pay back the interest on his huge debts.

The landlords and property owners were no less weighted down with debt. They did not get half the income from their lands, and were obliged to sell parts of their inheritance at a very low price to make a living. In short, almost all the members of the body politic were inert and almost paralyzed, and that is how the most flourishing, the most fertile, the largest Kingdom in Europe remained languishing and impoverished, for lack of understanding the secrets of credit and commerce.

Thanks to the new System, all the King's debts (except what he owes the Company of India, which advanced him very large loans) are paid—even with interest—and without having recourse to new taxes. His armies, his pensioners, his Crown officers, the salaries of all the positions in the magistracy, the royal house are also paid for. Handsome buildings were constructed for the military; the navy, which was almost ruined, is recovering; finally, the income of the King is increased, and thanks to the new administration of finances, he can increase them every year—not by overburdening his subjects, but by providing them with the means to enrich themselves, by protecting trade and favoring industry.

A great number of individuals have discharged their lands and paid their debts, and in a short while, all the debts of the King and his subjects will be paid off. Farmers [*laboureurs*°], craftsmen, and all those who live by their labor are employed; more than 70 ships have already been sent to India; the Eastern trade has increased; new colonies are being created in the West; domestic manufactures which are established and multiplied will support this two-fold and flourishing commerce everywhere.

Here is what this new System has already done to relieve France, after reordering the finances. What will not be done to reform the abuses in the magistracy, to support military power, and to rectify the administration of those three great rights of the sovereignty of the Prince? Do not all these advantages merit that we accept without a murmur the short-lived drawbacks which are inevitable in any great change? But those who have not yet delved into this issue wear themselves out with fears and worries. They would like to see the System started and completed all at once, whereas those who are well-informed about it consider rightly that anyone who opposes this implementation, or even who will not give his consent to it, is an enemy to himself and to his Homeland [Patrie°].

10

Cato's Letters

1721

Cato's Letters were written by Thomas Gordon and John Trenchard. Gordon was born in Scotland of obscure origins in the late seventeenth century. He may have acquired a law degree, perhaps at Edinburgh in 1716, but he earned his early living as a tutor in languages. Shortly after moving to London, he met the older Trenchard, who had been born in Somerset in 1662 and educated in the law at Trinity College in Dublin. Leaving law for a government position in 1690, Trenchard acquired a sizable enough fortune from an advantageous marriage and from inheritances to be able to devote himself to political writing. He became an MP from Taunton in 1722, which he remained until his death the next year. Among the topics on which he earned his early reputation were standing armies (1690s), church authority, and political liberty. His writings include *The Natural History of Superstition* (1709) and *The Independent Whig*, a journal that began publication in 1720. The occasion for the publication of *Cato's Letters* was the bursting of the South Sea Bubble in 1720. The work became one of the chief vehicles for conveying Lockean and radical Whig ideas on liberty throughout the English-speaking world in the eighteenth century. It began publication in *The London Journal* in late 1720 and continued toward the end of 1722.

The selection reproduced here comes from John Trenchard and
Thomas Gordon, "Trade and Naval Power the Offspring of Civil Liberty only, and cannot subsist without it" (Feb. 3, 1721), in *Cato's Letters*,
ed. Ronald Hamowy (Indianapolis: Liberty Fund, 1995), pp. 442–50, and
is reprinted with permission. The notes are by Hamowy.

Trade and Naval Power the Offspring of Civil Liberty Only, and Cannot Subsist Without It

Saturday, February 3, 1721

Sir,

I have in former letters begun to shew, by an induction of particulars, and
shall hereafter more fully shew, that population, riches, true religion,
virtue, magnanimity, arts, sciences, and learning, are the necessary effects and productions of liberty;[1] and shall spend this paper in proving,
that an extensive trade, navigation, and naval power, entirely flow from
the same source: In this case, if natural advantage and encouragements
be wanting, art, expence, and violence, are lost and thrown away. Nothing is more certain, than that trade cannot be forced; she is a coy and humorous dame, who must be won by flattery and allurements, and always
flies force and power; she is not confined to nations, sects, or climates,
but travels and wanders about the earth, till she fixes her residence where
she finds the best welcome and kindest reception; her contexture is so
nice and delicate, that she cannot breathe in a tyrannical air; will and
pleasure are so opposite to her nature, that but touch her with the sword,
and she dies: But if you give her gentle and kind entertainment, she is a

---

1. See especially Letters 59 through 63 (Dec. 30, 1721, to Jan. 27, 1721).

grateful and beneficent mistress; she will turn deserts into fruitful fields, villages into great cities, cottages into palaces, beggars into princes, convert cowards into heroes, blockheads into philosophers; will change the coverings of little worms into the richest brocades, the fleeces of harmless sheep into the pride and ornaments of kings, and by a further metamorphosis will transmute them again into armed hosts and haughty fleets.

Now it is absolutely impossible, from the nature of an arbitrary government, that she should enjoy security and protection, or indeed be free from violence, under it. There is not one man in a thousand that has the endowments and abilities necessary to govern a state, and much fewer yet that have just notions how to make trade and commerce useful and advantageous to it; and, amongst these, it is rare to find one who will forego all personal advantages, and devote himself and his labours wholly to his country's interest: But if such a phoenix should arise in any country, he will find it hard to get access to an arbitrary court, and much harder yet to grapple with and stem the raging corruptions in it, where virtue has nothing to do, and vice rides triumphant; where bribery, servile flattery, blind submission, riotous expence, and very often lust and unnatural prostitutions, are the ladders to greatness; which will certainly be supported by the same methods by which it is obtained.

What has a virtuous man to do, or what can he do, in such company? If he pity the people's calamities, he shall be called seditious; if he recommend any publick good, he shall be called preaching fool; if he should live soberly and virtuously himself, they will think him fit only to be sent to a cloister; if he do not flatter the prince and his superiors, he will be thought to envy their prosperity; if he presume to advise his prince to pursue his true interest, he will be esteemed a formidable enemy to the whole court, who will unite to destroy him: In fine, his virtues will be crimes, reproaches, and of dangerous consequence to those who have none. As jails pick up all the little pilfering rogues of a country, so such courts engross all the great ones; who have no business there but to grow rich, and to riot upon the publick calamities, to use all the means of oppression and rapine, to make hasty fortunes before the bow-string overtakes them, or a sudden favourite supplants them.

Now what encouragement or security can trade and industry receive

from such a crew of banditti? No privileges and immunities, or even protection, can be obtained but for money, and are always granted to such
who give most; and these again shall be curtailed, altered, abrogated, and
cancelled, upon the change of a minister, or of his inclinations, interest,
and caprices: Monopolies, exclusive companies, liberties of pre-emption,
&c. shall be obtained for bribes or favour, or in trust for great men, or vile
and worthless women. Some merchants shall be openly encouraged and
protected, and get exemptions from searches and duties, or shall be con-
nived at in escaping them; others shall be burdened, oppressed, man-
acled, stopped, and delayed, to extort presents, to wreak revenge, or to
give preference of markets to favourites. Governors of port-towns, or of
colonies, who have purchased their employments at court, shall be indulged and countenanced in making reprisals upon the traders, and to
enable them to satisfy the yearly presents due to minions: Admirals and
commanders of men of war shall press their sailors, to be paid for not doing it; and military officers and soldiers shall molest and interrupt them
in the course of their commerce and honest industry.

Nor shall it be in the power of the most vigilant, active and virtuous
prince, to prevent these and a thousand other daily oppressions; he must
see with his ministers' eyes, and hear with their ears; nor can there be any
access to him but by their means, and by their leave: Constant spies shall
watch and observe the first intentions, or least approaches to a complaint;
and the person injured shall be threatened, way-laid, imprisoned, perhaps
murdered; but if he escape all their treacheries, and can get to the ear of
his prince, it is great odds but he will be treated and punished as a calum-
niator, a false accuser, and a seditious disturber of his Majesty's government: No witness will dare to appear for him, many false ones will be sub-
orned against him; and the whole posse of ministers, officers, favourites,
parasites, pathicks,[2] strumpets, buffoons, fiddlers,[3] and pimps, will conspire to ruin him, as a common enemy to their common interests.

But if all these mischiefs could be avoided, the necessities of such a
prince, arising from the profusion and vast expence of his court, from his
foolish wars, and the depredations, embezzlements, and various thefts of

2. Pathics: catamites, that is, boys upon whom sodomy is performed.
3. Fiddlers: cheats.

his ministers and servants, will be always calling for new supplies, for new extortions, which must be raised by all the means by which they can be raised: New and sudden impositions shall be put upon trade, new loans be exacted from merchants; commodities of general use shall be bought up by the prince's order, perhaps upon trust, and afterwards retailed again at extravagant advantages: Merchants shall be encouraged to import their goods, upon promises of easy and gentle usage; these goods when imported shall be subjected to exorbitant impositions and customs, perhaps confiscated upon frivolous pretences. But if these, and infinite other oppressions, could be prevented for some time, by the vigilance of a wise prince, or the care of an able minister; yet there can be no probable security, or even hopes of the continuance of honest and prudent measures in such a government: For one wise prince so educated, there will be twenty foolish ones; and for one honest minister, there will be a thousand corrupt ones.

Under such natural disadvantages, perpetual uncertainties, or rather certain oppressions, no men will embark large stocks and extensive talents for business, breed up their children to precarious employments, build forts, or plant colonies, when the breath of a weak prince, or the caprice of a corrupt favourite, shall dash at once all their labours and their hopes; and therefore it is impossible that any trade can subsist long in such a government, but what is necessary to support the luxury and vices of a court; and even such trade is, for the most part, carried on by the stocks,[4] and for the advantage of free countries, and their own petty merchants are only factors to the others. True merchants are citizens of the world, and that is their country where they can live best and most secure; and whatever they can pick up and gather together in tyrannical governments, they remove to free ones. Tavernier[5] invested all the riches he had amassed by his long ramble over the world, in the barren rocks of

4. That is, the large trading companies whose capital is publicly subscribed.

5. Jean Baptiste Tavernier, Baron d'Aubonne (1605–1689), who authored an account of his travels: *Les six voyages de Jean Baptiste Tavernier . . . qu'il a fait en Turquie, en Perse et aux Indes* (2 vols.; Paris: Gervaise Clouzier, 1676–1677). The work was quickly translated into English as *The Six Voyages of John Baptista Tavernier . . . through Turkey, into Persia, and the East Indies, finished in the year 1670* (London: Printed for John Starkey and Moses Pitt, 1678), and it achieved considerable popularity.

Switzerland: And being asked by the last king of France, how it came to pass that he, who had seen the finest countries on the globe, came to lay out his fortune in the worst? He gave his haughty Majesty this short answer, that he was willing to have something which he could call his own.

As I think it is evident, by what I have said before, that trade cannot long subsist, much less flourish, in arbitrary governments; so there is so close and inseparable a connection between that and naval power, that I dare boldly affirm, that the latter can never arrive to any formidable height, and continue long in that situation, under such a state. Where there is an extensive trade; great numbers of able-bodied and courageous sailors, men bred up to fatigues, hardships, and hazards, and consequently soldiers by profession, are kept in constant pay; not only without any charge to the publick, but greatly to its benefit; not only by daily adding to its wealth and power, but by venting and employing abroad, to their country's honour and safety, those turbulent and unruly spirits that would be fuel for factions, and the tools and instruments of ambitious or discontented great men at home. These men are always ready at their country's call, to defend the profession which they live by, and with it the publick happiness: They are, and ever must be, in the publick interest, with which their own is so closely united; for they subsist by exporting the productions of the people's industry, which they constantly increase by so doing: They receive their pay from the merchants, a sort of men always in the interests of liberty, from which alone they can receive protection and encouragement. And as this race of men contribute vastly to the publick security and wealth, so they take nothing from it: They are not quartered up and down their native country, like the bands of despotick princes, to oppress their subjects, interrupt their industry, debauch their wives and daughters, insult their persons, to be examples of lewdness and prodigality, and to be always ready at hand to execute the bloody commands of a tyrant.

No monarch was ever yet powerful enough to keep as many seamen in constant pay at his own expence, as single cities have been able to do without any at all: The pay of a sailor, with his provision, is equal to that of a trooper in arbitrary governments; nor can they learn their trade, by taking the sea-air for a few summer months, and wafting about the coasts of their own country: They gain experience and boldness, by various and difficult voyages, by being constantly inured to hardships and dangers. Nor is it possible for single princes, with all their power and vigilance, to have such regular supplies of naval provisions, as trading countries must have always in store. There must be a regular and constant intercourse with the nations from whom these supplies come; a certain and regular method of paying for them; and constant demands will produce constant supplies. There are always numerous magazines in the hands of private merchants, ready for their own use or sale. There must be great numbers of shipwrights, anchor-smiths, rope and sail-makers, and infinite other artificers, sure always of constant employment; and who, if they are oppressed by one master, may go to another. There must be numbers of ships used for trade, that, upon occasions, may be employed for men of war, for transports, for fireships, and tenders. Now all these things, or scarce any of them, can ever be brought about by arbitrary courts; stores will be embezzled, exhausted, and worn out, before new ones are supplied; payments will not be punctually made; artificers will be discouraged, oppressed, and often left without employ: Every thing will be done at an exorbitant expence, and often not done when it is paid for; and when payments are made, the greatest part shall go in fees, or for bribes, or in secret trusts.

For these reasons, and many others, despotick monarchs, though infinitely powerful at land, yet could never rival Neptune, and extend their empire over the liquid world; for though great and vigorous efforts have been often made by these haughty tyrants of mankind, to subject that element to their ambition and their power, being taught by woeful experience, arising from perpetual losses and disappointments, of what vast importance that dominion was to unlimited and universal sovereignty; yet all their riches, applications, and pride, have never been able, in one instance, to effect it. Sometimes, indeed, trade, like a phantom, has made a faint appearance at an arbitrary court, but disappeared again at the first approach of the morning light: She is the portion of free states, is married to liberty, and ever flies the foul and polluted embraces of a tyrant.

The little state of Athens was always able to humble the pride, and put a check to the growing greatness, of the towering Persian monarchs, by their naval power; and when stripped of all their territories by land, and even their capital city, the seat of their commonwealth, yet had strength enough left to vanquish numerous fleets, which almost covered the sea, and to defeat an expedition carried on by armies that drank up rivers, and exhausted all the stores of the land.[6]

The single city of Venice has proved itself an over-match in naval power to the great Ottoman Empire, though possessed of so many islands, useful ports, environed with so many sea-coasts, and abounding with all sorts of stores necessary to navigation; and in the year fifty-six gave the Turks so signal an overthrow at the Dardanelles, as put that state in such a consternation, that they believed their empire at an end; and it is thought if the Venetians had pursued their victory, they had driven them out of Constantinople, and even out of Europe; for the Grand Seignior himself was preparing to fly into Asia.[7] The little island of Rhodes defended itself for some ages against the whole power of the Sultan, though encompassed by his dominions; and it was with great difficulty, hazard, and expence, that he at last overcame them,[8] and drove the inhabitants to Malta, where they have ever since braved his pride, and live upon the plunder of his subjects: And notwithstanding all his numerous and expensive efforts to share with the Christians the dominion of the sea; yet there are no other seeds or traces of it left through his great and extensive territories, but what are found in the free piratical states of Algiers, Tunis, and Tripoli.

Neither the Sophi[9] of Persia, the Great Mogul, the many kings who command the banks of the Ganges, nor all the haughty potentates of Asia and Africa, are able to contend at sea with the English or Dutch East-India Companies, or even to defend their subjects against but

6. The reference is to the battle of Salamis in 480 B.C., where the Athenian navy dealt a crushing defeat to the Persian fleet after most of central Attica, including Athens, had fallen before the Persian army.

7. In 1656, during the course of one of the many wars between the two powers over the eastern Mediterranean islands, the Venetian navy decisively defeated the Ottoman fleet in the Dardanelles and briefly threatened Constantinople itself.

8. Between 1480 and 1522, the Turks made several attempts against Rhodes, the stronghold of the Knights Hospitalers of St. John. Despite its immensely strong fortifications, the island finally fell to Ottoman forces in 1522.

9. The surname of the ruling dynasty of Persia from 1500 to 1736, hence the title of its emperor.

a few pirates, with all their population, and their mines of gold and diamonds.

Spain in all her pride, with the wealth of both Indies, with dominions so vast and extensive, that the sun rises and sets within them, and a sea-line, which if extended would environ the earth, yet was not able to dispute their title to that element with a few revolted provinces, who grew up through the course of an expensive war to that amazing greatness, that in less than a century they saw themselves, from a few fisher-towns encompassed with bogs and morasses, become a most formidable state, equal to the greatest potentates at sea, and to most at land; to have great kings in a distant world submit to be their vassals; and, in fine, to be protectors of that mighty nation from whom they revolted. Here is a stupendous instance of the effects of liberty, which neighbouring monarchs with twenty times the territory tremble at, and posterity will hardly believe.

France, with all its oeconomy, address, and power, with its utmost and most expensive efforts, and the assistance of neighbouring and even rival kings, has not been able to establish an empire upon that coy element. She saw it, like a mushroom, rise in a night, and wither again the next day. It is true, that at an immense expence and infinite labour, she got together a formidable fleet, and with it got victories, and took thousands of rival ships; yet every day grew weaker as her enemies grew stronger, and could never recover a single defeat, which in Holland would have been repaired in a few more weeks than the battle was days in fighting:[10] So impossible is it for art to contend with nature, and slavery to dispute the naval prize with liberty.

Sweden and Denmark, though possessed of the naval stores of Europe, nations who subsist by that commerce, and are constantly employed to build ships for their neighbours; yet are not able, with their

---

10. During the reign of Louis XIV, France saw the creation of a virtually new navy; while the nation possessed only twenty warships in 1661, by 1677 that number had increased to 270. Far from having quickly withered, the French navy continued as a powerful force. Indeed, during the first half of the eighteenth century, the French navy had clearly surpassed that of the Dutch and, outside of England, was the strongest in Europe.

united force, to equip, man out, and keep upon the sea for any considerable time, a fleet large enough to dispute with an English or Dutch
squadron: And I dare venture my reputation and skill in politicks, by
boldly asserting, that another vain and unnatural northern apparition[11]
will soon vanish and disappear again, like the morning-star at the glim-
mering of the sun, and every one shall ask, Where is it?

T   *I am, &c.*

11. The reference is to Russia, which had risen to the rank of a great power under Peter
the Great (d. 1725).

11

The Fable of the Bees
1723

BERNARD MANDEVILLE was born in Holland in 1670 into a family of physicians and naval officers. He received his degree of Doctor of Medicine at Leiden in 1691 and began to practice as a specialist in nerve and stomach disorders, his father's specialty. Perhaps after a tour of Europe, he ended up in London, where he soon learned the language and decided to stay. He married in 1699, fathered at least two children, and brought out his first English publication in 1703 (a book of fables in the La Fontaine tradition). He wrote works on medicine (*A Treatise of the Hypochondriack and Hysterick Passions*, 1711), poetry (*Wishes to a Godson, with Other Miscellany Poems*, 1712), and religious and political affairs (*Free Thoughts on Religion, the Church, and National Happiness*, 1720). He died in 1733.

His most famous work, *The Fable of the Bees, or Private Vices, Publick Benefits*, from which the present poem is taken, came out in more than half a dozen editions beginning in 1705 and became one of the most enduringly controversial works of the eighteenth century for its claims about the moral foundations of modern commercial society. The edition used here is *The Fable of the Bees*, edited by F. B. Kaye (Oxford: Clarendon Press, 1924; reprint, Liberty Fund, 1988), pp. 17–38. All notes but one brief bracketed addition are from the Kaye edition.

[1]

THE
GRUMBLING HIVE:
OR,
KNAVES *turn'd Honest.*

A Spacious Hive well stockt with Bees,
That liv'd in Luxury and Ease;
And yet as fam'd for Laws and Arms,
As yielding large and early Swarms;
Was counted the great Nursery
Of Sciences and Industry.
No Bees had better Government,
More Fickleness, or less Content:
They were not Slaves to Tyranny,
Nor rul'd by wild *Democracy;*
[2]   But Kings, that could not wrong, because
Their Power was circumscrib'd by Laws.

THESE Insects liv'd like Men, and all
Our Actions they perform'd in small:
They did whatever's done in Town,
And what belongs to Sword or Gown:
Tho' th' Artful Works, by nimble Slight
Of minute Limbs, 'scap'd Human Sight;
Yet we've no Engines, Labourers,
Ships, Castles, Arms, Artificers,
Craft, Science, Shop, or Instrument,
But they had an Equivalent:
Which, since their Language is unknown,
Must be call'd, as we do our own.
As grant, that among other Things,
They wanted Dice, yet they had Kings;
And those had Guards; from whence we may

Justly conclude, they had some Play;
Unless a Regiment be shewn
Of Soldiers, that make use of none.

VAST Numbers throng'd the fruitful Hive; [3]
Yet those vast Numbers made 'em thrive;
Millions endeavouring to supply
Each other's Lust and Vanity;
While other Millions were employ'd,
To see their Handy-works destroy'd;
They furnish'd half the Universe;
Yet had more Work than Labourers.
Some with vast Stocks, and little Pains,
Jump'd into Business of great Gains;
And some were damn'd to Sythes and Spades,
And all those hard laborious Trades;
Where willing Wretches daily sweat,
And wear out Strength and Limbs to eat:
(*A.*) While others follow'd Mysteries,
To which few Folks bind 'Prentices;
That want no Stock, but that of Brass,
And may set up without a Cross;[1]
As Sharpers, Parasites, Pimps, Players,
Pick-pockets, Coiners, Quacks, South-sayers,[2]
And all those, that in Enmity, [4]

---

1. Without money. A cross was a small coin.
2. Cf. Butler's posthumous *Upon the Weakness and Misery of Man:*

> . . . bawds, whores, and usurers,
> Pimps, scriv'ners, silenc'd ministers,
> That get estates by being undone
> For tender conscience, and have none,
> Like those that with their credit drive
> A trade, without a stock, and thrive. . . .

Had Mandeville perhaps seen a MS. of Butler's poem (published 1759)? The poem, incidentally, stated,

> Our holiest actions have been
> Th' effects of wickedness and sin . . .

With downright Working, cunningly
Convert to their own Use the Labour
Of their good-natur'd heedless Neighbour.
(*B.*) These were call'd Knaves, but bar the Name,
The grave Industrious were the same:
All Trades and Places knew some Cheat,
No Calling was without Deceit.

THE Lawyers, of whose Art the Basis
Was raising Feuds and splitting Cases,
Oppos'd all Registers, that Cheats
Might make more Work with dipt Estates;[3]
As wer't unlawful, that one's own,
Without a Law-Suit, should be known.
They kept off Hearings wilfully,
To finger the refreshing Fee;
And to defend a wicked Cause,
Examin'd and survey'd the Laws,
As Burglars Shops and Houses do,
To find out where they'd best break through.

[5]   PHYSICIANS valu'd Fame and Wealth
Above the drooping Patient's Health,
Or their own Skill: The greatest Part
Study'd, instead of Rules of Art,
Grave pensive Looks and dull Behaviour,
To gain th' Apothecary's Favour;
The Praise of Midwives, Priests, and all
That serv'd at Birth or Funeral.
To bear with th' ever-talking Tribe,
And hear my Lady's Aunt prescribe;
With formal Smile, and kind How d'ye,
To fawn on all the Family;

3. Mortgaged estates.

And, which of all the greatest Curse is,
T' endure th' Impertinence of Nurses.

AMONG the many Priests of *Jove*,
Hir'd to draw Blessings from Above,
Some few were Learn'd and Eloquent,
But thousands Hot and Ignorant:
Yet all pass'd Muster that could hide
Their Sloth, Lust, Avarice and Pride;
For which they were as fam'd as Tailors   [6]
For Cabbage, or for Brandy Sailors:
Some, meagre-look'd, and meanly clad,
Would mystically pray for Bread,
Meaning by that an ample Store,
Yet lit'rally received no more;
And, while these holy Drudges starv'd,
The lazy Ones, for which they serv'd,
Indulg'd their Ease, with all the Graces
Of Health and Plenty in their Faces.

(*C.*) THE Soldiers, that were forc'd to fight,
If they surviv'd, got Honour by't;
Tho' some, that shunn'd the bloody Fray,
Had Limbs shot off, that ran away:
Some valiant Gen'rals fought the Foe;
Others took Bribes to let them go:
Some ventur'd always where 'twas warm,
Lost now a Leg, and then an Arm;
Till quite disabled, and put by,
They liv'd on half their Salary;
While others never came in Play,   [7]
And staid at Home for double Pay.

THEIR Kings were serv'd, but Knavishly,
Cheated by their own Ministry;

Many, that for their Welfare slaved,
Robbing the very Crown they saved:
Pensions were small, and they liv'd high,
Yet boasted of their Honesty.
Calling, whene'er they strain'd their Right,
The slipp'ry Trick a Perquisite;
And when Folks understood their Cant,
They chang'd that for Emolument;
Unwilling to be short or plain,
In any thing concerning Gain;
(*D.*) For there was not a Bee but would
Get more, I won't say, than he should;
But than he dar'd to let them know,
(*E.*) That pay'd for't; as your Gamesters do,
That, tho' at fair Play, ne'er will own
Before the Losers what they've won.

[8]   BUT who can all their Frauds repeat?
The very Stuff, which in the Street
They sold for Dirt t'enrich the Ground,
Was often by the Buyers found
Sophisticated with a quarter
Of good-for-nothing Stones and Mortar;
Tho' *Flail* had little Cause to mutter,
Who sold the other Salt for Butter.

JUSTICE her self, fam'd for fair Dealing,
By Blindness had not lost her Feeling;
Her Left Hand, which the Scales should hold,
Had often dropt 'em, brib'd with Gold;
And, tho' she seem'd Impartial,
Where Punishment was corporal,
Pretended to a reg'lar Course,
In Murther, and all Crimes of Force;
Tho' some, first pillory'd for Cheating,
Were hang'd in Hemp of their own beating;

Yet, it was thought, the Sword she bore
Check'd but the Desp'rate and the Poor;
That, urg'd by meer Necessity,   [9]
Were ty'd up to the wretched Tree[4]
For Crimes, which not deserv'd that Fate,
But to secure the Rich and Great.

THUS every Part was full of Vice,
Yet the whole Mass a Paradise;
Flatter'd in Peace, and fear'd in Wars,
They were th' Esteem of Foreigners,
And lavish of their Wealth and Lives,
The Balance of all other Hives.
Such were the Blessings of that State;
Their Crimes conspir'd to make them Great:
(*F.*) And Virtue, who from Politicks
Had learn'd a Thousand Cunning Tricks,
Was, by their happy Influence,
Made Friends with Vice: And ever since,
(*G.*) The worst of all the Multitude
Did something for the Common Good.

THIS was the State's Craft, that maintain'd   [10]
The Whole of which each Part complain'd:
This, as in Musick Harmony,
Made Jarrings in the main agree;
(*H.*) Parties directly opposite,
Assist each other, as 'twere for Spight;
And Temp'rance with Sobriety,
Serve Drunkenness and Gluttony.

(*I.*) THE Root of Evil, Avarice,
That damn'd ill-natur'd baneful Vice,
Was Slave to Prodigality,

---

4. Cf. Livy i. 26: "infelici arbori reste suspendito"; also Cicero, *Pro C. Rabirio* iv. 13.

(*K.*) That noble Sin; (*L.*) whilst Luxury
Employ'd a Million of the Poor,
(*M.*) And odious Pride a Million more:
(*N.*) Envy it self, and Vanity,
Were Ministers of Industry;
Their darling Folly, Fickleness,
In Diet, Furniture and Dress,
That strange ridic'lous Vice, was made
The very Wheel that turn'd the Trade.

[11]   Their Laws and Clothes were equally
Objects of Mutability;
For, what was well done for a time,
In half a Year became a Crime;
Yet while they alter'd thus their Laws,
Still finding and correcting Flaws,
They mended by Inconstancy
Faults, which no Prudence could foresee.

THUS Vice nurs'd Ingenuity,
Which join'd with Time and Industry,
Had carry'd Life's Conveniencies,
(*O.*) It's real Pleasures, Comforts, Ease,
(*P.*) To such a Height, the very Poor
Liv'd better than the Rich before,[5]
And nothing could be added more.

How Vain is Mortal Happiness!
Had they but known the Bounds of Bliss;
And that Perfection here below
Is more than Gods can well bestow;

---

5. Of these lines and their elaboration in Remark P, I note two anticipations (not necessarily sources): ". . . a king of a large and fruitful territory there [America] feeds, lodges, and is clad worse than a day-labourer in England" (Locke, *Of Civil Government* II. v. 41); and ". . . a King of *India* is not so well lodg'd, and fed, and cloath'd, as a Day-labourer of *England*" (*Considerations on the East-India Trade,* in *Select Collection of Early English Tracts on Commerce,* ed. Political Economy Club, 1856, p. 594).

The Grumbling Brutes had been content   [12]
With Ministers and Government.
But they, at every ill Success,
Like Creatures lost without Redress,
Curs'd Politicians, Armies, Fleets;
While every one cry'd, *Damn the Cheats,*
And would, tho' conscious of his own,
In others barb'rously bear none.

ONE, that had got a Princely Store,
By cheating Master, King and Poor,
Dar'd cry aloud, *The Land must sink
For all its Fraud;* And whom d'ye think
The Sermonizing Rascal chid?
A Glover that sold Lamb for Kid.

THE least thing was not done amiss,
Or cross'd the Publick Business;
But all the Rogues cry'd brazenly,
Good Gods, Had we but Honesty!
Merc'ry smil'd at th' Impudence,   [13]
And others call'd it want of Sense,
Always to rail at what they lov'd:
But *Jove* with Indignation mov'd,
At last in Anger swore, *He'd rid
The bawling Hive of Fraud;* and did.
The very Moment it departs,
And Honesty fills all their Hearts;
There shews 'em, like th' Instructive Tree,
Those Crimes which they're asham'd to see;
Which now in Silence they confess,
By blushing at their Ugliness:
Like Children, that would hide their Faults,
And by their Colour own their Thoughts:
Imag'ning, when they're look'd upon,
That others see what they have done.

But, Oh ye Gods! What Consternation,
How vast and sudden was th' Alteration!
In half an Hour, the Nation round,
Meat fell a Peny in the Pound.

[14]   The Mask Hypocrisy's flung down,
From the great Statesman to the Clown:
And some in borrow'd Looks well known,
Appear'd like Strangers in their own.
The Bar was silent from that Day;
For now the willing Debtors pay,
Ev'n what's by Creditors forgot;
Who quitted them that had it not.
Those, that were in the Wrong, stood mute,
And dropt the patch'd vexatious Suit:
On which since nothing less can thrive,
Than Lawyers in an honest Hive,
All, except those that got enough,
With Inkhorns by their sides troop'd off.

Justice hang'd some, set others free;
And after Goal delivery,
Her Presence being no more requir'd,
With all her Train and Pomp retir'd.
First march'd some Smiths with Locks and Grates,
Fetters, and Doors with Iron Plates:

[15]   Next Goalers, Turnkeys and Assistants:
Before the Goddess, at some distance,
Her chief and faithful Minister,
'Squire Catch,[6] the Law's great Finisher,
Bore not th' imaginary Sword,[7]

---

6. "Jack Ketch" had become a generic term for executioners.

7. Probably the sword of justice, although a note in the French translation explains it differently (ed. 1750, i. 21): "On ne se sert dans les executions en *Angleterre* que de la hache pour trancher la tête, jamais de l'Epée. C'est pour cela qu'il donne le nom d'imaginaire à cette Epée qu'on attribue au Bourreau."

But his own Tools, an Ax and Cord:
Then on a Cloud the Hood-wink'd Fair,
JUSTICE her self was push'd by Air:
About her Chariot, and behind,
Were Serjeants, Bums[8] of every kind,
Tip-staffs, and all those Officers,
That squeeze a Living out of Tears.

THO' Physick liv'd, while Folks were ill,
None would prescribe, but Bees of skill,
Which through the Hive dispers'd so wide,
That none of them had need to ride;
Wav'd vain Disputes, and strove to free
The Patients of their Misery;
Left Drugs in cheating Countries grown,
And us'd the Product of their own;
Knowing the Gods sent no Disease   [16]
To Nations without Remedies.

THEIR Clergy rous'd from Laziness,
Laid not their Charge on Journey-Bees;[9]
But serv'd themselves, exempt from Vice,
The Gods with Pray'r and Sacrifice;
All those, that were unfit, or knew
Their Service might be spar'd, withdrew:
Nor was there Business for so many,
(If th' Honest stand in need of any,)
Few only with the High-Priest staid,
To whom the rest Obedience paid:
Himself employ'd in Holy Cares,
Resign'd to others State-Affairs.
He chas'd no Starv'ling from his Door,
Nor pinch'd the Wages of the Poor;

8. Bumbailiffs. [I.e., a bailiff employed in arrests.]
9. "Journeyman parson" was a slang term for a curate.

But at his House the Hungry's fed,
The Hireling finds unmeasur'd Bread,
The needy Trav'ler Board and Bed.

[17]   AMONG the King's great Ministers,
And all th' inferior Officers
The Change was great; (*Q.*) for frugally
They now liv'd on their Salary:
That a poor Bee should ten times come
To ask his Due, a trifling Sum,
And by some well-hir'd Clerk be made
To give a Crown, or ne'er be paid,
Would now be call'd a downright Cheat,
Tho' formerly a Perquisite.
All Places manag'd first by Three,
Who watch'd each other's Knavery,
And often for a Fellow-feeling,
Promoted one another's stealing,
Are happily supply'd by One,
By which some thousands more are gone.

(*R*) No Honour now could be content,
To live and owe for what was spent;
Liv'ries in Brokers Shops are hung,
They part with Coaches for a Song;
[18]   Sell stately Horses by whole Sets;
And Country-Houses, to pay Debts.

VAIN Cost is shunn'd as much as Fraud;
They have no Forces kept Abroad;
Laugh at th' Esteem of Foreigners,
And empty Glory got by Wars;
They fight, but for their Country's sake,
When Right or Liberty's at Stake.

Now mind the glorious Hive, and see
How Honesty and Trade agree.

The Shew is gone, it thins apace;
And looks with quite another Face.
For 'twas not only that They went,
By whom vast Sums were Yearly spent;
But Multitudes that liv'd on them,
Were daily forc'd to do the same.
In vain to other Trades they'd fly;
All were o'er-stock'd accordingly.

THE Price of Land and Houses falls;   [19]
Mirac'lous Palaces, whose Walls,
Like those of *Thebes,* were rais'd by Play,[10]
Are to be let; while the once gay,
Well-seated Houshold Gods would be
More pleas'd to expire in Flames, than see
The mean Inscription on the Door
Smile at the lofty ones they bore.
The building Trade is quite destroy'd,
Artificers are not employ'd;
(*S.*) No Limner for his Art is fam'd,
Stone-cutters, Carvers are not nam'd.

THOSE, that remain'd, grown temp'rate, strive,
Not how to spend, but how to live,
And, when they paid their Tavern Score,
Resolv'd to enter it no more:
No Vintner's Jilt in all the Hive
Could wear now Cloth of Gold, and thrive;
Nor *Torcol* such vast Sums advance,
For *Burgundy* and *Ortelans;*
The Courtier's gone, that with his Miss   [20]

---

10. A footnote in the French translation (ed. 1750, i. 27) says: "L'Auteur veut parler des bâtimens élevés pour l'Opera & la Comédie. *Amphion,* après avoir chassé *Cadmus* & sa *Femme* du lieu de leur demeure, y bâtit la Ville de *Thèbes,* en y attirant les pierres avec ordre & mesure, par l'harmonie merveilleuse de son divin Luth." It is possible, however, that Mandeville intended a pun on "Play" as meaning both music and gambling.

Supp'd at his House on *Christmas* Peas;
Spending as much in two Hours stay,
As keeps a Troop of Horse a Day.

THE haughty *Chloe,* to live Great,
Had made her (*T.*) Husband rob the State:
But now she sells her Furniture,
Which th' *Indies* had been ransack'd for;
Contracts th' expensive Bill of Fare,
And wears her strong Suit a whole Year:
The slight and fickle Age is past;
And Clothes, as well as Fashions, last.
Weavers, that join'd rich Silk with Plate,
And all the Trades subordinate,
Are gone. Still Peace and Plenty reign,
And every Thing is cheap, tho' plain:
Kind Nature, free from Gard'ners Force,
Allows all Fruits in her own Course;
But Rarities cannot be had,
Where Pains to get them are not paid.

[21]   As Pride and Luxury decrease,
So by degrees they leave the Seas.
Not Merchants now, but Companies
Remove whole Manufactories.
All Arts and Crafts neglected lie;
(*V.*) Content, the Bane of Industry,[11]
Makes 'em admire their homely Store,
And neither seek nor covet more.

---

11. Compare Locke's reflection: "When a man is perfectly content with the state he is in—which is when he is perfectly without any uneasiness—what industry, what action, what will is there left, but to continue in it? . . . And thus we see our all-wise Maker, suitably to our constitution and frame, and knowing what it is that determines the will, has put into man the uneasiness of hunger and thirst, and other natural desires, that return at their seasons, to move and determine their wills, for the preservation of themselves, and the continuation of their species" (*Essay concerning Human Understanding,* ed. Fraser, 1894, II. xxi. 34).

So few in the vast Hive remain,
The hundredth Part they can't maintain
Against th' Insults of numerous Foes;
Whom yet they valiantly oppose:
'Till some well-fenc'd Retreat is found,
And here they die or stand their Ground.
No Hireling in their Army's known;
But bravely fighting for their own,
Their Courage and Integrity
At last were crown'd with Victory.
They triumph'd not without their Cost,
For many Thousand Bees were lost.
Hard'ned with Toils and Exercise,   [22]
They counted Ease it self a Vice;
Which so improv'd their Temperance;
That, to avoid Extravagance,
They flew into a hollow Tree,
Blest with Content and Honesty.

The Moral   [23]

Then leave Complaints: Fools only strive
(*X.*) To make a Great an Honest Hive
(*Y.*) T' enjoy the World's Conveniencies,
Be fam'd in War, yet live in Ease,
Without great Vices, is a vain
EUTOPIA seated in the Brain.
Fraud, Luxury and Pride must live,
While we the Benefits receive:
Hunger's a dreadful Plague, no doubt,
Yet who digests or thrives without?
Do we not owe the Growth of Wine
To the dry shabby crooked Vine?
Which, while its Shoots neglected stood,
Chok'd other Plants, and ran to Wood;
But blest us with its noble Fruit,

As soon as it was ty'd and cut:
[24]   So Vice is beneficial found,
When it's by Justice lopt and bound;
Nay, where the People would be great,
As necessary to the State,
As Hunger is to make 'em eat.
Bare Virtue can't make Nations live
In Splendor; they, that would revive
A Golden Age, must be as free,
For Acorns, as for Honesty.

12

An Enquiry Whether a General Practice of Virtue Tends to the Wealth or Poverty, Benefit or Disadvantage of a People

1725

GEORGE BLEWHITT (or Bluett) is thought to be the author of the work anthologized here, though even that is not certain, and in any case not much is known about him. The book was perhaps the most sophisticated of the many polemical responses to the 1723 edition of Mandeville's *Fable of the Bees.* The work was divided into seven sections, including sections on topics such as dueling, prostitution, and charity schools, on all of which subjects Mandeville had written specifically.

The excerpt reprinted here is taken from *An Enquiry Whether a General Practice of Virtue Tends to the Wealth or Poverty, Benefit or Disadvantage of a People* (London: R. Wilkin, 1725). I reproduce the preface and section 1. Unbracketed notes are by the author; bracketed notes and material are by the present editor.

An Enquiry Whether a General Practice of VIRTUE Tends to the WEALTH or POVERTY, BENEFIT or DISADVANTAGE of *a People?*

In which the Pleas offered by the Author of the Fable of the Bees, or private Vices publick Benefits, *for the* Usefulness of VICE and ROGUERY *are considered.*

With some Thoughts concerning a Toleration *of* PUBLICK STEWS.

Hoc, de quo nunc agimus, id ipsum est, quod UTILE *appellatur: in quo lapsa Consuetudo deflexit de via sensimque eo deducta est, ut honestatem ab utilitate secernens, & constitueret honestum esse aliquid, quod utile non esset; & utile quod non honestum; qua nulla pernicies major hominum vitae potuit afferri.* Tull. de Offic. L. 2. 3.[1]

I would willingly ask in what Vice is profitable to *The Whole?* Not surely in Respect of heavenly Things, and such as are Divine by Nature: For it would be ridiculous [to say,] that were there not amongst Men, Malice, and Covetousness, and Lying, or that if we did not rob, plunder, slander and murther one another, the Sun would not run his appointed Course, nor the World enjoy its Seasons. It remains then that the Existence of Vice must be profitable for us and our Affairs,—[But] are we the more healthy for being vicious, or do we more abound with Necessaries? Or does Vice contribute anything to our Beauty and Strength? *Plutarch, of common Notions against the Stoicks.* Eng. Trans. [of *De Communibus notitiis adversus Stoicos.*] London 1704.

—What Difference is there between such Triflers and Ravers, and

---

1. [Now the subject I am to treat of is neither more nor less than what we call expediency; in which matter custom has so declined and gradually deviated from the right path, that, separating virtue from expediency, it has determined that some things may be virtue which are not expediency, and some expediency which are not virtue; than which doctrine nothing more pernicious can be introduced into human life. *Cicero's Three Books of Offices,* trans. Cyrus R. Edmonds (London: Bohn, 1853).]

those who say, that Intemperance was not brought forth unprofitably for Continence, nor Injustice for Justice? That so we may pray to the Gods, there may be always Wickedness: *Ibid.*

The Preface

The first Part of this Enquiry was drawn up at the Request of a Friend, who intended to write a general Discourse of the Grounds of Morality; and in that to consider the different Systems laid down in *the Fable of the Bees* and the *Characteristicks.*[2] To shew in Opposition to the one, that the shocking Image the Author has drawn of Mankind, and the moral Virtues they have hitherto thought it their Perfection to practise, was monstrous and unnatural; and in answer to the other, that neither is *Man* of so refined a Frame, or intended to be so, as to practise Virtue merely for its own Sake, or, if she were represented in a human Shape (as *Plato* said of Wisdom) immediately to fall in love with her, and that to so romantick a Degree, as to obey her severest Precepts, merely for the Pleasure of surveying the Beauty of her Person: In short, to prove (what it seems the Perverseness of some among us make it necessary should be proved) that *Men* in themselves are neither *Seraphims* nor *Devils.*

In the doing this, he proposed to consider the Objections the Author of *the Fable of the Bees* had urged against the Practice of Virtue: And finding that the most popular one was the Disadvantage it is pretended the Publick would lye under from the Loss of that Variety of Employments which now depend upon Vice and Roguery, what he designed by this Request to his Friend, was to see in a plain and distinct View, in what manner Trade and Employments would really be affected by a strict and general Practice of moral Duties. Upon perusal of that Paper, the Gentleman was pleased to disengage himself from so much of his Design as related to *the Fable of the Bees*, and lay the Burthen of it upon one much inferior to himself in those Abilities that must have recommended such a Treatise to the Favour of the Publick.

2. [Anthony Ashley Cooper, Earl of Shaftesbury (1671–1713), *Characteristicks of men, manners, opinions, times* (London, 1699, 1711, 1714).]

This Paper is now swelled to almost the Compass of a Book. But the Reader must not expect from hence a particular Answer to every thing that deserves Censure in *the Fable of the Bees*. The most tolerable Part of his Performance is a *borrowed* Satyr upon the *Follies* and *Vices* of Mankind, which the Author either mistakes himself, or is pleased to put upon the World for a Description of *human Nature*, and an Essay upon the Passions. There are other Passages so very low and indecent, that common Modesty will scarce allow an Answer to them. Among others to this Purpose let the Reader turn to p. 118,[3] where he is ridiculing the idle and extravagant Fears that ignorant and unexperienced People have upon them, from the Word *Enervate*. But for this I leave him to the Correction of his Brother *Anodyne*, and hope he will do him Justice in the next Edition of one of his late Pieces.

Such as his Book is, he says it has found its Patrons. But whether they are *Persons* either of the greatest *Probity* and *Virtue*, or the most *unquestionable good Sense*,[4] the Reader will be apt to guess from the Judgment he shall form of the Book itself in both these Respects; when he sees of what kind the Principles are which are recommended in it, and in how consistent a manner they are defended.

But whatever Notion the World may entertain of this Gentleman's Abilities, it ought to be allowed that they are well enough proportioned to the Task he has undertaken. There needs no great Wit, and much less Logick, to recommend the Practice of Vice. Treatises of Impiety will subsist, and find Applause from their own intrinsick Value, without the Gloss of good Sense to set them off. What Occasion is there for any exact Talent of reasoning to convince young Fellows, that in the midst of their Debauchery they are promoting the *publick Good?* That the Magistrate neglects his Duty to them in not providing better for their Pleasures, by tolerating a sufficient Number of Temples of *Venus*, where without the Trouble and Pains of employing People to bawd[5] for them, they may constantly offer up their Devotions? That if ever through a general

3. [Bernard Mandeville, *The Fable of the Bees*, ed. F. B. Kaye, 2 vols. (Oxford: Clarendon Press, 1924; reprint, Indianapolis: Liberty Fund, 1988), Remark (L.), 1:118. Bracketed references to Mandeville in this essay refer to the Kaye edition.]

4. P. 467. [1:405.]

5. [procure]

Practice of Virtue, or the want of good Government, they should fall under so great a Misfortune as to find a Scarcity of *English* Whores, it is the
proper Business of the Magistrate to look out and *procure* a sufficient
Number from foreign Parts? The Pupils such Lectures are designed for,
carry Inclinations about with them, that will easily excuse the want of a
good reasoning Head in their Tutor.

To those who are thoroughly acquainted with the Nature of *Trade,*
and the real Source of a national Wealth, a great deal less would have
been sufficient to shew the Mischiefs of Vice in general, and of Luxury
in particular. But for the sake of others I have been forced to follow him
thro' a tedious Repetition of the same thing in different Views.

The Account of his Opinions relating to the first Formation of Society, and the Origin of moral Virtues, is given with no other Design than
to prevent the Tediousness which a separate Answer to all the Absurdi-
ties he has fallen into would occasion. Indeed such an Answer is the less
necessary after what has been writ with so much Spirit and good Sense
upon this Subject already.[6]

It is a Saying of the Duke of *Rochefocault,* "That as wicked as Men are,
they never dare to profess themselves Enemies to Virtue; and when they
have a Mind to persecute it, they either pretend not to think it real, or
forge some Faults and lay to its Charge."[7] A Character, which if the
noble *Frenchman* drew for himself, is done with more Judgment than any
thing in his Book. But perhaps the same Principle of SELF-LOVE, he
had with so much Sagacity spied out in all the rest of Mankind, had shut
his Eyes against this lively Representation of himself.

It is not impossible however but this might be laid down as a Model
for the Observation of those who should write in the same Cause after
him, and to point out just how far it was proper for them to go in their
Attacks upon Virtue. This Model Mr. *Esprit*[8] has followed very closely,
and so, in the main, has the Author of *the Fable of the Bees:* But by leaving out sometimes the Restrictions their Notions were guarded with, or

6. Mr. *Law's* Remarks. [William Law, *Remarks upon a late Book, Entitled, the Fable of
the Bees* (1724).]
7. No. 556. Paris Edit. 1692.
8. La fausseté des Vertus humaines [Paris, 1678].

inserting others of his own, which rather expose than extenuate the Guilt of them, upon the whole, he has much outdone the Original. It is not only that most things are *not* Virtue, which the World take for such, but the Thing itself, we are told, is ridiculous in Theory, and mischievous in Practice.

As to what relates to Charity Schools, I have not presumed to give Notice in the Title Page that I have said any thing in Defence of them. Those Gentlemen who are the greatest Admirers of *the Fable of the Bees,* would hardly vouchsafe to look into a Book, which they found could treat of so ungraceful a Subject, as the Teaching poor Children to read, giving them Cloaths, and binding them Apprentices.

Section I

The different Parts of the Earth being endued with different Properties, and producing different Fruits for the Use of Mankind; and Men being naturally form'd with different Talents and Dispositions, and acquiring different Sorts of Skill in the Improvement of these; the Conveniency of Trade was found out as soon as there were any People in the World. Trade is nothing but an Exchange of Commodities, that is, of the Fruits of the Earth, either natural, or improv'd by Skill and Labour. Now Reason and Observation immediately taught them, that tho' no one Part of the Earth produced the Fruits of the whole, yet by Exchanging the Superfluities of one Sort, for what they wanted of others, the Defect might in a good Measure be supply'd. Trade therefore is a Contrivance to extend (as much as possible) the particular Benefits that any one Person or one People enjoys, to all People; and in effect to make each Portion of the Earth produce what the whole Earth produces. But these Advantages were soon carried further than bare Necessity pointed out to them. They found that less than all the Product of the Earth, and less than all their Labour would supply them with Necessaries and Conveniencies, and therefore naturally thought of adding to them the Elegancies or Ornaments of Life. From hence it will appear,

First, That the Wealth of a Country consists in a Soil that produces the greatest Plenty of the Necessaries, Conveniencies and Ornaments of

Living, or in the Returns of them by Trade. In order to enjoy which Advantages, the Community must have Hands enough to make the most of the natural Fruits of their Soil, to improve them by Skill and Labour, to secure Men in the Possession of them when they are obtain'd (with the Assistance of a mild Government) to exchange Commodities with one another, to furnish Foreigners with that Share of them that is not wanted at home, and to import in Exchange for them such of their Commodities as are wanted.

But Secondly, in forming a Comparison between the Wealth of one Country and that of another, we need only consider the Plenty of Ornaments there is in each; for the Necessaries and Conveniencies of Life are common to almost all People alike; it being absurd to say that a People should subsist without Necessaries, and very unlikely that any Community of Men should pitch upon so small or so barren a Portion of the Earth for their Residence, as by the Help of their Labour would not supply them with all the Conveniencies of Life. In this View therefore the Necessaries and Conveniencies of Life should not be consider'd as a Part of National Wealth any otherwise than as a Superfluity of them will procure Ornaments in return for them from those Countries, where 'tis their Interest either to neglect their own Soil, or to work up the Product of it for foreign Trade, rather than Home Consumption. What is common then to all Countries alike being thrown out of the Account, publick Wealth may be said to consist in the greatest Plenty of Ornaments.

These Advantages, the Author of *The Fable of the Bees* thinks no Society can enjoy, where there is a General Practice of Virtue. The Substance of what he says to this Purpose, is this:

"Since a Number of Men are employ'd and maintain'd by securing others in the Enjoyment of their Wealth or Property, which can only happen upon a Supposition of Wrong and Violence, all these must be left without Employment where there's an Universal Honesty. Therefore the Loss of this Labour is a Loss of Wealth to the Community, and the Maintenance of that vast Number of idle Hands, an unsupportable Charge and Burthen."

To judge of the Weight of this Objection, it must be consider'd, whether what is laid down in the first Position, be a true Account of National Wealth; whether it consists only in the Fruits of the Soil improv'd by Skill and Labour, and the Returns of them by Trade. If the Affirmative be true, 'tis necessary only there should be Hands enough to make the most of these Advantages, that is, to manure the Earth for the better and more plentiful Production of its Fruits, to draw forth and gather these Fruits, to improve them by Skill and Labour, and to exchange the Superfluities of them for such other Commodities as are wanted. By the Help of these Hands then, the Society will be as rich as *it can be,* and no sort of Labour that does not contribute to one of those Purposes, can add *at all* to their Wealth. For as to these Employments that are concern'd in the Security of Property, tho' they are necessary while Vice and Roguery subsist, yet they add no new Wealth to the Community; they only continue what is already got to the proper Owners. And as the Security of Possessions so gain'd gives Encouragement to Industry in the gaining them, 'tis upon that Account only that such Hands are instrumental in the Acquisition of National Wealth. But as these very Possessions would be much better secur'd by an Universal Honesty, so such an Honesty would be a much greater Encouragement to Industry, and consequently in a greater Degree contribute to the National Wealth. But this is carrying the Benefit of Universal Honesty further than is necessary in Answer to the Objection. 'Tis sufficient, at present, if it appears, that an entire Absence of Roguery, by which 'tis pretended so many Hands would be left idle, could not at all take off from the National Wealth.

It will be ask'd in Consequence of the second Part of the Argument, how these Men left without Employment can be maintained?

It has been prov'd already, that this Change in their Morals would not lessen the Wealth or Property of a People, and consequently there would be the *same* Fund of Provisions for the Maintenance of the *same* Number of People. We will allow then that such as are thus deprived of their Employments, have a Right to a Maintenance some way or other, and that the Society is under an Obligation to employ them, or (what comes to the same Thing), to maintain them unemployed.

It must be consider'd, that as every Man is oblig'd to be at some Expence, in fencing himself and his Property against Violence and Wrong, so this Expence would be entirely saved by a General Practice of Virtue; and the Savings of this Expence throughout the Community would be a Fund for the Maintenance of such as by this Means are grown useless.

This every one would chearfully contribute to the Payment of, on account of the compleat Security he has of enjoying the Remainder without Fear or Hazard.

Indeed in the present Situation of Affairs Idleness has a Tendency to Vice; but the Objection supposes an entire Absence of Vice. The Question here is not whether *Idleness* promotes *Vice,* but whether *Virtue* begets *Poverty.* It will be the same thing therefore to the Community, whether these Hands are employ'd in useless Labour, or maintain'd unemployed; for bare Employment is of no Use to the Publick, nor is it possible it should be.

I have known an Overseer of the Poor in the Country, when a lusty Fellow has complain'd to him of his want of Work, employ him for a whole Day together in turning a Grindstone, tho' nothing was all that while ground upon it. I believe it won't be said that the Parish was the richer for the Fellow's Labour; or that they might not as cheaply have paid him for sitting at home, or observing the Shapes of the Clouds. The Overseer however judg'd right; the Fellow grew asham'd of so senseless a Task, and soon found out a better Employment himself.

That somewhat like this would be the Case of the whole Community, is the next thing we shall endeavour to prove; that is, that all or great Numbers of those we have hitherto supposed would be useless from the want of their present Employment in providing against Roguery, would find other Employments: And as all the Skill and Labour exercis'd in these, would be just so much Addition to the publick Wealth; so it must be put to the Account of this Universal Honesty, that is, it will be a Proof that such Universal Honesty not only does not occasion any *Poverty,* but would greatly encrease a National *Wealth.*

In the first Place, there never was yet that Country in the World, where every Part of the Soil was so compleatly improv'd as not to be capable of much further Improvement. This of it self would employ vast Numbers, and all such further Improvement of the Soil would be an additional Wealth.

2dly, If Wealth consists in a Plenty of Ornaments, whatever adds to these is an Addition to Wealth. Now the Skill and Labour that might be employ'd in the Improvement of Commodities, or in adding to the Elegancies of Life, is almost infinite. The Arts of Painting, Carving,

Gilding, &c. might take up the Time, and supply Labour to all such as are now employ'd in Bolts, Locks and Fences. Such as are employ'd in teaching others their Duty, or pleading for their Rights, would, by their superior Skill and Understanding, be the Men of Wealth, and live in Elegance and Grandeur themselves, or in some Condition or other, contribute to those Advantages in their Neighbours.

There could be no Want of Employment then, supposing this great Change to be ever so sudden, and that a Miracle intervened to effect it at once. But this is setting the present Question in a very improper Light. When this is apply'd to Practice, and address'd to the Magistrate,[9] as a Rule to direct him in the Government of a Society, the Change must necessarily be supposed to be *gradual;* and then it will appear still plainer that there would necessarily arise a Succession of new Trades, or a greater Number of the present Trades that contribute to the ornamental Parts of Life, in Proportion as the Trades in providing against Roguery grew useless and wore off.

All the Consequences of an Universal Honesty will best appear from the following Case.

Suppose a Man possess'd of a large Flock of Sheep, who is oblig'd to be at a great Expence in making his Fences very strong, and in maintaining a Number of Shepherds to preserve them against the Wolves that abound in his Neighbourhood. Afterwards by the Care and Skill of the Government, or the Assistance of his Neighbours, the Wolves are all destroyed. Would the Countryman complain that by this Means his Servants were left without Employment? Or if he should, would not he be told, that his Expence, and not his Income, was lessen'd? Or if he was still oblig'd to maintain the *same* Servants, that they would contribute to his Profit by an Improvement of other Parts of his Farm; or if there was no Room for that, to his Conveniency and Grandeur, by adorning his House and Gardens; or by a better Attendance upon himself and Family? The worst that could happen from their Want of Employment being only that some of his Shepherds would be turned into Footmen, and

---

9. *In Answer to the Presentment of the Grand Jury, he says,* The Matter complain'd of (the Fable of the Bees) is manifestly address'd to Magistrates and Politicians, p. 469 ["A Vindication of the Book," 1:406]. N.B. *The last Edition is all along refer'd to.*

wait at their Master's Table, instead of watching his Flocks. In short, 'till his Acres grew fewer, or his Crops less plentiful, no one ill Consequence could follow from the Change.

Rogues and Plunderers are the *Wolves* of humane Society; and that People, as well as private Family, would be the most happy and wealthy, where the Employment for Fence-makers, Guards and Watchmen, and the *Occasion* for them were entirely at an End.

If it be objected that such a Morality would destroy a Part of Foreign Trade, because such as are now employed in building, exporting, &c. Ships of War, Ammunitions and other warlike Stores, which are occasion'd by Injustice and Oppression, would then have nothing to do; I answer, that warlike Stores, &c. being the Fences against the Plunder of other Societies, as Bolts, Locks and Barrs are against the Robberies of private Men, if such a Morality is suppos'd to be confin'd to one Nation, other Countries will still have Occasion for those Commodities; but supposing it Universal, their Commerce in the Ornaments of Life would be the greater, as their Demand for Provisions against those Mischiefs grew less.

To illustrate yet further, what has hitherto been said by another Instance that comes likewise within the Author's Scheme.[10]

Put the Case that by another Miracle the Use of Physick were to cease (as most of it, the learned Author thinks, would cease with common Roguery,[11] whilst a good Part of the Remainder would be left to subsist upon Folly); suppose all People were to enjoy a perfect State of Health 'till they died (for Sickness is a natural Evil, as Roguery is a moral one). Would any one scruple to pay Physicians as much to sit still, as he pays them at present for Advice and Physick, in Consideration of such a Blessing? Or wou'd the Publick suffer by their Idleness, or that of the Tradesmen dependant upon them? If the Evils themselves cease at the same Time that the Provisions against them are remov'd, 'tis impossible

---

10. P. 428. Evil moral as well as natural, is the solid Basis, the Life and Support of all Trades and Employments, without Exception. [The passage in the 1732 edition reads, "what we call Evil in this world, moral as well as natural, is the grand Principle that makes us sociable Creatures, the solid Basis, the Life and support of all Trades & Employments without exception." "A Search into the Nature of Society," 1:369.]

11. P. 5, & 15. [1:20–21, 29.]

any Loss or Inconvenience shou'd happen from the Alteration. If the Want of Employment be in it self a Grievance, let it be remembred, that tho' the universal Medicine would be worth very little, yet a large Field of Labour would still remain behind in squaring the Circle, finding out the Philosopher's Stone, or a perpetual Motion.

In the Instance now mention'd, 'tis certain, that a small Part of our Foreign, as well as Inland Trade, would be destroy'd. 'Twill be the same Thing in any more considerable Branch. As there would be no Occasion for the Importation of Drugs, it will be ask'd how that Quantity of our Goods, which is now exported in Exchange for them, can be dispos'd of? To suppose then the worst that could *possibly* happen, and that there is no other Vent for them, let there be as much Skill and Labour employ'd in working them up as there is now, and when they are ready for Exportation, either let them be destroy'd here, or shipped off immediately, and thrown over Board. *Goods burnt and sunk* [says the Author, in favour of Storms, Shipwrecks, &c.[12]] *are as beneficial to the Poor, as if they had safely arrived at their several Ports;* which then will appear more demonstrably true in the present Case, as the Substance of the Exporter or Employer of the Poor is not lessen'd by such an Accident. It will be ask'd, Who then shall pay for the Materials and Workmanship of them? The Property of those People whose Want of Drugs or Physick ceases, is increas'd by this means; or, which is the same Thing, their necessary Expences are lessen'd. These People wou'd think the Blessing of Health cheaply purchas'd at so small a Price; or as the Case is general, let the Publick pay it, and raise it upon the People in what Proportion they please. 'Tis plain, the whole Community would be as able to pay it as they are *now*, since no Part of their Wealth is lessen'd by the Change. Their natural Soil would be the same, while more Hands might be employ'd in making the utmost Advantages of it.

It would be too tedious to pursue this Observation thro' the several Branches of Trade that are now employ'd in providing against Vice and Roguery; but I believe enough has been said to convince the intelligent Reader, that the same Way of Reasoning will hold good universally in other Instances.

12. P. 421. [1:363–64.]

The Author makes Sickness, and such other *natural Evils,* a Part of the *solid Basis, the Life and Support of Trades and Employments,*[13] as much as *Moral* ones. In the same Manner the Inundations and Incroachments of the Sea, that some Countries are particularly liable to, are publick Benefits in that Country, as much as the Plunder and Incroachment of Rogues and Villains; for as many Hands may be employ'd in providing against those Natural Evils, as against Moral ones. What a vast Expence are the *Dutch* at every Year, in repairing their Dikes? Now according to him, a Project for saving this Expence ought to be lookt upon as a Plot against the Wealth and Safety of their Country, as it would certainly deprive a vast Number of Men of their present Employment. But if a rational feasible Project for this Purpose should meet with such a Reception, *the wise Rulers of that well-order'd Commonwealth*[14] would, in the Opinion of some People, forfeit a Share of their Reputation for good Policy. Suppose yet further, that such Hands were depriv'd of their present Employment ever so suddenly, that Providence shou'd in one Night's time raise Barriers against the Sea, that were to last as long as the World it self, in all Probability, these *wise Rulers* would not consider such a Miracle as a National Misfortune, but would find out ways enough to employ those Hands who now work in their Dikes, especially when, as the Author tells you, in some of their Provinces there's *Abundance of Ground lying waste* for want of Improvement.[15]

This Absurdity runs thro' his Book. *Evil moral as well as natural is the solid Basis,* &c. Not only all sorts of Vice and Roguery, *but the Necessities and Imperfections of Man, the various Inclemencies of Air and other Elements, the Treachery of Water, the Rage of Fire, the Sterility of the Earth,* Sickness and Disasters of all sorts; in short, all such Evils as the World call *Misfortunes,* come into his Account of *Publick Benefits. The Gifts of Munificence of Heaven, and all the Bounties and Benefits of Nature,* by *saving* a World of *Labour* and Pains, make us *poor.* But the *Inclemencies of Air and other Elements, Badness of Seasons, the Stubbornness and Sterility of the Earth,* are the great Source of Trades, and consequently of Wealth: They

---

13. P. 428. ["A Search," 1:369.]
14. P. 95. [Remark (H.), 1:96, where "City" appears instead of "Commonwealth."]
15. P. 205. [Remark (Q.), 1:188.]

rack our Invention, and so make us *rich*. The Loss of Limbs are vastly useful to a Society, or else there could have been no room for the Invention of wooden Legs, or the Practice of Surgery. If all People had their Sight in Perfection, the World had never had the Benefit of the curious Workmanship of Glass-eyes; and I take it upon me to prove, that if none were to walk upon their Feet, there would be more Stilts and Crutches in the Nation than there are now: And *the greater Variety there is of Wants, the larger Number of Individuals may find their private Interest* in supplying them.[16] The finding out the Longitude, for Instance, is one of the most impertinent mischievous Attempts that has hitherto employ'd the Care or Skill of Mankind. Instead of offering Rewards for it, every good Subject ought to beseech Providence to blast any traiterous Endeavours towards it, and to avert so heavy a Calamity as the Prevention of Ship-wrecks would bring upon us. If the Reader would see more of the same Strain of Politicks, let him read from Page 414 to 428, particularly 424 and 425, and the Vindication of them at the End.[17]

Upon the Whole, a People in the Circumstances *the Author* has represented his reform'd Hive,[18] that is, without any Vice or Roguery among them, would be wealthier than otherwise, as enjoying at least as many of the Necessaries and Conveniencies, and more of the Ornaments of Life; or in other Words, their Income would be at least as much, and their necessary Expences less. Whatever Complaints he may think fit to make, that Smiths, &c.[19] would starve, if there were no Roguery going forward, every Man would contribute to maintain those Engineers, not only in Idleness, but in Plenty and Affluence, provided he could be secure from the least Apprehension of Violence and Wrong of any kind; at least every Man *would*, that did not hope to thrive upon a general Plunder, to make himself Amends for the Injuries he received from some, by his greater Oppression of others. Besides, nothing can be so great an Encouragement to Industry, which is the Life of Trade, as *a Security*, that what a Man gets can never be wrested from him.

16. P. 465. ["A Vindication," 1:403.]

17. *See likewise the Index under the Word* Blessings, *the Place refer'd to (it seems) is to prove* Blessings *prejudicial.*

18. P. 13. [1:27.]

19. P. 82. [1:86.]

This Security is the chief End of Government; and if that particular Form of Government is the best calculated to promote the Trade and Wealth of a Country, and that People are the most happy, where the Properties of private Men are not liable to the Encroachments of arbitrary Rulers: *That* Form of Government, which could effectually secure Men from the Injustice and Wrongs of one another, should, one would think, be still more perfect. For the Tyranny of a Prince affects People in a more remote Degree than Robbery, Violence and Plunder among themselves. By such Practices they are thrown back into a State of Nature, which is much worse than a very bad Government. A Prince would do his People less Mischief if he oppress'd them *himself,* and prevented their oppressing *one another,* than if, by an indolent Behaviour and Remissness of Government (tho' he refrain'd from all Violence himself) he allow'd every Man to injure his Neighbour as he pleased. And yet a Statesman, who could fix this happy Model of Government, according to him, ought to be deemed an arrant Traitor to his Country, by rendring so many Smiths and Watchmen useless. The Author must not think to explain away the Badness or Absurdity of his Opinions, by saying, that such a Form of Government is *impossible;* that *to live*

> *Without great Vices, is a vain*
> Eutopia *seated in the Brain;*

an Excuse he seems to be laying in for in the *Moral,* as he calls it.[20] For wherever the Scheme was first *seated,* 'tis at present in *the Fable of the Bees.* He supposes *the Fact,* and then undertakes to shew you the Mischiefs of it. 'Tis only to disguise his main Design, that he employs his ingenious Raillery in ridiculing *Fools,* who *only strive*

> *To make a great an honest Hive,*

that is, for endeavouring at what is *impossible* to obtain. His real Sentiments appear, when he calls *the grumbling Hive* Rogues and Fools, for having by their impertinent Prayers procur'd *in Fact* such a State and Condition, and consequently such Ruin and Poverty. The *Knaves* are

---

20. P. 23. [1:36.]

actually *turned honest*,[21] a Curse which the great and good Gods sent
them in their Vengeance as the greatest they could inflict,

> —*All the Rogues cry'd brazenly,*
> Good Gods, had we but Honesty!
> Merc'ry *smil'd at the Impudence,*
> *And others call'd it Want of Sense;*

(tho' by the way, *Mercury* acts a little out of Character here; he might
with a better Grace have laugh'd at their want of Sense, than their want
of Modesty or Honesty, Qualities he was not very remarkable for himself) *but* Jove *mov'd with Indignation, at last swore in Anger*,[22]

> —He'd rid
> The bawling Hive of Fraud; AND DID.
> *The very Moment it departs,*
> *And Honesty fills all their Hearts.*

The Bees themselves immediately grew sensible of their *ugly* Transformation from Knavery to Honesty,

> —*In Silence they confess,*
> *By blushing at their Ugliness.*

Then comes the dreadful Account of Ruin and Desolation this Monster
Honesty brought with it;

> *But, oh you Gods! What Consternation,*
> *How vast and sudden was th' Alteration!*
> *In half an Hour the Nation round*
> *Meat fell a penny in the Pound,* &c.[23]

Till at last, finding themselves poor,

> —*To avoid Extravagance*
> *They flew into a hollow Tree,*
> *Blest with Content and Honesty.*[24]

21. The Title of the Fable itself is *The Grumbling Hive, or, Knaves turn'd honest.*
22. P. 13. ["The Grumbling Hive," 1:27; see above, p. 211.]
23. P. 13. [1:28; see above, p. 212.]
24. P. 22. [1:35; see above, p. 217.]

As this is an Excuse which the Author has very often Recourse to, I shall be oblig'd to take notice of it again in the Course of this Enquiry.

If what has been said be a true Account of national Wealth; if it consists wholly in the Product of the Soil improv'd by Skill and Labour, and the Returns of it by Trade, it will help us to discover another Mistake that some among us have run into; which is, that all Inventions to save Labour and Trouble, by the Help of which one Man may do the same Work in one Day, that would otherwise employ several Men for several Days, are prejudicial to the Publick. For whatever Labour is employ'd for other Purposes than the drawing out, improving, &c. the Product of the Soil, is utterly useless to the Publick; and consequently, if by the Help of new Inventions any piece of Work that now requires *two* Men, can be done in the same Time by *one* Man, all that Labour so sav'd would be so much real Gain to the Publick, as long as there is any room for the further Improvement of their Soil, or beautifying the Product of it, or extending their Commerce.

Tho' such an Universal Morality, as has been all along suppos'd, be impossible in Fact, without the Intervention of *a Miracle* (which one would wonder *the Author of the Fable* should have Recourse to for the Foundation of his Scheme) yet what has been said will hold equally true as to any less Improvement in Virtue, that the Care and Skill of the Magistrate can bring about; and 'tis in this *practical* View only that his Notions are of any Consequence to the World, or deserve to be consider'd.

It will be hard to guess, what Design *the Author* could have in publishing this System of Politicks. Has there been such a quick and sudden Progress in Morality of late Years here in *England,* as to occasion the starving great Numbers of People who were before employ'd in fencing against Roguery? For he tells you ENGLAND is the Country his *Hive* is intended to represent.[25] There are a great many thousand Acres of incultivated Land, which, at the Expence of Labour, would bring a large Accession of Wealth to the Kingdom; many Rivers might be made navigable, neglected Branches of Trade encourag'd to publick Advantage; and our publick Roads be kept in a much better Order. These are but a few

25. Preface, p. 4. ["Preface," 1:6, where it is implied but not stated that England is the subject.]

Instances that might be named, wherein the Labour of many thousands, according to his own Assertion,[26] might be usefully employed.

Tho' the Magistrate were to set about the Work of Reformation ever so heartily, I am afraid the Progress he could make, would not be so great as to enable him to make Draughts from such as are now employed in defending us against Roguery, large enough to supply these great Occasions; even tho' no new Trades were to arise, nor the Number of the present ones to encrease, that make for the ornamental Parts of Life, to afford Labour for such as would grow useless by a general Practice of Honesty. And yet till all this happens, and the Society is found to groan under the Weight and Misery of Virtue, one would think there should be no Occasion for such Lessons of Immorality. Has there been any insolent Attempt set on Foot to abridge Mankind of their natural Liberty of practising Vice and Wickedness, or to make Virtue and Religion fashionable among us? Can he, among the numberless Projects that have of late Years been offer'd for the Good of this Nation; tell us of any Schemes calculated to make the present or the future Age more honest or virtuous than former ones? I can think of but one, out of a great many that might be named to the contrary, I mean that of *Charity-Schools:* And 'tis greatly to the Honour of the Persons concerned in promoting these Seminaries of Virtue, that the same Book which attempts to prove *the more wicked and vicious Mankind are,* the better Subjects they are, *and the more useful Members of a Commonwealth,* should have in it a Treatise against those Charities. The Author might very well have changed Titles, and have called *the Fable* it self *an Argument against Charity-Schools.* For if *private Vices* are *publick Benefits,* 'tis a much better Argument against them, than any he has urged. But this will be considered more at large hereafter.

His Comparison of Wickedness in a Society to the Dirt of the Streets in *London,*[27] is nothing to his Purpose. The only way of reasoning that will hold here, is to say, that as the Wealth and Trade of the City of *London produce* some *Dirt* in the Streets, so will the Wealth of the Society

---

26. P. 364. There is above three or four hundred Years Work for a hundred thousand Poor, more than we have in this Island. [1:318.]

27. *See the Preface from* p. 9. *to* p. 11. *and* p. 471. ["Preface," 1:10–11, and "A Vindication," 1:408.]

produce some *Vice* and Wickedness in the People; which (if it proves any thing) is not an Argument for the *Usefulness* of *Vice*, but rather shews the *Inconvenience* of *Wealth*. To say, as the Dirt of the Streets is the *Effect* of the Wealth of the City, so Vice or Wickedness is the *Cause* of the Wealth of a Society, is a sort of Logick peculiar to himself.

This Comparison then is against him. For as a Project for the better cleansing the Streets would not, I presume, be lookt upon by the Inhabitants, as a Plot against the Trade and Wealth of the City: So the Extirpation of Vice in a Society would as little tend to the lessening the publick Wealth or Happiness; even tho' each could be so effectual, as that *the Blackguard and the Scavengers* in the *one* Case,[28] and Smiths[29] and Watchmen in the *other*, should be oblig'd to quit their present Employments, and the Expence of both be entirely saved.

But the Author thinks, however it might fare with lesser Communities, that *no Society can be raised into a rich and mighty Kingdom, or so raised subsist in their Wealth or Power for any considerable Time, without the Vices of Man.*[30] Now this Distinction he himself has effectually destroyed elsewhere. For if *what we call Evil in this World*, (the Expression looks as if he differ'd from the rest of the World in his Opinion of it) *moral as well as natural, is the grand Principle that makes us sociable Creatures, the solid Basis, the Life and Support of all Trades and Employments without Exception, that the Moment Evil ceases, the Society must be spoiled, if not totally dissolved*,[31] it will follow, that Evil is essential to the *Being* of Society, to lesser ones as well as greater. But to consider his Argument as it stands here.

As to the First Part of it, it will be readily allowed him, that History furnishes very few Instances of any wide Extent of Dominion, that was not *at first* procur'd by Methods very inconsistent with Virtue and Morality. The Conduct of an *Alexander* at the Head of his Army can as little be justified, as that of *Cartouche* and his Gang.[32] But then the

---

28. Preface, p. ii. ["Preface," 1:12.]
29. P. 82. [Remark (G.), 1:86.]
30. P. 225.
31. P. 428. ["A Search," 1:369.]
32. [Louis-Dominique Cartouche (1693–1721), a famous bandit. See note 36 of ch. 23 in this volume.]

utmost he can make of his Argument, will be this, that a Man cannot raise so large an Estate by being content with his own, as if he plunder'd his Neighbours, and had sufficient Power to back him in his Outrage, and that such Plunder can't happen without the Assistance of Vice and Roguery. In short, that it is impossible to be a mighty Robber, without being somewhat dishonest; a Discovery in which *Hamlet* has been beforehand with him.[33]

If he could have prov'd indeed that no body was the *poorer* for this *plunder'd Wealth*, it would have been a Secret worth communicating to the World; a Secret of great Use to justify the Conduct of Ministers of State.

But with regard to whole Societies he has yet a much harder Task. For besides the proving that no other Prince is the poorer for these plunder'd Territories, he must shew, before he can make the least Use of it, that a wide Extent of Dominion is necessary to the Wealth and Happiness of the People. And as to that, it must be consider'd, that the Happiness of a Community, is nothing but the Happiness of the private Individuals who compose it. To say, that a Community may be happy, where the private Individuals are unhappy, is to say, that an Army may be well cloathed, though every single Man in every Regiment were forc'd to go naked. 'Tis highly absurd to call a Nation happy and flourishing, only because it makes a Figure abroad, and is a Terrour to its Neighbours. For the greatest Power and Force that ever any Nation has possess'd, either to defend themselves, or to offend their Neighbours, has been of no real Use, but as they tended to make each Individual happy in his *private* Life, by securing to him the free and quiet Enjoyment of his own. If we are to judge by this Test, of the Use that new Acquisitions of Territories are to a Society, they will be far from serving the Purposes of the Author. Are private Men the more happy or the more wealthy, because their Sovereign has the Glory to be a Conqueror? It is not the Grandeur of the Prince, that makes the People happy; nor the Extent of his Dominions, that makes them rich. New Provinces may be bought or added every Year, and yet the Estates of private Men be not at all enlarg'd by it. If one Part of a Prince's Dominions grow the richer for any Addition to them,

---

33. *There's ne'er a Villain dwelling in all* Denmark, *but he's an arrant Knave.* Shakespear's Hamlet. [Act 1, scene 5, l. 127–28.]

it can only happen by draining the Wealth from other Parts. All Ages and Countries will afford Examples enough of this Truth. But to avoid giving Offence, I would choose to put the Reader in Mind of what has happen'd elsewhere, rather than of what *Englishmen* may be suppos'd to be more immediately concern'd in.

But when a mighty Kingdom is so raised, it is by no means true, that it can't subsist in its Wealth or Power, without the Assistance of *Vice.* I expect it will be said that Power must be supported by the Methods 'twas procured; but besides that this has no relation to *private* Vices, (no more indeed has the whole Objection) it can only be true as to the first *Conquerors themselves,* and will cease afterwards, when a long Possession, and a continued Submission to the Successors, have repair'd the want of Justice in the Title of the *Conqueror.* This, 'tis probable, has been the Case some time or other of every Kingdom in the World. When this Right is once acquir'd, Virtue and Morality don't exact a tame Submission to Injuries and Invasions from abroad, nor stand in the way to any publick Benefit or Happiness at home. Enough has been said to prove the Truth of the one already; and as to the *other,* Courage and a Love of Liberty have never yet been reckon'd among the Number of Vices.[34]

34. *See* p. 21. *of the Fable from these Words,* So few in the vast Hive, &c. ["Grumbling Hive," 1:35. See above, p. 217].

13

The Complete English Tradesman

1727

DANIEL DEFOE, a butcher's son, was born into a nonconformist family in London, probably in 1660 or 1661. He pursued but then abandoned the training for a dissenting minister. Instead, he went into business around 1685, becoming a liveryman in 1687–88. He participated in Monmouth's rebellion in 1685 and served in William's army in 1688. He became a hose factor in London, in which capacity he engaged in trade in France and Spain. He was not frugal in his expenses, however, and went bankrupt in 1697. He was a government accountant in the late 1690s. In the 1690s, he wrote numerous reform proposals on subjects such as a national bank, savings banks, and insurance. He changed his name from Foe to Defoe around 1703. By the time he was imprisoned in 1703 for "The Shortest Way with the Dissenters," a satire in favor of religious toleration, he had a wife and six children.

He wrote political works and served as a secret commissioner to Scotland for the government in the first decade of the 1700s. He was an anti-Jacobite pamphleteer in 1713 but was prosecuted by the Whigs for treasonable writings the same year; he was convicted of libel but freed by the efforts of Townsend, the secretary of state. He was the editor of the Jacobite *Mist's Journal,* 1717–24. His main works then proceeded in short order: *Robinson Crusoe* was published in 1719, *Moll Flanders* in 1722, and *Roxanna* in 1724. His *Journal of the Plague Year* came out in 1722, and *New Voyage Around the World* appeared in 1725. He also was the author of a large number of essays, pamphlets, travel pieces, and other works, including many that described the new commercial society that was emerging in England in his time, such as the influential *Plan of English Commerce.* He wrote more than 250 publications, and he died in 1731. Swift called him a "stupid illiterate scribbler."

Originally written in 1727, the work included here is from *The Complete English Tradesman* in *The Novels and Miscellaneous Works of Daniel Defoe,* edited by Sir Walter Scott (Oxford: Talboys, 1841), volume 17, chapter 25, pp. 241–53. The notes are by the present editor.

The Complete English Tradesman

Of the dignity of trade in England, more than in other countries. That England is the greatest trading country in the world; that our climate is the best to live in; that our men are the stoutest and best; that the tradesmen in England are not of the meanest of the people; that the wealth of the nation lies chiefly among them; that trade is a continual fund for supplying the decays in the rank of gentry; that an ordinary trader can spend more than a gentleman of 500l. a year; that an estate is a pond, but trade a spring; that the descendants of tradesmen here, for gallantry of spirit and greatness of soul, are not inferior to the descendants of the best families. Further hints to the ladies whose pride will not let them stoop to marry a tradesman. To trade, and not to conquest, is owing the present grandeur of the English nation. How much the landed interest owes to trade.

The instances which we have given in the last chapter, abundantly make for the honour of the British traders; and we may venture to say, at the same time, are very far from doing dishonour to the nobility who have from time to time entered into alliance with them; for it is very well known, that besides the benefit which we reap by being a trading nation, which is our principal glory, trade is a very different thing in England than it is in many other countries, and is carried on by persons who, both in their education and descent, are far from being the dregs of the people.

King Charles II., who was perhaps the prince of all the kings that ever reigned in England, who best understood the country and the people he governed, used to say, that the tradesmen were the only gentry in England. His majesty spoke it merrily, but it had a happy signification in it, such as was peculiar to the bright genius of that prince, who, though he was not the best governor, was the best acquainted with the world of all the princes of his age, if not of all the men in it; and I make no scruple to advance these three points in honour of our country; viz.—

1. That we are the greatest trading country in the world, because we have the greatest exportation of the growth and product of our land, and of the manufacture and labour of our people; and the greatest importation and consumption of the growth, product, and manufactures of other countries from abroad, of any nation in the world.

2. That our climate is the best and most agreeable to live in, because a man can be more out of doors in England than in other countries.

3. That our men are the stoutest and best, because, strip them naked from the waist upwards, and give them no weapons at all but their hands and heels, and turn them into a room or stage, and lock them in with the like number of other men of any nation, man for man, and they shall beat the best men you shall find in the world.

As so many of our noble and wealthy families, as we have shown, are raised by and derived from trade, so it is true, and indeed it cannot well be otherwise, that many of the younger branches of our gentry, and even of the nobility itself, have descended again into the spring from whence they flowed, and have become tradesmen; and thence it is that, as I said above, our tradesmen in England are not, as it generally is in other countries, always of the meanest of our people. Nor is trade itself in England, as it generally is in other countries, the meanest thing the men can turn their hand to; but, on the contrary, trade is the readiest way for men to raise their fortunes and families; and therefore it is a field for men of figure and of good families to enter upon.

N. B. By trade we must be understood to include navigation and foreign discoveries; because they are, generally speaking, all promoted and carried on by trade, and even by tradesmen, as well as merchants; and the tradesmen, as owners, are at this time as much concerned in shipping as the merchants, only the latter may be said to be the chief employers of the shipping.

Having thus done a particular piece of justice to ourselves, in the value we put upon trade and tradesmen in England, it reflects very much upon the understandings of those refined heads who pretend to depreciate that part of the nation which is so infinitely superior in wealth to the families who call themselves gentry, and so infinitely more numerous.

As to the wealth of the nation, that undoubtedly lies chiefly among the trading part of the people; and though there are a great many families raised within few years, in the late war,[1] by great employments and by great actions abroad, to the honour of the English gentry, yet how many more families among the tradesmen have been raised to immense estates, even during the same time, by the attending circumstances of the war; such as the clothing, the paying, the victualling and furnishing, &c., both army and navy. And by whom have the prodigious taxes been paid, the loans supplied, and money advanced upon all occasions? By whom are the banks and companies carried on, and on whom are the customs and excises levied? Have not the trade and tradesmen borne the burden of the war? And do they not still pay four millions a year interest for the public debts. On whom are the funds levied, and by whom the public credit supported? Is not trade the inexhausted fund of all funds, and upon which all the rest depend?

As is the trade, so in proportion are the tradesmen; and how wealthy are tradesmen in almost all the several parts of England, as well as in London? How common is it to see a tradesman go off the stage, even but from mere shopkeeping, with from ten to forty thousand pounds' estate to divide among his family! when, on the contrary, take the gentry in England, from one end to the other, except a few here and there, what with excessive high living, which is of late grown so much into a disease, and the other ordinary circumstances of families, we find few families of the lower gentry, that is to say from six or seven hundred a year down-

---

1. [The War of the Spanish Succession, 1701–14.]

wards, but they are in debt, and in necessitous circumstances, and a great many of greater estates also.

On the other hand, let any one who is acquainted with England, look but abroad into the several counties, especially near London, or within fifty miles of it; how are the ancient families worn out by time and family misfortunes, and the estates possessed by a new race of tradesmen, grown up into families of gentry, and established by the immense wealth gained, as I may say, behind the counter; that is, in the shop, the warehouse, and the counting-house.

How many noble seats, superior to the palaces of sovereign princes, in some countries, do we see erected within few miles of this city by tradesmen, or the sons of tradesmen, while the seats and castles of the ancient gentry, like their families, look worn out and fallen into decay! witness the noble house of sir John Eyles, himself a merchant, at Giddyhall, near Romford; sir Gregory Page, on Blackheath, the son of a brewer; sir Nathanael Mead, near Weal-green, his father a linendraper, with many others, too long to repeat; and, to crown all, the lord Castlemain's, now earl of Tilney, at Wanstead, his father, sir Josiah Child, originally a tradesman.

Again; in how superior a port or figure (as we now call it) do our tradesmen live, to what the middling gentry either do or can support! An ordinary tradesman now, not in the city only, but in the country, shall spend more money by the year, than a gentleman of four or five hundred pounds a year can do, and shall increase and lay up every year too; whereas the gentleman shall at the best stand stock still just where he began, nay, perhaps, decline: and as for the lower gentry, from a hundred pounds a year to three hundred, or thereabouts, though they are often as proud and high in their appearance as the other; as to them, I say, a shoemaker in London shall keep a better house, spend more money, clothe his family better, and yet grow rich too. It is evident where the difference lies; an estate's a pond, but trade's a spring: the first, if it keeps full, and the water wholesome, by the ordinary supplies and drains from the neighbouring grounds, it is well, and it is all that is expected; but the other is an inexhausted current, which not only fills the pond, and keeps it full, but is continually running over, and fills all the lower ponds and places about it.

This being the case in England, and our trade being so vastly great, it is no wonder that the tradesmen in England fills the lists of our nobility and gentry; no wonder that the gentlemen of the best families marry tradesmen's daughters, and put their younger sons apprentices to tradesmen; and how often do these younger sons come to buy the elder sons' estates, and restore the family, when the elder and head of the house, proving rakish and extravagant, has wasted his patrimony, and is obliged to make out the blessing of Israel's family, where the younger son bought the birthright, and the elder was doomed to serve him!

Trade is so far here from being inconsistent with a gentleman, that, in short, trade in England makes gentlemen, and has peopled this nation with gentlemen; for, after a generation or two, the tradesman's children, or at least their grandchildren, come to be as good gentlemen, statesmen, parliamentmen, privy-counsellors, judges, bishops, and noblemen, as those of the highest birth and the most ancient families; as we have shown. Nor do we find any defect either in the genius or capacities of the posterity of tradesmen, arising from any remains of mechanic blood, which, it is pretended, should influence them; but all the gallantry of spirit, greatness of soul, and all the generous principles that can be found in any of the ancient families, whose blood is the most untainted, as they call it, with the low mixtures of a mechanic race, are found in these; and, as is said before, they generally go beyond them in knowledge of the world, which is the best education.

We see the tradesmen of England, as they grow wealthy, coming every day to the herald's office to search for the coats of arms of their ancestors, in order to paint them upon their coaches, and engrave them upon their plate, embroider them upon their furniture, or carve them upon the pediments of their new houses; and how often do we see them trace the registers of their families up to the prime nobility, or the most ancient gentry of the kingdom!

In this search we find them often qualified to raise new families, if they do not descend from old; as was said of a certain tradesman of London, that if he could not find the ancient race of gentlemen, from which he came, he would begin a new race, who should be as good gentlemen as any that went before him.

Thus, in the late wars between England and France, how was our army full of excellent officers, who went from the shop, and behind the counter, into the camp, and who distinguished themselves there by their merits and gallant behaviour! And several such came to command regiments, and even to be general officers, and to gain as much reputation in the service as any; as colonel Pierce, Wood, Richards, and several others that may be named.

All this confirms what I have said before, viz., that trade in England neither is or ought to be levelled with what it is in other countries; or the tradesman depreciated as they are abroad, and as some of our gentry would pretend to do in England; but that as many of our best families rose from trade, so many branches of the best families in England, under the nobility, have stooped so low as to be put apprentices to tradesmen in London, and to set up and follow those trades when they have come out of their times, and have thought it no dishonour to their blood.

To bring this once more home to the ladies, who are scandalized at that mean step, which they call it, of marrying a tradesman, it may be told them, for their humiliation, that, however they think fit to act, sometimes those tradesmen come of better families than their own; and oftentimes, when they have refused them to their loss, those very tradesmen have married ladies of superior fortune to them, and have raised families of their own, who, in one generation, have been superior to those nice ladies both in dignity and estate; and have, to their great mortification, been ranked above them upon all public occasions.

The word "tradesmen," in England, does not sound so harsh as it does in other countries; and to say a gentleman-tradesman, is not so much nonsense as some people would persuade us to reckon it; and, indeed, the very name of an English tradesman, will and does already obtain in the world; and as our soldiers, by the late war, gained the reputation of being some of the best troops in the world; and our seamen are at this day, and very justly too, esteemed the best sailors in the world; so the English tradesman may be allowed to rank with the best gentlemen in Europe; and, as the prophet Isaiah said of the merchants of Tyre, that *her traffickers were the honourable of the earth,* Isa. xxiii. 8.

And hence it is natural to ask, whence comes all this to be so? How is it produced? War has not done it; no, nor so much as helped or assisted to it; it is not by any martial exploits; we have made no conquests abroad, added no new kingdoms to the British empire, reduced no neighbouring nations, or extended the possession of our monarchs into the properties of others; we have gained nothing by war and encroachment; we are butted and bounded just where we were in queen Elizabeth's time; the Dutch, the Flemings, the French, are in view of us, just as they were then; we have subjected no new provinces or people to our government; and, with few or no exceptions, we are almost, for dominion, where king Edward I. left us: nay, we have lost all the dominions which our ancient kings for some hundred of years held in France; such as the rich and powerful provinces of Normandy, Poictou, Gascoigne, Bretagne, and Aquitaine; and, instead of being enriched by war and victory, on the contrary, we have been torn in pieces by civil wars and rebellions, as well in Ireland as in England, and that several times, to the ruin of our richest families, and the slaughter of our nobility and gentry; nay, to the destruction even of monarchy itself, as in the long bloody wars between the houses of Lancaster and York,[2] the many rebellions of the Irish, as well in queen Elizabeth's time, as in king Charles I. time; and the fatal massacre, and almost extirpation of the English name in that kingdom; and, at last, the late rebellion in England, in which the monarch fell a sacrifice to the fury of the people, and monarchy itself gave way to tyranny and usurpation, for almost twenty years.[3]

These things prove abundantly that the greatness of the British nation is not owing to war and conquests, to enlarging its dominions by the sword, or subjecting the people of other countries to our power; but it is all owing to trade, to the increase of our commerce at home, and the extending it abroad.

It is owing to trade, that new discoveries have been made in lands unknown, and new settlements and plantations made, new colonies planted, and new governments formed, in the uninhabited islands, and the uncultivated continent of America; and those plantings and settlements have again enlarged and increased the trade, and thereby the wealth and power of the nation by whom they were discovered and planted; we have not increased our power, or the number of our subjects,

2. [The Wars of the Roses, 1455–85.]
3. [The English Civil War and Commonwealth, 1642–60.]

by subduing the nations which possess those countries, and incorporating them into our own; but have entirely planted our colonies, and peopled the countries with our own subjects, natives of this island; and, excepting the negroes, which we transport from Africa to America, as slaves to work in the sugar and tobacco plantations, all our colonies, as well in the islands, as on the continent of America, are entirely peopled from Great Britain and Ireland, and chiefly the former; the natives having either removed further up into the country, or, by their own folly and treachery raising war against us, been destroyed and cut off.

As trade has thus extended our colonies abroad, so it has (except those colonies) kept our people at home, where they are multiplied to that prodigious degree, and do still continue to multiply in such a manner, that, if it goes on so, time may come that all the lands in England will do little more than serve for gardens from them and to feed their cows, and their corn and cattle be supplied from Scotland and Ireland.

What is the reason that we see numbers of French, and of Scots, and Germans, in all the foreign nations in Europe, and especially filling up their armies and courts, and that you see few or no English there?

What is the reason that, when we want to raise armies, or to man navies, in England, we are obliged to press the seamen, and to make laws, and empower the justices of peace and magistrates of towns, to force men to go for soldiers, and enter into the service, or allure them by giving bounty-money as an encouragement to men to list themselves; whereas the people of other nations, and even the Scots and Irish, travel abroad and run into all the neighbour-nations, to seek service and to be admitted into their pay?

What is it but trade, the increase of business at home, and the employment of the poor in the business and manufactures of this kingdom, by which the poor get so good wages, and live so well, that they will not list for soldiers; and have so good pay in the merchants' service, that they will not serve on board the ships of war, unless they are forced to do it?

What is the reason that, in order to supply our colonies and plantations with people, besides the encouragement given in those colonies to all people that will come hither to plant and to settle, we are obliged to send away thither all our petty offenders, and all the criminals that we think fit to spare from the gallows, besides that we formerly called the kidnapping trade, that is to say, the arts made use of to wheedle and draw away young, vagrant, and indigent people, and people of desperate fortunes, to sell themselves, that is, bind themselves for servants, the number of which are very great?

It is poverty fills armies, mans navies, and peoples colonies; in vain the drums beat for soldiers to serve in the armies for fivepence a day, and the king's captains invite seamen to serve in the royal navy for twenty-three shillings per month, in a country where the ordinary labourer can have nine shillings a week for his labour, and the manufacturers earn from twelve to sixteen shillings a week for their work; and while trade gives thirty shillings per month wages to the seamen on board merchant-ships, men will always stay or go, as the pay gives them encouragement; and this is the reason why it has been so much more difficult to raise and recruit armies in England, than it has been in Scotland and Ireland, France and Germany.

The same trade that keeps our people at home, is the cause of the well-living of the people here; for as frugality is not the national virtue of England, so the people that get much, spend much; and as they work hard, so they live well, eat and drink well, clothe warm, and lodge soft; in a word, the working manufacturing people of England, eat the fat, drink the sweet, live better, and fare better, than the working poor of any other nation in Europe; they make better wages of their work, and spend more of the money upon their backs and bellies than in any other country. This expense of the poor, as it causes a prodigious consumption both of the provisions and of the manufactures of our country at home, so two things are undeniably the consequence of that part.

1. The consumption of provisions increases the rent and value of the lands; and this raises the gentlemen's estates, and that again increases the employment of people, and consequently the numbers of them, as well those that are employed in the husbandry of land, breeding and feeding of cattle, &c., as of servants to the gentlemen's families, who as their estates increase in value, so they increase their families and equipages.

2. As the people get greater wages, so they, I mean the same poorer part of the people, clothe better, and furnish better; and this increases the consumption of the very manufactures they make; then that consumption increases the quantity made; and this creates what we call inland

trade, by which innumerable families are employed, and the increase of the people maintained; and by which increase of trade and people the present growing prosperity of this nation is produced.

The whole glory and greatness of England then being thus raised by trade, it must be unaccountable folly and ignorance in us to lessen that one article in our own esteem, which is the only fountain from whence we all, take us as a nation, are raised, and by which we are enriched and maintained. The Scripture says, speaking of the riches and glory of the city of Tyre, which was indeed at that time the great port or emporium of the world for foreign commerce, from whence all the silks and fine manufactures of Persia and India were exported all over the western world, *that her merchants were princes,* and in another place, *by thy traffic thou hast increased thy riches,* Ezek. xxviii. 5. Certain it is, that our traffic has increased our riches; and it is also certain, that the flourishing of our manufacture is the foundation of all our traffic, as well our merchandise as our inland trade.

The inland trade of England is a thing not easily described; it would, in a word, take up a whole book by itself; it is the foundation of our wealth and greatness; it is the support of all our foreign trade, and of our manufacturing; and as I have hitherto written of the tradesmen who carry it on, I shall proceed with a brief discourse of the trade itself.

14

Plan for the Improvement of Commerce 1732?

Charles Irénée Castel, *abbé* de Saint-Pierre, was born into an old family in Normandy in 1658. After a Jesuit education, he entered holy orders. An early interest in the sciences led him to Paris, where he became well acquainted with many of the distinguished intellectuals of his time, including Nicole, Malebranche, Vertot, and Fontenelle, the latter of whom arranged for his selection to the Académie Française in 1695. He became a pensioner of the Duchess of Orléans in 1702. After attending the Treaty of Utrecht with the Cardinal of Polignac in 1712, he wrote and began to publish his *Projet de paix perpétuelle* in 1713 (described by Cardinal Dubois as "the dreams of a well-intentioned man"), the third volume of which came out in 1717 and was dedicated to the Duke of Orléans, then regent. His far-reaching attack on the reign of Louis XIV and scheme for constitutional reform, *Discours sur la polysynodie,* appeared in 1718. Though expelled unanimously by the Académie Française, he took refuge in the more receptive Club de l'Entresol, where he unleashed a continuing barrage of reform proposals during the existence of the Club, which was closed down by the prime minister Cardinal Fleury in 1731. Through the rest of his life, he lived either at his estate at Saint-Pierre-Eglise or at Chenonceaux, where Madame Dupin supported his ideas and where Rousseau regarded him sympathetically. Writings on the duel, on tax reform, on administrative reform, on poor relief, and on educational improvement had earned him the sobriquet "Solicitor for the public good" by the time of his death in 1743.

The brief excerpt here is "Observation I: L'Augmentation du Comerse augmentera le travail & l'industrie de la Nation," from *Projet pour perfectionner le Comerse,* in *Ouvrajes de politique,* 17 vols. (Rotterdam: J. D. Beman, 1733–41), 8:182–85.

Plan for the Improvement of Commerce

Observation I

The increase in trade will increase the work and industry of the Nation

All work is tedious, and when man sees that his work brings him nothing, or not enough, he remains idle and refrains from useless effort.

But where work is lucrative, men are willing to work, and they work much. Now where there is much trade going on, the merchants pay handsomely for manufactures and for the fruits of the earth; for as they carry them elsewhere, they sell them at a much higher price than they buy them for.

Inhabitants of cold countries have more needs; they lack more things. They need more clothes, and they need more heat. The roads are harder to maintain because of the rain. They need more buildings to protect them against the cold and the rain. It is thus not surprising that they are more hard-working than the inhabitants of warm countries; work itself is more tedious in warm countries. Hence it is not surprising that people closest to the Equator should be the laziest and least hard-working, and as a result less industrious than those who live in climates further removed from the Equator.

Work has four advantages for a family.

1. It brings in riches and goods.

2. It makes pleasures more palpable, for they are all the more perceptible as the person who tastes them is emerging from a difficult situation.

3. Work makes ills less palpable, for those who are already used to some pain feel other small pains less acutely.

4. Work habituates us to rules, discipline, and the observance of justice. For in work, the mind gets used to more attention, and the hard-working man, who is painstaking and rich, is more inclined to dispense justice—so that justice is done to him—than the lazy man who has nothing to lose.

One may conclude from this that that people which is the hardest-working will be the wealthiest, the most just, the easiest to govern, and the happiest.

Where there is much commerce, not only are the people happier and more industrious, but the wealthy themselves are more hard-working than elsewhere; the wealthiest merchants are never without occupation.

When the wealthy are hard-working, they make fewer useless expenses; for nothing teaches them the value of riches better than the pains and care they take in gaining them.

To reduce idleness and luxury expenses is to diminish the maladies of a state. Almost all types of goods and manufactures are part of maritime trade, either as transported goods or as consumer goods. Now the merchants who earn more from a commodity buy it at a higher price, and this describes the maritime merchants.

15

A Political Essay upon Commerce
1734

JEAN-FRANÇOIS MELON was born in 1675 into a judicial family and became a lawyer attached to the Parlement of Bordeaux. He came to be associated with the literary elite of the city and suggested the establishment of a literary circle. Under the protection of the Duke of La Force, that circle became a formal provincial academy in September 1712, with Melon as its secretary. Melon worked for La Force during the Regency and subsequently with the Guardian of the Seal d'Argenson, as well as with Cardinal Dubois, John Law, and the Duke of Orléans, whom he served as secretary and general financial adviser. According to Voltaire, it was Melon who persuaded the regent to recall Law from Venice to direct the administration's finances. Melon died in Paris in 1738.

The excerpt here comes from his only historically important work, *Essai politique sur le commerce* (1734), which was refuted by Dutot but praised by Voltaire in the midst of the latter's polemic over the "Mondain" (see chapter 16). I have used *A Political Essay upon Commerce*, translated by David Bindon (Dublin: Crampton, 1738), ch. 9, pp. 173–99, and have retained one or two of the more piquantly relevant of the translator's footnotes. The other notes, which are bracketed, are my own.

A Political Essay upon Commerce

Of Luxury

We are now led to the Consideration of Luxury, and its Workmen. A Subject, which hath given Occasion to many wild Declamations, that have oftener proceeded, from an envious and morose Temper, than from the true Principles of Reason, or a wise Severity of Manners.

If Men were so happy, as to regulate their Actions, according to the pure Maxims of Religion, they would not have Occasion for Laws. Duty would serve, as a Curb to Vice, and an Incitement to Virtue. But, unhappily for us, we are swayed by our Passions, and the Legislat[or], should only endeavour, to turn them to the best Advantage of the Community. Ambition maketh military Men valiant, and Traders are excited to work, by the Desire of Gain. The Expectation of being in a Condition to enjoy an easy, voluptuous Life, often influenceth both the one, and the other: And Luxury becometh an additional Incitement with them, to follow their several Occupations.

Luxury, is an extraordinary Sumptuousness, proceeding from the Riches, and Security of a Government. It will be always found attendant, upon every well-governed Society. Whoever findeth himself possessed of great Plenty, will be desirous to enjoy it. He hath, for this Purpose, several Cravings, which Persons not so rich as he, are not able to pay for; and these Cravings are always relative to Time, and to Persons. What was Luxury in the Days of our Fathers, is now very Common; and what is Luxury among us, will not be so, to our Posterity. Silk Stockings, were Luxury in the Days of *Henry* the Second; and *Delft-Ware,* is as much so, when compared to common *Earthen-Ware,* as *China* is, when compared to *Delft-Ware.*

The Peasant findeth Luxury in the Habitation of the Villager [*bourgeois*]; the Villager in the House of the Inhabitant of his Neighbour Town; who, on his Part, looketh upon himself, as unpolite, with respect to the Inhabitant of the Capital City; and he is yet more unpolite, when compared to the Courtier.

The Legislat[or] may judge the same way of Luxury, as [he] doth of Colonies. When a State hath the Number of Men necessary for tilling the Land, for War, and for Manufactures, it is of Use, that the Surplus, should employ themselves in works of Luxury. Because, there remaineth only this Employment for them, or they must be Idle; and, that it is of greater Advantage, to keep the Inhabitants, in the Place, where the Sovereignty is to be maintained, when they can earn a Livelihood, than to send them to the Colonies, where they labour only to promote Luxury. Sugar, Silk, Coffee, Tobacco, are new Luxuries, not known to the *Romans*. A People of the greatest Luxury, if we may believe the Declaimers of their Times, who were as peevish and satyrical, in Verse and Prose, as those of our Days.

In what Sense can it be said, that Luxury rendereth a Nation effeminate? This cannot relate to the Army. The Soldiers, and Subaltern Officers, are Strangers to Luxury, and it is not through the Magnificence of general Officers, that an Army hath been defeated. Ambitious Emulation, supports them, no less than it doth others. Is the Weakness of those numerous *Ottoman* and *Persian* Armies, to be attributed to Luxury, or to want of Emulation, and Discipline? Eastern Luxury, is an indolent Laziness, which enervates Courage, in a wretched Seraglio.

The *Spanish* Troops, much worse clad and more frugal, than any sumptuary Laws ever ordained, were not the more valiant for it; and when our Armies were beaten in the last War,[1] there was much less Plenty amongst them, than in the glittering Days of our Victories.

Luxury is, in some sort, the Destroyer of Sloth and Idleness. The sumptuous Man would soon see the End of his Riches, if he did not endeavour to preserve them, or to acquire more; and he is, by so much the more engaged, to perform the Duties of Society, as he is exposed to the Eyes of Envy.

And to pass from the Particular, to the General. The Luxury of a Nation, is confined to a thousand Men, relatively to twenty Million of others, who are as happy as they, when a good Polity makes them enjoy, in Quiet, the Fruit of their Labour. If Plowmen or Artificers, riot in Luxury, it must be supported, by the additional Labour of the Plowmen and

---

1. [The War of the Spanish Succession (1701–14).]

Artificers. This will always form a Circle, which rendereth Luxury, little to be feared, in a Nation.

Luxury may indeed be hurtful in War, by a great Train of Equipages, and Servants, who may incumber and occasion a Scarcity in the Army. For this Reason, the military Ordinance regulates the Equipages of the principal Officers: And the General, in some Cases, restrains them yet further; as Water is distributed by Measure, in a Siege, or in a Ship detained at Sea. In these Cases, it would be of Use to have fewer Men, but in the general Polity of a State, there cannot be too many.

Perhaps it is owing to Luxury, that Drunkeness, which is much more hurtful to Body and Mind, is not now so common, in Towns, and in the Army, as it was formerly.[2] Indeed, it seemeth to have retired into the Country, where Luxury is not yet arrived.

In a Common-wealth, where the Territory is of small Extent, and the People are obliged, in a great Measure, to live by their Labour, most Things are deemed Luxury. It is, but of late, that a Fiddle hath been admitted into * * *,[3] where it hath given great Offence, to the antient People, who complain, that all is lost. This resembleth rather a Community of Recluses, than a Society of Freemen. Accordingly, when a Citizen hath acquired a larger Fortune, than he is permitted to expend, he removeth to a Place where he can enjoy it with Freedom, and he depriveth his Country of his Person, and his Effects. In another Republick,[4] where Musick, and the Licentiousness of Women bear Sway, there are sumptuary Laws, restrained to the City only. Some say, that Luxury is allowed in the Country, in order to ruin the Citizens; others will have it, that it is prohibited in the City, to enrich these same Citizens. Uncertainty will always happen in Politicks, when they are not reduced to their plain and general Principles, which are susceptible, of all the Demonstration that Morality can admit.

Bread, is of absolute Necessity, and woollen Manufactures, are of second Necessity: But the white Bread, and the fine Cloth, introduced by

---

2. Drunkeness, is no part of *French* Luxury. It were to be wished, that we could make the same Observation with respect to *Ireland.*

3. [Geneva.]

4. [Probably Venice.]

Monsieur *Colbert*, would appear, as the highest Luxury, if we were not daily accustomed to make Use of them. The Term Luxury is an idle Name, which should never be employed, in Considerations on Polity, and Commerce: Because it conveyeth uncertain, confused, and false Ideas, the misapplication whereof, might stop Industry in its very Source.

When, in the last War,[5] the Privateers of our maritime Towns, returned home, laden with the Spoils of the Enemy, and displayed their Opulency, by extraordinary Profusions; every one strove, to fit out more Ships, in hopes of gaining wherewithal to support, the like Expences. This Incitement, produced the great Services, the Privateers performed to the State, and the astonishing Actions of the *Buccaniers*. If they had returned from those Expeditions, with empty Honour only, in common with that of all Soldiers and Sailors, can it be imagined, they would have gone again to Sea? Or that Emulation, would have excited others to follow them? Rigid *Sparta* was neither more conquering, nor better governed, nor did it produce greater Men, than voluptuous *Athens*. There are but four *Lacedemonians*, and there are seven *Athenians*, among the illustrious Men, whose Lives are wrote by *Plutarch*, without reckoning, *Socrates* and *Plato* who are omitted.

The sumptuary Laws of *Licurgus*, deserve no more Regard, than his other Institutions, which are so shocking to Modesty. How could he expect that the Members of his Community, who had no Knowledge of future Rewards, could support the ambitious Spirit of Acquisition, through a thousand Hardships, and a thousand Dangers, without the Hopes of augmenting their Portion, or diminishing their Labour? Glory alone, without those Advantages, which are inseparable from a happy Existence, is not a sufficient Spur for the Multitude. It would be ridiculous to form a Project to make all *France*, live in common. Would not such a Project be attributed, to a Genius, that had never passed, the Limits of a Village.

CATO, the great Advocate for sumptuary Laws among the *Romans*, being bred up in Villages, had acquired the Manners of them. He is represented to us, as an avaritious and intemperate Man; even as an Usurer and a Drunkard. The sumptuous *Lucullus*, a greater Commander, and as just a Man as he, was always liberal and beneficent. The Reformer, who

5. [The War of the Spanish Succession (1701–14).]

by the Severity of his Way, would also render Life more severe, may perhaps be revered by the Populace, but he will be slighted by wise Men,
who make it their Rule, to procure Ease and Comfort to Society.

Our sumptuary Laws have diminished, in proportion as our Polity
hath grown more perfect. There were only three or four made in the
Reign of the late King,[6] and they were concerning too rich Stuffs, and
too costly Works of Gold and Silver, and foreign Laces: And even these
Laws, as well as those made by his Predecessors, have been very seldom
carried into Execution. For, before they had put a Stop to one fashionable Luxury, Commerce introduced another, still greater, which made
the first to be easily forgotten. Thus Luxuries cannot subsist, but so long
as they are relative to Commerce.

We will mention some of those Ordinances, to shew how needless
they were, and what kind of Spirit directed the making of them.

CHARLEMAGNE forbids the wearing a *Sayon* of greater Value, than
twenty *Sols*, and a *Rochet* worth above thirty. The *Abbé de Vertot*, in-
formeth us, from the Treatise of Polity, wrote by *la Marre*,[7] that the
Sayon, was a *Vest*, over which the *Rochet* was wore. Thus the Coat and
Vest cost fifty *Sols*, which, according to the Encrease of the nominal
Value of Money, make the Weight of one hundred and eighty *Livres*, at
this Time. And if the Quantity of Money, at that time, be compared with
what it is at present, it may make a Sum ten times greater.

In *Fontanon*'s Collection of Ordinances, there is one, that limiteth,
"the largeness of Breeches, at two thirds in Compass, and above all the
Lining to be without Pockets, and not stuffed out with Horse-hair, Cotton, Flocks, or Wooll." And, with regard to the Frugality of Tables, it
was directed, "that there should not be, at Weddings, or Feasts, above
three Courses, of six Dishes each, and one Dish not to be double, that is
to say two Capons, or two Partridges, but there might be three Pidgeons,
or the Equivalent, as twelve Larks, &c. Prohibition to all Cooks to serve
up more, upon pain of a Fine, &c."[8]

That might, at least, regulate the Number of Guests for one Table. A

---

6. [I.e., Louis XIV.]

7. [Nicolas de La Mare (1639–1723), *Traité de la police* (Paris: Cot, 1705; repr. 1975).]

8. [Antoine Fontanon, *Les edicts et ordonnances des rois de France depuis Louis VI* (Paris:
Du Puys, 1585).]

Roman Tribune, regulated their Number to be, from three to nine. *Augustus* made a Law to allow twelve Guests, in Honour of the twelve great Divinities of *Paganism.* It is not worth while to relate so many trifling Things, and it is much less so, to search for, and examine them, in their first Source.

There was, in the Days of *Charles* V. a sort of Shoes, called *a la Poulaine,* the Toes of which, being very long, gave Occasion to People of fine Taste to contrive several Ornaments upon them, as Horns, Claws, and Nails. The Church cried out loudly against this Fashion, as being contrary to the Order of Nature, and disfiguring Man, in this Part of him. The Church condemned it, at the Council of *Paris,* in the Year 1212, and at the Council of *Angiers,* in the Year 1365, and in the Year 1368. King *Charles* suppressed them by Letters Patent, of which this is the Tenor.

"Prohibition to all Persons, of what Quality or Condition soever, upon pain of forfeiting ten *Florins,* to wear, hereafter, Shoes *a la Poulaine;* this Superfluity, being contrary to good Manners, in Derision of God, and the Church, through worldly Vanity, and extravagant Presumption." The Dates of the two Councils, and of the King's Ordinance, shew, that this Fashion lasted above one hundred and fifty Years. This Example, peculiar to our Nation, may give Room to suspect there was something more genteel in these kind of Shoes, than is represented. The Beak of Womens Shoes, hath, probably been saved, out of the general Shipwreck of the Shoes *a la Poulaine.*

Let us see at what Expence, Luxury was banished the Nation, during the first Race of our Kings. It is the *Abbe de Vertot,* who speaketh.[9] "A free, but savage Life; Ferocity of Manners, little Commerce with civiliz'd Nations, Ignorance of the Conveniencies of Life, contributed to keep Luxury from their Cottages; and we cannot form to our selves, a clearer, or more perfect Idea of those early Times, than by comparing them, with the kind of Life now led by the *Hurons,* and *Iroquois.*"[10] Yet the Author could not forbear, in the very same Dissertation, to declaim against Luxury.

---

9. [Abbé de Vertot (1655–1735), *Histoire des revolutions arrivées dans le gouvernement de la République romaine* (Paris: F. Barois, 1719).]

10. Let us observe, in this Place, that the Common People of *Ireland,* live in as wretched a Way, as the *Gauls* did during the first Race of their Kings. And as it is allowed,

The Degrees, are well enough distinguished, between the different Kinds of Necessities, and the Legislat[or] may very well rely thereupon. Workmen, will not be employed about Works for Luxury, until there be enough of the Commodities of second Necessity; and, in like manner, they will not be employed about these, until the Products of absolute Necessity, be fully supplied. There are twenty Million of Persons, who buy Bread; fewer Buyers of Stuffs; and yet fewer Purchasers of Linnen: And the Peasant doth not purchase Wine or Tobacco, until his more pressing Wants are satisfied.

What Matter is it to a State, if, through a foolish Vanity, a particular Person ruineth himself, by vying with his Neighbour, in Equipage? It is a Punishment he well deserveth. And Workmen, who are much more to be valued than he, are maintained thereby. What is said of a particular Person, may be applyed to a Family, and even to a Merchant, who is so imprudent, as to give a Credit, equally dangerous to both Parties, until the Law hath provided, for the speedy Payment of Debts. In a Regulation of K. *Charles* IX. for Moderation in Clothes, it is said, in the XVI Article. "And forasmuch as, the getting of Stuffs made of Silk upon Trust, hath encouraged People to run into those kinds of Superfluities in Dress, we enjoin all our Judges to refuse all Kinds of Process to Merchants, who, after Publication of these Presents, shall sell Stuffs made of Silk, upon Trust, to any Person whatsoever."

Is it the Business of the Legislat[or], to stop Industry by such a Law, to put a Restraint upon Liberty, reduce Workmen into dangerous Idleness, and take away a new Motive to Labour? Whatever is, in it self pernicious, should be always prohibited; but the Inconvenience that may follow from a Law, which is good in it self, ought to have no Weight with the Legislator. He acts, without respect of Persons, and what he doth, tends to the wel-fare of the greater Number. Why are the Laws against Duelling made so severe, as to extend even to the Punishing of a Person,

---

that the creating of Wants, is the likeliest Way to produce Industry in a People; and that, if our Peasants were accustomed to eat Beef, and wear Shoes, they would be more industrious; it seems to be the Business of all those, who wish to see this Country thrive, to procure comfortable Living among the lower Rank of People; and those of superior Degrees, will soon find the Benefit of it. To provide plentifully for the Poor, is to feed the Root, the Substance whereof, will shoot into the Branches and cause the Top to flourish.

who hath received the greatest Offence, but with an Intent to save the Lives of a greater Number of Persons.

The excessive Price paid for some trifling Provisions, which the Luxurious Man displayeth with Profusion, at an Entertainment, the Merit whereof, he would have to consist in the Expensiveness of it, is an Instance of the highest, and most ridiculous Kind of Luxury, and yet, why should this extravagant Expence be exclaimed against? The Money thus earned, would, if it lay in the Chest of the Luxurious Man, remain Dead to the Society. The Gardiner receiveth it, and hath deserved it, as a Recompence for his Labour, which is thereby excited again. His Children, almost naked, are thereby clothed; they eat Bread in Plenty, enjoy better Health, and labour with a cheerful Expectation. The same Money given to Beggars, would only serve to feed their Idleness and Debaucheries.

God forbid we should compare such a Manner of expending Sums of Money, with the great Motives of Charity, which giveth Assistance to shame-fac'd Poverty, and to Hospitals! Every other Virtue giveth Way, to this, the greatest of all Virtues, and which is always accompanied by Justice and Decency.[11] But, as we have already said, Men, are very rarely guided by the Rules of Religion. It is the Part of Religion, to endeavour to destroy Luxury, and it is the Business of the State, to make an Advantage of it: And when we mentioned frivolous Declamations, we did not mean the Declamations which are made from the Pulpit, but those which resemble the Satyrs of the Pagans.

There are some other Motives to Luxury of a lower Nature, which the Legislat[or] might likewise make Advantage of. A Man, who layeth out Money in building and adorning a magnificent Palace, doth nothing that is contrary to the State, or to Morality: But he cannot expect to have Honours paid him by the Publick, for so doing, because what he doth, is only for his own private Use. But he, who repaireth a High-Road, or buildeth Fountains, Aquaeducts and the like, would deserve honourable Marks of his Beneficence, by Statues, or by some other Distinctions, which might excite a new Emulation among the People.

Publick Shews, cannot be too great, too magnificent, or too frequent.

11. [*Bienfaisance,* or "beneficence".]

It is a kind of Traffick, whereby *France,* always maketh Advantage, and never loseth.

Luxury ought not to be confounded with the wearing of the *Indian* Goods, prohibited by the *Council of Trade;* For this Prohibition, is not so much, on Account of the Richness of those Goods, as to encourage the Consumption of much richer Stuffs of our own Manufacture.

We ought to believe this Prohibition to be useful, because it is so constantly continued, and perhaps upon good Experience. But the Way it is executed, is attended with so many Contrarieties, that one is at a Loss to know, what to think of it. The *Company of the Indies,* hath the sole Right of importing these Goods, and is not allowed to sell them, but in order to be carried to foreign Countries: And this is executed, at least in Appearance: For what Goods are found contrary to this Law, are publickly burnt.

And nevertheless, those Goods are to be met with every where. This must be, by Means of our Neighbours; and thus, they gain the Advantage of this rich Commerce, of which we have all the Trouble, by long and dangerous Voyages; And to which, the poor fraudulent Dealers, half tollerated and half punished, become at length the Victims.

The Alternative is evident. The Use of these Goods, is either of Advantage, or Disadvantage to us. In the first Case, let them be allowed, and we shall have them in Plenty, and enjoy the Profits of them. In the other Case, execute the Law with Rigour, and we shall reap the Benefit of the Prohibition, by the Consumption of our own Manufactures. If, by a Distinction more subtil, than solid, it is believed there must be a certain Quantity, to supply what Manufactures of our own, may be wanting, let the Quantity be determined, at more, or at less, and let our own People sell that Quantity. To say, that this is impracticable, must proceed from not knowing the force of Laws.

Stuffs, and Linnens, serve for clothing, and their Beauty and Fineness, seem to make them more convenient; but, Diamonds serve only, to dress up a Head, or to incumber a Finger with a vain Lustre. They do not stand in the Place of any Product of our Labour, or make up for the Want of any Merchandize. The fine Diamonds, which are of an excessive Price, can scarcely be distinguished from our false Stones. Diamonds are brought from very distant Countries, and we pay Silver for them: But we do not go on Purpose, and at great Expence, to seek them. It is a part of general Commerce, and Diamonds make a new Value of Circulation, which is received through all the World.

The Sovereign, who possesseth the Diamond Mines, hath not Men enough to defend his Territories, neither against his Neighbours, nor against the *European* Settlements. It is to him, that the Diamond Mines are hurtful. He employeth in them, thirty thousand Men, whose Days are shortned by this painful Labour, and who might be more usefully employed as Soldiers or Plowmen.

The Diamonds lately discovered in the *Brazils,* will, more certainly, beat down the Value of those of *India,* than they will encrease the Riches of that Colony. The Price of Diamonds must necessarily decrease, because their Quantity encreaseth and is not consumed. Sugars, and other Provisions, must keep up to a Price, because the annual Consumption of them encreaseth, in Proportion to their Produce.

16

"The Worldling"
1736

FRANÇOIS-MARIE AROUET, known from an early age as Voltaire, was born in Paris in 1694. Though he was primarily a playwright, poet, and writer (he described himself in his autobiography as the author of *La Henriade,* an epic poem on the French King Henry IV), he turned increasingly in his later years to questions of social and political reform. Although he is most famous for his interventions on matters of religious toleration such as the case of Calas (1760s), his writings also embraced questions of economic and financial policy. In the *Lettres anglaises* (*Philosophical Letters*) of 1732, the *Dictionnaire philosophique* (*Philosophical Dictionary*) of 1764, and *L'homme aux quarante écus* (*Man of Forty Crowns*) of 1768, for example, he expressed some of his views on these topics.

By 1778, Voltaire had become the leading literary and intellectual figure in France, arguably in Europe, and was welcomed triumphantly back to Paris for the first time in nearly thirty years, shortly before his death.

The works included here are "Le Mondain" (literally, "The man of the world," translated here as "The Worldling") and "La Défense du mondain" (translated here as "The Man of the World"), from 1736 and 1738, as well as "Sur le luxe et le commerce" (translated here as "On Commerce and Luxury"), also from 1738. I use *The Works of Voltaire,* edited by Tobias Smollett and translated by William Fleming (New York: E. R. Du Mont, 1901), 42 vols. "The Worldling" appears in volume 36, pp. 84–88. Bracketed notes are by the present editor; unbracketed ones are from the Smollett edition.

The Worldling.[1]

Others may with regret complain
That 'tis not fair Astrea's[2] reign,
That the famed golden age is o'er
That Saturn, Rhea rule no more:
Or, to speak in another style,
That Eden's groves no longer smile.
For my part, I thank Nature sage,
That she has placed me in this age:
Religionists may rail in vain;
I own, I like this age profane;
I love the pleasures of a court;
I love the arts of every sort;
Magnificence, fine buildings, strike me;
In this, each man of sense is like me.
I have, I own, a worldly mind,
That's pleased abundance here to find;
Abundance, mother of all arts,
Which with new wants new joys imparts
The treasures of the earth and main,
With all the creatures they contain:
These, luxury and pleasures raise;
This iron age brings happy days.

---

1. This poem was written in 1736. It is a piece of humor founded upon philosophy and the public good.
2. [Roman goddess of justice who presided over a golden age.]

Needful superfluous things appear;
They have joined together either sphere.
See how that fleet, with canvas wings,
From Texel, Bordeaux, London brings,
By happy commerce to our shores,
All Indus, and all Ganges stores;
Whilst France, that pierced the Turkish lines,
Sultans make drunk with rich French wines.
Just at the time of Nature's birth,
Dark ignorance o'erspread the earth;
None then in wealth surpassed the rest,
For naught the human race possessed.
Of clothes, their bodies then were bare,
They nothing had, and could not share:
Then too they sober were and sage,
Martialo[3] lived not in that age.
Eve, first formed by the hand divine,
Never so much as tasted wine.
Do you our ancestors admire,
Because they wore no rich attire?
Ease was like wealth to them unknown,
Was't virtue? ignorance alone.
Would any fool, had he a bed,
On the bare ground have laid his head?
My fruit-eating first father, say,
In Eden how rolled time away?
Did you work for the human race,
And clasp dame Eve with close embrace!
Own that your nails you could not pare,
And that you wore disordered hair,
That you were swarthy in complexion,
And that your amorous affection
Had very little better in't
Than downright animal instinct.

3. The author of a treatise entitled "The French Cook."

Both weary of the marriage yoke
You supped each night beneath an oak
On millet, water, and on mast,
And having finished your repast,
On the ground you were forced to lie,
Exposed to the inclement sky:
Such in the state of simple nature
Is man, a helpless, wretched creature.
Would you know in this cursed age,
Against which zealots so much rage,
To what men blessed with taste attend
In cities, how their time they spend?
The arts that charm the human mind
All at his house a welcome find;
In building it, the architect
No grace passed over with neglect.
To adorn the rooms, at once combine
Poussin, Correggio the divine,[4]
Their works on every panel placed
Are in rich golden frames incased.
His statues show Bouchardon's skill,[5]
Plate of Germain, his sideboards fill.
The Gobelin tapestry, whose dye
Can with the painter's pencil vie,
With gayest coloring appear
As ornaments on every pier.
From the superb salon are seen
Gardens with Cyprian myrtle green.
I see the sporting waters rise
By jets d'eau[6] almost to the skies.
But see the master's self approach

4. [Nicolas Poussin (1594–1665) and Antonio Correggio (c. 1490–1534) were famous painters.]
5. [Edmé Bouchardon (1698–1762) was a classical sculptor.]
6. [I.e., bursts of water.]

And mount into his gilded coach,
A house in motion, to the eyes
It seems as through the streets it flies.
I see him through transparent glasses
Loll at his ease as on he passes.
Two pliant and elastic springs
Carry him like a pair of wings.
At Bath, his polished skin inhales
Perfumes, sweet as Arabian gales.
Camargot[7] at the approach of night
Julia, Goffin by turns invite.
Love kind and bounteous on him pours
Of choicest favors plenteous showers.
To the opera house he must repair,
Dance, song and music charm him there.
The painter's art to strike the sight,
Does there with that blest art unite;
The yet more soft, persuasive skill,
Which can the soul with pleasure thrill.
He may to damn an opera go,
And yet perforce admire Rameau.[8]
The cheerful supper next invites
To luxury's less refined delights.
How exquisite those sauces flavor!
Of those ragouts I like the savor.
The man who can in cookery shine,
May well be deemed a man divine.
Chloris[9] and Aegle at each course
Serve me with wine, whose mighty force
Makes the cork from the bottle fly
Like lightning darting from the sky.
Bounce! to the ceiling it ascends,

---

7. [Marie-Anne Cupis de Camargo (1710–70) was a famous ballerina.]
8. [Jean-Philippe Rameau (1683–1764) was an influential music theorist and composer.]
9. [Chloris was a nymph who was transformed into the goddess Flora.]

And laughter the apartment rends.
In this froth, just observers see
The emblem of French vivacity.
The following day new joys inspires,
It brings new pleasures and desires.
Mentor, Telemachus[10] descant
Upon frugality, and vaunt
Your Ithaca and your Salentum
To ancient Greeks, since they content them:
Since Greeks in abstinence could find
Ample supplies of every kind.
The work, though not replete with fire,
I for its elegance admire:
But I'll be whipped Salentum through
If thither I my bliss pursue.
Garden of Eden, much renowned,
Since there the devil and fruit were found.
Huetius, Calmet,[11] learned and bold,
Inquired where Eden lay of old:
I am not so critically nice,
Paris to me's a paradise.

10. [Telemachus was Odysseus's son; Mentor was his wise counselor.]
    11. [Pierre-Daniel Huet (1630–1721) was a prolific scholar of Church history; Augustin Calmet (1672–1757) was a Benedictine biblical scholar.]

17

"The Man of the World"
1738

THIS POEM is an "apology for luxury" written by Voltaire (see headnote to chapter 16). The edition used here is *The Works of Voltaire,* edited by Tobias Smollett and translated by William Fleming, 42 vols. (New York: E. R. Du Mont, 1901), 36:170–74. Bracketed notes are by the present editor; unbracketed ones are from the Smollett edition.

The Man of the World[1]

An Apology for Luxury

At dinner, 'twas one day my case
By a rank bigot to have place,
Who said, I on it might depend
That hell would have me in the end;
And he an angel heaven's host in

1. This piece was written as a defense of the "Mondain" (see "The Worldling"), which had been prosecuted.

Would loudly laugh to see me roasting.
Roasting for what? "Why for your crimes;
You've told us in some impious rhymes
That Adam, ere the days of sin,
Was oft with rain wet to the skin;
That he his time most dully spent,
Ate fruit, and drank the element;
That he his nails could never pare;
And that he was not over fair.
You Epicurus' doctrine[2] teach,
And for luxurious pleasures preach."
Having these words in passion said,
He swallowed wine like amber red;
Wine, which by its taste confessed
The grape from whence the juice was pressed.
And I, while crimson stained his face,
Addressed the saint brimful of grace:
"Religious sir, whence comes this wine?
I own its gusto is divine."
"This wine is from Canary brought,"
Said he, "and should be nectar thought;
It is in every respect
A liquor fit for the elect."
"That coffee which when full refection
The feast has given, so helps digestion,
Whence comes it?" "It from heaven descended,
A gift by God for me intended."
"But sure 'twas in Arabia sought
By men, and thence with trouble brought.
Both porcelain and chinaware
For you men labor to prepare;
'Twas baked, and with a thousand dyes
Diversified, to please your eyes;
That silver, where such art's displayed,

2. [I.e., that pleasure is the highest good.]

Of which cups, salvers, plates are made,
Which with mild lustre faintly shines,
Was dug from Potosi's rich mines.[3]
For thee the world at work has been,
That thou at ease might vent thy spleen
Against that world, which for thy pleasure
Has quite exhausted all its treasure.
Thou real worldling, learn to know
Thyself, and some indulgence show
To others, whom so much you blame
For vices, whilst you have the same.
Know luxury, which destroys a state
That's poor, enriches one that's great;
That pomp and splendor deemed so vain,
Are proofs still of a prosperous reign.
The rich can spend his ample store;
The poor is grasping still at more.
On you cascades now fix your sight,
In them the Naiads[4] take delight;
See how those floods of water roam
Covering the marble with a foam.
These waves give moisture to the fields,
Earth beautified more rich crops yields.
But should this source be once decayed,
The grass would wither, flowers would fade.
Thus wealth, in France and Britain's states,
Through various channels circulates.
Excess prevails, the great are vain,
Their follies oft the poor maintain;
And Industry, whom opulence hires,
To riches by slow steps aspires.
I hear a staunch, pedantic train
Of pleasure's ill effects complain,

3. [Potosi: Southern Bolivian site of silver discoveries in the sixteenth century.]
4. [Naiads, freshwater nymphs.]

Who Dionysius, Dion cite,
Plutarch and Horace the polite,[5]
And cry that Curius, and a score
Of consuls ending in 'us' more,
Tilled the earth during war's alarms,
And managed both the plow and arms;
That corn which flourished in the land,
Was sown by a victorious hand.
'Tis well, sirs, and I am content
To such relations to assent.
But tell me, should the gods incite
Auteuil against Vaugirard to fight,[6]
Must not the victor from the field
Returning home his land have tilled?
Rome the august was heretofore
A hole like Auteuil, nothing more.
When those chiefs, from god Mars descended,
Attacked a meadow or defended,
When to the field they took their way,
Their standard was a truss of hay.[7]
Jove's image wooden under Tullus
Was beaten gold when lived Lucullus.[8]
Then don't bestow fair virtue's prize
On what from poverty had rise.
France flourished by wise Colbert's[9] care,
When once a dunce, intent to spare,
Presumed the progress to oppose
Of arts, by which famed Lyons rose,

---

5. [Dionysius or Bacchus, god of joy and of wine; Plutarch (46?–?120) and Horace (65–8 B.C.) were known for their sobriety.]

6. [Perhaps a reference to two neighborhoods in Paris.]

7. A handful of hay at the end of a pole, called Manipulus, was the first standard of the Romans.

8. [May refer to Tullus, King of Rome c. 665 B.C. Lucullus (c. 110–56 B.C.) was a Roman general noted for the extravagance of his retirement.]

9. [Jean-Baptiste Colbert (1621–83), leading royal minister under Louis XIV, 1661–83.]

And by cursed avarice possessed
Had industry and arts suppressed;
That minister, as wise as great,
By luxury enriched the state.
He the great source of arts increased,
From north to south, from west to east.
Our neighbors all with envy fired
Paid dear for genius they admired.
A monarch's portrait here I'll draw,
Rome, Paris, Pekin, such ne'er saw;
'Tis Solomon, that king who shone
A Plato, while he filled a throne;
Who all things was to know allowed,
From hyssop to the cedar proud;
In luxury he surpassed mankind,
With glittering gold his palace shined.
All various pleasures he could taste,
A thousand beauties he embraced.
With beauties he was well supplied;
Give me but one, I'm satisfied.
One's full enough for me; but I
Cannot with sage or monarch vie."
Thus speaking, I perceived each guest
To approve of my discourse professed.
Sir Piety no more replied,
But, laughing, still the bottle plied.
While all, who well knew what I meant,
Seemed to my reasons to assent.

18

"On Commerce and Luxury"
1738

THIS ESSAY is Voltaire's contribution to the public controversy over the Law system that broke out in the late 1730s, especially after the publication of Melon's 1734 essay (see chapter 15). The edition used here is *The Works of Voltaire*, edited by Tobias Smollett and translated by William Fleming, 42 vols. (New York: E. R. Du Mont, 1901), 37:211–18. Bracketed notes are by the present editor; unbracketed ones are from the Smollett edition.

On Commerce and Luxury

Within the last twenty years commerce has been better understood in France than it had ever before been, from the reign of Pharamond to that of Louis XIV.[1] Before this period it was a secret art, a kind of chemistry in the hands of three or four persons, who actually made gold, but without communicating the secret by which they had been enriched. The

1. [Pharamond, a legendary Frankish chieftain; Louis XIV (1638–1715), King of France.]

body of the nation were in such profound ignorance of this important secret that we had neither minister nor magistrate that knew what the words "annuities," "principal," "exchange," or "dividend" meant. It was destined that a Scotchman called John Law[2] should come into France and overturn the whole economy of our government to instruct us. He had the courage, in the most horrible confusion of our finances, and in the time of a most dreadful famine, to establish a bank and an India company. This was giving a vomit to the sick; we took too much, and convulsions were the consequence: but, at length, from the ruins of his system, we had left us an India company, with a capital amounting to the sum of fifty millions of livres. What had been the case had we taken a moderate dose of that salutary medicine? In my opinion, the state had certainly been the most vigorous and powerful in the whole world.

There prevailed still among us, at the time when the present India company was established, a prejudice so very strong that the Sorbonne declared the sharing of dividends of actions usurious. In the same manner the German printers, who came to establish their art in France, were, in 1570, accused of witchcraft.

We Frenchmen, there is no denying it, have come very late into everything. Our first steps in the arts have been to thwart the introduction of those truths which came to us from abroad: we defended theses against the circulation of the blood, after it had been demonstrated in England; against the revolution of the earth, which had been made evident in Germany; not even the most salutary remedies have escaped being proscribed by an arret. To discover any new truths, to propose anything of general use to mankind is a sure step to persecution. John Law, that Scotchman to whom we owe our India company, and all we know of commerce, was driven out of France, and died in misery at Venice; and yet, although we had scarcely three hundred merchant ships of any burden when he proposed his system, we have now—in 1738—over eighteen hundred. Though we owe them all to him, we are yet exceedingly ungrateful to the memory of our benefactor.

The principles of commerce are known at present to all the world: we are beginning to have good books on that subject. The essay "*Sur le*

2. [See chapter 9 in this volume.]

Commerce," of Melon, is the work of a man of sense, a good citizen, and an excellent philosopher:[3] it has a tincture of the spirit of his age; and I do not think that even in the time of M. Colbert, there were two persons in France capable of producing such a work. There are, however, a number of errors in that excellent book; so great progress as he has made in the road to truth was no easy matter: it is a service done to the public to point out the mistakes that happen in a useful book. It is indeed in such only we should look for them. It is showing respect to a good work to contradict it; a bad one does not deserve that honor.

The following observations are such as seem contrary to truth:

1. He says those countries in which are the greatest number of beggars are the most barbarous. I believe there is no city more civilized than Paris, and where at the same time there are more beggars. This is a vermin that attach themselves to riches; the drones run from the extremities of the kingdom to Paris, in order to lay opulence and good nature under contribution. This is an abuse difficult to root out, but which proves only that there are wretches in such a country, who prefer begging to getting their livelihood by honest industry. This may be a proof of wealth and negligence, but by no means of barbarity.

2. He repeats in several places that Spain would be more powerful without America. He grounds his observations on the depopulation of Spain, and on the weakness under which that state has long languished. This notion of America weakening Spain is to be met with in a hundred different authors. But had they given themselves the trouble to reflect that the treasures of America were the cement of the power of Charles V., and that by their means Philip II. would have been master of Europe, if Henry the Great, Elizabeth, and the princes of Orange had not been heroes, those authors would have been of a different way of thinking.[4] It has been imagined that the Spanish monarchy has been in a manner annihilated, because their kings Philip III., Philip IV., and Charles II. were either unfortunate or weak princes.[5] But let us see how this monarchy has

---

3. [See chapter 15 in this volume.]

4. [Charles V, Habsburg Emperor (r. 1519–55); Philip II, King of Spain (r. 1555–98); Henry IV, King of France (r. 1589–1610); Queen Elizabeth I of Great Britain (r. 1558–1603); the princes of Orange ruled the Dutch state.]

5. [Philip III (r. 1598–1621), Philip IV (r. 1621–65), Charles II (r. 1665–1700).]

resumed new life under Cardinal Alberoni;[6] let us cast our eyes toward Africa and Italy, those theatres of the conquests of the present Spanish government, and we shall be forced to own that nations are just what kings and ministers make them. Courage, fortitude, industry, every talent remains buried till some great genius appears, who rouses and sets them in motion. The capitol is at present inhabited by Recollets, and chaplets are now distributed on the spot where vanquished kings followed the chariot of Paulus Aemilius.[7] Let but an emperor take up his residence in Rome, and let this emperor be a Julius Caesar, every Roman will become a Caesar with him.

As to the depopulation of Spain, it is not nearly so great as what it is given out to be: and even after all, this kingdom, and the states of America depending on it, are at this time so many provinces of the same empire, which are separated only by a space that may be sailed over in two months. In a word, their treasures become ours, by a necessary and unavoidable circulation. Their cochineal, their quinine, their mines of Mexico and Peru, are ours, and by the same means our manufactures are Spanish. Had America been a burden to them, is it to be thought they would have persisted so long in denying admittance into that country to strangers? Do people preserve with so much care the principle and source of ruin, after having had two hundred years to consider it?

3. He says that the loss of their soldiers is not the most fatal consequence in their wars; that a hundred thousand men are a very small number in comparison to twenty millions; but that an increase of taxes renders twenty millions of persons miserable. I will grant him twenty millions of souls in France; but I will not admit that it is better to have a hundred thousand soldiers cut to pieces than to put the rest of the nation to an additional expense in taxes. This is not all; here is a strange and fatal miscalculation. Louis XIV. had, reckoning the whole body of the marine, four hundred and forty thousand men in pay during the war in 1701.[8] The Roman Empire never had such a numerous army on foot. It has been observed that about one-fifth of an army is destroyed by the end

6. [Julio Cardinal Alberoni (1664–1752), leading official under Philip V.]
7. [Paulus Aemilius, consul in 168 B.C., when he defeated Perseus, King of Macedonia.]
8. [War of the Spanish Succession.]

of a campaign by disease, accidents, fire, and sword. Here then are eighty-eight thousand men destroyed each year; therefore, at the expiration of ten years, the state has lost eight hundred and eighty thousand men, together with all the children they would have procreated in that time. At present, if France contains about eighteen millions of souls, take away about one-half for the women, together with all the old men, the children, the clergy, the monks, the magistrates, and those who are necessary to carry on manufactures and to till the ground, what number remains for the defence of the nation? In eighteen millions you will hardly find eighteen hundred thousand men, and the war in ten years is supposed to have destroyed nearly nine hundred thousand. Thus the war destroys one-half a nation's men capable of bearing arms in her defence; and you say a new impost is more disastrous to a nation than the death of so many of her best people.

After correcting these inadvertencies, which the author would have corrected himself, permit me to consider what he has advanced on freedom of commerce, on manufactures, on exchange, and chiefly with regard to luxury. This wise apology for luxury is by so much the more estimable in this author, and has so much the more force from his mouth, as his life was that of a philosopher.[9]

What then is luxury? It is a word without any precise idea, much such another expression as when we say the eastern and western hemispheres: in fact, there is no such thing as east and west; there is no fixed point where the earth rises and sets; or, if you will, every point on it is at the same time east and west. It is the same with regard to luxury; for either there is no such thing, or else it is in all places alike. Lead us back to those times when our grandfathers wore no shirts. Had anyone told them that they must wear finer and lighter stuffs than the finest cloth, white as snow, and must change them every day; and even after they were a little dirty must, with a composition prepared with great art, restore them to their former lustre; everybody would cry out, "What luxury! What effeminacy! Such a magnificence as this is hardly sufferable in a king. You want to corrupt our manners and ruin the nation." Do they understand by luxury the expense of an opulent person? Must he then live like the poor, he whose

9. [Melon's chapter on luxury is chapter 15 in the present volume.]

profusion alone is sufficient to maintain the poor? Expensiveness should be the thermometer of a private man's fortune, as general luxury is the infallible mark of a powerful and flourishing empire. It was under Charlemagne, Francis I., and under the ministry of the great Colbert,[10] and the present administration, that men lived at the greatest expense; that is to say, that the arts were encouraged and cultivated.

What would the tart, the satirical la Bruyére[11] be at? What means this affected misanthrope, by crying out: "Our ancestors knew not what it was to prefer taste to utility; they were never known to light themselves with waxen tapers; this was a commodity reserved for the altar and the royal palace. They were never heard to say: 'Let my horses be put to my coach'; good pewter shone on their tables and side-boards; their silver was laid up in their coffers," etc. Is not this a very pleasant eulogium of our forefathers, to say they had neither taste, industry, neatness, nor plenty? Their silver was laid up in their coffers. Were this really true, it was certainly the greatest folly imaginable. Money is made for circulation, to bring the secrets of art to light, and to purchase the industry and labors of men: he who hoards it is a bad citizen, and even a bad economist. It is by circulating it that we render ourselves useful to our country and to ourselves. Will men never grow weary of commending the follies of antiquity, with a view to ridicule the advantages of our own times?

This work of Melon has produced another by M. Dutot,[12] which is preferable, both in point of depth and justness of reasoning. This work of M. Dutot is likely to give birth to another, which will probably carry the palm from both the others, as it is the production of a statesman. Never was the study of the belles-lettres so closely connected with that of the revenues, which is an additional merit in the age in which we live.

10. [Charlemagne (742–814), Holy Roman Emperor; Francis I (r. 1515–47), King of France; Jean-Baptiste Colbert (1619–83), finance minister under Louis XIV.]

11. [Jean de La Bruyère (1645–96), *Charactères* (1688–96).]

12. [Dutot, *Réflexions politiques sur les finances et le commerce* (La Haye: V. & A. Prevost, 1738), 2 vols.]

19

Spectacle of Nature
1746

Noël-Antoine Pluche was born in 1688. After completing his studies, he became a professor first of humanities, then of rhetoric in his hometown of Rheims, before taking holy orders. The Bishop of Laon made him director of the *collège* (secondary school), an offer he accepted partly to escape the controversy that arose around him for his refusal to swear adherence to the bull *Unigenitus* (1713). After a *lettre de cachet*° was prepared against him, he was provided with private tutorial positions by both Gasville (royal intendant of Rouen) and the Englishman Lord Stafford. After a chance discovery of information useful to the Crown, he was offered a lucrative priory by Cardinal Fleury—which he refused on principle because of his continued refusal to sign *Unigenitus*. Still, his teachings and writings began to gain some notoriety. He became deaf, retired in 1749 to Varenne-Saint-Maur, and died of apoplexy in 1761.

His major work, *Spectacle de la nature*, was an eight-volume study of life and creation that was translated into virtually all European languages, still appearing in abridged editions in the early nineteenth century. His other works include *Histoire du ciel* (1739), *La Méchanique des langues* (1751), and *Concorde de la Géographie des différents âges* (1765), as well as works on Holy Scripture and French royal coronation ceremonies.

The present excerpt is a new translation of the full text of the twenty-fifth "Entretien," or "Conversation," the one devoted to commerce and which first appeared in 1746, from *Spectacle de la Nature* (Paris: La Veuve Estienne,

1732–51), 8 vols., 7:439–47. It offers an example of how a popular writer viewed the place of commerce in the education of a well-bred Frenchman.

Spectacle of Nature

Whatever is gathered and fashioned by the arts for our use is conveyed to us by commerce thanks to exchanges or ordered compensations. All our previous conversations constitute virtually a running exposé of the raw materials of commerce, and there is no point in going over it again. A few of those very conversations dealt with the places where there is the greatest trade, and in particular with the current distribution of the commerce of both our Companies and our European Colonies on the various continents.

As far as the most ordinary and at the same time most lovely processes of commerce are concerned, I know, my dear friend, that your upbringing has been too good to deprive you of the advantage of knowing them. You know their merit and the way they work, because you have had instructors who, besides the study of literature and nature, always took care to reserve an exercise for the study of society's needs and the means to fulfill them. For you, the currencies, weights and measures of the ancients have been reduced to current values, and the values that are used among us have been compared clearly enough to those in current use among our neighbors. How many times have I seen you coming back from a friend's house—a merchant—giving me a faithful report of what a currency exchange and bill of exchange is, and telling me how one can transfer a payment from one place to another without taking the risks which are inseparable from the transfer of funds? I have heard you making a clear distinction between the fair benefits of currency exchange and the illegal interest required beyond a capital that has been lent out. I have heard you present the reasons which are put forward to defend arbitrary usury, and then describe them as empty words. For we find security only in the rules laid down by the Church and invariably supported by the worldly courts, both to focus the mind and to close the door on cupidity. I have seen you grasp firmly the wise principle which supports peace in society by giving preference to the teachings of the Church over mere reasoning; for the rule of the Church prevents the destruction of individuals through the fair restraint in profit, whereas cupidity—of even the most obnoxious kind—always saves itself under the protection of false philosophy. It seduces itself. It masks its own ugliness by claiming it shelters those in need. Cupidity never acts without allowing itself some reasoning, which is often specious, but always frivolous because it lacks security.

We have not failed to show you the great advantage in transferring your money to Lyon, Rome or London, with a bill addressed to your correspondent so as to withdraw your sum from a banker or a merchant living on site. We have informed you of the subsequent use you can make of this bill of exchange, in transferring it to others as a commodity of genuine quality. We have also informed you of the care one takes to protest when the person who is in charge of the payments refuses to make them. Finally, you were informed of all the risks and limits necessary in a commerce of paper money, which may help the first few operations between trustworthy people, but which degenerates as it becomes a common currency. For metallic currency is a real commodity and a solid compensation which can make up for everything. But paper money is worth nothing more than a piece of leather, which has no real value or use in itself; the credit which had been given to it by the guarantee of a few individuals who had given their names to it gets suddenly destroyed because either the credit or the fortunes of these individuals collapses.

Because you could neither learn these processes through the practice of commerce, nor always have the lessons of your gentle merchant [*négociant°*] at will, I have often seen you supplementing or obviating the need for his instructions by reading the *Treatise on Commerce* by Samuel Richard, and sometimes *The Perfect Tradesman* by Jacques Savary, and more ordinarily *The Dictionary of Commerce*, which was written by his two sons—one of them an Inspector of our factories, the other a Canon of St.-Maur, a very good writer and an even better citizen.[1] There is no book less fitting to satisfy a mind accustomed to the abstractions of metaphysics. There is none more attractive for those who have been filled by a judicious instructor with a taste for the mundane sciences and a tender love of the welfare of society. You have often spent nights and days either stopping at the trade fairs of Archangel, Lyon, Bander-Abbas, or Portobello, or keeping busy with a problem in natural history, or dealing with the way merchants organize their account books, with the way their payments are done, with the rules of their association, with the expeditious methods used to settle their quarrels with the other merchants before the Judge-Consul, or with the custom of guaranteeing what is sent out to sea by an insurance company by giving five, six, or seven per cent on the returns; so that as there are more successful returns than shipwrecks or losses, the profit is great for the insurers, and the insured enjoy perfect tranquillity.

I will not forget the reflection you made one day on the charming variety in this book, and on the great necessity of knowing most of the things it contains. You said people claim that a few of the memoirs the Savarys based their work on can be improved. I hope and wish for it; but as of now it is the best philosophy available.

May all good minds become philosophers after your fashion, and learn either in this book or elsewhere how to serve the society for which we are made. Making people happy by the ease of communications and the proliferation of aids of which they have an ever-renewed need—either in a high position or in a subordinate one—this is certainly the most pleasant philosophy. It is precisely this which makes a true citizen, but at the same time, it is the definition of the spirit of commerce.

The hope for a legitimate profit may be a spur in all social conditions, but it is not the characteristic which distinguishes the skilled trader

---

1. [The references are to Samuel Ricard, *Traité général du commerce* (Amsterdam, 1700), Jacques Savary (1622–90), *Le Parfait négociant* (Paris, 1675), Jacques Savary des Brûlons (1657–1716) and Philémon-Louis Savary (1654–1721), *Dictionnaire universel du commerce* (Paris, 1723).]

[*négociant*°] from the orator or the artist. Love of the most sordid gain may ensconce itself in the Fleur-de-lis or embark for the Coromandel;[2] but it is the spirit of justice and peace which makes the true magistrate, and it is the passion to provide his country with the enjoyment of what it desires that makes a trader [*négociant*] highly esteemed. A skilled merchant [*commerçant*°] is more than a good citizen. The extent of his services turns him, as it were, into a statesman; and of all the sciences, his is, after religion, the one whose progress one must most strongly desire.

If it were merely a question of an honest pleasure, "a general trader of good sense," Mr. Addison says, "is pleasanter company than a general scholar."[3] We are very happy to have the assistance of books. They are the first supplement of the experience we lack. But the ancients and not a few moderns put in their books what they had heard of or what they thought rather than what they had seen or experienced. We are far from despising them: what pains do we not take to understand them? But it is clear that those who have seen and practiced things are by rights our first libraries.

I admit that books like that written by Pliny may help us even in their false accusations if we take care to clarify and rectify everything with the assistance of witnesses, guarantors, and experience; but when we listen to an experienced trader [*négociant*], we draw from the source. The knowledge we gain in this way is distorted neither by the multiplication of accounts, nor by the mingling of others' thoughts. He himself is the sure commentator as well as the faithful guarantor of what he reports. He has seen it: the fear of misunderstandings has kept him attentive to everything, and what has this fear not taught him?

The disposition of the seas, coasts and provinces; the measurement of distances; the roads' dangers; national needs and interests; the laws and customs of places; the dominant trends; the ways to vary one's behavior according to the persons and customs; local productions, natural curiosities, modern inventions; whether to provide hitherto unknown aids or to improve upon what is already in use; and in addition to this pleas-

2. [The references are to the emblem of the French monarchy and to a part of the Eastern coast of India.]

3. [*The Spectator* no. 2 (Mar. 2, 1711); the piece appears to have been written by Steele.]

ant knowledge, the origins, preparations and exchanges of all the materials that are in use—these are the subjects of discussion for a skilled trader [*commerçant*]. His good mind has had him draw benefits from everything, but the diversity of objects, and the necessity of wisely resolving each new situation, have extended his natural understanding no less than they have embellished his conversation.

You see, Sir, that there is more than pleasure to hope for from such a man. He is the compass of society. Everybody asks for his advice or arbitration. He is the soul of the enterprises of his family and his city. How many mere traders [*négociants°*] have we seen who became counsellors to the wisest ministers, and were even appreciated by our kings who subsequently entrusted them with the best negotiations and accorded them nobility!

I would have innumerable observations to make here about the high opinion we should have of commerce, about the means of training perfect merchants [*commerçants*], about the usefulness of travel and the best method of turning it to account, and about the various people whose inclinations we should turn towards commerce. But instead of telling you my thoughts about this—which have little authority—I will report to you the conversation I witnessed a few days ago. The whole of it dealt with the questions which you and I both are keen to have explained on this matter. And maybe it will make a greater impression on your mind, because it took place between two men of uncommonly refined judgement—one a highly distinguished nobleman, the other a merchant [*marchand°*] accomplished in the finest enterprises.

20

Spirit of the Laws
1748

CHARLES DE SECONDAT, Baron of La Brède and of Montesquieu, was born in 1689. He came from a judicial family and became a lawyer in Bordeaux as well as a judge in its local *parlement*. His 1721 work *The Persian Letters*, an epistolary novel concerning the travels to France and Europe of some Persian noblemen, was one of the founding literary productions of the French Enlightenment, with its oblique social satire and its comparative exploration of human customs and human nature. It had sufficient impact to secure his entry into the Académie Française in 1728. His *Considerations on the causes of the greatness of the Romans and their decline* (1734) also made a sizable impact on contemporaries, but it was *Esprit des lois* (1748) that assured his immortality. That work, on which he labored for twenty years, was an exploration of the history of the law and its relations to social and political systems. It contains, among many other things, an interpretation of the English parliamentary system that was destined to be highly influential on both sides of the Atlantic. He popularized the notion that an English parliamentary system based on checks and balances, and on a systemic separation of powers, was crucial to liberty. The book was condemned, to his great dismay, by the Parlement of Paris. He died in 1755.

The excerpt contained here is the full text of book 20, which is devoted to commerce. It is from *The Spirit of the Laws*, ed. and trans. Anne M. Cohler, Carolyn Basia Miller, and Harold Samuel Stone (© Cambridge

University Press 1989), bk. 20, pp. 337–53; reprinted with the permission of Cambridge University Press. Unbracketed notes are by Montesquieu; those in brackets are by the Cambridge editors.

On the Laws in Their Relation to Commerce, Considered in Its Nature and Its Distinctions

> That which great Atlas taught.
> VIRGIL, *Aeneid* [1.741]

Invocation to the Muses[1]

Virgins of the Pierian Mount,[2] do you hear the name I give you? Inspire me. I have run a long course. I am crushed by pain, fatigue, and worry. Give my spirit the calm and the gentleness that now flee from me. You are never as divine as when you lead to wisdom and truth through pleasure.

But if you do not want to soften the harshness of my labors, conceal the labor itself. Make it so that I meditate though I appear to feel. Make it so that one is instructed though I do not teach and that, when I announce useful things, one believes that I knew nothing and that you told me everything.

When the waters of your spring come forth from your beloved rock,

---

1. [We have placed the "Invocation to the Muses" at the beginning of Book 20, as Montesquieu originally intended.]
2. "Speak on, O ye Pierian maidens, if it be proper for me to call you maidens" [L.]. [Juvenal, *Satires* (4.35–36).]

they rise into the air not to fall back again but to flow over the meadow; they are your delight because they are the delight of the shepherds.

Charming Muses, if you cast me but a single glance, everyone will read my works, and what was not intended as an amusement will be a pleasure.

Divine Muses, I sense that you inspire me, not just what is sung in Tempe with the pipes or what is repeated at Delos on the lyre. You also want me to make reason speak. It is the noblest, the most perfect, the most exquisite of our senses.

Chapter 1

On commerce

The following material would require more extensive treatment, but the nature of this work does not permit it. I should like to glide on a tranquil river; I am dragged along by a torrent.

Commerce cures destructive prejudices, and it is an almost general rule that everywhere there are gentle mores,[3] there is commerce and that everywhere there is commerce, there are gentle mores.

Therefore, one should not be surprised if our mores are less fierce than they were formerly. Commerce has spread knowledge of the mores of all nations everywhere; they have been compared to each other, and good things have resulted from this.

One can say that the laws of commerce perfect mores for the same reason that these same laws ruin mores. Commerce corrupts pure mores,[4] and this was the subject of Plato's complaints; it polishes and softens barbarous mores, as we see every day.

---

3. [Although *doux* can be translated as "soft," "gentle," with its less pejorative and more descriptive tone, is most appropriate to Montesquieu's meaning.]

4. Caesar says of the Gauls that the proximity and commerce of Marseilles had spoiled them so that they, who had formerly always vanquished the Germans, had become inferior to them. [Gaius Julius Caesar] *De bello Gallico*, bk. 6 [6.24].

Chapter 2

On the spirit of commerce

The natural effect of commerce is to lead to peace. Two nations that trade with each other become reciprocally dependent; if one has an interest in buying, the other has an interest in selling, and all unions are founded on mutual needs.

But, if the spirit of commerce unites nations, it does not unite individuals in the same way. We see that in countries[5] where one is affected only by the spirit of commerce, there is traffic in all human activities and all moral virtues; the smallest things, those required by humanity, are done or given for money.

The spirit of commerce produces in men a certain feeling for exact justice, opposed on the one hand to banditry and on the other to those moral virtues that make it so that one does not always discuss one's own interests alone and that one can neglect them for those of others.

By contrast, total absence of commerce produces the banditry that Aristotle puts among the ways of acquiring. Its spirit is not contrary to certain moral virtues; for example, hospitality, so rare among commercial countries, is notable among bandit peoples.

It is a sacrilege among the Germans, says Tacitus, to close one's house to any man whether known or unknown. Anyone who has offered hospitality to a stranger will point him to another house where there is similar hospitality,[6] and he will be received there with the same humanity. But, after the Germans had founded kingdoms, hospitality became burdensome to them. This is shown by two laws in the code of the Burgundians:[7] the one imposes a penalty on any barbarian who would point a stranger to the house of a Roman and the other rules that anyone who receives a stranger will be compensated by the inhabitants, each according to his share.

---

5. Holland.
6. "The one who was just now the host directs the guest to another host" [L.]. [Tacitus] *Germania* [21]. See also [Gaius Julius] Caesar, *De bello Gallico*, bk. 6 [6.23.9].
7. [*Leges Burgundionum*] tit. 38 [38.7].

Chapter 3

On the poverty of peoples

There are two sorts of poor peoples: some are made so by the harshness of the government, and these people are capable of almost no virtue because their poverty is a part of their servitude; the others are poor only because they have disdained or because they did not know the comforts of life, and these last can do great things because this poverty is a part of their liberty.

Chapter 4

On commerce in the various governments

Commerce is related to the constitution. In government by one alone, it is ordinarily founded on luxury, and though it is also founded on real needs, its principal object is to procure for the nation engaging in it all that serves its arrogance, its delights, and its fancies. In government by many, it is more often founded on economy. Traders, eyeing all the nations of the earth, take to one what they bring from another. This is how the republics of Tyre, Carthage, Marseilles, Florence, Venice, and Holland engaged in commerce.

This kind of traffic concerns the government of many by its nature and monarchical government on occasion. For, as it is founded only on the practice of gaining little and even of gaining less than any other nation and of being compensated only by gaining continually, it is scarcely possible for it to be done by a people among whom luxury is established who spend much and who see only great objects.

In keeping with these ideas, Cicero said so well:[8] "I do not like a people to be both the rulers and the clerks of the universe." Indeed, one would have to assume that each individual in this state and even the

---

8. "I do not wish the same people to be both the ruler and customs officer for the world" [L.] [Cicero, *De republica* 4.7].

whole state always had a head full of both great projects and small ones, which is contradictory.

Yet the greatest enterprises are also undertaken in those states which subsist by economic commerce, and they show a daring not to be found in monarchies: here is the reason for it.

One commerce leads to another, the small to the middling, the middling to the great, and he who earlier desired to gain little arrives at a position where he has no less of a desire to gain a great deal.

Moreover, the great enterprises of the traders are always necessarily mixed with public business. But, public business is for the most part as suspect to the merchants in monarchies as it appears safe to them in republican states. Therefore, great commercial enterprises are not for monarchies, but for the government by many.

In short, one's belief that one's prosperity is more certain in these states makes one undertake everything, and because one believes that what one has acquired is secure, one dares to expose it in order to acquire more; only the means for acquisition are at risk; now, men expect much of their fortune.

I do not mean that any monarchies are totally excluded from economic commerce, but they are less inclined to it by its nature; I do not mean that the republics we know are entirely without the commerce of luxury, but it is less related to their constitution.

As for the despotic state, it is useless to talk about it. General rule: in a nation that is in servitude, one works more to preserve than to acquire; in a free nation, one works more to acquire than to preserve.

Chapter 5

On peoples who have engaged in economic commerce

Marseilles, a necessary retreat in the midst of a stormy sea, Marseilles, where all the winds, the shoals, and the coastline order ships to put in, was frequented by sea-faring people. The barrenness[9] of its territory

---

9. Justin [*Epitoma historiarum Philippicarum*], bk. 43, chap. 3 [43.3.5].

made its citizens decide on economic commerce. They had to be hard-working in order to replace that which nature refused them; just, in order to live among the barbarian nations that were to make their prosperity; moderate, in order for their government always to be tranquil; finally, of frugal mores, in order to live always by a commerce that they would the more surely preserve the less it was advantageous to them.

It has been seen everywhere that violence and harassment have brought forth economic commerce among men who are constrained to hide in marshes, on islands, on the shoals, and even among dangerous reefs. Thus were Tyre, Venice, and the Dutch towns founded; fugitives found security there. They had to live; they drew their livelihood from the whole universe.

Chapter 6

Some effects of a great navigation

It sometimes happens that a nation that engages in economic commerce, needing the commodities of one country to serve as a basis for procuring the commodities of another, is satisfied to gain very little and sometimes nothing on the former, in the expectation or the certainty of gaining much on the latter. Thus, when Holland almost alone traded from the south of Europe to the north, the French wines, which it carried to the north, in a way served it only as a base for its commerce in the north.

It is known that in Holland certain kinds of commodities imported from a distance often sell for no more than they cost where they come from. Here is the reason given: a captain who needs ballast in his ship will take on marble; he needs wood for packing his cargo, he will buy it; and provided he loses nothing on it, he will believe he has done well. Thus, Holland also has its quarries and its forests.

Not only can a commerce that produces nothing be useful, but so can even a disadvantageous commerce. I have heard that in Holland whale-hunting generally speaking almost never returns what it costs; but those who have been employed in building the ship, those who have provided the rigging, the gear, and the provisions, are also those who take the principal interest in the hunt. Even if they lose on the hunt, they have come out ahead on the equipage. This commerce is a kind of lottery, and each one is seduced by the hope of a lucky number. Everyone loves to play, and the most sober[10] people willingly enter the play when it does not have the appearance of gambling, with all its irregularities, its violence, its dissipation, the loss of time, and even of life.

Chapter 7

The spirit of England concerning commerce

Almost none of England's tariffs with other nations are regular; tariffs change, so to speak, with each parliament, as it lifts or imposes particular duties. England has also wanted to preserve its independence in this matter. Sovereignly jealous of the commerce that is done there, it binds itself with few treaties and depends only on its laws.

Other nations have made commercial interests give way to political interests: England has always made its political interests give way to the interests of its commerce.

This is the people in the world who have best known how to take advantage of each of these three great things at the same time: religion, commerce, and liberty.

Chapter 8

How economic commerce has sometimes been hampered

In certain monarchies, laws have been made which serve to lower the states that engage in economic commerce. They have been forbidden to supply commodities other than those produced in their country; they have been permitted to trade only with ships built in their own country.

The state imposing these laws must be able to engage in the commerce

---

10. [Les plus sages.]

easily itself; otherwise, it would do itself at least an equal wrong. It is better to deal with a nation that requires little and that the needs of commerce render somewhat dependent; with a nation that knows where to place all superfluous commodities due to the breadth of its views or its business; that is rich and can itself take many products; that will pay promptly for them; that has, so to speak, necessities for being faithful; that is peaceful on principle; that seeks to gain, and not to conquer: it is better, I say, to deal with this nation than with others that are ever rivals and would not offer all these advantages.

Chapter 9

On exclusion in commerce

The true maxim is to exclude no nation from one's commerce without great reasons. The Japanese trade with only two nations, the Chinese and the Dutch. The Chinese[11] earn a thousand percent on sugar and sometimes as much on return commodities. The Dutch make about the same profit. Any nation that is guided by the maxims of the Japanese will necessarily be deceived. It is competition that puts a just price on goods and establishes the true relations between them.

Still less should a state subject itself to selling its commodity to but a single nation on the pretext that it will take all of it at a certain price. For their grain, the Poles made this bargain with the town of Danzig; many kings of the Indies have similar contracts with the Dutch for spices.[12] These agreements are appropriate only for a poor nation, which willingly abandons the expectation of becoming rich, provided it has secured its sustenance, or for nations whose servitude consists in renouncing the use of the things nature has given them or in using these things to engage in a disadvantageous commerce.

11. Father [Jean Baptiste] du Halde [*Description de l'Empire de la Chine*], vol. 2, p. 170 ["Du commerce du Chinois," 2, 205–206 H; 2, 170 P; 2, 297 L.].
12. This was first established by the Portuguese. François Pyrard, *Voyages*, pt. 2, chap. 15 [vol. 2, pt. 1, chap. 15; 2, 204–205; 1887–1890 edn].

Chapter 10

Establishment proper to economic commerce

In states that engage in economic commerce, one has fortunately established banks, which, by means of their credit, have formed new signs of values. But it would be wrong to introduce them into states that carry on a commerce of luxury. To put them into countries governed by one alone is to assume silver on one side and power on the other: that is, on the one side, the faculty of having everything without any power, and, on the other, power with the faculty of having nothing at all. In such a government, there has never been anyone but the prince who has obtained or has been able to obtain a treasury, and wherever there is a treasury, as soon as it is excessive, it immediately becomes the prince's.

For the same reason, trading companies that associate for the sake of a certain commerce are rarely suited to the government by one alone. The nature of these companies is to give to individual wealth the force of public wealth. But in these states this force can be found only in the hands of the prince. I would go further: trading companies do not always suit states where there is economic commerce; and, if the business is not so large as to be beyond the reach of individuals, it is better not to hamper the liberty of commerce by exclusive privileges.

Chapter 11

Continuation of the same subject

In states that engage in economic commerce, one can establish a free[13] port. The economy of the state, which always follows the frugality of individuals, gives its economic commerce a soul, so to speak. What it loses in taxes by the establishment considered here is offset by what it can draw from the republic in wealth made by industriousness. But in

13. [*Franc.*]

monarchical government such establishments would be contrary to reason; their only effect would be to relieve luxury of the weight of imposts. It would deprive itself of the sole good this luxury can procure and of the only bridle that, in such a constitution, it can have.

Chapter 12

On the liberty of commerce

Liberty of commerce is not a faculty granted to traders to do what they want; this would instead be the servitude of commerce. That which hampers those who engage in commerce does not, for all that, hamper commerce. It is in countries of liberty that the trader finds innumerable obstacles; the laws never thwart him less than in countries of servitude.

England prohibits the export of its wool; it wants coal brought to the capital by sea; it does not permit the export of horses unless they are gelded; the ships[14] from its colonies that trade in Europe are to anchor in England. It hampers the trader, but it does so in favor of commerce.

Chapter 13

What destroys that liberty

Where there is commerce there are customs houses. The object of commerce is to export and import commodities in favor of the state, and the object of the customs houses is a certain duty[15] on that same exporting, also in favor of the state. Therefore, the state must be neutral between its customs houses and its commerce and must arrange that these two

---

14. Navigation Act of 1660 [*The Statutes of the Realm*, 12 Car., vol. 2, chap. 18; 5, 246–250; 1963 edn; consider the Act of Interregnum, October 9, 1651]. It was only in wartime that those [merchants] of Boston and Philadelphia sent the vessels carrying their goods directly to the Mediterranean.

15. [*Droit.*]

things never thwart one another; then one enjoys the liberty of commerce there.

The farming of the customs[16] destroys commerce by its injustices and harassments and by the excess of what it imposes, but independently of that it also destroys it further by the difficulties to which it gives rise and the formalities it requires. In England, where customs are imposed directly,[17] there is a singular ease in trade: a word in writing accomplishes the greatest business; the merchant does not have to waste an infinite time and have specified agents in order to conclude all the difficulties brought up by the tax-farmers or to submit to them.

Chapter 14

On the loss of commerce that entails the confiscation of commodities

The Magna Carta of England forbids in the event of war the seizure and confiscation of the commodities of foreign traders, except as a reprisal. It is a fine thing for the English nation to have made this one of the articles of its liberty.

In the war Spain waged against the English in 1740, a law was made[18] that punished with death those who introduced English commodities into the Spanish states;[19] it imposed this same penalty on those who carried Spanish commodities to the English states. Such an ordinance can find, I believe, no other model than the laws of Japan. It runs counter to our mores, to the spirit of commerce, and to the harmony that should prevail in proportioning penalties; it confuses all ideas, making a state crime of what is only a violation of the police.

16. [*La finance* here means the work of the *financiers*, tax-farmers, in regard to customs.]
17. [*Régie.*]
18. Published at Cadiz in March 1740. [See Jean Rousset de Missy, *Les Procès entre l'Espagne et Grande-Bretagne*, vol. 13, Supplement of the *Recueil historique*, Declaration of War, November 28, 1739; p. 252; 1756 edn.]
19. [Here *états*, "states," are what we today would call the Spanish colonies.]

Chapter 15

On corporal constraint

Solon[20] ordered that there would no longer be corporal obligations for civil debts in Athens. He drew this law from Egypt;[21] Bocchoris had made it, and Sesostris had revived it.

This law is good for ordinary civil business,[22] but we are right not to observe it in commercial business. For as traders are obliged to entrust great sums for often quite short periods of time, to give them and take them back again, the debtor must fulfill his engagements at the appointed time; this assumes corporal constraint.

In business deriving from ordinary civil contracts, the law should not provide for corporal constraint because it makes more of the liberty of one citizen than of the convenience of another. But, in agreements that derive from commerce, the law should make more of public convenience than of the liberty of a citizen; this does not prevent the restrictions and limitations that humanity and a good police can require.

Chapter 16

A fine law

The law of Geneva that excludes from magistracies and even from entry to the Great Council the children of those who have lived or who have died insolvent, unless the children discharge their father's debts, is a very good one. It has the effect of building up trust in traders, in magistrates, and in the city itself. Here again, confidence in an individual has the force of public confidence.

20. Plutarch [*Moralia*], *De vitando aere alieno* [828f].
21. Diodorus Siculus [*Bibliotheca historica*], bk. 1, pt. 2, chap. 3 [1.79].
22. Those Greek legislators were blameworthy who had forbidden taking a man's weapons and cart as securities but had permitted taking the man himself. Diodorus Siculus [*Bibliotheca historica*], bk. 1, pt. 2, chap. 3 [1.79.5].

Chapter 17

A law of Rhodes

The Rhodians went further. Sextus Empiricus[23] says that there a son could not be excused from paying his father's debts by renouncing his inheritance. This law of Rhodes was given to a republic founded on commerce: now, I believe that reasons drawn from commerce itself should have set this limitation, that the debts contracted by the father after his son had begun to carry on the commerce would not affect the goods acquired by the son. A merchant should always know his obligations and conduct himself at every moment in accordance with the state of his fortune.

Chapter 18

On judges for commerce

Xenophon, in his book, *Ways and Means*,[24] wanted one to reward those prefects of commerce who dispatched proceedings most quickly. He felt the need for our commercial jurisdiction.[25]

Commercial business is only slightly susceptible to formalities. The actions of one day have to be followed the next day by others of the same nature. Therefore, they must be decided every day. It is otherwise in the actions of life that have much influence on the future, but which happen rarely. One usually marries only once; one does not make bequests or testaments every day; one comes of age only once.

Plato[26] says that, in a town where there is no maritime commerce, half the number of civil laws are needed, and this is very true. Commerce

---

23. [Sextus Empiricus, *Pyrrhoeia*] *Hippotiposes*, bk. 1, chap. 14 [1.149].
24. [Xenophon, *Ways and Means* 3.3.]
25. [*Jurisdiction consulaire.*]
26. [Plato] *Laws*, bk. 8 [842c–d].

brings into a country different sorts of peoples, a great number of agreements, kinds of goods, and ways of acquisition.

Thus, in a commercial town there are fewer judges and more laws.

Chapter 19

That the prince should not engage in commerce

Theophilus,[27] on seeing a ship which carried commodities for his wife Theodora, had it burned. "I am the emperor," he told her, "and you make me a shipmaster. How can the poor people earn a living if we too ply their trade?" He could have added: who will restrain us if we make monopolies? Who will require us to fulfill our engagements? The courtiers will want to do our commerce; they will be more avid and more unjust than we. The people have trust in our justice; they have none in our opulence; the many imposts that make their misery[28] are certain proofs of our own.

Chapter 20

Continuation of the same subject

When the Portuguese and Castilians dominated the East Indies, commerce had such rich branches that their princes did not fail to seize them. This ruined their establishments in those parts.

The viceroy of Goa granted exclusive privileges to individuals. One has no trust in such people; commerce is interrupted by the perpetual change of those to whom it is entrusted; no one manages this commerce or is concerned that one leaves only ruins to one's heir; the profit stays in the hands of individuals and is not spread out enough.

27. [Johannes] Zonaras [*Epitome historiarum* 25.25.41–42].
28. [Here *misère* means both "misery" and "poverty."]

Chapter 21

On commerce by the nobility in a monarchy

It is against the spirit of commerce for the nobility to engage in it in a monarchy. "That would be pernicious for the towns," say the emperors Honorius and Theodosius,[29] "and would take away the ease with which merchants and plebeians buy and sell."

It is against the spirit of monarchy for the nobility to engage in commerce. The usage that permitted commerce to the nobility in England is one of the things that most contributed to weakening monarchical government there.

Chapter 22

A particular reflection

People who are struck by what is practiced in some states think there should be laws in France engaging the nobles to carry on commerce. This would be the way to destroy the nobility, without being of any utility to commerce. The practice of this country is very wise; traders are not nobles, but they may become nobles. They can have the expectation of becoming noble without the drawback of being nobles. They have no surer way of quitting their profession than to do it well or to do it successfully: something usually linked to prosperity.

The laws ordering each man to stay in his profession and to pass it down to his children are and can be useful only in despotic states,[30] where none can or should be rivals.

Let it not be said that each man will follow his profession better when

---

29. Law "Nobiliores," *Code* [*Corpus Juris Civilis, Code* 4.63.3] *de commerciis et mercatoribus,* and the last law of *de rescindenda venditione* [*Corpus Juris Civilis, Code* 4.44].
30. Indeed, they are often established that way.

he cannot leave it for another. I say that a profession will be better pursued when those who have excelled in it can expect to attain another.

When nobility can be acquired with silver, it greatly encourages
traders to put themselves in a position to attain it. I am not examining
whether it is good thus to give the prize of virtue to wealth; there are governments in which this can be quite useful.

In France, that estate of the robe lying between the great nobility and
the people, which, without having the brilliance of the former, has all its
privileges; that estate which leaves individuals at mid-level while the
body, the depository of the laws, is glorified; that estate in which one has
no way to distinguish oneself but by prosperity and virtue; an honorable
profession, but one which always lets a more distinguished one be seen:
that altogether warlike nobility, who think that, whatever degree of
wealth one has, one's fortune is yet to be made but that it is shameful to
increase one's goods if one does not begin by dissipating them; that part
of the nation who always serve with their capital goods; who, when they
are ruined, give their place to others who will serve with their capital
again; who go to war so that no one will dare to say they did not go; who
expect honors when they cannot expect wealth, and when they do not get
wealth, console themselves because they have acquired honor: all these
things have necessarily contributed to the greatness of the kingdom.
And if, over the past two or three centuries, the kingdom has endlessly
increased its power, this must be attributed to the goodness of its laws
and not to fortune, which does not have this sort of consistency.[31]

Chapter 23

Those nations for whom it is
disadvantageous to engage in commerce

Wealth consists in land or in movable effects; the land of each country is
usually possessed by its inhabitants. Most states have laws that discour-

---

31. [*Ces sortes de constance.*]

age foreigners from acquiring their lands; only the presence of the master can increase their value; therefore, this kind of wealth belongs to each state particularly. But movable effects, such as silver, notes, letters of exchange, shares in companies, ships, and all commodities, belong to the whole world, which, in this regard comprises but a single state of which all societies are members; the people that possess the most of such movable effects in the universe are the richest. Some states have an immense number of them; they acquire them by their produce, by the labor of their workers, by their industry, by their discoveries, even by chance. The avarice of nations disputes the movables of the whole universe. There may be a state so unhappy that it will be deprived of the movable effects of other countries and also even of almost all its own; the owners of its land will be but the colonists of foreigners. This state will lack everything and will be able to acquire nothing; it would be far better for it to have commerce with no nation in the world; in these circumstances commerce has led to poverty.

A country which always sends out fewer commodities or less produce than it receives puts itself in equilibrium by impoverishing itself; it will receive ever less, until, in extreme poverty, it receives nothing.

In commercial countries, silver that has suddenly vanished comes back because the states that received it owe it; in the states of which we speak, silver never comes back because those who have taken it owe nothing.

Poland will serve here as our example. It has almost none of the things we call the movable effects of the universe except the grain of its fields. A few lords possess whole provinces; they oppress the plowman in order to have a greater quantity of grain to send to foreigners and procure for themselves the things their luxury demands. If Poland had commerce with no nation, its people would be happier. Its important men, who would have only their grain, would give it to their peasants for them to live on; excessively large domains would be burdensome to them, they would divide them among their peasants; as everyone would have skins or wools from his herds, there would no longer be an immense expense in making clothing; the important men, who always love luxury and who would be able to find it only in their own country, would encourage the poor in their work. I say that this nation would flourish more, unless it became barbarous; something that the laws could prevent.

Now let us consider Japan. The excessive quantity of what it can accept produces the excess of what it can send out: things will be in equilibrium as if imports and exports were moderate, and besides, this kind of inflation[32] will produce a thousand advantages for the state; there will be more consumption, more things on which the arts can be exercised, more men employed, more means of acquiring power. In cases in which one needs prompt aid, a state that is so filled can give it more quickly than another. It is hard when a country does not have superfluous things, but it is the nature of commerce to make superfluous things useful and useful ones necessary. Therefore, the state will be able to give the necessary things to a greater number of its subjects.

Let us say, therefore, that it is not the nations who need nothing that lose by carrying on commerce; it is those who need everything. It is not the peoples who have enough among themselves but those who have nothing at home who find it advantageous to trade with no one.

32. [*Enflure*, "inflation," means blown up like a balloon.]

21

On Money

1751

FERDINANDO, ABATE GALIANI, was born to the family of a royal auditor in Naples in 1728. He showed early interest in philosophy, history,
and especially economic theory and history. His dissertation on money
in the age of Troy for the University of Naples was praised by his teachers and led to the publication of his precocious *Della moneta* (1751). He
also translated Locke's essays on monetary topics. He was possessed of
an imaginatively playful spirit. On one occasion, as revenge for not being allowed to address the whole assembly of the university (on the
ground that he was too young at twenty-one), he published a collection
of parodies by himself and some friends in the styles of its offending faculty. A new government's policies caused an increase in the money
supply in Naples and therefore in prevailing prices. That was the occasion for his *Della moneta*.

Offers by the Archbishop of Tarento for benefices led him to take minor orders, hence his normal title of *abate* (or *abbé* to his many French
friends). A grand tour of Italy followed, and the volumes of correspondence that then arose and that continued throughout his life are a veri-
table history of Italian letters at this time. He returned from his first trip
abroad in 1753. He became secretary of state and of the royal household,
and then ambassador to France in 1759. It did not take him long to become a fixture in the salons of Paris, and he was a special friend of Louise
d'Epinay, whose correspondence with him is a key source for the period.
After the Physiocrats succeeded in pushing through a decree allowing

the free trade and export of grain (1764), Galiani conceived an opposition to those policies and drafted his most famous and influential work, *Dialogues sur le commerce des bleds* (1769), published with the help of his friend Diderot in 1770. By that time, he had been called back to Naples. He died in 1787.

The work excerpted here is "Statement of the principles from which the value of all things arises," from *On Money* (1751), ed. and trans. Peter R. Toscano (Ann Arbor, Mich.: University Microfilms, 1977, reprinted by permission of ProQuest Information and Learning), bk. 1, ch. 2, pp. 19–37, 287, 388–90. (See xi–xii of the Toscano volume for questions about the authorship of the work.) The work was revised by the author for a second edition in 1780. Symboled footnotes are by Galiani and are to the first edition unless otherwise indicated; unbracketed footnotes are by Toscano, bracketed material by the present editor.

On Money

Statement of the principles from which the value of all things arises. Of utility and scarcity, the established principles of value. Reply to many objections.

The acquisition of gold and silver, of which the most precious money is made, has always been—and is now—the ultimate goal of the multitudes. At the same time, it is the source of loathing and contempt for those who arrogate to themselves the venerable name of sage. Of these contrary opinions the first is often base and sometimes poorly controlled; the second is generally unjust or not very sincere. Moreover, since those who are interested in accumulating the metals usually overvalue them, while their detractors tend to undervalue them, none value them legitimately and reasonably. Many regard the prices of the metals as purely arbitrary and imaginary. These persons believe such prices arise out of common error and are passed on to us along with our education. Describing price in derogatory terms, such people refer to it variously as folly, fraud, or madness; they regard price as unreal. Others, more discreetly, believe that the common consensus of men has caused them, for their greater convenience, to adopt the common use of money, for the first time giving the metals a value they do not intrinsically possess. Few understand that the just price and value of the metals has been fixed and firmly established by their very nature and by the disposition of human minds. Under these circumstances, the reader will have to decide for himself where the truth resides before continuing. He must bear in mind that in each step in the discussion of extrinsic value, the augmentation of the value of money, interest, exchange, and the proportions of money— reference is always made to an intrinsic, certain, and natural value.

Aristotle, a great genius and a man of wonder, has laid bare many fine considerations concerning the nature of money as, for example, in *Customs*, Chapter Seven, Book Five where he has written as follows:

τὸ νόμισα γέγονε κατὰ συνθήκην, καὶ διὰ τοῦτο τοὔνομα ἔχει νόμισμα, ὅτι οὐ φύσει, ἀλλὰ νομῷ ἐστὶ, καὶ ἐφ' ἡμῖν μεταβάλλειν, καὶ ποιῆσαι ἄχρησον:

Ex convento successit nummus, atque ob hanc causam νόμισμα *vocabitur (a Graecis) nempe a lege, quia non natura, sed lege valeat, sitque in nostra potestate eum immutare, inutilemque reddere.*[1]

This is repeated in Chapter Six, Book One of *Politics*. If this philosopher has ever been heeded in his teachings more than is appropriate, it would be in this matter, to our detriment. Following his master, Bishop Covarruvias, for example, proceeds in this manner:

Si non natura ipsa, sed a Principe valorem numismata accipiunt, & ab ipso legem revocante inutilia effici possunt, profecto non tanti estimatur materia ipsa auri vel argenti, quantum numus ipse; cum si tanti estimaretur natura ipsa non lege praetium haberet.[2]

Aristotelians, which includes Moralists and Jurisconsults, reason in the same way. It is obvious how correct such conclusions are. Given the truth of such a principle, I should not wish any to have to demonstrate by direct experience just how fatal and productive of grief such considerations can be. These opinions cannot be contradicted without destroying their very basis. Hence, I do not know, or even begin to understand, how it could be possible that such writers as John Locke, Davanzati,[3] Broggia,[4]

---

1. This is probably rendered into English best by W. D. Ross, as follows, ". . . money has become by convention a sort of representative of demand; and this is why it has the name 'money' (νόμισμα)—because it exists not by nature but by law (νόμος) and it is in our power to change it and make it useless." Aristotle, *Nicomachean Ethics*, trans. W. D. Ross, "The Works of Aristotle," 2, *Great Books*, 9:381. See also [Alberto Merola, ed., *Della moneta e scritti inediti*, by Ferdinando Galiani (Milan: Feltrinelli, 1963)], p. 37, notes 3 & 4; and Aristotle, *Politics*, trans. Benjamin Jowett, "The Works of Aristotle," 2, *Great Books*, 9:Book I, pp. 437–548.

2. Merola, ed., op. cit., pp. 37–38, note 4, where the Latin is rendered into Italian, and is attributed to the fifteenth-century canonist Diego Covarrubias y Leiva (1512–1577).

3. [Bernardo] Davanzati (1529–1606).

4. [Carlo Antonio] Broggia (1683–1763).

the authors respectively of the works *Sul commercio*[5] and of *Dello spirito delle leggi,*[6] among others, could have had contrary sentiments so firmly established on so false a foundation, without ever denying the first principle. They were not aware either of the weakness of the latter or the instability of the former. For this reason, I myself, more than all others, have done my utmost to show—with every study I have made—what I have long believed. Namely, that not only the metals comprising money but every other worldly thing, barring none, has its natural value derived from certain, general, and invariant principles; that neither whimsy, law, nor princes, nor anything else can violate these principles and their effects. Finally, concerning value, the Scholastics have said: *passive se habent.*[7]

Any edifice built on these foundations will be durable and everlasting. I trust my readers will pardon any verbosity here, given the importance of the subject. It would be wrong to consider me responsible for so great a truth, should any be inclined to do so; the responsibility belongs instead to the infinite number of writers who have either failed to understand, or have not wished to demonstrate it.

The value of things, in general, is defined by many as the esteem which men have for such things. Perhaps, these words do not evoke an idea which is as clear or as distinct as it might be. One might say that *esteem or value, as conceived by an individual, is an idea of proportion between the possession of one thing and another.* If we say that ten bushels of grain are worth as much as a cask of wine, we are expressing a proportion of equality between possession of one thing and the other. It follows that because men are always most careful not to be defrauded of their own pleasures, one thing exchanges for another, and, consequently, equality involves neither loss nor fraud.

It can be seen from what I have said that the value of things varies as men's ideas and needs vary. Since some things are more generally

---

5. [The reference is to Melon, *Essai politique sur le Commerce* (1734), chapter 15 in this volume.]

6. The reference is, no doubt, to Montesquieu's *De l'Esprit des lois, i.e., The Spirit of the Laws,* trans. Thomas Nugent, revised by J. V. Prichard, *Great Books,* 38.

7. Generally: must maintain a certain passivity.

enjoyed and demanded than others, they have a value which is called current; other things have a value only because of the desire of those who wish to have them and those who can provide them.

Value, then, is a ratio which is, in turn, composed of two other ratios expressed by the names *utility* and *scarcity*. Allow me to explain my understanding of value with some examples, in order to avoid any confusion over words. Obviously, air and water, which are the most useful things for human life, have no value at all, because they are not scarce. A small bag of sand from the shores of Japan, on the other hand, would be a rare thing, but since it has no particular utility, it would also have no value.

Some will wonder what great utility one would possibly find in many things which have very high prices. This is a natural and frequently asked question which makes men appear foolish and irrational. It also destroys the basis on which the science of money rests. It will, therefore, be necessary to explore the utility of things and its measurement in more general terms. If utility does not depend on principles which are certain, then there can be no principles on which the prices of things are based either. Where there is no certainty or any means of demonstrating it, there is no science.

Utility is the ability a thing has to provide us with happiness. Man is a mixture of passions which move him with unequal force. Pleasure consists of gratifying these passions; and happiness is the acquisition of pleasure. But, I am not an Epicurean, and do not wish to appear to be one; permit me, therefore, to elaborate on some points in the argument introduced which must be refuted.

The gratification of a passion which stimulates and arouses another passion is not a true pleasure. Indeed, if the trouble caused by it is greater than the pleasure itself, then the pleasure should be abhorred as a true pain and an evil. If the pain is less than the pleasure, however, it is a benefit, though reduced in intensity and duration. This view, therefore, considers the pleasures of this life without reference to the other, eternal life, as though one and the other could possibly be considered with the same admiration. It is obvious to us, thanks to Providence, that after this life we shall live another, the pleasures and pains of which are closely connected with our behavior in the present life. Now, without altering anything I have just said, note that true and perfect pleasures are pleasures which produce no pain in that life. Those pleasures which produce pain in that life are always false and deceitful pleasures, since the difference between the pleasures and pains of this life and that is infinite, however large the enjoyment of this and small the pain of that might be. Had this assertion been made by all concerned, the ancient dispute between Epicureans and Stoics—that is, between delight and virtue—could not have arisen. Either the Stoics would have been totally incorrect in their view or it would have been clear that the differences between the two are simply verbal differences.

To return to where I left off, utility is anything which produces a true pleasure, something which gratifies the excitement of the passions. Our passions are not just the desires to eat, drink, and sleep, however; these are just the first or primary passions. Once satisfied, these give rise to others which are just as strong. For man is so constituted that once he has satisfied one desire, another springs up in its place, always exciting him with an intensity equal to the first. He is, therefore, perpetually agitated in this manner, never quite succeeding in the achievement of full gratification. For this reason, it is incorrect to say that the only things which are useful are those which are required for the primary needs of life. Nor can any limits or frontiers be found between things we need and things we do not need. It is an ultimate truth that just as a thing is attained and, consequently, as soon as one ceases to need it, a person begins to crave something else.

Once man has satisfied the passions which appear in the human mind, passions which he holds in common with beasts and which are needed for survival of the individual and of the species, then nothing moves him more vehemently or more strongly than the desire to distinguish himself from others, and to be superior to them. This is prior even to self-love; it is the very source of action in us, and surpasses every other passion. Those things which are of use to, and which satisfy us, have the greatest value, superceding every other pleasure and, often, the security of life itself. Men seek food when they have none with the same justification as they seek titles of nobility, once they have been provided with food. Life is miserable and sad when we are hungry, but it can be just as miserable and sad when we are not held in high esteem or noticed. Indeed, sometimes the latter unhappiness is so much greater that we are more disposed to die or to place ourselves in a situation in which we risk the loss of life itself, than to go on living unhappily without the respect of others.

What is more just, therefore, than to acquire something of great utility, even with great privation and labor, as long as it produces a great many pleasures? If the feeling of pleasure derived from the reverence and high esteem in which others hold us should be ridiculed, this would constitute a reproach against our nature, which has provided us with a disposition of mind which we could not otherwise have acquired for ourselves, and which—like hunger, thirst, and the need for sleep—we neither should nor can defend or explain to anyone.

Some philosophers are contemptuous of riches and of the esteem of others; such philosophers have also trampled dignity underfoot. They are not honest when they say they hold such a position because these things bring them no pleasure! They have only spoken and behaved in this manner because of the security they were already enjoying, the security of knowing that they were enthusiastically applauded and commended by the public, even after they had revealed their contempt for public acclaim.*

The things which bring us respect are, therefore, deservedly valued most highly. Among those most often cited are dignity, titles, honors, nobility, and the power to command. Close behind these is a variety of things which have at all times been sought after by men because of their beauty. Those who have had the good fortune to acquire these and to adorn their persons with them have been, at the same time, admired and envied. These are: gems, rare stones, certain skins, the most beautiful metals such as gold and silver, and certain works of art embodying both a great deal of effort and great beauty. According to some, these bodies, which add dignity to the awkward appearance of people, have also come to provide the superiority which is a source of the most considerable satisfaction, as I have already indicated. Hence, the value of such things is deservedly great. Indeed, even kings owe the greater part of the veneration of their subjects to the external magnificence which always sur-

---

* It is known that the "display" or "pomposity" of Diogenes was greater than that of Plato.

rounds them. Deprived of these trappings, kings would retain only powers and gifts of mind which they had formerly; they have come to realize that the reverence shown them has been greatly reduced in such circumstances. Consequently, those powers which possess less true force and authority seek to regulate, with more attention to external pomp, the ideas of men among whom the august and magnificent are often nothing more than exaggerated nonentities. This is formally called, with words taken from the Scholastics and very appropriately adopted, which mean, in effect, "*id quod non est, neque nihil, neque aliquid.*"[8]

If the desire to make a good appearance generates in men affection for these fairest and most beautiful products of nature, then the more ardent desire to appear beautiful makes these bodies even more valuable to women and children. Women constitute half of the human race and exist only, or in large part, solely for our propagation and breeding. They do not have any other value and merit than the love they arouse in men. And because this attribute is almost entirely derived from beauty, women have no greater duty than to appear attractive in the eyes of men. How useful they are as ornaments is attested to by common consensus. Hence, if the value of women arises from their amiableness, which is, in turn, enhanced by ornaments, it is reasonable to conclude that the value of ornaments must be great indeed.

As for children, they require the most tender care of parents. Men know of no other way to show this tender love than to make the object loved more desired and charming in their view. Thus, a man will not be moved to adorn his children except by the desire to satisfy a woman.

This is how it has come about that the most beautiful metals were first collected, with great difficulty, from the sands of the rivers and, later, from the very bowels of the earth. It is still true that nations which are known to be rich in these metals, such as Mexico and Peru, hold nothing—except gems—in higher esteem than gold and silver. And insofar as they hold such trifles as glass and steel in higher esteem, what I have just said would be confirmed, not denied. For it would be the beauty that

---

8. According to Merola, ed., op. cit., p. 42, note 10: "that which is neither nothing nor anything." Italics in original. See also [Galiani, 1751], p. 32.

results from our toil which enchants people. Inasmuch as the beauty of glass and crystal results from art rather than from nature, their value varies only insofar as nature varies their scarcity, which because it was unknown to the Americans cannot be regarded as a contradiction of what I have demonstrated.

The greater portion of mankind reasons, as does Bernardo Davanzati, that "A natural lamb is more noble than one of gold, but how much less is it valued?" I reply to him as follows. If a natural lamb were as rare as one of gold, its price would be higher than that of the golden lamb, to the degree that its utility and the necessity for it exceeded those of the golden lamb. Such people imagine that value is derived from one principle alone, and not from many which join together to form a compound reason. I hear others say, "A pound of bread is more useful than a pound of gold." To this I reply that this is a shameful paralogism derived from not knowing that "more useful" and "less useful" are relative terms, and that they are measured according to the different conditions of different people. To a person who has neither bread nor wine, bread is surely the more useful; an examination of the facts of this case would confirm this assertion because one will not find anyone who would choose gold and forgo bread to die of hunger. Those who dig in the mines, for example, never forget to eat and sleep. Nonetheless, there is nothing more useless than bread for one who is sated. In this case it makes sense for a person to satisfy other drives. The precious metals are the handmaidens of luxury, but only when the primary needs are already satisfied. It is for this reason, Davanzati asserts, that:

> an egg worth half a grain of gold would have kept Count Ugolino from starving to death, even after ten days in his tower prison. All the gold in the world would not have matched it in value.

Davanzati badly confuses the difference in value between an egg to one who is not in danger of starving to death, and the needs of Count Ugolino. On what basis does he conclude that the count would not have paid even as much as a thousand grains of gold for the real egg? Though not aware of it, Davanzati himself provided evidence of this error a little later on when he said:

Though a mouse is a most loathsome creature, one was sold for two hundred florins in the siege of Casilino. And this was not actually dear, because the seller* died of hunger, while the buyer lived.

Note that he was agreed, thanks to heaven, at least in this instance, that dear and cheap are relative terms.

Some find it strange that precisely the most useful things have a low value, while the less useful have a great and excessive value. Such persons should be reminded that the world is well constituted just for our welfare. What amazing good fortune! In general, utility is never matched with scarcity. Indeed, the more the basic utility of a thing increases, the greater the abundance in which it is found: hence, its value cannot be great. Those things which are needed to sustain life are profusely distributed over the entire world; they either have no value at all or have value to a very moderate degree. Many draw false conclusions, regarding my purpose, from these considerations; some unjustly regard my judgement with contempt. My desire to do good should rather evoke prayers to God, feelings of self-abasement; such an intention should be blessed at every turn. But few do this.

Many philosophers may, perhaps, say to me that although the value of gems and their scarcity spring from the nature of humans, as I have already demonstrated, these concepts do not cease to seem to them as ridiculous and miserable madness. To whom I reply: I wonder whether they could ever find any other human thing which does not appear this way to them! Nothing is likely to divert them from this opinion. But I would like the good philosopher—after he has rid himself of earthly deceptions and after having virtually dehumanized himself and has so raised himself above the others that he is able to laugh at us poor mortals and amuse himself—when he has then separated himself from these ideas and returned down here to mix in society—which will, of course, force the needs of life upon him—I would like him to return as a common man and not as a philosopher. That smile, which healed his soul, while he was philosophizing, would disturb his work and also the work

---

*Plin. lib. *8.* c. *57.* Front[inus, *The Stratagems*]. lib. *4.* c. *5.* [20.] Valer. lib. *7.* c. *6.*

of others now that he must labor. It is better that these concepts remain locked in his mind. For as he understands and deplores—together with his peers—that man is not very much superior to brutes (which I concede), he will by attempting to improve them only make them worse. This is an impossible enterprise for him. If men are guided to perfect virtue by our divine religion, then our teachers are assisted by supernatural and divine power; if examples of the highest perfection are seen among us, these works come from heavenly grace and not from human nature. He who is thus armed comes to perfect us—and well he can. For philosophy is not capable of doing this! We have seen Stoics, who have wished to render men perfectly virtuous, and have instead rendered them fiercely proud; others have wished to make them silent and contemplative but have, instead, made them gluttonous; those who would see them as poor, have brutalized them; and, finally, wishing to purge them of prejudice, Diogenes has ended by establishing an infamous race of dogs. But, alas, they have finally let us live in peace. They have left to the metals and precious stones the value they have, whatever it may be.

No longer, then, can Horace proclaim:

> Vel nos in mare proximum
> Gemmas & lapides aurum & inutile
> Summi materiem mali
> mittamus.[9]

Since we have been able to advance, without suffering, by means of these otherwise useless bodies, from a primitive life in which we literally devoured each other to a civilized state in which we live peacefully, by trade, we need not return, in the name of wisdom, to the barbarism from which we have, by the grace of God, been happily delivered. The community of man can only improve its ideas within certain limits; attempts made to exceed these limits of the order of things will destroy and corrupt man.

---

9. The proclamation, attributed to Horace, is translated from Latin into Italian, in Merola, ed., op. cit., p. 46, note 17. I have, in turn, translated it into English as: "Let us cast into the nearest sea the gems and precious stones, and even gold, which are useless, and are the cause of the worst evils." See [Galiani, 1751], p. 37.

Leaving these considerations aside, considerations spawned out of superficial and imperfect ideas, we conclude at once that those substances which enhance the respect of men, increase the beauty of women and the amiability of children are useful and deservedly precious. The important consequence that gold and silver had value as metals, before becoming money, follows from this. I will treat this subject at greater length in the next chapter; here I have spoken of value in general and have explained what I understand utility to mean. I turn now to a discussion of scarcity.

Scarcity refers to the proportion between the quantity of a thing and the use which is made of it. Use is not so much the destruction as the employment of a thing, where its employment by one person, and the satisfaction of his desires, precludes the satisfaction of another person's desires. Assume, for example, that one hundred paintings are offered for sale. If some gentleman should buy fifty of them, the paintings would become about twice as rare, not because they are consumed, but because they have been withdrawn from the market or, as some might say, they are no longer a part of trade. It is true, however, that the destruction of a thing raises its price more than its removal from trade. This is because its destruction completely eliminates all hope, while its removal preserves its value in accordance with the probability that the thing will be used and returned again to circulation and trade. This merits more serious consideration.

Turning now to the discussion of quantity, two classes may be distinguished. For some things, quantity depends upon the different degrees of abundance with which nature provides them. For others, it depends on the different amounts of labor employed upon them. The first class is formed by a group of things which are reproduced after a short time and which are expended as they are consumed. This group consists of animals and of the fruits of the earth. With the same work, their harvest may be as much as eight or ten times more than it was just a short time earlier, depending on differences in climate. Plenty, obviously, does not depend on human will but on the circumstances of climate and of the elements.

Another class includes certain bodies such as minerals, stones, and marble, different amounts of which are scattered throughout the world, though their total does not vary from year to year. But the amount mined does vary according to our wishes. More of this class of bodies can be extracted from the earth as more people are put to work on them; thus, in order to determine the amount produced, one needs only compute the labor, for the quantity of these things always corresponds to this labor. Of course, I really do not believe that new metals and gems are not regenerated in their great natural laboratory, but their creation is very slow compared to their destruction and it is, therefore, not necessary to take this into account.

I turn next to a discussion of labor. This alone gives things value whether they are entirely works of art, such as paintings, sculptures, carvings, *et cetera,* or such things as minerals, stones, wild fruit trees, and so on. The quantity of the material in these bodies contributes to value in no other manner except that it increases or reduces work. Thus, should one inquire why gold is worth more than sand, despite the fact that gold and sand are found mixed together on the banks of many rivers, he should be reminded that he could easily fill his sack with sand in just a quarter of an hour, but that it would take him many years to gather the very scarce grains of gold.

One must keep three things in mind in connection with the calculation of labor: the number of people, or the population; time; and the different prices of those who work. I shall discuss first the number of people.

Certainly, no one works except to live, nor can one work without sustenance. For example, the work of fifty persons is needed for the manufacture of a bale of cloth, beginning with the clipped wool and continuing on through the state in which it is displayed at a shop. The cloth will be worth more than the wool it contains. Its price is equal to the cost of food for the fifty persons, for a time equal to the period of time involved in the work. For example, if twenty men are employed for an entire day, ten for half a day, and twenty for three days, the value of the cloth produced is equal to enough food to feed a man for eighty-five days. Twenty of these days will be earned by the first, five by the second, and sixty by the third. This obviously assumes that these persons all have equal compensation. So much for population.

Time includes not only the period actually involved in the work but also the period during which a person is at rest, because he must eat even during that period. This is because the work of an individual is interrupted either by law or because of the very nature of the arts, and not simply by slothfulness of the individual. Laziness is not so general in a nation that it would have a significance equal to that of laws and customs. Similarly, feast days among those people who observe them without working, make things more costly than they would otherwise be. Consider, for example, a man who works 300 days in a year and produces 100 pairs of shoes. The value of the shoes must correspond to his subsistence for an entire year. Another man producing 120 pairs while working 360 days, will sell his product for one-fifth less, since it is not necessary for the latter to earn any greater wage, while producing 120 pairs of shoes, than the first man received for his 100 pairs.

There are, in addition, some types of labor which cannot, by nature, exert themselves constantly. The fine arts belong to this group. I do not believe there is a sculptor or musician who works more than one-hundred days a year. So much time is needed to determine where employment can be found, in order to get started, for travel, and so on. Therefore, their work is properly worth more.

Finally, I would add the diverse lengths of time it takes different men to begin to enjoy profit from their work. For this reason, those arts and studies which require a great deal of time and expense to master must be higher in price. These are no different than pine timber and some walnut trees which, because of the length of time they take to grow, are worth more than poplars and elms. So much for time.

A correct appraisal of the value of different human talents, from which various prices of labor result, is a more difficult matter. This concerns a question about which less is known. I will discuss my thoughts on it here without knowing whether others believe as I do, since I have not found any other writer who has discussed this matter. I would certainly be pleased if anyone who knows better, or simply just thinks differently, would refute any of my arguments with logic and candor.

I think the value of human talents is appraised by the same means as the value of inanimate things; that is, by the same principles of scarcity and utility considered together. Different men are providentially disposed to different occupations at the time of birth. Although these are not equally scarce, they correspond to human needs with remarkable wisdom. For example, of a thousand men, six hundred are only fit for agriculture, three hundred inclined to the various manufacturing arts, fifty to the richer trades, and another fifty disposed to succeed in different studies and disciplines. Granting this, the worth of a man of letters compared to a peasant would be in inverse proportion to these figures, or as six hundred to fifty: he will be twelve times better. Consequently, it is not utility alone which determines prices. This is why the good Lord has willed that men who practice the most useful arts be born in large numbers. Since these are the very bread and wine of mankind, their value cannot be great. Learning and wisdom, on the other hand, are like gems among talents, and these deservedly have the highest prices.

Note, here, that scarcity should not be valued according to the proportions in which talents are provided, but instead in accordance with how rapidly different talents come to maturity. Consequently, the price of a talent is greater, the greater the difficulties of bringing it to a degree in which the talent is important and worthy of such a price. Great generals such as Prince Eugene or Marshall Turenne, command an unlimited price compared to a simple soldier. This is not so much because nature produces few men as able as these, as because wherever military victories are reported these same few men find themselves in the fortunate circumstance of being present, practicing their skills. Nature behaves here as it does in the case of seeds and plants. Almost anticipating a great loss between sowing the seed and harvesting the plants which finally blossom, nature provides a much greater quantity of seeds, depositing more of them into the earth than the number of plants which finally bloom. Or, a plant is worth more than the seed from which it springs.

Reflecting on these sound principles, one notes how brilliantly the wisdom of human judges gleams. Everything is valued in measure. Wealth does not fall to a person except as payment for the just value of his work, although he can give his wealth to a person who is not worthy of acquiring it. For example, no family exists, indeed, there is no man, who can boast of wealth which has not been obtained either by merit or as a gift originally obtained on the basis of merit. Such a gift is referred to simply as a gift, when it is made in life, or as an inheritance, if given after death. But in either case, if one were to examine the early history of the wealth which someone might have received undeservedly, he would observe that it was originally acquired wholly on the basis of merit. Though it is true that, in this connection, it is often necessary to ignore scores of persons for long periods of time, reason will show that, in the end, even these exceptions will fit this group.

Some would assert that merit, or virtue, often goes unrewarded—that it is madness to deny the frequent existence of the most atrocious acts of injustice. But note the false reasoning here. First, there is no need to refer to some professions as synonymous with virtue or kindness, just because they may be scarce and acquired only with great difficulty; virtue or kindness may not be able to produce either true utility or true pleasure for the multitudes. Prices are made by the many, not by the few.

Second, bear in mind that since man is made up of virtues and vices taken together, there is no way of rewarding a man's virtues without at the same time also rewarding his vices, despite the fact that one will never find vice exalted by anyone. These defects only occasionally fail to get in his way; barring such defects, he would surely have achieved greater success.

Third, always bear in mind that possession of skill in obtaining employment is one matter. To know how to perform the duties of a position well is quite another. The first consists merely of the arts of being pleasing to persons responsible for filling the position, whether the position involved be military or civilian. On the other hand, the skills required to perform different employments are never the same, depending on the various needs of different offices. In any event, no one has ever acquired employment which he is not worthy of being able to secure. It would be well if, when the science of acquiring a position is not joined with the ability of filling it well, a person were held responsible for the consequences and regarded as undeserving of the position. Men regard as worthy only the ability to employ well the talents which one may have. Anything else will either not be virtuous or will not require skill for the application of any labor. Consequently, they refer to as an injustice what is not an injustice at all. But, we must not include here those who are able to acquire some high office, either as a favor from others, which is tantamount to a gift among living persons, or because of birth, which is a bequest from one's ancestors. I am aware that this argument extends beyond the confines of this work, but because this has appeared to me to be a useful subject, worthy of careful reflection, I have not been able to restrain myself from dealing with it. I beg my readers' indulgence. How pleased I would be if he should share my view. Nevertheless, I fear that few will agree with me, so much do men prefer to protect themselves from committing an error and to accuse others of doing so.

Enough has now been said of the principles from which value is derived. It has been seen that since these principles are certain, invariant, universal, and based on the order and nature of earthly matters—nothing among us is arbitrary and accidental, all is necessarily order and harmony. Values vary from one thing to another, but not capriciously. Their very variation is orderly, with exact and immutable rules. These values are ideal; but those ideas of ours which are based on need and pleasure are part of man's internal makeup. They contain within them the ideas of justice and stability.

An exception to what I have just said would appear to be required here. Sometimes fashion affects our ideas and values. As for the sense in which the word fashion is intended, after considerable thought I have found it possible to give it only one definition. *Fashion is a malady of the cerebrum common to the nations of Europe, because of which many things are rendered of little value simply because they are not new.* This is an illness of the mind which rules over but few things. To find some rationality in it, you would have to say that a good part of such tastes results from imitation of the customs of more dominant nations.

Having said this much about fashion, it is necessary that I define its limits, which I shall do now, in order not to have to do it in a less appropriate place.

Fashion is entirely in the realm of the beautiful; none of it is in the useful. As a result, when a thing which is more useful and convenient is in fashion, I do not think of it as fashionable but as an improvement of the arts and of the comforts of life. Beauty is divided into two classes. One is founded on certain ideas engraved on our minds at birth. The other consists, though it does not seem to, of things which only appear beautiful out of habit of mind, or custom. The power of fashion is extended only over the second class, which is greater by far than the first. It is appropriate, therefore, to say that the beauty of gems and of gold and silver is universally established on the constitution of our minds, no part of it ever having succumbed to fashion, for it could not. Hence, the prices of such things are always recognized to be great and unique. Nevertheless, none of my observations are altered by fashion, which only varies the utility of things as the pleasure enjoyed by using them varies. The rest remain the same.

I will complete my remarks by discussing the value of unique things and of monopoly, that is, of those things which cannot be made by others, like the statue of *Venere de' Medici,* or those which become unique because of the unity of sellers. I have often found that even the wisest writers describe the value of these commodities as being infinite. But of all words that come from the mouths of those who reason about mortal things so often, I can think of none that is more inappropriate than infinite. These writers have, perhaps, wished to say indefinite, but even this is inappropriate, for I believe every human thing has order and limits. Indefinite is no less alien to these limits than infinite. These things, then, have limits. Their prices always correspond to the needs and desires of the buyer joined together to form a compound ratio with the esteem of the seller. Hence, at times, their value can even be equal to nothing. Moreover, it is always regulated, although it may not be everywhere the same.

It may, perhaps, seem to many that from the observations made thus far it is easy to determine the value of all things. But to believe this is to close one's mind on the matter prematurely. It is most difficult, often impossible, for us to draw such a conclusion from principles thus established, which logicians would call *a priori.* Because, we would have to establish, for certain, that because scarcity and value depend on consumption, consumption likewise corresponds to, and varies with, value. The problem is rendered indeterminate by this relationship, as it always is, when two unknown quantities which have some relationship between them are set against each other.

That differences of consumption emerge from price is obvious, if one recalls that aside from the air we breathe and the soil we stand upon, man regards nothing else as an absolute and eternal necessity. He must feed himself, but not with any food in particular or any sooner than with any other. Air and earth are not scarce, nor do they have value of any kind. Man can abstain from the consumption of other things, more easily for some than for others; and he is willing to do so in proportion to the discomfort, work, and cost of acquisition of a thing. Those which are worth less are, therefore, taken for consumption more readily. Consumption is, therefore, regulated by price; price, in turn, arises out of scarcity.

Price, on the other hand, is regulated by the exhaustion of a commodity. Because if, for example, 50 thousand casks of wine were being consumed in a nation, at the same time that a similar quantity was being produced, and if suddenly a military contingent should appear in the nation, then the price of wine would rise, because now people would be drinking more of it.

Some find an unalterable relationship here, a vicious circle. They would be able to solve this problem if only they would reflect on what I have already said. That is, in many instances, scarcity and abundance suddenly reverse places due to external causes, without man's interference but, instead, because of seasonal changes. In such cases, prices follow scarcity and, although men possess unequal wealth, purchase of certain commodities always corresponds to a certain degree of wealth. Should these commodities fall in price, even those of less wealth would purchase them. If their prices should rise, those who formerly used them, would begin to abstain from their use. This is supported by many observations. For example, in good growing seasons, in the kingdom of Naples, a total of approximately 15 million *tumoli** of grain are consumed annually. We know from experience that occasionally, in the most fertile years, as many as 6 or 7 million more *tumoli* of grain, than usual, are harvested. Moreover, export is never more than 1.5 million, nor is the amount stored for their later use greater. On the contrary, in barren years it is certain that no more than 8 million have been harvested, and we have not imported more than a million from abroad. Nor has the amount stored from previous years come to 2 million. For this reason, in years of plenty, incomparably more grain is consumed, otherwise used up and sown, and smaller quantities in calamitous years. This is why the limits on consumption are fixed more by price than by the number of *tumoli*.†

---

*A *tumolo* is a measure equivalent to three Neapolitan cubic feet, less one fiftieth part.

†Until the year 1750, the year in which this book was written, the price of grain in the provinces was under ten *carlini*, in good years, and was regarded as dear if it rose to thirteen *carlini*. Now prices are considerably changed, and the price of grain is between twelve and fourteen *carlini* in fertile years, between seventeen and nineteen in years of normal production. The most extraordinarily poor harvest of 1763 caused this considerable alteration to begin. [1780 edition]

Every year, for example, the kingdom consumes 13 million ducats worth of grain. This is always the same whether this sum purchases as many as 15 or as few as 10 million *tumoli*.

Changes in the scarcity of goods, whose production is not subject to variation, have no other extrinsic reason but *fashion*. Precious metals, however, (and, due to their regal beauty, gems) are not subject to such capricious changes in tastes or to such variations in production. They, therefore, have constant prices more so than any other product. Their production varies in accordance with the discovery of richer mines, as in the case of the American discoveries. This is why their value fell as their use rose. It was this increased use which prevented their value from falling as much as their abundance would have required. For it is from this relationship that the great and most useful effect of the proportional equilibrium of all things has arisen. This equilibrium, in its turn, conforms neatly with the proper abundance of both the comforts of life and worldly happiness, although not from human prudence and virtue but from the lowest stimuli of all—private gain. For, in spite of ourselves, due to His infinite love of mankind, Providence has so arranged all things that our base passions are often ordered for the benefit of all. I shall endeavor to explain how this has come about.

Let us suppose that a country which is thoroughly Mohammedan in customs and religion should adopt the religion and customs of Christianity. Few grapevines would be found in such a country, because Mohammedans are forbidden from drinking wine, and I suppose they would have been obeying this law. But now, wine would quickly be rendered dear in price because of its scarcity; and merchants would begin to import a great deal of wine from abroad. Soon, however, because all would wish to enjoy such high profits, many new vines would be planted, so much wine would be imported, that everyone would end by gaining only a just profit. Thus, things always arrange themselves at some common level, such is their intrinsic nature. Frequently, the size of a population even grows so much in this way that, though first drawn to this type of industry by the example of the first producers who entered the industry and by the earliest rumors, they impetuously turn to it, albeit so belatedly, that value falls below a just level. But then, as each person pays the penalty of his rashness, all begin to withdraw from the industry, and the just limit of value is restored anew.

Two great consequences are drawn from this. First, one should not pay particular attention to the first movements of things, but only to permanent and fixed states. It is in the latter that order and sameness are found, just as water in a bowl finds its own level after some disturbance has caused a disoriented and irregular tossing about. Secondly, nature provides no examples of phenomena which display infinite changes. A certain moral gravity, which all things possess, always draws them from an infinite linear path and pulls them into one which, though perpetual, is circular and finite.

I have applied what I have said here to money, hundreds of times. As a result, my readers have fixed it in their minds. They have, consequently, been persuaded that the laws of commerce correspond with no less exactness to the laws of gravity and the laws of fluids. The desire for gain, or the desire to live happily, is to man what gravity is to physics. Once this is given, all physical laws of matter can be verified perfectly, by one who knows how, to the ethical principles of our lives.

22

"An Enquiry into the Causes of the Late Increase of Robbers"
1751

THE ENGLISH AUTHOR Henry Fielding was born into a relatively illustrious family in 1707. He studied law at Leiden but also wrote plays, his first production appearing in 1728. A crackdown on licentious theater spelled an end to his theatrical career in 1737. He received his law degree in 1740, though he continued to write. He imitated *The Spectator* with his own journal, *The Champion,* in 1741. His parody of Richardson's *Pamela,* entitled *Joseph Andrews,* appeared in 1742 and was a great success. His *Tom Jones* appeared in 1749. Through the intercession of his school friend Lyttelton, he was introduced to the Duke of Bedford and shortly thereafter was made justice of the peace in 1748 for Westminster. The work included here is one of several Fielding wrote while he served as magistrate, and it led to legal restrictions on gin drinking in the summer of 1751. Hogarth's famous engraving "Gin Lane" is visual testimony to its influence. In June of 1754, he sailed to Lisbon for health reasons, where he died some weeks later.

 I reprint with permission "An Enquiry into the Causes of the Late Increase of Robbers" (1751), from *The Wesleyan Edition of the Works of Henry Fielding,* vol. 6, edited by Malvin R. Zirker (Middletown, Conn.: Wesleyan University Press, 1988), Preface, Introduction, and Section I, pp. 65–84. Numbered notes are by the Wesleyan editor; symboled notes are by

Fielding; material by the current editor is marked "Ed." For ease of reference, I append the modern editor's list of abbreviations (pp. xv–xvi).

An Enquiry into the Causes of the Late Increase of Robbers

The Preface

There is nothing so much talked of, and so little understood in this Country, as the *Constitution*.[1] It is a Word in the Mouth of every Man;[2] and yet when we come to discourse of the Matter, there is no Subject on which our Ideas are more confused and perplexed.[3] Some, when they speak of the Constitution, confine their Notions to the Law; others to the Legislature; others, again, to the governing or executive "Part; and many there are, who jumble all these together in one Idea. One Error, however, is common to them all: for all seem to have the Conception of something

---

1. The constitution was a constant topic in *The Craftsman* and other opposition as well as ministerial journals and pamphlets especially in the 1730s. But here Fielding may be thinking particularly of Montesquieu's *Esprit des Lois* (1748) which was translated into English in 1750. Extracts dealing with the English constitution had appeared in the *Monthly Review* for July and Oct. 1749 (see F. T. H. Fletcher, *Montesquieu and English Politics* [London, 1939], pp. 17 ff.). Or, he may be harking back to the period 1745–47 when, in *The True Patriot, The Jacobite's Journal*, and related writings, he campaigned vigorously against the "Jacobite" conception of an "old constitution": "that is, the Constitution as it existed under . . . James the Second" ("A Proper Answer," *JJ* p. 88). Fielding also mentions Montesquieu in *CGJ* no. 15 (i. 224) and the *Voyage to Lisbon*, p. 49.

2. E.g. the bailiff in *Amelia* (VIII. ii. 70) who defines "liberty" for Booth: "'Oh, 'tis a fine thing, 'tis a very fine thing, and the constitution of England.'"

3. Fielding echoes III. x. 2, 3 ("Of the abuse of words"), of Locke's *Essay Concerning Human Understanding* (*Works*, 5th edn. [London, 1751], i. 228: Baker, no. 456). He quotes from these sections at length in *CGJ* no. 4 (i. 153). Cf. *The Champion* for 17 Jan. 1739/40 and 27 Mar. 1740.

uniform and permanent, as if the Constitution of *England* partook rather of the Nature of the Soil than of the Climate, and was as fixed and constant as the former, not as changing and variable as the latter.[4]

Now in this Word, *The Constitution,* are included the original and fundamental Law of the Kingdom, from whence all Powers are derived, and by which they are circumscribed; all legislative and executive Authority; all those municipal Provisions which are commonly called *The Laws;* and, *lastly,* the Customs, Manners, and Habits of the People. These, joined together, do, I apprehend, form the Political, as the several Members of the Body, the animal Oeconomy, with the Humours and Habit, compose that which is called the Natural Constitution.

The *Greek* Philosophy will, perhaps, help us to a better Idea: for neither will the several constituent Parts, nor the Contexture of the whole, given an adequate Notion of the Word. By the *Constitution* is, indeed, rather meant something which results from the Order and Disposition of the whole; something resembling that Harmony for which the *Theban* in *Plato's Phaedo* contends; which he calls ἀόρατόν τι καὶ ἀσώματον, *something invisible and incorporeal.*[5] For many of the *Greeks* imagined the Soul to result from the κρᾶσις or Composition of the Parts of the Body[6] when these were properly tempered together, as Harmony doth from the proper Composition of the several Parts in a well tuned

---

4. The idea that climate affects a nation's culture is old (e.g. Aristotle, *Politics,* VII. vii. 1.) but that it affects political constitutions was particularly topical because of Montesquieu's comments in Bk. XIV of *Esprit des Lois,* "Of Laws in Relation to the Nature of the Climate." Bolingbroke too had remarked, "Now, tho the true interest of several states may be the same in many respects, yet is there always some difference to be perceived, by a discerning eye, both in these interests, and in the manner of pursuing them; a difference that arises from the situation of countries, from the character of people, from the nature of government, and even from that of climate and soil" (*The Idea of a Patriot King,* ed. Sydney W. Jackman [Indianapolis, 1965], p. 64). *The Idea of a Patriot King* was first published by Bolingbroke (with *A Letter on the Spirit of Patriotism*) in 1749 (Baker, no. 243). Cf. *The Champion,* 15 Dec. 1739.

5. *Phaedo,* sect. 36. Socrates refutes the idea of the soul as a harmony and Simmias the Theban, who had advanced it in opposition to Socrates' argument for the soul's immortality, recants.

6. E.g. Phaedo's auditor, Echecrates of Philius, who says, "the doctrine that the soul is a kind of harmony has always had . . . a wonderful hold upon me" (*Phaedo,* sect. 38 [Loeb]).

musical Instrument: In the same manner, from the Disposition of the several Parts in a State, arises that which we call the *Constitution*.

In this Disposition the Laws have so considerable a Share, that, as no Man can perfectly understand the whole, without knowing the Parts of which it is composed, it follows, that, to have a just Notion of our Constitution, without a competent Knowledge of the Laws, is impossible. Without this, the reading over our Historians may afford Amusement, but will very little instruct us in the true Essentials of our Constitution. Nor will this Knowledge alone serve our Purpose. The mere Lawyer, however skilful in his Profession, who is not versed in the Genius, Manners, and Habits of the People, makes but a wretched Politician. Hence the Historian, who is ignorant of our Law, and the Lawyer who is ignorant of our History, have agreed in that common Error, remarked above, of considering our Constitution as something fixed and permanent: for the exterior Form of Government (however the People are changed) still, in a great Degree, remains what it was; and the same, notwithstanding all its Alterations, may be said of the Law.

To explain this a little farther: From the Original of the Lower House of Parliament to this Day, the Supreme Power hath been vested in the King and the Two Houses of Parliament. These Two Houses have, each at different Times, carried very different Weights in the Balance, and yet the Form of Government remained still one and the same: So hath it happened to the Law; the same Courts of Justice, the same Form of Trials, &c. have preserved the Notion of Identity, tho', in real Truth, the present Governing Powers, and the present legal Provisions, bear so little Resemblance to those of our Ancestors in the Reign of King *John*, or indeed in later Times, that could any Lawyer or Statesman of those Days be recalled to Life, he would make, I believe, a very indifferent Figure in *Westminster-hall,*[7] or in any of the Parts there adjacent.

To perceive the Alterations in our Constitution doth, in fact, require a pretty just Knowledge both of the People and of the Laws: for either of these may be greatly changed, without producing any immediate Effect on the other. The Alterations in the great Wheels of State abovemen-

---

7. Where the three common-law courts of King's Bench, Common Pleas, and Exchequer sat during term time.

tioned, which are so visible in our Historians, are not noticed in our Laws, as very few of the great Changes in the Law have fallen under the Eye of our Historians.

Many of both Kinds have appeared in our Constitution; but I shall at present confine myself to one only, as being that which principally relates to the Subject of the following Treatise.

If the Constitution, as I above asserted, be the Result of the Disposition of the several Parts before mentioned, it follows, that this Disposition can never be altered, without producing a proportional Change in the Constitution. "If the Soul (says *Simmias* in *Plato*) be a Harmony resulting from the Disposition of the corporeal Parts, it follows, that when this Disposition is confounded, and the Body is torn by Diseases or other Evils, the Soul immediately (whatever be her Divinity) must perish."[8] This will be apparent, if we cast our Eyes a Moment towards the animal Oeconomy; and it is no less true in the political.

The Customs, Manners, and Habits of the People, do, as I have said, form one Part of the Political Constitution; if these are altered therefore, this must be changed likewise; and here, as in the Natural Body, the Disorder of any Part will, in its Consequence, affect the whole.[9]

One known Division of the People in this Nation is into the Nobility, the Gentry, and the Commonalty. What Alterations have happened among the two former of these, I shall not at present enquire; but that the last, in their Customs, Manners, and Habits, are greatly changed from what they were, I think to make appear.

If we look into the earliest Ages, we shall find the Condition of this Third Part to have been very low and mean. The highest Order of this

---

8. *Phaedo*, sect. 36.

9. That the constitution or state was a harmony or organism arising from the balanced arrangement of its parts which disproportion (or unnatural growth) destroyed, was a commonplace: e.g. "The *disproportionate increase of a part* of the state is also an occasion which leads to constitutional changes. The analogy of the body is instructive. The body is composed of parts, and it must grow proportionately if symmetry is to be maintained. Otherwise it perishes . . . or again it may sometimes change into the form of some other animal . . . The same is true of a state" (Aristotle, *Politics*, V. iii. 6). Cf. Cicero, *De re-publica*, II. xlii; Locke, *The Second Treatise of Government*, XIII, sects. 157–58; Pope, *An Essay on Man*, iii. 283 ff.; and Bolingbroke (who follows Machiavelli), *The Idea of a Patriot King*, p. 35.

Rank, before the Conquest, were those Tenants in Socage, who held their Lands by the Service of the Plough; who, as *Lyttleton* tells us, "were to come with their Plough for certain Days in the Year, to plow and sow the Demesne of the Lords;"[10] as the Villains, saith the same Author, "were to carry and recarry the Dung of his Lord, spread it upon his Land, and to perform such like Services."[11]

This latter was rightly accounted a slavish Tenure. The Villains were indeed considered in Law as a Kind of Chattle belonging to their Masters: for though these had not the Power of Life and Death over them, nor even of maiming them with Impunity,[12] yet these Villains had not even the Capacity of purchasing Lands or Goods; but the Lord, on such Purchase, might enter into the one, and seize the other for his own Use. And as for the Land which they held in Villenage, tho' Lord *Coke* says, it was not only held at the Will of the Lord, but according to the Custom of the Manor; yet, in antient Times, if the Lord ejected them, they were manifestly without Remedy.[13]

And as to the former, tho' they were accounted Freemen, yet were they obliged to swear Fealty to their Lord; and tho' Mr. *Rapin* be mistaken, when he says they could not alienate their Land, (for before the Statute of *Magna Charta, Chap.* 32. they could have given or sold the whole, but without any Alteration of the Tenure)[14] yet was the Estate of these but very mean. "Tho' they are called Freemen (says Lord *Coke*), yet they ploughed, harrowed, reaped, and mowed, &c. for the lord;" and *Bracton, Dicuntur Socmanni eo quod deputati sunt tantummodo ad culturam.*[15]

---

10. Sir Edward Coke, *I Inst.*, fo. 87a.

11. Ibid., fo. 116b.

12. Cf. Rapin, "Among the Anglo-Saxons, the lords had not the power of life and death over their slaves. Nay, the laws provided, they should not cripple or maim them without incurring a penalty" ii. 14.

13. Coke, *I Inst.*, fo. 119b.

14. By ch. 32 of the Magna Charta a freeman was enabled to sell part of his land, the buyer assuming an appropriate obligation to the lord of the fee. Previously, as Fielding indicates, he could alienate only the whole. Rapin had stated that tenants in socage "were possessed only of what they called socland, or lands of the plough, which they could not alienate, because they were properly but farmers" (ii. 13).

15. *I Inst.*, fo. 86b: "And sometimes they are called liberi homines, qui tamen arabant, herciabant, falcabant, and metebant, &c." Coke cites the same passage from Bracton (*De*

Besides such as were bound by their Tenures to the Service of Agriculture, the Number of Freemen below the Degree of Gentry, and who got their Livelihood in the Mercantile or Mechanical Way, was very inconsiderable. As to the Servants, they were chiefly bound by Tenure, and those of the lower Sort differed very little from Slaves.

That this Estate of the Commonalty is greatly changed, is apparent; and to this Alteration many Causes in subsequent Ages have contributed.

First, The Oath of Fealty, or Fidelity, which of old Time was administered with great Ceremony, became afterwards to be omitted; and though this Fealty still remained incident to every Socage Tenure, yet the Omission of the Form was not without its Consequences; for, as Lord *Coke* says, speaking of Homage, *Prudent Antiquity did, for the more Solemnity and better Memory and Observation of that which is to be done, express Substances under Ceremonies.*[16]

2dly, Whereas in the antient Tenures the principal Reservation was of personal Services from the inferior Tenants, the Rent being generally trifling, such as Hens, Capons, Roses, Spurs, Hawks, &c. afterwards the Avarice or Necessity of the Lords incited them to convert these for the most part into Money, which tended greatly to weaken the Power of the Lord, and to raise the Freedom and Independency of the Tenant.

3dly, The dismembering Manors by Leases for Years, as it flowed from the same Sources, so it produced the same Effects. These were probably very rare before the Reign of *Edward* I. at which time the Statute of *Glocester* secured the Estate of this Tenant.[17]

4thly, The Estate of the Villain or Copyholder seems clearly, as I have said, to have originally been holden only at the Will of the Lord; but the Law was afterwards altered, and in the Reign of *Edward* IV. some of the best Judges were of Opinion, that if the Copyholder was unlawfully

---

Legibus, ed. Thorne, p. 226): "[The term socage is derived from *socus,* a plough, and thus tenants who hold in socage] may be called sokemen because, so it seems, they are deputed to agricultural work only."

16. *I Inst.,* fo. 65b.

17. "The Statute of Glocester [6 Edw. I; 1278] gave the Lessee for yeares some remedy by Way of receipt, and a triall Whether the Demandant did move the plea by good right or collusion, and if it were found by collusion then the termor should injoy his tearme . . ." *I Inst.,* fo. 46b.

ejected by his Lord, he should have an Action of Trespass against him at the Common Law.[18]

From this Time the Estate of the Copyholder (which, as *Briton* tells us, was formerly a base Tenure) began to grow into Repute, and, though still distinguished in some Privileges from a Freehold, became the Possession of many opulent and powerful Persons.[19]

By these and such like Means the Commonalty, by Degrees, shook off their Vassalage, and became more and more independent on their Superiors. Even Servants, in Process of Time, acquired a State of Freedom and Independency, unknown to this Rank in any other Nation; and which, as the Law now stands, is inconsistent with a servile Condition.

But nothing hath wrought such an Alteration in this Order of People, as the Introduction of Trade.[20] This hath indeed given a new Face to the whole Nation, hath in a great measure subverted the former State of Affairs, and hath almost totally changed the Manners, Customs, and Habits of the People, more especially of the lower Sort. The Narrowness

18. Fielding follows Coke, *I Inst.* 1. ix ("Tenant by Coppie"), sect. 77.

19. Coke (*I Inst.*, fo. 58b) notes that both Bracton and Littleton use the phrase "base tenure" to describe the estate of the copyholder. The relevant part of *Britton* (ed. Nichols, ii. 13–14) does not use this phrase but his description of the estate agrees with the others. On the limitation of a copyhold estate, Rapin notes, "For as of old villains were not reckoned as members of the commonwealth, but part and parcel of their owner's substance, so were they therefore excluded from any share in the legislature, and their successors still continue without any right to vote at elections, by virtue of their copyholds" (ii. 15 n. u). *Britton:* a late 13th-century legal work (authorship unknown) based on Bracton. That it was in Law French instead of Latin contributed to its influence.

20. Fielding generally shared his contemporaries' respect for the industrious merchant though, considering the hapless Heartfree, he ought to have agreed with Johnson's blunt observation, "trade could not be managed by those who manage it, if it had much difficulty" (*Life*, ed. Hill and Powell, iii. 382). Fielding's most enthusiastic encomium on trade appears in the *Voyage to Lisbon:* "There is . . . nothing so useful to man in general, nor so beneficial to particular societies and individuals, as trade. This is that *alma mater,* at whose plentiful breast all mankind are nourished. It is true, like other parents, she is not always equally indulgent to all her children; but tho' she gives to her favourites a vast proportion of redundancy and superfluity, there are very few whom she refuses to supply with the conveniencies, and none with the necessaries of life" (p. 60). But it is clear from the present context that he was not at ease with an institution that could produce a "riotous independent Butcher or Baker, with two or three thousand Pounds in his Pocket." For a fuller discussion of the contradictions in Fielding's social attitudes, see Zirker, *Social Pamphlets, passim.*

of their Fortune is changed into Wealth; the Simplicity of their Manners into Craft; their Frugality into Luxury; their Humility into Pride, and their Subjection into Equality.[21]

The Philosopher, perhaps, will think this a bad Exchange, and may be inclined to cry out with the Poet,

> ———Saevior armis
> Luxuria incubuit.———
> Nullum crimen abest, facinusque libidinis, ex quo
> Paupertas Romana perit.[22]

Again,

> Prima peregrinos obscoena pecunia mores
> Intulit, & turpi fregerunt saecula luxu
> Divitiae molles.———[23]

But the Politician finds many Emoluments to compensate all the moral Evils introduced by Trade, by which the Grandeur and Power of the Nation is carried to a Pitch that it could never otherwise have reached; Arts and Sciences are improved, and human Life is embellished with every Ornament, and furnished with every Comfort which it is capable of tasting.[24]

---

21. Fielding's treatment of the "commonalty" provoked some angry response.

22. Juvenal, *Satires*, vi. 291–94: "Luxury, more deadly than any foe had laid his hand upon us . . . Since the day when Roman poverty perished, no deed of crime or lust has been wanting to us" (Loeb).

23. Ibid., 298–300: "Filthy lucre first brought in amongst us foreign ways; wealth enervated and corrupted the ages with foul indulgences" (Loeb). Fielding's burlesque translation of Juvenal's lines may be found in *Miscellanies* (1743), pp. 115–17, ll. 440–43 and 448–51. He quotes these lines in a similar context in *A Dialogue between a Gentleman from London . . . and an Honest Alderman:* "Indeed, to speak a bold political Truth, some Degree of Corruption always hath attended, and always will attend a rich and flourishing Nation. The virtuous Principles on which the *Roman* Commonwealth was founded, excluded this no longer than 'till Wealth flowed in upon them. Their Satyrist, you remember, introduces his Complaints of their Corruption by these Words . . ." (*JJ* p. 31).

24. Although the emphasis in Mandeville is on "luxury" as a spur to trade ("Luxury / employed a Million of the Poor, / And odious Pride a Million more," and see, especially, "Remark L" of *The Fable of the Bees*) rather than as an effect of trade, he undoubtedly provides the best gloss on Fielding's acknowledgement of the benefits of commerce. Moreover, arguing against national frugality, Mandeville anticipates closely Fielding's point

In all these Assertions he is right; but surely he forgets himself a little, when he joins the Philosopher in lamenting the Introduction of Luxury as a casual Evil; for as Riches are the *certain* Consequence of Trade, so is Luxury the no less *certain* Consequence of Riches; Nay, Trade and Luxury do indeed support each other; and this latter, in its turn, becomes as useful to Trade, as Trade had been before to the Support of Luxury.[25]

To prevent this Consequence therefore of a flourishing Commerce is totally to change the Nature of Things, and to separate the Effect from the Cause. A Matter as impossible in the Political Body as in the Natural. Vices and Diseases, with like Physical Necessity, arise from certain Habits in both; and to restrain and palliate the evil Consequences, is all that lies within the Reach of Art. How far it is the Business of the Politician to interfere in the Case of Luxury, we have attempted to shew in the following Treatise.

Now, to conceive that so great a Change as this in the People should produce no Change in the Constitution, is to discover, I think, as great Ignorance as would appear in the Physician, who should assert, that the whole State of the Blood may be entirely altered from poor to rich, from cool to inflamed, without producing any Alteration in the Constitution of the Man.

To put this in the clearest Light: There appear to me to be Four Sorts of Political Power; that of Bodily Strength, that of the Mind, the Power of the Purse, and the Power of the Sword. Under the Second of these Divisions may be ranged all the Art of the Legislator and Politician, all the Power of Laws and Government. These do constitute the Civil Power;

---

here: ". . . promote Navigation, cherish the Merchant, and encourage Trade in every Branch of it; this will bring Riches, and where they are, Arts and Sciences will soon follow, and by the Help of what I have named and good Management, it is that Politicians can make a People potent, renown'd and flourishing" (*Fable*, ed. F. B. Kaye [Oxford, 1924], i. 184–85). Though Fielding's few allusions, explicit or implicit, to Mandeville are uniformly hostile, he echoes many of Mandeville's social attitudes in the pamphlets reprinted in this volume. See, for example, the *Proposal*, p. 228.

25. Cf. Mandeville, *Fable*, i. 185: "Great Wealth and Foreign Treasure will ever scorn to come among Men, unless you'll admit their inseparable Companions, Avarice and Luxury: Where Trade is considerable Fraud will intrude. . . . and . . . while Man advances in Knowledge, and his Manners are polish'd, we must expect to see at the same time his desires enlarg'd, his Appetites refin'd, and his Vices increas'd."

and a State may then be said to be in good Order, when all the other Powers are subservient to this; when they own its superior Excellence and Energy, pay it a ready Obedience, and all unite in Support of its Rule.

But so far are these Powers from paying such voluntary Submission, that they are all extremely apt to rebel, and to assert their own Superiority; but none is more rebellious in its Nature, or more difficult to be governed, than that of the Purse or Money. Self-opinion, Arrogance, Insolence, and Impatience of Rule, are its almost inseparable Companions.

Now if these Assertions are true, what an immense Accession of this Power hath accrued to the Commonalty by the Increase of Trade? for tho' the other Orders have acquired an Addition by the same Means, this is not in the same Proportion, as every Reader, who will revolve the Proposition but a Moment in his own Mind, must be satisfied.

And what may we hence conclude? Is that Civil Power, which was adapted to the Government of this Order of People in that State in which they were at the Conquest, capable of ruling them in their present Situation? Hath this Civil Power kept equal Pace with them in the Increase of its Force, or hath it not rather, by the Remissness of the Magistrate, lost much of its antient Energy? Where is now that Power of the Sheriff, which could formerly awaken and arm a whole County in an Instant? Where is that *Posse Comitatus,* which attended at his Beck?[26] What is become of the Constitutions of *Alfred,* which the Reader will find set forth at large in the following Treatise? What of the antient Conservators of the Peace?[27] Have the Justices, on whom this whole Power devolves, an Authority sufficient for the Purpose? In some Counties, perhaps, you may find an overgrown Tyrant, who lords it over his

26. The decline of the power of the office of sheriff (and his court) began in the 13th century and continued through the 19th until "All that remains of his once extensive powers over the military and police forces of the shire is his power to call out the posse comitatus [power of the county]" (Holdsworth, i. 68). This decline reflects in part the crown's desire to see its law administered by its own appointees, i.e., justices of the peace, whose powers, especially since the 16th century, increased until "lawyers abandoned all hope of describing [their] duties in any methodic fashion, and the alphabet [became] the one possible connecting thread" (ibid., i. 286).

27. I. Edw. III, st. 2. c. 16 (1327) established provisions for the appointment of conservators of the peace in each county who, as Fielding indicates, were replaced by justices of the peace (c. 1363).

Neighbours and Tenants with despotic Sway, and who is as regardless of the Law as he is ignorant of it;[28] but as to the Magistrate of a less Fortune, and more Knowledge, every riotous independent Butcher or Baker, with two or three thousand Pounds in his Pocket, laughs at his Power, and every Pettyfogger makes him tremble.[29]

It is a common and popular Complaint, that the Justices of Peace have already too much Power. Indeed a very little is too much, if it be abused; but, in truth, this Complaint proceeds from a Mistake of Business for Power: The Business of the Justice is indeed multiplied by a great Number of Statutes; but I know not of any (the Riot Act perhaps excepted) which hath at all enlarged his Power. And what the Force of that Act is, and how able the Magistrate is, by means of the Civil Power alone, to execute it in any popular Commotion, I have myself experienced.[30] But when a Mob of Chairmen or Servants, or a Gang of Thieves and Sharpers, are almost too big for the Civil Authority to suppress, what must be the Case in a seditious Tumult, or general Riot of the People?

From what hath been said, I may, I think, conclude, that the Constitution of this Country is altered from its antient State.

2*dly*, That the Power of the Commonalty hath received an immense Addition; and that the Civil Power having not increased, but decreased, in the same Proportion, is not able to govern them.

What may and must be the Consequences of this, as well as what Remedy can be applied to it, I leave to the Consideration of others: I have proceeded far enough already on the Subject, to draw sufficient Ill-will on myself, from unmeaning or ill-meaning People, who either do not foresee the mischievous Tendency of a total Relaxation of Government, or who have some private wicked Purpose to effect from public Confusion.

28. Epitomized among Fielding's representations of the type by Squire Western, whose excesses had produced "two informations exhibited against him in the King's Bench" and whose clerk prevents him from sending Honour Blackwell to Bridewell "only for Ill-breeding" (*Tom Jones*, VII. ix. 357).

29. Cf. the "vile Petty-fogger" in *Tom Jones* (VIII. viii. 431–32) who was "without Sense or Knowledge of any Kind; one of those who may be termed Train-bearers to the Law; a Sort of Supernumeraries in the Profession, who are the Hackneys of Attornies, and will ride more Miles for half a Crown, than a Post-boy."

30. Referring to the riots described in *Bosavern Penlez*. See especially Fielding's discussion of the Riot Act, ibid., p. 42 ff.

In plain Truth, the principal Design of this whole Work, is to rouse the CIVIL Power from its present lethargic State. A Design which alike opposes those wild Notions of Liberty that are inconsistent with all Government, and those pernicious Schemes of Government, which are destructive of true Liberty. However contrary indeed these Principles may seem to each other, they have both the same common Interest; or, rather, the former are the wretched Tools of the latter: for Anarchy is almost sure to end in some kind of Tyranny.[31]

Dr. *Middleton,* in his Life of *Cicero,* hath a fine Observation to my present Purpose, with which I will conclude this Preface.

"From the Railleries of the *Romans* (says he) on the *Barbarity and Misery of our Island,* one cannot help reflecting on the surprising Fate and Revolutions of Kingdoms: how *Rome,* once the Mistress of the World, the Seat of Arts, Empire and Glory, now lies sunk in Sloth, Ignorance and Poverty; enslaved to the most cruel, as well as to the most contemptible of Tyrants, *Superstition and Religious Imposture:* while this remote Country, anciently the Jest and Contempt of *the polite Romans,* is

---

31. For a description of the progress of excessive liberty to anarchy to tyranny, see Plato, *Republic,* viii. 562–64. Fielding's comments on abuses and misconceptions of liberty are especially frequent in the last ten years of his career. Recurrent are (1) the insistence that vulgar conceptions of liberty are vague or quite empty of meaning, e.g. in the *Voyage to Lisbon* where he condemns "the vague and uncertain use of a word called Liberty, of which, as scarce any two men with whom I have ever conversed, seem to have one and the same idea, I am inclined to doubt whether there be any simple universal notion represented by this word, or whether it conveys any [clear] or . . . determinate idea" (p. 82; cf. *Amelia,* VII. ii. 70, and note the duplication of Lockean rhetoric here and on p. 65 of the *Enquiry* and p. 15 of *A Dialogue between a Gentleman from London . . . and an Honest Alderman*); (2) the conviction that the lower classes (and writers of newspapers) demand and exercise a license that will lead to anarchy and tyranny (e.g. *A Dialogue,* p. 15; *Covent-Garden Journal* no. 47; the *Proposal,* p. 267; and the *Charge, passim*); and (3) the negative definition of liberty as "the Enjoyment of all those Privileges which the Law allows" (*A Dialogue,* p. 15, and cf. *JJ* no. 46, the *Voyage to Lisbon,* p. 83, and the *Charge,* p. 18). Fielding's definition of liberty is essentially in accord with Locke's in the *Second Treatise of Government:* "Freedom then is not what Sir Robert Filmer tells us 'a liberty for every one to do what he lists, to live as he pleases, and not to be tied by any laws'; but freedom of men under government is to have a standing rule to live by, common to every one of that society and made by the legislative power erected in it, a liberty to follow my own will in all things where the rule prescribes not . . ." (iv. 22; and see vi. 57 and vii. 94). Fielding's emphasis, however, is on fear of revolution and license, presumably because of the revolt of 1745 and his experience as magistrate.

become the happy Seat of Liberty, Plenty, and Letters; flourishing in all the Arts and Refinements of Civil Life; yet running perhaps the same Course, which *Rome* itself had run before it; from virtuous Industry to Wealth; from Wealth to Luxury; from Luxury to an Impatience of Discipline and Corruption of Morals; till by a total Degeneracy and Loss of Virtue, being grown ripe for Destruction, it falls a Prey at last to some hardy Oppressor, and, with the Loss of Liberty, losing every thing else, that is valuable, sinks gradually again into its original Barbarism."[32]

Introduction

The great Increase of Robberies within these few Years, is an Evil which to me appears to deserve some attention; and the rather as it seems (tho' already become so flagrant) not yet to have arrived to that Height of which it is capable, and which it is likely to attain: For Diseases in the Political, as in the Natural Body, seldom fail going on to their Crisis, especially when nourished and encouraged by Faults in the Constitution. In Fact, I make no Doubt, but that the Streets of this Town, and the Roads leading to it, will shortly be impassable without the utmost Hazard; nor are we threatned with seeing less dangerous Gangs of Rogues among us, than those which the *Italians* call the Banditi.[33]

32. *The Life of Marcus Tullius Cicero.* (1741; London, 1810), ii. 110–11. In *Shamela*, Fielding had mocked Conyers Middleton's dedication of his *Cicero* to Hervey, but in *Joseph Andrews* (III. vi. 239), he implies respect for the *Life* itself by invoking the muse "who hadst no Hand in that Dedication, and Preface, or the Translations which thou wouldst willingly have struck out of the Life of *Cicero.*"

33. For Fielding's pursuit of these gangs, see General Introduction, p. lv ff. Though complaints about increasing crime are common throughout the 18th century, they were particularly shrill in the years following the Peace of Aix-la-Chapelle when 34,000 men were discharged from the navy and 20,000 from the army: "the reduction of the army and navy had thrown on society, a vast body of men, unfitted for the habits and pursuits of ordinary life; and the transition from war to peace, had been attended by a considerable increase of crime" (William Coxe, *Memoirs of the Administration of the right Honourable Henry Pelham* [London, 1829], ii. 112). There is abundant supporting evidence, e.g. Rapin, *History of England* (1759), xxi. 398 ff. and 420; Smollett, *History of England*, 3rd edn. (London, 1760), x. 368. The extent of the government's concern over the disbanded military is marked by its offer of land grants and other benefits to those who would em-

Should this ever happen to be the Case, we shall have sufficient Reason to lament that Remissness by which this Evil was suffered to grow to so great a Height. All Distempers, if I may once more resume the Allusion, the sooner they are opposed, admit of the easier and the safer Cure.³⁴ The great Difficulty of extirpating desperate Gangs of Robbers, when once collected into a Body, appears from our own History in former Times.³⁵ *France* hath given us a later Example in the long Reign of *Cartouche*,³⁶ and his Banditi; and this under an absolute Monarchy, which affords much more speedy and efficacious Remedies against these political Disorders, than can be administred in a free State, whose Forms of Correction are extremely slow and incertain, and whose Punishments are the mildest and the most void of Terror of any other in the known World.

For my own Part, I cannot help regarding these Depredations in a most serious Light: Nor can I help wondering that a Nation so jealous of her Liberties, that from the slightest Cause, and often without any Cause at all, we are always murmuring at our Superiors, should tamely and quietly support the Invasion of her Properties by a few of the lowest and vilest among us: Doth not this Situation in reality level us with the most enslaved Countries? If I am to be assaulted and pillaged, and

---

igrate to Nova Scotia. According to Rapin (xxi. 400–401), "3,750 persons and families entered themselves for Nova Scotia."

34. Doctors in both *Joseph Andrews* (I. xiv. 63) and *Tom Jones* (V. vii. 240) cite the appropriate tag from Persius (*Satires*, iii. 64). From *Tom Jones:* "Surely the Gentlemen of the *Aesculapian* Art are in the Right in advising, that the Moment the Disease is entered at one Door, the Physician should be introduced at the other; what else is meant by that old Adage: *Venienti occurrite Morbo?* 'Oppose a Distemper at its first Approach.'"

35. Probably a reference to the "Gang of Rogues then called *Roberdsmen*" cited in Section VI, below, p. 136.

36. Cartouche's career is described in the anonymous *Life and Actions of Lewis Dominique Cartouche: Who was broke Alive upon the Wheel at Paris Nov. 28, 1721 N.S., Trans. from the French* (London, 1722). Cartouche, like Sheppard, Turpin, and Wild, captured the public imagination and his exploits, according to the translator, were described regularly in the *Gazette*. Fielding's allusion to him is apposite because his gang had been established shortly after the Peace of Utrecht and was composed largely of disbanded soldiers and officers. Cartouche had been in the army himself. He terrorized Paris from the Peace of Utrecht to 1719: "The Highways were as unsafe as the City, and daily Attacks were made upon Coaches" (p. 36).

plundered; if I can neither sleep in my own House, nor walk the Streets, nor travel in safety; is not my Condition almost equally bad whether a licenced or unlicenced Rogue, a Dragoon or a Robber, be the Person who assaults and plunders me? The only Difference which I can perceive is, that the latter Evil appears to be more easy to remove.

If this be, as I clearly think it is, the Case, surely there are few Matters of more general Concern than to put an immediate End to these Outrages, which are already become so notorious, and which, as I have observed, do seem to threaten us with such a dangerous Increase. What indeed may not the Public apprehend, when they are informed as an unquestionable Fact, that there is at this Time a great Gang of Rogues, whose Number falls little short of a Hundred, who are incorporated in one Body, have Officers and a Treasury; and have reduced Theft and Robbery into a regular System. There are of this Society of Men who appear in all Disguises, and mix in most Companies. Nor are they better versed in every Art of Cheating, Thieving, and Robbing, than they are armed with every Method of evading the Law, if they should ever be discovered, and an Attempt made to bring them to Justice. Here, if they fail in rescuing the Prisoner, or (which seldom happens) in bribing or deterring the Prosecutor, they have for their last Resource some rotten Members of the Law to forge a Defence for them, and a great Number of false Witnesses ready to support it.[37]

Having seen the most convincing Proofs of all this, I cannot help thinking it high Time to put some stop to the further Progress of such impudent and audacious Insults, not only on the Properties of the Subject, but on the National Justice, and on the Laws themselves. The Means of accomplishing this (the best which suggest themselves to me) I shall submit to the public Consideration, after having first enquired into the Causes of the present Growth of this Evil, and whence we have great Reason to apprehend its further Increase. Some of these I am too well versed in the Affairs of this World to expect to see removed; but there are others, which without being over sanguine, we may hope to

---

37. I have not found any evidence to confirm Fielding's description in this paragraph of such a highly organized gang of criminals. He may be alluding to thieves associated with the organization of receivers of stolen goods he describes in Section V, below, p. 126.

remedy; and thus perhaps one ill Consequence, at least, of the more stubborn political Diseases, may cease.

Section I

Of too frequent and expensive Diversions among the Lower Kind of People

First then, I think, that the vast Torrent of Luxury which of late Years hath poured itself into this Nation, hath greatly contributed to produce, among many others, the Mischief I here complain of. I aim not here to satirize the Great, among whom Luxury is probably rather a moral than a political Evil. But Vices no more than Diseases will stop with them; for bad Habits are as infectious by Example, as the Plague itself by Contact. In free Countries, at least, it is a Branch of Liberty claimed by the People to be as wicked and as profligate as their Superiors. Thus while the Nobleman will emulate the Grandeur of a Prince; and the Gentleman will aspire to the proper State of the Nobleman; the Tradesman steps from behind his Counter into the vacant Place of the Gentleman. Nor doth the Confusion end here: It reaches the very Dregs of the People, who aspiring still to a Degree beyond that which belongs to them, and not being able by the Fruits of honest Labour to support the State which they affect, they disdain the Wages to which their Industry would intitle them; and abandoning themselves to Idleness, the more simple and poor-spirited betake themselves to a State of Starving and Beggary, while those of more Art and Courage become Thieves, Sharpers and Robbers.[38]

Could Luxury be confined to the Palaces of the Great, the Society would not perhaps be much affected with it; at least, the Mischiefs which I am now intending to obviate can never be the Consequence. For tho', perhaps, there is not more of real Virtue in the higher State, yet the Sense

38. Fielding frequently observed that the vices of the rich corrupt the manners of the poor (e.g., the maid's defense of her slip with the Merry Andrew on the Puppet-show stage in *Tom Jones* [XII. vi. 641]: "If I am a Wh—e . . . my Betters are so as well as I. What was the fine Lady in the Puppet-show just now? I suppose she did not lie all Night out from her Husband for nothing)." The rhetorical "train" which traces the progress of luxury or vice downward through the social ranks was commonplace in writings on the poor (for instances, see Zirker, *Social Pamphlets*, pp. 74–75).

of Honour is there more general and prevalent.[39] But there is a much
stronger Reason. The Means bear no Proportion to the End: For the
Loss of Thousands, or of a great Estate, is not to be relieved or supplied
by any Means of common Theft or Robbery.—With regard to such Evils
therefore the Legislature might be justified in leaving the Punishment,
as well as the pernicious Consequence, to end in the Misery, Distress,
and sometimes utter Ruin of a private Family. But when this Vice de-
scends downward to the Tradesman, the Mechanic, and the Labourer, it
is certain to engender many political Mischiefs, and among the rest is
most evidently the Parent of Theft and Robbery, to which not only the
Motive of Want but of Shame conduces: For there is no greater Degree
of Shame than the Tradesman generally feels at the first Inability to
make his regular Payments; nor is there any Difficulty which he would
not undergo to avoid it. Here then the Highway promises, and hath, I
doubt not, often given Relief. Nay I remember very lately a Highwayman who confessed several Robberies before me, his Motive to which,
he assured me, (and so it appeared) was to pay a Bill that was shortly to
become due.[40] In this Case therefore the Public becomes interested, and
consequently the Legislature is obliged to interpose.

To give a final Blow to Luxury by any general Prohibition, if it would
be adviseable, is by no Means possible. To say the Truth, bad Habits in
the Body Politic, especially if of any Duration, are seldom to be wholly
eradicated. Palliatives alone are to be applied; and these too in a free

39. The faintness of this qualification is underlined by the narrator's ironical statement in *Tom Jones* (XVIII. xi. 964) that Lord Fellamar was "strictly a Man of Honour,
and would by no Means have been guilty of an Action which the World in general would
have condemned."

40. *Select Trials* reports on thirteen trials "for the Highway" held at the Old Bailey
Sessions between Sept. 1748 and Sept. 1750. The thirteen accused (an inaccurate number
in so far as the trial accounts make clear that many of these highwaymen had accomplices
still at large) were all found guilty and hanged. They were for the most part young, poor,
and menially employed, if employed at all. Five were seamen, six, Irishmen. Two were
women (a barmaid and a prostitute). Only James Macleane, known as the "Gentleman
Highwayman," even approximately fits the figure of bourgeois pathos Fielding sketches
here. After a varied career, Macleane had married an industrious woman who kept their
grocer and chandler shop afloat. After her death, he wasted their funds and took to the
highway (*Select Trials*, ii. 36 ff.). Gentleman-like highwaymen may still be found in *Moll
Flanders*, *Tom Jones*, and *Humphry Clinker*, but they could rarely be seen in 18th-century
London.

Constitution must be of the gentlest Kind, and as much as possible adapted to the Taste and Genius of the People.

The gentlest Method which I know, and at the same Time perhaps one of the most effectual, of stopping the Progress of Vice, is by removing the Temptation. Now the two great Motives to Luxury, in the Mind of Man, are Vanity and Voluptuousness. The former of these operates but little in this Regard with the lower Order of People. I do not mean that they have less of this Passion than their Betters; but the apparent Impossibility of gratifying it this Way deters them, and diverts at least this Passion into another Channel; for we find it puts them rather on vying with each other in the Reputation of Wealth, than in the outward Appearance of Show and Grandeur. Voluptuousness or the Love of Pleasure is that alone which leads them into Luxury. Here then the Temptation is with all possible Care to be withdrawn from them.

Now what greater Temptation can there be to Voluptuousness, than a Place where every Sense and Appetite of which it is compounded, are fed and delighted; where the Eyes are feasted with Show, and the Ears with Music, and where Gluttony and Drunkenness are allured by every Kind of Dainty; nay where the finest Women are exposed to View, and where the meanest Person who can dress himself clean, may in some Degree mix with his Betters, and thus perhaps satisfy his Vanity as well as his Love of Pleasure?

It may possibly be said that these Diversions are cheap: I answer, that is one Objection I have to them: Was the Price as high as that of a Ridotto,[41] or an Opera,[42] it would, like these Diversions, be confined to the higher People only; besides the Cheapness is really a Delusion. Unthinking Men are often deceived into Expence, as I once knew an honest Gentleman who carried his Wife and two Daughters to a Masquerade,[43]

---

41. "An entertainment or social assembly consisting of music and dancing. Introduced into England in the year 1722, at the Opera House in the Haymarket" (*OED*).

42. The customary price of a theater ticket was five shillings for a box seat, two and six for the pit; for the opera in the 1740s, either seat was half a guinea, though prices varied. See Arthur H. Scouten, *The London Stage, 1729–1747*, pp. lxv and lxix. In *Evelina* Mr Branghton is amazed at the high price of opera tickets.

43. By the 1720s the Masquerade, which was essentially a costume ball, had been established at the Opera House by "Count" Heidegger, and by 1751 masquerades had long been the object of rebuke such as Dr Harrison makes in *Amelia:* "though perhaps they may not be as some represent them, such brothels of vice and debauchery as would

being told that he could have four Tickets for four Guineas; but found afterwards, that in Dresses, Masques, Chairs, &c. the Night's Entertainment cost him almost Twelve. I am convinced that many thousands of
honest Tradesmen have found their Expences exceed their Computation
in a much greater Proportion. And the Sum of seven or eight Shillings
(which is a very moderate Allowance for the Entertainment of the smallest Family) repeated once or twice a Week through a Summer, will make
too large a Deduction from the reasonable Profits of any low Mechanic.

Besides the actual Expence in attending these Places of Pleasure, the
Loss of Time and Neglect of Business are Consequences which the inferior Tradesman can by no Means support. To be born for no other Purpose than to consume the Fruits of the Earth is the Privilege (if it may be
called a Privilege) of very few.[44] The greater Part of Mankind must sweat
hard to produce them, or Society will no longer answer the Purposes for
which it was ordained. *Six Days shalt thou labour*, was the positive Command of God in his own Republic. A Severity, however, which the Divine Wisdom was pleased somewhat to relax; and appointed certain
Times of Rest and Recreation for his People. Such were the *Feast of the
unleavened Bread*, the *Feast of the Weeks*, and the *Feast of the Tabernacles*.
On which Occasions it is written, *Thou shall rejoice before the Lord thy
God, thou and thy Son and thy Daughter, and thy Servant, and thy Maid,
and the Levite that is within thy Gates, and the Stranger, and the Fatherless,
and the Widow.**

All other Nations have imitated this divine Institution. It is true
among the *Greeks*, arising from the Nature of their Superstition, there

---

* *Exod.* Chap. xxxiv. *Deut.* Chap. xvi.

impeach the character of every virtuous woman who was seen at them, [they] are certainly . . . scenes of riot, disorder, and intemperance, very improper to be frequented by
a chaste and sober Christian matron" (X. iv. 200–201). Battestin (*Tom Jones*, XIII. vi.
708 n.) notes Fielding's attacks on masquerades in *The Masquerade* (1728), *The Champion*
(19 Feb. 1739/40), *Miss Lucy in Town* (1742), and the *Charge*. Pat Rogers also provides useful information about masquerades in *Henry Fielding, a Biography* (New York, 1979),
pp. 21–22.

44. Horace's phrase, "*Fruges consumere nati*" (*Epistles*, I. ii. 27) is cited playfully in *Tom
Jones* (III. ii. 120). Jonathan Wild, justifying his right to booty he has not won, remarks,
"It is well said of us, the higher Order of Mortals, that we are born only to devour the
Fruits of the Earth; and it may be as well said of the lower Class, they are born only to
produce them for us" (I. viii. 26).

were many Festivals; yet scarce any of these were universal, and few attended with any other than religious Ceremonies.* The *Roman* Calendar is thinner strewed with these Seasons of Idleness. Indeed there seems to have been one only Kind of universal Sport and Revelling amongst them, which they called the *Saturnalia,* when much too great Indulgence was given to all Kinds of Licentiousness. Public Scenes of Rendezvous they had none. As to the *Grecian* Women, it is well known they were almost intirely confined to their own Houses;[45] where the very Entertainment of their finest Ladies was only Works of the finer Sort. And the *Romans,* by the *Orchian* Law, which was made among many others for the Suppression of Luxury, and was published in the third Year of *Cato's* Censorship, thought proper to limit the Number of Persons who were to assemble even at any private Feast.† Nay the Exhibitions of the Theatre were suffered only at particular Seasons, and on Holydays.

Nor are our own Laws silent on this Head, with Regard at least to the lower Sort of People, whose Diversions have been confined to certain stated Times. Mr. *Pulton*‡ speaking of those Games and Assemblies of the People which are lawful, says, that they are lawful at certain Places

---

* The Gods, says *Plato,* pitying the laborious Condition to which Men were born, appointed holy Rites to themselves, as Seasons of Rest to Men; and gave them the Muses, with *Apollo* their Leader and *Bacchus,* to assist in the Celebrations, &c. *De Leg.* I. ii. p. 787. *Edit Ficini.*[46]

† *Macrob. Saturnalia.* lib. 2. c. xiii. *Note,* This RIOT ACT passed in one of the freest Ages of the *Roman* Republic.[47]

‡ *De Pace,* fol. 25.

45. As was noted, for example, in Charles Rollin, *Ancient History:* "[Grecian] ladies were very reserved, seldom appeared in public, had separate apartments, called *Gynaecea,* and never ate at table with the men when strangers were present" (Philadelphia, 1825; English trans. London, 1732), i. 53.

46. *De Legibus,* II. iii. 653 in the received text: "The gods, however, took pity on the human race, born to suffer as it was, and gave it relief in the form of religious festivals to serve as periods of rest from its labours. They gave us the Muses, with Apollo their leader, and Dionysus; by having these gods to share their holidays, men were to be made whole again, and thanks to them, we find refreshment in the celebration of these festivals." Plato was skeptical, however, of this traditional view, and argued that drinking parties (a synecdoche for recreation generally) should inculcate virtue or be abolished.

47. Macrobius, *Saturnalia,* iii. 17 (trans. Percival Vaughn Davies [New York, 1969], p. 241): "The Orchian Law [was] proposed . . . in the third year after the appointment of Cato as censor. . . . its main provisions prescribed the permissible number of guests at a meal."

and Seasons of the Year, allowed by old and ancient Customs.[48] The Statute of *Hen.* VIII.* goes farther, and expresly enacts, that no Manner of Artificer or Craftsman of any Handicraft or Occupation, Husband-man, Apprentice, &c. shall play at the Tables, Tennis, Dice, Cards, Bowls, &c. out of *Christmas* under the Penalty of 20s.

Thus we find that by divine as well as human Institution, as well by our own Laws as those of other Countries, the Diversions of the People have been limited and restrained to certain Seasons: Under which Limitations, *Seneca* calls these Diversions the necessary Temperament of Labour. "Some Remission (says he) must be given to our Minds, which will spring up the better, and more brisk from Rest. It is with the Mind as with a fruitful Field, whose Fertility will be exhausted if we give it no Intermission. The same will accrue to the Mind by incessant Labours, whereas both from gentle Remission will acquire Strength. From constant Labour arises a certain Dulness and Languor of the Spirits; nor would Men with such Eagerness affect them, if Sport and Merriment had not a natural Sweetness inherent in themselves; the frequent Use of which however will destroy all Gravity and Force in our Minds. Sleep is necessary to our Refreshment, but if this be continued Night and Day, it will become Death. There is a great Difference between the Remission of any Thing and its Dissolution. Lawgivers, therefore, instituted certain Holydays, that the People might be compelled by Law to Merriment, interposing this as a necessary Temperament to their Labours."†[49]

Thus the *Greek* and *Latin* Philosopher, tho' they derive the Institution differently, the one alledging a divine and the other a human Original, both agree that a necessary Relaxation from Labour was the only End for which Diversion was invented and allowed to the People. This Institution, as the former of these great Writers tells us, was grosly perverted even in his Time; but surely neither then, nor in any Age or Nation, un-

---

* 33 *Hen.* VIII. c. ix.
† Sen. *De Tranquill. Animi.* p. 167. *Edit. Lips.*

48. Ferdinando Pulton also lists a number of common games and pastimes that are always legally enjoyed, "for these assemblies be not made with the intent to break or disturbe the Peace" (*de Pace*, fo. 25a). He cites 33 Hen. VIII, c. 8 & 9. For Pulton, see *Charge*, p. 24.

49. Apparently Fielding's translation from Seneca's "The Tranqvilitie and Peace of the Minde" (see *Works*, trans. T. Lodge [London, 1614], p. 653). Fielding owned a 1615 edition, ed. Justus Lipsius (Baker, no. 476).

til now, was this Perversion carried to so scandalous an Excess as it is at present in this Kingdom, and especially in and near the Metropolis, where the Places of Pleasure are almost become numberless: for besides those great Scenes of Rendezvous, where the Nobleman and his Taylor, the Lady of Quality and her Tirewoman, meet together and form one common Assembly, what an immense Variety of Places have this Town and its Neighbourhood set apart for the Amusement of the lowest Order of the People; and where the Master of the House, or Wells, or Garden, may be said to angle only in the Kennels, where baiting with the vilest Materials, he catches only the thoughtless and tasteless Rabble? And these are carried on, not on a single Day, or in a single Week; but all of them during half, and some during the whole Year.[50]

If a Computation was made of the Money expended in these Temples of Idleness by the Artificer, the Handicraft, the Apprentice, and even the common Labourer, the Sum would appear excessive; but without putting myself to that Trouble, I believe the Reader will permit me to conclude that it is much greater than such Persons can or ought to afford; especially as Idleness, its necessary Attendant, adds greatly to the Debtor's Side in the Account; and that the necessary Consequence must be Ruin to many, who from being useful Members of the Society will become a heavy Burden or absolute Nuisance to the Public. It being indeed a certain Method to fill the Streets with Beggars, and the Goals with Debtors and Thieves.

That this Branch of Luxury hath grown to its present Height, is owing partly to a Defect in the Laws; and this Defect may, with great Decency

---

50. *Humphry Clinker* (1771) provides a useful gloss on this passage. In his tirade against London (letter dated 29 May) Matthew Bramble complains that the "hod-keeper, the low mechanic, the tapster, the publican, the shop-keeper, the pettifogger, the citizen, the courtier, *all tread upon the kibes of one another*" and that "the gayest places of public entertainment are filled with fashionable figures; which, upon inquiry, will be found to be journeymen taylors, serving-men, and abigails, disguised like their betters." He cites Ranelagh and Vauxhall, "the court, the opera, the theatre, and the masquerade," and "other public gardens of inferior note." For the proliferation of these latter, see Sir Walter Besant, *London in the Eighteenth Century* (London, 1925), pp. 412 ff.; and M. Dorothy George, "London and the Life of the Town," in *Johnson's England*, ed. A. S. Turberville (London, 1933), i. 189 ff. Both Warwock Wroth, *The London Pleasure Gardens* (London, 1896) and E. Beresford Chancellor, *The Pleasure Haunts of London* (London, 1925) contain abundant information on public places of entertainment.

and Respect to the Legislature, be very truly imputed to the Recency of the Evil; for as our Ancestors knew it not, they may be well excused for not having foreseen and guarded against it. If therefore it should seem now necessary to be retrenched, a new Law will, I apprehend, be necessary for that Purpose; the Powers of the Magistrate being scarce extensive enough, under any Provision extant, to destroy a Hydra now become so pregnant and dangerous. And it would be too dangerous as well as too invidious a Task to oppose the mad Humours of the Populace, by the Force of any doubtful obsolete Law; which, as I have hinted before, could not have been directly levelled at a Vice which did not exist at a Time when the Law was made.

But while I am recommending some Restraint of this Branch of Luxury, which surely appears to be necessary, I would be understood to aim at the Retrenchment only, not at the Extirpation of Diversion; nay, and in this Restraint, I confine myself entirely to the lower Order of People. Pleasure always hath been, and always will be, the principal Business of Persons of Fashion and Fortune, and more especially of the Ladies, for whom I have infinitely too great an Honour and Respect to rob them of any their least Amusement. Let them have their Plays, Operas, and Oratorios, their Masquerades and Ridottos; their Assemblies, Drums, Routs, Riots, and Hurricanes;[51] their *Ranelagh* and *Vauxhall*, their *Bath, Tunbridge, Bristol, Scarborough,* and *Cheltenham;*[52] and let them have their Beaus and Danglers to attend them at all these; it is the only Use

51. In *Tom Jones* (XVII. vi. 898) Fielding defines a drum as "an Assembly of well dressed Persons of both Sexes, most of whom play at Cards, and the rest do nothing at all; while the Mistress of the House performs the Part of the Landlady at an Inn." Besant quotes an 18th-century definition of a drum: "a riotous assembly of fashionable people of both sexes at a private house; not unaptly styled a drum, from the noise and emptiness of the entertainment. There are also drum-major, rout, tempest, and hurricane, differing only in degrees of multitude and uproar, as the significant name of each declares" (*London in the Eighteenth Century,* p. 404).

52. In a paper contributed to the *Rambler* (no. 97, 19 Feb. 1751) just about a month after the publication of the *Enquiry,* Samuel Richardson bemoans the extravagance of country town assemblies at "Tunbridge, Bath, Cheltenham, Scarborough!" Like Fielding, he connects "places of open resort, and general entertainment, which fill every quarter of the metropolis, . . . Breakfasting-places, dining-places; routs, drums, concerts, balls, plays, operas, masquerades" with "public sales of the goods of broken housekeepers, which the general dissoluteness of manners has contributed to make very frequent."

for which such Beaus are fit; and I have seen in the Course of my Life, that it is the only one to which by sensible Women they are applied.[53]

In Diversion, as in many other Particulars, the upper Part of Life is distinguished from the Lower. Let the Great therefore answer for the Employment of their Time, to themselves, or to their spiritual Governors. The Society will receive some temporal Advantage from their Luxury. The more Toys which Children of all Ages consume, the brisker will be the Circulation of Money, and the greater the Increase of Trade.[54]

The Business of the Politician is only to prevent the Contagion from spreading to the useful Part of Mankind, the ΕΠΙΠΟΝΟΝ ΠΕΦΥΚΟΣ ΓΕΝΟΣ,*[55] and this is the Business of Persons of Fashion and Fortune too, in order that the Labour and Industry of the rest may administer to their Pleasures, and furnish them with the Means of Luxury. To the upper Part of Mankind Time is an Enemy, and (as they themselves often confess) their chief Labour is to kill it; whereas, with the others, Time and Money are almost synonymous; and as they have very little of each to spare, it becomes the Legislature, as much as possible, to suppress all Temptations whereby they may be induced too profusely to squander either the one or the other; since all such Profusion must be repaired at the Cost of the Public.

Such Places of Pleasure, therefore, as are totally set apart for the Use of the Great World, I meddle not with. And though *Ranelagh* and *Vauxhall*, by reason of their Price,[56] are not entirely appropriated to the People of Fashion, yet they are seldom frequented by any below the middle Rank; and a strict Regard to Decency is preserved in them both. But

---

* Plato.

53. Fielding's persistent scorn for fashionable life is perhaps summed up by his comment in "An Essay on Conversation" (*Miscellanies* [1743], p. 140): "If Men were to be rightly estimated, and divided into subordinate Classes, according to the superior Excellence of their several Natures, perhaps the lowest class of either Sex would be properly assigned to those two Disgracers of the human Species, commonly called a Beau, and a fine Lady." Cf. *A Proposal*, below, p. 272.

54. Cf. *A Proposal*, p. 228.

55. *De Legibus*, II. iii. 653: [mankind] "born to misery." Fielding quotes from the same passage he cites above, p. 80 n. 6 [p. 349 n. 46 in this volume—Ed.].

56. In the 1730s the price of admission to Vauxhall was one shilling. The admission price to Ranelagh, first opened in 1742, varied from one shilling to a guinea, depending on the entertainment offered.

surely two such Places are sufficient to contain all those who have any Title to spend their Time in this idle, though otherwise innocent Way. Nor should such a Fashion be allowed to spread into every Village round *London,* and by degrees all over the Kingdom; by which means, not only Idleness, but all Kinds of Immorality, will be encouraged.

I cannot dismiss this Head, without mentioning a notorious Nuisance which hath lately arisen in this Town; I mean, those Balls where Men and Women of loose Reputation meet in disguised Habits. As to the Masquerade in the *Hay-market,*[57] I have nothing to say; I really think it a silly rather than a vicious Entertainment: But the Case is very different with these inferiour Masquerades; for these are indeed no other than the Temples of Drunkenness, Lewdness, and all Kind of Debauchery.

Abbreviations

Amelia	Henry Fielding. *Amelia,* ed. W. H. Henley. London, 1903.
Baker	*A Catalogue of the Entire and Valuable Library of the Late Henry Fielding, Esq; . . . sold by Auction by Samuel Baker.* [London, 1755.]
BL	British Library.
Blackstone, *Comm.*	Sir William Blackstone. *Commentaries on the Laws of England; in Four Books* (London, 1765–9), ed. Thomas M. Cooley. Chicago, 1872.
Bosavern Penlez	Henry Fielding. *A True State of the Case of Bosavern Penlez.* London, 1749.
Bracton	Henry of Bratton. *De Legibus et consuetudinibus Angliae,* ed. George E. Woodbine. 2 vols., Cambridge, Mass., 1968–.
CGJ	Henry Fielding. *The Covent-Garden Journal,* ed. Gerard Edward Jensen. 2 vols., New Haven, Conn., 1915.

57. Alluding to "Count" Heidegger's masquerade at the Opera House in the Hay-market (see above, p. 79 n. 3) [pp. 347–48 n. 43 in this volume—Ed.].

Charge	Henry Fielding. *A Charge Delivered to the Grand Jury . . . for the City and Liberty of Westminster.* London, 1749.
Coke, *Inst.*	Sir Edward Coke. *The Institutes of the Laws of England.* Four Parts. London, 1628–44.
Cross	Wilbur L. Cross. *The History of Henry Fielding.* 3 vols., New Haven, Conn., 1918.
DNB	*Dictionary of National Biography.*
Dudden	F. Homes Dudden. *Henry Fielding, his Life, Works, and Times.* 2 vols., Oxford, 1952.
ECS	*Eighteenth-Century Studies.*
ELH	*English Literary History.*
Elizabeth Canning	Henry Fielding. *A Clear State of the Case of Elizabeth Canning.* London, 1753.
Enquiry	Henry Fielding. *An Enquiry Into the Causes of the late Increase of Robbers, &c. with some Proposals for Remedying this Growing Evil.* London, 1751.
Examples of Providence	Henry Fielding. *Examples of the Interposition of Providence in the Detection and Punishment of Murder.* London, 1752.
GM	*The Gentleman's Magazine.* London, 1731–1914.
Godden	G. M. Godden. *Henry Fielding, A Memoir.* London, 1910.
Hale	Sir Matthew Hale. *Historia Placitorum Coronae,* ed. Sollom Emlyn. 2 vols., London, 1736.
Hawkins	William Hawkins. *A Treatise of the Pleas of the Crown.* 2nd edition. 2 vols., London, 1724, 1726.
Henley	*The Complete Works of Henry Fielding, Esq. With an Essay on the Life, Genius and Achievement of the Author, by William Ernest Henley, LL.D.* 16 vols., London, 1903.
Holdsworth	Sir William Holdsworth. *A History of English Criminal Law.* 16 vols., London, 1922–66.
JHC	*Journals of the House of Commons.*

JJ	Henry Fielding. *The Jacobite's Journal and Related Writings*, ed. W. B. Coley. Oxford and Middletown, Conn., 1975.
Jonathan Wild	Henry Fielding. *Jonathan Wild*, ed. W. E. Henley. London, 1903.
Jones	B. Maelor Jones. *Henry Fielding, Novelist and Magistrate*. London, 1933.
Joseph Andrews	Henry Fielding. *Joseph Andrews*, ed. Martin C. Battestin. Oxford and Middletown, Conn., 1967.
Loeb	The Loeb Classical Library.
Miscellanies (1743)	*Miscellanies, by Henry Fielding Esq; Volume One*, ed. Henry Knight Miller. Oxford and Middletown, Conn., 1972.
MP	*Modern Philology.*
N&Q	*Notes and Queries.*
OED	*Oxford English Dictionary.*
PMLA	*Publications of the Modern Language Association.*
PQ	*Philological Quarterly.*
Proposal	*A Proposal for making an Effectual Provision for the Poor, for Amending their Morals, and for Rendering them Useful Members of Society.*
Radzinowicz	Leon Radzinowicz. *A History of English Criminal Law and its Administration from 1750.* 4 vols., London, 1948–68.
Rapin	M. Rapin de Thoyras. *The History of England*, trans. Nicholas Tindal. 4th edition. 21 vols., London, 1757.
RES	*Review of English Studies.*
Sedgwick	Romney Sedgwick. *The History of Parliament: The House of Commons, 1715–1754.* 2 vols., New York, 1970.
Select Trials	*Select Trials . . . at the Sessions-House in the Old-Bailey.* 4 vols., London, 1764.

State Trials	T. B. Howell. *Complete Collection of State Trials and Proceedings for High Treason and Other Crimes and Misdemeanors from the Earliest Period.* 33 vols., London, 1809–26.
Statutes at Large	*The Statutes at Large, from Magna Charta to . . . 1761,* ed. Danby Pickering. Cambridge, 1762.
Tom Jones	Henry Fielding. *Tom Jones,* ed. Martin C. Battestin. 2 vols., Oxford and Middletown, Conn., 1974.
TP	Henry Fielding. *The True Patriot,* ed. Miriam Austin Locke. University of Alabama, 1964.
Voyage to Lisbon	Henry Fielding. *The Journal of a Voyage to Lisbon,* ed. Harold E. Pagliaro. New York, 1963.
Zirker, *Social Pamphlets*	Malvin R. Zirker, Jr. *Fielding's Social Pamphlets.* Berkeley and Los Angeles, 1966.

23

"Of Refinement in the Arts"
1752

THE SCOTTISH PHILOSOPHER David Hume was born in 1711 into a family of modest landed wealth. After writing his masterpiece, *Treatise on Human Nature*, in 1739, which he complained "fell dead-born from the press," Hume turned his talents to writings that would be more accessible to worldly as well as philosophical audiences. Thus, in the 1740s, he came out with a very successful and influential collection of *Essays Moral, Political and Literary*, from which the present essay is taken, which he continued to revise and expand in the 1750s. In 1752, he became librarian for the Faculty of Advocates in Edinburgh.

Hume was a friend of Adam Smith, who was twelve years his junior and who acknowledged his debt both to Hume's general philosophy and to his essays on economic subjects, such as the one chosen here. Hume also wrote a justly influential *History of England* (beginning in 1754) as well as important philosophical works such as *Philosophical Essays Concerning Human Understanding* (1748), *An Enquiry Concerning the Principles of Morals* (1751), and *Dialogues Concerning Natural Religion* (published posthumously). A notorious atheist, he died without recanting his religious views and was publicly eulogized by Adam Smith in 1776.

"Of Refinement in the Arts" is the later title of an essay originally published in 1752 under the title "Of Luxury." It contains some of his most far-reaching observations on the character of "commercial society." It is reprinted here with permission from *Essays Moral, Political and Literary,* edited by Eugene F. Miller (Indianapolis: Liberty Fund, 1987), pp. 268–80. Unbracketed notes are by Hume, bracketed ones by Miller.

Of Refinement in the Arts

Luxury is a word of an uncertain signification, and may be taken in a good as well as in a bad sense. In general, it means great refinement in the gratification of the senses; and any degree of it may be innocent or blameable, according to the age, or country, or condition of the person. The bounds between the virtue and the vice cannot here be exactly fixed, more than in other moral subjects. To imagine, that the gratifying of any sense, or the indulging of any delicacy in meat, drink, or apparel, is of it-self a vice, can never enter into a head, that is not disordered by the fren-zies of enthusiasm. I have, indeed, heard of a monk abroad, who, because the windows of his cell opened upon a noble prospect, made a *covenant with his eyes* never to turn that way, or receive so sensual a gratification. And such is the crime of drinking CHAMPAGNE or BURGUNDY, prefer-ably to small beer or porter. These indulgences are only vices, when they are pursued at the expence of some virtue, as liberality or charity; in like manner as they are follies, when for them a man ruins his fortune, and reduces himself to want and beggary. Where they entrench upon no virtue, but leave ample subject whence to provide for friends, family, and every proper object of generosity or compassion, they are entirely inno-cent, and have in every age been acknowledged such by almost all moral-ists. To be entirely occupied with the luxury of the table, for instance, without any relish for the pleasures of ambition, study, or conversation, is a mark of stupidity, and is incompatible with any vigour of temper or genius. To confine one's expence entirely to such a gratification, with-out regard to friends or family, is an indication of a heart destitute of humanity or benevolence. But if a man reserve time sufficient for all laudable pursuits, and money sufficient for all generous purposes, he is free from every shadow of blame or reproach.

Since luxury may be considered either as innocent or blameable, one may be surprized at those preposterous opinions, which have been entertained concerning it; while men of libertine principles bestow praises even on vicious luxury, and represent it as highly advantageous to society; and on the other hand, men of severe morals blame even the most innocent luxury, and represent it as the source of all the corruptions, disorders, and factions, incident to civil government. We shall here endeavour to correct both these extremes, by proving, *first,* that the ages of refinement are both the happiest and most virtuous; *secondly,* that wherever luxury ceases to be innocent, it also ceases to be beneficial; and when carried a degree too far, is a quality pernicious, though perhaps not the most pernicious, to political society.

To prove the first point, we need but consider the effects of refinement both on *private* and on *public* life. Human happiness, according to the most received notions, seems to consist in three ingredients; action, pleasure, and indolence: And though these ingredients ought to be mixed in different proportions, according to the particular disposition of the person; yet no one ingredient can be entirely wanting, without destroying, in some measure, the relish of the whole composition. Indolence or repose, indeed, seems not of itself to contribute much to our enjoyment; but, like sleep, is requisite as an indulgence to the weakness of human nature, which cannot support an uninterrupted course of business or pleasure. That quick march of the spirits, which takes a man from himself, and chiefly gives satisfaction, does in the end exhaust the mind, and requires some intervals of repose, which, though agreeable for a moment, yet, if prolonged, beget a languor and lethargy, that destroys all enjoyment. Education, custom, and example, have a mighty influence in turning the mind to any of these pursuits; and it must be owned, that, where they promote a relish for action and pleasure, they are so far favourable to human happiness. In times when industry and the arts flourish, men are kept in perpetual occupation, and enjoy, as their reward, the occupation itself, as well as those pleasures which are the fruit of their labour. The mind acquires new vigour; enlarges its powers and faculties; and by an assiduity in honest industry, both satisfies its natural appetites, and prevents the growth of unnatural ones, which commonly spring up, when nourished by ease and idleness. Banish those arts from society, you deprive men both of action and of pleasure; and leaving nothing but indolence in their place, you even destroy the relish of indolence, which never is agreeable, but when it succeeds to labour, and recruits the spirits, exhausted by too much application and fatigue.

Another advantage of industry and of refinements in the mechanical arts, is, that they commonly produce some refinements in the liberal; nor can one be carried to perfection, without being accompanied, in some degree, with the other. The same age, which produces great philosophers and politicians, renowned generals and poets, usually abounds with skilful weavers, and ship-carpenters. We cannot reasonably expect, that a piece of woollen cloth will be wrought to perfection in a nation, which is ignorant of astronomy, or where ethics are neglected. The spirit of the age affects all the arts; and the minds of men, being once roused from their lethargy, and put into a fermentation, turn themselves on all sides, and carry improvements into every art and science. Profound ignorance is totally banished, and men enjoy the privilege of rational creatures, to think as well as to act, to cultivate the pleasures of the mind as well as those of the body.

The more these refined arts advance, the more sociable men become: nor is it possible, that, when enriched with science, and possessed of a fund of conversation, they should be contented to remain in solitude, or live with their fellow-citizens in that distant manner, which is peculiar to ignorant and barbarous nations. They flock into cities; love to receive and communicate knowledge; to show their wit or their breeding; their taste in conversation or living, in clothes or furniture. Curiosity allures the wise; vanity the foolish; and pleasure both. Particular clubs and societies are every where formed: Both sexes meet in an easy and sociable manner; and the tempers of men, as well as their behaviour, refine apace. So that, beside the improvements which they receive from knowledge and the liberal arts, it is impossible but they must feel an encrease of humanity, from the very habit of conversing together, and contributing to each other's pleasure and entertainment. Thus *industry, knowledge,* and *humanity,* are linked together by an indissoluble chain, and are found, from experience as well as reason, to be peculiar to the more polished, and, what are commonly denominated, the more luxurious ages.

Nor are these advantages attended with disadvantages, that bear any proportion to them. The more men refine upon pleasure, the less will they indulge in excesses of any kind; because nothing is more destructive to true pleasure than such excesses. One may safely affirm, that the TAR-TARS[1] are oftener guilty of beastly gluttony, when they feast on their dead horses, than EUROPEAN courtiers with all their refinements of cookery. And if libertine love, or even infidelity to the marriage-bed, be more frequent in polite ages, when it is often regarded only as a piece of gallantry; drunkenness, on the other hand, is much less common: A vice more odious, and more pernicious both to mind and body. And in this matter I would appeal, not only to an OVID or a PETRONIUS,[2] but to a SENECA or a CATO. We know, that CAESAR, during CATILINE's conspiracy, being necessitated to put into CATO's hands a *billet-doux*, which discovered an intrigue with SERVILIA, CATO's own sister, that stern philosopher threw it back to him with indignation; and in the bitterness of his wrath, gave him the appellation of drunkard, as a term more opprobrious than that with which he could more justly have reproached him.[3]

But industry, knowledge, and humanity, are not advantageous in private life alone: They diffuse their beneficial influence on the *public,* and render the government as great and flourishing as they make individuals happy and prosperous. The encrease and consumption of all the commodities, which serve to the ornament and pleasure of life, are advantageous to society; because, at the same time that they multiply those innocent gratifications to individuals, they are a kind of *storehouse* of labour, which, in the exigencies of state, may be turned to the public service. In

1. [The name Tartars was applied generally to nomads of the Asian steppes and deserts, including Mongols and Turks.]

2. [Petronius (died A.D. 65), an intimate of Nero and his official "arbiter of taste," is probably author of the satirical novel known as the *Satyricon,* a surviving portion of which describes the absurd conduct of a wealthy freedman, Trimalchio, as he becomes increasingly drunk at a banquet.]

3. [See Plutarch, *Lives,* in the life of Cato the Younger, sec. 24. Cato threw the note back to Caesar with the words "Take it, thou sot" (Loeb translation by Bernadotte Perrin).]

a nation, where there is no demand for such superfluities, men sink into indolence, lose all enjoyment of life, and are useless to the public, which cannot maintain or support its fleets and armies, from the industry of such slothful members.

The bounds of all the EUROPEAN kingdoms are, at present, nearly the same they were two hundred years ago: But what a difference is there in the power and grandeur of those kingdoms? Which can be ascribed to nothing but the encrease of art and industry. When CHARLES VIII. of FRANCE invaded ITALY, he carried with him about 20,000 men: Yet this armament so exhausted the nation, as we learn from GUICCIARDIN, that for some years it was not able to make so great an effort.[4] The late king of FRANCE, in time of war, kept in pay above 400,000 men;[5] though from MAZARINE's death to his own, he was engaged in a course of wars that lasted near thirty years.

This industry is much promoted by the knowledge inseparable from ages of art and refinement; as, on the other hand, this knowledge enables the public to make the best advantage of the industry of its subjects. Laws, order, police, discipline; these can never be carried to any degree of perfection, before human reason has refined itself by exercise, and by an application to the more vulgar arts, at least, of commerce and manufacture. Can we expect, that a government will be well modelled by a people, who know not how to make a spinning-wheel, or to employ a loom to advantage? Not to mention, that all ignorant ages are infested with superstition, which throws the government off its bias, and disturbs men in the pursuit of their interest and happiness.

Knowledge in the arts of government naturally begets mildness and moderation, by instructing men in the advantages of humane maxims above rigour and severity, which drive subjects into rebellion, and make the return to submission impracticable, by cutting off all hopes of

4. [Francesco Guicciardini (1483–1540), *Storia d'Italia* (History of Italy), bks. 1–3.]

5. The inscription on the PLACE-DE-VENDOME says 440,000. [Hume refers in the text to Louis XIV, who died in 1715. Louis had assumed absolute power upon the death of his minister, the Cardinal Mazarin, in 1661. Louis-Joseph, duc de Vendôme, was one of the king's leading generals during the War of the Grand Alliance (1689–97) and the early years of the War of the Spanish Succession (1701–14). England was allied against France in both wars.]

pardon. When the tempers of men are softened as well as their knowledge improved, this humanity appears still more conspicuous, and is the chief characteristic which distinguishes a civilized age from times of barbarity and ignorance. Factions are then less inveterate, revolutions less tragical, authority less severe, and seditions less frequent. Even foreign wars abate of their cruelty; and after the field of battle, where honour and interest steel men against compassion as well as fear, the combatants divest themselves of the brute, and resume the man.

Nor need we fear, that men, by losing their ferocity, will lose their martial spirit, or become less undaunted and vigorous in defence of their country or their liberty. The arts have no such effect in enervating either the mind or body. On the contrary, industry, their inseparable attendant, adds new force to both. And if anger, which is said to be the whetstone of courage, loses somewhat of its asperity, by politeness and refinement; a sense of honour, which is a stronger, more constant, and more governable principle, acquires fresh vigour by that elevation of genius which arises from knowledge and a good education. Add to this, that courage can neither have any duration, nor be of any use, when not accompanied with discipline and martial skill, which are seldom found among a barbarous people. The ancients remarked, that DATAMES was the only barbarian that ever knew the art of war.[6] And PYRRHUS, seeing the ROMANS marshal their army with some art and skill, said with surprize, *These barbarians have nothing barbarous in their discipline!*[7] It is observable, that, as the old ROMANS, by applying themselves solely to war, were almost the only uncivilized people that ever possessed military dis-

6. [Datames was a Persian commander and satrap who led a rebellion against Artaxerxes II around 362 B.C. He is praised by Cornelius Nepos (100?–24? B.C.) as the bravest and most prudent of all the barbarian commanders, except for the two Carthaginians Hamilcar and Hannibal. See *De Viris Illustribus* (Lives of illustrious men), in the life of Datames.]

7. [Pyrrhus, the greatest king of Epirus (the "mainland" north and west of Greece, in present-day Albania), fought against the Romans between 280 and 275 B.C. The statement quoted by Hume was made before the battle of Heraclea. See Plutarch, *Lives,* in the life of Pyrrhus, sec. 16. After winning the battle at high cost, Pyrrhus remarked, "If I win a victory in one more battle with the Romans, I shall not have left a single soldier of those who crossed over with me" (Diodorus, *Library of History* 22.6.2; Loeb translation by Francis R. Walton). Hence the phrase *Pyrrhic victory.*]

cipline; so the modern ITALIANS are the only civilized people, among EUROPEANS, that ever wanted courage and a martial spirit. Those who would ascribe this effeminacy of the ITALIANS to their luxury, or politeness, or application to the arts, need but consider the FRENCH and ENGLISH, whose bravery is as uncontestable, as their love for the arts, and their assiduity in commerce. The ITALIAN historians give us a more satisfactory reason for this degeneracy of their countrymen. They shew us how the sword was dropped at once by all the ITALIAN sovereigns; while the VENETIAN aristocracy was jealous of its subjects, the FLORENTINE democracy applied itself entirely to commerce; ROME was governed by priests, and NAPLES by women. War then became the business of soldiers of fortune, who spared one another, and to the astonishment of the world, could engage a whole day in what they called a battle, and return at night to their camp, without the least bloodshed.

What has chiefly induced severe moralists to declaim against refinement in the arts, is the example of ancient ROME, which, joining, to its poverty and rusticity, virtue and public spirit, rose to such a surprizing height of grandeur and liberty; but having learned from its conquered provinces the ASIATIC luxury, fell into every kind of corruption; whence arose sedition and civil wars, attended at last with the total loss of liberty. All the LATIN classics, whom we peruse in our infancy, are full of these sentiments, and universally ascribe the ruin of their state to the arts and riches imported from the East: Insomuch that SALLUST represents a taste for painting as a vice, no less than lewdness and drinking. And so popular were these sentiments, during the later ages of the republic, that this author abounds in praises of the old rigid ROMAN virtue, though himself the most egregious instance of modern luxury and corruption; speaks contemptuously of the GRECIAN eloquence, though the most elegant writer in the world; nay, employs preposterous digressions and declamations to this purpose, though a model of taste and correctness.[8]

But it would be easy to prove, that these writers mistook the cause of

8. [See Sallust, *The War with Catiline,* secs. 6–12. Sallust took advantage of his position as provincial governor of Nova Africa to amass great riches, and he escaped prosecution only by bribery. After retiring to his luxurious gardens in Rome to write history, he admitted in his works that he had once been driven to vice by ambition.]

the disorders in the ROMAN state, and ascribed to luxury and the arts, what really proceeded from an ill modelled government, and the unlimited extent of conquests. Refinement on the pleasures and conveniencies of life has no natural tendency to beget venality and corruption. The value, which all men put upon any particular pleasure, depends on comparison and experience; nor is a porter less greedy of money, which he spends on bacon and brandy, than a courtier, who purchases champagne and ortolans. Riches are valuable at all times, and to all men; because they always purchase pleasures, such as men are accustomed to, and desire: Nor can any thing restrain or regulate the love of money, but a sense of honour and virtue; which, if it be not nearly equal at all times, will naturally abound most in ages of knowledge and refinement.

Of all EUROPEAN kingdoms, POLAND seems the most defective in the arts of war as well as peace, mechanical as well as liberal; yet it is there that venality and corruption do most prevail. The nobles seem to have preserved their crown elective for no other purpose, than regularly to sell it to the highest bidder. This is almost the only species of commerce, with which that people are acquainted.

The liberties of ENGLAND, so far from decaying since the improvements in the arts, have never flourished so much as during that period. And though corruption may seem to encrease of late years; this is chiefly to be ascribed to our established liberty, when our princes have found the impossibility of governing without parliaments, or of terrifying parliaments by the phantom of prerogative.[9] Not to mention, that this corruption or venality prevails much more among the electors than the elected; and therefore cannot justly be ascribed to any refinements in luxury.

If we consider the matter in a proper light, we shall find, that a progress in the arts is rather favourable to liberty, and has a natural tendency to preserve, if not produce a free government. In rude unpolished nations, where the arts are neglected, all labour is bestowed on the culti-

---

9. [Prerogative refers to the executive powers of the Crown and, more broadly, to its supposed right even to disobey the law if this is required for the public safety. The royal prerogative was brought under parliamentary control by constitutional developments of the seventeenth century.]

vation of the ground; and the whole society is divided into two classes, proprietors of land, and their vassals or tenants. The latter are necessarily dependent, and fitted for slavery and subjection; especially where they possess no riches, and are not valued for their knowledge in agriculture; as must always be the case where the arts are neglected. The former naturally erect themselves into petty tyrants; and must either submit to an absolute master, for the sake of peace and order; or if they will preserve their independency, like the ancient barons, they must fall into feuds and contests among themselves, and throw the whole society into such confusion, as is perhaps worse than the most despotic government. But where luxury nourishes commerce and industry, the peasants, by a proper cultivation of the land, become rich and independent; while the tradesmen and merchants acquire a share of the property, and draw authority and consideration to that middling rank of men, who are the best and firmest basis of public liberty. These submit not to slavery, like the peasants, from poverty and meanness of spirit; and having no hopes of tyrannizing over others, like the barons, they are not tempted, for the sake of that gratification, to submit to the tyranny of their sovereign. They covet equal laws, which may secure their property, and preserve them from monarchical, as well as aristocratical tyranny.

The lower house is the support of our popular government; and all the world acknowledges, that it owed its chief influence and consideration to the encrease of commerce, which threw such a balance of property into the hands of the commons. How inconsistent then is it to blame so violently a refinement in the arts, and to represent it as the bane of liberty and public spirit!

To declaim against present times, and magnify the virtue of remote ancestors, is a propensity almost inherent in human nature: And as the sentiments and opinions of civilized ages alone are transmitted to posterity, hence it is that we meet with so many severe judgments pronounced against luxury, and even science; and hence it is that at present we give so ready an assent to them. But the fallacy is easily perceived, by comparing different nations that are contemporaries; where we both judge more impartially, and can better set in opposition those manners, with which we are sufficiently acquainted. Treachery and cruelty, the most pernicious and most odious of all vices, seem peculiar to uncivilized ages; and by the refined GREEKS and ROMANS were ascribed to all the barbarous nations, which surrounded them. They might justly, therefore, have presumed, that their own ancestors, so highly celebrated, possessed no greater virtue, and were as much inferior to their posterity in honour and humanity, as in taste and science. An ancient FRANK or SAXON may be highly extolled: But I believe every man would think his life or fortune much less secure in the hands of a MOOR or TARTAR, than in those of a FRENCH or ENGLISH gentleman, the rank of men the most civilized in the most civilized nations.

We come now to the *second* position which we proposed to illustrate, to wit, that, as innocent luxury, or a refinement in the arts and conveniencies of life, is advantageous to the public; so wherever luxury ceases to be innocent, it also ceases to be beneficial; and when carried a degree farther, begins to be a quality pernicious, though, perhaps, not the most pernicious, to political society.

Let us consider what we call vicious luxury. No gratification, however sensual, can of itself be esteemed vicious. A gratification is only vicious, when it engrosses all a man's expence, and leaves no ability for such acts of duty and generosity as are required by his situation and fortune. Suppose, that he correct the vice, and employ part of his expence in the education of his children, in the support of his friends, and in relieving the poor; would any prejudice result to society? On the contrary, the same consumption would arise; and that labour, which, at present, is employed only in producing a slender gratification to one man, would relieve the necessitous, and bestow satisfaction on hundreds. The same care and toil that raise a dish of peas at CHRISTMAS, would give bread to a whole family during six months. To say, that, without a vicious luxury, the labour would not have been employed at all, is only to say, that there is some other defect in human nature, such as indolence, selfishness, inattention to others, for which luxury, in some measure, provides a remedy; as one poison may be an antidote to another. But virtue, like wholesome food, is better than poisons, however corrected.

Suppose the same number of men, that are at present in GREAT BRITAIN, with the same soil and climate; I ask, is it not possible for them to be happier, by the most perfect way of life that can be imagined, and by the greatest reformation that Omnipotence itself could work in their temper and disposition? To assert, that they cannot, appears evidently ridiculous. As the land is able to maintain more than all its present inhabitants, they could never, in such a UTOPIAN state, feel any other ills than those which arise from bodily sickness; and these are not the half of human miseries. All other ills spring from some vice, either in ourselves or others; and even many of our diseases proceed from the same origin. Remove the vices, and the ills follow. You must only take care to remove all the vices. If you remove part, you may render the matter worse. By banishing *vicious* luxury, without curing sloth and an indifference to others, you only diminish industry in the state, and add nothing to men's charity or their generosity. Let us, therefore, rest contented with asserting, that two opposite vices in a state may be more advantageous than either of them alone; but let us never pronounce vice in itself advantageous. Is it not very inconsistent for an author to assert in one page, that moral distinctions are inventions of politicians for public interest; and in the next page maintain, that vice is advantageous to the public?[10] And indeed it seems upon any system of morality, little less than a contradiction in terms, to talk of a vice, which is in general beneficial to society.

I thought this reasoning necessary, in order to give some light to a philosophical question, which has been much disputed in ENGLAND. I call it a *philosophical* question, not a *political* one. For whatever may be the consequence of such a miraculous transformation of mankind, as would endow them with every species of virtue, and free them from every species of vice; this concerns not the magistrate, who aims only at possibilities. He cannot cure every vice by substituting a virtue in its place. Very often he can only cure one vice by another; and in that case, he ought to prefer what is least pernicious to society. Luxury, when excessive, is the source of many ills; but is in general preferable to sloth and

---

10. Fable of the Bees. [Bernard de Mandeville (1670–1733), *The Fable of the Bees: or, Private Vices, Publick Benefits* (1714; enlarged editions in 1723 and 1728–29). See especially the section entitled "An Enquiry into the Origin of Moral Virtue."]

idleness, which would commonly succeed in its place, and are more hurtful both to private persons and to the public. When sloth reigns, a mean
uncultivated way of life prevails amongst individuals, without society,
without enjoyment. And if the sovereign, in such a situation, demands
the service of his subjects, the labour of the state suffices only to furnish
the necessaries of life to the labourers, and can afford nothing to those
who are employed in the public service.

24

"Mémoire"
1753

Jacques-Claude-Marie-Vincent de Gournay was one of the leading figures in the liberal movement in France in the middle of the eighteenth century. He was born into a business family in 1712. Early in life, he participated in the family business, making extended trips abroad and learning about long-distance trade. Through these activities, he became involved in government, and by 1751 he was made intendant of commerce of France. While holding this position for the next seven years, he also actively promoted free-market policies both among the *philosophe* protégés he attracted around him, such as Morellet and Turgot, and in his patronage of the publication and translation of significant tracts in the growing economic literature of the time. He is probably most famous for having coined, or at least popularized, the French expression "laissez-faire" as a statement of his policy prescriptions. Though he did little systematic writing himself, he translated Josiah Child's *Discourse of Trade*, which he and his circle regarded as of seminal importance (see chapter 3). Gournay died in 1759 and was warmly eulogized in the same year by his leading follower, Turgot (see chapter 29).

The work included here is one of many manuscript memoirs he wrote while intendant of commerce. Though hardly a polished literary production, it offers a fair sample of the general tendencies of his thinking. It is translated here for the first time from "Mémoire (untitled)" (1753), in *Mémoires et lettres de Vincent de Gournay*, edited by Takumi Tsuda (Tokyo:

Kikokuniya, 1993), pp. 39–63, which is used with permission. Unbracketed notes are by the author, bracketed ones by the present editor.

Mémoire

In all countries around the world, there are only two categories of people who contribute to increase wealth—first, the farmers [*laboureurs°*] because they till the land and get the produce from it; and secondly, the workers, craftsmen, seamen and merchants, thanks to their industriousness and trade. As all other occupations obtain nothing from the land and derive no new wealth from foreign countries, it is fair to say that those who practice these occupations live at the expense of the fruit of the labor of the farmers, craftsmen, seamen, and merchants.

One must remove from the number of farmers, workers, craftsmen, seamen or merchants who are or could be in France:

300,000	monks, priests or nuns,
200,000	soldiers,
40,000	men who dispense justice or enforce the law,
58,000	clerks who collect taxes, fees, and so on,
2,000	*taille°* collectors, head clerks, deputy farmers, contractors in food, fodder and hospitals, general tax collectors, farmers-generals, businessmen, and so on,
200,000	people of independent means, who live on the income they derive from the King and from individuals, without doing anything,
150,000	footmen,
1,800,000	vagrants and idlers—men as well as women and children—who are constantly wandering and begging throughout the kingdom because they are unemployed.

2,750,000

So here are 2,750,000 people, who are supported by others, and who necessarily live at the expense of the farmers, and of the merchants, workers and craftsmen, for it is well-known that these are the only two sources of wealth in any State.

In a country where there would be 18 million people, the proportion would be 11 to 72, so that out of 72 people, there would necessarily be 11 people who would do nothing, and who would be fed, clothed, and enriched at the expense of the 72 [sic] others.

But if there were only 12 million people instead of 18 million, the burden would be even heavier; for out of 48 people, there would necessarily be 11 people who would do nothing, and who would be fed, clothed, and enriched at the expense of the 48 others. It must be noted that, among those different categories of people, monks and nuns are not only fed and clothed at the expense of others, but they do not contribute to the increase in population.

And it must be noted that the 200,000 soldiers are almost in the same situation.

And it must be noted that the prodigious number of financiers and people who aspire to become such—together with the great size of their fortunes and the rapidity with which they have become rich—throw the nation into a prodigious contempt towards all other occupations. As a result, everyone thinks only of becoming a financier, and individuals, in order to plunge themselves into finance, keep on abandoning farming, trade, the arts and professions—which are, however, the only sources of wealth and abundance for the nation.

The 200,000 people of private means [*rentiers*°] who do nothing do not contribute to the increase in the State's wealth through any work, and since they lead a soft and idle life whose ease they would be afraid of altering through marriage, they remain celibate—a situation which has become so common nowadays that the kingdom cannot fail to grow weaker and poorer in population compared to foreign countries where marriage is much more frequent.

Footmen are so prodigiously numerous that they form so many arms which are not used for tilling the land or for the arts, and in most cases, given to living in idleness and debauchery, they end their days in city hospitals, and rarely give back to the countryside what it lost when they left it.

It must be reckoned that, out of the 1,800,000 beggars and vagrants, a tenth die annually from starvation or destitution—that is to say, 180,000 people per year. Besides, those poor wretches rarely get married, and if they do, their children are soon smothered by the destitution they were born in.

And if we assume that, out of those 1,800,000 idlers and vagrants who live in the Kingdom, only one thousand each year go to foreign countries, where they are provided with employment, there results again a double loss for us, because foreign countries are strengthened by what we lose.

According to those general observations, we are going to try to examine how much it costs the nation to have 2,750,000 people clothed, fed and maintained.

The 300,000 regular clergy—men and women, rich and poor—cost 500 l. per year for their food and clothes, i.e.	150,000,000[1]
For the 200,000 soldiers, the pensions, officers' salaries and so on amount—at the rate of 10 s. a day—to 182 l. per year, i.e.	36,500,000
The 40,000 dispensers of justice, including bailiffs and policemen, cost the nation at least 500 l. a year in forced gratuities and transaction costs, i.e.	20,000,000
The 58,000 clerks working in the kingdom to collect fees and taxes of all kinds cost 600 l. per year, i.e.	34,800,000
The 1,920 *taille°* collectors, head clerks, deputy tax-farmers, contractors in food, fodder and hospitals, and the people described as having a vested interest in the affairs of the King cost 10,000 l. per year in salaries and profits, i.e.	19,200,000
The 40 general tax collectors cost 50,000 l. per year—this evaluation is done on a basis of 10%, and all the costs of the general tax collectors are assessed at 500,000 l. each—i.e.	2,000,000
The 40 farmers-general cost 120,000 l. per year in directors' fees, interest on advances and profits, i.e.	4,800,000

1. [During this period, 12 *deniers* equaled one *sou* or *sol,* and 20 *sous* equaled one *livre,* or pound.]

The 200,000 individuals living on their incomes [*ren-tiers°*] and depending on the King as well as on private
individuals cost 3,000 l. each, i.e.   600,000,000
The 150,000 footmen, both in Paris and in the pro-
vinces, cost only 300 l. for food and clothes, i.e.   45,000,000
The 1,800,000 vagrants—men, women and children—
who cannot survive below the 3 s. per day which they
receive as alms, or which they steal, cost 54 l. 15 s. per
year, i.e.   98,550,000
                                                          1,010,850,000

If the 2,750,000 people the nation supports are, as we have seen, deducted from the 18 million people who supposedly compose the nation,
there will remain 15,250,000 people who, in order to have the 2,750,000
others fed, clothed and enriched, will have to pay 66 l. 5 s. per person, in
compulsory and voluntary contributions of all sorts, and regardless of
what they have to spend for their food and their own support. And if we
reckon that, among the 15,250,000 people who supposedly contribute to
the support of the 2,750,000 others, there are always many old people,
children, women and girls who do nothing[2]—even though they do not
beg—we will recognize that the burden of the part of the nation which
actually works and is active is even heavier than what is being assumed.

One can sense, without having to point it out, that if the nation were
composed only of 12 million people instead of 18 million people, the burden would be even heavier.[3]

Since the clergy in England are less numerous and less wealthy than
in France, and since the English do not have as many soldiers, financiers,

---

2. Because men have denied them [i.e., the women and girls] access to innumerable
occupations for which they would be as well-suited as themselves.

3. If we assumed (even though we do not believe it) that the capital
stock of France were twice that of England, that would amount to 48
million; and if we assumed that those sums yielded 10% every year as is
reckoned in financial circles, the total revenue of the Kingdom would
amount to   4,800,000,000
If, in order to support 2,750,000 people according to the chart
above, the State must spend   1,010,850,000
Their maintenance would thus cost 4s 3d per *livre* every year on the total income of
the Kingdom. If the income of the Kingdom is not that high, taxes are even heavier.

and people administering justice—which are the occupations living at the expense of others—as we do, England as a result can have and indeed does have fewer beggars and more farmers, seamen, workers and merchants (which are the occupations that produce wealth and acquire some of it for the nation) than we do or could have.

It thus arises that in England—since compared to France, the idle part of the nation that lives at the expense of the rest is less numerous than the working and active part—the burden is lighter for the active and working part than in France; so that, because all the clergymen, soldiers, dispensers of justice, clerks, beggars and so on in England are less numerous than those in similar occupations in France, it must necessarily be the case that each farmer, worker, seaman, merchant and so on pays less than in France to have the clergy, soldiers, dispensers of justice, financiers, beggars and so on fed, clothed and maintained.

The same argument we develop here about England could be developed about Germany[4] in comparison with us.

If, then, the proportion of people hired, fed, clothed and maintained at the expense of the active and working part of the nation—which is composed of the farmers, workers and merchants—is greater in France than in England and in Germany, it must be that we have fewer farmers and so on, and that they are more heavily burdened in our country than in England and in Germany. And since we have fewer farmers, and since they are more heavily burdened here than in neighboring countries, it must be that farming is less widespread, and that every day many of our farmers abandon the land to become beggars. Therefore, one should not be surprised if the number of our crops is decreasing, whereas the number of our beggars is increasing.

Farming and commerce are, as we have shown, the only two sources of wealth for any State; thus, if these occupations are exercised by fewer people in France than in England, it necessarily follows that capital in France increases far less in proportion, and far more slowly than in England; and since more activity, more trade and more money attract people, then England must surely attract our people, whereas we do not attract hers.

---

4. [The word is "l' Allemagne," but Vincent de Gournay seems to refer to Prussia, as is suggested below.]

Besides, the fact that there are more people employed in commerce in England must necessarily have broadened the horizons of commerce there; broader commercial horizons have enabled people to expand circulation; a wider and more rapid circulation in England must enable it to increase its capital more than is the case in France, where there is always an infinity of riches which do not circulate for lack of value to represent them.

Thus, the number of people and the sum of monetary wealth surely increases each year much more in England than in France.

If we consider how many more people and how much more trade Germany has acquired in the last 20 years, and if we consider that during that time, we have gained no more people and no new branch of trade, it follows that we are becoming poorer in men and commerce compared to Germany.

The result of the evidence we have gathered here is that, since our most powerful neighbors are more populous and wealthier every year—whereas we are not becoming more populous, and as such, are not getting wealthier—we must conclude that we are getting weaker and poorer compared to our most powerful neighbors.

We certainly did not draw this picture in order to prove that, in France, there should only be farmers, seamen, workers and merchants; we know that in every State, there must be ministers for religion and for the teaching of those who profess it, soldiers to defend the State, people who apply themselves to the study of laws and to the administration of justice, and so on; and the more populous a State is, the more the numbers of people exercising these professions must be proportioned to it.

We just want to underline that, because occupations like farmer, seaman, worker and merchant are the most useful to society and the only sources of strength and wealth for any State, one must encourage these as best one can, and limit the number of the others to prevent them from extending beyond what is necessary.

But the exact opposite has been happening from 1685 till today.[5] The nation is deeply weakened by 30 years of wars we have waged against all Europe, and by an emigration that has gone on for 68 years.

5. [That is, since the Revocation of the Edict of Nantes, which had extended a limited toleration to the French Protestant (Huguenot) minority.]

And yet, people claim that, in 1685, there were not half as many clerks and assistants as there are today; so the burden is heavier even though the nation is smaller.

Everything has its counterpart. If it is more attractive to be a clerk, a footman or a beggar than to farm the land, then by necessity the number of those people increases, and the number of farmers, who hire them, decreases. If one wants the lands of the kingdom to be farmed, one must make sure that farming them is found more attractive than being a clerk, a footman or a beggar, so that farmers may hire people among the clerks, footmen, and beggars.

The proof that the State would gain much if it encouraged farming and if it banished everything that keeps people away from work and constrains industry, is highly palpable.

We reckoned that the 1,800,000 beggars who supposedly are in the Kingdom cost the working part of the nation only 98,550,000 l.—each of them costing 3 s. per day. And if, because we encouraged farming and industry, those 1,800,000 beggars strove to work (and there is no doubt they would if one made work soft and easy for them) and earned only 5 s. per day, it would amount to . . . . .164,250,000 l. per year, which would be so much gain for the nation, and would moreover from then onwards spare the 98,550,000 l. these beggars presently cost; so the nation would gain . . . . .262,800,000 l.

But the gains the nation would acquire in this way would be all the greater, since not only would those 1,800,000 people no longer cost anything, but they would even pay their share of the support for the clergy, soldiers, dispensers of justice—who are and must be supported at the expense of the nation—and that would make the burden all the lighter for the rest [of the taxpayers].[6]

If we now try to determine the increase in wealth in France by considering the four visible signs which prove it in England, we shall see that:

6. 1,800 thousand beggars, earning 5 s a day, would earn   164,250,000
Because those people do not earn anything today, they cannot consume anything, and as a result do not contribute anything; but if they earned they would consume, and if they would pay to the King a consumption tax amounting to even a 20th of their earnings, the King would get   8,212,500

1. Since the interest rate has not diminished since the war, and is even higher than before the war, we are less rich than we were before the war.[7]

2. People claim that, before the war, we had more than 80,000 classified seamen, and that today they hardly number 70,000; so our merchant marine has diminished since the war, and if our merchant marine has diminished, our trade must be as well.

3. Rents in general are not increasing in the provinces and are even decreasing in a few of our sea ports.

4. In the provinces one finds lands to buy at five per cent and the quantity of even seigneurial lands offered for sale proves that they are a burden to the landlords.

Now, since the Kingdom is not witnessing an increase in the number of people, in agriculture, shipping and trade, the value of all goods in those occupations cannot increase; it can only decrease just like the number of our people, our shipping and our trade.

If one judged the wealth of the Kingdom by that of Paris and of the opulent subjects, as well as by that of the financiers, it would be like judging the portliness and health of a man when looking at him on the side of his inflammation.

Here are particular observations on the navy, the colonies and the trade of the English in general, in comparison with our navy, colonies and trade, in order to prove the general observations made above.

The royal navy in England amounts to 200 thousand tons.

It is doubtful that the French one with everything included could amount to 60 thousand tons.

If we assume that we have in France 70,000 classified seamen, and that we use 18 men to sail a ship of 140 tons, our merchant marine would be composed of ships—large and small—amounting to at most 544,444 tons, which, after being divided by 140, would give a result of 3,889 merchant ships.

It must be noted that, since the English sail with fewer men than we, they would use at most 14 men to sail a 140-ton ship, so that with 70,000 seamen, they would sail 5,000 ships, whereas we sail only 3,889.

7. [The reference is probably to the War of the Austrian Succession, 1740–48.]

This difference gives them an infinite advantage over us; i.e., because equipping their ships is cheaper for them, and because they sail with fewer men and more ships, they are able to sail more than we do, to convey goods more cheaply than we do, and as a consequence to cut off our shipping everywhere.

Those who are prejudiced toward our way of equipping ships say that we lose fewer ships than the English. This is true, but it is not because we put more men on them, but because we have a third as many ships as they; it is less the number of seamen which ensures navigation than their knowledge and their skill; now fewer seamen on a ship learn their profession better and more quickly than if you have a greater number of seamen, for there are always some who depend on others and who are unproductive [literally, "useless mouths"]. Besides, if there are more men on fewer ships, it necessarily increases the costs of navigation and limits trade.

If the English have three times more ships than we do, we have at least four times more clerks than they do in the service of our navy, so that we have less profit and higher costs.

Our two islands of Martinique and Santo Domingo provide us now with more sugar, more indigo and more coffee than the English can derive from their colonies; and these are the two islands which have contributed most to support our shipping for the last 30 years; but the land which produces the indigo and the sugar can wear out there as it did in Barbados, in Jamaica and in the English islands.

In addition to these products, the English take from their colonies cotton, hemp, masts, timber, tobacco, rice, wheat, logwood, drugs used for dyeing, tar, resin, oil, plates of whales caught by the inhabitants of their northern-most colonies, boards made out of cedar, walnut and other woods used for the marquetry of oak casks.

Except for cotton, which is also produced by our colonies, we extract from them neither tobacco, nor rice, nor timber, nor hemp, nor tar, etc.—even though they could produce all that just like the English colonies; and since all those things have a great volume they occupy a prodigious number of ships.

Because we do not derive those commodities from our colonies, and because we do not receive them from our own ships and yet consume a great quantity of them—buying them from the English themselves or from the Dutch—it follows that *we* contribute for the most part to the power and growth of the English colonies, and that *we* for the most part pay and maintain the British and Dutch navies which bring us all those commodities.

For 20 years the British colonies have witnessed a prodigious increase in men and lands under cultivation; since that time, they have established and are still establishing settlements, both in Southern and in Northern America; Liverpool alone carries more black slaves to America than all the French harbors combined.

As far as we are concerned, we have not established new settlements in America for 20 years, or at least, they have not helped to increase our supplies and our shipping. Louisiana and Guyana are almost as little cultivated as they were 20 years ago; the former still does not supply us with tobacco or rice, which we buy from the British; and in the latter, more than half the population does not know it belongs to the King, because nothing is worth anything over there, and nothing comes from there.

If, while the British strengthen themselves in America and see their men, cultivable lands and shipping increase, we derive from it no men, no cultivable lands and no shipping, we are therefore becoming visibly weaker compared to the English in America.

According to a list printed in London in 1747, there were 2,700 wholesale merchants there, who would go and attend the Stock Exchange; if we consider all together the wholesalers, merchants and so on, who gather in the stock exchanges in Paris, Lyon and all the cities of the Kingdom where there are stock exchanges or currency markets, I doubt we have 2,700 people.

According to the *Complete English Tradesman*, which was printed in London for the fifth time in 1745, the English have 2 million people trading both wholesale and retail in England alone without Scotland; and that does not include pedlars, manufacturers, innkeepers and so on.

One reckons that England without Scotland has 8 million people; so there would be a fourth of the nation employed in trade.

It is a mistake to believe that London is almost the only trading city in England.

Bristol
Liverpool
Hull
Yarmouth
Plymouth
Lynn
Deal
Newcastle

} have each more vessels and more shipping done and maintained by their own vessels than the city of Nantes.

In the current parliamentary session, the British have proposed a law to make the nation grow, and they have passed four laws to extend trade.

The first law, which looks to naturalize the Jews and to incorporate them into the body of the nation, has been desired and proposed for more than 80 years as a way to enlarge and fortify the nation and extend its trade.

As far as we are concerned, it has been 68 years since the revocation of the Edict of Nantes started to cause a great number of the King's subjects to emigrate—an emigration which continues even today, and which, while weakening us, strengthens the British and the Germans; we still have not found any means either to stop the malady which devours us, or to make up for the men we have lost and are losing every day by acquiring new subjects for the King.

As far as the four laws passed to extend navigation and trade are concerned,

The 1st aims at extending trade in the Levant.

The 2nd aims at encouraging more and more herring fishing.

The 3rd aims at admitting Irish wool freely through all the harbors in England—a wool which could get in before only through a small number of set harbors.

The 4th aims at encouraging and extending even further the manufacture of silk.

As far as we are concerned, for 50 years we have passed innumerable laws which tend to limit trade, and I only know two which tend to increase it.

The first suppresses export fees on a few of the goods manufactured by us, as well as import fees on a few raw materials (the special rights of the city of Lyon lead one to regret that this exemption could not have been extended to silk).

The other deals with the incentives bestowed by the King in order to favor the plantation of mulberry trees and improve the drawing of silk.

As for the laws tending to limit trade and shipping in our country, they are numerous. Among them, there are the many regulations which have been made for 50 years on manufactures; the seizures and fines, the visitations to the manufacturers which are ordered by those regulations are so many things tending to hamper the work of the factory, and thus to repulse people from work, in as much as they put any man who dares undertake to work and cease living at the expense of others under the risk of paying a fine, which he would not have incurred if he had remained idle.

If we examine well the spirit of our regulations, we will see that they are all designed to favor the consumer at the expense of the worker. Is this not because, since the regulations have only been drafted by consumers, they have only considered their own convenience without bothering about that of the worker?

We were all born with needs, tastes and passions to fulfill; all those things necessarily lead to consumption, so that consumption is natural and does not need to be encouraged.

But we were not born as workers; one becomes a worker through labor. So it is work one must encourage by making it accessible to all—and as easy and gentle as possible. Then in its turn it triggers consumption, presenting the worker with more varied and more numerous objects, which answer to the various preferences of the consumer.

The purpose one must set oneself in passing laws regarding trade is naturally to extend trade; one proceeds toward this goal if these laws are able to convince the greatest number of idle consumers to become workers, because they increase production; and that is how active trade is born, without harming consumption, considering that—in order to become workers—people do not lose the quality of consumer they had when they were born.

But the laws on trade lead us away from the purpose we set ourselves, if they are such as to convince the greatest number of people to remain idle instead of becoming workers.

In order to pass good laws on manufacturing, one should take more care of what might favor the worker than of what concerns the consumer; for it is the business of the worker to find a consumer, or else he has worked in vain.

Consumers always complain about the workers' mischief, and never talk about their own strangeness.[8] They want to buy good merchandise with their eyes closed, and without making the effort they should make in order not to be deceived; now everything that regulations grant to the satisfaction and laziness of the consumers, they take away from the freedom of the workers.

Regulations are said to have been made in order to prevent people from being deceived; but the public does not purchase as a body; and we have not been put in charge of its business. The public is nothing else than individuals, each of whom buys either for his own consumption, or to trade; in both cases, he knows better than anyone else what is convenient for him, so let us leave him alone [*laissons donc le faire*].

A country where the number of workers and people laboring in production is infinitely higher than that of consumers is a country which will trade actively and become wealthier.

Labor is thus a capital stock which money only represents. Hence it is labor and not money which is the wealth of the State; everything that restricts labor, and which puts people off it impoverishes the State, as it takes away from work people who would be willing to devote themselves to it.

The regulations giving instructions are thus very useful because they say how one must work; those mentioning penalties are harmful, because they put people off work. The only rule one should abide by is to affix the label—which indicates what one means by good quality—to the fabric which is in accordance with the regulation, and to refuse it to that which is not; we are convinced that all the other functions of the inspectors create more beggars than they wrest from idleness.

The principal laws which limit trade and shipping are the Letters-Patent of 1717, which fix trade with our colonies only to certain ports and

---

8. One must suppose that every man who undertakes a commercial transaction knows or should know each other's merchandise, and the multiplicity of laws and formalities that have been introduced under the pretext of preventing the buyer from being deceived are as much a cost of this transaction, as would be laws and administration uniquely constituted for social relations, as if one supposed everyone was blind.

oblige ships to sail back to practically the same ports as those they left. The effect of this constraint is to restrict shipping to our own colonies, and therefore to increase the temptations for the British and the Dutch to engage in smuggling there.

The exclusive privilege Marseilles has to trade in the Levant still contributes much to diminish our shipping and trade. England, by according the capability of trading in the Levant to a greater number of its subjects[9]—as it has just done in the current parliamentary session—is going to increase its trade there even more, and limit ours, if we do not hurry to give them the greatest number of competitors possible by extending our trade to all the ports of the Kingdom. It is as easy to sail from Bayonne, Le Havre, Nantes, St. Malo to Constantinople or Smyrna, as it is from London or Amsterdam. Our ships from the Ponant will bring to the Turks fabrics as well as innumerable other commodities which they have received up to now only from the British or Dutch, as it were. The silks and other goods they will bring back into the West of France at an even cheaper rate and more frequently than in the past will enable us to create new manufactures and increase their number—providing us again with new weapons against those commercial rivals of ours. Besides, the people from the Ponant, while bringing some woollen cloth to the Turks—even though they do so in competition with the people from Marseilles and Languedoc—will only increase the number of pieces of French woollen cloth in opposition to the progress and consumption of British woollen cloth. Hence if we allow the people from the Ponant to trade in the Levant, we shall give far less to the rivals of Marseilles or Languedoc than to the rivals of the British and the Dutch.

Besides, our ships from the Ponant [i.e., the West], which sail in the Levant in competition with those from Marseilles, will oblige one another to sail more cheaply; and this shall extend our shipping as efficiently as cheap prices extend our manufactures.

What did the inhabitants living on the coast from Bayonne to Dunkerque—i.e., a distance of 300 leagues—do to the State to merit being prevented from trading in the Levant with their commodities and

9. By virtue of this law, every inhabitant of Great Britain is allowed to establish himself in the Levant by making a one-time payment of 20 pounds sterling.

their ships? With this interdiction do we not deprive them of a source of occupation we thus leave to Holland or England?

What is a merchant from the Ponant supposed to do when he does not have good catches of fish, when the trade with our colonies is unfruitful and that with Spain overburdened? What do we want him to use his money and his work for? Are the world and what it consumes thus limited to this small range of objects? And when we have set for our merchants the small number of ways they may exchange their riches and their skills at the same time and all together, have we not exposed them to become glutted and to lose in one day what took them many efforts and much time to acquire? And are not the losses we impute to their ignorance and greed rather the necessary effect of the small extent of the scope we have let them sail?

If, instead of all this and in keeping with the increase in their wealth in one branch of trade, we had opened new branches for them where they could have put a part of what they had acquired in the former, and if they had been allowed to try a new branch after having grown tired of one, our trade and shipping would have traced more varied paths and would have enabled us to know sources we do not believe possible because we have not yet allowed them to try.

We have extended the capability of trading with our colonies to almost all our coasts, and I am complaining about the fact that this capability is still far too limited because a few ports have been excluded; however, we have limited the capability of trading in the Levant—i.e., countries that are infinitely larger, more populous, and thus able to consume much more than our colonies—to a single place in the Kingdom. It is in vain, in such a strange situation, that we look for the proportion, the reasoning and, most of all, the calculating spirit which must govern the conduct of trade rather than titles, possessions and ancient customs, where their ancientness alone can be adduced.

The biggest exports of woollen cloth Marseilles has managed each year for 30 years to the Levant are hardly enough to clothe 200 thousand people. What does this quantity represent compared to the numberless inhabitants to clothe in Turkey or Persia, where our woollen cloth has found an outlet? How can we be fearful of sending too much woollen cloth to the Levant?

Besides, since the raw material makes up only a quarter of the value of a piece of cloth which is dyed and manufactured, it is proven that, when, as individuals, our merchants who send it lose 20% as they sell it, the State would still earn much, because what is lost for the individual merchant is paid to other subjects of the King, and is thus not lost to the State.

What is called the arrangements—i.e., fixing the number of pieces of woollen cloth a manufacturer can make and ship to the Levant, fixing the price and the number of people who may sell it—necessarily tends to diminish the number of merchants, manufacturers and workers, and ruins our wholesalers by depriving them of their calculating spirit and of the necessity to calculate. Therefore those arrangements tend to increase the number of beggars in our country.

Forbidding foreigners to sell our woollen cloth destined to the Levant under the pretext that they themselves sell it to the Turks is equally extraordinary, and also tends to limit trade as surely as would forbidding the merchants from Rouen, Morlaix and St. Malo to sell cloth to the British and the Dutch under the pretext that it harms the sale of those the French merchants send to Cádiz or the Indies in ships and galleons. It amounts to insulting the great Colbert to think that, because he set a few limits to our trade, he intended them to last forever; it was enough to have drawn our commerce out of nothing and led it to the point where he left it. He probably reckoned that it would be easy to take it further after him, and to make sure that there would be no province in the Kingdom that would not benefit from it, and that could not one day communicate with all the nations of the world with its shipping and output.

Since the British need foreign silk as we do, they have opened all their ports to receive it, and as we have said previously, they are occupied in the current parliamentary session with the means to encourage its use and extend its production.

We have the same need for silk, but its entry into our country is limited to only two routes—i.e., Marseilles and Lyon—which turns silk into a more expensive material for our manufactures (which could otherwise obtain it through a shorter and less expensive way), and which has made all the cities on this side of Lyon become dependent on that city, causing them much harm. As silk is a second source of occupation, it seems that one could not open too many channels to spread through the provinces.

The exclusive privilege of passage the cities of Lyon and Marseilles demand and maintain vehemently is founded on titles and a possession of more than 300 years, which dates back to a time when we had neither trade nor rivals.

If one wishes to evaluate the progress that the manufacturing of silk has made in England over the past 70 years, one must note that before 1685 no cloth, as it were, was made in their country, and that according to the *British Merchant,* they would then get it every year from our country for a sum of 12 to 14 million.

In an essay printed in London in 1719 requesting the repression of the use of cloths from the Indies, a British author named Claude Rey, a silk merchant, put forward that as early as that time the silk industry was approaching 12,000 powerlooms in Great Britain.

The author of another book printed in 1728 entitled *Plan of English Commerce* establishes that at that time the silk industry of England manufactured up to a value of 2 million pounds sterling every year—i.e., 48 million of our money, about 30 million of which are consumed within Great Britain, and the 18 million that are left are sold and sent to foreign countries.[10]

The same author also confirms that in 1728 the English withdrew less than 120 thousand pounds sterling in silk fabric—or 2,880,000 liv. in our money—either from France or from Italy.

There is no doubt that, from 1728 to the present, the manufacture of silk has grown considerably in England.

Here, roughly speaking, is the current situation of silk manufacture in our country.

In Lyon, according to the Report of the consulate dating back to February 4th, 1753, there are . . . . 10,000 looms

According to the Report of the Inspectors $\begin{cases} \text{in Tours} & 1,300 \\ \text{in Nîmes} & 1,500 \end{cases}$

In Paris it is assumed that there are at most 1,000

In Marseilles   200

I.e.   14,000 looms

10. [The references are to Charles King, *The British Merchant, or, Commerce preserved* (London, 1713–14, 1720, 1721); Claudius Rey, *The weavers' true case* (London, 1719); Daniel Defoe, *A Plan of the English Commerce* (London, 1728; repr. 1974).]

One must note that the manufacture of silk was already flourishing in France in 1685, whereas it did not exist, as it were, in England; thus, the progress the English have made in this area is more substantial than ours.

It is likely that in their silk manufacturing, the English include stockings and hosiery, which counts for much also in our country. Thus, in order to properly evaluate the strength of both manufactures, one should know not only the number of power looms we have to make silk fabrics, but also looms used to make stockings and other works made purely of silk.

But it is even more important to examine which of the two manufactures is likely to grow more in the future.

I am afraid it is the English, even though we have an advantage they do not have—i.e., we have silks in our country. Here is why:

1. The population of England increases every day.
2. Apprenticeships there are shorter than in our country.
3. Native English do not pay any rights of production [*droits de maîtrise*].[11]
4. Silk comes into England through all its harbors, and no fee has to be paid for fabrics inside the Kingdom when going from one province to another.
5. The main manufacture being set up in a London suburb, it can more easily spread beyond than in Lyon, where it is concentrated inside the city.
6. The same man may have as many looms as he likes.
7. There is plenty of money in England at 3%, whereas there is scarcely any in Lyon at 13%. If the manufacture of silk grows in England more quickly than in our country, there will thus be fewer idlers and beggars in England than in our country with each passing day.

In the past 20 years, the British have greatly expanded their whale and cod fishing; the law they have just passed to encourage herring fishing is going to create even more opportunities; as a result, this branch will reduce even more the number of beggars in their country.

As far as we are concerned, for 20 years we have not passed any law

---

11. [These were conditions and expenses associated with the privilege of becoming a master guildsman.]

either to acquire a share in whale fishing, or to increase herring fishing; cod fishing is even decreasing, because in our own country we treat our own fish as foreign. As a result, this abundant source of occupation has not reduced the number of beggars in our country compared to what it was 20 years ago.

A sure means to limit trade in foreign countries is to extend and facilitate it in one's own country. This is what the English clearly understood when, in the current parliamentary session, they decided to open all their ports to receive Irish wool; the more they receive it in their country and the more they work on it, the less wool there will be in Ireland to be brought to us. The result of this will be another increase in employment in their country and a decrease in work in our country; there will be fewer beggars in their country and more in ours.

For 70 years, the English have prodigiously limited the consumption of our fabrics in their country; we used to sell it to them for up to £600,000, i.e., 14 million of our money in 1685, according to the *British Merchant;* in reducing the consumption of our fabrics in their country, they have attracted those from Germany, and established manufactures in Scotland and Ireland. The latter especially make considerable progress, so that there is more employment and fewer beggars in their country. By reducing the consumption of our fabrics in their country, they have reduced the number of people who, in France, would live at their expense. There must thus be fewer people in France today who are kept occupied by the English, as opposed to when they used to consume great quantities of our fabrics. Therefore the English owe us less today than they used to back then, and provide a living for fewer people than they used to. Thus, there must be more beggars in our country today than there used to be.

It has been proven by the treatise against usury written by the knight Thomas Culpeper (printed in London in 1621) that we then provided the English with much wheat, and that we would sell them such great quantities and at so cheap a rate that our wheat would prevent theirs from being sold in their home market. It is only too obvious that things have greatly changed between them and us, since we not only have not provided them with any wheat for 50 years, but turn to them for our subsistence. Thus, cultivation has grown much in their country and has prodigiously decreased in ours; as a result, there is more employment in their country and more beggars in ours.

As the grain trade is constantly free in England, there are a great many people who constantly occupy themselves with it, so that it is a great source of employment in their country. In France the trade and circulation of grain is so often hindered even from one province to another, and those who take care of it are so often viewed askance and sometimes even subjected to search, that few people devote themselves to it. So here is a source of employment missing in our country, and thus more idlers.

It is said that grain must be kept in the Kingdom; however, it is often dangerous to keep some in one's own home. How does one make sense of this?

All the management of grain in England seems devised according to the interests of the farmer, and it does not seem that one pays attention to the consumer; so it is not surprising that there is much farming done there.

In our country, the management of grain seems devised only to serve the interests of the consumers who, always afraid of running short, can only think in terms of restrictions and regulations, whose first effect however is to stifle production; so it is not surprising that in France little farming is done.

If, while the English grow and acquire daily more men, more lands under cultivation, more fish, more shipping, more commerce and trade, we do not get more men, more lands, more fish, more shipping, more commerce and trade, we thus become notably poorer and weaker compared to the English.

The country compared to which we are growing thus weaker is hardly a third the size of France and [...] of the people who currently pay nothing to it and live at the expense of its other subjects.

We are convinced that this total is much higher than the one that emerges all over the Kingdom under the name of industry, as well as the taxes paid by the corporate bodies [*communautés*].

25

"Luxury, Commerce, and the Arts"
1754

JEAN-JACQUES ROUSSEAU was one of the leading intellectual figures in Europe in the middle of the eighteenth century. Though born in Geneva in 1712 into an artisanal family, he left home while a teenager and made his way up the social ladder in France, first as a music copyist, then as a writer. He befriended Diderot in particular just when the *Encyclopédie* was being created, and contributed some articles to that work. His *Discourse on the Arts and Sciences* (1750), the winning entry in a competition promoted by the provincial academy of Dijon, was an instant sensation. His *Discourse on the Origins of Inequality Among Men*, also written for a prize competition (though not the winner), came out in 1754 and was a more complex and controversial work. These general attacks on progress and modern civilization were at first regarded as mere paradox by some of his *philosophe* friends; only in the late 1750s did he become estranged from them—partly for personal reasons, as Rousseau was possessed of a prickly and hypersensitive personality. Among his other famous works were *Letter to d'Alembert on the Theatre* (1758), which precipitated the break in his friendship with Diderot and his circle, *Emile, or on Education* (1762), and especially *The Social Contract* (1762), one of the most influential works of political theory in the modern world. He also wrote constitutional projects for Corsica and Poland, as well as a *Discourse on Political Economy*. He eventually went mad, produced little in his later years, and died in 1778.

The work translated here for the first time was chosen for its obscurity and its concise representativeness of Rousseau's thinking. It was an unpolished manuscript published for the first time as "Le Luxe, le commerce et les arts," in *Oeuvres complètes de Jean-Jacques Rousseau,* vol. 3, edited by B. Gagnebin, M. Raymond, and Robert Derathé (Paris: Gallimard, 1964), pp. 516–24 and 1529–32. Both the text and the unbracketed notes are © Gallimard, 1964, and are used with permission; bracketed material is by the present editor.

Luxury, Commerce, and the Arts[2]

If men could recognize how much more dangerous it is for them to be mistaken than it is useful for them to have knowledge, they would be less eager to listen to the teachings of the philosophers; and the Philosophers would be more cautious about dispensing them, if they could sense that

1. In his previous writings—in particular, or so it seems, in the first version of the *Discourse on Inequality*, with the *Responses* to the King of Poland and to Mr. Bordes— Rousseau had considered the issues of luxury, commerce and arts "in relation to morals." Here he examines them from a political point of view "in relation to the prosperity of the State." The reflections included in this fragment are a result of his reading of "several modern writers," and concern mainly "two men [who] have taken it upon themselves to-day to overthrow all the economic maxims of the ancient politicians to replace them with a brand new system of government." Since they are contemporary authors, Rousseau, as usual, does not give their names. One may think that he refers to J.-F. Melon (*Essai Politique sur le Commerce,* first edition, 1734, 2nd edition, 1736 [see chapter 15 in this volume]), who was denounced in the *Response to M. Bordes* as the author of a "poisonous doctrine," and to David Hume, whose *Essays* on commerce, luxury ("Refinement in the Arts"), and money had been published in 1752 and translated into French the following year [see chapter 23]. One could also think of "The Worldling" and the "Apology for Luxury" [see chapters 16 and 17], but the words used by Rousseau ("two men trying to become famous with uncommon opinions") are enough to show that Voltaire is not referred to in this text—at least not directly.

one bad line of reasoning would diminish their reputations more than a hundred truths they discovered could add to it. The best use one can make of Philosophy is to have it destroy the evils it has given birth to, even if in the process one has to destroy the good (if there is any) caused by it. For in what is added to the simple light of reason and the pure feelings of nature, it is still better to remove the good than to let the evil be. It would be to the advantage of society if philosophers were to organize their work so that, after many Books and disputes, they found themselves mutually refuted, with everything null and void. It is true that we would not know anything then, but we would agree upon that in good faith, and in the search for truth, we would have truly taken all the steps one must take backwards from error to ignorance.[2] In order to work towards this salutary aim, I shall endeavor to examine a few questions of ethics and politics hashed out and settled by several modern Writers, and which deal with subjects on which I have been obliged to meditate. In this way, I also hope to develop certain Theorems which a fear of digression led me to put forward without proof in other writings. But since in all this I wish rather to attack mistakes than to establish new truths, I honestly confess that, when the works of my adversaries cease to exist, mine will be perfectly useless. I do not mean to be the guide of my contemporaries; I am merely warning them when I see someone who leads them astray; and I would not have to bother them with my opinions if nobody took it upon himself to be their leader.

The issue I wish to examine here deals with luxury, commerce and the arts, not exactly in relation to morals as I did previously, but with a new perspective and in relation to the prosperity of the State.

All the ancients regarded luxury as a sign that morals were corrupted, and that the government was weak. Sumptuary Laws[3] are almost as old as polities. The Egyptians had them, the Hebrews received some from their legislators; they can even be found in Persia; as for the Greeks, the

2. Cf. *Emile*, book III: "Because the more men know the more they are mistaken, the only means of avoiding errors is ignorance."

3. Rousseau does not believe in their efficacy: "it is not with sumptuary laws that one manages to entirely suppress luxury," he writes in *Considerations on the Polish government*.

deep contempt they had for Asian pomp was the best sumptuary law they could have had.

This contempt was even more palpable among the Romans. For them, the luxury and magnificence of the other nations were true objects of ridicule, and the use they made of them in their triumphs was much more likely to ridicule all the vain pomp of the defeated Peoples than to give the conquerors the desire to imitate it.[4]

It was natural that commerce should be tainted with the contempt felt towards luxury. The Romans despised it, the Greeks left it to Foreigners; mechanical arts were exercised almost solely by Slaves, and the liberal arts themselves required a great superiority in talent for those who exercised them in order to be deemed respectable—even though they never acquired such respectability in Rome during the entire time of the Republic. In short, in the countries where money was despised, all the means to earn some had always something ignominious about them.[5]

When these Peoples started to degenerate, when vanity and love of pleasure succeeded that of homeland [*patrie°*] and virtue, vice and indolence came in from everywhere, and there was only luxury and money to satisfy them. Individuals became wealthier; commerce and the arts blossomed, and the State soon perished.[6]

However, during the time of the greatest depravity, philosophers and

---

4. Cf. *Considerations on the Polish government:* "Romans would display much luxury in their triumphs. But it was the luxury of the conquered; the more it shone, the less it seduced people. Its brightness itself was a lesson for the Romans. The captive Kings were tied with chains of gold and precious stones. That's luxury of course." One can find a slightly different remark in *Discourse on Political Economy:* "The hat of a citizen who had been freed from slavery, the civic crown of the man who had saved somebody else's life— that is what was looked upon with the greatest delight in the pomp of triumphs; and it must be noted that among the crowns used to praise great battle deeds, only the civic crown and that of victors were made of herbs and leaves; all the others were only made of gold."

5. According to *Considerations on the Polish government,* one of the means to create a free, peaceful and sensible nation is "to turn money into something despicable, and if possible, useless."

6. Cf. *Discourse on Inequality,* footnote IX: "From Society and the luxury to which it gives birth arise the liberal and mechanical arts, commerce, letters, and all those superfluities which make industry flourish, enrich and ruin nations."

politicians never ceased to protest loudly against all those disorders whose effects they could foresee. Nobody contradicted them, and nobody corrected them. All agreed that their reasoning was sound, and all behaved so as to make it look even better. Those declaimers themselves seemed to pick out the flaws of the Peoples only to make theirs more inexcusable. They publicly blamed the vices whose examples they would have shown if they had not been warned against them.

Therefore, in indulging in a behavior that was opposed to their own maxims, people did not stop paying tribute to truth. It is thus that all nations at all times have agreed in condemning luxury (even when giving themselves over to it), and that during such a long succession of centuries, no Philosopher has dared to contradict public opinion.

I do not claim to take advantage of this universal agreement to support the view I am about to develop. I know that Philosophy, as it adopts the proofs of Philosophers, does without their testimonies, and that reason does not care about authority. But as I know from experience that the word Paradox can be detrimental to propositions that have been proven,[7] I am most pleased to take this resource away at the outset from those who will have none other to combat what I have to prove. I am thus warning them that the opinion which I attack must be called a paradox, which is as extraordinary as it is ridiculous and pernicious; and by refuting this soft, effeminate Philosophy, whose convenient maxims have acquired so many sectarians among us, I am only joining in the cry of all nations and pleading the cause of common sense and of society.

Finally, after so many centuries, two men who strove to become famous with uncommon opinions, which could flatter the taste for illusion, dared today to overthrow all the economic maxims of ancient politics, and to substitute a system of government which is entirely new and so brilliant that it was difficult not to be seduced by it. Besides, since their own interests did very well out of it, it became another way to achieve success in a century when nobody cares any longer about the public good, and when this ridiculously profaned term serves only as an excuse for Tyrants and as a pretext for thieves.

---

7. Here one must remember the famous sentence of the author in the second book of *Emile:* "I would rather be a man of paradox than a man of prejudice."

2

In order to think clearly on the question at stake, I would first like to fix some sure and clear principles which nobody can reasonably deny, and which serve as a base for all my research. Otherwise, if, instead of definitions, each of us has only vague ideas, developed according to our own whim and fancy, we will never know very well what is meant by the words "happiness" and "prosperity" for a people.

Before talking about the means of making a people happy and prosperous, let us try and determine what constitutes the glory and felicity of a people, and what sure signs will enable us to know that a people finds itself in such a condition.

I am deeply aware of the fact that this question will seem hardly embarrassing to most modern men of politics. For one of them will tell me without hesitation that that happiest nation lies where all the arts are best cultivated; another that it lies where commerce flourishes the most; another, where there is the most money; and the majority where all these advantages are joined to the highest degree. But let us first examine whether or not these definitions are correct.

First, as for commerce and the arts, it is obvious—even in the system I combat—that these are rather the means used to achieve State prosperity than the essence of that prosperity. For I do not believe that, to demonstrate the happiness of a nation, any man would presume to advance as proof that it is composed of workers and merchants.[8] And even though I were to admit that workers and merchants are necessary to satisfy public needs, it will never follow that the nation is happy, since one can prove—as I shall below—that commerce and the arts, while providing for a few imaginary needs, produce a much greater number of real ones.[9]

Perhaps one will object that the arts, manufactures and commerce do

---

8. For Rousseau, a happy nation is "a people of farmers," composed of "countryfolk." He advises Corsica to "keep a rustic system, and only to change it when the Island will no longer be large enough" (*Constitutional Project for Corsica*).

9. At the end of the paragraph one reads the following words which have been crossed out: *The most solid advantage a nation can derive from its industry is to attract money from foreign countries.*

not so much aim at providing for the individual conveniences of citizens as to enrich the State, either through the introduction of foreign money or through the circulation of the money already there. Therefore it would follow that the entire happiness of a people consists in being rich in specie—an issue I still have to examine.

As gold and silver are merely the signs representing the things for which they have been exchanged, they have properly speaking no absolute value, and it is not even up to the Sovereign to give them one.[10] For when the Prince orders for instance that a silver coin having such and such a weight, and bearing such and such a mark should be worth so many *livres* or *sols*, he fixes a denomination for commerce and nothing more. One crown is thus worth so many *livres*, or one florin is worth precisely so many *sols*. But it is clear that the price of the *sol* or the *livre*—and thus of the florin or the crown—will remain as variable as it was before, and that it will rise or fall not according to the will of the Prince, but through entirely separate causes. All operations made to fix the values of currencies are thus only imaginary; or if they have some real effects, it is only upon annual income, pensions and all payments that are fixed only in the ideal denominations of *livres*, crowns or similar currencies. Therefore, when the Prince raises the price of currencies, it is a sham through which he deceives his creditors; and when he lowers it, it is another sham through which he deceives his debtors. But since the prices of all commodities rise or fall according to the changes made in the currencies, the same relationship always prevails in commerce between the sign and the thing represented. What I am saying here about cash also applies to the worth of the gold or silver mark fixed by a public edict. This price is only what the flow of commerce makes it; and regardless of all the edicts, the same variations appear depending on whether business is going well or not.

Even though money has no real value in itself, it assumes one by tacit convention in every country where it is used, and this value varies according to the combination of causes which serve to determine it. These causes can be reduced to three main ones—i.e., 1st, the abundance or

10. Cf. *A Constitutional Project for Corsica:* "Money is not only a sign; it is a relative sign which has a real effect only because it is unequally distributed." A similar statement is made in *Considerations on the Polish government:* "As a matter of fact, money is not wealth, it is only a sign of it. It is not the sign which must be multiplied, but what it represents."

scarcity of specie, 2nd, the abundance or scarcity of foodstuffs and other goods, 3rd, the amount of circulation, which depends on the quantity of exchanges, that is to say on the vigor of commerce. According to the way those three things are combined in a country, money can reach an exorbitant price or fall to virtually nothing. As a result, a State may find itself in such a situation that even with a great quantity of money, it would still remain very poor and lack the bare necessities. On the contrary, it could be deprived of money while still being very wealthy thanks to the abundance of all the things other peoples are obliged to spend their money on.[11]

One must add to this first observation a second one, no less important and directly if not immediately implicated in the first. For there are many distinctions one must make between the exclusive wealth of a few individuals, and that which is common to a whole nation.[12] Since the words poor and rich are relative, there are poor people only because there are rich people, and in more than one sense. For the moment I limit myself to the relation between the two ideas. One calls a man wealthy when he has more possessions than the majority of people is used to having, and one calls him poor not only when he does not have enough to live on, but also when he has less than others.[13] Such revolutions may take place in society that the same man may be alternately wealthy and poor, without increasing or decreasing his fortune. The same can be said of nations whether considered individually or compared to one another. Therefore each people takes hardly less care—if a bit less overtly—to harm the advantages of its neighbors than to work on its own. Mankind is thus sacrificed to the national interest by bodies politic, just as it is sacrificed

11. According to Rousseau, the true prosperity of the State does not lie in its pecuniary wealth, but in its independence or its economic autarchy.

12. Here Rousseau tackles the problem of the distribution of wealth, and through this, he tackles his favorite issue—that of inequality.

13. In *Considerations on the Polish government* the principle according to which wealth is relative only applies to pecuniary wealth. Rousseau writes, "Pecuniary wealth is only relative, and according to relations which may change because of thousands of reasons, one can be successively rich and poor with the same amount of money, but not with commodities in kind. For as they are immediately useful to men, they also have absolute values, which do not depend on commercial dealings." It is true that different aspects of the question are looked upon, depending on whether one studies it strictly from an economic point of view as here, or whether one considers it from a slightly different point of view as in our fragment—i.e., that of social psychology.

every day to the spirit of property by individuals. However, one cannot easily imagine how the poverty of one country can contribute to the well-being of the inhabitants of another.

Let us assume that, after long and painful efforts, a people manages to fulfill its plans in this regard, and that it has ruined all its neighbors and piled up for itself as much gold and silver as there is in the rest of the world. And let us see what will result from this public prosperity for the individual happiness of the citizens. First, if this wealth is equally distributed, it could surely not remain in that situation, or it would certainly be as if nonexistent for those who possess it; for in everything beyond the bare necessities, the advantages of fortune are only felt because of differences. Thus, if according to this hypothesis, all these treasures were destroyed in a single night, while foodstuffs and other goods were not spoiled, nobody would mind this loss, and it would be scarcely noticed the following day.

But fixing our attention on so fanciful an hypothesis—i.e., the equal distribution of wealth[14]—would be taking too much advantage of time. This equality cannot be accepted—even as an hypothesis—because it is not in the nature of things, and I believe that any sensible reader will have anticipated this reflection.

As soon as the use of gold was known to men, they all strove to pile up a great quantity of it. Naturally, success had to correspond to the various degrees of industriousness and avidity of the competitors—in other words, they had to be deeply unequal. This first inequality, combined with avarice and with the talents which had produced it, must have increased even more through its own strength; for one of the vices[15] of existing societies is that the difficulty to acquire anything always increases according to needs, and that the surplus the wealthy have is itself what enables them to deprive the poor of the bare necessities. It is an axiom in business as well as in physics that one makes nothing with nothing. Money is the true seed of money, and the first crown is infinitely harder to earn than the second million.[16] Besides, thefts are punished only when

14. Cf. *Social Contract*, book II, chapter II: "As far as equality is concerned, this word does not imply that the degrees of power and wealth are absolutely the same."

15. A first version of this was: *What shows best the extravagance of existing societies . . .*

16. These phrases can be found almost verbatim in *Political Economy:* "One does nothing with nothing; it is true in business as well as in Physics. Money is the seed of money,

necessity makes them forgivable; they cost honor and life to the poor man, and bring glory and fortune to the wealthy man. A destitute man who takes a crown from a harsh man sated with gold in order to have bread is a thief led to the gallows, whereas honored citizens peacefully quench their thirst with the blood of the craftsman and the farmer.[17] And the monopolies of the trader and the embezzlements of the tax-gatherer bear the names of useful talents and ensure those exercising them that they have the favor of the Prince and the esteem of the public. That is how the wealth of a whole nation makes the opulence of a few individuals at the expense of the public, and how the treasures of millionaires increase the destitution of the citizenry. For in that forced, monstrous inequality, it follows that the sensuousness of the wealthy devours in delights the substance of the people, and blows their way only a dry, stale, brown bread at the cost of sweat and servitude.

If we add to this that the prices of all things inevitably increase because of the abundance of specie and especially the scarcity of foodstuffs— which must result in such a situation as I will prove—we shall see how easy it is to demonstrate that the more money a State has, the more poor people it must have, and the more the poor must suffer.

Now since commerce and the arts are only proofs of human need in a nation, and since money is not a proof of true wealth, it follows that the combination of all these things is not a proof of happiness, either.

To set aside other useless reckonings, one must distinguish between the means individuals use to try to become happy—each according to his character and inclinations—and those the social body can put to use for the same purpose. For as society can neither foresee nor satisfy the different desires of the people who compose it, it does not take care of that, but only provides for the common defense and security. And as far as subsistence is concerned, it takes care to enable individuals to provide for their own needs, so that all the commitments the confederation can take

---

and the first pistole is sometimes more difficult to earn than the second million." One might be tempted to infer from the similarities between these texts that the fragment was written before the *Political Economy,* which borrows this passage from it. But obviously it is just a conjecture.

17. The same image is used in the fragment *On the State of War:* "I see . . . a crowd of people who are starving, who are overburdened with labor and hunger, and whose blood and tears are drunk by the wealthy man."

towards the confederates are reduced to these two—peace and abundance. As long as by the word peace one means the security peace creates externally and the manners and morals [*moeurs°*] which create peace within, but also the freedom without which there is no true peace.[18] For tyranny and slavery are obviously states of war,[19] and it is easy to prove that a slave[20] who kills his master sins against neither natural law nor international law.

As far as abundance is concerned, this word does not refer to a situation in which a few individuals gorge themselves while the rest are obliged to resort to them to get their subsistence at the price they want. Nor do I refer to this other hypothetical and impossible situation (at least in the long run) in which everyone would find something to satisfy all his needs near at hand without any work and effort. I refer, rather, to the situation in which all the bare necessities of life are gathered in the country in such quantities that everyone can through his work easily amass everything he needs for his maintenance.[21]

18. Rousseau always protested against those, like Hobbes, who wanted to turn "civil tranquillity" into the aim of civil society. According to him, there is no true peace without freedom. To a certain extent and despite what has been said, Rousseau remains closer to Locke than to any other theoretician of his time.

19. In the *Social Contract* (book I, chapter IV), Rousseau states that "the state of war continues to subsist" between master and slave. He is still more explicit in the first version of the book (book I, chapter V): "As soon as the subjugated people can overthrow the yoke that has been imposed on it by force and get rid of its master—that is to say its enemy—it must do it if it can. And when it gets its legitimate freedom back, it only uses the right to wage war, which persists as long as the violence it allows takes place."

20. The manuscript had originally the word *slavery*, which is obviously a *lapsus*.

21. One knows how vigorously Rousseau condemns idleness in the third book of *Emile:* "Outside of society, the isolated man owes nothing to anyone; he has a right to live as he pleases. But in society, where he necessarily lives at the expense of others, he owes them in work the price of his maintenance; this is without exception. To work is therefore an indispensable duty for social man. Rich or poor, powerful or feeble, any idle citizen is a thief." No idle citizens—that will therefore be the maxim of any well-ordered State. The obligation to work must however have its counterpart in the profitability of work. Men must be able to secure their subsistence and independence with their manual work. Here then is one of the most modern and revolutionary aspects of the social thought of Rousseau. He wanted to free the world of labor from the domination of the idle.

26

A View of the Manner in Which Trade and Civil Liberty Support Each Other
1756

NOT MUCH IS KNOWN about William Hazeland. It seems that he had a Master of Arts degree and that he was a schoolmaster in Middlesex. The writing reproduced here in its entirety was a prize-winning dissertation at Cambridge in 1755 and was read before the university. It offers an articulate example of the political implications that could be attributed to commerce at that time. It does not appear that Hazeland published any other works. His dates of birth and death are not known. The work was never reprinted, and the edition used is thus the original: *A View of the Manner in Which Trade and Civil Liberty Support Each Other* (London: Beecroft, 1756). All bracketed notes are by the present editor; the others are Hazeland's.

A View of the Manner in Which Trade and Civil Liberty Support Each Other

An established Liberty, and an extensive well-conducted Commerce, are the surest foundations, and most effectual means, of national happiness, that any political union of mankind can procure. The ancients, who knew how to value the former of these advantages, and enterprized the noblest designs for the support of their freedom, appear to have had but imperfect views of Trade; and not at all to have considered the very important influence that each of these principles hath on the other. So far from it, that a rigorous prohibition of all kinds of commercial intercourse with foreigners was among the fundamental maxims of one of their most famous republics. The defect of modern policy, as to this particular, seemeth to lie the other way. Most of the civilized nations of the world are now become attentive to the beneficial effects of commerce, and shew a disposition to neglect none of the advantages of their situation, and native commodities: but the spirit of Liberty is, in the mean time, suffered to languish and decline. We have lately seen an instance of a trading nation,[1] who, in order to promote their commercial views, took the rare expedient of delivering up the charter of their Liberties into the hands of the Sovereign: acting herein a direct counter-part to the *Spartan* institution, before noted. It must be a strange concurrence of accidents, that can give a prosperous turn to such narrow schemes of policy, as oppose, or even separate, the interests of Liberty and Trade. As long as things proceed in their ordinary course, the safety of both must consist in their union. Let each of them be pursued as an end independent of the other, they have perhaps an equal right to this distinction; and they will be found eventually to concur in affording each other the surest aid and support.

If this be the characteristic of our happy Administration, 'tis a glorious peculiarity, and will not fail to continue to the nation all the good effects that can arise from such causes; that is, in short, all the blessings

---

1. Denmark.

which a nation can enjoy. Our business is to enquire into the nature of this friendly coalition, and to point out the mutual assistance of Liberty and Commerce.

I

'Tis a maxim which nothing but scepticism ever controverted, "That power must always follow property." Immense riches on the one hand, and on the other excessive indigence—what plainer indications of despotism and slavery? Who ever thought of so much as a legal establishment, where the Sovereign was the only proprietor? You must give the subject his *Focus* and *Penates*,[2] something that he may call his own, before he can be inspired with a zeal for his country, or can understand a constitution. In the states of old, wherein land was the only source of wealth, the *Agrarian law* was ever the favorite object of the republican party, as the firmest support of civil freedom. The share which the subjects can command of the national stock, will hold a due proportion to their weight in the balance of power.

But it is not only relative, but absolute poverty, that is inauspicious to Liberty. In the *Roman* republic, by virtue of the *Valerian law*,[3] the right of electing magistrates by the votes of the tribes and the tribunitian authority,[4] the supreme power was actually vested in the people. And yet their wretched indigence produced such a dependence, as obliged the brave spirits of the Plebeians to yield to an usurped Oligarchy, the power which the constitution gave themselves; and to maintain, for more than two centuries, an unsuccessful struggle with slavery, at the time they were nominally possessed of freedom. The establishment of a military stipend at length relieved the poor husbandmen from the necessity of

2. [I.e., Hearth and household gods.]

3. [Lucius Valerius Poplicola Potitus, consul with Horatius Barbatus in 449 B.C., when (according to Livy 3.55.3 ff.) these laws took effect.]

4. The Aristocratical institution of the centuries is no objection to what is here asserted. For as the *Comitia Tributa* were still allowed, after that other usage took place, that is as much as the present argument requires.

mortgaging their estates; and a flow of foreign success, particularly the important conquest of *Veii*,[5] having enriched, in some measure, every citizen; they grew easy in their fortunes, felt their independency, and pushed every advantage of their form of government. The state took its natural turn; the prize of honour and power became open to the merit of every competitor, Plebeians filled the exalted stations of Consul and Dictator, and would not be denied the Praetor's Chair and Augur's Staff.

Wealth in the subject, then, is the natural poize against arbitrary power in the state; a weight which, as it prevails, will forever draw and incline the revolving constitution, till it settle at the centre of Liberty. But Wealth is the peculiar gift of Trade: an art invented to relieve the distresses of mankind, that operates by producing all kinds of affluence, and whose certain effect is riches. And, what is most to the present purpose, its benefits are immediately conferred on the industrious, who are the more indigent part of every community. Among these it erects a monied interest, a new species of property intirely its own creation, that lifts the humble vassal within sight of his haughty lord, and, by dispersing among numbers the means of power, gives the people a taste and an ability to be free. Meanwhile the Great take no alarm at this growing rival, but pleased with those refinements and elegancies of fashionable life, introduced by Trade, and enriched by it in their turn, thro' the increase of their rents, which must ensue on the improvement of native commodities, they encourage and support the friend of Liberty, which in the end must prove fatal to their power. For Liberty makes its advances no less after Trade is become a general concern, after the government and governed are alike in its interest, than during the first steps of its progress. In that former period, the basis of freedom is laid, by the removal of absolute indigence; in the latter, that vast disproportion of property is corrected, which hinders the superstructure. For a continual addition of wealth, communicated alike thro' all the various stations of civil life, must hasten the several heaps to a level; must bring the fortunes of fellow citizens towards that unattainable limit of equality near which all the safe-guards of freedom lie.

1. It is here obvious to remark, how much better calculated for the in-

5. [Southernmost of the great Etruscan cities, it is 16 km. north of Rome.]

terests of freedom this commercial arithmetic of multiplication is, that regulates the national property, by increasing every particular person's share, than that *Agrarian* division, projected by the ancients to serve the same purpose. For, supposing both of these to be means equally effectual, the latter, which does violence to the possessions of all the most powerful men in the state, can never be brought about but by a military force, which is the least eligible of all revolutions. Whereas commerce works its effect by the most peaceful, popular, and beneficial methods, and, as we have seen before, will naturally obtain and avail itself of the patronage of the Great. Let it be added, that the *Agrarian law*, by removing all the rewards of industry and application, must produce a general idleness and inactivity; an event which will inevitably beggar the public, and thereby expose its liberties to the danger of a foreign conquest, at the same time that such a depravity of manners furnishes the fairest occasion to domestic usurpation: While Commerce sufficiently precludes the avenues of both. For by its vast augmentation of the national wealth, and by means of the number of laborious hands it employs, that are always ready to be turn'd to the public service, it affords the surest barrier against hostilities from abroad; and it is also vitally concerned to nourish and support an habit of industry, a disposition the most tenacious of its rights and jealous of tyranny.

2. This effect of Commerce, which we have been considering, will likewise furnish a very strong objection against a method which still prevails in the conduct of Trade, tho' its other disadvantages be notorious; I mean the custom of erecting companies of merchants, indulged with exclusive privileges. Such monopolies, by confining within a few hands the vast profits of an extensive Trade, must tend to destroy that equilibrium of property, which Commerce is particularly circumstanced for promoting. Which is more especially a grievance, because, as that enormous wealth is amass'd only in consequence of the exclusive power, with which these societies are arm'd by the Government, they will probably be ready, on all emergencies, to unhoard their immense treasures in behalf of their supporters: so that, under this management, Trade becomes a dangerous engine of State-policy, directly pointed against Liberty.

Such establishments are in the monied interest something like those *Gothic* institutions in the property of land which prevail in most parts of

Europe: by which a large inheritance is confined to a succession of single heirs, exclusive perhaps of a numerous race of relations, who are thereby left destitute and dependent on the great Lord of the family. While a free and open Trade, like a *Kentish* yeomanry, distributing the patrimony alike among all its children, enriches a whole posterity, and gives none of them an opportunity to oppress and ruin the rest. For no sooner are the profits arising from any particular branch of Trade become excessive, but the vigilant Spirit of Emulation puts forth a number of competitors to share the Golden fleece. The contest for gain is as warm as for glory. Diligence, skill, and oeconomy, the whole militia of Trade, are all exerted to the utmost; and, by cutting into many different chanels the overflowing stream of wealth, the torrent soon subsides within its proper bounds.

It hath been hinted already, that the manners introduced by Trade are a considerable furtherance of Liberty. I would place in this view, that general improvement in the arts of life, that refinement in the public taste and sentiments, in short all those intellectual and moral acquirements that are duly to be ascribed to Commerce. The contrast between civil life, in that degree of perfection to which it is carried in some countries, and the unenlightened rudeness of human society, before it had learnt the use of laws and government, is too violent to give pleasure by the description. The opposition is not much less glaring of civil society uncultivated by Commerce (if such a state be indeed supposeable) when set against the improved condition of mankind, where Trade has flourished. That wide experience of men and things which this affords, that active enterprising spirit which it cherishes, those encouragements of genius and invention that are proposed by it, have changed ignorance, barbarity, and inhospitable distrust into mutual confidence, arts and humanity; have given rise to all that is useful and ornamental in human nature. For a proof of this let us recur to the history of the *Egyptians* and *Phoenicians,* the most ancient trading nations upon record, who are likewise honor'd by their posterity as the sacred fountains whence all kinds of knowledge and civility were at first derived. Now after the views of mankind have been thus enlarged, when arts are become common, and science is far advanced; is it unnatural to imagine, that the theory of government would at length come to be considered, and sooner or later, as occasions were favourable or adverse, the forms of it be corrected and improved? In fact, the *Grecians,* the most faithful disciples of *Egypt* and *Phoenicia* in the liberal arts, tho' not equally adepts in Trade, no sooner became famous for those accomplishments, than their monarchies began to totter, and they exhibited in their several states more models of a free-government than have since appeared in the world.

Thus the progression of these internal effects of Trade, towards that last and greatest of mental improvements, a true political knowledge and sense of Liberty, is analogous to the order of its external operations before considered. For as it was there seen to create and dispense an affluence of fortune, even to those inconsiderable members of a community to whom property was a thing unknown; so here, in like manner, it raises, enlarges, and opens the stock of intellectual treasure, calls forth sentiments that had never been felt, and virtues that had no objects. And as in the former case the great accession of wealth to the indigent, that is of power to the weak, brings down that extravagant superiority, which supported the throne of despotism, and riveted the chains of slavery; so, in the latter, when the light of knowledge and experience is risen in the mind, it shines thro' that antient veil, the thin texture of prejudice and superstition, that had sanctified establish'd forms, and made kings revered as gods. In short, both conspiring to the same mighty end, the one of these means only strengthens the hand to execute, what the other moves the heart to wish, and teaches the head to design.

Here then I shall rest the first part of our enquiry. For it is presumed, that the manner in which Trade promotes Liberty is that we have been describing: namely, by the production of a monied interest, which emancipates the meaner people from their subjection to the land-owners, who are otherwise their natural masters: and, by giving rise to that refinement in manners, which would at length bring men acquainted with the true nature of civil government, and the desireableness of civil freedom.

II

Let us now turn to the other side of the prospect, and see what are those circumstances, in the nature of a free-government, that render it particularly advantageous to Commerce.

1. And here the first object that strikes us is, that *security of property* which the laws of such a state afford its subjects. In an absolute monarchy it is commonly unsafe to be rich. The exigencies of state, or the caprice of power, will too often induce the Sovereign, whose will is uncontrollable, to catch at the readiest means of raising supplies, which is, by seizing wealth where it may be found already amassed. And whether this be claimed, together with the person of the owner, by a furious *Lettre de cachet*,° or asked on the insidious pretext of a loan, it is an hardship equally felt and apprehended. Whether the sternness of a *Turkish Basha*,[6] or the address of a *French* Comptroller of Finances, be the guise of the executioner, the stroke is equally fatal to Commercial industry—Sensible of the ill effect such precedents must ever have upon Trade, the wisest Monarchs have practised all the arts of persuasion, to quiet the fears and suspicions of this useful stranger, and have courted her stay by numberless grants and immunities. Their delusions have sometimes succeeded. But, however the watchful, jealous look, which Trade is observed to wear in such Governments, shews, that she considers herself all the while in an enemy's country, ready to withdraw upon any sudden alarm. What numbers of Merchants and Manufacturers left their settlements in the *Netherlands,* on account of the tyrannous exactions of *Philip* the Second, to take refuge under the milder auspices of a *British* Government! And in a later period, how was *France* depopulated of its ingenious artists, by the persecutions of *Lewis* the Fourteenth! Instances of this sort are unknown to a state where the Prerogative is restrained by law; where, if the meanest subject feel the hand of oppression, the whole power of the constitution is prepared to do him right. Now, as the safe and quiet enjoyment of his accumulated wealth must be supposed the principal end and reward that encourages the Merchant to dare the hazards and expense of Trade, it may be concluded, that the Government wherein this is best secured, must naturally be the seat of Traffic.

2. In the next place, that equable distribution of property, which is necessary to a free government, but inconsistent with the more absolute forms, will be found no inconsiderable advantage to Trade. Whatever we suppose to be the state of arts and refinement in a nation, it is probable

6. [A high Ottoman official, similar to a provincial governor; also spelled "Pasha."]

that there will be greater expense, a larger consumption of the subjects of Commerce, where the fortunes of men are nearly upon a level, than if they were exceedingly disproportionate. Every man, in that case, is possessed of a competency, will have some little taste for what is convenient, and may give encouragement by his demands to several branches of Trade. And the men of fashion and figure, whose more enlarged desires require a more expensive gratification, will form a very considerable part of the community. But where the whole people are rich or poor to an extreme, exceedingly the greater part must confine their wants to the bare supply of nature, and that at the cheapest rate she can be served. Buying and selling enter but little into their concerns. They must prepare their own food, and make their own cloathing. Their houses are built, furnished, and inhabited by the same persons. If you suppose that the aggregate of wealth, which is possessed by the Grandees, and scattered by them on a refined luxury, will make up the other's defect, it is certainly a mistake. For wherever this immense disparity of condition subsists, the national wealth will always be less, than in consequence of a more uniform dispersion. When all the laborious part of a people are slaves, or hirelings, it is folly to expect the same increase, as if every little field was cultivated by its proper owner, who should himself receive the fruits of his own industry. There is not, therefore, the same foundation for expense under such an arbitrary dispensation, neither are there the same motives and occasions to call it forth. For greatness is always retired and unsociable. The men of exalted stations in despotic governments seldom meet with their equals, do not mix so frequently in public assemblies, or join in that familiar intercourse of amusement and conversation, so common with the moderate quality of more equal Governments. So that the active principle of emulation, which is excited by comparison, and continually prompts these to refinement and novelty in all the articles of expense, operates but weakly on those, who, notwithstanding the encomiums of flatterers and dependents on their splendor and magnificence, are never sumptuous, in proportion to their estates, to the same degree as their inferiors. Now it is the great home-consumption of their several manufactures which gives rise, in any country, to the particular arts of Trade. Where this demand is slackened and abated, less attention will be given to those pursuits, fewer people will care to be initiated in such mysteries; and consequently there will not be kept up[7] that emulous struggle, those perpetual trials of skill among artificers, which are necessary to bring their works to any degree of perfection.

The cause under consideration operates yet another way, to the benefit of Trade. For, by means of the modest inequality in the fortunes of free-citizens, the mercantile part of a nation will be left in possession of greater portions of wealth than can fall to the share of numbers, where the sceptre of Monarchy is wielded. This will enable them to maintain more extensive manufactories, and to pursue useful inventions; enterprising spirits will not here be deterr'd from any hopeful experiments, by the dread of ruin in case of failure. And, which is no immaterial point, their larger stocks will allow them to be content with smaller profits than will satisfy their less opulent rivals. Now in absolute governments, the men of fortune are all men of family. These will be afraid of degrading themselves by an application to Commerce. Their high blood would be polluted by such mean mechanical industry. And their poor vassals, who have no such restraints, are in too abject a condition to be capable of carrying on any work of difficulty and expense. In consequence of this, the rich will always find their native manufactures but miserable, imperfect attempts, compared with those of more expert foreigners. These therefore will be purchased at any rate, to the entire discouragement and destruction of the Trade at home. And as this character will extend to almost every thing that is exquisite in the manual arts, and which respects

7. The effect of this generous strife is beautifully described by *Hesiod*.

Ἥτε καὶ ἀπάλαμόν περ ὁμῶς ἐπὶ εργον ἔγειρεν.
Εἰς ἕτερον γάρ τίς τε ἰδὼν ἔργοιο χατίζων
Πλούσιον, ὃς σπεύδει μὲν ἀρώμεναι ἠδὲ φυτεύειν
Οἶκόν τ' εὖ θέσθαι· ζηλοῖ δέ τε γείτονα γείτων
Εἰς ἄφενος σπεύδοντ'· ἀγαθὴ δ' Ἔρις ἥδε βροτοῖσιν.
Καὶ κεραμεὺς κεραμεῖ κοτέει καὶ τέκτονι τέκτων,
Καὶ πτωχὸς πτωχῷ φθονέει καὶ ἀοιδὸς ἀοιδῷ.

Εργα καὶ Ἡμερ.

["For any one when idle having looked upon another being rich, he, I say, makes haste to plough and to plant, and well to order his house; for neighbour rivals neighbour, when hastening toward riches; but this contention is good for mortals. Both potter is jealous of potter, and craftsman of craftsman; and poor man has a grudge against poor man, and poet against poet." "Works and Days," in *The Works of Hesiod, Callimachus, and Theognis*, trans. James Davies Banks (London: Bohn's Classical Library, 1889), 74–75 (ll. 20–26).]

the gratifications of refined and polite life; the state is hereby deprived of all the ingenious labor that should supply this demand, and must pay for its costly elegancies in ready cash or unwrought materials, directly against the balance of Trade. This ruinous inversion of exchange, (which, according to the happy expression of a celebrated writer, is a Commerce of luxury, not of oeconomy)[8] is remarkably exemplified in *Poland.* An instance not to be passed over, as being particularly adapted to ascertain the principles, and confirm the reasoning used on this head. For the government of this nation is absolute even to despotism. The Nobility, tho' almost entire masters of the national property, are observed to live in less splendor than in the more moderate courts of *Europe.* The bulk of the people are immersed in the deepest poverty and slavery. They have hardly any sort of manufactures of their own workmanship; and corn, which is their only staple commodity, brings no return of gain into the state, but barely counterpoises the heavy account of their foreign expenses.

3. Let it be remembered, as a further advantage which Trade derives from a free government, that Republics have always been observed to be more populous than Monarchies. This fact is verified by the experience of all ages, and holds true, not only in commercial states, wherein other causes may have concurred to increase the number of inhabitants; but was remarkably seen in the *Spartan* commonwealth of old, and the *Swiss* cantons of modern times. These are perhaps the only examples of republics that have supported themselves without the aids of Trade. And they are no less remarkable for their populousness; the former having sent forth more colonies than any other city of *Greece,* and the latter at this day furnishing all *Europe* with artificers, soldiers, and servants. This prolific quality is perhaps no more than a consequence of those two circumstances in the nature of a free government before insisted on. For where *property is so fairly distributed,* it is certain that a greater number of persons may be maintained out of the same fund, than upon any other supposition. If the balance preponderate on one side with a barren superfluity, it must leave in the other scale a wretched deficiency, that cuts off the prospects of many, and the support of more. But when to *the possession*

8. [See Montesquieu, *Spirit of the Laws,* bk. 20, ch. 4, 5, 8, 10; see chapter 20 above.]

of a competency there is added *the assurance* of preserving it ourselves, and transmitting it to our posterity, what impediment shall interpose to prevent the closing of the *Hymeneal* tye? When conjugal ease and peace is thus secured, what should hinder the social appetite from operating to its full extent? It is true the happiness of mankind is but very imperfectly defined from external circumstances; as being principally influenced by the prevailing sentiments, manners, and habits of thinking. So that this principle may appear too precarious, to be the sole foundation of so important a conclusion. But this matter, tho' curious, would detain us too long by a further disquisition. It is enough, that the truth of the fact is beyond dispute. I shall briefly consider one or two of its consequences, as they appear to affect the growth of Trade. *First,* It is evident that populousness must increase the natural consumption of commodities and manufactures: not merely in proportion to the augmentation of people, but infinitely beyond this, from the influence of fashion, which subsists and flourishes by means of well frequented neighbourhoods, and by enlarging the sphere of our wants, gives encouragement to every kind of artificial productions. *Secondly,* It furnishes a constant supply of hands to be employed in all the numberless exigencies of Commerce. It is to be supposed, that the Tradesmen, in every country, originally consisted of such persons as, having no property in land, and being too numerous to find employment in agriculture, or the raising of commodities, made themselves necessary to the others, by their ingenious contrivances to alter and apply to various uses the effects of nature, that is, by the invention of manufactures. Now if it happen that the number of inhabitants in the same place be increased according to any rate, the number of this sort of men, who are at leisure to prosecute the arts of Trade, will be augmented in a much higher proportion. For there is no need of supposing the land-owners to be at all more numerous after this change. And tho' a larger quantity of commodities must be raised by the husbandmen, to supply the increasing consumption; yet the labor of a very few additional hands, thus employed, will be sufficient to answer the necessities of many. So that the bulk of this swarm of new people must fall into the division of Traders. In large and long-established governments, where it is not so easy to estimate the comparative increase of the several orders, the same causes still subsisting, must produce the same variations. So that wherever the people are very numerous in proportion to the extent of their territory, there will always be a store of vacant hands that will naturally addict° themselves to every sort of commercial industry. Want will oblige them to exert their faculties, and emulation will prompt them to excell. Here then will be found the greatest abundance, and the greatest perfection of rare manufactures. This is the glory of Trade. For it lays up for the public an exhaustless stock of useful labor, and gives an universal value to the works of its artists, which renders them real treasure to the possessors. *Lastly,* It prevents an excessive growth in the price of labor, which is the gauge that must regulate the profits of all foreign Trade. When by a great overbalance, the quantity of current coin in a nation is considerably augmented, it is a common, tho' by no means a necessary consequence, that the prices of labor, and other commodities, should be enhanced. Thus the Merchants of poorer countries are enabled to undersell the rich at all foreign markets, and, in the end, to ruin their Trade. But an increase of mechanical hands, proportioned to the increasing species, will prevent this mischief. For were the money which circulates in any of the chanels of Trade doubled, trebled, or quadrupled, if the labor which is respectively employed in the several manufactures belonging to those kinds be also augmented in like manner, there will remain the same proportion as before between money and wares, which is the only circumstance which determines their price. Was it never known, when the great profits and increasing demands that have been made of any particular manufacture had tempted too great a number of adventurers to engage therein, that, the quantity of goods produced being too great for the vent, the prices of them, and of the several sorts of labor employed in preparing them, have been so far from rising, that they have *sunk?* But no more of this; for the subject of populousness would require a fuller exposition than can here be attempted.

Let it suffice, then, that we have discovered three several branches in which the ingrafted interest of Trade grows up, and flourishes on the stem of Liberty. Forasmuch as by *populousness,* and by a *similarity of fortunes,* which are the genuine produce of Freedom, Commerce is created, improved and perfected; and by the establishment of *Laws above the controll of Prerogative,*° which constitutes the very being of Freedom, the fruits and acquirements of Commerce are secured to their owners.

After this review of the connection and happy correspondence sub-sisting between the effects of these two potent principles, which have been the subject of our enquiry, we can no longer ascribe it to chance, that *Venice, Genoa, England* and *Holland* have been the chief trading na-tions in modern history; but are left to wonder, even with astonishment, that *Spain* and *Portugal* should still be found playing with the chains of arbitrary power, and *France* in vain struggling to break them.

27

The Commercial Nobility
1756

GABRIEL FRANÇOIS, *abbé* Coyer, was a French man of letters and worldly cleric born in 1707. He entered the Society of Jesus, studying humanities and philosophy until he left the order in 1736. He then became private tutor to the young Duke of Bouillon (Prince of Turenne at the time) in 1741. There followed public functions that saw him in attendance at some battles of the War of the Austrian Succession (1740–48). His many works include a history of the Polish king Jan Sobieski, travel accounts of Holland and Italy, a study of ancient religions, *belles-lettres*, and a popular attack on the guild system, *Chinki*. He became a member of the Royal Academy of England and the Academy of Nancy. It is said that when he visited Voltaire at Ferney and announced his desire to return each year for three months, Voltaire replied that whereas Don Quixote had mistaken inns for castles, Coyer was mistaking castles for inns. He died in 1782.

The excerpt here is from his controversial tract *La Noblesse commerçante* (London: Duchesne, 1756), which precipitated a huge pamphlet war on the question of whether the legal impediments to noblemen engaging in trade should be lifted. This excerpt provides Coyer's treatment of the question of the basic honor of the activity of commerce. Unbracketed notes are by the author, bracketed ones by the present editor.

The Commercial Nobility

If I only had to address reason to open trade to the nobility, soon all its doors would be wide open to them. But one must again deal with prejudices; it is they which rule the world. Czar Peter [r. 1697–1725] had more trouble getting the Muscovites to cut their beards than turning them into men. However, there are prejudices we have overcome, which is a reason for hope. We no longer believe, as our ancestors did, that dissecting the human body is a sacrilege, or that a dead person who has not made a bequest to the Church should be refused burial. Our senators are no longer buried dressed as Cordeliers[1] in order to reach Heaven. Astrology has lost its credit; sorcerers have disappeared. Ghosts have become ridiculous, trial by combat has been abolished, and we have abandoned the judgment of God by ordeal of fire and water. I have mentioned these religious prejudices because they are very difficult to subdue; victory is sweet. Here are other laurels: The nobles themselves, so attached to the errors gratifying their nobility, have cast off many of them. They no longer pride themselves on their ignorance; they have abandoned the closed space,[2] and our multicolored knights no longer roam the world fighting for their ladies.

Still, let us listen to Prejudice. He would have something to complain about if one condemned him without listening to him: *"the honor of the nobility is highly delicate, wouldn't trade be an offence against it?"*

This honor, however delicate it may be, is clad in the livery of the great nobles, serves in their stables or in their antechambers; a title of Page or Stable boy puts a veneer on those functions performed by servants. If only words are needed to dignify trade in the eyes of the nobility, our language will provide some, and all the more easily in that trade has nothing servile about it; it depends on only the state and itself.

Neither the Marquis of Lassay nor the President of Montesquieu has ever suggested that trade dishonors the nobility.[3] Such language would

---

1. [A branch of Franciscan friars.]

2. [I.e., of the tournament.]

3. [Armand de Madaillan de Lesparre, Marquis de Lassay (1652–1738), "Réflexions de M. le Marquis de Lassé [sic], mort en 1738," in *Mercure de France*, vol. 2, Dec. 1754, and Montesquieu, *Spirit of the Laws*, bk. 20, ch. 21; in chapter 20 in this volume.]

have dishonored them. Who does hold this view? The Great, on whom fortune always smiles, and who hardly bother if others cry; frivolous souls, who take image for substance, titles and vanity for honor. Who else? Wandering knights, better known these days for their industry than for their prowess, and who are a useless and often dangerous burden to the families they frequent. Let us compare them with Messrs. *Rousseau and Paignan* from Sedan, with Mr. *Julienne* from Paris, active citizens whose fortunes make the fortunes of so many others, and who nourish the arts as well as men. On which side are honor, decency, substance, dignity, true nobility? Here is something I acknowledge: As long as games, pleasures, fantastic expenditures, pomp, and uselessness maintain an air of nobility about them, commerce will not adopt them. If it plays, it does so after hard work. If it indulges in pleasure, it does so after privation. If it spends, it does so wisely. If it gives, it has paid its debts. If it summons the delights of the arts in its house, its family has plenty to live on, and the worker [*ou-vrier*] does not wait for his wage. Finally, if it displays magnificence, neither the People nor the Great can reproach it because it is neither nourished by injustice nor inflated by pomp. As far as uselessness is concerned, it wants nothing to do with this idol of good company.

Prejudice is going to dig in the remnants of Antiquity, and shake its powder on Trade to tarnish it. *Egyptians, Jews, several Greek Republics and the Romans despised Commerce,* or so it says. Heavens! If we wanted to mimick the Ancients in everything, we would do some wonderful things! We would marry our sisters as in Egypt; we would repudiate and stone our wives to death as in Judea; we would make them common property as in Sparta; we would expose and kill our deformed children together with our youngest daughters as in early Rome; we would cut an insolvent debtor to pieces.

But is it truly proven that the Ancients regarded commerce with contempt? Because of its religion and morals, Egypt first broke off all communication with foreigners. Judea too made up a separate people. All the earth was profane for an Egyptian and a Jew, who in turn were profane to one another. But this zeal did not hold out very long against the advantages of commerce. Eventually, the navies of both nations were fighting over the riches of Africa and Asia. As for the Greeks, it is true that Sparta relegated trade to the slaves, an affront that commerce shared with agriculture and the fine arts. But I can find Greeks opposed to

Greeks. Athens and Corinth yielded nothing to Sparta in their valuation of things and in their respect for the proprieties; both shone in their trade. And if Rome neglected trade as long as she was busy breaking scepters and spilling the blood of nations, she embraced it as soon as she could breathe again. Blissful Arabia attracted Roman citizens.[4] This "king-people" became a "merchant-people"; a hundred and twenty Ships sailed annually to the Indies, returning loaded with merchandise worth up to fifty million Sesterces.[5]

Let no one object that the Claudian law forbade patricians to trade, as if it were indecent. Surely I would not advise our senators to join together the balance of trade with that of justice; they are busy maintaining public order. But here is what I would say to this subordinate group of people who constantly strive to forge weapons for petty quarrels, and who only survive by devouring the citizenry: Enrich yourselves [*Enrichissez-vous*] and do some good for the state through honest means—engage in trade! Neither will I preach to our soldiers, who have already put their courage to the test, or whose courage will be put to the test by propitious circumstances, to renounce the sword for trade. But I will urge that nobility which is even larger, and which is condemned to idleness by misfortunes, to associate themselves with the fortunes and labors of the merchants.

It is difficult getting to the bottom of the judgment of the Ancients on the dignity of commerce. The Romans for instance had a law which confounded female shopkeepers with slaves, innkeepers, and actresses;[6] another law gave the title of Roman citizen to a slave who had done a considerable trade for six years, in order to fill the warehouses of Rome.[7] This was to ennoble the slave because he had done something noble. So why condemn the woman who had a shop? When Cicero speaks of the "commerce of economy," he does not like the fact that the same people should be at the same time the ruler and the factor of the universe.[8] And

4. Pliny [the Elder], Bk. 6, Ch. XXVIII.
5. Ibid., Ch. XXIII, & Strabo [*The Geography*], bk. 2.
6. Leg. 5, de naturalibus Liberis.
7. Ulpian, Sueton[ius, *De vita Caesarum*], in Claudi[us].
8. Nolo eundem populum Imperatorem & portitorem esse terrarum. [Montesquieu had cited the same passage in *Spirit of the Laws*, bk. 20, ch. 4; in chapter 20 in this volume.]

in another passage, he praises wholesale trade,[9] as if the commerce of economy did not offer just as worthy objects as the commerce of luxury. In this area, one should not take one's bearings from Rome in the time of Cicero; a City where people cared only about elections, campaigns and trials, a state which wanted only to dominate others through force of arms, was easily blind to the importance and dignity of trade.

In any discussion, it is essential to distinguish between times. There are times when the greatest geniuses do not look in a certain direction. Caesar and Charlemagne, dazzled by conquests, did not see commerce. And when circumstances change, different ideas emerge.

Among the Jews, David said: "Because I did not know trade, I shall be in the glory of God." Solomon—the wisest man of all—and the Holy King Josephat thought they could enter into the glory of God while sending merchant ships into the Red Sea. The prophet Ezechiel reproached the city of Tyre with having soiled itself through trade.[10] Isaiah ranks her above all cities—*It is the Queen of the Sea, whose merchants are princes, whose agents are the Great of the earth.*[11]

Early Christianity had Doctors who left commerce with the honorable reputation it had; others condemned it. Saint Chrysostomus, with anathema near at hand, decided without further ado that *a merchant can hardly, can never please God*; from which he concludes that no Christian should be a merchant, or if he wishes so, he should be cast out of the Temple.[12] If one had followed that piece of advice, Constantinople and the Saint himself would have died of starvation.

Among the Moderns, one finds no more harmony of sentiment. *Bodin*[13] and *Tiraqueau*[14] forbid the nobility to trade; *Baldus* urges them to do so as if it were something useful and proper.[15] If the question is

---

9. [Cicero], Bk. 1, de Officiis.

10. By the multitude of thy merchandise, thy inner parts were filled with iniquity. Ch. 28.

11. Who hath taken this counsel against Tyre, which was formerly crowned, whose merchants were princes, and her traders the nobles of the earth? Ch. 23.

12. In 2. part homil. in Matth. 21[:12].

13. Bk. 5 Reipubl[ica].

14. [André Tiraqueau (1480–1558), *Tractatus de nobilitate et jure primogeniorum* (1543),] Ch. 23.

15. [Baldus de Ubaldis (1327–1400)], In rubricis de Clericis peregrina.

submitted to Italy, to Denmark, to England, to Holland, the nobles themselves resolve it in favor of trade, whereas the Germans and the Polish cry foul. The Chevalier de la Roque,[16] who tells us about these conflicting opinions in a treatise which was written deliberately to ensure the honor and the prerogatives of the nobility, declares himself highly in favor of involving them in trade.

French nobles, dare to think on your own! Or if you want others to decide for you, decide according to the facts. *Solon* was as worthy as a nobleman from Beauce or Picardie. He was the descendant of Codrus, the last king of Athens, and before giving laws to the Athenians, he regained his fortune through trade.[17] Plutarch says,[18] "in those times, there was no handywork which was shameful, no art, no trade which caused divisions among men; merchandise in particular was honorable because it opened trade with the barbaric nations, provided the means to strike friendships and alliances with kings, and taught innumerable things that would have been ignored without it." I do not know if *Protus* had letters of nobility; this merchant dared to found Marseille, which has contributed to our wealth for so many centuries.[19] *Cato* the censor was certainly from a respectable family; Kings had implored him to protect them before he was even a consul. Besides, his scrupulous austerity as far as virtue and honor were concerned is well-known. As a matter of fact, he had increased his patrimony through commerce.[20] I will speak neither of *Hippocratus* the mathematician, nor of the wise *Thales,* nor of the divine *Plato,* all of whom engaged in trade.[21] It is not surprising that philosophers and wise men should have suspected nothing disgraceful in such an honorable occupation. But Rome comes back to mind and what do I see? *Pertinax,* you are engaging in commerce[22] and soon you shall carry the imperial crown! The emperor Caracalla had not done any trade, but he honored

16. [Gilles André de La Roque (1598–1686), *Le Traité de la noblesse* (Paris, 1678).]
17. Plutarch, [L]ife of Solon.
18. Ibid.
19. Ibid.
20. Plutarch, [L]ife of Cato.
21. Plutarch, [L]ife of Solon.
22. History of the Commerce [and Navigation] of the Ancients [1716], by M. [Pierre-Daniel] Huet, Ch. LVII.

merchants; he gave them a marked proof of this in the massacre of Alexandria: everybody—nobles, priests, magistrates, warriors—was put to the sword, but he spared the merchants.

Open the archives of the world and you will find that Trade was honored by all nations during their golden age [*beau siècle*]—in Egypt under Ptolemy Philadelphus, in Judea under Solomon, in Athens under Pericles, in Carthage under Hanno, in Florence under Cosimo de' Medici, in Great Britain under Elizabeth, in Holland under the banners of liberty, in Russia under Peter the Great. Your own nation, whose censure you unwisely fear, has been inviting you to engage in trade for a long time now.

28

An Estimate of the Manners and
Principles of the Times
1757

JOHN BROWN, the son of a parish priest, was born in 1715. He went to
Cambridge in 1732, where he passed with distinction in 1735. He took orders shortly thereafter and was made a minor canon and lecturer. He defended the Whig cause both in the battle of Carlisle in 1745 and in published sermons, and he was made chaplain to the dean of York in 1747. In
a eulogistic essay, he praised Pope's literary executor, Warburton, who
then became a sort of literary patron to him. At Warburton's suggestion,
he wrote an essay in 1751 on Shaftesbury's *Characteristics,* which was later
admired by Mill for its utilitarian bent; it went through five editions by
1764. He also wrote tragedies and works on music, poetry, dialogues, and
literary histories, and he announced an eight-volume "Principles of
Christian Legislation" that never appeared. Toward the end of his life,
he was approached by advisers to Catherine II of Russia about establishing an educational system there. Catherine invited him to St. Petersburg;
he prepared to go, but doctors and friends prevailed upon him to spare
his fragile health the rigors of a Russian winter. On September 23, 1766,
he committed suicide by cutting his own throat, an act feared by his
friends for many years.

An Estimate of the Manners and Principles of the Times (1757; 7th ed.,
London, 1758) was by far his most famous and popular work, going
through seven editions in one year. Cowper says in his *Table-Talk,* "The

inestimable estimate of Brown / rose like a paper kite and charmed the town." All of part three is reproduced here. Unbracketed notes are by the author, bracketed ones by the editor.

━━━━━━━━━━

An Estimate of the Manners and Principles of the Times

Part III. Of the Sources of these Manners and Principles

Section I

Of a general Mistake on this Subject

The public Effects of our Manners and Principles here enumerated, begin now to appear too manifest in our public Miscarriages, to be any longer derided. The Nation stands aghast at it's own Misfortunes: But, like a Man starting suddenly from Sleep, by the Noise of some approaching Ruin, knows neither whence it comes, nor how to avoid it.

In Proof of this, we need only look into the late Instructions from Constituents to Representatives. These we see, seldom look farther than the immediate and incidental Occasion of each particular Misconduct: While the grand general Principles in which these Misconducts have been chiefly founded, are neither seen, nor suspected: Nay, an impartial Enquiry will probably convince us, that while they strike at the Shoots and Branches, they feed the Root from whence these Misconducts have been originally derived.

For it seems to be the ruling Maxim of this Age and Nation, that if our Trade and Wealth are but increased, we are powerful, happy, and secure: And in estimating the real Strength of the Kingdom, the sole Question for many Years hath been, "What Commerce and Riches the Nation is possessed of?" A Question, which an ancient Lawgiver would have laughed at.

There never was a more fatal Error more greedily embraced by any People.

Section II

Of the Effects of exorbitant Trade and Wealth on Manners

By Wealth is understood, every kind of useful Possession; or Money, which is it's Sign, and may be converted into it.

By Commerce is understood the Exchange of Wealth, for mutual Benefit.

The Effects of Commerce on Manners have by most Writers, I think, been considered as *uniform*. Even the sage and amiable MONTESQUIEU says only, in general Terms, "That Commerce polishes Manners, but corrupts Manners."[1] Whereas, from a candid View of it's Nature and Effects, we shall probably find, that in it's first and middle Stages it is beneficent; in it's last, dangerous and fatal.

If we view Commerce in its first Stages, we shall see, that it supplies mutual Necessities, prevents mutual Wants, extends mutual Knowledge, eradicats mutual Prejudice, and spreads mutual Humanity.

If we view it in its middle and more advanced Period, we shall see, it provides Conveniencies, increaseth Numbers, coins Money, gives Birth to Arts and Science, creates equal Laws, diffuses general Plenty and general Happiness.

If we view it in it's third and highest Stage, we shall see it change it's Nature and Effects. It brings in Superfluity and vast Wealth; begets Avarice, gross Luxury, or effeminate Refinement among the higher Ranks, together with general Loss of Principle.

Concerning the two first Stages of Commerce, I shall have no Dispute with the present Times: Its Benefits are generally acknowledged. The dangerous Effects of it's Exorbitance or Excess have not yet been sufficiently developed.

---

1. L'Esprit des Loix, l. xx. c. 1. [See chapter 20 in this volume.]

That Commerce in it's Excess brings a general Superfluity of Goods, that this general Superfluity settles in particular Hands into vast Wealth, will be readily acknowledged.

The next Step is, to consider how vast Wealth naturally produces Avarice, Luxury, or Effeminacy, according to the Genius or Circumstances of the People among whom it comes.

Industry, in it's first Stages, is *frugal* not *ungenerous:* It's End being that of Self-Preservation and moderate Enjoyment, it's little Superfluities are often employed in Acts of Generosity and Beneficence. But the daily Increase of Wealth by Industry naturally increases the *Love* of Wealth. The Passion for Money, being founded, not in Sense, but Imagination, admits of no Satiety: like those which are called the natural Passions. Thus the Habit of saving Money, beyond every other Habit, gathers Strength by continued Gratification. The Attention of the whole Man is immediately turned upon it; and every other Pursuit held light when compared with the Increase of Wealth. Hence the natural Character of the Trader, when his final Prospect is the Acquisition of Wealth is that of *Industry* and *Avarice.*

What is true, in this Respect, of *trading Men,* is true of *trading Nations.* If their Commerce be that of Oeconomy in the Extreme, if the last Object of their Pursuit be Wealth for it's own Sake, if the Leaders of such a People be *commercial,* the Character of that People, and it's Leaders, will be found in *Industry* and *Avarice.* But if a trading Nation hath a large *Territory* sufficient to create a *Landed Interest,* Commerce will produce very different Effects. For as it multiplies Inhabitants, and brings in Wealth, it naturally increases the Value of landed Estates. Barren Grounds are cultivated, and cultivated Spots are made more fertile. Hence a vast Accession of Income to the Nobility and Gentry.

These Ranks of Men being not bred up to Habits of Industry; on the contrary, their increased Rents coming in unsought for, and their Time being often a Load upon them, thro' want of Capacity and Employment, the Habit of *Indulgence* comes on, and grows of Course. Additional Wealth gives the Power to gratify every Desire that rises, Leisure improves these Desires into Habits; thus Money is at length considered as no more than the Means of Gratification; and hence the genuine Character of a rich Nobility or Gentry, is that of Expence and Luxury.

But the first Essays of Luxury, like those of every other Art, are coarse and rude: The natural Character of Luxury, therefore, is to refine by Degrees: Especially, when assisted by Commerce, it advances apace into Refinement. For Commerce searches every Shore and Climate for it's Supplies; and Art is studious, because rewarded, in arranging and applying these Materials to the most exquisite and delicate Use. Thus every coarse Mode of Pleasure is by Degrees despised; new Habits of higher Indulgence come on: gross Luxury is banished, and Effeminacy takes it's Place.

But Luxury, in this *last* Period, being exhausted in it's Course; and turned, for want of new Objects of Indulgence, into Debility and Languor, would expire or sleep, were it not awakened by another Passion, which again calls it into Action. Nothing is so natural to effeminate Minds, as *Vanity*. This rouses the luxurious and debilitated Soul, and the Arts of pleasurable Enjoyment are now pushed to their highest Degree, by the Spirit of delicate Emulation.

Thus the whole Attention of the Mind is centred on *Brillancy* and *Indulgence:* Money, tho' despised as an *End,* is greedily sought as a *Means:* And *Self,* under a different Appearance from the trading Spirit, takes equal Possession of the Soul.

Thus as the Character of a State altogether commercial in the highest Degree, is that of Industry and Avarice; so, in a Nation of extended Territory, where Commerce is in it's highest Period, while its trading Members retain their Habits of Industry and Avarice, the natural Character of it's landed Ranks, it's Nobility and Gentry, is that of "a vain, luxurious, and selfish Effeminacy."

We speak here of the simple and proper Effects of Trade and Wealth, uncontrouled by opposite Manners or Principles; which, it is to be observed, never existed probably, at least in the mixed State, in their full Extent: Individuals there are, and will be, in almost every State and Period, who are influenced by dissimilar Manners or Principles: There are Traders who are generous; Nobles and Gentry whose ultimate Passion is for Gold: But such Exceptions affect not the general Principle: And tho' these incidental Mixtures *Weaken* the different Colours of different Ranks or States, yet still the different Colours remain in their Nature distinct and invariable.

'Tis probable, the Reader will have discovered, that this Reasoning is strengthened by, or rather built upon, the Examples of two neighbour Nations; one wholly commercial, that of *Holland:* The other a mixed State, compounded of a commercial and landed Interest; I mean *our own.* And to say the Truth; no two Nations perhaps ever existed, which approached so near to the full and proper Effects of the Causes here alledged.

It will appear immediately why the Genius of the Republic of *Holland* is here annalysed into its first Principles; which are simply, those of Industry and the Love of Gain.

In the mean Time, we may justly conclude from this Argument, that the exorbitant Trade and Wealth of *England* sufficiently account for it's present *Effeminacy.*

Section III

Of the Effects of exorbitant Trade and Wealth on the religious Principle

Such therefore are the ruling Manners which may naturally be expected in a Nation thus circumstanced, unless they be counteracted by opposite Principles: 'Tis now Time to consider the natural Effects of exorbitant Trade and Wealth, on all these salutary Principles by which these effeminate Manners can most effectually be controuled.

Let us still carry the two characteristic States of *Holland* and *England,* in our Eye. Whether, then, we view the commercial State, where the Love of Money rules; or the mixed State, where the Love of Money rules; or the mixed State, where vain Effeminacy predominates; we shall find both these national Characters have but a bad Aspect and Influence on every Kind of Principle. Let us first consider that of Religion.

Avarice seems not, in it's own Nature, prone to destroy *speculative* religious Belief; but effectually to extinguish *active* religious Principle.

It tends not to destroy speculative Belief, because this Effect must be a Work of Application, Time, and Labour: Now the Labour of Avarice is naturally bent on it's main Object, *Money;* therefore, to waste this Labour on the Propagation of the unprofitable and fruitless Doctrines of Irreligion, must ever be contrary to it's ruling Character.

But Avarice naturally tends to the Destruction of active religious Principles; because this is chiefly a Matter of *habitual Impression;* and therefore, in order to accomplish it's Destruction, nothing more is necessary than to *forget.* Now this requires no positive act or Labour of the Mind, but is the natural Result from an attentive Pursuit of the favourite Object, *Money.*

Hence, in a mere commercial State, actuated by the Love of Gain, religion is not railed at or disputed against, but only *neglected* and *forgot.* And thus the *genuine Trader,* who never questioned the Articles of his national Faith at home, scruples not to forswear *Christianity,* and tread upon the Cross in *Japan,* and returns the same good *Christian* as he went.

But in the mixed State, where national Effeminacy forms the *primary,* and Avarice only the *secondary* Character, the Effects of exorbitant Trade and Wealth on religious Principle, will be widely different.

Lord VERULAM[2] hath some where observed, that "Times of Atheism are civil Times." He had been much nearer the Truth, had he affirmed, that "Civil Times are Times of Atheism." He mistook the Cause for the Effect.

This Effect of national Luxury and Refinement, in producing national Irreligion, is not difficult to account for. In some Periods of a State, Opinions controul Manners; but in most Periods, Manners controul Opinions. Where the ruling Manners coincide with the common Good, as in the middle Period of a State, there we commonly find that a rational and beneficent System of Religion prevails: This comes to pass, because the Principles of the received Religion contradict not the ruling Manners.

But in the State and Period of Luxury or Refinement, active religious Principle is lost thro' the attentive Pursuit of *Pleasure;* as in the commercial State, it is lost thro' the attentive Pursuit of *Gain.*

And *speculative* Belief, in this Period must naturally be lost along with *practical;* because *Leisure* and *Literature* having opened the Field of *Disputation,* Vice as well as Virtue will of course arm herself with every Weapon of Preservation and Defence. Luxury therefore will generally list under the Banner of Irreligion; because Religion condemns her Manners; Irreligion suffers, or approves them.

2. [I.e., Francis Bacon (1561–1626).]

To confirm the Truth of this Reasoning, we need only observe, that in the Period of refined Luxury, *few* but they who are involved in the *Vices*, are involved in the *Irreligion* of the Times.

One Exception, however, must be made, with Regard to the *Writers* against Religion. For *these*, though they *promote*, yet are not often *involved* in the common Degeneracy. This Fact hath been regarded as unaccountable: that *sober* Men of Morals apparently *unblameable*, should madly unhinge the great Principle of Religion and Society, without any visible Motive or Advantage. But by looking a little farther into human Nature, we shall easily resolve this seeming Paradox. These Writers are generally Men of Speculation and Industry; and therefore though they give themselves up to the Dictates of their ruling Passion, yet that ruling Passion commonly leads to the Tract of *abstemious* Manners. That Desire of *Distinction* and *Superiority*, so natural to Man, breaks out in a thousand various and fantastic Shapes, and in each of these, according as it is directed, becomes a Virtue or a Vice. In Times of Luxury and Dissipation therefore, when every Tenet of Irreligion is greedily embraced, what Road to *present Applause* can lie so open and secure, as that of disgracing religious Belief? Especially if the Writer help forward the Vices of the Times, by *relaxing Morals*, as well as *destroying Principles*. Such a Writer can have little else to do, but to new model the Paradoxes of ancient *Scepticism*, in order to *figure it* in the World, and be regarded by the Smatterers in Literature and Adepts in Folly, as a Prodigy of Parts and Learning. Thus his *Vanity* becomes deeply criminal, and is execrated by the Wise and Good, because it is gratified at the Expence of his Country's Welfare. But the *Consolation* which degenerate Manners received from his fatal Tenets, is repaid by eager *Praise:* And *Vice* impatiently drinks in and *applauds* his hoarse and boding voice, while like a *Raven,* he sits croaking universal Death, Despair, and Annihilation to the human Kind.

Thus, where Manners and Religion are opposed, nothing is so natural, as that the *one* should bear down the *other*. If Religion destroy not the ruling Manners, *these* will gather Strength, and destroy Religion. Especially, in a Country where Freedom is established, and Manners lost through the Exorbitance of Wealth, the Duration of religious Principles can be but short. Despotism arms itself with Terror; and by checking the open and avowed *Profession,* checks in a certain Degree the *Progress* of *Impiety.* Whereas it must be acknowledged and lamented, as one of the unalterable Defects of a free Government that *Opinion* must have its Course. The Disease is bad; but the Cure would be fatal. Thus Freedom is compelled to admit an *Enemy,* who under the Pretence and Form of an *Ally,* often proves her *Destroyer.*

Section IV

Of the Effects of exorbitant Trade and Wealth on the Principle of Honour

In the mixed State, where Luxury and Effeminacy form the ruling Character of a People, the Excess of Trade and Wealth naturally tends to weaken or destroy the Principle of *Honour,* by fixing the Desire of Applause, and the Fear of Shame, on improper and ridiculous Objects. Instead of the Good of others, or the Happiness of the Public, the Object of Pursuit naturally sinks into some unmanly and trifling Circumstance: The Vanity of Dress, Entertainments, Equipage, Furniture, of course takes Possession of the Heart.

But in the pure commercial State, where the Love of Gain predominates among the higher Ranks, the Desire of Applause and Fear of Shame are not *perverted,* but *extinguished.* The Lust of Gold swallows up every other Passion: And a Nation of this Character can without Emotion stand the Laughter and Contempt of *Europe,* and say with the Miser,

> Populus me sibilat; at mihi plaudo
> Ipse Domi, simulac Nummos contemplor in Arca.[3]

In whatever Shape, therefore, the Passion for Applause appear, whether it assume the fantastic Form of Vanity, the more solemn one of Pride, or the steady and elevated Desire of rational Esteem; we shall find this Excess of national Avarice tends to its Extinction. A great Writer in-

---

3. ["The people hiss me, but at home I clap my hands for myself, once I gaze on the moneys in my chest." *Horace: Satires, Epistles, and Ars Poetica,* trans. H. Rushton Faircloth (Harvard: Loeb Library, 1929), ll. 66–67.]

deed hath told us, that "Vanity creates Industry;"[4] which is true: Notwithstanding this, we have seen above, that Industry in the Excess naturally begets Avarice; and Avarice in the Excess works a total Change in the Soul, and expels that Vanity which gave it birth.

The same great Writer hath told us, "that Pride destroys Industry;"[5] the Reverse of which holds equally true: "that Industry destroys Pride:" We speak here of Pride in the blameable Sense, as when it riseth into blind and overbearing *Insolence*. Industry in the moderate Degree tends to destroy this contemptuous Spirit, by introducing Knowledge and Equality: And in this Respect, as in most others, is attended with excellent Effects.

But the Spirit of Trade in its Excess, by introducing Avarice, destroys the Desire of *rational Esteem*. In Confirmation of this, we need only cast our Eyes on the HOLLANDERS and CHINESE, among whom the trading Spirit is almost in its unmixed Perfection: The one is the most *mercenary*, the other the most *thieving* of all Nations.

Section V

Of their Effects on public Spirit

This Part of our Subject needs little Investigation. For both in the commercial and mixed State, it appears, that exorbitant Trade and Wealth tend naturally to turn all the Attention of Individuals on *selfish* Gratification.

Therefore they must of course generally tend to destroy the principle of public Spirit: because *this* implies, that our Attention and Regard is turned on *others*.

In the commercial State, Avarice represents *Wealth*, in the mixed State Effeminacy represents *Pleasure*, as the *chief Good*. Both these Delusions tend to the Extinction of public Spirit.

These Delusions create a new Train of Wants, Fears, Hopes, and

4. L'Esprit des Loix, l. xix. c. 9.
5. Ibid.

Wishes: All these terminating in selfish Regard, naturally destroy every Effort of generous and public Principle.

Section VI

Farther Remarks on this Subject

In Consequence of these Remarks, some farther Distinctions will arise.

Thus, the religious Principle will *seem* to exist in the commercial State, where Avarice forms the national Character; while in the mixed State where Luxury and Effeminacy predominate, it is evidently destroyed. The Reason is, that in the first, although active Principle is lost, speculative Belief is not controverted: whereas, in the latter, not only active principle is lost, but Religion itself (if such a State be free) is publickly insulted and derided. Thus in *Holland,* Religion *seems* yet to exist; while in *England* it is evidently destroyed.

On the contrary, the Principle of Honour will seem to exist in the mixed State, where luxurious Effeminacy forms the primary Character of the Nation; while in the commercial State, where Avarice predominates, the Principle is evidently no more. The Reason is, that in the former, the Love of Applause and Fear of Shame are not wholly destroyed, but perverted, and turned upon unworthy Objects; while in the latter, the Passion itself is totally extinguished. Thus the faint Appearance of Honour yet remains in *England,* while in *Holland* it is manifestly destroyed.

But as modern *Dutch* Religion, and modern *English* Honour, seem no more than the Ghosts of departed Principles, so they have precisely those Effects which may reasonably be expected from such shadowy Non-Entities.

Again: The Colours or Characters of Industry and Avarice will naturally be *strong* in the commercial State: because, being almost wholly unmixed with Manners of a dissimilar Nature, the ruling Genius of the State is left uncontrouled, to its proper Operations and Effects.

But in the mixed State, where Industry and Love of Gain form the Character of the *secondary* Ranks; Dissipation and Effeminacy, of the *higher;* there the two separate Characters, by the Force of incidental

Coalition and Example, will always influence each other in a certain Degree. Some ambitious Traders will aspire to luxurious Effeminacy: Some, of the higher Orders, will descend to Industry and Merchandise. Thus each Rank must be tinctured with a Colour different from its own; and hence, the general Colour or Character of each of these Ranks, will, in some measure be controuled and *weakened.*

This Circumstance is favourable to the mixed State, beyond that which is purely commercial; as it checks in a certain Degree the Virulence of the Excess; and produceth a national Character in some Measure approaching that of more moderate Trade and Wealth.

Hence too it follows, that a State purely commercial, when once arrived at the Period of exorbitant Wealth, will naturally degenerate *faster* than that which is compounded of Commerce and Luxury. For whatever Causes check the ruling Manners in their *Degree,* will check them in their *Consequences.*

But beyond this, there is another Reason, why the State purely commercial will degenerate faster than the mixed State. In the commercial State, the ruling Manners go Hand in Hand with the Exorbitance of Wealth; because the Love of Gain, which forms the leading Character, being likewise the leading Motive, must be even prior to this Exorbitance in the Order of our Ideas: and therefore, in it's Effects, must be at least contemporary.

But in the mixed State, there will always be a short Period between the national Exorbitance of Wealth, and the national Increase of luxurious Effeminacy: because Manners, once got into a certain Track, are not at once thrown out of it. There must be a short Period, before the leading Parts of the Nation can *feel* their Increase of Wealth; and after this, another Period, before new and more refined Modes of Pleasure can be invented.

Hence a neighbouring Republic seems to have well nigh filled up the Measure of its Iniquities; while *ours,* as yet, are only rising towards the *Brim.*

Lastly; though the ruling Manners of such a mixed State are luxurious and effeminate, yet its public Measures will be *commercial.* First, because, Commerce is the Hand-Maid of *Wealth,* and therefore of *Pleasure.* Secondly, because the Idea of national Strength as well as Happiness, being degenerated into that of Wealth and external Good, Commerce will above all Things be naturally encouraged, because it is the means of procuring them.

Section VII

A Review of the Argument

Thus our present exorbitant Degree of Trade and Wealth, in a mixed State like that of *England,* naturally tends to produce luxurious and effeminate Manners in the higher Ranks, together with a general Defect of *Principle.* And as the internal Strength of a Nation will always depend chiefly on the Manners and Principles of it's leading Members, so these effeminate Manners and this Defect of Principle operate powerfully, and fatally, on the national Conduct and Affairs. They have produced a general Incapacity, have weakened the national Spirit of Defence, have heightened the national Disunion: And this national Disunion, besides it's proper and immediate Effects, being founded in Avarice for the Ends of Dissipation, hath again weakened the small Remainder of publick Capacity and Defence; and thus seems to have fitted us for a Prey to the Insults and Invasions of our most powerful Enemy.

Section VIII

An Objection considered

Tho' this Estimate may appear *just* to those who take an enlarged View of Things in their Principles and Consequences; yet I am not ignorant of certain Maxims, generally approved, and hardly even disputed among modern Politicians, which if true, would weaken or overturn these accumulated Proofs.

The capital Maxim, which seems to include the rest, is this; "That vast Trade and Wealth, above all things make a Nation powerful and invincible, as they increase it's Numbers, enable it to pay it's Fleets and Armies, provide continual Supplies for War; and thus, in the End tire out and defeat every Enemy, whose Wealth and Commerce are inferior."

The Examination of this Maxim will throw many strong collateral Lights upon our main Subject.

First it affirms, "That Trade and Wealth make a Nation strong, because they make it populous." This indeed is true of the first and second Periods of Trade and Wealth; That it is true of the *third* or *highest* Period, of which *England* is now possessed, may very reasonably be questioned. In the first Period, Industry is chiefly employed in cultivating the Lands, in encreasing, manufacturing, and exchanging the Produce of the Mother Country. These Branches of Trade call for vast additional Numbers of Hands; and hence an Increase of Numbers naturally ariseth.

The same Effect takes Place in the second Period of Trade; so far as home Productions are *exchanged* for foreign ones. This Stage of Commerce brings on a fresh Demand of Artificers of new and various Kinds, produces an Increase of Labour, and therefore of Inhabitants.

But in the third or highest Period of Trade, of which *England* is now possessed, there are very extensive Branches of Commerce, which brings no new Accession of Numbers to the Comonwealth. I mean, all those Branches of Commerce, where *Money* is sent and exchanged for *foreign* Goods. This Species of Trade occasions little Increase of *Labour,* and therefore less of *Numbers;* except only of those few who navigate the Vessels thus employed, to their respective Ports. And as this kind of Trade will always grow and predominate, in proportion as a Nation becomes more luxurious and effeminate, so for this Reason the highest Stage of Trade is not naturally attended with the highest Increase of Labour, nor consequently of *Numbers,* as is commonly imagined. Besides this, in the refined Period, additional Art and Experience in Labour prevent, in some Measure, the Increase of Numbers. By the Invention of Machines, an equal Degree both of Tillage and Trade is carried on by fewer Hands, than in the simpler Periods; and therefore the Increase of Numbers is by no means proportional to the Increase of Commerce and Wealth.

But these are far from being the only Considerations worth our Notice on this Subject. For when we speak of any Stage of Trade, we must in Reason take in *every* Circumstance which naturally attends it. There are other Causes, therefore, why Numbers increase not, but rather naturally *diminish,* in the highest Period of Trade and Wealth.

For *first*, the Vanity and Effeminacy which this exorbitant Pitch of Wealth brings on, lessens the Desire of Marriage.

Secondly, the Intemperance and Disease which this Period of Trade naturally produceth among the *lower Ranks* in great Cities, bring on in some Degree an Impotence of Propagation.

Thirdly, This Debility is always attended with a Shortness of Life, both in the Parents and the Offspring; and therefore a still farther Diminution of Numbers follows on the whole.

Matter of Fact confirms these Reasonings; and lies open to every Man's Observation. Since the first Increase of Tillage and Home-manufactures, the Increase of Inhabitants hath been great in *England*: Since the vast Increase of foreign Commerce, the Increase of Numbers is hardly perceivable. Nay, there is great Reason to believe, that upon the whole, the Nation is less populous than it was fifty Years ago, tho' it's Trade perhaps is doubled. Some trading Towns indeed are better peopled, but others are thinned by the Flux of Commerce. The Metrop-olis seems to augment in its Dimensions: But it appears, by the best Cal-culations, that it's Numbers are diminished; And as to the Villages thro' *England*, there is great Reason to believe, they are in general at a Stand, and many of them thinner of Inhabitants than in the Beginning of this Century. 'Tis hard to obtain Certainty in this Particular, without a gen-eral Examination and Comparison. But it appears by the Registers of some *Country* Parishes, which I have looked into, that from the Year 1550 to 1710 the Number of Inhabitants increased gradually; the two Extremes being to each other, as 57 to 72; and that from 1710 to the present Time, the Number has been at a Stand, if not rather diminished.

But suppose, what there is no Reason to believe, that our present Ex-cess of Trade and Overflow of Wealth have in some Degree increased our *Numbers*, yet it will probably appear, that they have as much, at least, im-paired our *bodily Strength*. For as *Temperance* is the ruling Character of the middle Stage of Commerce, so is *Intemperance* of the highest. Hence, Health and Strength prevail in the first; Disease and Debility in the lat-ter. This is universally confirmed by Fact: Villages abounding with Health, commercial Cities with Disease. So that an Army taken from the Villages, with equal Commanders, Arms, and Discipline, would drive the same Number of debilitated Gin-drinkers, like a Flock of Geese before them.

The Author of the *Fable of the Bees* made his Boast, that the Wisdom of the Legislature had, upon his Plan, adopted the Encouragement of this pernicious Liquid: But the same Wisdom hath upon Trial been obliged to *discourage* the Use of this malignant Spirit; as they found that it ruined the Health, and shortened the Lives, of half the lower Ranks in *London.*

And all good Men hope that the Time will come, when this infernal Potion will be laid under such Discouragements, as may amount to a general Prohibition. The Necessity of such a Reformation grows greater every Day, not only in *London,* but throughout the Kingdom. For in some Villages in *England* there is now a greater Quantity of Gin consumed than of Ale.

But to quit these inferior Considerations, tho' they all unite in confirming the Theory here advanced; the Weight of the Reply lies indeed in another Circumstance: For altho' we should admit (what is not true) that our present Exorbitance of Trade and Wealth increased our Numbers and bodily Force, yet as the real and essential Strength of a Nation consists in the Manners and Principles of it's *leading Part;* and as our present Excess of Trade and Wealth hath produced such fatal Effects on these Manners and Principles; no Increase of Numbers in the inferior Ranks can possibly make amends for this internal and capital Defect. Such a Nation can, at best, only resemble a large *Body,* actuated (yet hardly actuated) by an incapable, a vain, a dastardly, and effeminate *Soul.*

But the Maxim we are engaged to obviate, alledges farther, that "This exorbitant Increase of Trade and Wealth enables a Nation to pay it's Fleets and Armies, and afford continual Supplies for War." Yet, even this Part of the Maxim, in it's modern Acceptation, is far beyond the Truth.

For under the present Stage of Trade, the Increase of Wealth is by no means equally or proportionally diffused: The Trader reaps the main Profit: after him, the Landlord, in a lower Degree: But the common Artificer, and still more the common Labourer, gain little by the exorbitant Advance of Trade: It is true, their Wages are increased; but so are the Prices of Provisions too: and therefore they are no richer than before.

Now Taxes and public Supplies are raised upon the Consumer: and as it appears from hence, that only a few of the Consumers are made richer by the Exorbitance of Trade, it follows, that not the Nation in general, but a select Number of Individuals only, are made more capable of contributing to those supplies, which are levied without Distinction on the *whole*. Would they who reap the plenteous Harvest of foreign Trade, generously allot their proportional and extraordinary Gains to the Service of the Public, we should then indeed be furnished with a *new* Argument in Favour of Commerce in it's highest Pitch.

Farther: As the labouring Ranks are little or nothing enriched by the exorbitant Degree of Trade, so it often happens that even the higher Ranks, and the Nation in general, are not *more*, nay perhaps less enabled to contribute to the public Supplies, than when possessed of Wealth in a more moderate Degree. For we have seen, in the Progress of this Estimate, that the natural Effect of an Increase of Wealth, is an Increase of Luxury, Vanity, and Expence; which, if it outrun the Increase of Wealth, as in it's Nature it tends to do, instead of Riches will bring on public Poverty. For the Ability or Wealth of a People, considered in their Capacity for raising Supplies, consists not in the Largeness of their Income, but in the Proportion of their Expences to their Income: It consists not in "what they *have*," but "what they can *Spare?*" Hence it appears, that a Nation may be at once very *rich*, and very *poor;* rich in Income, but poor thro' Extravagance. And as national Extravagance is the natural Effect of an Overflow of Wealth, so national Indigence is it's most natural and final Consequence. How far this is our present Situation, can hardly be necessary to affirm.

To this Argument it may possibly be objected that if great Wealth is but among us, new Imposts will naturally *force* it into Circulation. That the more the Artificers and Labourers are taxed, the more their Wages will increase, and consequently their Ability to bear the increasing Taxes: And that as to the higher Ranks, exorbitant Wealth *enables* them still better to endure additional Imposts, because these deprive the Great of nothing but the Superfluities of Vanity and Luxury.

To this it is replied, that in Case of additional Taxes, tho' the Poor *must* indeed increase their Wages in order to subsist, yet this Increase never takes Place, till they are compelled by the last *Necessity* and *Want:* The natural Consequence of which must be Murmurs, Sedition, and Tumults. With Regard to the higher Ranks, a parallel Reply may suffice: For in the refined Period, when Manners and Principles are lost, the Luxuries of Life become *Necessaries* among the Great; and therefore will be as obstinately adhered to, and quitted with the same Reluctance, as Food and Cloathing by the *Poor.* The Consequence therefore must be the same; a general Discontent and Disaffection to the Government, among the higher Ranks of Life.

Is not all this confirmed by evident Facts; There is at present in this Nation a Mass of Wealth at least twelve Times more than the publick Debt: Yet we are reduced to the sad Necessity of plunging deeper every Day. What is the Reason? No Ministry dares to provoke and exasperate a luxurious and selfish Nation, by demanding such Sums, as every one has the *Power* had he but the *Will,* to bestow.

But beyond all this, will any Man of Sense assert, that the Circumstance of *paying* an Army or a Fleet, is the one thing that will decide a War? 'Tis true, indeed, Provisions, Arms, Ammunition are necessary; and therefore *Wealth,* because it procures them. But will a General or Admiral therefore gain the Victory, only because his Men are furnished with Provisions, Arms, and Ammunition? If not, what can Trade or Wealth do, towards making a Nation victorious? Again, therefore, let me remind my Countrymen, that the capital Question still remains, not, "who shall *pay,*" but "who shall *fight?*"

There is a trite Observation on Foot, indeed, drawn from the best political Writers ill understood, that "the Principles of War are wholly changed; and that not the Nation who has the best *Troops,* but the longest *Purse,* will in the End obtain the Victory." This, in the modern Application of it, is a most dangerous Maxim. It naturally tends to extinguish military Skill, as well as Honour: And will inevitably sink the People that maintains it, into a Nation of defenseless and Money-getting Cowards.

It must be confessed that Doctor DAVENANT, the most able Writer on these Subjects, hath affirmed, "That now, the whole Art of War is in a Manner reduced to Money; and now-a-day, that Prince who can best find Money to feed, cloath, and pay his Army, not he that hath the most valiant Troops, is surest of Success and Conquest."[6] This Declaration, which is now stolen and retailed for new, by every modern Dabler in Politics, has had the usual Fortune of these kind of Thefts, to be misunderstood: as may appear from the general Tenor of the Doctor's Writings. To shew this, two Instances, out of many may suffice. Even when speaking on the Benefits of foreign Trade, he warns us, as if he had foreseen all that has befallen, or is likely to befall us. For he says, "If a trading and rich People are grown soft and luxurious, their Wealth will invite over to them Invaders from Abroad, and their being *effeminate* will make the Conquest easy."[7] And again, in Terms yet stronger: "In succeeding Times our Manners may come to be depraved; and when this happens, all Sorts of Miseries will invade us: The whole Wealth of the Kingdom will not be sufficient for it's Defence."[8]

Thus, what he and other sensible Writers have affirmed under proper Restrictions, and upon Supposition that a Nation maintained it's Manners and Principles, is now advanced absolutely, and without Restriction, as if Manners and Principles, military and naval Skill and Courage, had no Part, or at least no essential Part, in the Success of War.

These shallow Politicians, therefore, might well be put in Mind of the Maxim of a warlike Prince, when his Ministers dissuaded him from attacking a wealthy Enemy, because he wanted Money to pay his Troops. "My Enemies, said he, are rich, luxurious, and effeminate; my Troops are valiant and hardy; my Officers brave and honourable; they shall plant *my* Standard in my Enemy's Country, and then *my Enemy shall pay them.*"

We have lately seen this military Conduct followed by a brave King, in the Electorate of *Saxony:* We ourselves have formerly pursued it on the Plains of *Agincourt* and *Cressi:* The *French* are now pursuing it on the Plains of *America:* And if we hold to our dastardly Maxim, they will pursue it on the Plains of *Salisbury.*

Thus the boasted modern Maxim which we proposed to obviate,

6. Ways and Means, p. 27. [Charles Davenant (1656–1714), *An essay upon ways and means of supplying the war* (London: Tonson, 1695), 2 vols.]

7. Dav[enant] on Trade, v. ii, p. 13.

8. Ibid. p. 317.

seems void of Truth in every Branch of it: As it appears from this View, that without the internal Strength which Manners and Principles produce, the most exorbitant Trade and Wealth can never be the Foundation of a successful War; or give us any rational Prospect, either of *Victory* or *Self-Defence*.

Section IX

Another Objection considered

Such then are the natural Effects of exorbitant Trade and Wealth, unless counteracted by opposite Manners or Principles. The History of our own Nation would confirm these Truths in a most striking and particular Manner, were it within the proposed Limits of this Estimate, to enter so large a Field of Enquiry. We should there see, that Manners and Principles have always prevailed, and baffled the most sanguine Attempts of Wealth, when set in Competition with them. This System would be found supported by a vast Variety of Events, from the Reign of *Elizabeth* to the present Times. But this might perhaps be regarded as a Research rather curious than necessary; since a single Reflection on the present State of the Kingdom may seem to stand in the Place of a thousand Proofs.

At present therefore, we shall not touch on this Enquiry; but rather proceed to remove another Objection, which may seem to overturn the Theory here proposed.

For it is urged, that *France* is an Exception to the Truth of these Remarks: inasmuch as, in the midst of a large and extensive Commerce, which brings in a vast Accession of Wealth, she still retains her Principles and Power.

The Fact objected is true: But the Consequence follows not; because the Trade of *France* is limited and controuled by such Accidents, as prevent it's most dangerous and ruinous Effects on Government.

The *Poverty* of its *Noblesse* or leading Ranks, who are often possessed of sounding Titles without any Realities annexed, as it prevents them from reaping that Increase of Wealth which naturally ariseth to a rich Landed Gentry from an Increase of Commerce, so it naturally drives them to the Profession of *Arms*, as the necessary Means of Support: This strengthens and supports their Monarchy; which, finding it's Advantage from this Disposition to Arms, naturally gratifies this military Spirit in it's *Noblesse*, and gives it Exercise and Encouragement by frequent Wars.

Hence the national Spirit of the *French Noblesse* hath long been military, in the highest Degree.

With Regard to Commerce, it's Growth in *France* hath been but late: Meeting therefore with this established Spirit of Arms in the leading Ranks, it hath not as yet been able to controul it. Commerce indeed is encouraged; but so encouraged, as not to destroy the leading Principle of their Monarchy. To this End, the Ranks of the Kingdom are kept essentially distinguished; and while the People are allured to Trade by every Kind of Motive, the *Noblesse* or Gentry are, in Honour, prohibited from Commerce. It was indeed formerly proposed in *France*, that the *Noblesse* should be drawn down to Trade[.] But, whether thro' deep and consummate Policy, or thro' the Principle of Honour itself, working blindly for it's own Preservation, the dangerous Proposal was *weakly* or *wisely* rejected. Whenever this Overture meets with Acceptance and Success, tho' it may seem for a while to give Vigour to their State, yet from that Period we may date the Downfall of *France*. Their effeminate Manners, now controuled by *Oeconomy* and the Love of *Glory*, will, like ours, degenerate into *Profusion* and the Love of *Gold*.

On the contrary; Trade, tho' encouraged, is by the ruling Principles of this great Monarchy, kept within it's proper Limits; and while the Merchant traverseth Seas in Pursuit of *Gain*, the Gentleman does the same in Pursuit of *Glory*. Thus the two incompatible Provinces are kept distinct; and hence, while the *French* vie with us in *Trade*, they tower above us in *Principle*.

Nay their very trading Settlements among foreign Nations are actuated by this ruling Principle in such a Manner, as to give a Splendor to their Monarchy and Commerce in the most barbarous Climates.[9] Thus,

---

9. Numerous Proofs might be given of this: At present it may suffice to take one from a very fine Book lately published. "It is usual among the *French* of *Alexandria* to shew an extreme Respect for their Consul. In order to make him more considerable in the Eyes of the *Turks*, and of the other Nations, they endeavour to give an high Idea of his Person, and to illustrate his Birth in such a Manner, that it is not their Fault, if he is not consid-

while *we* are poorly influenced by a sorry and mercantile Maxim, first broached by a trading Minister, "that the *Interest* of a Nation is it's *truest* Honour;" the *French* conduct themselves on an opposite and higher Principle, "that the *Honour* of a Nation is its truest Interest."

In Confirmation of what is here advanced, we need only cast our Eyes on the Fortune and Fate of *France*, during the present Century. In the last War, she was exhausted, tho' victorious: In the former, she was both beaten and exhausted: In both these Instances, it was weakly thought by every superficial Politician in *England*, that because we had exhausted the Men and Money, we had destroyed the Power of *France*. Experience hath told us the Reverse: The Spirit of Honour and Union working at the Root, soon restored those Branches that War had swept away, and have at length shot them into their former Vigour and Luxuriancy.

Hence then, we may learn an important Truth: "That no incidental Events can make a Nation *little*, while the Principles remain that made it *great*."

Section X

The Conclusion

From these accumulated Proofs, then it seems evident, that our present effeminate Manners and Defect of Principle have arisen from our exorbitant Trade and Wealth, left without Check, to their natural Operations and uncontrouled Influence. And that these Manners, and this Defect of Principle, by weakening or destroying the national Capacity, Spirit of Defence, and Union, have produced such a general Debility as naturally leads to Destruction.

We might now proceed to confirm these Reasonings, by Examples drawn from History. For there is hardly an ancient or modern State of

---

ered as issued from the Blood Royal. If by Chance he take a Tour to *Rosetto*, he carries a white Flag at the Mast of his Pinnace; and when he goes out of the Port, as likewise when he returns into it, he is saluted by a general Discharge of the Cannon of the *French* Vessels." NORDEN's Travels in *Egypt* and *Nubia*, Vol. i. p. 29. [Peter Templeman (1711–69) and Frederick Lewis Norden (1708–42), *Travels in Egypt and Nubia* (London: Davis & Reymers, 1757), 2 vols.]

any Note recorded in Story, which would not in one Respect or other, confirm the leading Principles on which this Argument is built.

In these, throughout their several Periods, we should see *Trade* and *Wealth,* or (what is in this respect equivalent) *Conquest* and *Opulence,* taking their Progress: At one Period, polishing and strengthening: at another, refining, corrupting, weakening, destroying, the State that gave them Entrance: Working indeed in different Ways, and under a Variety of Appearances: by Avarice, by Faction, by Effeminacy, by Profligacy; by a Mixture and Combination of all these Evils: sometimes dividing a Nation against itself; at others, quelling it's Spirit, and leaving it an easy Prey to the first Invader: Sometimes checked by a rising Patriot, or counterworked by national Misfortunes: In one Country corrupting Manners; in another, Principles; in a third, both Manners and Principles: rendering one People blind, another cowardly, another treacherous to itself: Stealing secretly and insensibly on one Nation; overwhelming another in sudden Destruction.

But to enlarge on these Subjects in that vague and undistinguishing Manner, which most Writers have pursued in treating them, tho' it might carry the *Appearance* of Reasoning, would in Truth be no more than *Declamation* in Disguise. And to develope and unravel the Particularity of Causes and Effects, thro' all their Variety of Combination and mutual Influence, as it would extend this Estimate beyond it's designed Limits, must be left to make a Part of some future Enquiry.

The *Character, Effects,* and *Sources* of our Manners and Principles, being thus laid open, the Writer had it in his Thoughts to have proceeded to the Consideration of "*their most practicable Remedies.*" But as the Closet-*Projects* of retired and speculative Men, often *are,* and always are *regarded,* as *chimerical:* he was therefore unwilling, at present, to hazard the Discredit of such an Attempt.

However, lest his Attempt should be deemed more visionary than perhaps it is, he judged it not improper to hint at some of the leading Principles on which it is built. And with this View, the following Reflections are submitted to the Consideration of the Public.

The World has been long amused with a trite and hacknied Comparison between the Life of Man, and that of States; in which it is pretended that they both proceed in the same irrevocable Manner; from Infancy to

Maturity, from Maturity to Death: A Comparison, perhaps as ground-less as it is common. The human Body contains, in its very Texture, the Seeds of certain Dissolution. That is, tho' you set aside all the possible Accidents arising from Intemperance, from the Influence of the Elements, the Climate, and every other external and contingent Cause, the human Frame itself, after a certain Period, would grow into Rigidity; the Fluids would decrease, the Solids accumulate, the Arteries *ossify*, the Blood stagnate, and the Wheels of Life stand still.

But in Societies, of whatever Kind, there seems no such necessary or essential Tendency to Dissolution. The human Body is *naturally* mortal; the political, only so by *Accident:* Internal Disorders or Diseases may arise; External Violence may attack or overpower: but these Causes, tho' always to be expected, are wholly incidental: the first is precisely of the same Nature as Intemperance, the second as the Influence of the external Elements, on the human Body. But there appears nothing in the internal Construction of any State, that tends inevitably to Dissolution, analogous to those Causes in the human Frame, which lead to certain Death.

This Observation seems confirmed by History: Where you see States, which, after being sunk in Corruption and Debility, have been brought back to the Vigour of their first Principles: But you must have recourse to Fables, for medicated Old Age, restored to Infancy or Youth.

29

"In Praise of Gournay"
1759

ANNE-ROBERT-JACQUES TURGOT, Baron of Aulne, hailed from one
of France's oldest and most prestigious families. Born in Paris in 1727,
Turgot distinguished himself at the Sorbonne and became one of the
leading protégés of the liberal intendant of commerce of the time, Vincent de Gournay. In the 1750s, he drafted a number of highly original
works on the historical evolution of the human mind and on economic
development, among other things, and acquired the reputation as a poly-
math genius. After composing several articles for the *Encyclopédie* in the
1750s on topics as varied as etymology and market-fairs, he dissociated
himself from the project in the aftermath of the controversy of 1758 that
led to its temporary suppression. In 1761, he became provincial *intendant*
for Limousin, where he remained for thirteen years, developing a reputation for reformist vigor and effectiveness in an undynamic province.
During that period, he became the leading exponent of free trade in
grain, though his relations with the Physiocrat school that made that position a matter of dogma were cool. In 1774, he was elevated to controller-
general of France, in which position he attempted to implement on a national scale the reforms he had reflected on, described, and attempted
locally for many years. His far-reaching reforms, such as the abolition of
the guilds, met with a backlash, and he was disgraced and forced from
office nineteen months later in early 1776. He died in 1781.

"In Praise of Gournay" was Turgot's eulogy for the deceased intendant
of commerce and was prepared for the popular periodical *Le Mercure* in

August 1759. The edition used here is *The Economics of A. R. J. Turgot,* ed. P. D. Groenewegen (© 1977 by Martinus Nijhoff, The Hague, Netherlands), pp. 20–42; reprinted with the kind permission of Kluwer Academic Publishers. All notes are by the Nijhoff editor; material in brackets is by the present editor.

In Praise of Gournay
(Eloge de Gournay)

Letter from Turgot to Marmontel[1]
Paris, 22 July, 1759

I have certainly not forgotten, sir, the note on the late M. de Gournay, which I promised you. I even counted on giving it to you last Monday, at Mme. Geoffrin's,[2] but, not having found you there, and believing you to be in no great hurry, moreover, I took it back home, with the idea that perhaps I would have the time to complete the draft of the eulogy which I would like to make of this excellent citizen.

Since you can wait no longer, I am sending you an outline of it, sketched in great haste, which may yet be able to help you write it, and which you will undoubtedly use in a manner which does much greater justice to his glory than my efforts.

You are aware of my affection.

---

1. Jean François Marmontel (1723–1799), French writer and contributor to the *Encyclopédie*. He prepared the official eulogy of Gournay by having extracts of Turgot's eulogy printed in *Le Mercure*, August, 1759, No. 8; the first full edition of this work did not appear till the 19th century when it was included in Du Pont's edition of Turgot's works. (See III, pp. 321–375.)

2. Marie Thérèse Rodet Geoffrin (1699–1777), famous for her salon, which Turgot frequented.

Jean Claude Marie Vincent, Seigneur de Gournay, honorary councillor of the Grand Council, and honorary Intendant of Commerce, died at Paris, June 27 (1759) at the age of forty-seven.[3]

He was born in St. Malo in May 1712. His father was Claude Vincent, one of the most important merchants of that town, and Secretary Royal.

His parents destined him for a commercial life, and sent him to Cadiz in 1729, when he was only just seventeen.

Left to his own devices at this early age, he was yet able to avoid the perils and frivolity which are but too common at that age, and, during his entire stay in Cadiz, his life was divided between study, the work of his business, and the numerous connections which his business required and which his personal merit soon procured him.

Through diligence and alertness he found time to enrich his mind with a mass of useful knowledge, without yet neglecting that higher literature, but it was, above all, to the science of commerce that he felt himself drawn and to which he directed his mind in all its vigour. To compare the products of nature and those of the arts in man in different climes, to arrive at the value of these different products, or, in other words, their relationship with the needs and wealth of people at home and abroad, the costs of transport which vary according to the nature of the commodities and the diversity of the routes, the many duties to which they are subject, etc., etc.; in short, to comprehend in its full scope, and to follow in its continual upheavals, the condition of natural production, of industry, of population, of wealth, of finance, of the needs and even the vagaries of fashion in all the nations that are united by commerce, in order to theorise profitably on the basis of a thorough study of all these details—this is to be concerned with the science of trade, as a merchant and constitutes only a part of the science of commerce. But to discover the causes and effects of that multitude of upheavals in all their diversity, to search out the elemental forces whose action, always in combination with, and sometimes disguised by, local circumstances, directs

---

3. Turgot made two errors in this official description. Gournay's name was Jacques Claude Marie and not Jean Claude Marie, and his title was M. le Marquis de Gournay and not simply Sieur de Gournay. See G. Schelle, *Vincent de Gournay*, pp. 17, 24 which remains the standard biography.

all the transactions of commerce; to recognise those special and basic laws, founded in Nature itself, by which all the values existent in commerce are balanced against each other and settle at a certain value, just as bodies left to themselves take their place, unaided, according to their specific gravity; to discern those complicated relations which link commerce with all the branches of political economy; to perceive the interdependence of commerce and agriculture, the influence of the one and the other on the wealth, the population, and the strength of states, their intimate connection with the laws and customs, and with all the processes of the government, especially with the distribution of its finances; to weigh the assistance which commerce receives from the Navy and that which it renders to it in return, the changes it produces in the respective interests of States, and the weight it places in the political balance of nations; in fine, to select, from among chance events and principles of administration adopted by the different nations of Europe, the true causes of their progress or of their decline in commerce—this is to approach the subject as a philosopher and a statesman.

If his position in life caused M. Vincent to concern himself with the science of commerce as under the first of these two points of view, his vast and penetrating intellect did not allow him to confine himself to this.

To the enlightenment which he drew from his own experience and his reflections, he added a reading of the best works on this subject produced by the different nations of Europe, and particularly by the English nation—the richest of all in such works, and with whose language he familiarised himself for this reason. The works which he read with most pleasure, and whose doctrine he most appreciated, were the Treatises of the famous Josiah Child[4] (which he afterwards translated into French) and the Memoirs of the Grand Pensionary, Johan de Witt.[5] We know that these two great men are considered (the one in England, the other

---

4. Sir Josiah Child (1630–1699), English merchant and economist. The treatise to which Turgot refers is his *New Discourse Upon Trade* (1690) which Gournay had translated into French [see chapter 3 in this volume].

5. Johan de Witt (1623–1672), prominent Dutch statesman. The treatise to which Turgot refers is the *Political Maxims of the State of Holland . . . by John de Witt, pensionary of Holland;* first Dutch edition in 1662, first English edition in 1702, the first French edition was published in 1709 under the title *Mémoires de Jean de Witt* [see chapter 2 above].

in Holland) as the legislators of commerce; that their principles have become national principles, and that the observance of these principles is regarded as one of the sources of the vast superiority in commerce which these two nations have acquired over all the other powers. M. Vincent constantly found verification of these simple and enlightened principles in the practice of an extensive business. He made them his own, without foreseeing that he was destined one day to spread their light through France, and to merit from his own country the same tribute of gratitude which England and Holland pay to those two benefactors of their nation and humanity. His talents and knowledge, together with the most perfect integrity, assured M. Vincent the admiration and the confidence of that multitude of merchants that commerce brings together at Cadiz from all parts of Europe, while at the same time his charming manners procured him their friendship. He soon enjoyed there an esteem unusual for his age, and which the natives of the country, his own compatriots, and the foreigners there, were equally eager to bestow upon him.

During his stay in Cadiz he had paid several visits to the Court of Spain, and to the various provinces of that kingdom.

In 1744, some commercial enterprises which had to be arranged with the Government brought him to France, and in contact with the Comte de Maurepas,[6] then Minister of Navy, who soon discovered M. Vincent's worth.

After leaving Spain, M. Vincent resolved to spend some years travelling through the different parts of Europe in order to increase his knowledge, as well as to extend his correspondences and to form connections favourable to the business he intended to pursue. He visited Hamburg and travelled through Holland and England. Everywhere he made observations and collected notes on the state of commerce and shipping, and on the principles of administration adopted by the different nations in respect to those great objects. During his travels, he maintained an uninterrupted correspondence with M. de Maurepas, whom he ac-

---

6. Jean Frédéric Phélypeaux, Comte de Maurepas (1701–1781), Minister for the Navy and Colonies (1723–1749). On the accession of Louis XVI he became First Minister, and on the advice of his wife and Abbé de Véri invited Turgot to the ministry, first of the Navy, then of Finances.

quainted with the knowledge which he was gathering. Everywhere, he made a favourable impression, and attracted the goodwill of the most considerable merchants, of men of great distinction in all walks of life, and of the ministers of foreign powers who were resident in the places through which he travelled. The Court of Vienna, as well as that of Berlin sought to procure his services, and made him very enticing proposals, but he rejected them. He had no other intention than to continue in business and to return to Spain, after having again seen Germany and Italy, when an unforeseen event interrupted his projects and brought him back to his own country.

M. Jametz de Villebarre, his business partner and friend, died in 1746, and being without children, made M. Vincent his sole heir. The latter was in England when he received this news; he returned to France. The amount of his fortune was sufficient for his modest needs; he felt he should settle in his own country and he gave up commerce in 1748. He then took his name from his estate of Gournay, which was included in the legacy he received from M. de Villebarre. The minister[7] was aware how useful his knowledge of commerce might prove to the administration of that important sector. The court had planned to send him to the general peace discussions being held at Breda,[8] not unlike M. Ménager, who in 1711, had been sent to the conferences which preceded the Treaty of Utrecht, in order to discuss the commercial aspects of our interests. The changes which occurred in the conferences did not permit this wise project to be executed, but M. de Maurepas adhered to his original desire to make the talents of M. de Gournay useful to the government; he advised him to consider the prospects of a position as Intendant of Commerce, and to enter, in the meantime, one of the higher Courts. Consequently, in 1749, M. de Gournay purchased the office of councillor in the Grand Council. When an Intendancy of Commerce fell vacant in 1751, M. de Machault,[9] who was also most familiar with the merits of M. de Gournay, had that office conferred on him. From this time onwards, his

7. I.e. de Maurepas, see above, p. 22, n. 6 [p. 452 n. 6 in this volume].

8. In 1748, at the end of the War of Austrian Succession. The peace treaty itself was signed at Aix-la-Chapelle in the same year.

9. M. de Machault d'Arnouville (1701–1794). Intendant of Hainaut (1743–1745), President of the Ministry of Commerce (1745), Contrôleur-Général des finances (1745–1750).

life was devoted to public affairs: his entry into the Ministry of Commerce appears to have marked the beginning of a period of profound change. During twenty years of experience in a wide and varied trade, in his frequent visits to the most competent merchants of Holland and England, in the reading of the most highly esteemed authors of these two nations, in his careful observation of the causes of their prosperity, M. de Gournay had formulated principles which appeared to be new to some of the magistrates of whom the Ministry of Commerce was composed— M. de Gournay was of the opinion that every man who works deserves the gratitude of the public. He was astonished to find that a citizen could neither manufacture nor sell anything without having bought the right to do so by entering a corporation or guild at great expense, and that, after having bought this right, it was still sometimes necessary to have a law suit, to determine whether by entering this or that corporation he had acquired the right to manufacture precisely this or that article. He thought that a workman who had manufactured a piece of cloth had made a real addition to the stock of wealth in the State; that if this cloth happened to be inferior to others, there might yet be found among his customers somebody to whom this inferiority would be more suitable than a more expensive perfection. He could not see why this piece of cloth, for failing to conform to certain regulations, should be cut up into fragments of three ells in length, and why the unfortunate man who had made it should be ordered to pay a penalty, enough to reduce him and his family to poverty.[10] He could not conceive why a workman, when making a piece of cloth, should be exposed to risks and expenses from which an idle man was exempt. He could not see of what use it might be that a manufactured piece of cloth should involve legal procedures and tedious discussions in order to establish whether it conformed to an extensive system of regulation, often difficult to understand, nor did he think that such discussions ought to be held between a manufacturer who cannot read and an inspector who cannot manufacture, nor that that inspector should yet be the final judge of the fortune of the unlucky man, etc.

M. de Gournay found it equally strange that, in a kingdom in which

10. For a full description of some of these regulations, see E. F. Heckscher, *Mercantilism*, second edition, London, 1955, I, pp. 157–166.

the order of succession was determined simply by custom, and in which the question of applying the death sentence to certain crimes was still left to the discretion of the courts, the government should have deigned to regulate by special legislation the length and breadth of each piece of cloth,[11] the number of threads it was to contain, and to hallow with the seal of the legislature four volumes in quarto filled with these important details, and in addition innumerable statutes, dictated by the spirit of monopoly, the whole purpose of which were to discourage industry, to concentrate trade within the hands of a few people by multiplying formalities and charges, by subjecting industry to apprenticeships and journeymanships (*compagnonnages*) of ten years in some trades which can be learned in ten days, by excluding those who were not sons of masters, or those born outside a certain class, and by prohibiting the employment of women in the manufacture of cloth, etc., etc.

He had not imagined that in a kingdom subject to the same prince, all towns looked on each other as enemies, that they would assume the right to prohibit work within their precincts to other Frenchmen, classifying them as *foreigners*, to oppose the sale or the free transit of commodities of a neighbouring province—and thereby for the sake of some fleeting interest, to contend against the general interest of the State, etc., etc.

He was no less astonished to see the government concern itself in regulating the circulation of each commodity, in proscribing one kind of industry in order to encourage another, in subjecting to special constraints the sale of the provisions most necessary to life, in forbidding the setting up of stores of a product whose crop varies from year to year and whose consumption is nearly always the same, in forbidding the exportation of an article subject to depreciation, and to see the government expect to secure the abundance of corn by making the condition of the farm labourer more uncertain and more unhappy than that of all other men, etc.

M. de Gournay was well aware that several of the abuses to which he was opposed had existed in former times in a large part of Europe, and that vestiges of them still remained even in England; but he also knew that the English government had abolished part of them; that, if some

---

11. E. F. Heckscher, *Mercantilism*, I, pp. 160–161, where the first five rules in the regulations for the weaving of woollen cloth are quoted.

still remained, far from adopting them as useful institutions, that government tried to restrict them, and to prevent them from spreading, and continued to tolerate them only because the republican constitution sometimes places obstacles in the path of reform of certain abuses when these abuses can be corrected only by an authority which is always mistrusted by the people, even if it is used to their own advantage. Finally, he knew that for more than a century, all enlightened minds, whether in Holland or in England, had regarded these abuses as remnants of mediaeval barbarism and of the weakness of all the governments which had known neither the importance of public liberty, nor how to protect it against the invasions of the spirit of monopoly and of particular interests.

For twenty years, M. de Gournay had himself carried out, and had seen carried out, the greatest commerce on earth without having had occasion to learn, other than from books, of the existence of all those laws to which he saw so much importance attached, and therefore he did not believe that he would be taken for an *innovator* and a *man of systems*, when all he did was to develop those principles which experience had taught him, and which he saw unanimously recognised by the most enlightened merchants with whom he was associated.

These principles, which others styled as a *new system,* to him appeared to be no more than the maxims of the plainest common sense. This whole so-called *system* was founded on this maxim, that in general every man knows his own interest better than another to whom it is of no concern.

Hence he concluded that when the interest of individuals is precisely the same as the general interest, every man ought best to be left at liberty to do what he likes. Now, in the case of unrestrained commerce, M. de Gournay thought it impossible for the individual interest not to concur with the general interest.[12]

Commerce can be connected with the general interest, or, what is the same thing, the State can interest itself in commerce, in two respects only. As protector of the individuals who compose it, it is in its interest that no one should be able to inflict any great injustice on another, against which the latter has no protection. Next in its capacity as a political unit forced to defend itself against foreign invasions, it is in the in-

---

12. Cf. Charles Davenant, *Discourses on the Publick Revenues* (1698) in *Works* (edited by Charles Whitworth), London, 1771, I, p. 146.

terest of the State that the stock of its wealth and the annual product of the soil and of industry should be as great as possible. In both respects, the State has a special interest in protecting the value of the necessities of life from those sudden shocks which, by plunging the people into the horrors of famine, may endanger public tranquility and the safety of citizens and magistrates. Now, it is clear that the interest of all the individuals, kept free from restraint of any kind, necessarily fulfils all these conditions of general usefulness.

As for the first object, that in trade no one should injure another, it is evidently sufficient that the government should always protect the natural liberty of the buyer to buy, and of the seller to sell. For if the buyer is always the one who decides whether to buy or not, it is certain that he will select among all the sellers the man who will give him at the best price the merchandise that suits him best. It is no less certain that every seller, it being his chief interest to gain preference over his competitors, will sell in general the best merchandise at the lowest possible price, in order to attract customers. It is not true therefore that a merchant may be interested in deception—unless he has some exclusive privilege.

But if the government limits the number of sellers by exclusive privileges or otherwise, it is certain that the consumer will be wronged and that the seller, certain of selling, will compel him to buy bad articles at a high price.

If, on the contrary, it is the number of buyers which is diminished, by the exclusion of foreigners or of certain other persons, then the seller is wronged, and, if the injury is carried to the point where the price does not compensate him, with profit, for the costs and risk, he will cease to produce the commodity in such abundance, and scarcity will result.

The general freedom of buying and selling is therefore the only means of assuring, on the one hand, the seller of a price sufficient to encourage production, and on the other hand, the consumer, of the best merchandise at the lowest price. This is not to say that in particular instances we may not find a cheating merchant and a duped consumer; but the cheated consumer will learn by experience and will cease to frequent the cheating merchant, who will fall into discredit and thus will be punished for his fraudulence; and this will never happen very often, because generally men will be enlightened upon their evident self-interest.

To expect the government to prevent such fraud from ever occurring would be like wanting it to provide cushions for all the children who might fall. To assume it to be possible to prevent successfully, by regulation, all possible malpractices of this kind, is to sacrifice to a chimerical perfection the whole progress of industry; it is to restrict the imagination of artificers to the narrow limits of the familiar; it is to forbid them all new experiments; to renounce even the hope of competing with the foreigners in the making of the new products which they invent daily, since, as they do not conform to our regulations, our workmen cannot imitate these articles without first having obtained permission from the government, that is to say, often after the foreign factories, having profited by the first eagerness of the consumer for this novelty, have already replaced it with something else. It means forgetting that the execution of these regulations is always entrusted to men who may have all the more interest in fraud or in conniving at fraud since the fraud which they might commit would be covered in some way by the seal of public authority and by the confidence which this seal inspires, in the consumers. It is also to forget that these regulations, these inspectors, these offices for inspection and marking, always involve expenses, and that these expenses are always a tax on the merchandise, and as a result overcharge the domestic consumer and discourage the foreign buyer. Thus, with obvious injustice, commerce, and consequently the nation, are charged with a heavy burden to save a few idle people the trouble of instructing themselves or of making enquiries to avoid being cheated. To suppose all consumers to be dupes, and all merchants and manufacturers to be cheats, has the effect of authorising them to be so, and of degrading all the working members of the community.

As for the second object for the Government in this connection, which is to procure for the nation the greatest possible stock of wealth, is it not evident that since the only real wealth of the State is the annual output of its land and of the industry of its inhabitants, its wealth will be at its greatest when the produce of each acre of land, and of the industry of each individual is carried to the highest possible level? And is it not evident that each proprietor has more interest than any other person in drawing from his land the greatest possible return? That every individual has the same interest in gaining by his work as much money as possible? It is equally obvious that the employment of the soil or of industry which yields the greatest revenue to each proprietor or to each inhabitant will always be the one that is of the greatest advantage to the State, because the sum which the State can use annually for its needs is always an aliquot part of the total revenue which is annually produced in the State, and because the sum of these revenues is composed of the net revenue of each estate and of the product of the industry of each individual—if then, instead of leaving all this to private interests, the government takes it upon itself to prescribe to each what he must do, clearly all the benefits individuals lose because of the constraints imposed upon them, will represent an equal deduction from the total net revenue produced in the State each year.

To imagine that the State should encourage the earth to bring forth one kind of produce rather than another, that it ought to establish certain types of manufactures rather than some others; that consequently it ought to prohibit the production of some goods and order that of others; to forbid certain kinds of industry for fear of injuring other kinds; to claim to sustain manufacturing, when it is at the expense of agriculture by forcibly maintaining the price of provisions below their natural level; to establish certain manufactures at the expense of the Treasury; to heap privileges on them, favours, exclusions of all manufactures of the same kind for the purpose of procuring for the manufacturers a profit which it is assumed they could not obtain by the natural sale of their products: all this is to misunderstand greatly the true advantages of commerce; it is to forget that no commercial transaction can be anything other than reciprocal, and that, therefore, the desire to sell everything to the foreigners and to buy nothing from them, is absurd.

There is no need to prove that each individual is the only competent judge of this most advantageous use of his lands and of his labour. He alone has the particular knowledge without which the most enlightened man could only argue blindly. He alone has an experience which is all the more reliable since it is limited to a single object. He learns by repeated trials, by his successes, by his losses, and he acquires a feeling for it which is much more ingenious than the theoretical knowledge of the indifferent observer because it is stimulated by want.

If the objection is raised that apart from exchange value, the State may also be interested in being as little dependent as possible on other states for the commodities of prime necessity; firstly, all that this proves is that, although both freedom of industry and freedom of trade in the produce of the soil, are very precious, freedom of trade in the produce of the soil is yet the more essential; secondly, it will always be true that greater wealth and a larger population will give the State in question the means of ensuring its independence in a much more reliable manner. Besides, that suggestion is purely speculative; a large State always produces everything and with regard to a smaller one, a bad harvest would soon wreck this fine scheme of independence.

As for the third object, which may interest the State in two respects, both as protector of the individuals whom it must put in the way of earning a comfortable living by their own labour, and as a political body interested in preventing the domestic troubles which a famine could cause, this matter has been developed so clearly in the work of M. Herbert,[13] and in the article *Corn* by M. Quesnay,[14] that I refrain from discussing it here, since M. Marmontel knows these two works thoroughly.

It follows from this discussion that, in all respects in which commerce may interest the State, unrestrained individual interest will always produce the public welfare more surely than the operations of government, which are always faulty and of necessity directed by a hazy and dubious theory.

M. de Gournay concluded that the only aim the administration should set for itself was: firstly, to restore to all branches of commerce that precious liberty they had lost through the prejudices of ages of ignorance, through the ease with which the Government fell in with particular interests, and the desire for a misplaced perfection; secondly, to grant the right to work to all members of the State, for the purpose of exciting the greatest competition in the market, which will infallibly produce the greatest perfection in manufacture, and the most advantageous price to the buyers; thirdly, to give at the same time as many competitors as possible to the buyer by opening for the seller all the outlets for his

---

13. Claude-Jacques Herbert, *Essai sur la police des grains, sur leur prix, et sur les effets de l'agriculture*, Londres, 1753.

14. François Quesnay, "Grains," first published in the *Encyclopédie* in 1757. See *Quesnay et la Physiocratie*, II, pp. 459–510.

commodity, which is the only means of assuring labour its reward, and of perpetuating production, which has this reward as its sole object.

Besides this, the government should plan to remove those obstacles which retard the progress of industry by diminishing the extent and the certainty of its profits. M. de Gournay considered the chief of these obstacles to be the high interest of money,[15] which, by offering to all owners of capital the means of spending their lives without working, encourages luxury and idleness and withdraws from commerce the riches and industry of a multitude of citizens, rendering them unproductive to the State; which excludes the nation from all branches of commerce not yielding one or two per cent more than the current rate of interest; which consequently gives foreigners the exclusive privilege of all these branches of commerce, and enables them to gain preference over us in almost all other countries by lowering the price more than we would afford to do; which gives the inhabitants of our colonies a powerful reason to engage in smuggling, and in this way weakens the natural affection they ought to have for the mother country; which alone would secure for the Dutch and the Hanse towns the carrying trade of all of Europe including even France itself; which, every year, makes us tributaries to the foreigners by the high rates we pay on their loans to us; which, finally, withdraws from cultivation all those lands which would not yield more than five per cent, since it is possible, to obtain the same return with the same capital, without working. But similarly, he believed that the dealings in capital itself, which have this rate of interest as their price, can be made to regulate this price equitably and with all necessary economy only, as in the case of all commerce, by competition and by mutual liberty, and that the government could best bring this about by, on the one hand abstaining from making laws whenever agreements can serve this purpose, and on the other hand, by not swelling the number of debtors and consumers of capital whether by borrowing or by not repaying punctually.[16]

Another kind of obstacle to the progress of industry which M. de

15. Cf. Turgot, "Remarks on the Notes to the Translation of Child," section 1.
16. The last sentence of this paragraph is not in the original manuscript but was included by Du Pont in his edition of Turgot's works. (Note by G. Schelle.)

Gournay considered could not be cleared away too soon was that multiplicity of taxes which, owing to the necessity of meeting the requirements of the State, had been imposed upon labour of every kind, entailing vexatious modes of collection which were often more onerous than the taxes themselves; the arbitrary nature of the *taille*,° the multiplicity of dues on every sort of merchandise, the complexity of tariffs, the inequality of these dues in the different provinces, the innumerable customs houses at the frontier of these provinces, the frequency of inspections and the importunity of enquiries necessary to provide against fraud, the necessity of relying on the solitary testimony of mercenary men of low character for proof of these frauds; the interminable disputes, so fatal to commerce that almost any merchant would prefer, in this respect, a disadvantageous arrangement to a law suit, no matter how obvious the justice of his case. Finally, he condemned the impenetrable obscurity and mystery resulting from this complexity of local dues and regulations published at different dates, an obscurity which is always interpreted in favour of revenue and against commerce. He condemned the excessive duties, the evils of smuggling, the loss of a multitude of citizens which this entails, etc., etc., etc.

Public finance is necessary, since the State needs revenue; but agriculture and commerce, or rather agriculture animated by commerce, is the ultimate source of these revenues. Thus public finance should not be prejudicial to commerce, since it would at the same time harm itself. These two interests are of necessity united, and if a conflict of interests seems to exist, it is perhaps because we have confused the interests of finance as related to the State and the monarchy, which are eternal, with the interests of the financiers, who, being charged with the collection of the revenues for a certain period only, prefer to increase present revenue rather than to conserve the source which produces this revenue. Add to this the dubious and fortuitous way in which this hydra of all types of duties has taken shape, i.e. by the successive gathering together of a multitude of fiefs and sovereignties, and the conservation of the taxes which each individual sovereign used to enjoy, while the urgency of the kingdom's needs has never left time to reform this chaos by establishing a uniform system of duties. Finally, there are the facilities which public finance has had at all times of making its voice heard, to the prejudice of commerce.

The fiscal authority consists of a body of accredited men, whose prestige varies with the urgency of the needs of the State. They are always occupied with a single object, never distracted nor negligent, resident in the capital and in constant touch with the government. The merchants, on the other hand, occupied each with his individual objective, dispersed in the provinces, without fame or protection, without a central meeting place, are only able to raise a feeble and solitary voice in any given case, a voice that is inevitably stifled both by the number and the prestige of their adversaries, and by the opportunities the latter have of engaging skilled writers in the defence of their interests. If the merchant agrees to abandon the care of his affairs in order to hold a litigation rather than to surrender his rights, the odds are high against him, and even if he wins, he still remains at the mercy of a powerful body which has, through the rigour of the laws which it has suggested to the ministry, an easy means of crushing the merchant; for (and this is not one of the least abuses), there exist several laws of this type which are impossible to execute and which the tax farmers only use to ensure the submission of individuals, by threatening a rigorous application of them.

M. de Gournay thought that the Board of Trade would be of much greater use if, rather than managing commerce, which ought to go its own way, it protected commerce against the activities of the public revenue. He would have liked the needs of the State to be such that they would allow commerce to be delivered from all kinds of duties. He believed that a nation fortunate enough to have reached this point would necessarily draw to itself the greater part of the commerce of Europe. He believed that all taxes, of whatever kind they may be, are, in the final analysis, paid by the landowner, who sells by so much the less the produce of his land, and that if all the taxes were assessed on landed property, the proprietors and the kingdom would thereby gain all that was now absorbed in the cost of administration, the unproductive employment of men now wasted in tax collection, in smuggling, or in preventing it, without even counting the immense gain from the increase in riches and value that would result from the increase in commerce.

There exist also some obstacles to the progress of industry that arise from our customs, from our prejudices, from some of our civil laws, but the two which are most disastrous I have already discussed, and the others would entail too much detail. Besides, M. de Gournay did not

pretend to limit the duties of the government towards commerce strictly
to that of maintaining its free course and removing the obstacles that oppose the improvement of industry. He was also quite convinced of the
usefulness of the encouragements that could be given to industry[17] either
by recompensing the authors of useful inventions, or by encouraging, by
prizes or gratuities, a competition among artisans to attain perfection.
He knew that even when industry enjoyed the most complete freedom,
these measures are often useful in hastening its natural progress, and that
they are essential above all when the fear of constraints has not been
completely dispelled and still slows down its development. But he could
not give his approval when these encouragements could conceivably
stand in the way of new progress through prohibitions and exclusive advantages. It was only with great reservations that he supported loans by
the government, and he preferred other encouragements: rewards in
proportion to production, and prizes designed to attain perfection in
work, in short, marks of distinction and all measures which encourage
competition among a greater number of men.

This, more or less, expresses M. de Gournay's attitude towards the administration of commerce; these are the principles which he constantly
applied to all the matters discussed at the Board of Trade from the moment he entered it. As he had no idea of creating a new system, he was
satisfied to develop only what was necessary to support his opinions in
regard to each particular affair; but it was not long before the consistency
and fruitfulness of his principles were recognised, and soon he had to
countenance a mass of challenges.

He gave himself with pleasure to these discussions which could only
elucidate the subject and in one way or another produce a knowledge of
the truth. Free from all selfish interest, from all personal ambition, he
lacked even that slavery to his opinions which self-love might have induced. All he lived for, and aspired to, was the public welfare; thus his
opinions were expressed with as much modesty as courage. Equally
incapable of taking an overbearing tone, and of speaking against his

---

17. Cf. Turgot "Remarks on the Notes to the Translation of Child," where he argued
in section IX: "I doubt strongly that the regulations would be useful even for the original
establishment of manufacturers."

opinion, he delivered his sentiments in a straightforward manner which derived all its power from the strength of his reasoning. He skilfully put his ideas within the grasp of all minds, stating his principles with a kind of luminous precision, and emphasising them by a sensible use of some well chosen examples. When he was contradicted, he listened with patience; however sharp the attack might be, he never discarded his customary politeness and gentleness, nor did he lose anything of the presence of mind and composure necessary to fathom completely the artful reasoning advanced against him.

His simple eloquence, animated by that engaging earnestness which pervades the discourse of a virtuous man who is deeply persuaded that he is upholding the cause of the public welfare, never detracted from the soundness of the discussion; sometimes it was seasoned with a harmless jest which was all the more pleasant since it was never pointless.

His zeal was gentle because it was purged of all self-esteem; but it was not therefore any the less earnest, for love of the public welfare gripped him.

He was convincing without being excessively attached to his opinions; his mind, always without bias, was constantly ready to receive fresh enlightenment; sometimes he did change his mind on important matters, and there was nothing to suggest that his previous opinion had in the least delayed that sudden impression which the proffered truth makes on one as fairminded as he.

He had the good fortune to find in M. Trudaine,[18] who was even then at the head of the administration of commerce, the same love of truth and of the public welfare that motivated himself. Since at that stage he had developed his ideas only as occasion arose during business discussion or in conversation, M. Trudaine urged him to give as it were an outline of his doctrine. It was with this in mind that he translated in 1752 the treatises on trade and the interest of money by Sir Josiah Child and Sir Thomas Culpeper. He added a great many interesting remarks in which he thoroughly examined and discussed the principles of the text, and clarified them by applying them to the most important questions of

---

18. Daniel Charles Trudaine (1703–1769), Intendant of Reom (1730–43), Director of Roads and Bridges (1743–69). His son, Jean Charles Trudaine (1733–1777), was Intendant-Général des Finances in 1769. Both were friends of Turgot.

commerce. These remarks formed a work as considerable as that of the English authors, and M. de Gournay counted on having them printed together. He printed only the text however, in 1754: reasons, which no longer exist, then prevented the printing of the commentary.[19]

His reputation became well established, and his zeal communicated itself to others. It is to the ardour with which he sought to direct all men of talent with whom he was acquainted to the study of commerce and political economy, and to the ease with which he communicated all the knowledge he acquired, that we owe that propitious fermentation of thought on these important questions that has taken place these last few years, and which sprang up two or three years after M. de Gournay had been Intendant of Commerce. Since then, it has already presented us with several works[20] filled with laborious research and profound views, works that have cleared our nation of the charge of frivolity which it had not failed to incur by its indifference to those studies which are the most truly useful.

In spite of the opposition which he had to endure, M. de Gournay often tasted the satisfaction of succeeding in eradicating part of the abuses which he was attacking, and above all, of weakening the authority of those archaic principles which even then had to be relaxed as to the rigour and the extent of their application in order to withstand his attacks. However difficult people may have found it to embrace his principles to their full extent, his insight, his experience, the general esteem of the merchants for him personally, the unimpeachable purity of his

---

19. Together with Butel-Dumont and published in 1754 under the title *Traité sur le commerce et les avantages qui résultent de la réduction de l'intérêt d'argent*, par Josiah Child bart., *avec un petit traité contre l'usure* par Sir Thomas Culpeper. The notes and explanations by Gournay were not published at the time for reasons explained by Turgot and appear to have been lost. See Palgrave, *Dictionary of Political Economy*, II, p. 236.

20. These "several works" to which Turgot refers would presumably include: Forbonnais, *Elémens du Commerce*, published in 1754; Forbonnais, *Divers mémoires sur le commerce*, published in 1756; (Ange Goudar), *Les Intérêts de la France mal entendus, dans les branches de l'agriculture, de la population, des finances, du commerce, de la marine & de l'industrie*, published in 1756; Simon Cliquot de Blervache, *Considérations sur le commerce, et en particulier sur les compagnées, sociétés, et maîtrises*, published in 1758. This last work is reputed to have been written with Gournay's advice and guidance. Turgot may also have referred to the articles appearing in the *Journal économique* whose first series appeared from 1751 to 1757, while the second series started in 1758 and finished in 1772.

views, these things inevitably earned him the confidence of the minister and the respect even of those who yet fought against his ideas.

His zeal induced him to make plans to tour the kingdom in order to see for himself the state of commerce and of manufactures, and to discover the reason for the rise or decay of each branch of trade,[21] the abuses, the needs, the resources of each type. He started the execution of his plan in 1753 and departed in July. From that time up to December he traversed Bourgogne, Lyonnais, Dauphiné, Provence, upper and lower Languedoc, and returned finally by way of Lyon.

In 1754, he was unable to travel because of a tumour situated on his back, which he had cut out twice, and which had to be burned out the third time with the help of caustics, at the beginning of 1755. He resumed his travels in 1755 and made a tour of inspection of La Rochelle, Bordeaux, Montauban, the remainder of Guyenne and Bayonne. In 1756 he followed the course of the Loire from Orléans to Nantes, travelled through Maine, Anjou, the coast of Bretagne from Nantes to Saint-Malo, and returned to Rennes for the sitting of the States in 1756. The deterioration of his health did not permit him to make any further journeys.

At each step he found further reasons to confirm him in his principles, and new arguments against the restriction of commerce against which he was fighting. He took up the complaints of the friendless, poor manufacturer who, unable to write and to present his claims in plausible arguments, and having no representative at the Court, has always been the victim of a government misguided by interested men to whom he was forced to appeal. M. de Gournay applied himself to uncovering the hidden interests which had called for those allegedly useful rules whose sole object it was to put the poor more and more at the mercy of the rich. The fruits of his travels were the reform of an infinite number of abuses of this kind; a knowledge of the true state of the provinces giving more certainty and better direction to the operations of the Ministry; a more exact appreciation of complaints and requests; the facility which was afforded to the people and to the simple artisans of making known their own complaints; finally, a fresh spirit of emulation in all branches of commerce which M. de Gournay was able to spread by his persuasive

---

21. Turgot accompanied Gournay on several of these tours of inspection. See Dakin, *Turgot and the Ancien Régime in France*, p. 18.

eloquence, by the exactness with which he stated his ideas and by the happy contagion of his patriotic zeal.

He sought to inspire in the magistrates and notable persons in the places he visited a zeal for the prosperity of their town or their district; he interviewed men of letters, suggested subjects for treatment, and urged them to direct their studies towards questions of commerce, agriculture and all economic matters.

It is partly to his suggestions and to the zeal which he had inspired at the sittings of the States of Bretagne during his stay at Rennes in 1756 that the Society[22] for the Perfection of Agriculture, Commerce and Industry, established in Bretagne under the protection of the States and the auspices of the Duke d'Aiguillon,[23] owes its existence. This society was the first of its kind to be formed in France. Its programme, which is connected with the municipal administration of the province, was drawn up by M. de Montaudouin, a merchant from Nantes.

M. de Gournay knew how to adapt himself to the degree of intelligence of his audience, and he answered the absurd objections—dictated by ignorance—with the same suavity and exactness with which he answered the bitter opposition, dictated by quite different principles, in Paris.

Full of respect for all those persons charged with the administration of the provinces which he visited, he gave them no occasion to think that his mission could cast the least shadow on their authority. Always forgetting himself, sacrificing himself without effort for the benefit of the objective, it was as far as possible through them and with them that he acted; he seemed only to supplement their zeal, and he often credited them in the presence of the minister with his own ideas. By this conduct, if he did not always succeed in convincing them of his principles, he at least always won their friendship.

The life of M. de Gournay does not offer any other outstanding event during the time that he continued as Intendant of Commerce. Ever occupied with the functions of his office, never missing any opportunity to put forward some useful ideas, or to spread light among the public, there

22. *Société d'Agriculture de Bretagne;* for further details of Gournay's association with this society see Palgrave, *Dictionary of Political Economy,* II, p. 236.

23. Duc d'Aiguillon (1720–1788), Administrator of Bretagne (1753–1770), Foreign Minister in the Maupeou government (1770–1774).

is hardly an important question on commerce or political economy on which he has not written several notes or reasoned letters. He devoted himself to this sort of work with a type of prodigality, producing nearly always, on every occasion, new papers, without referring his audience to the earlier ones he had written. He did not try to evade the trouble of re-discovering ideas which he had already expressed, or the unpleasantness of repeating himself. The reason for this manner of working was the small value which he attached to what he had composed, and his total unawareness of any literary repute. Overflowing with his salutary and fruitful principles, he applied them to every question with the greatest ease. Completely preoccupied with propagating some useful idea, he did not think of himself as a writer. Free from personal attachment to what he had written, he gave it over, without reservations, to all those who wished to instruct themselves, or to write, on these matters, and more of-ten than not he did not even keep copies of what he had written. These fragments, jotted down in haste and forgotten by him, are nevertheless precious, even if regarded purely from the point of view of composition: his writings, like his conversation, was characterised by a natural elo-quence, a lucid precision when expounding his principles, a remarkable art of presenting them from all types of viewpoints, of adapting them for all minds and of having them appreciated by examples which were al-ways just right, and whose very rightness was often striking; a politeness which never failed, and a shrewd logic in the discussion of objections; finally, a patriotic and humane tone, which was unintentional and there-fore all the more genuine.

M. de Gournay did not content himself with advocating his ideas through writing or speech: to command respect for the ideas he thought useful he applied the same activity, the same warmth and the same per-severance which an ambitious man puts into the pursuit of his own interests. Incapable of losing heart when the cause was a worthy one, he did not hesitate to push his efforts to the point of obtrusiveness. No proprietor of our isles has clamoured with as much zeal for the freedom of trade for neutral vessels in our colonies during the war.[24] His solicita-tions were all the more animated and pressing because he demanded

---

24. I.e. the Seven Years' War (1756–1763) in which France supported Austria against Prussia and England.

nothing for himself, even to the extent that he died without receiving any favour from the court.

Meanwhile, as he occupied himself solely with public work, his own fortune, as well as his health, had wasted away. He had sustained losses on the funds which he had left in Spain, and the state of his affairs forced him to leave his position as Intendant of Commerce in 1758. Some important people who knew how useful he was suggested that he ask the Court for some favours for himself which would compensate him for the losses he had sustained. He replied: "that he did not esteem himself sufficiently to believe that the State had to buy his services, that he had always looked upon similar favours as a dangerous practice, especially in the circumstances in which the State was situated, and that he did not desire to be reproached for being a party to exceptions to his own principles in his own interest." He added, "that he did not believe himself to be excused by his retirement from occupying himself with objectives useful for the well-being of trade." For this reason, he requested to keep his seat at the Board of Trade, with the title *honorary*, which was accorded to him.

Some time previously, he had similarly sold his Office of Councillor at the Grand Council, but had kept the title of *honorary councillor.*

Retirement did not deprive M. de Gournay of his importance. His zeal was not lessened because of it, his insight could still be as useful as ever. M. de Silhouette,[25] whose regard for M. de Gournay speaks in praise of both of them, resolved, as soon as he had become Contrôleur-général, to remove from retirement a man whose talents and zeal were so fitted to furthering his own designs. He began by inviting him to be present at the conference which the Intendants of Commerce held every week with the Contrôleur-général, and at which M. de Gournay had ceased to be present. He also intended him to take up one of the positions of Royal Commissioner to the General-Farm.[26] In this office, M. de Gournay would have been in a position to appraise the reciprocal complaints of commerce and finance, and to search for a means of rec-

25. M. Etienne de Silhouette (1709–1767), who was Contrôleur-Général from March to November 1759.

26. I.e. the agency for collecting indirect taxation on behalf of the crown on a commission basis.

onciling these two interests of the State as far as possible, but he was not able to profit from this token of esteem of M. de Silhouette. When this proposition was put to him he had already been stricken by the illness of which he died.

His health had been deteriorating for a long time. After spending carnival time at his estate of Gournay, he returned with a pain in the hip he at first took for sciatica. For a time the pain gradually grew worse, and at the end of two months a tumour was discovered which appeared to be the source of the trouble, but several different attempted cures could not dissipate it. Weakness and emaciation increased. The waters had been suggested, but he was not strong enough to undertake the journey; a slow fever was consuming him. A last effort was made with the use of a resolvent which was regarded as more potent, but no sooner was it applied, than M. de Gournay lapsed into a violent fever accompanied by delirium. This state of affairs lasted for three days; at the end of this time, he regained consciousness, of which he made use to make his will and to receive the last rites of the church. He died that same evening.

In the year . . . [27] he married Clothilde Verduc, and he lived in great harmony with her. No children resulted from this marriage.

M. de Gournay would merit the gratitude of the nation even if it would have been obliged to him only for having contributed more than any other person to the directing of minds towards economic knowledge. This glory would be secured for him even if his principles were still liable to opposition; and truth would always have profited from the discussion of matters to which he had given occasion for debate. Posterity will decide between him and his adversaries. But until the nation delivers its judgement, the honour of being the first to diffuse the principles of Child and of Johan de Witt may be confidently claimed in his memory. And, if one day these principles are adopted for commerce by our administration, if they will ever be for France what they have been for Holland and England, that is, a source of abundance and prosperity, our descendants will know that gratitude for it is due to M. de Gournay.

27. This is left blank in the French text. The date of marriage between Gournay and Clothilde Verduc was apparently not known to Turgot. In fact, Gournay was married in 1748, on his retirement from trade.

The opposition which his principles encountered has led some people to portray M. de Gournay as a fanatic and a *man of systems*. This phrase, *a man of systems,* has become a type of weapon in use by all those who are biased or interested in maintaining some abuse, and directed against all those who propose changes in the *status quo*.

The philosophers of recent times have indeed, with as much strength as reason, striven against the spirit of *systems*. They understood by this term those arbitrary suppositions with the help of which it is attempted to explain all phenomena and which actually explain them all equally, because they do not explain any; that lack of observation, that overhasty reliance on obscure analogies by which a particular fact is rashly transformed into a general principle, and the whole is judged by a superficial glance at a part; that blind presumption which relates all it does not know to the little it knows; which, dazzled by an idea or a principle, sees it everywhere, like the eye, fatigued by an intense look at the sun, casts its image on all the objects to which it directs itself; which wants to know all, explain all, arrange all, and which, ignorant of the inexhaustible variety of nature, claims to subjugate it to its arbitrary and limited methods, and tries to circumscribe the infinite in order to embrace it.

But when men of the world in their turn condemn *systems*, it is not in the philosophic sense. These men, accustomed to receive all opinions, one after the other, like a mirror reflects all images without retaining them, accustomed to find everything probable without ever being convinced, to ignore the intimate connection of effects with their causes, to contradict themselves constantly without being aware of it or placing any importance on it, these men cannot help but be astonished when they meet with a man who is inwardly convinced of a truth, and deduces consequences from it with the rigour of exact logic. Today they will listen to him, tomorrow they will listen to entirely contrary propositions, and they will be surprised not to see in him the same flexibility. They do not hesitate to call him a fanatic and a *man of systems*. Thus, although in their language the word system applies to an opinion adopted after mature consideration, supported by proofs and consistent in its consequences, they none the less take it amiss because the little attention of which they are capable does not enable them to judge the reasons, and does not offer them any opinion to which they can refer constantly or which is clearly related to a particular principle.

Yet it is true that all thinkers have a *system,* that a man who has no system or logical connection between his ideas must either be an imbecile or a madman.[28] Never mind. The two senses of the word system are confused, and he who has a system in the sense of the men of the world, that is, a settled opinion resulting from a chain of observations, will incur the reproaches made by the philosophers to the spirit of systems taken in quite a different sense, that of an opinion not founded on sufficient observation.

Taking the word system in the popular sense, M. de Gournay, undoubtedly, was a man of systems, since he had a viewpoint to which he was strongly attached. His adversaries were all men *of systems,* as much as he was, since they held an opinion contrary to his.

But if the word *system* is taken in the philosophical sense, which I first developed, nobody was further removed from that than he. On the contrary, he would rather have had the right to lay this reproach at the door of the principles against which he fought, since his whole doctrine was founded on the complete impossibility of directing, by invariant rules and by continuous inspection a multitude of transactions which by their immensity alone could not be fully known, and which, moreover, are continually dependent on a multitude of ever changing circumstances which cannot be managed or even foreseen; and since he therefore wanted the administration not to attempt to lead everybody by the hand, and not to claim the ability to do so, but rather to let them go their way and rely more on the natural motive of self interest, than on the external and artificial restraints of regulations which were always arbitrary in spirit and often so in application. If arbitrariness and a mania for fitting facts to ideas rather than ideas to the facts are the distinguishing marks of the spirit of *systems,* then assuredly M. de Gournay was not a *man of systems.*

He was even less so as far as an obstinate attachment to his ideas was concerned. The humility with which he held them proved strongly that he was not conceited about them and that he upheld them only as a citizen. It can be said that few men have been as perfectly free as he was

28. This sentence was changed by Du Pont in his edition of Turgot's works. It should apparently read as follows: "In this last sense, it is however true that everybody who thinks has a *system* and that a system cannot be a matter for reproach, seeing that a system can only be confounded by an opposite system." (Note by G. Schelle.)

from that type of vanity which shuts the door on new ideas. He searched for new information as if he knew nothing, and was ready to examine every assertion as if he had never held any opinion to the contrary.

It must also be said that this so-called system of M. de Gournay had this peculiarity that its general principles have been adopted by nearly the whole world; that at all times the desire of commerce among all the nations has been expressed by those two words: *freedom* and *protection,* but above all freedom. M. le Gendre's phrase to M. Colbert is well known: laissez-nous faire.[29] Often M. de Gournay differed from the men who treated him as a man of systems only in this: that he objected with the strictness of a just and righteous heart, to the exceptions which they allowed in favour of their own interests.

For example, the world is full of people who condemn exclusive privileges, but who believe that there are certain commodities for which they are necessary. This exception is generally based on their personal interest, or on that of individuals with whom these people are connected. Thus the majority of people is by nature well disposed towards the sweet principles of commercial freedom. But nearly all, either through interest, or through habit, or through subordination, insert some small modifications or exceptions.

M. de Gournay, in objecting to any exception in particular, had the majority with him, but by objecting to all exceptions at the same time, he ranged against him all the people who each wanted one exception, even though they were not united on the type of exception they desired. The result of this was a misleading unanimity of feeling against his principles, and an almost universal imputation of the title of *man of systems* against him personally.

This imputation was seized upon as a rallying cry by those who were turned into his adversaries because of envy or an excessive zeal for their

---

29. Possibly François Legendre, author of *L'Arithmétique et sa perfection selon l'usage des Financiers, Banquiers, et Marchands* which was published in several editions between 1657 and 1687, who is here credited by Turgot of having coined the phrase "Laissez-nous faire." According to Oncken, *Die Maxime Laissez-faire et Laissez-passer,* this remark was probably made to Colbert in about 1680. See Palgrave, *Dictionary of Political Economy,* II, p. 534; while for a detailed discussion of the origin of the phrase, "laissez-faire, laissez-passer," see G. Schelle, *Vincent de Gournay,* pp. 214–217.

own opinion, and gave them the excuse to oppose him as a solid body, instead of the empty shadow they really were, of which any man less zealous for the public welfare and less indifferent to his own interests, would have been terrified.

Opposition only served to stimulate his courage. He knew that by declaring the universality of his principles less candidly, and by failing to acknowledge all the remote consequences which derived therefrom, by being a party to some slight modifications, he would have evaded this dreaded title of a *man of systems* and would have escaped the bias which people endeavoured to propagate against him. But he believed in the usefulness of developing principles to their fullest extent, and he wanted the nation to instruct herself; and only the clearest exposition of the truth could instruct her. He thought that such circumspection would be useful only to himself, and he held himself of no account.

It is not true that he believed, as several people alleged he did, that there was no need for any moderation in the reform of abuses; he knew how necessary it was to prepare all improvements, how dangerous too sudden shocks are; but he thought that the necessary moderation should be in the action and not in the thought. He did not desire to have the whole old edifice knocked down before the foundations of the new one had been moulded, but he wanted an extensive plan to be drawn up before this task was started, to avoid acting blindly either in destroying, or conserving, or in reconstructing.

Finally, to M. de Gournay's very personal glory, there was his virtue, which was so well known that in spite of all the opposition which he had to endure, not the least shadow of suspicion ever tarnished the brightness of his reputation even for a moment. This virtue did not falter all through his life. Based on a deep feeling of justice and philanthropy, it made him a kindly and modest man, forbearing in society, irreproachable and even austere in his conduct and principles, but austere only for himself; even tempered at home, busy in his family circle to make all those around him happy, always ready to sacrifice, obligingly, all that he did not regard as duty. In public life he showed himself free from all self interest, ambition, and almost entirely free from love of glory, and yet, none the less active for it, nor less indefatigable, nor less ingenious in the pursuit of the fulfilment of his designs, whose sole objective was the general welfare. He was a citizen completely occupied with the prosperity and glory of his country and the happiness of mankind. Humanity was one of the motives which tied him most to what was called his *system*. He most vigorously reproached his opponents for the principle of always favouring the rich and idle part of society at the expense of the poor and industrious part.

It is unfortunate in a way that men commendable for the most deserving virtues, and who are most truly useful to the world, are most unfavourably endowed in the distribution of fame. Posterity considers almost exclusively those actions which take place in public and which are dazzling, and it is perhaps more sensitive to their brilliance than to their usefulness. But, even if we assume its judgement to be always equitable in this respect, the motives and the spirit which produce these actions and which alone can lend them the mark of virtue, are ignored. The finer details are lost in the narrative of history, like the glow of a complexion and the delicacy of features vanish under the painter's colours. Only lifeless brush strokes remain, and actions whose character is misjudged. Sometimes spite and sometimes flattery interpret them at their pleasure, and only too often succeed in making posterity's verdict fluctuate between the purest virtue, and clever vice masked as virtue.

This misjudgement never occurs while these people are still living, and there is an interval of time when spite in vain attempts to tarnish a well known virtue and when flattery that would offer undeserved honours can be repelled. This moment passes with the life of the person. Therefore the only means of ensuring, for that small number of men whose virtue is generally recognised, the continuation of the general esteem which they deserve, and of catching the fragrance of virtue which surrounds them, is to call forth the testimony of the present generation, and to call recent events to bear witness. In rendering this deserved public homage to the virtue of M. de Gournay, we feel sure that no voice will be lifted against us.

30

"Luxury"
1764

THE POET Jean-François, Marquis de Saint-Lambert, was born into a poor and obscure noble family in 1716. After a Jesuit education, he served in the infantry and for the king of Poland. Stationed at Lunéville, he was acquainted with Voltaire, fell in love with his mistress Emilie du Châtelet, and sired a child by her. When she died in childbirth (1749), he gained notoriety and moved to Paris, where his poetry began to attract attention. Voltaire described his now-obscure *Les Saisons* as "the only work in our century that will pass into posterity." In the Seven Years War, he became a colonel for the French army, though an attack of paralysis led him to leave the military career for good in 1758, and instead pursue a life of letters. He was friendly with the *Encyclopédie* circle, including Diderot, Mme. Geoffrin, d'Holbach, Grimm, Mme. d'Epinay, and especially Mme. d'Houdetot, with whom he had an affair that was celebrated for its dignity and fidelity until his death nearly half a century later. His plays and, especially, his highly scientific and philosophic poetry led to his selection by the Académie Française in 1770, where he became influential. His *Catéchisme universel*, a lengthy work on the origins and nature of human morality, won the grand prize for *morale* at the Institut in 1810. Saint-Lambert died in 1803.

The work translated here for the first time is his *Encyclopédie* essay on luxury (1764). It was immediately reproduced as a free-standing *Essai sur le luxe* and published the same year. The edition used is Diderot, d'Alembert, et al., eds., *Encyclopédie*, 17 vols. (Paris: Briasson, 1751–65), 8:763–71.

All notes and explanatory material are by the present editor and are in brackets. Where stylistic considerations permit, we have translated *moeurs*° as "manners and morals." Otherwise, we chose one term or the other according to context.

─────────────

Luxury

LUXURY: It defines the use one makes of wealth and industry to procure a pleasant existence.

The first cause of luxury is our dissatisfaction with our situation, our desire to be better off, which is and must be in all men. This is the cause of their passions, their virtues and their vices. That desire unfailingly makes them love and seek wealth. Therefore, the desire to enrich oneself is and must be among the resources of any government not founded on equality and common property. Now, the main object of that desire must be luxury. There is thus luxury in all states and in all societies. The savage has his hammock which he buys with pelts; the European has his sofa and his bed. Our women put on red and diamonds; the women of Florida put on blue and glass beads.

Luxury has always been the subject of the declamations of the Moralists, who have censured it with more moroseness than insight, and recently it has been the subject of praise by a few men of politics who have talked about it more as merchants or clerks than as philosophers or statesmen.

They have said that luxury contributed to the growth of population.

According to Livy [*History of Rome*], Italy at the height of the republic's grandeur and luxury had less than half the population it had when it was divided into small republics almost devoid of luxury and industry.

They have said that luxury enriches states.

There are few states where there is greater luxury than Portugal. And yet, with the resources of its soil, its situation, and its colonies, Portugal is less wealthy than Holland, which does not have the same advantages, and whose manners and morals [*moeurs*°] are dominated by frugality and simplicity.

They have said that luxury facilitates the circulation of money.

France is today one of the nations where there is the greatest luxury, and one rightly complains there about the lack of circulation for money, which goes from the provinces into the capital without flowing back from the capital into the provinces.

They have said that luxury softens manners and spreads the private virtues.

There is much luxury in Japan, yet manners and morals are still atrocious there. There were more private virtues in Rome and Athens, more humanity and beneficence when both were poor than in the period of their luxury.

They have said that luxury was favorable to the progress of knowledge and the fine arts.

What progress did knowledge and the fine arts make among the Sybarites, the Lydians, and the Tonkinites [i.e., the Vietnamese]?

They have said that luxury increases both the strength of nations and the happiness of citizens.

Under Cyrus, the Persians had little luxury, and they subjugated the rich and industrious Assyrians. As they became rich and emerged as the people among whom luxury was most prevalent, the Persians were subjugated by the Macedonians, a poor people. Savages overthrew or usurped the empires of the Romans, and those of some caliphs of India or China. As far as the happiness of citizens is concerned, if luxury provides more conveniences and pleasures, you shall see—if you travel over Europe and Asia—that at least it does not do so to the greatest number of citizens.

The censors of luxury are also contradicted by the facts.

They say there is no luxury without extreme inequality of wealth, that is to say without the people living in misery, and a few men in abundance. But this disproportion is not always to be found in the countries where there is the greatest luxury; it can be found in Poland and in other countries where there is less luxury than in Bern or Geneva, where the people live in affluence.

They say that luxury leads to a sacrifice of the useful for the agreeable arts, and that it ruins the countryside as it gathers people in the cities.

Lombardy and Flanders are full of luxury, and of beautiful cities; and yet the farmers are wealthy there, the lands cultivated and well-populated. There is little luxury in Spain, and agriculture is neglected; most of the useful arts are neglected there.

They say that luxury contributes to depopulation.

For a century, luxury and population in England have increased in similar proportions; moreover, England has populated some immense colonies.

They say that luxury weakens courage.

Under the commands of Luxembourg, Villars, and the count of Saxe,[1] the French—a people living in the greatest luxury known—showed themselves to be the most courageous. Under Sylla, Caesar, and Lucullus, the prodigious luxury of the Romans carried over into their armies detracted nothing from their courage.

They say that luxury kills the feelings of honor and love of country.

To prove the contrary, I will cite the spirit of honor and the luxury of the French in the finest years of Louis XIV's reign, and since then, I will cite the fanaticism for the homeland [*patrie*°], enthusiasm for virtue, and love of glory that now characterize the English nation.

I do not claim to gather here all the good and bad things that have been said about luxury. I limit myself to stating the main forms of praise or blame and to showing that history contradicts both.

The most moderate philosophers who have written against luxury have claimed that it was harmful to states only when it was excessive, and they have located this excess in the greater number of objects and means that it involves, that is, in the number and perfection of the arts, in this period when industry is making the greatest progress, which accustoms nations to enjoy innumerable commodities and pleasures, and renders them necessities. Finally, these philosophers saw the dangers of luxury only in the wealthiest and most enlightened nations. But it was not diffi-

---

1. [Christian-Louis de Montmorency-Luxembourg, Claude-Louis-Hector Villars (1658–1734), and Hermann Maurice, Count of Saxe (1696–1750), important military leaders in France.]

cult for philosophers who had more logic and more spirit than those moderate men to prove to them that luxury had been harmful to poor and almost barbaric nations. And step by step, it followed that people wanted to put men back into the woods and into a certain primitive state—which has never existed and cannot exist—so that men would avoid the inconveniences of luxury.

Until now the apologists of luxury have offered no solid answer to those who, following the flow of events, the rise and decline of empires, have seen that luxury was increasing by degrees together with nations, that morals were becoming corrupted, and that empires were weakening, declining, and falling.

We have the examples of the Egyptians, the Persians, the Greeks, the Romans, the Arabs, the Chinese, and so on, whose luxury increased in tandem with their grandeur, and who from the moment of their greatest luxury never ceased losing their virtues and power.

These examples are more effective in proving the dangers of luxury than are the reasons its apologists put forward to justify it. As a result, the most commonly held opinion today is that luxury must be there to drag nations out of weakness and obscurity, to give them a strength, consistency, and wealth that put them above other nations. And this luxury must constantly increase to allow the progress of the arts, industry, and trade, as well as to lead nations to that level of maturity that is necessarily followed by their decline and eventually their destruction. This opinion is quite general, and even Mr. Hume is not far removed from it.[2]

How is it that none of the philosophers and men of politics who have dealt with luxury in their speculations have ever said to themselves that, when nations begin to take shape, one is and must be more attached to the principles of government; that in newly created societies, all laws and regulations are important to the members of that society, provided it was established freely; and that if it was not, all laws and regulations are supported by the power of the legislator, whose views have not yet changed, and whose means are not diminished in terms of strength or number; finally, that the personal interests of each citizen—which are almost everywhere in opposition to the common interest, and which constantly

2. [See Hume's "Of Refinement in the Arts," chapter 23 in this volume.]

tend to drift away from it—had had less time and fewer means to be in opposition to it. As a result, it is more mingled with it; and therefore in newly created societies, there must be more morals and virtues, and a more patriotic spirit, than in ancient societies.

But also when nations first emerged, reason, intelligence, and industry made less progress; there was less wealth and luxury, fewer arts, and fewer means to procure a pleasant life by the toil of others, and inevitably there was poverty and simplicity.

Because it is part of the nature of men and things that governments should become corrupted with time, and that states should grow wealthier with time, arts then improve and luxury increases.

Have we not been considering as cause and effect things that, without being cause and effect, can be encountered together and proceed at almost the same pace?

Have not private interests—without being turned into a love of wealth and pleasures, i.e., those passions leading to luxury—led now magistrates, now the king or the people to make changes in the constitution of the state, which became corrupted because of them? Or is it not a fact that those private interests, habits, and prejudices have prevented changes that had become necessary because of changing circumstances? And finally, is it not a fact that in the constitution, in the administration, there are mistakes and flaws that, apart from any luxury, have corrupted governments and led to the decline of empires?

The ancient Persians, who were poor and virtuous under Cyrus, conquered Asia, brought back luxury, and became corrupted. But were they corrupted because they conquered Asia or because they brought back luxury? Was it not the extent of their domination that changed their morals? Was it not impossible for good order or any kind of order to survive in so large an empire? Was Persia not destined to sink into the abyss of despotism? Why should we search for other causes of corruption wherever we see despotism?

Despotism is the arbitrary power of one over a great number with the aid of a small number, but the despot cannot obtain arbitrary power without corrupting that small number.

Athens is said to have lost its strength and virtue after the Peloponnesian war, the era of its wealth and luxury. I find a real cause for the decline of Athens in the power of the people and the debasement of the senate. When I see the executive and legislative powers in the hands of a blind multitude, and when at the same time I see the Areopagus[3] powerless, I then judge that the republic of Athens could have kept neither its power nor its good order. It was in abasing the Areopagus, not in raising the theaters, that Pericles lost Athens. As for the manners of that republic, it still kept them for a long time, and during the war that destroyed it, it lacked prudence more than virtue, good sense rather than morals.

The example of ancient Rome, referred to by the censors of luxury with so much confidence, would not embarrass me any more. I would first observe the virtues of Rome, the strength and simplicity of its manners, emerging from its government and its situation. But this government surely brought the Romans some anxiety and some turmoil. It rendered war necessary for them, and war strengthened their morals and fostered their fanatical patriotism. I would see that when Carneades [213–129 B.C.] came to Rome, and when statues from Corinth and Athens were brought there, there were two parties in Rome, one of which was destined to subjugate the other as soon as the state had nothing more to fear from abroad. I would see that in that immense empire, the victorious party was destined to lead it either to despotism or to anarchy. And even if one had never seen in Rome the luxury or wealth of Antioch or Carthage, nor the philosophers and masterworks of Greece, the Roman republic—designed only for ceaseless aggrandizement—would have nevertheless fallen at the moment of its greatness.

It seems to me that if one cited Asia, plunged in luxury, poverty, and vice, to prove the dangers of luxury, I would ask someone to show me a single nation in Asia (China excepted) where the government cared about the morals and happiness of a great number of its subjects.

I would not be more embarrassed by those who—to prove that luxury corrupts morals and reduces courage—would point to modern Italy, which lives in luxury and which is indeed not warlike. I would tell them that if one leaves aside the military spirit, which is not part of the Italian character, that character is as worthy as those of other nations. Nowhere

3. [I.e., the highest judicial court of the city.]

will you find more humanity and beneficence; nowhere does social life have more charms than in Italy; nowhere are the private virtues more deeply cultivated. I would say that Italy, subject to the authority partly of a clergy that preaches only peace, and partly of a republic whose purpose is tranquillity, absolutely cannot be warlike. I would even say that it would be useless for them to be that way; that men and nations have very little of the virtues that are useless to them; that she is not united under a single government; and finally that, because Italy is surrounded by four great powers—namely, Turkey, the House of Austria, France, and Spain—Italy could not possibly resist any of these great powers, whatever its manners might be. Therefore it should concern itself with civil laws, the administration, the arts, and everything that can make life peaceful and agreeable. I would conclude by saying that it is not luxury but its situation and the nature of its governments which prevent Italy from having strong morals and war-like virtues.

After seeing that luxury could not have been the cause of either the fall or the prosperity of empires or the characters of certain nations, I would examine whether luxury should not be relative to the situations of peoples, to their types of productions, and to the situations and types of productions of their neighbors.

I would say that the Dutch, who are the makers and providers of nations, must preserve their frugality, without which they could not provide the freights of their ships at low rates and carry the commodities of the world.

I would say that if the Swiss derived from France and Italy many wines, gold and silk fabrics, paintings, statues, and precious stones, they would not derive from their sterile lands enough with which to pay back foreign countries; and they will be allowed to enjoy a great luxury only when their industry has made up for the scarcity of the country's production.

If one assumed that in Spain, in Portugal, in France, the land was badly tilled, and that manufactures of primary or secondary necessity were neglected, those nations would still be able to maintain a great deal of luxury.

Thanks to its mines in Brazil, its wines, and its colonies in Africa and

Asia, Portugal will always have something to provide foreign countries and will be able to rank among the rich nations.

However little labor or farming is done there and in its colonies, Spain will always have the productions of the fertile countries under its domination in two worlds; and the rich mines of Mexico and Potosi will support the luxury of the court and of superstition there.

France, after abandoning its agriculture and its manufactures of primary and secondary necessity, would still have branches of commerce overflowing with wealth. Pepper from India, sugar and coffee from its colonies, its oils and wines would provide it with exchanges with foreign countries, from which it would derive part of its luxury. It would support this luxury even more by its fashions; this nation, which has long been admired by Europe, is still imitated by it today. If ever its luxury was excessive compared to the product of its lands and its manufactures of primary and secondary necessity, this luxury would be its own remedy; it would nurture innumerable fashion workers and would delay the ruin of the state.

I would conclude from these observations and reflections that luxury is opposed to or favorable to the wealth of nations depending on whether it consumes more or less of the produce of their lands and industry, whether it consumes the produce of the lands and industry of foreign countries; that it should have more or fewer objects, depending on whether these nations have more or fewer resources. In this regard, luxury is for peoples what it is for individuals; the multitude of gratifications must be in keeping with the means to enjoy them.

I would see that this desire to enjoy on the part of the wealthy, and the desire to become wealthy on the part of those who have only the bare necessities, must stir up the arts and every kind of industry. That is the first effect of the instincts and passions that lead us to luxury and of luxury itself. These new arts and this growth in industry give the people new means of subsistence, and they must therefore increase the population; without luxury, there are fewer exchanges and less trade; without trade, nations must be less populated, and the nation that has only farmers within it must have fewer people than the one that maintains farmers, seamen, and textile workers. Sicily, which has but little luxury, is one of the most fertile countries on earth; it is ruled by a moderate government, yet it is neither wealthy nor populated.

After seeing that the passions that inspire luxury and luxury itself can be profitable to the wealth and population of states, I still do not see how this luxury and these passions could be opposed to manners and morals. However, I cannot deny that in a few regions of the world there are nations that have the greatest commerce and the greatest luxury but that lose every day some of their inhabitants and some of their manners and morals.

If there were a government established on the basis of perfect equality and uniformity of morals, manners, and status among its citizens—somehow like the governments of Sparta, Crete, and a few peoples we call Savages—it is certain that the desire to enrich oneself could not be innocent there. Anyone who wished to enjoy a greater fortune than his fellow citizens would have already stopped loving the laws of his country and would no longer be virtuous within his heart.

But in our modern governments where the constitution and civil laws encourage and ensure property, in our large states that must be wealthy to maintain their greatness and their power, it seems that anyone who strives to become wealthier is useful to the state, and that anyone who is wealthy and wants to enjoy his life is a reasonable person. How is it conceivable that some citizens, as they seek to enrich themselves and enjoy their wealth, ruin the state and lose their morality?

One must remember the main objectives of government to resolve this difficulty.

Governments must protect the property of each citizen. But since they must aim at maintaining the whole and at ensuring the advantages of the greatest number of people while maintaining and even arousing the love of property and the desire to increase and to enjoy it among the citizens, they must also maintain and arouse a spirit of community—a patriotic spirit. They must pay attention to the ways in which the citizens want to enrich themselves and to the ways they are able to enjoy their riches. The means people use to enrich themselves must contribute to the state's wealth, and the ways people enjoy their riches must be useful to the state. Each property must serve the community. The well-being of one category of citizens must not be sacrificed to the well-being of another. Finally, luxury and the passions leading to it must be subordinated to a spirit of community and to the goods of the community.

The passions leading to luxury are not the only ones necessary in citizens; they must be joined to other passions—ambition, love of glory, honor.

All these passions must be subordinated to a spirit of community; it alone can maintain them in order, and without it, they would lead to frequent injustices and wreak havoc.

None of these passions must destroy the others; there must be a balance between them. If luxury had extinguished these passions, it would have become licentious and harmful, and then it would not have been in accordance with a spirit of community; but it remains subordinated to that spirit unless the administration has severed the link between them, unless the administration has destroyed the spirit of community in a nation where there is wealth, industry, and luxury.

Finally, wherever I see that luxury is dissolute, wherever I see the desire for wealth and its use running contrary to good morals and to the good of the state, I will say that the spirit of community—that necessary basis upon which all the motivating forces of society must act—was dashed because of the errors of government. I shall say that luxury, which is useful under a good administration, becomes dangerous only through the ignorance and ill will of the administrators. And I shall examine luxury in nations where good order is in force and in those where it has become weak.

First, I see how agriculture was abandoned in Italy under the first emperors and how all the provinces in the centre of the Roman empire became covered with parks, country cottages, planted woods, and large roads. I say to myself that before freedom was lost and the constitution overthrown, the leading senators—devoured by love of their homeland and devoted to increasing its strength and population—would never have bought the possessions of farmers to turn them into objects of luxury, and would never have converted their useful farms into country cottages. I am even convinced that if the Italian countryside had not been parcelled out several times among the soldiers of Sylla, Caesar, and Augustus, who did not bother to cultivate it, Italy would have preserved its agriculture for a long time, even under the emperors.

I then turn my focus to kingdoms where the greatest luxury reigns and where the countryside has become a desert. But before ascribing this misfortune to the luxury of the cities, I ask myself how the administrators of those kingdoms acted, and I see that their conduct has led to the depopulation so often attributed to luxury, and to the abuse of luxury itself.

If in those countries the inhabitants of the countryside were overburdened with taxes and tasks [*corvées*];[4] if they often felt anxiety and humiliation from the abuse of a legitimate authority; if the circulation of their commodities were stopped by monopolies; if those mistakes and others I will not mention here were made, a part of the rural population would leave to seek their livelihood in the cities. Those wretches found luxury there and, by devoting themselves to its service, have managed to live in their homeland. As luxury kept the inhabitants of the countryside occupied in the cities, it merely delayed the depopulation of the state; I say "delayed" and not "prevented," because there are few marriages in destitute parts of the countryside, and even fewer among that category of men who seek refuge from the countryside in the cities. They arrive there to learn the crafts that create luxury, and they need a long time before they are able to support their families through their work. They miss opportunities when nature strongly calls to the union of the sexes, and debauchery diverts them even more from a legitimate union. Those who decide to take on a master are always in an uncertain situation. They have neither the time nor the willpower to get married; but if one of them becomes established, he owes it to the luxury and prodigality of the opulent.

The oppressiveness of the countryside suffices to account for an extreme inequality of wealth whose origin is attributed to luxury—even though the latter alone could on the contrary restore a sort of equilibrium of fortunes. The peasant who is oppressed is no longer a landowner; he sells his forefathers' land to the master he gave himself, and all the possessions of the state pass imperceptibly to an ever smaller number of hands.

In a country where the government falls into such great mistakes, it is not luxury that extinguishes the love of one's country or makes the wretched citizens hate it; other citizens are taught that those who run the

---

4. [The *corvée* was a compulsory labor burden imposed by the local lord or by the state in Old Regime France.]

country are indifferent about its fate, and that is enough to ensure that no one will love it with ardor.

There are countries where government has taken other measures to increase the inequalities of wealth and where exclusive privileges were given to, and maintained for, the directors of several manufactures, several citizens for the exploitation of colonies, and a few companies so that they alone could maintain a wealthy trade. In other countries, those mistakes were compounded by another—that of making the financial, legally binding charges excessively lucrative.

All these means gave birth to odious and sudden fortunes. If the fortunate men who made them had not lived in the capital before becoming rich, they would have come there afterward, as the center of power and pleasures. The only things left to desire are credit and gratifications [*jouissances*], and they seek those in the capital. One must see what the gathering of so many opulent men in the same place brings about.

People in society constantly compare themselves with one another. They endlessly try to establish the idea of their superiority, first in their own minds, and then in the minds of others. This rivalry becomes more intense between men of similar qualities. There is only one government—that of Sparta—that made wealth useless, where men could not boast about their wealth. As soon as men make a virtue of their wealth, they must make an effort to appear wealthy; so that, for every category of men, there must come to be expenses excessive for each individual, and thus emerges a luxury that we describe as being of pure decorum [*de bienséance*]. Without that immense superfluity, each class believes it is destitute.

It must be observed that, almost all over Europe, the competition to appear wealthy and the respect for wealth must have emerged independently of the quite natural causes I have just discussed. In barbarous times, when trade was unknown and crude manufactures could not enrich their makers, only land represented wealth, and the only opulent men were the great landlords. Now, those great landlords were "lords of fiefs." The laws of the fiefs—the right to be the only ones to possess certain things—kept wealth in the hands of the noblemen. But as the progress of trade, industry, and luxury created, as it were, a new type of wealth shared by the commoner, the people, accustomed to respecting wealth in their superiors, respected it in their equals as well. They believed that they could equal the great by imitating their pomp; the great believed that they were witnessing the end of the hierarchy that had raised them above the people. They increased their expenses to preserve their distinctions, and it was at that very moment that this decorum luxury [*luxe de bienséance*] became costly for all classes and dangerous for manners and morals. That situation turned the desire to enrich oneself into an excessive cupidity; in a few countries, it became the ruling passion and suppressed the noble passions that were supposed not to destroy it, but to rule it.

When extreme cupidity motivates all hearts, fits of virtuous enthusiasm disappear, and extreme cupidity does not exist without the most excessively possessive spirit; then the soul dies, because it dies when it focuses on itself.

The hard-up government can reward only with huge sums of money those it used to reward with small marks of honor.

Taxes, already multiplied, are further multiplied and become a burden on land and essential industry, which is easier to tax than luxury—either because with its constant vicissitudes it escapes the government or because the wealthiest have the credit to free themselves from taxes so that it is morally impossible for them not to have more credit than they should have. The more their fortunes are sudden, excessive, and founded on abuse, the more they need credit and the means to obtain it. They attempt, successfully, to corrupt those whose task is to repress them.

In a republic, they tempt the magistrates and administrators; in a monarchy, they offer pleasures and wealth to the nobility, guardian of the nation's spirit and morals, as the magistrates are guardians of the laws.

One of the effects of the credit of wealthy people when wealth is unequally divided—an effect of the lavish use of wealth, an effect of the need we have of wealthy men, of the authority they have, of the pleasantness of their company—is the confusion of ranks I have already spoken about. It is thus that the tone, the decency, the distinction of each class, which do more to preserve the spirit of each class than one may think, are lost. When one no longer holds to the marks of one's rank, one is no longer attached to the general order. It is when one no longer wants to perform the duties of rank that one neglects the external appearances, tone, and manners that would recall the idea of these duties one has toward others and oneself. Besides, one rules a people neither by reasonings nor by definitions; one must make an impression upon the senses and announce with distinctive marks the sovereign, the great, magistrates, and clergymen. Their external appearance must express power, goodness, gravity, and sanctity—what a man of a certain class, or a citizen clad in a certain dignity is or should be. As a result, if wealth were used to give the trappings of young lords to magistrates, the paraphernalia of indolence and affected costumes to warriors, dissolute airs to priests, the array of grandeur to simple citizens, that would necessarily weaken the impression that the presence of the men destined to rule the people are supposed to make upon them. With the proprieties of each class, one would witness the erasure of the general order down to the slightest trace; nothing could remind the wealthy of their duties, and everything would urge them to enjoy life.

From a moral point of view, it is inevitable that the use of wealth be contrary to good order, manners, and morals. When wealth is acquired without work through abuse, the *nouveaux riches* rapidly enjoy their quick fortunes, and at first they become used to idleness and to the need for frivolous dissipations. As they are hateful to most of their fellow citizens, to whom they were unfairly preferred, and whose own fortunes they hindered, they do not try to obtain what they cannot hope to obtain—their esteem and good wishes. It is especially the fortunes of monopolists, administrators, and collectors of public funds that are the most odious, and thus most susceptible to abuse. After sacrificing one's virtue and reputation for honesty to the desire of enriching oneself, one scarcely bothers to make virtuous use of one's wealth; one tries to conceal the origin of one's family and fortune under the pomp and display of luxury; one tries to lose in pleasures the memory of what one has done and what one has been.

Under the first emperors, men from a class other than those I have just discussed were gathered in Rome, where they had just brought back the spoils from the subjugated provinces. Patricians succeeded one another in the government of these provinces; many did not even live there but merely travelled there a few times. The quaestors would steal for themselves and for the proconsuls, whom the emperors liked to keep in Rome, especially if they belonged to powerful families. There, the patricians could hope neither to receive credit nor to take part in the government, which was in the hands of emancipated slaves, so they gave themselves over to indolence and pleasures. Senators who bought security with debasement no longer displayed the strength and pride of ancient Rome. It was not luxury that had degraded them—it was tyranny, just as the passion for spectacles would not have found senators and emperors mounting a stage if that passion had not been preceded and aroused by the perfect disregard for any order, any decency, and any dignity.

If there were governments whose legislators had kept the great too much in the capital; if the latter had responsibilities, commands, and so on that gave them nothing to do; if they were not obliged to perform great services to merit their positions and honors; if emulation in work and virtues were not aroused within them; finally, if they were allowed to forget what they owed their homeland, contented in their wealth and status, they would abuse it in idleness.

In several countries in Europe, there is a type of property that demands neither care nor maintenance from its owners—the national debts. In big cities, this type of possession is likely to increase the disorders that are the necessary effects of extreme opulence combined with idleness.

See what kind of character luxury takes from those abuses, mistakes, and circumstances that nations find themselves in; and see what the characters of the different orders must be in such a nation.

Among the inhabitants of the countryside, there are no lofty feelings, little of that courage that attaches to self-esteem and to the awareness of one's powers. Their bodies are not strong. They have no love of a country that is for them only the scene of their debasement and of their tears. Among the craftsmen in the cities, there is the same meanness of spirit; they are too close to those who despise them to feel any self-respect. Their bodies, enervated by sedentary labor, are not capable of withstanding fatigue. In a government in which the majority of people groan under oppression, the laws, which ensure the security of all in a well-regulated government, are only an obstacle that deprives the majority of the hope for a better condition. They must desire greater license rather than the reestablishment of an order that says: here is the people; there are the other classes.

The intermediary class between the people and the great, composed of the main artisans of luxury—financiers, traders, and almost all those who occupy secondary positions in society—constantly works to move from a meager fortune to a greater one. Schemes and mischief are often its tools. When the habit of honest feelings no longer keeps within reasonable limits the cupidity and boundless love of what we call pleasures, when good order and worthy examples do not inspire people with abiding respect for honesty, the second order of the state usually combines the vices of the first and last orders.

As for the great, the wealthy without function, the decorated without occupation, their only motive is to escape boredom, which—as it does not even impart taste—leads the soul from one object to another, which amuses it without fulfilling or occupying it. In such a situation, one experiences not enthusiasm, but bursts of joy for anything that promises pleasure. In that flow of fashion, fantasy, and amusement, which do not last at all and which destroy one another, souls lose even the strength to enjoy things, and they become as incapable of feeling the grand and the beautiful as of producing it. Then, the point is no longer to know who is more estimable, Corbulo or Trasea, but rather who will receive preference, Pilade or Bathyllus.[5] It is then that Ovid's *Medea,* [Rufus] Varius's *Thyestes,* and the plays of Terence are abandoned for the farces of [Decimus] Laberius [105–43 B.C.]. Political and military talents progressively decline, as do philosophy, eloquence, and all the arts of imitation. Frivolous men who do nothing but enjoy themselves have exhausted the beautiful and now seek the extraordinary. Then, uncertainty, affectation, and childishness invade ideas of perfection; small souls amazed and humiliated by the powerful and the strong prefer people who are petty, farcical, ridiculous, and affected. The talented who are most encouraged are those who flatter vice and bad taste, and they perpetuate the general disorder, which was not brought about by luxury, but which instead corrupted luxury, manners, and morals.

5. [Gnaeus Domitius Corbulo (d. A.D. 67) was a Roman general who restored control over Armenia; P. Clodio Trasea Peto was a Stoic Senator who committed suicide rather than be executed by Nero in A.D. 66. Bathyllus was an Alexandrian youth noted for his graceful pantomime dancing; Pilade was a pantomime dancer in the Augustan age. Saint-Lambert appears to be drawing on a passage from Juvenal, *Satires*, 6.63.]

Disordered luxury destroys itself, exhausts its sources, and dries up its channels.

The idle men who wish to pass from one luxury to another without interval seek out the productions and industry from all corners of the globe; the works of their nations pass out of fashion in their countries, and craftsmen become discouraged. Egypt, the African coasts, Greece, Syria, and Spain provided Romans with luxury under the first emperors, and that was not enough.

The taste for excessive expense, spread to all classes of citizens, leads workers to demand excessive prices for their work. Apart from a taste for expense, they are obliged to raise the price of labor, because they live in great, opulent cities, where the bare necessities are never cheap. Soon, poorer nations of simpler manners produce the same things; and since they retail them at lower cost, they are the preferred retailers. The very industry of the nation—the industry of luxury—decreases; its power diminishes; its cities become depopulated; its wealth goes abroad, and in general, it is left with indolence, languor, and a habit of slavery.

After examining the character of a nation in which certain abuses reign in the government, after seeing that the vices of those nations are the effects less of luxury than of those abuses, let us now determine what must be the national spirit of a people that has all the luxury possible, but in which order is also kept by a wise and vigorous government, which pays equal attention to preserving both the true riches of the state and its manners and morals.

Those riches and manners are the fruit of the affluence of the majority, and especially the close attention the government pays to conduct all its operations for the common good—without exception of class or person—and to constantly display those righteous intentions to the public.

Everywhere, this majority is or should be composed of the inhabitants of the countryside—of farmers [*cultivateurs*°]. To be affluent, they must be industrious; to be industrious, they must be able to hope their work will earn a good living, and they must desire that it will. Those peoples sunk in apathy willingly make do with the bare necessities, such as the inhabitants of those fertile countries where nature offers everything and where everything languishes if the legislator does not introduce vanity and, in due course, a bit of luxury. In villages and small market towns, there must be manufactures of implements, fabrics, and so on, which are necessary for the upkeep and even the coarse finery of the country people. Those manufactures will increase further the affluence and the population there. That was the plan of the great Colbert, who was too often accused of wanting to make the French a merely commercial nation.

When the inhabitants of the countryside are treated well, the number of proprietors imperceptibly increases among them; the extreme distance and base dependence of the poor upon the rich diminishes. As a result, those people will have lofty feelings, courage, strength of soul, robust bodies, and love of country; they will show respect and attachment for the magistrates, a prince, a [social] order, and laws to which they owe their well-being and their tranquillity. People tremble less before their lord, but they fear for their consciences, the loss of their possessions, their honor, and their tranquillity. They will sell their work to the wealthy at a high price, and the son of the honorable farmer [*laboureur°*] will not leave the noble work of his forefathers so easily to be sullied by the liveries and the contempt of the opulent man.

If the exclusive privileges I have talked about had not been granted, if the financial system did not enable people to amass riches, if the government did not encourage the corruption of the great, there would be fewer opulent men living in the capital, and those who did would not be idle; there would be few great fortunes, and no sudden ones; the means of enrichment, shared more widely among the citizens, would parcel out the riches naturally; extreme poverty and extreme wealth would be equally rare.

When men accustomed to work make great fortunes slowly and by degrees, they preserve a taste for work; few pleasures can distract them, because they enjoy work itself, and because a long time in strenuous occupations and in managing a moderate fortune have given them a love of orderliness and a moderation in their pleasures.

When men make their fortunes by honest means, they maintain their honesty; they maintain that self-respect that prevents them from giving themselves over to a thousand fantasies. When a man has served his fellow-citizens through the acquisition of wealth, or by bringing new resources to the state, or by making a useful industry flourish, he knows his fortune is less envied than honored; and as he relies on the esteem and benevolence of his fellow citizens, he wants to keep both.

Among the city people—and, to a small extent, those in the country-side—there will be a certain search for commodities, and even for a decorum luxury. But it will always be attached to usefulness; and the love of this luxury will never degenerate into mad emulation.

In the second class of citizens, there will be a spirit of order and an aptitude for discussion that come naturally to people who take care of their own business. This class of citizens will look for something solid even in their amusements. They will be proud because bad morals will not have debased them. They will be jealous of the great who will not have corrupted them; they will keep an eye on their conduct and will be flattered to explain things to them. It is they who will spread the wisdom that will reach down to the people and up to the great.

The latter will have duties; those devoting themselves to war—which is their status—will learn it in armies and on the frontier; those intending to be part of government will spend a long time learning about it with diligence; and if financial rewards are never piled up by those performing the greatest services, if great positions, posts, or commands are never given to birth without service, if they are never without function, the great will not lose the feeling and the capacity for enlightenment in frivolous and idle luxury. Less tormented by boredom, they will wear out neither their own imagination nor those of their flatterers in the search for puerile pleasures and fantastic fashions. They will not display an excessive pomp, because they will have real prerogatives and a true merit for which the public will hold them to account. Less concentrated together, and with fewer opulent people by their side, their decorum luxury will not be excessive. Witnessing the interest that government takes in maintaining the order and well-being of the state, they will become attached to both order and well-being. They will inspire love of country and all the feelings of a severe and virtuous honor. They will be attached to the decency of manners and morals, and they will have the bearing and the tone of their condition.

Then, neither destitution nor the need for excessive expense will prevent marriages, and the population will increase; that is how one supports oneself, and how luxury and the wealth of the nation are maintained. This luxury is a representation, a convenience, and a fantasy; in all its different aspects, it combines all the arts that are simply useful and all the fine arts. But it will be kept within just limits by a spirit of community, a dedication to duties, a continual occupation that will leave no one in constant need of pleasure. It will be parcelled out, like wealth. And all the manners of enjoyment, all the objects most opposed to one another, will not be possessed by the same citizen. The different branches of luxury and its different objects will thus be set according to differences in status; the soldier will have beautiful weapons and expensive horses; he will be refined when he equips the troops entrusted to him. In his luxury, the magistrate will maintain the gravity of his estate; his luxury will be dignified and moderate. The merchant and financier will be refined in their conveniences. All classes will sense the importance of the fine arts and will enjoy them. But these fine arts will bring the minds of the citizens back to patriotic feelings and true virtues; they will not be merely objects of dissipation for them, but will present them with lessons and models. Wealthy people whose souls are lofty will elevate the souls of artists. They will not ask the latter for an affected Galatea, little Daphnis, a Magdalena, or a Jerome.[6] But they will suggest that they should represent Saint Hilary dangerously injured, as he shows his son the great Turenne lost for the fatherland.[7]

Such was the use of the fine arts in Greece before its governments became corrupted. It is still the way they are often used in Europe in wise nations that have not deviated from the principles of their constitutions. France has had Pigalle make a tombstone for the general who has just covered her with glory; her temples are full of monuments built for citizens who honored her; her painters have often sanctified their brushes by portraying men of virtue. England had the castle of Blenheim built to the glory of the duke of Marlborough;[8] her poets and orators constantly

6. [Galatea was one of the Nereids, or sea nymphs; Daphnis was a shepherd and nymph.]

7. [Henri de la Tour d'Auvergne, Viscount of Turenne (1611–75), marshal of France and hero of the Thirty Years War in its latter phases.]

8. [John Churchill, Duke of Marlborough (1650–1722), hero of the War of the Spanish Succession against Louis XIV.]

sing the praises of their illustrious fellow citizens, already so rewarded by the voice of the nation and the honors bestowed by the government. What strength, what patriotic feelings, what loftiness, what love of honesty, good order, and humanity are found in the poetry of Corneille, Addison, Pope, and Voltaire! If a poet sometimes celebrates indolence and voluptuousness, his lines become expressions used by a happy people in times of temporary exhilaration, which does not divert it from its occupations and duties.

Eloquence is marked by the feelings of a well-governed people; by its force and its charms it rekindles patriotic feelings when they are disappearing. Philosophy, which deals with the nature of man, politics, and morals, strives to spread useful knowledge about all parts of administration and its main duties, and to show society its solid foundations, which only error could undo. Let us revive within ourselves the love of country, of good order, and of laws. The fine arts will stop being debased, as they are when devoted to superstition and debauchery. They will deal with subjects useful to morals, and will treat them with force and nobility.

The use of wealth dictated by a patriotic spirit is not limited to base personal interests and false, childish pleasures, and luxury is not opposed to the duties of father, husband, friend, and man. When a rich man sees two poor young people whom he has just had married, and when he sees them happy on the threshold of their cottage, it delights him more deeply, more purely, and more durably than when he sees the ensemble of Salmacis and Hermaphroditis placed in his garden.[9] I do not believe that in a well-run state, and one therefore where love of country prevails, piles of money from China should make their owners as happy as is the citizen who willingly contributes out of his own fortune to the maintenance of a public road.

Luxury is not excessive in the multitude of its ends and means. Luxury is rarely excessive in England, even though in that nation, there are all the types of pleasure that industry can add to nature, as well as many rich individuals who procure them. Luxury has become excessive in France only since the misfortunes of the war of 1700 disturbed the

---

9. [Salmacis was a water nymph; Hermaphroditis was the son of Hermes and Aphrodite.]

finances and caused some abuses. There was more luxury in the finest years of the age of Louis XIV than in 1720, and [yet] in 1720 that luxury was more excessive.

Luxury is excessive whenever individuals sacrifice their duties and the interests of the nation to their own pomp, conveniences, or whims. And individuals are only led toward this excess by flaws in the constitution or errors in administration. In this regard, whether nations are rich or poor, enlightened or barbarous, does not matter; manners and morals will be depraved and luxury will take on their character as long as love of country and useful passions are not maintained. The people will prove to be weak, lazy, weary, and apathetic. The empire of Morocco is neither civilized nor enlightened nor rich; and [yet] a few fanatics who have been hired by the emperor, oppressing the people in his name and for themselves, have turned the people into a vile herd of slaves. Under the weak and abusive reigns of Philip III [r. 1598–1621], Philip IV [r. 1621–65], and Charles II [r. 1665–1700], the Spanish were ignorant and poor, lacking strong morals as they lacked industry; the only virtues they had kept were those religion must give, and even in their armies, there was a luxury devoid of good taste as well as an extreme poverty. In countries where a crude luxury prevails, without refinement or enlightenment, harsh and unfair treatments that the weakest endure everywhere at the hands of the strongest are more atrocious. Everyone knows about the horrors of feudal government and about the luxury of the nobles at that time. On the banks of the Orinoco,[10] mothers are filled with joy when they can secretly drown or poison their daughters, so as to shield them from the labors to which they are condemned by the ferocious laziness and savage luxury of their husbands.

A little emir, a nabab, and their main officers crush the people to maintain their numerous seraglios. A petty German sovereign ruins agriculture by the quantity of game he supports on his estates. A savage woman sells her children to buy a few ornaments and some brandy. Among civilized people, a mother makes lavish expenses and leaves her children without inheritance. In Europe, a young nobleman forgets the duties of status and indulges in our polite tastes and our arts. In Africa,

10. [A river in Venezuela.]

a young black prince spends his days sowing reeds and dancing. There you have what passes for luxury in those countries where morals become corrupted. But it takes on the character of nations rather than creates it; it is sometimes effeminate like them, and sometimes cruel and barbarous. I think that it is still better for peoples to obey frivolous epicureans than savage warriors, and better to nurture the luxury of enlightened, voluptuous rogues than that of ignorant heroic thieves.

Since the desires to enrich oneself and to enjoy one's riches are part of human nature as soon as man is in society; since those desires support, enrich, and vivify all large societies; since luxury is a good and by itself does no harm, it is essential that neither the philosopher nor the sovereign attack luxury in and of itself.

The sovereign will remedy the abuses and excesses that luxury may have attained when he reforms the errors or flaws in the constitution or the administration that have led to them.

In a country where wealth has been amassed in great quantities in a capital and is shared only among a few citizens who doubtless enjoy the greatest luxury, it would be completely absurd suddenly to oblige the opulent to diminish their luxury. That would shut off the channels by which wealth may circulate from rich to poor and reduce innumerable citizens who live on luxury to despair. Or else those citizens—craftsmen less attached to their homeland than farmers—would go abroad *en masse.*

With so widespread a commerce, such universal industry, a multitude of sophisticated arts, do not hope to return Europe to ancient simplicity; that would take it back to weakness and barbarism. I will demonstrate elsewhere how luxury adds to the happiness of humanity. I am proud that it follows from this article that luxury contributes to the grandeur and power of states, and that it must be encouraged, enlightened, and directed.

There is only one type of sumptuary law that is not absurd; namely, a law that taxes a branch of luxury derived from abroad or a branch of luxury that would give preference to one type of industry at the expense of others. There are even times when that law could be dangerous.

Any other sumptuary law is totally useless. When wealth is too unequal, when the rich are idle, when the patriotic spirit is extinguished, luxury will constantly pass from one abuse to another. If you suppress one of its means to exist, it will find a replacement opposed to the general good.

Princes who did not see the true causes of change in manners and morals have attacked this or that object of luxury—conveniences, fantasies, fine arts, philosophy; all have been forbidden in turn by Greek and Roman emperors. None of them wanted to see that luxury does not create manners and morals, but takes on their character as well as that of the government.

The first operation to put luxury back in order and reestablish the equilibrium of wealth is to bring relief to the countryside. A contemporary prince has, in my view, made a great mistake in forbidding the farmers of his country to settle in the cities. It is only when their situation is pleasant that it may be made a necessity, and then one may tax the surplus produced by luxury craftsmen without consequence, when they return to the countryside.

One must diminish the number of inhabitants in the capital only little by little, and only by obliging the men on site to take care of the duties that call them to the provinces.

If the rich must be separated, wealth must be divided. But I am not proposing agrarian laws, new divisions of property, or violent means. That there be an end to exclusive privileges for certain manufactures and certain types of commerce; that state finance be less lucrative; that expenses and profits be less concentrated in the same hands; that idleness be punished by shame or by loss of employment: Without attacking luxury itself, without even disturbing the wealthy very much, you will see wealth imperceptibly parcelled out and increased, and luxury increased and parcelled out like it, and everything restored to order. I sense that most of the truths contained in this article should be treated at greater length. But I compressed everything because I am writing an article and not a book. I beg my readers to rid themselves alike of the prejudices of Sparta and of Sybaris.[11] And if they apply a few points presented in this work to their age or to their nation, I beg them to consider their nation and their age the way I did—without favorable or unfavorable preconceptions, without fanaticism, and without personal bias [*sans humeur*].

---

11. [Sybaris, whose inhabitants were known for their luxurious living, is now Taranto, a city in southern Italy.]

31

A View of the Progress
of Society in Europe
1766

WILLIAM ROBERTSON was born in Scotland in 1721, the son of a Presbyterian minister. He entered Edinburgh University in 1733 and received his license to preach in June 1741. When both his parents died days apart in 1745, he delayed his marriage and took care of his younger siblings. His reputation for scholarship and for speaking ability grew, and in 1754 he was one of the original members of the Select Society, which included Hume, Smith, Ferguson, Monboddo, and Kames, among others. Though he would not attend the theater himself, he defended his friend John Home's play *Douglas* when it was condemned by the clergy (1756–57). He became a doctor of divinity in 1759, and his *History of Scotland* appeared in that year. Burke, Gibbon, and d'Holbach were among its admirers. A series of important church positions then ensued, leading to moderator of the general assembly, which post he held for sixteen years, starting in 1763. Simultaneously, he was principal of Edinburgh University, where he would govern for thirty-one years. His *History of Charles V* was published in 1762. Though some of his erstwhile friends did not like it as well as the Scottish history, it was well received on the Continent, by Voltaire and Catherine II of Russia, among others. His *History of America* was a sequel and appeared to great acclaim in 1777. He also wrote a work on ancient knowledge of India in 1784. The Academies of Madrid, Padua, and St. Petersburg honored him for his efforts. He died in 1793.

The excerpt here is section 10, with note xxix, of his *A View of the Progress of Society in Europe*. This was the introductory volume to the *History of Charles V* (Philadelphia: Bell, 1770), 3 vols., 1:66–70, 272–84. The note, which is at least as substantive as the text and is a distinctive feature of Robertson's method as an historian, is by the author and has been retained without revision.

A View of the Progress of Society in Europe

X. The progress of commerce had considerable influence in polishing the manners of the European nations, and in leading them to order, equal laws, and humanity. The wants of men, in the original and most simple state of society, are so few, and their desires so limited, that they rest contented with the natural productions of their climate and soil, or with what they can add to these by their own rude industry. They have no superfluities to dispose of, and few necessities that demand a supply. Every little community subsisting on its own domestick stock, and satisfied with it, is either unacquainted with the states around it, or at variance with them. Society and manners must be considerably improved, and many provisions must be made for public order and personal security, before a liberal intercourse can take place between different nations. We find, accordingly, that the first effect of the settlement of the barbarians in the Empire, was to divide those nations which the Roman power had united. Europe was broken into many separate communities. The communication between these divided states ceased almost totally during several centuries. Navigation was dangerous in seas infested by pirates; nor could strangers trust to a friendly reception in the ports of uncivilized nations. Even between distant parts of the same kingdom, the intercourse was rare and difficult. The lawless rapine of banditti, together with the avowed exactions of the nobles, scarce less formidable and oppressive, rendered a journey of any length a perilous enterprize. Fixed to the spot in which they resided, the greater part of the inhabitants of Europe lost, in a great measure, the knowledge of remote regions, and were unacquainted with their names, their situations, their climates, and their commodities.

Various causes, contributed to revive the spirit of commerce, and to renew in some degree the intercourse between different nations. The Italians, by their connection with Constantinople and other cities of the Greek empire, preserved in their own country some relish for the precious commodities, and curious manufactures of the East. They communicated some knowledge of these to the countries contiguous in Italy. This commerce, however, was extremely limited, nor was the intercourse considerable which it occasioned between different nations. The Crusades, by leading multitudes from every corner of Europe into Asia, opened a more extensive communication between the East and West, which subsisted for two centuries; and though the object of these expeditions was conquest and not commerce; though the issue of them proved as unfortunate, as the motives for undertaking them were wild and enthusiastic, their commercial effects, as hath been shewn, were both beneficial and permanent. During the continuance of the Crusades, the great cities in Italy and in other countries of Europe acquired liberty, and together with it such privileges as rendered them respectable and independent communities. Thus, in every state there was formed a new order of citizens, to whom commerce presented itself as their proper object, and opened to them a certain path to wealth and dignity. Soon after the close of the Holy war, the mariner's compass was invented, which, by rendering navigation more secure as well as more adventrous, facilitated the communication between remote nations, and brought them nearer to each other.

The Italian States, during the same period, established a regular commerce with the East in the ports of Egypt, and drew from thence all the rich products of the Indies. They introduced into their own territories manufactures of various kinds, and carried them on with great ingenuity and vigour. They attempted new arts; and transplanted from warmer climates, to which they had been hitherto deemed peculiar, several natural productions which now furnish the materials of a lucrative and extended commerce. All these commodities, whether imported from Asia, or produced by their own skill, they disposed of to great advantage among the other people of Europe, who began to acquire some taste of elegance unknown to their ancestors, or despised by them. During the twelfth and thirteenth centuries, the commerce of Europe was almost entirely in the hands of the Italians, more commonly known in those ages by the name of Lombards. Companies or societies of Lombard merchants settled in every different kingdom. They were taken under the immediate protection of the several governments. They enjoyed extensive privileges and immunities. The operation of the ancient barbarous laws concerning strangers was suspended with respect to them. They became the carriers, the manufacturers, and the bankers of all Europe.

While the Italians, in the south of Europe, cultivated trade with such industry and success, the commercial spirit awakened in the north, towards the middle of the thirteenth century. As the nations around the Baltick were, at that time, extremely barbarous, and infested that sea with their piracies, this obliged the cities of Lubeck and Hamburgh, soon after they began to open some trade with these people, to enter into a league of mutual defence. They derived such advantages from this union, that other towns acceded to their confederacy, and, in a short time, eighty of the most considerable cities scattered through those vast countries which stretch from the bottom of the Baltick to Cologne on the Rhine, joined in the famous Hanseatick league, which became so formidable, that its alliance was courted, and its enmity was dreaded by the greatest monarchs. The members of this powerful association formed the first systematick plan of commerce known in the middle ages, and conducted it by common laws enacted in their general assemblies. They supplied the rest of Europe with naval stores, and pitched on different towns, the most eminent of which was Bruges in Flanders, where they established staples in which their commerce was regularly carried on. Thither the Lombards brought the productions of India, together with the manufactures of Italy, and exchanged them for the more bulky, but not less useful commodities of the North. The Hanseatick merchants disposed of the cargoes which they received from the Lombards, in the ports of the Baltick, or carried them up the great rivers into the interior parts of Germany.

This regular intercourse opened between the North and South of Europe, made them sensible of their mutual wants, and created such new and vast demands for commodities of every kind, that it excited among the inhabitants of the Netherlands a more vigorous spirit in carrying on the two great manufactures of wool and flax, which seem to have been considerable in that country as far back as the age of Charlemagne. As Bruges became the centre of communication between the Lombard and Hanseatick merchants, the Flemings traded with both in that city to such extent as well as advantage, as spread among them a general habit of industry, which long rendered Flanders and the adjacent provinces the most opulent, the most populous, and best cultivated countries in Europe.

Struck with the flourishing state of these provinces, of which he discerned the true cause, Edward III. of England endeavoured to excite a spirit of industry among his own subjects, who, blind to the advantages of their situation, and ignorant of the source from which opulence was destined to flow into their country, totally neglected commerce, and did not even attempt those manufactures, the materials of which they furnished to foreigners. By alluring Flemish artisans to settle in his dominions, as well as by many wise laws for the encouragement and regulation of trade, he gave a beginning to the woolen manufactures of England, and first turned the active and enterprizing genius of his people towards those arts which have raised the English to the highest rank among commercial nations.

This increase of commerce, and of intercourse between nations, how inconsiderable soever it may appear in respect of their rapid and extensive progress during the last and present age, seems vast, when we compare it with the state of both in Europe previous to the twelfth century. It did not fail of producing great effects. Commerce tends to wear off those prejudices which maintain distinction and animosity between nations. It softens and polishes the manners of men. It unites them, by one of the strongest of all ties, the desire of supplying their mutual wants. It disposes them to peace, by establishing in every state an order of citizens bound by their interest to be the guardians of public tranquillity. As soon as the commercial spirit begins to acquire vigour, and to gain an ascendant in any society, we discover a new genius in its policy, its alliances, its wars, and its negociations. Conspicuous proofs of this occur in the history of the Italian States, of the Hanseatick league, and the cities of the Netherlands during the period under review. In proportion as commerce made its way into the different countries of Europe, they successively turned their attention to those objects, and adopted those manners, which occupy and distinguish polished nations.

Note XXIX

The great variety of subjects which I have endeavoured to illustrate, and the extent of this upon which I now enter, will justify my adopting the words of M. de Montesquieu, when he begins to treat of commerce. "The subject which follows would require to be discussed more at large, but the nature of this work does not permit it. I wish to glide on a tranquil stream; but I am hurried along by a torrent."

Many proofs occur in history of the little intercourse between nations during the middle ages. Towards the close of the tenth century, Count Bouchard intending to found a monastery at St. Maur des Fosses, near Paris, applied to an Abbot of Clugny in Burgundy, famous for his sanctity, intreating him to conduct the monks thither. The language in which he addressed that holy man is singular: He tells him that he had undertaken the labour of such a great journey; that he was fatigued with the length of it, therefore hoped to obtain his request, and that his journey into such a distant country should not be in vain. The answer of the abbot is still more extraordinary: He refused to comply with his desire, as it would be extreamly fatiguing to go along with him into a strange and unknown region. Vita Burchardi venerabiles Comites ap. Bouquet Rec. des Hist. vol. x. p. 351. Even so late as the beginning of the twelfth century, the monks of Ferrieres in the diocese of Sens did not know that there was such a city as Tournay in Flanders; and the monks of St. Martin of Tournay, were equally unacquainted with the situation of Ferrieres. A transaction in which they were both concerned, made it necessary for them to have some intercourse. The mutual interest of both monasteries prompted each to find out the situation of the other. After a long search, which is particularly described, the discovery was made by accident. He- rimannus Abbas de Restauratione St. Martini Tornacensis ap. Dacher. Spicel. vol. xii. p. 400. The ignorance of the middle ages with respect to the situation and geography of remote countries was still more remark- able. The most ancient geographical chart which now remains as a mon- ument of the state of that science in Europe during the middle ages, is found in a manuscript of the Chronique de St. Denys. There the three parts of the earth then known are so represented, that Jerusalem is placed in the middle of the globe, and Alexandria appears to be as near to it as Nazareth. Mem. de l'Acad. des Belles Lettres, tom. xvi. p. 185. There seem to have been no inns or houses of entertainment for the reception of travellers during the middle ages. Murat. Antiq. Ital. vol. iii. p. 581, &c. This is a proof of the little intercourse which took place between different nations. Among people whose manners are simple, and who are seldom visited by strangers, hospitality is a virtue of the first rank. This duty of hospitality was so necessary in that state of society which took place during the middle ages, that it was not considered as one of those virtues which men may practise or not, according to the temper of their minds, and the generosity of their hearts. Hospitality was enforced by statutes, and those who neglected this duty were liable to punishment. Quicumque hospiti venienti lectum, aut focum negaverit, trium selido- rum inlatione mulctetur, Leg. Burgund. tit. xxxviii. § 1. Si quis homini aliquo pergenti in itinere mansionem vetaverit sexaginta solidos com- ponat in publico. Capitul. lib. vi. § 82. This increase of the penalty, at a period so long after that in which the laws of the Burgundians were pub- lished, and when the state of society was much improved, is very re- markable. Other laws of the same purport are collected by Jo. Fred. Po- lac Systema Jurisprud. Germanicae, Lips. 1733. p. 75. The laws of the Slavi were more rigorous than any that he mentions; they ordained, "that the moveables of an inhospitable person should be confiscated, and his house burnt. They were even so solicitous for the entertainment of strangers, that they permitted the landlord to steal for the entertainment of his guest." Quot noctu furatus fueris, cras appone hospitibus. Rerum Mecleburgicar. lib. viii. a Mat. Jo. Beehr. Lips. 1751. p. 50. In conse- quence of these laws or of that state of society which made it proper to enact them, hospitality abounded while the intercourse among men was inconsiderable, and secured the stranger a kind reception under every roof where he chose to take shelter. This too proves clearly, that the intercourse among men was rare, for as soon as this increased, what was a pleasure became a burden, and the entertaining of travellers was converted into a branch of commerce.

But the laws of the middle ages afford a proof still more convincing of the small intercourse between different nations. The genius of the Feudal system, as well as the spirit of jealousy which always accompanies ignorance, joined in discouraging strangers from settling in any country. If a person removed from one province in a kingdom to another, he was bound within a year and a day, to acknowledge himself the vassal of the baron in whose estate he settled; if he neglected to do so, he became liable to a penalty; and if at his death he neglected to leave a certain legacy to the baron within whose territories he resided, all his goods were confiscated. The hardships imposed on foreigners settling in a strange country, were still more intolerable. In more early times, the superior lord of any territory, in which a foreigner settled, might seize his person, and reduce him to servitude. Very striking instances of this occur in the history of the middle ages. The cruel depredations of the Normans in the ninth century, obliged many inhabitants of the maritime provinces of France, to fly into the interior parts of the kingdom. But instead of being received with that humanity to which their wretched condition entitled them, they were reduced to a state of servitude. Both the civil and ecclesiastical powers found it necessary to interpose, in order to put a stop to this barbarous practice. Potgiesser, de Statu Servor. lib. i. c. 1. § 16. In other countries, the laws permitted the inhabitants of the maritime provinces, to reduce such as were shipwrecked on their coast, to servitude. Ibid. § 17. This barbarous custom prevailed in other countries of Europe. The practice of seizing the goods of persons who had been shipwrecked, and of confiscating as the property of the lord on whose manor they were thrown, seems to have been universal. De Westphalen Monum. inedita Rer. Germ. vol. iv. p. 907, &c. et Du Cange, voc *Laganum,* Beehr. Rer. Mecleb. lib. p. 512. Among the ancient Welsh, three sorts of persons, a madman, a stranger, and a leper, might be killed with impunity. Leges Hoel Dda, quoted in observat. on the Statutes, chiefly the more ancient,

p. 22. M. de Lauriere produces several ancient deeds which prove, that in different provinces of France, strangers became the slaves of the lord on whose lands they settled. Glossaire du Droit Francois, Art. *Aubaine,* p. 92. Beaumanoir says, "that there are several places in France, in which, if a stranger fixes his residence for a year and a day, he becomes the slave of the lord of the manor. Coust. De Beauv. ch. 45. p. 254. But as a practice so contrary to humanity could not subsist, the superior lords found it necessary to rest satisfied with levying certain annual taxes from aliens, by imposing upon them some extraordinary duties or services. But when any stranger died, he could not convey his effects by a will; and all his real as well as personal estate fell to the king, or to the lord of the barony, to the exclusion of his natural heirs. This is termed in France Droit d'Aubaine. Pref. de Laurier. Ordon. tom. i. p. 15. Brussel. tom. ii. p. 944. Du Cange, voc. *Albani.* Pasquier Recherches, p. 367. This practice of confiscating the effects of strangers upon their death, was very ancient. It is mentioned, though very obscurely, in a law of Charlemagne, A.D. 813. Capitul. Baluz. p. 507. § 5. Not only persons who were born in a foreign country were subject to the Droit d'Aubaine, but even such as removed from one diocese to another, or from the lands of one baron to another. Brussel. vol. ii. p. 947, 949. It is scarce possible to conceive any law more unfavourable to the intercourse between nations. Something similar to it, however, may be found in the ancient laws of every kingdom in Europe. With respect to Italy, see Murat. Ant. vol. ii. p. 14. It is no small disgrace to the French jurisprudence, that this barbarous, inhospitable custom, should still remain in a nation so highly civilized.

The confusion and outrage which abounded under a feeble form of government, incapable of framing or executing salutary laws, rendered the communication between the different provinces of the same kingdom extremely dangerous. It appears from a letter of Lupus, abbot of Ferrieres, in the ninth century, that the highways were so much infested by banditti, that it was necessary for travellers to form themselves into companies or caravans, that they might be safe from the assaults of robbers. Bouquet Recueil des Hist. vol. vii. 515. The numerous regulations published by Charles the Bald in the same century, discover the frequency of these disorders; and such acts of violence were become so common, that by many they were hardly considered as criminal; and for this reason, the inferior judges called Centenarii, were required to take an oath, that they would neither commit any robbery themselves, nor protect such as were guilty of that crime. Capitul. edit. Baluz. vol. ii. p. 63, 68. The historians of the ninth and tenth centuries give pathetic descriptions of these disorders. Some remarkable passages to this purpose are collected by Mat. Jo. Beehr. Rer. Mecleb. lib. viii. p. 603. They became so frequent and audacious, that the authority of the civil magistrate was unable to repress them. The ecclesiastical jurisdiction was called in to aid it. Councils were held with great solemnity, the bodies of the saints were brought thither, and in presence of the sacred reliques, anathemas were denounced against robbers, and other violators of the publick peace. Bouquet Recueil des Hist. tom. x. p. 360, 431, 536. One of these forms of excommunication issued A.D. 988, is still preserved, and is so singular, and composed with eloquence of such a peculiar kind, that it will not perhaps appear unworthy of a place here. After the usual introduction, and mentioning the outrage which gave occasion to the anathema, it runs thus, "Obtenebrescant occuli vesstri, qui concupiverunt; arescant manus, quae rapuerunt; debilitentur omnia membra, quae adjuverunt. Semper laboretis, nec requiem inveniatis, fructuque vestri laboris privemini. Formidetis, & paveatis, à facie persequentis, & non persequentis hostis, ut tabescendo deficiatis. Sit portio vestra cum Juda traditore Domini, in terra mortis et tenebrarum; donec corda vestra ad satisfactionem plenam convertantur. Ne cessent a vobis hae malidictiones, scelerum vestroram persecutrices, quamdiu permanebitis in peccato pervasionis. Amen. Fiat, Fiat." Bouquet. Ib. p. 517.

With respect to the progress of commerce which I have described, it may be observed that the Italian states carried on some commerce with the cities of the Greek empire, as early as the age of Charlemagne, and imported into their own country the rich commodities of the east. Murat. Antiq. Ital. vol. ii. p. 882. In the tenth century, the Venetians had opened a trade with Alexandria in Egypt. Ibid. The inhabitants of Amalphi and Pisa had likewise extended their trade to the same ports. Murat. Ib. p. 884, 885. The effects of the Crusades in increasing the wealth and commerce of the Italian states, and particularly that which they carried on with the East, I have already explained in this volume. They not only imported the Indian commodities from the East, but established manufactures of curious fabric in their own country. Several of these are enumerated by Muratori in his Dissertations concerning the *arts* and the *weaving* of the middle ages. Antiq. Ital. vol. ii. p. 349, 399. They made great progress particularly in the manufacture of silk, which had long been peculiar to the eastern provinces of Asia. Silk stuffs were of such high price in ancient Rome, that only a few persons of the first rank were able to purchase them. Under Aurelian, A.D. 270, a pound of silk was equal in value to a pound of gold. Absit ut auro fila pensentur. Libra enim auri tunc libra serici fuit. Vopiscus in Aureliano. Justinian, in the sixth century, introduced the art of rearing silk-worms into Greece, which rendered the commodity somewhat more plentiful, though still it was of such great value, as to remain an article of luxury or magnificence, reserved only for persons of the first order, or for public solemnities. Roger I. King of Sicily, about the year 1130, carried off a number of artificers in the silk trade from Athens, and settling them in Palermo, introduced the culture of silk into his kingdom, from which it was communicated to other parts of Italy. Gianon. Hist. of Naples, b. xi. c. 7. This seems to have rendered silk so common that about the middle of the fourteenth century, a thousand citizens of Genoa appeared in one procession clad in silk robes. Sugar is likewise a production of the East. Some plants of the sugar-cane were brought from Asia; and the first attempt to cultivate them in Sicily was made about the middle of the twelfth century. From thence they were transplanted into the southern provinces of Spain. From Spain they were carried to the Canary and Madeira isles, and at length into the new world. Ludovico Guicciardini, in enumerating the goods imported into Antwerp, about the year 1560, mentions the sugar which they received from Spain and Portugal as a considerable article. He describes that as the product of the Madeira and Canary islands. Descritt. de Paesi Bassi, p. 180, 181. The sugar-cane was either not introduced into the West-Indies at that time, or the cultivation of it was not so considerable as to furnish an article in commerce. In the middle ages, though sugar was not raised in such quantities, or employed for so many purposes, as to become one of the common necessaries of life, it appears to have been a considerable article in the commerce of the Italian states.

These various commodities with which the Italians furnished the other nations of Europe, procured them a favourable reception in every kingdom. They were established in France in the thirteenth century with most extensive immunities. They not only obtained every indulgence favourable to their commerce, but personal rights and privileges were granted to them, which the natives of the kingdom did not enjoy. Ordon. tom. iv. p. 688. By a special proviso, they were exempted from the droit d'aubaine. Ibid. p. 670. As the Lombards engrossed the trade of every kingdom in which they settled, they became masters of its cash. Money of course was in their hands not only a sign of the value of their commodities, but became an object of commerce itself. They dealt largely as bankers. In an ordinance, A.D. 1295, we find them stiled *mercatores* and *campsores*. They carried on this as well as other branches of their commerce with somewhat of that rapacious spirit which is natural to monopolizers, who are not restrained by the concurrence of rivals. An absurd opinion, which prevailed in the middle ages, was, however, in some measure, the cause, of their exorbitant demands, and may be pleaded in apology for them. Commerce cannot be carried on with advantage unless the persons who lend a sum are allowed a certain premium for the use of their money, and as a compensation for the risk which they run in permitting another to traffick with their stock. This premium is fixed by law in all commercial countries, and is called the legal interest of money. But the Fathers of the church preposterously applied the prohibitions of usury in scripture to the payment of legal interest, and condemned it as a sin. The schoolmen, misled by Aristotle, whose sentiments they followed implicitly, and without examination, adopted the same error, and enforced it. Blackstone's Commentaries on the laws of England, vol. ii. p. 455. Thus the Lombards found themselves engaged in a traffick which was deemed criminal and odious. They were liable to punishment if detected. They were not satisfied, therefore, with that moderate premium, which they might have claimed, if their trade had been open and authorised by law. They exacted a sum proportional to the danger and infamy of a discovery. Accordingly, we find that it was usual for them to demand twenty per cent. for the use of money in the thirteenth century. Murat. Antiq. Ital. vol. i. p. 893. About the beginning of that century, the countess of Flanders was obliged to borrow money in order to pay her husband's ransom. She procured the sum requisite, either from Italian merchants or from Jews. The lowest interest which she paid to them was above twenty per cent. and some of them exacted near thirty. Martene and Durand. Thesaur. Anecdotorum. vol. i. p. 886. In the fourteenth century, A.D. 1311, Philip IV. fixed the interest which might be legally exacted in the fairs of Champagne at twenty per cent. Ordonan. tom. i. p. 484. The interest of money in Aragon was somewhat lower. James I. A.D. 1242. fixed it by law at eighteen per cent. Petr. de Marca. *Marca* sive Limes Hispan, app. 1433. As late as the year 1490, it appears that the interest of money in Piacentia, was at the rate of forty per cent. This is the more extraordinary, because at that time the commerce of the Italian States was become considerable. Memoire Storiche de Piacenza, tom. viii. p. 134. Piac. 1760. It appears from Lud. Guicciardini, that Charles V. had fixed the rate of interest in his dominions in the Low Countries at twelve per cent. and at the time when he wrote about the year 1560, it was not uncommon to exact more than that sum. He complains of this as exorbitant, and points out its bad effects both on agriculture and commerce. Descritt. di Paesi Bassi, p. 172. This high interest of money, is alone a proof that the profits on commerce were exorbitant.—The Lombards were likewise established in England, in the thirteenth century, and a considerable street in the city of London still bears their name. They enjoyed great privileges, and carried on an extensive commerce, particularly as bankers. See Anderson's Chronol. Deduction, vol. i. p. 137, 160, 204, 231, where the statutes or other authorities, which confirm this are quoted. But the chief mart for Italian commodities was at Bruges. Navigation was then so imperfect, that a voyage between the Baltick and Mediterranean could not be performed in one summer. For that reason, a magazine or storehouse half way between the commercial cities in the North, and those in Italy became necessary. Bruges was pitched upon as the most convenient station. That choice introduced vast wealth into the Low-Countries. Bruges was at once the staple for English wool; for the woolen and linnen manufactures of the Netherlands; for the naval stores, and other bulky commodities of the north; and for the Indian commodities, as well as domestick productions imported by the Italian States. The extent of its commerce in Indian goods with Venice alone appears from one fact. In the year 1318, five Venetian galeasses laden with Indian commodities arrived at Bruges, in order to dispose of their cargoes at the fair. L. Guic. Descritt. di Paesi Bassi, p. 174. Galeasses were vessels of very considerable burthen. It was the greatest emporium in all Europe. Many proofs of this occur in the historians and records of the thirteenth and fourteenth centuries. But instead of multiplying quotations, I shall refer my readers to Anderson, vol. i. p. 12, 137, 213, 246. The nature of this work prevents me from entering into any long details, but there are some detached facts, which give an high idea of the wealth both of the Flemish and Italian commercial states. The Duke of Brabant contracted his daughter to the Black Prince, son of Edward III. of England, A.D. 1339, and gave her a portion which would amount to three hundred thousand pounds of our present money. Rymer's Faedera, vol. v. p. 113. John Galeazzo Visconti Duke of Milan concluded a treaty of marriage between his daughter and Lionel Duke of Clarence Edward's third son, A.D. 1367, and granted a portion equal to two hundred thousand pounds of our present money. Rymer Faeder. vol. vi. p. 547. These exorbitant sums so far exceeding what was then granted by the most powerful monarchs, and which appear extraordinary even in the present age, when the wealth of Europe is so much increased, must have arisen from the riches which flowed into these countries from their extensive and lucrative commerce. The first source of wealth to the towns situated on the Baltick sea, seems to have been the herring fishery; the shoals of herring frequenting at that time the coasts of Sweden and Denmark, in the same manner as they now resort to the British coasts. The effects of this fishery are thus described by an author of the thirteenth century. The Danes, says he, who were formerly clad in the poor garb of sailors, are now cloathed in scarlet, purple and fine linen. For they abound with wealth flowing from their annual fishery on the coast of Schonen; so that all nations resort to them, bringing their gold, silver and precious commodities, that they may purchase herrings, which the divine bounty bestows upon them. Arnoldus Lubecensis ap. Conring. de Urbib. German. § 87.

The Hanseatick league is the most powerful commercial confederacy known in history. Its origin towards the close of the twelfth century, and the objects of its union, are described by Knipscildt Tractatus Historico-Politico Juridicus de Juribus Civitat. Imper. lib. i. cap. 4. Anderson has mentioned the chief facts with respect to their commercial progress, the extent of the privileges which they obtained in different countries, their successful wars with several monarchs, as well as the spirit and zeal with which they contended for those liberties and rights, without which it is impossible to carry on commerce to advantage. The vigorous efforts of a society attentive only to commercial objects, could not fail of diffusing over Europe new and more liberal ideas concerning justice and order wherever they settled.

In England the progress of commerce was extremely slow; and the causes of this are obvious. During the Saxon heptarchy, England, split into many petty kingdoms, which were perpetually at variance with each other, exposed to the fierce incursions of the Danes, and other northern pirates, and sunk in barbarity and ignorance, was in no condition to cultivate commerce, or to pursue any system of useful and salutary policy. When a better prospect began to open by the union of the kingdom under one monarch, the Norman conquest took place. This occasioned such a violent shock, and such a sudden and total revolution of property, that the nation did not recover from it during several reigns. By the time that the constitution began to acquire some stability, and the English had so incorporated with their conquerors as to become one people, the nation engaged with no less ardour than imprudence in support of their monarch's pretensions to the crown of France, and long wasted its vigour and genius in its wild efforts to conquer that kingdom. When by ill success and repeated disappointments, a period was at last put to this fatal frenzy, and the nation beginning to enjoy some repose, had leisure to breathe and to gather new strength, the destructive wars between the houses of York and Lancaster broke out, and involved the kingdom in the worst of all calamities. Thus, besides the common obstructions of commerce occasioned by the nature of the feudal government, and the state of manners during the middle ages, its progress in England was retarded by peculiar causes. Such a succession of events adverse to the commercial spirit was sufficient to have checked its growth, although every other circumstance had favoured it. The English were accordingly one of the last nations in Europe who availed themselves of their natural commercial advantages. Before the reign of Edward III. all the wool of England except a small quantity wrought into course cloths for home consumption, was sold to the Flemings or Lombards, and manufactured by them. Though

Edward, A.D. 1326, began to allure some of the Flemish weavers to settle in England, it was long before the English were capable of fabricating cloth for foreign markets, and the export of unwrought wool still continued to be the chief article of their commerce. Anderson passim. All foreign commodities were brought into England by the Lombard or Hanseatick merchants. The English ports were frequented by ships both from the north and south of Europe, and they tamely allowed foreigners to reap all the profits arising from the supply of their wants. The first commercial treaty of England on record, is that with Haquin King of Norway, A.D. 1217. Anders. vol. i. p. 108. But they did not venture to trade in their own ships to the Baltick until the beginning of the fourteenth century. Ib. 151. It was after the middle of the fifteenth before they sent any ships into the mediterranean. Ib. p. 177. Nor was it long before this period that their vessels visited the ports of Spain or Portugal. But though I have pointed out the slow progress of the English commerce, as a fact little attended to, and yet meriting consideration; the concourse of foreigners to the ports of England, together with the communication among all the different countries in Europe, which went on increasing from the beginning of the twelfth century, is sufficient to justify all the observations and reasonings in the text concerning the influence of commerce on the state of manners, and of society.

32

Reflections on the Formation and the Distribution of Wealth
1766

For a summary of Turgot's life, see "In Praise of Gournay" (chapter 29). The work excerpted here, *Reflections on the Formation and the Distribution of Wealth,* is as close as Turgot came to writing a polished masterpiece. Written in the 1760s, it contains far-reaching discussions of topics such as money, exchange, value, and capital investment in agriculture, all set in a distinctive historical framework not dissimilar to that of Scottish historians such as Robertson and Millar. It is known that Turgot discussed economic matters with Adam Smith during the latter's sojourn in France in the 1760s and that he corresponded with Hume, who was in Paris from late 1763 to 1766, during the same decade. He also wrote the work during the Physiocrats' period of greatest creativity and influence. Though the work was completed by the end of 1766, it did not appear in print until 1770.

The edition used here is from Ronald Meek, ed., *Turgot on Progress, Sociology and Economics* (Cambridge University Press, 1973), pp. 134–74, © Cambridge University Press 1973, reprinted with the permission of Cambridge University Press. The excerpt chosen begins just before section XXXI on the "birth of commerce" and ends with a general statement on the wealth of a nation. The one bracketed note is by the present editor.

Reflections on the Formation and the Distribution of Wealth

28

Recapitulation of the different methods of turning land to account.

I have just enumerated five different methods by which Proprietors have been able, in exempting themselves from the labour of cultivation, to turn their estates to account by means of the hands of others.

The first, by workmen paid fixed wages.

The second, by slaves.

The third, by giving up the estate for a rent.

The fourth, by giving up to the Cultivator a particular share, usually one-half, of the fruits, the Proprietor undertaking to make the advances involved in cultivation.

The fifth, by letting out the land to Farmers who undertake to make all the advances involved in cultivation, and who bind themselves to pay the Proprietor, for the number of years agreed upon, an unvarying revenue.

Of these five methods, the first is too expensive, and is very rarely put into use; the second can find a place only in countries which are still ignorant and barbarous; the third is less a method of turning one's property to account than a surrender of one's property in return for a debt claim on the estate, so that the old Proprietor, properly speaking, is no more than a creditor of the new one.

The two last methods of cultivation are those most generally used: that is, cultivation by *Métayers°* in poor countries, and cultivation by Farmers in more wealthy countries.

29

Of capitals in general, and of the revenue of money.

There is another way of being wealthy without working and without possessing land of which I have not yet spoken. It is necessary to explain its origin and its relation with the rest of the system of the distribution of wealth in society, of which I have just sketched the outlines. This way consists in living on what is called the revenue of one's money, or on the interest which is derived from money put out on loan.

30

Of the use of gold and silver in commerce.

Silver and gold are two commodities like others, and less valuable than many others since they are of no use for the real needs of life. In order to explain how these two metals have become the pledge representing all kinds of wealth, what influence they exercise in the business of commerce, and how they enter into the composition of fortunes, we must go back a little and retrace our steps.

31

Birth of Commerce. Principle of the valuation of exchangeable things.

Reciprocal need led to the introduction of the exchange of what one possessed for what one did not possess; men exchanged one kind of produce for another, and produce for labour. In these exchanges it was necessary that the two parties should agree about the quality and the quantity of each of the things that were exchanged. In this agreement it is natural that each should desire to receive as much and to give as little as he can; and since both are equally masters of what they have to give in the exchange, it is up to each of them to balance the attachment he has for the commodity he gives against the desire he has for the commodity he wants to receive, and in accordance with this to fix on the quantity of each of the things exchanged. If they are not in agreement, they will have to draw nearer one another by yielding a little on both sides, offering more and contenting themselves with less. Let us suppose that one of the parties is in need of corn and the other of wine, and that they agree to exchange *one bushel of corn* for *six quarts of wine*. It is obvious that each of the parties regards *one bushel of corn* and *six quarts of wine* as exact equivalents, and that in this particular exchange the price of *one bushel* of corn is *six quarts* of wine, and the price of *six quarts* of wine is *one bushel* of corn. But in another exchange between other men this price will be different, according to whether one of the parties has a more or less urgent need for the other's commodity; and *one bushel* of corn will possibly be exchanged for *eight quarts* of wine, while in another case *one bushel* will be exchanged for only *four quarts*. Now it is obvious that no one of these three prices any more than another can be regarded as the true price of the bushel of corn, since for each of the contracting parties the wine which he received was the equivalent of the corn which he gave: in a word, so long as we consider each exchange as isolated and standing on its own, the value of each of the things exchanged has no other measure than the need or the desire of the contracting parties, balanced on one side and the other, and is fixed by nothing but the agreement of their will.

32

How the current value comes to be established in the exchange of commodities.

However, it often happens that several Individuals have wine to offer to the man who has corn: if one of these is not willing to give any more than *four quarts* for a *bushel,* the Proprietor of the corn will not give him his corn if he comes to learn that someone else will give him *six quarts* or *eight* for the same *bushel.* If the first man wants to have corn, he will be forced to raise the price to the level of the one who offers more. The Sellers of wine gain on their side from the competition between the Sellers of corn: no one decides to part with his commodity until he has compared the different offers that are made to him of the commodity which he needs, and he gives preference to the highest offer. The value of corn and wine is no longer haggled over by two isolated Individuals with reference to their reciprocal needs and resources; it is fixed as a result of the balancing of the needs and resources of the whole body of Sellers of corn with those of the whole body of Sellers of wine. For someone who would willingly give *eight quarts* of wine for *one bushel* of corn will in fact only give *four* if he comes to learn that a Proprietor of corn is willing to give *two bushels* of corn for *eight quarts*. The price which represents an average between the different offers and the different demands will become the current price to which all the Buyers and Sellers will adapt themselves in their exchanges; and it will be true to say that *six quarts* of wine are the equivalent of *one bushel* of corn for everyone if that is the average price, until a lowering of offers on one side or of demands on the other brings about a change in this valuation.

33

Commerce gives to each commodity a current value, relative to each of the other commodities, from which it follows that every commodity is the equivalent of a certain quantity of every other commodity, and may be regarded as a pledge which represents it.

Corn is exchanged not only for wine, but also for all the other things which the proprietors of corn may need—for wood, leather, wool, cotton, etc.; and what applies to wine applies to every other particular commodity. If *one bushel* of corn is the equivalent of *six quarts* of wine, and *one sheep* is the equivalent of *three bushels* of corn, this same *sheep* will be the equivalent of *eighteen quarts* of wine. The man who has corn and needs wine may without disadvantage exchange his corn for a sheep, in order afterwards to exchange this sheep for the wine that he needs.

34

Each commodity can serve as a scale or common measure with which to compare the value of all others.

It follows from this that in a country where Commerce is very brisk, where there are many products and much consumption, and where there are many offers and demands for all kinds of commodities, each kind will have a current price relatively to every other kind; that is, a certain quantity of one will be equivalent to a certain quantity of each of the others. Thus the same quantity of corn which is worth eighteen quarts of wine will also be worth one sheep, one piece of dressed leather, and a certain quantity of iron; and in commerce all these things will have an equal value. To express and make known the value of any particular thing, it is clear that it is sufficient to state the quantity of any other known commodity which would be regarded as its equivalent. Thus in order to make known what a piece of leather of a particular size is worth, we may say indifferently that it is worth *three bushels of corn* or *eighteen quarts of wine*. In the same way we may express the value of a certain quantity of wine by the number of sheep or bushels of corn which it is worth in Commerce.

We see by this that all the different kinds of commodities that can be objects of Commerce measure one another, so to speak; that each may serve as a common measure or scale of comparison to which to relate the values of all the others; and in like manner each commodity becomes, in the hands of the one who possesses it, a means of procuring all the others, a kind of universal pledge.

35

Every commodity does not present an equally convenient scale of values. Preference was bound to be given in practice to those which are not susceptible to any great difference in quality and thus have a value which is in the main relative to their number or quantity.

But although all commodities essentially possess this property of representing all the others, of being able to serve as a common measure to express their value, and as a universal pledge for procuring all of them by means of exchange, not all can be employed with the same facility for these two purposes. The more a commodity is susceptible to changes in value when its quality changes, the more difficult it is to make it serve as a scale to which to relate the value of other commodities. For example, if *eighteen quarts* of *Anjou* wine are the equivalent of *one sheep, eighteen quarts* of *Cape* wine may be equivalent of *eighteen sheep*. Thus one who, in order to make known the value of a sheep, should say that it was worth eighteen quarts of wine would be using language which was equivocal and conveyed no precise idea, unless he added a lengthy explanation, which would be very inconvenient. So men were bound to choose for their scale of comparison, in preference to others, those commodities which, being more commonly in use and thus having a more generally known value, were more like one another, and whose value was therefore more relative to their number or quantity than to their quality.

36

Failing an exact correspondence between value and number or quantity, people make up for it by means of an average valuation which becomes a sort of ideal money.

In a country where there is only one breed of sheep, the value of a fleece or that of a sheep can easily be taken as the common measure of values, and people will say that a barrel of wine or a piece of material is worth a certain number of fleeces or sheep. It is true that there is some disparity between sheep, but when it is a question of selling sheep care is taken to evaluate this disparity, and to reckon, for example, two lambs as equal to one sheep. When it is a question of valuing any other commodity, people take as their unit the common value of a sheep of average age and average condition. In this way, the statement of values in terms of sheep becomes as it were a conventional language, and the words *one sheep* in the language of commerce simply signify a certain value which in the minds of those who hear them convey the idea not only of a sheep but also of a certain quantity of each of the more common commodities which are regarded as the equivalent of this value; and this expression will end up by referring to a fictitious and abstract value rather than to a real sheep; with the result that if by chance a large number of sheep die, so that in order to get one it becomes necessary to give twice as much corn or wine as one formerly gave, people will say that *one sheep* is worth *two sheep* rather than alter the expression for all other values to which they have become accustomed.

37

Examples of these average valuations which become an ideal expression of values.

The commerce of every Nation presents us with quite a number of examples of these fictitious valuations in terms of commodities which are only, so to speak, a conventional language for the expression of their value. Thus the Cooks of Paris and the Fishmongers who supply large establishments generally sell *by the piece.* A fat pullet is reckoned as one piece; a chicken as half a piece, more or less according to the season, and so on. In the trade of Negro slaves to the American Colonies, a cargo of Negroes is sold at the rate of so much per head of Negro, an *Indes piece.* The women and children are valued in such a way that, for example, three children, or one woman and one child, are reckoned as one head of Negro. The valuation is increased or diminished in proportion to the strength or other qualities of the slaves, so that a particular slave may be reckoned as *two head of Negro.*

The *Mandingo* Negroes, who carry on a trade in gold dust with the Arabian Merchants, relate all their commodities to a fictitious scale of which the parts are called *macutes,* so that they tell the Merchants that they will give them so many *macutes* in gold. They also value the commodities they receive in terms of *macutes,* and their haggling with the Merchants turns on this valuation. Similarly in Holland they reckon in terms of *Bank florins,* which are only fictitious money and which in commerce have sometimes a higher and sometimes a lower value than the money called *florins.*

38

Every commodity is a pledge which is representative of all the objects of Commerce; but it is more or less convenient in use according to whether it is more or less easy to transport and to keep without deterioration.

The variation in the quality of commodities, and in their price in accordance with this quality, which renders them more or less suitable than others to serve as a common measure, also to a greater or lesser extent stands in the way of their being a representative pledge of all other commodities of the same value. But so far as this latter property is concerned there is also a very great difference between the different kinds of commodities. It is obvious, for example, that a man who possesses a piece of cloth is much surer of being able to procure himself a certain quantity of corn when he wants it, than if he had a barrel of wine of the same value; for the wine is subject to an infinity of accidents which are capable of depriving him of the whole of its value in an instant.

39

Every commodity has the two essential properties of money, to measure and to represent all value; and, in this sense, every commodity is money.

These two properties of serving as a common measure of all values and of being a representative pledge of all commodities of the same value, embody all that constitutes the essence and utility of what is called money; and it follows from the account I have just given that all commodities are in certain respects *money*, and share in these two essential properties to a greater or lesser extent in accordance with their particular nature. All are more or less suitable to serve as a common measure in proportion as they are in more general use, of a more similar quality, and more easy to divide into parts of equal value. All are more or less suitable to be a universal pledge of exchanges in proportion as they are less susceptible to diminution and deterioration in their quantity or quality.

40

Conversely, all money is essentially a commodity.

One can take as a common measure of value only that which itself has a value, that which is received in Commerce in exchange for other values; and there is no pledge universally representative of a value except another of equal value. A purely conventional money is thus an impossibility.

41

Different articles are capable of serving and have in fact served as ordinary money.

A number of Nations have adopted as a common measure of value, in their language and in their Commerce, different articles of a more or less precious character. Even today there are certain Barbarous Peoples which make use of a type of small shell called *Cowrie*. I remember having seen at College apricot stones exchanged and passed as a kind of money among the Scholars, who made use of them in playing various games. I have already spoken of evaluation in terms of head of cattle. We find traces of this in the Laws of the ancient Germanic Nations which destroyed the Roman Empire. The early Romans, or at any rate their ancestors the Latins, also made use of it. It is asserted that the first coins which were struck in copper represented the value of a sheep, and bore the impression of that animal, and that it is from this that the word *pecunia* has come, from *pecus*. This conjecture has a great deal of probability.

42

The Metals, and above all gold and silver, are more suitable for this purpose than any other substance; and why.

We have now arrived at the introduction of the precious metals into Commerce. All the metals, as they have been discovered, have been accepted in exchanges in proportion to their real utility. Their brilliance has caused them to be sought for to serve as ornaments; their malleability and solidity have rendered them suitable for making vessels which are lighter and more durable than those made of clay. But these substances could not be brought into Commerce without almost immediately becoming the universal Money. A piece of any metal, of whatever kind, has exactly the same qualities as any other piece of the same metal, provided that it is equally pure: the ease with which one metal can, by different operations of Chemistry, be separated from others with which it may be alloyed, always makes it possible to reduce them to the degree of purity, or, as it is called, *to the title*, which is desired: and then the value of the metal can only vary according to its weight. Thus in expressing the value of each commodity in terms of the weight of the metal which is given in exchange for it, we have the clearest, the most convenient, and the most potentially precise expression of all values; and consequently it is impossible that it should not in practice be preferred to every other. Nor are the metals any less suitable than other commodities to become the universal pledge of all the values they are capable of measuring: since they are capable of being divided in every imaginable way, there is no object of Commerce whose value, whether great or small, cannot be exactly paid for by a certain quantity of metal. To this advantage of lending themselves to every kind of division, they add that of being imperishable; and those which are rare, like silver and gold, have a very great value in a very inconsiderable weight and bulk.

These two metals, then, are of all commodities the easiest to verify as to their quality, to divide as to their quantity, to keep for a long period without deterioration, and to transport everywhere at the least cost. Everyone who has a surplus commodity, and who is not at the moment in need of another commodity for his use, will therefore hasten to exchange it for money, with which he is more certain than with anything else to be able to procure the commodity he wants at the moment he needs it.

43

Gold and silver are constituted as money, and universal money, through the nature of things, independently of any agreement and any law.

Thus we have gold and silver constituted as money, and universal money, and this without any arbitrary agreement between men, and without the intervention of any law, but through the nature of things. They are not, as many people have thought, signs of values: they themselves have a value. If they are capable of being the measure and the pledge of other values, they have this property in common with all other objects which have a value in Commerce. They differ from them only because being at once more divisible, more imperishable, and more easy to transport than

the other commodities, it is more convenient to employ them to measure
and to represent values.

44

The other metals are employed in these uses only in a subsidiary capacity.

All the metals would be capable of being employed as money. But those
that are very common have too little value in too great a bulk to be employed in the everyday exchanges of Commerce. Copper, silver, and gold
are the only ones which have been brought into regular use. And even
copper, except among a few Peoples whom neither mines nor Commerce
have yet been able to provide with a sufficient quantity of gold and silver,
has always served only in exchanges of the smallest values.

45

The use of gold and silver as money has increased their value as materials.

It would have been impossible for the eagerness with which everyone
sought to exchange his surplus commodities for gold or silver, rather than
for any other commodities, not to have greatly increased the value of these
two metals in Commerce. As a result of this they have become even more
suitable for their employment as pledge and common measure.

46

*Variations in the value of gold and silver as compared with the other objects
of Commerce, and with one another.*

This value is susceptible to change, and does in fact change continually,
so that the same quantity of metal which used to correspond to a particular quantity of such and such a commodity ceases to correspond to it,
and more or less money is required to represent the same commodity.
When more is required we say that the commodity is dearer, and when
less is required we say that it is cheaper; but we could just as well say that

it is the money which is cheaper in the first case and dearer in the second. Not only do silver and gold vary in price when compared with all other commodities, but they also vary in price when compared with one another, in proportion to the extent that they are more or less abundant. It is well known that in Europe today we give from *fourteen* to *fifteen ounces of silver* for *one ounce of gold,* whereas in earlier times only *ten* to *eleven ounces of silver* were given for *one ounce of gold.* Even today in China they give only about *twelve ounces of silver* to get *one ounce of gold,* so that there is a very great advantage in taking silver to China in order to exchange it for gold to bring back to Europe. It is obvious that in the long run this Commerce is bound to render gold more common in Europe and more scarce in China, and that the values of these two metals must in the end be brought back everywhere into the same proportion.

A thousand different causes concur to determine at each moment the values of commodities and to cause them continually to vary when compared either with one another or with money. The same causes determine the value of money and cause it to vary when compared either with the value of each individual commodity or with the totality of the other values which are currently the subjects of Commerce. It would not be possible to disentangle these different causes and to treat of their effects without going into very extensive and very difficult detail, and I shall refrain from entering upon such a discussion.

47

The practice of making payments in money gave rise to the distinction between the Seller and the Buyer.

To the extent that men became familiar with the practice of valuing everything in money, of exchanging all their surplus for money, and of exchanging money only for things which were useful or pleasing to them at the moment, they became accustomed to consider the exchanges of Commerce from a new point of view. They distinguished between two persons, the Seller and the Buyer. The Seller was the one who gave the commodity for the money, and the Buyer was the one who gave the money to get the commodity.

48

The use of money greatly facilitated the separation of different labours as between the different Members of Society.

The more that money came to stand for everything else, the more possible it became for each person, by devoting himself entirely to that type of cultivation or industry which he had chosen, to relieve himself of all worry about providing for his other needs, and to think only about how to obtain as much money as he could through the sale of his produce or his labour, in the complete certainty that with this money he would be able to get all the rest. It was in this way that the use of money prodigiously accelerated the progress of Society.

49

Of the reserve of annual produce, accumulated to form capitals.

As soon as men were found whose ownership of land assured them of an annual revenue more than sufficient to meet all their needs, there were bound to be found men who, either because they were anxious about the future or merely because they were prudent, put into reserve a portion of what they gathered in each year, whether to guard against possible accidents or to increase their well-being. When the produce which they gathered in was difficult to keep, they must have sought to obtain for themselves in exchange objects of a more durable nature whose value would not be lost with time, or which could be employed in such a fashion as to obtain profits which would more than make up for the deterioration.

50

Movable wealth; accumulation of money.

Possessions of this kind, resulting from the accumulation of unconsumed annual produce, are known by the name of *movable wealth*. Furniture, houses, plate, commodities in store, the tools of each trade, and live-stock constitute wealth of this kind. It is obvious that men worked hard to obtain as much as they could of this kind of wealth, before they became acquainted with money; but it is no less clear that as soon as it became known, as soon as it was established, that money was the most imperishable of all objects of Commerce and the easiest to keep without inconvenience, it could not fail to be sought after above all other things by anyone who wanted to accumulate. It was not only the Proprietors of land who accumulated their surplus in this way. Although the profits of industry, unlike the revenues of the land, are not a gift of nature, and although the man engaged in industry gets from his labour only the price which is given to him for it by the one who pays his wages; although the latter economises as much as possible in paying these wages, and although competition forces the man engaged in industry to content himself with a price lower than he would like—it is nevertheless certain that this competition was never so extensive or so keen in all the different branches of labour as at any time to prevent a man who was more skilful, more energetic, and above all more economical than others in his personal consumption, from being able to earn a little more than was required for the subsistence of himself and his family, and from putting this surplus into reserve in order to build up a little stock of money.

51

Movable wealth is an indispensable prerequisite for all kinds of remunerative work.

It is also necessary that in every trade the Workmen, or the Entrepreneurs who set them to work, should have a certain fund of movable wealth accumulated beforehand. Here we are again obliged to retrace our steps in order to recall a number of matters which were to begin with indicated only in passing, when we were talking about the division of the different occupations and the different means by which the Proprietors could turn their estates to account, because we could not at that stage have explained them properly without breaking the thread of ideas.

52

Necessity of advances in cultivation.

Every kind of work, whether in cultivation, in industry, or in commerce, requires advances. Even if one should work the land with one's hands, sowing would be necessary before reaping; one would have to live until after the harvest. The more that cultivation is perfected and the more energetic it becomes, the larger are these advances. There is need of live-stock, implements of husbandry, and buildings in which to keep the live-stock and to store the produce; it is necessary to pay a number of people proportionate to the extent of the undertaking and enable them to subsist until the harvest. It is only by means of substantial advances that we can obtain rich harvests, and that the land yields a large revenue. In every trade, whatever it may be, it is necessary beforehand that the Workman should have tools, and that he should have an adequate quantity of the materials upon which he is to work; it is necessary that he should be able to subsist while waiting for the sale of his products.

53

First advances furnished by the land while still uncultivated.

It is always the land which is the primary and unique source of all wealth: it is the land which through cultivation produces all revenue; and it was the land which provided the first fund of advances prior to all cultivation. The first Cultivator took the seeds he sowed from plants which the earth had produced of itself; while waiting for the harvest, he lived by hunting and fishing, and upon wild fruits. His tools were the branches of trees uprooted in the forests, shaped with edged stones which he sharpened on other stones; he himself captured in the chase animals wandering in the woods, or caused them to fall into his traps; he brought them into subjection and domesticated them, using them at first for his food and then to assist him in his labour. This primary fund grew little by little. Live-stock, especially, were of all kinds of movable wealth the most sought after in these early times, and the kind which it was easiest to accumulate: they die, but they reproduce themselves, and the wealth embodied in them is in a way imperishable. This fund, moreover, increases simply by the process of generation, and yields an annual product, in the form either of milk foods, or of wool, hides, and other materials which, together with the wood procured in the forests, constituted the first fund for the works of industry.

54

Live-stock, movable wealth even prior to the cultivation of land.

In a time when a large amount of land was still uncultivated and belonged to no one, it was possible to possess live-stock without being a Proprietor of land. It is even probable that men almost everywhere began to gather flocks and herds and to live on their produce before they devoted themselves to the more arduous labour of cultivation. It would seem that the Nations which were the earliest to cultivate the land were those who found in their Country species of animals which were more susceptible to domestication, and who as a result of this were led from the restless, nomadic life of Peoples who live by hunting and fishing to the more tranquil life of Pastoral Peoples. Pastoral life requires a longer period of residence in one and the same place; it affords more leisure, and more opportunity to study the differences between soils and to observe the course of nature in the production of those plants which serve for the support of live-stock. Perhaps this is the reason why the Asiatic Nations were the first to cultivate the land, and why the Peoples of America have remained for such a long time in the Savage state.

55

Another kind of movable wealth, and of advances of cultivation: Slaves.

Slaves were another kind of movable wealth, procured at first by violent means and later by way of Commerce and exchange. Those who possessed a large number of slaves employed them not only in the cultivation of land but also in the different branches of industry. The ease with which these two kinds of wealth could be accumulated almost without limit and made use of even independently of land, made it possible to evaluate the land itself and to compare its value with that of movable wealth.

56

Movable wealth has an exchangeable value in relation to the land itself.

A man who had a large amount of land but no live-stock or slaves would certainly make an advantageous bargain if he surrendered a portion of his land to a man who gave him in exchange cattle and slaves to cultivate the remainder. It was mainly in this way that landed estates themselves entered into Commerce and acquired a value comparable with that of all other commodities. If *four bushels* of corn, the net product of an acre of land, were worth *six sheep,* the acre itself which produced them could be transferred at a certain value, larger than this, it is true, but always easily determined in the same manner as the price of every other commodity; that is, at first by haggling between the two contracting parties, and then in accordance with the current price which is established by the competition of those who want to exchange land for live-stock and those who want to part with live-stock to get land. It is in accordance with this current price that land is evaluated when a Debtor is sued by his Creditor and is forced to give up his estate to him.

57

Evaluation of land in accordance with the proportion which the revenue bears to the amount of movable wealth, or the value for which it is exchanged: this proportion is what is called the number of years' purchase of the land.

It is obvious that if a piece of land which produces a revenue equivalent to *six sheep* can be sold for a certain value, which can always be expressed by a number of *sheep* equivalent to this value, this number will bear a definite proportion to the number *six,* and will contain it a certain number of times. The price of an estate will then be simply a certain number of times its revenue; *twenty times* if the price is *120 sheep; thirty times* if it is *180 sheep.* Thus the current price of land is regulated by the proportion which the value of the estate bears to the value of the revenue, and the number of times that the price of the estate contains the revenue is called *the number of years' purchase of the land.* Land is sold at *twenty years' purchase,* at *thirty years' purchase, forty,* etc., when twenty, thirty, or forty times its revenue is paid in order to acquire it. It is also obvious that this price, or this number of years' purchase, will necessarily vary according to whether there is a greater or lesser number of people who want to sell or buy land, just as the price of all other commodities varies in accordance with the differing proportion between supply and demand.

58

Every capital in the form of money, or every sum of values of whatever kind, is the equivalent of a piece of land producing a revenue equal to a particular fraction of this sum. First employment of capitals. Purchase of a landed estate.

Let us now go back to the period following the introduction of money. The ease with which money could be accumulated soon made it the most sought after form of movable wealth, and afforded the means of continuously increasing the quantity of it by the simple method of economy. Anyone who, whether in the form of revenue from his land, or of wages for his labour or his industry, receives each year more value than he needs to spend, can put this surplus into reserve and accumulate it: these accumulated values are what is called *a capital.* The faint-hearted Miser, who fears that he may come to lack the necessities of life in an uncertain future, amasses money only in order to set his mind at rest about this, and keeps it in a hoard. If the dangers he foresaw were realised, and he were forced through poverty to live every year on his treasure, or if a prodigal Heir were to spend it bit by bit, this treasure would soon be exhausted and the capital entirely lost to the Possessor. But the latter can make use of it in a much more advantageous way. Since a landed estate of a certain revenue is only the equivalent of a sum of values equal to that revenue multiplied a certain number of times, it follows that any sum of values whatever is the equivalent of a landed estate producing a revenue equal to a particular fraction of that sum. It is a matter of complete indifference whether this sum of values or this capital consists of a mass of metal or of any other thing, since money represents all kinds of value, just as all kinds of value represent money. The Possessor of a *capital* may therefore, in the first place, employ it in the purchase of land; but there are also other courses open to him.

59

Another employment of money, in the advances of manufacturing and industrial enterprises.

I have already noted that all kinds of work, whether in cultivation or in industry, required advances. And I have shown how the land, by means of the fruits and plants which it produced of itself for the nourishment of men and animals, and by means of the trees from which men formed their first tools, provided the first advances of cultivation, and even of the first hand-made products which each man might fashion for his own use. For example, it was the land which provided the stone, the clay, and the wood from which the first houses were constructed; and, before the separation of occupations, when the same man who cultivated the land provided for his other needs by his own labour, no other advances were necessary. But when a large part of Society came to have nothing but their own hands to support them, it was very necessary that those who thus lived on wages should begin by having something in advance, either to procure the materials upon which they worked, or to enable them to live while waiting for the payment of their wages.

60

Further points about the use of capital advances in industrial enterprises, about their returns, and about the profit they ought to yield.

In the earliest times he who set men to work provided the materials himself and paid from day to day the wages of the Workman. It was the Cultivator or the Proprietor himself who gave to the Spinner the hemp he had gathered in, and maintained her while she was working: then he passed the yarn to a Weaver to whom he paid every day the agreed wage. But insubstantial daily advances of this kind can suffice only in the case of crude manual labour. A large number of Arts, and even of Arts engaged in by the poorest Members of Society, require that the same material should pass through many different hands, and undergo for a very long time very difficult and diverse preparations. I have already mentioned the preparation of the hides from which shoes are made: anyone who has seen a Tanner's works will appreciate the absolute impossibility of one poor man, or even several poor men, providing themselves with hides, lime, tan, tools, etc., getting the buildings which are necessary for the operation of a Tannery erected, and living for several months until the leather is sold. In this Art and in many others, is it not necessary that those who work at it should have learned the trade before venturing to touch the material, which they would spoil in their first attempts? Here, then, another advance is indispensable. And who, in the next place, will collect together the materials for the work, and the ingredients and tools necessary for their preparation? Who will get canals, markets, and buildings of all kinds constructed? Who will make it possible for this great number of Workmen to live until the leather is sold, when no one of them could prepare a single hide on his own, and when the profit from the sale of a single hide could not afford subsistence for any one of them? Who will defray the costs of the instruction of Pupils and Apprentices? Who will obtain for them the means of subsistence during the period until they are taught, enabling them to pass step by step from labour which is easy and proportioned to their age to tasks which require the greatest vigour and ability? It will be one of those Possessors of *capitals,* or of movable accumulated values, who will use them, partly as advances for construction and the purchase of materials, and partly as the daily wages of the Workmen who work them up. He it is who will wait until the sale of the leather returns to him not only all his advances, but also a profit sufficient to compensate him for what his money would have been worth to him if he had employed it in the acquisition of an estate, and, in addition, for the wages due for his work, his trouble, his risks, and his ability itself; for there is no doubt that if the profit were the same he would have preferred to live without any exertion on the revenue of an estate which he could have acquired with the same capital. As fast as this capital is returned to him through the sale of the products, he employs it in making new purchases in order to supply and maintain his Factory by means of this continual circulation: he lives on his profits, and he puts into reserve what he is able to save, in order to increase his capital and invest it in his enterprise, adding to the amount of his advances so as to add still further to his profits.

61

Subdivision of the industrial stipendiary Class into capitalist Entrepreneurs and ordinary Workmen.

Thus the whole Class which is engaged in meeting the different needs of Society with the vast variety of industrial products finds itself, so to speak, subdivided into two orders: that of the Entrepreneurs, Manufacturers, and Masters who are all possessors of large capitals which they turn to account by setting to work, through the medium of their advances, the second order, which consists of ordinary Artisans who possess no property but their own hands, who advance nothing but their daily labour, and who receive no profit but their wages.

62

Another employment of capitals, in the advances of Agricultural enterprises. Observations on the use, the return, and the indispensable profits of capitals in Agricultural enterprises.

In speaking first of the employment of capitals in Manufacturing enterprises, my aim was to present a more striking example of the necessity and effect of large advances, and of the process of their circulation. But in doing this I have to some extent reversed the natural order of things, which would have required me to begin by speaking about agricultural enterprises, which similarly cannot come into being or be enlarged or become profitable except through the medium of large advances. It is the Possessors of large capitals who, in order to turn them to account in agricultural enterprises, take leases of land, paying the Proprietors a high rent for it and undertaking to make all the advances of cultivation. Their situation must be the same as that of the Entrepreneurs of Factories: like them, they must make the first advances of the enterprise, provide themselves with cattle, horses, and implements of husbandry, and purchase the first seed; like them, they must maintain and feed the Carters, Reapers, Threshers, Servants, and Workmen of all kinds who possess nothing but their hands, advance nothing but their labour, and earn nothing but their wages. And like them, they must get in, over and above the return of their capital, i.e., of all the original and annual advances, (1) a profit equal to the revenue they could acquire with their capital without any labour; (2) the wages and the price of their labour, their risks, and their industry; (3) the means of annually making up for the wear and tear of the items of property employed in their enterprise—the live-stock that die, the implements that wear out, etc. All this must be deducted from the price of the produce of the land; the surplus serves the Cultivator for paying the Proprietor for the permission the latter has given him to make use of his land for the establishment of his enterprise. This is the price of the lease, the revenue of the Proprietor, the *net product;* for everything which the land produces up to the amount of the return of the advances and the profits of every kind accruing to him who makes them cannot be regarded as a *revenue,* but only as a *return of the costs of cultivation,* since if the Cultivator did not get these back he would take good care not to employ his wealth and his toil in cultivating the land of another.

63

The competition of Capitalist Entrepreneurs in agriculture establishes the current price of leases, and large-scale cultivation.

The competition of wealthy agricultural Entrepreneurs establishes the current price of leases in proportion to the fertility of the land and the price at which its produce is sold, always in accordance with the calculation which the Farmers make of their costs and of the profits which they ought to draw from their advances: they are unable to give the Proprietor more than the surplus. But when competition between them is very keen, they give him the whole of this surplus, since the Proprietor will let his land only to the man who offers the highest rent.

64

The lack of Capitalist Entrepreneurs in agriculture confines the working of land to small-scale cultivation.

When, on the other hand, there are no wealthy men at all who have large capitals to put into agricultural enterprises; when, owing to the low price of the produce of the land or to any other cause, the crops are not sufficient to ensure to the Entrepreneurs, over and above the return of their capital, profits at least equal to those which they would derive from their money if they employed it in any other way, no Farmers at all will be found willing to take the land on lease. The Proprietors are forced to get it cultivated by Husbandmen or *Métayers* who are not in a position to make any advances or to carry on proper cultivation. The Proprietor himself makes scanty advances which yield him a very scanty revenue: if the land happens to belong to a Proprietor who is poor, or in debt, or neglectful, or to a widow or a Minor, it remains uncultivated. This is the true cause of the difference upon which I have already remarked between the Provinces in which the land is cultivated by wealthy Farmers, as in Normandy and the Isle of France, and those in which it is cultivated only by poor *Métayers,* as in Limousin, L'Angoumois, Le Bourbonnais, and many others.

65

Subdivision of the Class of Cultivators into Entrepreneurs or Farmers, and ordinary Wage-earners, Hands or Day-labourers.

Hence it follows that the Class of Cultivators, like that of Manufacturers, is divided into two orders of men, that of the Entrepreneurs or Capitalists who make all the advances, and that of the ordinary Workmen on wages. We also see that it is capitals alone which establish and maintain great Agricultural enterprises, which give the land, so to speak, an invariable rental value, and which ensure to the Proprietors a revenue which is always regular and as high as it is possible for it to be.

66

Fourth employment of capitals, in the advances of Commercial enterprises. Necessity for the intervention of Merchants, properly so-called, between the Producers of commodities and the Consumers.

The Entrepreneurs, whether in agriculture or in Manufacture, get back their advances and their profits only through the sale of the fruits of the earth or of the manufactured products. It is always the needs and *the means* of the Consumer which set the price at the sale; but the Consumer does not always need the thing which is manufactured or produced at the moment when the harvest is brought in or the work finished. However, the entrepreneurs need their capitals to be returned to them immediately and regularly in order to reinvest them in their enterprises. Harvesting must be followed without a break by ploughing and sowing; the Workmen in a Manufactory must be kept continuously employed, work on new products must begin as fast as the old ones are completed, and materials must be replaced as fast as they are used up. One cannot with impunity interrupt the work of an established enterprise, and resume it again just when one wishes. Thus the Entrepreneur has the greatest possible interest in getting his capital returned to him very quickly through the sale of his crops or his products: on the other hand, the Consumer has an interest in finding the things which he needs when and where he wants them; it would be extremely inconvenient for him if he were obliged to buy his provisions for a whole year at the moment when the harvest was brought in. Among the objects of common consumption there are many which require long and costly labours, which can be profitably undertaken only upon a very large quantity of materials—so large that the consumption of a small number of men or of a district of limited area may not be sufficient to absorb the output of a single Manufactory. Enterprises where the work is of this kind, therefore, must necessarily be few in number, at a considerable distance from one another, and consequently very far from the homes of the majority of the consumers. There is no man above the level of extreme poverty who is not in a position to consume a number of things which are gathered in or manufactured only in places far removed from his home and equally far removed from one another. A man who could not obtain the objects of his consumption except by buying them directly from the hands of him who had gathered them in or manufactured them would either go without a good many things, or spend his whole life in travel.

This two-fold interest which the Producer and the Consumer have, the first in finding an opportunity to sell and the second in finding an opportunity to buy, yet without wasting precious time in waiting for a Purchaser or in seeking out a Seller, was bound to suggest to third parties that they might act as intermediaries between the one and the other. And this is the purpose of the profession of the Merchant, who buys commodities from the hands of the Producer in order to accumulate them or put them in a warehouse, where the Consumer comes to get what he wants. By this means the Entrepreneur, assured of a market and of the return of his capital, devotes himself without anxiety and without any letting-up to producing further goods, and the Consumer finds within his reach, and at any moment, the things of which he stands in need.

67

Different orders of Merchants. All have this in common, that they buy in order to resell; and that their traffic depends upon advances which have to be returned with a profit, in order to be newly invested in the enterprise.

From the Woman who offers her herbs for sale in the market-place, up to the Ship-owner of Nantes or Cadiz who carries on his sales and purchases as far away as India and America, the profession of a merchant, or what is properly called commerce, is divided into an infinity of branches, and, so to speak, of degrees. One merchant confines himself to laying in a stock of one or of several kinds of commodities which he sells in his shop to all who come there. Another goes and sells particular commodities in a place where they are lacking, in order to bring back from there in exchange commodities which are produced there and which are lacking in the place from which he set out. One makes his exchanges in his own neighbourhood and by himself; another through the medium of Correspondents, and by the agency of Carriers whom he pays, sends out, and causes to go from one Province to another, from one Kingdom to another Kingdom, from Europe to Asia, and from Asia to Europe. One sells his commodities in small portions to each of the individuals who consume them; another sells only large quantities at a time to other Merchants who resell them at retail to the Consumers. But they all have this in common, that they *buy in order to resell,* and that their first purchases constitute an advance which is returned to them only in the course of time. It has to be returned to them, as in the case of the advances of the Entrepreneurs in Agriculture and manufacture, not only in its entirety within a certain period in order to be reinvested in new purchases, but also (1) with a profit equal to the revenue they could acquire with their capital without any labour; and (2) with the wages and the price of their labour, their risks, and their industry. Without the assurance of this return and these indispensable profits, no Merchant would undertake Commerce, and no one could continue in it: it is from this point of view that he regulates his behaviour in making his purchases, when he calculates the quantity and the price of the things which he can expect to sell in a certain time. The Retailer learns by experience, and by the success of limited trials undertaken with caution, what is the approximate quantity of the needs of the Consumers he is in a position to supply. The trader, from his Correspondence, acquires knowledge of the abundance or scarcity and the price of commodities in the different Regions to which he extends his Commerce: he directs his speculative activities accordingly, sending the commodities from the place where they are at a low price to those where they are selling at a higher one; it being understood, of course, that the costs of Carriage enter into the calculation of the advances which have to be returned to him.

Since Commerce is necessary, and since it is impossible to undertake any commerce without advances which are proportionate to its extent, we have here another employment of movable wealth, a new use which the possessor of a mass of values put into reserve and accumulated, of a sum of money, in a word of *a capital,* can put it to in order to procure his subsistence and to increase, if possible, his wealth.

68

True idea of the circulation of money.

We see, from what has just been said, how the cultivation of the land, manufactures of all kinds, and all the branches of commerce depend upon a mass of capitals, or movable accumulated wealth, which, having been first advanced by the Entrepreneurs in each of these different classes of work, must return to them every year with a regular profit; that is, the capital to be reinvested and newly advanced in the continuation of the same enterprises, and the profit to provide for the more or less comfortable subsistence of the Entrepreneurs. It is this continual advance and return of capitals which constitutes *what ought to be called the circulation of money;* that useful and productive circulation which enlivens all the work of society, which maintains movement and life in the body politic, and which is with good reason compared to the circulation of blood in the animal body. For if, through any disarrangement, whatever it may be, in the order of the expenditure of the different classes of society, the Entrepreneurs cease to get back their advances together with the profit which they have a right to expect from them, it is obvious that they will be obliged to reduce their enterprises; that the amount of labour, the amount of consumption of the fruits of the earth, and the amount of production and of revenue will be reduced in like measure; that poverty will take the place of wealth, and that ordinary Workmen, ceasing to find employment, will sink into the most extreme destitution.

69

All enterprises, above all those in manufacture and commerce, must have been very limited before the introduction of gold and silver into commerce.

It is hardly necessary to note that enterprises of all kinds, but especially those in manufacture and even more those in commerce, must have been very limited before the introduction of gold and silver into commerce, since it was almost impossible to accumulate large capitals, and even more difficult to multiply and divide payments as much as is necessary to facilitate and increase exchanges to the extent required by a thriving commerce and circulation. The cultivation of the land alone could maintain itself to some extent, because live-stock constitute the principal object of the advances which it requires; moreover, it is probable that there was then no agricultural Entrepreneur other than the Proprietor. As to the arts of all kinds, they must have languished very greatly before the introduction of money. They were limited to the crudest kinds of work, for which the Proprietors made the advances by feeding the Workmen and providing them with materials, or which they caused to be carried on at home by their Servants.

70

Capitals being as necessary to all enterprises as labour and industry, the industrious man willingly shares the profits of his enterprise with the Capitalist who supplies him with the funds he needs.

Since capitals are the indispensable basis of every remunerative enterprise, and since with money one can set up agricultural workshops, establish factories, or found a commercial undertaking, the profits from which when frugally accumulated and put into reserve become new capitals; since, in a word, money is the principal means of attracting money, those who are industrious and like work but have no capital at all, or who do not have enough for the enterprises which they want to establish, have no difficulty in deciding to give up to the Possessors of capitals or money who are willing to entrust them with it, a portion of the profits which they expect to get in over and above the return of their advances.

71

Fifth employment of capitals: the loan at interest. Nature of the loan.

The possessors of money balance the risk which their capital may run if the enterprise should not succeed, against the advantage of enjoying a regular profit without any labour; and they are guided by this in demanding a greater or smaller amount of profit or interest on their money, or in agreeing to lend it at the interest which is offered to them by the Borrower. Here is another outlet which is open to the Possessor of money, the loan at interest, or trade in money. For there must be no mistake about it: the loan at interest is nothing at all but a trading transaction in which the Lender is a man who sells the use of his money, and the Borrower a man who buys it; in exactly the same way as the Proprietor of a piece of land and a Farmer respectively sell and buy the use of an estate which is being leased. This is perfectly expressed by the name which the Latins gave to the interest on loaned money—*usura pecuniae,* words of which the French translation has become odious in consequence of the false ideas which have been adopted about interest on money.

72

False ideas about the loan at interest.

The price of the loan is by no means based, as might be imagined, on the profit the Borrower expects to make with the capital of which he buys the use. This price is determined, like the price of all commodities, by the haggling which takes place between the seller and the buyer, by the balance of supply and demand. People borrow with every kind of design and for every kind of motive. One man borrows to establish an enterprise which will make his fortune, another to buy a piece of land, one to pay a gaming debt, one to make up for the loss of his revenue of which some accident has deprived him, and one to enable himself to live until he is able to earn something by his labour; but all these motives which influence the borrower are a matter of complete indifference to the lender. The latter is concerned about two things only, the interest which he will receive, and the security of his capital. He does not worry about the use which the borrower will make of it, any more than a merchant concerns himself about the use which the purchaser will make of the commodities he sells to him.

73

Errors of the Schoolmen refuted.

It is because they have not seen the loan at interest in its true light that certain moralists, more inflexible than enlightened, have sought to have it looked upon as a crime. The scholastic Theologians concluded, from the fact that money produces nothing by itself, that it was unjust to demand interest for money put out on loan. Full of their preconceptions, they fancied that their doctrine was sanctioned by this passage from the Gospel: *mutuum date nihil inde sperantes.*[1] Those Theologians who adopted more reasonable principles on the subject of interest were subjected to the sharpest reproaches from the Writers who belonged to the opposite party.

Nevertheless it needs only a little reflection to appreciate the shallowness of the pretexts which have been used to condemn the loan at interest. The loan is a reciprocal contract, which is freely entered into by the two parties and which they make only because it is advantageous to them. It is obvious that if the lender finds an advantage in receiving a payment for the hire of his money, the borrower is equally interested in finding the money of which he stands in need, as is shown by the fact that he makes up his mind to borrow this money and to pay for the hire of it.

---

1. ["Lend, not hoping for gain." Luke 6:35]

But in accordance with what principle can one conceive of any element of crime in a contract which is advantageous to the two parties, with which both are content, and which certainly does not injure anyone else? To say that the lender takes unfair advantage of the borrower's need for money in order to demand interest on it is to speak as absurdly as if one should say that a baker who demands money for the bread that he sells takes unfair advantage of the purchaser's need for it. If in the latter case the money is the equivalent of the bread which the purchaser receives, the money which the borrower receives today is equally the equivalent of the capital and the interest which he promises to return at the end of a certain time: for it is in fact an advantage to the borrower to have during this interval the money of which he stands in need, and it is a disadvantage to the lender to be deprived of it. This disadvantage is appraisable, and it is appraised: the *interest* is its price. This price is bound to be still higher if the lender runs the risk of losing his capital through the insolvency of the borrower. The bargain, therefore, is a perfectly equal one on each side, and is consequently justifiable. Money considered as a physical substance, as a mass of metal, produces nothing; but money employed as advances in agricultural, manufacturing, and commercial enterprises procures a certain profit; with money one can acquire a piece of land and procure a revenue for oneself: thus the person who lends his money does not simply give up the barren possession of that money, but deprives himself of the profit or revenue which he could have procured for himself, and the interest which compensates him for this deprivation cannot be regarded as unjust. The Schoolmen, forced to defer to these considerations, allowed that interest on money could be taken provided that the capital was alienated, that is, provided that the lender renounced the right to demand the repayment of his money at a certain time, and left the borrower free to keep it as long as he wished while simply paying interest on it. The reason put forward for their toleration of this was that then the interest was no longer something derived from the lending-out of a sum of money: it was an annuity which one purchased with a sum of money, just as one purchased a piece of land. This was a petty subterfuge to which they had recourse in order that they might concede the absolute necessity of lending operations in the course of the affairs of Society, without frankly acknowledging the falsity of the principles according to

which they had condemned them. But this stipulation about the alienation of capital is by no means an advantage to the borrower, who still remains charged with the debt until he has repaid this capital, and whose
property is always liable as security for this capital. It is even a positive
disadvantage, in that he finds it more difficult to borrow money when he
needs it; for a man who would willingly agree to lend for a year or two a
sum of money with which he plans to buy a piece of land, would not be
willing to lend it for an indefinite period. Moreover, if one is allowed to
sell one's money in return for a perpetual annuity, why should one not be
allowed to let it out for a certain number of years, in return for an annuity which will continue only for that number of years? If an annuity of
1,000 francs a year is the equivalent of a sum of *20,000 francs* to the man
who keeps that sum in perpetuity, 1,000 francs will be the equivalent
each year of the possession of that sum during a year.

74

True foundation of the interest on money.

A man, then, is as justified in letting out his money as he is in selling it;
and the possessor of money may do either one or the other, not only because the money is the equivalent of a revenue and a means for procuring him a revenue, not only because the lender loses during the term of
the loan the revenue which he would have been able to procure, not only
because he risks his capital, not only because the borrower may employ
it in advantageous purchases or in enterprises from which he will derive
large profits: the Proprietor of money may justifiably draw interest on it
in accordance with a principle which is more general and more decisive.
Even if none of the foregoing were the case, he would nevertheless be
justified in demanding interest on the loan, simply for the reason that his
money is his own. Since it is his own, he is free to keep it; there is no obligation at all upon him to lend it out: if then he does lend it out, he may
attach to his loan whatever condition he wishes. In doing this he does no
wrong to the borrower, since the latter acquiesces in the condition, and
has no kind of right to the sum lent. The profit that a man may obtain

with the money is no doubt one of the commonest motives influencing the borrower to borrow at interest; it is one of the sources of the ease with which he finds himself able to pay this interest, but this is not at all what gives a right to the lender to demand it; for that, it is enough that his money is his own, and this right is inseparable from property. He who buys bread does so in order to feed himself; but the right which the Baker has to demand a price for it is quite independent of this use of the bread: it is the same right which he would have to sell him stones—a right founded solely upon the fact that since the bread is his own, nobody has a right to oblige him to give it away for nothing.

75

Reply to an objection.

This reflection enables us to appreciate how false is the application made by the rigorists of the passage *Mutuum date, nihil inde sperantes,* and how far it departs from the meaning of the Gospel. This passage is clear when it is understood, as it is by moderate and reasonable Theologians, as a precept of charity. All men ought to come to one another's assistance: a wealthy man who saw his fellow-creature in want and sold him his assistance instead of relieving his distress would be failing alike in the duties of Christianity and in those of humanity. In circumstances such as these charity does not simply prescribe lending without interest: it commands us to lend, and even to give, if necessary. To make of this precept of charity a precept of rigorous justice is equally repugnant to reason and to the meaning of the text. Those whom I am attacking here do not claim that it is a duty of justice to lend one's money; they must therefore agree that the first words of the passage, *mutuum date,* embody no more than a principle of charity. Why then, I ask, do they say that the close of the passage should be interpreted as a duty of justice? What, shall the lending itself not be a rigorous precept, but its accessory, the condition of the loan, be made into one? If so, men would in effect be being told this: "You are free to lend or not to lend; but, if you lend, take care that you do not accept any interest on your money; even if a Merchant should ask a loan from you for an enterprise from which he expects to make large profits, it would be a crime for you to take the interest which he offers you; it is absolutely necessary that you should either lend to him gratuitously or not lend to him at all. You have indeed one means of making interest justifiable—you can lend your capital for an indefinite period and renounce the right to demand its repayment, which your debtor may make when he wishes or when he can. If you find that this has drawbacks on the grounds of security, or if you foresee that you are going to need your money in a certain number of years, the only course you can take is not to lend: it is better to allow this Merchant to miss the most precious opportunity than to commit a sin in order to help him to take advantage of it." That is what has been discovered in these five words, *mutuum date, nihil inde sperantes,* when they have been interpreted with the preconceptions created by a false metaphysics. Everyone who reads this text without prejudice will see what it really means: "*As men, as Christians, you are all brothers and all friends: act towards one another as brothers and as friends; help one another in your necessities; let your purses be open to one another, and do not sell the assistance which you mutually owe to one another by demanding interest on a loan which charity makes it your duty to give.*" That is the true meaning of the passage in question. The obligation to lend without interest and the obligation to lend are clearly related to one another: they are of the same order, and both of them set forth a duty of charity and not a precept of rigorous justice applicable to all cases in which lending may take place.

76

The rate of interest ought to be fixed, like the prices of all commodities, by nothing but the course of trade alone.

I have already said that the price of borrowed money is regulated, like that of all other commodities, by the balance of supply and demand: thus, when there is a large number of borrowers who are in need of money, interest on money becomes higher; when there is a large number of possessors of money who are offering to lend it, interest falls. Thus it is once again a mistake to believe that interest on money in commerce ought to be fixed by the laws of Princes. It is a current price, fixed like that of all other commodities. This price varies a little according to the greater or smaller degree of security which the lender has that he will not lose his capital; but with equal security it must rise or fall in proportion to the abundance and the need; and the law ought no more to fix the rate of interest on money than it ought to regulate the price of any of the other commodities which are in circulation in commerce.

77

Money in commerce has two distinct valuations: one expresses the quantity of money which is given to obtain different kinds of commodities; the other expresses the relation which a sum of money bears to the interest which it yields according to the course of trade.

It will appear from this explanation of the manner in which money is sold or let out for an annual interest that there are two ways of valuing money in commerce. In purchases and sales, a certain weight of money represents a certain quantity of values or of commodities of all kinds: for example, an ounce of silver is the equivalent of a certain quantity of corn, or of a certain number of days' labour. In lending, and in trade in money, a capital is the equivalent of an annual payment equal to a fixed proportion of this capital; and conversely an annual payment represents a capital equal to the amount of this annual payment multiplied a certain number of times, according to whether interest is at a higher or lower number of years' purchase.

78

These two valuations are independent of one another, and are regulated by quite different principles.

These two different appraisals have much less connection and depend much less upon one another than one would at first sight be tempted to believe. Money may be very plentiful in everyday commerce, it may have very little value there, and it may correspond to a very small quantity of commodities, while at the same time interest on money may be at a very high level.

Let us assume that with *one million ounces of silver* at present circulating in commerce, *one ounce of silver* is given on the market for a measure of corn. Let us now assume that there is brought into the State, by some means or other, *a second million* ounces of silver, and that this increase is distributed to everyone in the same proportion as the first million, so that the man who formerly had two ounces of silver now has four. The money, considered as a mass of metal, will certainly diminish in price, or, what amounts to the same thing, commodities will be paid for at a dearer price; and, in order to obtain the measure of corn which was formerly bought for one ounce of silver, it will be necessary to give a good deal more silver—perhaps *two ounces* instead of *one*. But it will by no means follow from this that interest on money will fall, if all this money is brought to the market and employed in the current expenditure of those who possess it, as we have assumed that the first million ounces of silver were; for interest on money falls only when there is more money to lend, relative to the needs of borrowers, than there was before. But the money which people bring to the market is not for lending at all; it is the money which is put into reserve, the accumulated capitals, that are lent; and so far from the increase in the money in the market, or the lowering of its price relative to the commodities entering into everyday commerce, infallibly and as a direct consequence leading to a fall in the interest on money, it may on the contrary happen that the very cause which increases the amount of money in the market, and which increases the prices of other commodities by lowering the price of money, is precisely the cause which increases the price of money, or the rate of interest.

Indeed, let us assume for a moment that all the wealthy men in a nation, instead of saving out of their revenues or their annual profits, should spend the whole of them; that, not content with spending the whole of their revenue, they should spend their capital; that a man who has 100,000 francs in money, instead of employing it in a profitable manner or lending it out, should consume it bit by bit in frivolous expenditure: it is clear that on the one hand there will be more money employed in current purchases, for the satisfaction of the needs or whims of each individual, and that consequently its price will fall; while on the other hand there will certainly be much less money available for lending; and, since many people will be ruined, there will probably also be more borrowers. Interest on money will therefore rise, while money will become more plentiful in the market and will fall in price there, and precisely for the same reason.

We shall cease to be surprised at this apparent inconsistency if we remember that the money which is offered in the market to obtain corn is that which is spent every day to satisfy one's needs, and that the money which is offered on loan is precisely that which is held back from one's everyday expenditure to be put into reserve and used to create capitals.

79

In the valuation of money relative to commodities, it is the money considered as metal which is the subject of the appraisal. In the valuation of the number of years' purchase of money, it is the use of the money during a given period which is the subject of the appraisal.

In the market, a measure of corn is balanced against a certain weight of silver; it is a quantity of silver which is purchased with the commodity; it is this quantity which is appraised, and which is compared with the different values of other things. In the loan at interest, the subject of the appraisal is the use of a certain quantity of values during a certain period. It is no longer a mass of silver which is compared with a mass of corn; it is now a mass of values which is compared with a determinate proportion of itself, the latter becoming the price of the use of this mass during a certain period. Whether *20,000 ounces of silver* are the equivalent in the market of *20,000 measures of corn,* or only of *10,000,* the use of these 20,000 ounces of silver during one year will in the loan market be worth not less than a *twentieth* part of the principal sum, or *1,000 ounces of silver,* if interest is at *twenty years' purchase.*

80

The rate of interest depends directly upon the relation between the demand of the borrowers and the supply of the lenders, and this relation depends mainly upon the quantity of movable wealth which is accumulated as a result of saving out of revenues and annual products in order to create capitals, whether these capitals exist in the form of money or of any other kind of effects which have a value in commerce.

The price of silver in the market is relative only to the quantity of this metal employed in current exchanges; but the rate of interest is relative to the quantity of values accumulated and put into reserve in order to create capitals. It is immaterial whether these values are in the form of the money metal or of other effects, provided that these effects are easily convertible into money. It is far from being the case that the mass of the monetary metal which exists in a State is as large as the sum of values which is lent at interest in the course of a year: but all the capitals in the form of equipment, commodities, implements, and live-stock take the place of this money and represent it. A paper signed by a man who is well known to have effects worth *100,000 francs,* and who promises to pay *100,000 francs* at such and such a date, passes up to that date for 100,000 francs: all the capitals of the man who has signed this note answer for the payment, whatever the nature of the effects which he has in his possession, provided that they have a value of *100,000 francs.* Thus it is not the quantity of money existing in the form of metal which causes interest on money to rise or fall, or which brings into commerce a greater supply of money to lend; it is solely the sum of capitals to be found in commerce, that is, the current sum of movable values of all kinds, accumulated and saved bit by bit out of revenues and profits, in order to be employed to obtain for their possessor new revenues and new profits. It is these accumulated savings which are offered to borrowers; and the more there are of them the lower will interest on money be, at any rate if the number of borrowers is not increased in proportion.

81

The spirit of economy in a nation continually increases the sum of capitals; luxury continually tends to destroy them.

The spirit of economy in a nation continually tends to increase the sum of its capitals, to increase the number of lenders, and to diminish the number of borrowers. The habit of luxury has exactly the opposite effect; and from what has already been said about the use of capitals in all the enterprises of agriculture, industry, or commerce one can judge whether luxury enriches a nation or whether it impoverishes it.

82

The fall in interest proves that in general economy has prevailed over luxury in Europe.

Since for several centuries interest on money has continually been diminishing in Europe, it must be concluded that the spirit of economy has been more general than the spirit of luxury. It is only men who are already wealthy who give themselves up to luxury; and, among the wealthy, all those who are sensible limit themselves to spending their revenue, and take great care not to break into their capitals. Those who wish to become wealthy are much more numerous in a nation than those who are already wealthy; but in the present state of things, when all the land is occupied, there is only one way to become wealthy, and that is to possess or to obtain for oneself, by whatever means, a revenue or annual profit over and above what is absolutely necessary for one's subsistence, and to put this surplus into reserve each year in order to create a capital, by means of which one may obtain an increase in revenue or annual profit, which may again be saved and converted into capital. Thus there are large numbers of men who are interested in and engaged in amassing capitals.

83

Recapitulation of the five different methods of employing capitals.

I have listed five different methods of employing capitals, or of investing them profitably.

The first is to buy a landed estate which brings in a certain revenue.

The second is to invest one's money in agricultural enterprises, by taking a lease of land, the produce of which ought to yield, over and above the rent, the interest on the advances and the reward for the labour of the man who devotes both his wealth and his trouble to its cultivation.

The third is to invest one's capital in industrial or manufacturing enterprises.

The fourth is to invest it in commercial enterprises.

And the fifth is to lend it to those who are in need of it, at an annual interest.

84

Influence upon one another of the different employments of money.

It is obvious that the annual products which can be derived from capitals invested in these different employments are mutually limited by one another, and that all are relative to the existing rate of interest on money.

85

Money invested in land is bound to bring in least.

The man who invests his money in the purchase of an estate which is let out to a completely solvent Farmer obtains for himself a revenue whose receipt involves him in very little trouble, and which he can spend in the most agreeable manner by giving free rein to all his tastes. He has in addition the advantage of acquiring that form of property the possession of which above all others is the most assured against every kind of accident.

Thus one must pay a higher price for a given revenue obtained from land, or be content with a smaller revenue from the investment of a given capital.

86

Money placed on loan is bound to bring in a little more than the revenue of land purchased with an equal capital.

The man who lends his money at interest enjoys it even more peaceably and freely than the possessor of land; but the insolvency of his debtor is capable of bringing about the loss of his capital. Thus he will not be content with an interest equal to the revenue of the land which he could buy with the same capital. Interest on money placed on loan must therefore be higher than the revenue from an estate purchased with the same capital; for if the lender found an estate for sale with a revenue equal to the interest, he would prefer that employment of his money.

87

Money invested in agricultural, manufacturing, and commercial enterprises is bound to bring in more than the interest on money placed on loan.

For a similar reason, money employed in agriculture, industry, and commerce ought to bring in a profit which is greater than the revenue of the same capital when employed in the purchase of land, or the interest on the same amount of money placed on loan; for since these employments require, besides the capital which is advanced, a great deal of trouble and labour, if they were not more remunerative it would be much better to obtain a revenue of equal amount which could be enjoyed without having to do anything. Thus it is necessary that the entrepreneur, over and above the interest on his capital, should every year draw a profit which compensates him for his trouble, his labour, his talent, and his risks, and which in addition provides him with the means to make good the annual wear and tear of his advances, which he is obliged from the very first to convert into effects which are susceptible to deterioration, and which are moreover exposed to all kinds of accidents.

88

Nevertheless the products of these different employments mutually limit one another, and in spite of their inequality are kept in a kind of equilibrium.

Thus the different employments of capitals bring in very unequal products; but this inequality does not prevent their having a reciprocal influence on one another, nor the establishment of a kind of equilibrium between them, like that between two liquids of unequal gravity which come into contact with one another at the base of an inverted siphon whose two branches they occupy: they will not be on a level, but the height of one cannot increase without the other also rising in the opposite branch.

Let us assume that a very large number of proprietors of estates suddenly want to sell them. It is obvious that the price of land will fall, and that one will be able to acquire a greater revenue by the expenditure of a smaller sum. This cannot happen without interest on money becoming higher, for the possessors of money will prefer to buy land rather than to lend at an interest which is no higher than the revenue of the land which they could purchase. If, then, borrowers want to have money, they will be obliged to pay a higher price for it. If interest on money becomes higher, people will prefer to lend it out rather than to turn it to account in a more troublesome and risky manner in agricultural, industrial, and commercial enterprises; and only those enterprises will be embarked upon which bring in, over and above the wages of the labour, a profit much greater than the rate of interest on money placed on loan. In a word, as soon as the profits resulting from one employment of money, whatever it may be, increase or diminish, capitals either turn in its direction and are withdrawn from the other employments, or are withdrawn from it and turn in the direction of the other employments; and this necessarily alters in each of these employments the ratio between the capital and the annual product. In general, money converted into landed property brings in less than money placed on loan, and money placed on loan brings in less than money employed in enterprises involving work; but whatever the manner in which money is employed, its product cannot increase or diminish without all the other employments experiencing a proportionate increase or diminution.

89

The current interest on money is the thermometer by which one may judge of the abundance or scarcity of capitals; it is the measure of the extent to which a Nation can carry its agricultural, manufacturing, and commercial enterprises.

The current interest on money placed on loan can thus be regarded as a kind of thermometer of the abundance or scarcity of capitals in a Nation, and of the extent of the enterprises of all kinds in which it may engage. It is obvious that the lower the interest on money is, the greater will be the value of land. A man who has an annual income of 50,000 livres, when land is sold at only twenty years' purchase, owns wealth to the value of only one million, whereas he owns two millions if land is sold at forty years' purchase. If interest is at five per cent, all uncleared land whose product would not bring in five per cent, over and above the replacement of the advances and compensation for the Cultivator's trouble, will remain uncultivated. No manufacturing or commercial enterprise which will not bring in five per cent, over and above the wages and the equivalent of the trouble and risks of the Entrepreneur, will exist. If there is a neighbouring Nation in which interest is at only two per cent, then not only will it carry on all the trade from which the Nation where interest is at five per cent finds itself excluded, but in addition, since its manufacturers and merchants are able to content themselves with a lower profit, they will put their commodities on all the markets at a lower price, and attract to themselves an almost exclusive trade in all those goods in respect of which neither particular circumstances nor excessive costs of carriage are able to keep the trade in the hands of the nation where money is at five per cent.

90

Influence of the rate of interest on money on all remunerative enterprises.

The rate of interest may be regarded as a kind of water-level, below which all labour, all cultivation, all industry, and all commerce come to an end. It is like a sea spread over a vast region: the summits of the mountains rise above the waters, and form fertile and cultivated islands. If this sea should happen to roll back, to the extent that its level falls the land on the slopes is revealed, and then the plains and the valleys, and they are covered with every kind of produce. It is enough that the water should rise or fall by a foot to inundate huge tracts or open them up for cultivation. It is the abundance of capitals which gives life to all enterprises; and a low rate of interest on money is at one and the same time the effect and the sign of an abundance of capitals.

91

The total Wealth of a nation is composed of (1) the net revenue of all the landed property multiplied by the rate at which land is sold; and (2) the sum of all the movable wealth which exists in the nation.

Landed estates are the equivalent of a capital equal to their annual revenue multiplied by the number of years' purchase at which land is currently sold. Thus if we add up the revenue of all the land, that is, the net revenue which it yields to the proprietors and to all those who share in its ownership, such as the Seigneur who collects the dues, the Priest who collects the tithes, and the Sovereign who collects the taxes; if, I say, we add up all these sums, and multiply them by the rate at which land is sold, we shall have the total of the Nation's wealth in the form of landed property. To obtain the grand total of a Nation's wealth, we must also include its movable wealth, consisting of the sum of the capitals which are employed in all the agricultural, industrial, and commercial enterprises, and which never come out of them, since all the advances in every kind of enterprise have to return continually to the entrepreneurs in order to be continually reinvested in the enterprise, which, without this, could not be continued. It would be a very gross error to confuse the immense mass of this movable wealth with the mass of money which exists in a State; the latter is a very small thing in comparison. To be convinced of this, it is enough to remember the immense quantity of live-stock, implements, and seed which constitute the advances of Agriculture; the materials, tools, equipment, and commodities of all kinds which fill the work-rooms, shops, and warehouses of every Manufacturer, every Merchant, and every Trader; and one will then realise that in the grand total of the wealth, both landed and movable, of a Nation, money in the form of specie makes only a very small part. But since all forms of wealth are continually exchangeable with money, they all represent money, and money represents them all.

33

On the Origin and Progress of
a New Science
1768

PIERRE SAMUEL DU PONT DE NEMOURS, born in 1739, was the son of a Parisian clockmaker. A brilliant student from an early age, he was interested in everything from the natural sciences to literature. After coming to the attention of the Physiocrats in 1763, he quickly became active in editing the propaganda organs of the school, such as *Journal d'Agriculture* and *Ephémérides du citoyen*. He collaborated with provincial intendants such as Turgot in Limoges, and gained notoriety abroad among such rulers as Gustavus III of Sweden, Catherine II of Russia, the Margrave of Baden (who made him a counselor), and the king of Poland (who made him an education official). He became an intimate of Turgot in the 1760s, and especially during his ministry of 1774–76; he later edited Turgot's works, though not always faithfully.

After a brief exile upon Turgot's disgrace in 1776, he was charged by Vergennes with drafting a trade treaty with England and with supervising the diplomatic recognition of the new American republic. He became general commissioner of commerce in the 1780s. Elected a deputy to the Third Estate in the upheavals of 1789, he took positions during the Revolution that may be generally described as liberal but royalist—supporting the abolition of the hated salt tax (*gabelle*) but using his own journal to declaim against the radical drift of events that led to the seizure of the royal family in the *coup d'état* of August 10, 1792. His opposition to the death sentence against the king (January 1793) led to a warrant for his arrest that summer, by which time he was in hiding. He was eventually arrested but was saved by the fall of Robespierre (July 1794).

During the Directory he took up the cause of the parents of *émigrés*. Arrested again and his presses smashed, he fled to the United States with his two sons, settling in New Jersey, where he farmed and planned a colony for persecuted *émigrés*. Vice President Jefferson had him draft a plan for public education. Under Napoleon, he returned to France in 1802, becoming president of the Chamber of Commerce. Scholarly and philanthropic works now occupied much of his time, though his well-known opposition to Napoleon's regime led to his selection as secretary of the provisional government in 1814 and counselor of state under the restoration monarchy. During Napoleon's brief return in 1815, however, the elderly man fled to Delaware to rejoin his sons. During bouts of insomnia, he translated Ariosto. He died in 1817; his son Eleutherius founded the industrial chemical company DuPont de Nemours.

The work translated here for the first time, *On the Origin and Progress of a New Science,* was first published in 1768. It is arguably the clearest, most concise introduction to the full range of Physiocratic thinking on the nature of an enlightened, interdependent, exchange-based economy and its moral and political implications. Even so, there are a number of terms that appear with self-conscious repetitiveness throughout the work, the most notable perhaps being *évidence,* by which the Physiocrats meant something like "self-evidence" or the quality of being self-evident. We have translated it in different ways here, depending on the context, but have signaled its appearance where necessary. The edition used is A. Dubois, ed., *De l'origine et des progrès d'une science nouvelle* (Paris: Geuthner, 1910; repr. from 1768 ed.). Unbracketed notes are by the author; bracketed notes are by the present editor.

On the Origin and Progress
of a New Science

If, from one end of the world to the other, one casts a philosophical glance at the history of the most wonderful sciences, and if one considers how they emerged and came to be extended and improved, one will be surprised to note that that happened in the midst of the greatest obstacles, the most stubborn prejudices, the most bitter contradictions, the most formidable oppositions. One will find *Confucius* chased and threatened with death in China, *Pythagoras* obliged to conceal his doctrine behind a mysterious veil and to hide the truth from the people in order to preserve the freedom to develop it for a few adepts, *Democritus* thought to be mad and treated as such by the Abderitians, *Socrates* drinking hemlock, *Galileo* in the chains of the Inquisition, *Descartes* forced to seek refuge in the North, *Wolff* banished and sacrificed for eighteen years to the schemes of the *Langes* and the *Strahlers,* etc.[1]

"Everything has been said," "Everything is known," "Do we claim that we are more clever than our fathers?" are banalities which laziness, ignorance, and vanity have in every age and every country loudly opposed to anyone who had the audacity, the genius, the talent, the good fortune to search for, uncover, and reveal useful truths.

It has been said many times that man is a credulous animal. That was a mistake. One should have said that children are credulous and man is opinionated. You will find no man who believes something different from what he learned in his tender youth—thoughtlessly and without sufficient grounds. It is, as I say, not a question of credulity, but of rou-

---

1. [The reference is to Confucius (551–479? B.C.); Pythagoras (c. 582–c. 507 B.C.); Democritus (c. 460–c. 370 B.C.), a Greek philosopher from Abdera, hence the reference to the Abderitians; Socrates (469–399 B.C.); Galileo Galilei (1564–1642), the Italian physicist, astronomer, and mathematician; and René Descartes (1596–1650), the French philosopher, mathematician, and scientist. The remainder of the paragraph probably refers to the important German philosopher Christian Wolff (1679–1754), the criticism of him by Joachim Lange (1670–1744), *Neue Schriften über die Angegebene Irrthümer welche in der Philosophie des . . . Wolffs enthalten seyn sollen* (Leipzig, 1736), and Christian Augustin Ernst Strähler (fl. 1754), *Kurze doch gründliche Widerlegung* (1754).]

tine and obstinacy. Look at a mature man; you cannot help noting that, far from being credulous, he falls rather on the opposite extreme. His soul is closed to new ideas. He is prone to deny everything he does not understand. Whether truth or error, he combats equally everything he has not heard of. There are a few exceptions concerning very superior men; but the very nature of those exceptions shows how rare they are.

Therefore, one should not be surprised, still less irritated when one meets people—even famous and studious people—who, carried away by the obvious facts they know, and conceiving only vague ideas of what they do not know, believe they are nearing the limits of possible human knowledge, and do not imagine that there might be a new science in Europe.

If one of those clever people said to you: "What are we lacking? What do we not know? We can measure the sky and the earth. We observe their revolutions. We calculate their movements. We forecast eclipses. We weigh the atmosphere. We know, assess, and use the force of the winds and waters. We have discovered that active fluid that, diversely found inside all bodies, constantly and with prodigious force disperses all its parts, while also—as it surrounds all bodies—compressing those parts and through its immense effort keeping them in the position bestowed upon them by Nature. In more than one case, we know how to govern the powerful action of this first motion and to imitate fire and thunder. All the properties of beings seem to be instruments prepared for our intelligence. We apply to our own use weight, motion, and the way one arises from the other. The greatest burdens are raised in the air by our weak, frail hands. A mineral transmits to iron a natural attraction toward a certain point on the globe, and that is enough to mark out a route on the immensity of the seas." One should warmly applaud such grand ideas. And if you asked this same man what should be done to have a flourishing, wealthy, powerful political society, so that the families and the individuals which compose it should be as happy as possible? And if he answered: "This is not the subject of an exact science, and depends on innumerable variable conditions, which are difficult to sort out and assess," you should not find this answer ridiculous, because it appears natural and sensible to those who utter it in good faith; and when you suggest questions people are not familiar with, it is up to you to judge in advance how few people know what they have not been taught by their

Masters. Just imagine that Montesquieu himself, worthy in all respects to educate mankind, has told us, like someone else, that the principles of Government must change according to the form of its constitution. Imagine that he had not taught us what is the primitive basis and the common object of any government's constitution, and yet you saw that great man use almost alone the extreme sharpness and superior sagacity of his mind to search for and invent particular reasons for the given cases.

However, men did not randomly gather into civil societies. It is not without reason that they extended the natural chain of reciprocal duties and submitted to a sovereign authority. They had and still have a purpose that is essentially marked by their nature to behave in that way. Now, their physical constitutions, and those of the other beings surrounding them, do not permit that the means for achieving this end be arbitrary; for there can be nothing arbitrary in physical acts aiming at a determined end. You cannot reach a point unless you take the road leading to it.

Therefore, there is one necessary path to approach as closely as possible to the object of associations among men, and of the formation of bodies politic. There is thus one order—natural, essential, and general—which comprises the laws that are constitutive and fundamental to all societies; one order from which societies cannot deviate without losing their status as societies, without the political order losing its coherence, without its members finding themselves more or less disunited and in a violent situation; one order that could not be entirely abandoned without dissolving society and eventually completely destroying mankind.

Here is what *Montesquieu* did not know. Here is what minor writers—the so-called political authors, who thought they could follow in the footsteps of this great genius—were even further from grasping than he. Here is what many worthy men well learned in all the fields of knowledge we listed at the beginning of this essay know absolutely nothing about.

Ignorance, like all things in this world, tends to feed on itself. Our [ignorance] about those most important of all truths for men united in societies was supported and nurtured by a great number of external causes that it is unnecessary to develop here. We do not know how long it would have lasted; but one may infer from the resistance it offers today to the emerging enlightenment that it was of hardy temperament.

Thirteen years ago or so, a man of great genius,[2] who was used to profound meditations, and was already known for his excellent works and successes in an art where the greatest skill consists in observing and respecting nature, divined that nature does not limit its physical laws to those that have been studied up to now in our schools and in our Academies; and that when it gives ants, bees, and beavers the capacity to submit themselves by common accord and from their own interests to a good, stable, and uniform government, it does not deny man the capacity to raise himself to the enjoyment of the same advantage. Animated by the importance of this insight, and by the prospect of the great consequences to be drawn from it, he devoted all the intelligence of his mind to search for physical laws relating to society, and he eventually managed to reach the unshakable basis of those laws, to grasp them all together, to show how they derived from one another, and to extract and demonstrate their results. All this was a brand new doctrine, far removed from the prejudices adopted by general ignorance and far beyond the grasp of the common man, whose habit as a child of stuffing his memory prevents him from using his judgment.

And yet the time was not completely unpropitious for publishing that doctrine. The famous M. de Gournay, Intendant of Commerce,[3] guided like Quesnay only by the soundness of his genius, arrived at the same time, though by a different route, at many of the same practical results. He began to present them to the supreme Administrators, and, by his conversations and advice, to train young and worthy Magistrates who are today the honor and hope of the Nation; whereas *Quesnay* contributed to the *Encyclopédie* the words "Farmers" and "Grains," the first public works in which he began to present the Science he had discovered. Soon afterward, he invented the *Economic Chart* [*Tableau économique*]—that astonishing formula, which describes the birth, distribution, and reproduction of riches, and which enables us to calculate so surely, rapidly, and

2. François Quesnay, Squire, former permanent Secretary of the Royal Academy of Surgeons, member of the Royal Academy of Sciences, of the Royal Society of London, of the Academy of Lyon, etc., etc. First ordinary Physician and Adviser of the King.

3. [See chapters 24 and 29 in the present volume.]

accurately the effect of all operations relating to riches. That formula, its explanation, and the *General principles of economic government,* which the Author added, were printed with learned footnotes in the Château de Versailles in 1758.[4]

Three men equally worthy of being friends of the inventor of the Science and the Economic Chart—M. de Gournay, M. *le Marquis* de Mirabeau, and M. Mercier de la Riviere[5]—became intimate friends with him at that time. There was every reason to hope for a rapid progress of the new Science from the cooperation of three such talented men with its creator. But an early death prevented M. de Gournay from fulfilling the wishes and making the happiness of his country. M. de la Riviere was appointed *Intendant of Martinique,* and his zeal and diligence in serving his country with useful operations, constantly guided by the luminous principles he was familiar with, did not enable him during his whole term of office to occupy himself with transmitting to others the evidence of those principles which guided his immense daily work. The virtuous Friend of Mankind remained the only one to assist the creative spirit of this most useful Science to the human race by publicly retracting errors which had escaped him in his Treatise on Population. This was a generous deed, which was enough to serve as a scale to compare the strong mind, honest heart, and noble soul of this true citizen on the one hand, and the weakness, base pride, and deceitful ploys of a few contemporary writers on the other, whose errors were greater and much more dangerous, but who—even haunted by obvious facts [*évidences*]—wanted to convince their readers that they had never been wrong, and that they had no responsibility toward anyone for knowing truths contradicting their previous opinions, which they try in vain today to combine.

The *Friend of Mankind* had not only to admit that he had mistaken consequences for principles; he had to correct his errors by publishing truths. That is what he did. His fruitful pen produced a *New Introduc-*

---

4. Those works can be found with a *Treatise on Natural Order,* a few *Issues,* and a few *Economic Dialogues,* by the same author, in a collection entitled, *Physiocracy,* published by Merlin, Rue de la Harpe, Paris.

5. [Victor Riqueti, Marquis de Mirabeau (1715–89), chief protégé of Quesnay and author of *L'Ami des hommes,* hence the sobriquet "friend of mankind"; Pierre-Paul Le Mercier de la Rivière (1720?–1793 or 1794).]

tion to his *Report on Provincial Estates,* a refutation of the critical review *someone working in Finance* had written about that report, an eloquent *Speech on Agriculture* addressed to the Society of Bern, an excellent work on *Compulsory Labor,* explanatory comments on the *Economic Chart,* the *Theory of Taxation,* the *Rural Philosophy,* etc., etc.[6] A few Authors, trained by his lessons and by those of the Master he had adopted, and carried away by the obviousness [*évidence*] of their doctrine, started to follow in their footsteps. Whole Bodies, and respectable Bodies—the Académie des Sciences et Belles-Lettres in Caen, the Société Royale in Orléans— studied the new Science and proclaimed themselves its defenders.

That was the situation for this Science, unknown for so long, when M. de la Riviere came back from Martinique, to hasten and quicken its progress. Soon he had resumed the research that had occupied him before his journey. In passing, he added a few Reports to the Journal on Commerce under the name of M. G., and eventually wrote the Book entitled: *The natural and essential Order of political Societies,* which has just been published by *Dessaint, rue du Foin S. Jacques,* in Paris. This excellent Book keeps in its eloquent and closely argued Logic the very *order* it exposes to its Readers. Always clear and evident for strong minds, he has the supreme art of making himself understood by weak minds, by seizing how the most neglected truths are intimately linked to the most well-known truths. He presents their union with an evidence so naive that everyone imagines that he is the first to have thought of things he never dreamed about. It is this sublime naiveté—which destroys sophisms, and irresistibly drives *évidence* into your head—that the Friends of the Author call *the simplicities of M. de la Rivière.* Each of these *simplicities* is a stroke of genius.

I would be very happy if I could present here justly, clearly, and rapidly the main truths, whose chain—discovered by Doctor Quesnay—is so exceptionally well and clearly developed in that sublime Book. The deep conviction they have brought to my soul for so long prevents me from resisting the desire to attempt this enterprise, which may be beyond

6. Since then he has published the Summary of that great and profound work under the title *Elements of Rural Philosophy.* Copies of it can be found at Desaint, Bookshop, rue du Foin S. Jacques.

my capacities. But before yielding to this pressing desire, I think I must warn my Readers with a reflection I will draw from the August 1766 issue of the old *Journal of Agriculture, Commerce and Finance,* p. 88:[7] *It would be as imprudent to judge a work by even the best and most faithful extract as to judge the beauty of a painting by the outline of its copy, or a body by its skeleton.*

Section 1

There is a natural Society, which preceded any convention among men, and is founded on their constitution, their physical needs, and their evident common interest.

In that primitive state, men have reciprocal rights and duties with an *absolute* justice, because they are of physical nature, and therefore *absolute* for their existence.

There are no rights without duties, and no duties without rights.

The *rights* of each man, anterior to all convention, are the *liberty* to provide for his subsistence and well-being, and the *property* in his person and in the things acquired by the labor of his person.

His *duties* are to work to provide for his needs, and to respect the liberty, the personal property, and the mobile property of others.

Conventions can be made among men only for the acknowledgment and mutual guarantee of those rights and duties established by God himself.

There is thus a natural and essential order, to which social conventions are subjected, and that order is the one assuring men gathered in society the *enjoyment of all their rights by the observance of all their duties.* The exact and universal submission to that order is the sole condition, from which people may expect with certainty to have their share in all the advantages society can procure.

7. What we call the *former* Journal de l'Agriculture, du Commerce et des Finances, began in 1765, and ended in November 1766. The *new one* began in December 1766. It is known that both periodicals resemble each other only by their title.

Section 2

The spontaneous productions of the earth and water are not enough either to maintain a large population or to provide men with all the satisfactions they like to enjoy.

However, the nature of man leads him inevitably to propagate his species, to procure his enjoyments, and to avoid sufferings and privations as much as possible.

Therefore, nature gives men the art of multiplying productions and agriculture to improve his condition, and to provide abundantly for the needs of growing families.

Agriculture can only be established by preparatory work and capital investment [*avances foncieres*], essential preliminaries to annual operations. Those investments must be perpetually maintained, and expenses must be perpetually renewed; that is what we properly call agriculture [*culture*].

Before tilling the land, one must cut trees, rid the ground of woods, pull out their roots; one must let out stagnant waters or waters that wash the soil between two lands; one must prepare buildings to store harvests, etc. etc.

In using his *own self* and his *mobile resources* for the works and expenses preparatory to cultivation, man acquires the *ownership* of the land he has worked on. If he was deprived of that land, his work and the resources he used for tilling it would be taken away from him; that would be a violation of his *personal property* and of his *mobile property*.

By acquiring *ownership of the land,* man acquires the *ownership of the fruit* produced by that land. This ownership of the fruit is the purpose of all the expense and work done to acquire or create landed property. Without it, nobody would engage in such work and expense; there would be no Landlords, and the land would lie fallow, to the great detriment of the present and future population.

If man, having become a landlord through the lawful use of his personal and mobile properties, associates himself with another man to continue cultivating his land; or even if, after all those expenses, he arranges with someone else who takes care of all expenses of cultivation properly speaking, a convention will be freely and naturally agreed upon, by which each Contracting party will enjoy a portion of the produce proportionate to his work and expense. As a result, the right to personal and mobile property of both will be wholly preserved.

Section 3

We have just seen that, independent of capital investment [*avances foncieres*], agriculture requires a constant stock of funds that, together with the land, form as it were the raw material of its operations—such as the plowing implements, carriages, working animals, and beasts providing manure for the land, etc., etc.

Those *primitive investments* in farming are perishable, and subject to sundry accidents. They must be constantly maintained, repaired, and renewed.

One must also cover the *annual expenses* demanded by wages and by the maintenance of all the men and animals whose work contributes to the exploitation of the lands.

It is therefore absolutely necessary that every year a sufficient sum be deducted on the value of the crops to maintain the *primitive investments*, and to provide for the *annual expenses of cultivation* for the following year; otherwise, farming would notably and progressively perish, and a proportionate decrease in the mass of renewable production and in the population would inevitably follow.

It is also necessary that this sum withdrawn on crops in favor of the long term, should not be so strictly measured by current expenses, so that it leaves Farmers [*cultivateurs*°] no means of withstanding great hazards caused by bad weather, such as frost, hail, blight, flooding, etc.; otherwise, those unavoidable accidents would deprive Farmers of the capacity to continue their work, and would destroy not only the crops of that year, but those of the following years as well.

Those sums, which must be devoted every year to perpetuate the harvests, are what are called the *farmers' withholdings* [*reprises des cultivateurs*].

The desire to assure a return on them is the purpose of the free agreements agricultural entrepreneurs make with Landlords.

Section 4

When farmers' withholdings—those sums necessary to pay the expenses of farming for the following year and to maintain the investment funds that permanently exist in the form of cattle, implements, etc.; those sums whose annual use for tilling the land is imperiously required and determined by Nature—have been deducted from the harvest, there remains what is called the *net profit*.

This *net profit* is the share of *landed property*. It is the cost of expenses and operations for clearing, drying out, planting, building, etc.—everything done to ensure that the land can be tilled.

The greater this *net profit* is, the more advantageous it is to be a Landlord.

The more advantageous it is to be a Landlord, the more people you will find who devote money and work to create, acquire, extend, and improve landed properties.

The more people employ money and work to create or improve landed properties, the more farming is extended and improved.

The more farming is extended and improved, the more consumable production appears every year.

The more consumable productions are multiplied, the more men are able to procure satisfactions, and as a result, the happier they are.

The happier men are, the more the population grows.

That is how the prosperity of the whole of mankind is linked to the greatest possible *net profit*, to the best possible condition of the Landlords.

Section 5

To achieve the greatest possible *net profit*, all works that lead to the growth and turnover of production must be done with as little expense as possible.

For these operations to be done with the least expense possible, there must be the greatest possible competition among those who make the investments and who bear the strain of that work. For with competition, each one strives to economize on his work expenses in order to deserve preference, and general economizing turns to the profit of all.

To assure the greatest competition among those who do the work, and among those who have the work done, there must be the greatest possible liberty in the use of all personal, movable, and landed properties, and the greatest possible security in the possession of what one acquires by the use of those properties.

One cannot in any way impede the free use of one's personal, movable, or landed properties without diminishing the net profit of farming, and therefore the interest one has in farming, and therefore farming itself, and therefore the stock of consumable productions, and therefore the population.

To commit that offence would be to declare war on one's fellow creatures, to violate the rights and fail in the duties established by the Creator, to oppose his Decrees as much as our weakness allows it, and to commit a human and divine crime of treason [*lèse-majesté*].

The general liberty of enjoying entirely one's property rights necessarily implies in each individual an entire security in the enjoyment of them, and prohibits—by the clear light of evidence—any use of the capacities of some against the properties of others.

There is no property without liberty; there is no liberty without security.

Section 6

To have the greatest possible liberty in the use of personal, movable, and landed properties, and the greatest possible security in enjoying them, men gathered in society must mutually guarantee and reciprocally protect those properties with all their physical strength.

That guarantee and that mutual protection actually constitute *society.*

Section 7

If, to preserve the mutual guarantee of property rights, all men had to keep vigil over the defense of their possessions and those of others, they would be in a condition less advantageous than the primitive state in which each one had only to maintain his own property. Therefore, there must be a tutelary authority that is vigilant for all, while each individual does his business.

For that authority to perform the duty it is entrusted with, it must be sovereign, and armed with a force superior to all the obstacles it could encounter.

It must also be unique. The idea that there could be several authorities in the same State is completely absurd. If they are equal, there is no authority; there can only be more or less anarchy. If one of them is superior, that one is the authority; the others are nothing.

Section 8

The sovereign authority is not established to *make Laws;* for *Laws* are already made by the hand of the one who created *rights* and *duties*.

The *social Laws* established by the Supreme Being prescribe only the preservation of *property rights*, and of the *liberty* that is inseparable from it.

The Sovereign Ordinances called *Positive Laws* must only be *declaratory acts of those Laws essential to social order.*

If Sovereign Ordinances were contradictory to the *Laws of social order,* if they forbade the respect of property, if they commanded the burning of crops, if they prescribed the sacrifice of small children, they would not be *Laws,* they would be insane acts which would not be obligatory for anyone.

There is thus a natural and unimpeachable Judge of the Sovereign Ordinances; and that Judge is *the evidence of their conformity or opposition to the natural Laws of social order.*

One must have extreme respect for and complete obedience to the Laws, because they are advantageous for all, and because men would be obliged to submit to them through an *intimate religious conviction*, even if those laws had not been promulgated by the Sovereign, and even if he had not used all the power of his beneficent authority to have them observed.

Sovereigns are obliged to promulgate the *natural Laws essential to social order by positive Decrees,* and they have the right to carry out that sacred function. As they are the guardians of all social forces, only they may *declare open war* on behalf of society upon those who violate its members' rights.

Thus, what we call *legislative power,* which is not that of *creating,* but that of *declaring Laws,* and of assuring their observance, belongs exclusively to the Sovereign; for the *executive Power* belongs exclusively to the Sovereign, by the very nature of sovereignty.

These two powers cannot be separated without disorder; for the right to command would become useless without the power to be obeyed.

Section 9

Because the Sovereign has the legislative and the executive power, the function of judging citizens is incompatible with Sovereignty.

It is incompatible with Sovereignty; for judging how the law should be applied to particular cases entails an investigation into innumerable particular facts, which the Sovereign cannot accomplish.

It is incompatible with Sovereignty; for it would deprive Sovereignty and the Laws of their sacred character. It would expose the Sovereign to all possible seductions, and to the perpetual suspicion of all possible seductions. One would no longer know if he spoke as a Legislator or as a Judge. There would no longer be any true *positive Laws,* and all Decrees would be considered as momentary wishes.

It is incompatible with Sovereignty; for when any Sovereign were mistaken in his Judgment—as it is inevitable that any Judge will be sometimes given facts that are equivocal or difficult to certify—and all the more so for any Sovereign (who never has the leisure to examine sufficiently a case considering the numerous cases he is overwhelmed with), there would be no one to appeal to. And for having wanted to dispense justice, the Sovereign would then be deprived of the Power to have justice be dispensed.

There must therefore be Magistrates who are set up to apply the Laws, to examine disputes between Individuals—and even between the Sovereign as the protector of the Public, and Individuals accused of violating public order—and to declare after sufficient examination that *such and such a person* is *in such and such a case, on which the Law has pronounced.*

To assure that it is evident that the magistrates have sufficiently examined the cases submitted to their judgment, they must be subjected to forms which constantly demonstrate this examination.

The right to establish those forms belongs to the Sovereign, as a branch of positive legislation.

Section 10

As Magistrates being charged with judging according to positive Laws and in conformity with prescribed rules fixed by positive Laws, and having to make decisions concerning the property, lives, and honor of their fellow citizens, they are religiously obliged to begin by judging positive Laws.

It is evident that a Magistrate would be culpable if he decided to deliver verdicts against his fellow men according to Laws that were *evidently unfair.*

Therefore, before setting themselves to judge according to Decrees, magistrates must compare the positive Decrees with the Laws of *essential Justice,* which regulate the rights and duties of each and are therefore the basis of social order.

Ignorance does not justify magistrates in not performing this examination and this comparison; for ignorance itself is a capital crime in a man who takes up a solemn office requiring *essentially* that those performing it not be ignorant.

Section 11

The examination Magistrates are obliged to perform should not harm the Sovereign authority; for Sovereign authority is such only because it is the depository of public forces, so that it has no other interest than increasing the available forces with the best positive Laws.

Sovereign authority is the depository of public forces and commands them, because the common interest carries such evidence that it wins over all wills.

It is that combining of wills and forces that constitutes the Sovereign power and authority.

That is why what is advantageous to the Subjects increases the power and authority of Sovereigns.

It would gravely insult Sovereigns by assuming them to be both unjust and insane, to suppose that they wanted to diminish their power and authority, by disuniting through evident injustices the wills and forces naturally inclined to support them.

When an error escapes Sovereigns in their positive Decrees, it can only be involuntary; and magistrates serve them usefully, faithfully, and religiously in having them note these involuntary errors.

Section 12

In order that magistrates fulfill this duty that is inseparable from their position—i.e., the important function of verifying positive Decrees by comparing them to *natural Laws essential to social order*—they must, as we noted, be deeply instructed in those primitive laws that are fundamental to any society.

To ensure that magistrates are enlightened and well-informed about the natural laws of social order, one must be able to judge their level of study and their capacity in this regard.

To be able to judge the Magistrates' capacities, the Nation itself must be very enlightened about the reciprocal rights and duties of men united in society, and about the physical laws concerning the reproduction and distribution of riches.

To ensure that the Nation is sufficiently enlightened about those natural laws, a general public instruction about them must be established, and doctrinal works in that field must be favored; so that the least of the citizens can know at least a little bit about them, and that all those who claim to be promoted to any sort of dignity have a deep, accurate, and complete knowledge of them.

Section 13

The Sovereign authority can only fulfill its tutelary duties, guarantee everyone's property by forces superior to all those who would violate it, and cover the expenses of distributive justice and public instruction, by making expenditures—and considerable ones at that.

Society must therefore pay out those expenses, which are *essential* to preserve Society, to respect order, and to maintain the rights of property.

The portion of wealth paying for those public expenses is called *Taxes*.

Taxes, as the preservers of property, are the great link, the federative knot, the *sacred bond* of society. This is such an important matter that we will devote several paragraphs to explaining the natural laws concerning it.

Section 14

It is not up to men to fix taxes according to their caprice; taxes have a foundation and a form *essentially* established by the natural order.

By "*it does not depend on men,*" one means enlightened and reasonable men; for no one disputes that the ignorant are capable of falling into great errors. But then natural laws submit them to very harsh punishments inevitably attached to those errors, and that is all one means here.

Taxes must provide for ever recurring expenses; therefore they can only be collected from ever recurring riches.

Taxes should not even fall equally on all renewable riches. Nature denied those called the "farmers' withholdings" (see section 3) the capacity to contribute to Taxes; for it has imperiously imposed upon them the law of being used to maintain and preserve agriculture, under pain of seeing the progressive destruction of farming, crops, population, and Empires.

The share of harvests called *net profit* (see section 4) is thus the only one that may contribute to Taxes—the only one nature has decreed is appropriate to pay for them.

It is therefore part of the *essence* of Taxes to be a portion of the *net profit* of agriculture.

Section 15

The purpose of Taxes is the preservation of property rights and the liberty of man in all their primitive and natural extent. Such preservation is the only way to ensure the proliferation of wealth and population.

Any form of taxes that would restrain property and the liberty of man, and that would necessarily diminish wealth and population, would then be manifestly opposed to the purpose of Taxes.

If Taxes on persons, commodities, expenses, and consumption were established, the collection of these taxes would be very expensive; their existence would impede the freedom of human work, and would necessarily increase the cost of Commerce and agriculture (see section 5).

This increase in the cost of commerce and agriculture, these high taxes between production and consumption, would not increase the wealth of any buyer or consumer, and could not lead anyone to spend more than his income.

They would thus force buyers to make bad offers for goods and raw materials, because of the taxes, the expensive collection of the taxes, and the increase in intermediary expenses that taxes and their collection would occasion for commerce and manufacturing.

They would thus necessarily diminish as much the cost of all first-hand sales.

The farmers [*cultivateurs*°] who make these sales would find themselves in *deficit* in their revenues, equal to the whole decrease in the price of their goods and raw materials.

They would thus be obliged to abandon the tilling of bad or mediocre lands, which, before the decrease in prices, had yielded very little or nothing beyond the expenses paid for tilling them, and which, because of that decrease in the value of the harvest, could no longer defray the necessary costs of cultivating them. This would lead to a first and palpable diminution in the stock of subsistence goods, in the well-being of the People, and soon in the population.

Farmers would also be obliged to withdraw a sum equal to the *deficit* in their revenues either from their landed incomes, or from the expenses in cultivation.

If farmers could withdraw that sum from their landed incomes (as would be fair, for those incomes are the only *available* ones, whereas the farmers' withholdings are *essentially* mortgaged to the tasks of reproduction), it is evident that in that case these landlords would bear the whole of the taxes on people, on operations, on goods, on commodities, as well as the expenses multiplied due to tax collection, and the decrease in value and the difficulties these taxes would create for the harvests.

It is equally evident that, in this case, the landlords would face higher expenses than if they had directly paid the treasury out of their income, without collection expenses, and without a decrease in the value of the production which represents the basis of their income—a sum equal to the one the Sovereign would withdraw from indirect taxes.

If farmers had commitments toward landlords that obliged them to pay them a fixed sum every year, they would be reduced to withdrawing expenditures from farming, because of the loss they would endure with the decrease in the prices of products, and the payment of indirect taxes and collection expenses they would be obliged to make.

Withdrawing productive expenditures would inevitably lead to a decrease in production. For the expenses necessary for farming are a *sine qua non* for harvests. These expenses cannot be eliminated without eliminating the crops; they cannot be diminished, without the harvests diminishing accordingly.

If the leases that engaged the farmers toward the landlords had to go for several more years, and if the former could not cancel them, degradation would become progressive, and all the more rapid as farmers would be obliged to pay the same rent and the same taxes *every year* on a crop weakened *every year* because of those expenses which farmers could only pay by cutting *every year* the expenditures for farming.

This degradation, which would be so fearsome for the population, would in the end fall upon the landlords and the Sovereign, either by the ruin of the agricultural entrepreneurs or by the expiration of their leases.

Those agricultural entrepreneurs still able to renew their leases, instructed by experience, would make such conditions as to compensate themselves for their losses, or at least to avoid them in the future. As their diminished means would not allow them to run their farms as profitably as in the past, they would commit themselves only because of the incapacity brought about by the loss of some of their riches, the decrease in the prices of their first-hand sales, and the excess indirect taxes and collection costs.

The impoverishment of these agricultural entrepreneurs, and the ruin of those others who would no longer have the capacity to make advances for disbursements on their farms, would divert rich men from devoting themselves to a profession that would offer them only the prospect of losing their fortunes. The farming of the majority of lands would be abandoned to unfortunate laborers [*manouvriers*] without means whom the landlords would be obliged to support. Then it would be impossible to get strong beasts to perform tasks with strength and dispatch, as well as enough cattle to provide manure for the lands; there would be a dearth of the necessary fertilizers; there would not be enough repairs, and buildings and ditches would not be sufficiently maintained, etc.; the harvests, means of subsistence, population, the *net profit* that constitutes landlords' wealth, the public income that can only be a share of that *net profit* (see previous section), the power of the Sovereign, which is based on public income—all that would be almost entirely extinguished.

Indirect taxes, poor peasants. Poor peasants, poor kingdom. Poor kingdom, poor sovereign.

Section 16

We have extended the previous paragraph to give an idea of the misfortunes Nations are exposed to, when they believe they can govern themselves or be governed arbitrarily; whereas nature has surrounded us with supreme Laws, and with a physical and inviolable chain of causes and effects that leaves our intelligence and our liberty merely the task of studying them, conforming our behavior to them, so that we may benefit from the advantages they offer us, and avoid the evils they would inevitably attract to us if we refused or neglected to enlighten ourselves about the order they constitute, and to submit ourselves to what it prescribes for us.

We have just seen that, when one wants to take an indirect route to levying taxes, they are still eventually paid by the *net profit* of landed capital. But they are paid in a way that is disastrous and much more costly for the landlords. They impede the liberty and restrict the property of citizens. They decrease the prices of products for first-hand sales. They diminish the stock of products, and even more the gross income of the territory. They bring misery and depopulation. They ruin by degrees agriculture, farmers, landlords, the Nation, and the Sovereign.

It is thus evident that indirect taxes would be entirely contrary to the purposes of taxes, of the establishment of Sovereign authority, and of Society.

It is thus evident that taxes must be directly collected on the net profit available from the landed capital. For then it will not disturb the legitimate and necessary schemes of the farmers, for whom it is a matter of indifference to pay part of the net profit to the Sovereign or to the landlords. The liberty of operations will remain wholly intact, and the prices of crops for the first sale will not diminish; for the order of expenditure will not be changed, and nothing will prevent them from returning directly to the land to put its products on sale, and the tutelary authority will merely replace the landlords in the disbursement of part of the available profit.

It remains only to examine what rules Nature indicates for the direct collection of the share that must go for taxes in the net profit of the territory.

Section 17

First, it is evident that with net profit, the proportion of taxes cannot be arbitrary.

It cannot be arbitrary on the part of the Sovereign authority; for then the Sovereign could invade all properties, he would no longer be regarded as their protector, people would be more inclined to distrust him rather than to obey him, and he would soon have no more authority.

That proportion must not be arbitrary on the part of the landlords either; for in moments of ignorance, a misunderstood interest could lead them to reduce the public revenue so as to harm the cohesiveness of

Society and the security of its constitution based on the preservation of property.

It is also evident that taxes cannot be invariably fixed to a determined sum of money. For a public revenue sufficient for a weak and beginning society would not be enough for an extended and wealthier society that has cleared and exploited a large territory. And the revenue necessary for a flourishing society would also become excessive, onerous, and destructive for that same society if exterior conditions or political errors reduce the *net profit* of agriculture, and thus bring it back to its state of primitive weakness.

It is a most fearsome opinion that leads to the belief that any State has to defend itself by submitting itself to taxes capable of paying for a public force roughly equal to that of the neighboring Peoples. This prejudice, which has increased and multiplied taxes in weak and poor Nations, for no other reason than weakness and poverty themselves, has caused the most dreadful evils the human species has ever experienced. Because of it, property has been sacrificed, and the foundations of society sapped, under pretext of protecting property and maintaining society. Because of it, taxes have become arbitrary, and have known no limits but those a disordered imagination have given to ceaselessly exaggerated public necessity. It would have led people to wish against Nature for the Prince *of Monaco* to have a revenue capable of balancing the power of the King *of France*.

Taxes must thus be proportioned not to the so-called needs of States, but to their available wealth. As soon as one deviates from this rule, no rule at all will be acknowledged; and Empires will soon be led to that terrible epoch, when the nation does not care whether its territory is devastated by the enemy or by the tax collectors.

The proportion of taxes in relation to net profit, which constitutes the sole available wealth (see section 4), must ensure that the fate of the landlords be the best possible, and that their condition be preferable to any other in society. For if any other status were preferable to that of landlord, people would all turn to that other status. They would neglect to use their mobile wealth to create, improve, and maintain landed properties, but would devote them to other operations and enterprises. Then the buildings necessary to farming—barns, stables, presses, etc.—would fall into ruin; plantations would be abandoned; trees would be chopped down; enclosures would deteriorate; ditches would be filled in; waters would become stagnant on the lands; marshes and fallow land would replace crops; the harvests, net profit, and taxes themselves would perish progressively and inevitably.

This legitimate and natural proportion of taxes with the net profit covering them establishes itself in an emerging society. For it is these landlords, pressed by the necessity of submitting to the tutelary authority they raise among them to guarantee one another in the enjoyment of their possessions, who voluntarily and out of their own interest devote part of the net profit of their domains to cover the expenses due to administration of that protecting authority.

That is how taxes, far from being opposed to the rights of landlords, are on the contrary a usage of their property rights.

It is even a profitable usage of the rights of landlords, for thanks to the security this institution gives to properties and to liberty, landlords can extend and multiply their operations, and infinitely increase agriculture and the products of their lands.

And if we claim that the tutelary authority will perpetually remain co-owner of the net profit of agriculture, according to the proportion fixed by evidence of the quota that taxes must represent to offer the greatest security to society, and to assure the best possible conditions for landlords—and preferable to any other in society—we constitute the most advantageous possible form of taxes for the Sovereign and the Nation.

This way, taxes are naturally proportioned to the real needs of society, since they increase as the population growth, occasioned by the progress of agriculture and the increase in *net profit*, requires an increase in public expenditures devoted to preserve good order and to protect property.

This way, farmers pay the value of the *net profit*, by their free and voluntary engagements, to those who are their owners. It is a great advantage for them that part of that net profit should pass into the hands of the Sovereign authority; for it is the only way to enable that authority to protect their property rights. And they do not have to pay for that; for they have no right of property on the *net profit*, and they are obliged by competition to take full account of whom it belongs to, and they do not mind if part of that *net profit* is called *tax*, while the other is called *farming costs* [*fermage*], provided they are not burdened with more than the *net profit*, and that their farmers' withholdings are always clear, intact, and assured.

This way, landlords who seem to pay income taxes, pay it in fact on an increase in available wealth or in *net profit* that would not exist without the implementation of taxes; for only the security that taxes provide for property could underwrite and favor the enterprises and operations by which farming was able to produce a net profit, however modest.

This way, taxes, to which a proportioned share of *net profit* belongs, are thus a great advantage for landlords; for they extend the wealth and satisfactions they can enjoy. It is a sort of inalienable common property. It is not part of any of the contracts landlords agree upon together. When they buy and sell lands, they do not buy or sell taxes, they only dispose of the share of the land that is theirs—the taxes being already levied. Thus, those taxes exist no more at the expense of any given landlord than the right other landlords have on the lands bordering his.

This way, taxes are a great advantage for the class of people who subsist only by wages; for they enable them to be certain of the full enjoyment of their rights of personal and mobile property. And they are in no way charged for this; far from withdrawing anything from the wages, or from the facility of earning them, taxes increase gross wages by increasing riches, which results from the entire assurance of property rights.

This way, the freedom of human work is the greatest possible. The competition among those who have the work performed, and among those who perform the work, is the greatest possible; the condition of the landlords is the best possible; the multiplication of riches and of net profit is the quickest possible. As a result, public revenue, which is always proportioned to the constantly increasing *net profit,* is the greatest possible.

This way, the tutelary authority enjoys the entire use of the sums devoted to public revenue; for collection expenses are reduced to nothing, or almost nothing, just as the expenses for the collection of rent [*fermages*] cost nothing to the Nation.

This way, any sort of contestation between the guardians of authority and the subjects is banned for ever; for once the proportion of taxes is established and well-known, arithmetic is sufficient to decide *with sovereign power* what is each person's share in the *net profit* of the territory.

This way, then, the greatest possible public revenue, increasing daily, is the most profitable one possible for all members of society, is onerous to no one, costs nothing to anyone, and is paid for by no one.

This way, finally, the Sovereign authority is in a perfect community of interests with the nation. The income of the latter could not perish, or the Prince, alerted by the decrease in his own revenue, would be spurred by the most pressing motives to put an end to the disorder that destroys the riches of his subjects and his own, and on the contrary to take the most efficacious measures to increase both.

Section 18

The community of interests between the Sovereign and the nation, manifestly established by the proportionate sharing of the net profit of the territory, is the surest guarantee that the laws of the natural order will be observed.

It is impossible that a Sovereign, convinced by arithmetic that he can increase his riches—and thus his power—only by the prosperity of his subjects, would not be exceedingly careful to be informed about everything that could increase the comfort and happiness of his people, as well as very diligent about preserving his people's free enjoyment of all their property rights.

Wherever a bad constitution makes this community of interests less visible, and where the guardians of public authority could or believed they could make money, at least for a while, independently from the Nation, public instruction about the natural laws—whose *observance* can alone ensure better conditions for princes and Peoples—would soon be neglected. One could even reach a point of finding few or even no Magistrates well informed about those laws. Everything would be abandoned to a torrent of prejudices, to the whims of opinion, to the ruses of a dark and arbitrary politics. One could forget what *property* and *liberty* mean. Riches would diminish because of this fatal lapse of memory. Ruinous expedients could be considered part of the usual regime, momentarily concealing from the Sovereign the degradation they contributed, leading society to weakness and ruin, and Government to poverty and impotence—all this long before it realized how necessary it was to bring an effective remedy to a disorder so fatal to itself and to the Nation.

Section 19

This community so necessary between the governing and the governed parts of the State, which puts the greatest interest of the Sovereign in the increase in the net profit of the lands subjected to his rule, and without which no nation may be said to have a constantly prosperous administration, shows us what form Sovereign authority must have, and in whose hands that authority may properly be entrusted. For any form of government that did not include that perfect and visible community of interests between those exercising Sovereign authority and those subjected to it, would evidently be a form forbidden by the laws of the natural order, the most profitable one possible for men gathered in society.

It is evident that a democratic Sovereign cannot exercise his authority by himself, and that he may only make use of it by appointing Commissioners and Representatives to exercise this authority. These representatives, charged with exercising the authority of a democratic Sovereign, are individuals whose functions are necessarily temporary. These *temporary* representatives cannot have a *perpetual* community of interests with the nation. These individuals have or at least may have exclusive private interests opposed to the *observance* of public order and the public interest. Their administration is thus not recommended by the natural order, and cannot strengthen the bonds of society through the union of the interest of the guardians of authority with that of the rest of the Nation.

The same can be said about an aristocratic Sovereign. The members composing it are also individuals who have lands and families, whose exclusive private interests can often be in opposition to the interests of other landlords subjected to their rule, and are thus naturally dearer to aristocrats than the interest of property-owners, which constitutes the public interest.

The same can be said about an elective Monarch. This Prince also has lands and a family that belong to him as an individual, that exist independent of his sovereignty, and that will remain after his sovereignty has passed. He thus has an exclusive private interest in using the power entrusted to him to improve and extend his domains, to enlarge and enrich his family. If this interest is opposed to that of the public revenue and the private incomes of the Nation, the prince will be exposed to perpetual temptations, which can often become ruinous.

It is not that great virtue and genius in an elective Monarch, in the aristocratic Sovereign, or in the Representatives of a democratic Sovereign—together with sufficient enlightenment in the nation about the rights of property and of liberty—cannot ensure for a while the prosperity of the societies subjected to these different forms of Government. But great genius and virtue are personal qualities that are not always transmitted from one Prince to his successor, and that are rarely extended to a great number of people at the same time. When supreme Administrators lack them in these imperfect Governments, they can be easily seduced by their exclusive private interest. In that case, the enlightenment of the Nation can seem fearsome to them. In that case, the nation necessarily becomes less enlightened than it should be, and than it would be if the current and visible interest of the guardians of authority was to extend and favor public instruction about the natural order. In that case, ignorance contributes to maintain dissension among interests, and to render it more dangerous.

Only with hereditary monarchs can personal and private, current and future interests be intimately, perceptibly, and manifestly linked to the interests of their Nations, by their co-ownership of all *net profits* of the territory subjected to their rule.

It is true that only this co-ownership can effect a perfect community of interests between a Monarch, even hereditary, and his People. For if this Monarch, instead of that joint ownership, had lands to exploit for supplying revenues for the public expenses, he could not perform the duties of a landlord on such a vast extent of land, and to support the revenue from them, he would have only the ruinous resource of favoring his lands to the detriment of those of his subjects. This domanial Monarch would be in a situation vis-à-vis his nation absolutely incompatible with the exercise of Sovereign authority.

But hereditary Monarchy presents the most perfect form of Government when it is combined with the implementation of the joint ownership of the public in the *net profit* of all landed capital, in such proportion that the treasury revenue is the greatest possible, while the situation of the landlords remains the best possible in society.

Section 20

A hereditary Monarch, associated with his Nation through the proportional sharing of the *net profit* of landed capital, has a visible interest in the *net profit* being the greatest possible.

He thus has a visible interest in the conditions necessary to the greatest possible net profit being completely fulfilled.

He has a visible interest in competition being as great as possible in all the operations contributing directly or indirectly to the formation of this net profit.

He has a visible interest in the liberty of any kind of trade, domestic or foreign, being complete.

He has a visible interest in the enjoyment of all rights of personal, movable, and landed property being assured.

He has a visible interest in the use of those rights being informed by the most enlightened, most extensive, most universal, and most strongly encouraged public instruction.

He has a visible interest that this general instruction about the *laws of the natural order* should form his Magistrates, whose knowledge and virtue he depends on to examine and decide according to these *laws* how his sovereign authority should be applied in specific cases to maintain property, on whose product his income is based.

He has a visible interest that these studious and skillful Magistrates compare the positive laws he is obliged to promulgate with the divine laws of the natural order, so as to warn him if some error detrimental to his revenue should escape him in his Ordinances. For even the positive laws that seem furthest removed from fiscal laws, cannot but concern the revenue of a co-proprietary Monarch.

They are necessarily either in conformity with or contrary to the natural laws; either favorable or harmful to property and to the liberty inseparable from it.

If they are in conformity with the laws of the natural order, and favorable to property and liberty, they motivate men to put the greatest activity into their work, by leaving the field open to the licit interest of everyone, and by assuring everyone that he will collect the fruits of his labor. They thus extend agriculture, multiply riches, increase the *net profit*, and as a result the revenue of the Sovereign that is proportioned to that *net profit*.

If they are contrary to the laws of order, and harmful to property and liberty, they throw discouragement into the hearts of men, by making them feel powerless and by encumbering their labors with complications. They restrict agriculture, diminish riches and the *net profit*, and thus the Sovereign's revenue.

As a result there is no positive Ordinance, of which one could not ask this question: *is the point to increase our harvests, to raise our children, and to increase the Prince's revenue, or is it to burn our harvests, stifle our offspring, and ruin the public Finances?*

The solution to that question, discussed to a point of manifestness by the Magistrates, will always remind a hereditary and co-proprietary Monarch of his true will. For one cannot envision a Sovereign or even a man who could want to harm others without profit, much less where there is a manifest loss for him and his descendants. This would assume a decision without a reason, an effect without a cause, or rather a decision contrary to reason, an effect contrary to its cause; this would assume a complete absurdity.

Section 21

Here then is a summary of all the social institutions founded on the natural order, on the physical constitution of men and of the other Beings in their midst.

Personal Property established by Nature, and by the physical necessity every individual is under to dispose of all his personal faculties to obtain the things appropriate to fulfill his needs, on pain of suffering or death.

The freedom to work, inseparable from personal property of which it constitutes a part.

Movable property, which is merely personal property itself, considered in its usage, its purpose, and its necessary extension to all the things acquired by personal work.

Freedom of exchange, of trade, of the use of one's wealth, inseparable from personal and movable property.

Agriculture, a use of personal property, movable property, and the liberty that is inseparable from both; a profitable and necessary use, essential for the growth of the population by the multiplication of the products necessary for men's subsistence.

Landed property, a necessary consequence of agriculture, which is merely the preservation of one's personal and movable property used for the preparatory work and expenses essential for ensuring the land is cultivable.

Freedom in the use of the land, in the type of farming, in all the conventions related to the exploitation, concession, retrocession, exchange, and sale of one's land, inseparable from landed property.

Natural division of the harvest into the *farmers' withholdings,* or riches whose use must serve to perpetuate agriculture, on pain of diminishing population and harvests; and *net profit,* or disposable wealth whose volume determines the prosperity of society, and whose use is left to the will and interests of the landowners, and which constitutes for them the legitimate and natural price of the expenses they incurred and the operations they undertook to ensure that the land would be cultivable.

Security, without which property and liberty would be merely rights and not facts, without which the *net profit* would soon be destroyed, without which agriculture itself could not survive.

Tutelary and sovereign Authority to procure the security absolutely necessary for property and liberty. It fulfills this important function by promulgating and executing the laws of the natural order, so that property and liberty may be well established.

Magistrates, for deciding how the laws of the natural order must be applied in particular cases, as they are reduced to positive laws by the sovereign authority. They also have the imperious duty of comparing the Ordinances of Sovereigns with the laws of essential justice, before venturing to take these positive Ordinances as the standard of their judgments.

Public Instruction favored so that the citizens, sovereign authority, and the Magistrates never lose sight of the invariable laws of the natural order, and are never misled by the prestige of opinion, or by the attractions of exclusive private interests that, once they become *exclusive,* are always misunderstood.

Public revenue, to constitute the strength and power necessary to Sovereign authority, to cover the expenses of its protective ministry, of the important functions of the Magistrates, and of the public instruction essential to the laws of the natural order.

Direct Taxes, or rather the sharing of the net profit of the territory between the landowners and the Sovereign authority, so that public revenue is formed in such a way that it does not restrain property or liberty, and thus is not destructive.

Essential and necessary proportion of direct tax to the net profit, so that it provides to society the greatest possible public revenue, and thus the greatest possible degree of security, while still ensuring that the fate of the landowners remains the best available in the society.

Hereditary Monarchy, to ensure that all the current and future interests of the depository of sovereign authority be intimately linked with those of society through the proportional sharing of the *net profit.*

SUCH IS THE SUMMARY of that doctrine, which, following the Nature of man, exposes the laws necessary to a Government made for man, and appropriate for man in all climates and countries—a Government that has survived for four thousand years in China under the Tropic of Cancer, and which the genius of a Great Empress[8] is going to establish for the happiness of her subjects in the midst of the Northern ice; a Government that is manifestly most advantageous for Peoples, since it assures them the full and complete enjoyment of all their natural rights, and the greatest possible abundance in the things appropriate for their needs; and manifestly most advantageous to Kings, since it provides them with the greatest possible wealth and authority.

It is only in such a simple and natural Government that Sovereigns are

---

8. [The reference is to Catherine II (the Great) of Russia (r. 1762–96).]

truly *despots*,[9] that they can do everything they want for their own good, which is inseparably and manifestly linked to that of the nations they govern. To ask for more for them would be to harm and insult them. The privilege of hurting oneself belongs only to madmen, and dementia is not made for the Throne. If we assumed that madness could touch the Throne, it would hardly be harmful for the Sovereign unfortunate enough to suffer from it, or for his subjects, as long as Nations were sufficiently informed about the Laws of order, and as long as Magistrates were watched over by public evidence and thus obliged to be faithful to their duties toward the Prince and toward the People. And yet, the Sovereign who was co-proprietor of the net profit of an enlightened Empire governed by the laws of the natural order would be nonetheless a despot, as far as man can be; for when he wants to increase his revenue and his power, he is sure to find all the wills and all the forces of his subjects disposed to support him, and to hear them say to everyone: *Blessed be the Prince who wants to increase our wealth and our income.*

A government which harmonizes so perfectly the interests of all men, which guarantees so well all their reciprocal rights and duties, which leads them so necessarily to the procurement of the greatest satisfactions of which they are capable, is manifestly the best Government one can imagine—the Government prescribed to men by the natural order.

Could it be believed, however, that, despite the manifestness of the Sovereign truths that we have tried to expose and follow here, and that

---

9. The word *despot* refers, as is shown by its etymology, to the person *who disposes as he wills.* In applying it, as several famous Moderns have, to arbitrary Sovereigns, one has overlooked that the term implied a contradiction with the idea that one wanted to express; for these arbitrary Sovereigns, whom the vulgar ignorant believe to be *despots,* and who can be ignorant enough to believe it themselves, cannot nevertheless *dispose* of anything, or at least of very little. They are the servants of their servants, the slaves of the fleeting opinions of their people, the feeble playthings of their Soldiers. They can do almost nothing for their own good, or for the good of others. They can improve their servile and dangerous situation only by renouncing their so-called *despotism.* They are thus not true *despots.* To give them that title is to fail in the Metaphysics of language, and manifestly not to use the proper word. This error, although it escaped the attention of magnificent geniuses, is nonetheless an error. That is why we must alter our terminology now that a serious analysis and a scrupulous dissection of ideas make us feel the necessity of expressing ourselves more exactly.

reveal to us the laws of this *physiocratic* Government,[10] there are still men, still writers, and even writers who claim they have studied these truths, who nonetheless persist in asserting that God has not established a natural order that must serve as the standard for society? Or that if he has, it is not true that men can know that order and submit themselves to it? Or at least that if they could, it is not true that each of them should take the initiative in this direction? No, without doubt, this could not be believed, and posterity, which will not see their writings, will be surprised to learn that *I could name up to three of them.* They should be pitied, if they truly doubt that God has given laws to all beings; or if, compelled by experience to avow that we can know with certainty innumerable natural laws of scant importance to us, they nonetheless think that we can acquire no certain knowledge of those that are most crucial for our existence and happiness. They are to be pitied if they are truly unfortunate enough not to sense that man is a reasonable animal capable of being guided by his manifest interest. But if they spared no maneuvers to delay the progress of research on such important matters; if they diffused the most bitter hostility in their writings; if they burdened with odious accusations peaceful men who work with zeal for the sole purpose of contributing to the happiness of the human species; if they tried, though in vain, to cast suspicion—in the eyes of the administration—on virtuous citizens whose every wish and every study aims only at the glory of the Prince and the prosperity of the State, they should be pitied still more. The activity, the numerous efforts caused by a misunderstood pride, and by base private interests in opposition to manifestly useful truths, serve only to bury deeper and deeper those who abandon themselves to the mire of contempt and of public indignation.

---

10. [I.e., government by the laws of *physis*, or nature.]

34

Dialogues on the Grain Trade
1769

FOR A SUMMARY of Galiani's life, see the excerpt from *On Money* (chapter 21). The publication in 1770 of *Dialogues sur le commerce des bleds* (*Dialogues on the Grain Trade*) caused a firestorm; free-market friends cried betrayal, and one of them, *abbé* Morellet, attacked him in a lengthy 1770 pamphlet (censored until a change of government made possible its publication in 1774). Galiani pursued this polemic in a brief parody, *La bagarre*, which has been rediscovered only in the twentieth century.

In 1764, the French government passed an edict designed to assure the free export of grain. In the midst of an economic crisis in 1768, and a general controversy over the wisdom of the 1764 edict, Galiani's *Dialogues* was the most influential critique. The dialogue involves three characters. The Marquis is a socially well-connected conformist proud of having read all the latest and most fashionable writings—mostly by the Physiocrats—on economic policy. The Knight (Chevalier) was a well-traveled gentleman who had been away from Paris since 1764 and who prided himself on having read none of the Physiocrats' writings, and on resting his economic judgments upon his travels and observations alone. He certainly represents the views of the author. The President, who enters the conversation midway through the work, serves as a foil who facilitates the conversation.

The present excerpt from the seventh of the eight dialogues was chosen because it provides both a convenient summary of the core discussion up to that point and a sample of the distinctive narrative and rhetorical style of the author. The translation is based on the 1770 London edition of *Dialogues sur le commerce des bleds,* pp. 200–212. All notes are by the present editor.

———

Dialogues on the Grain Trade

The Marquis

And what were we supposed to do to encourage agriculture and make it flourish?

The Knight

Oh, you want to know too many things at the same time. Let us continue . . .

The Marquis

You want to continue, and I am stopping you. I still feel sore about this bet you unfairly won, and I am asking for revenge. I want to bet.

The Knight

On what?

The Marquis

Listen carefully. This time I am definitely betting that you are against the [free] export [of grain]; that you agree with me on the fact that we must withdraw the Edict [of 1764],[1] and go back to our former situation—as I told you when you trapped me with a comparison that was pleasing but had nothing to do with what we were saying.

1. [The Royal Edict of July 19, 1764, went far toward explicitly guaranteeing the free export of grain, though the Physiocrats sometimes claimed that it did not go far enough; see "Lettre de M. Le Trosne, Avocat du Roi à Orléans, sur la nécessité de l'entière liberté du commerce des grains," in *Ephémérides du citoyen,* vol. 4 (Nov. 1767).]

The Knight
Will you bet a lot?

The Marquis
Everything you'd like! One scruple stops me, though, and it is that I am betting for real; I can read it in your eyes.

The Knight
And will the President bet as well?

The President
I would be tempted.

The Knight
On what grounds?

The President
Here they are: You have proven to us that we must not let France export grain other than the real surplus of an ordinary year. You have then proven to us that it was very doubtful that this surplus existed, and that nobody knew about it or could have known about it until now. And you ended up concluding that it would be better that way, because the purpose of any good government must be the increase in a population that would consume all the harvest, and not the increase in the latter's departure to foreign countries. After setting up that purpose, you left us uncertain about the choice of means. But you had us consider [several facts].

First, the weight and volume of grain, in increasing transportation costs, decreases the profit in trade. Second, the difficulty of preservation in transit increases the losses and risks even more. Third, the same problem remains if it is kept in storage, which obliges the trader either to suffer waste, or to sell hastily, and thus miss opportunities to sell at a high price. Fourth, one always encounters the most adverse season when the grain must necessarily be sold without being able to wait for the good season. Fifth, it [the grain trade] is neither the treasure nor the wealth of any country in particular; as it comes from everywhere, and may run out everywhere, this trade—always vague, uncertain, fortuitous, and short-lived—is not fixed in regular channels or subject to a steady and continuous turnover; so that this trade—which is not as quiet as others—looks more like looting than like an honest trade. Sixth, since it is abandoned by most merchants, whether from lack of means or of courage, it is automatically reduced to a monopoly, if one wants to trade wholesale with foreign countries. On the contrary, the domestic retail trade in grain is teeming with cleverness, fraud, and petty cheating. Its technical details, swallowing honest gains, force one into illicit conduct. Seventh, grain purchases under current conditions are impracticable, and in general, it is almost impossible to effect them without arousing complaints and disturbing whole provinces. There are no human means to balance, on the one hand, the secret of extraordinary commissions that must be maintained with salesmen, and on the other, the necessity not to let ordinary supplies run out or become expensive on a market that has just been caught off guard, as it were. Eighth, if purchasing is tedious, the internal turnover is even longer, more inconvenient, tangled in detail, and exceedingly prone to loss and waste. So many intermediaries harm the true usefulness of trade, which should only aim at enriching and encouraging the productive class. The number of hazards—as it increases proportionally to the number of different hands that handle this trade—raises the price by at least a third above ordinary cost. Finally, because the innumerable methods that are required to transform grain into bread prevent the farmer from selling it directly to the consumer, they leave him with only a very meager benefit from high prices. Therefore, in conclusion, it must be said that, if bread is the object ranked first among the needs of men, it is ranked last as far as commercial profit is concerned. If it is the dearest to the administration, it is the most unrewarding, the most often treacherous and costly for the trader; it is the most indispensable, but also the least reliable way for each state to become rich when it sells to its neighbors. The current condition of all purely agricultural nations, which you have described for us, is striking proof. According to the very coherent chain of reflections you have just presented to us— and I must confess that most of them were new to me—what other conclusion would you draw, except that we must completely abandon the system of export adopted by the economists?[2]

The Knight

But will you bet?

The President

I am not bold enough for that.

The Knight

And you are right, because you would have lost. Marquis, it pains me to say so, but to tell you the truth—and this will be my final word—I am in favor of free export.

The Marquis

You mean against, don't you?

The Knight

I am in favor, not against.

The Marquis

You are pulling our leg as usual. This can't be possible.

The Knight

It is just as I tell you, though.

The Marquis

But on what grounds?

The Knight

Before sharing them with you, I want to tell you a little story.

2. ["Economists" was at that time a synonym for the Physiocrats, such as Quesnay and Mirabeau. For an introduction to their doctrine, see the essay by Du Pont de Nemours, chapter 33 of this volume.]

The Marquis
You have good ones sometimes. Let's hear this one.

The Knight
A few years ago in Rome, there was a young Abbot, whom I knew well. His family was fairly rich, and his mother deeply wanted him to become a Prelate. So he was bought a prelacy, and as soon as he had taken holy orders, he was given a position as a magistrate in one of the courts of Rome, called the *Buon governo*. It is roughly like the Châtelet in Paris.[3] On the day he was to start his term of office, luck would have it that a case that had become famous because of quite extraordinary circumstances was about to come before the court. (It dealt with the validity of a will.) It was the talk of the town; people looked forward to the judgment of that Court. It was composed of only twelve Prelates. In serious cases, each Judge writes his opinion and reads it aloud; and it is customary in Rome to let the verdict of each Judge leak out; no one makes a mystery out of it as in other countries. Now you must know that our man was an idiot.

The Marquis
Who? The young Prelate?

The Knight
Yes, the young Prelate was still a fool, even though he was already a Prelate, and as a result, he did not want to look like it. He felt strongly that he had to shine in his début, that everybody would talk about his "voto," and that he had to make his reputation for insight and knowledge on this fortunate occasion. Therefore, without thinking twice (for he did not beat about the bush), he had a famous Lawyer, whom he strongly urged to give him something good, whatever the price might be, write a verdict for him. He wanted it to be well filled with quotations and extracts from Latin authors—and the best ones. The Lawyer, an honest man, did his best. Justinian, Gratian, the Gloss, Accursius, and

---

3. [I.e., a court of common civil and criminal pleas, of first instance.]

Cujas—every one of them was resorted to,[4] and it must be acknowledged that the opinion he received in writing was magnificent. It proved as clear as daylight that the will had to be quashed. On the very morning of that fateful judgment day, the Lawyer brought this writing to his Lordship, who received it with transports of enthusiasm, gratitude, and reward; he then perused the verdict two or three times to be able to read it smoothly, declaimed it a little in his bedroom, folded it, pocketed it, had his horses harnessed, and set off for the Palace, head held high. He felt in possession of something that would allow him to aspire to immortality. But one is never aware of everything, and one cannot avoid one's destiny. Unfortunately for him that day, he was not the first person to pronounce himself. Two Prelates were to speak before him, and both pronounced themselves in favor of the validity of the will. What a disaster! Faced with this unexpected blow, our man was in despair. The idea hit him that all the other Judges would pronounce themselves for the will, and that he would remain alone with his verdict. What shame! What ridicule! The whole town would say he was alone! This prospect made him blush, blanch, and tremble. He swore and cursed inwardly: "Damn, that treacherous Lawyer! He deceived me, tricked me, even though I paid him well. The rogue! He makes me stand out from the rest." He then realized what a drawback it was to have only one verdict. He said to himself: "Ah, how foolish of me! How much would it have cost me to order the two opposing verdicts so as to use them as occasion warranted? Just a little more money, what would it have mattered? When one's honor is at stake, one must know how to spend without stinting." But all his useless regrets fell on his afflicted heart, and he had no time left for anything; he had to accept it, the fateful hour of his reading was drawing closer. And yet what to do? What side to take? What is to become of him? He could very well say in a nutshell that he agreed with the Prelates who had preceded him; but the verdict, that lovely, costly verdict—what would become of it? Everyone would say that he had not

4. [The Eastern Roman Emperor Justinian I (r. 527–65) codified Roman Law in the Corpus Juris Civilis; Gratian was an Italian legal scholar whose *Decretum* (c. 1140) synthesized Church law; Francesco Accursius (1182–1260) was a Bolognese legal scholar who compiled a glossary of the whole body of law; Jacques Cujas (1522–90) was a French jurist and close student of the Corpus Juris Civilis.]

studied the case, that he had no verdict, and everyone would have it wrong, since he had it in his pocket. Finally despair gave him courage, and he bravely made up his mind; he took his paper out, read it loudly and clearly, with grace and dignity, without changing anything in it. The only thing was that, when he came to the solemn words of the conclusion, instead of saying, "I am for quashing the will," he said, "I am for the validity of the will." The Cardinal, who presided over the Court and suspected nothing, believed it was a misunderstanding, and said immediately: "Surely, my Lord, you are mistaken, you mean you are for quashing it." Our Prelate modestly replied: "I beg your pardon, your Honor, I am for the will." The Cardinal answered: "But how is that? You have just proven the contrary." Our man kept repeating: "It does not matter, your Honor, I am for the will. I agree with these gentlemen who were for it too." They all looked at one another, puzzled, scarcely daring to believe their ears. Everyone asked him questions in turn: Why? How? By what reasoning? He continued to answer to everyone that he was for the will. Finally, he let out a few barely articulate words, saying that he did not want to be the talk of the town for his lonesome opinion. His neighbor heard the words, understood the enigma, and discovered that in his own mind, he was unbelievably convinced that one had to have the same opinions as everyone else, just as one had to have the same clothes.

The Marquis

Ah, my good Sir, now I've got you. You knew you were greatly suspected of making up your stories on the spur of the moment; for this occasion I am convinced of it. Your story was too convenient. To tell you the truth, as soon as you uttered the words, "I am for [free] export," I said to myself: "What is that? Surely the Knight sees that he would be the only man of wit [*homme d'esprit*], the only man of good company who would be against free export, he is completely ashamed of being on his own, and he has decided to follow the crowd for fear of being anathematized."

The Knight

So you do not believe that I have more wit than that Prelate? Well, I assure you that the story is true, and that I told it to you on purpose, so as to forestall your suspicions. I will never be afraid to hold my opinions alone—even against the whole of nature. If, after distrusting my reasoning for a long time, I was firmly certain about my opinion, I would not fear to say it either, even at the risk of being deafened by the shouts that would rise against me. But the reason why I favor freedom of export is surely due neither to the smile of favor upon my conformity, nor to the pleasure of being ranked among the witty [*gens d'esprit*], admitted into good company by the sole title of exportationist. I have other reasons for committing myself to it.

The President, to the Knight

If the marquis wished to amuse himself and joke around for a little while, do not doubt that he saw as well as I that, even if you gave us innumerable reflections on the nature of grain which no one had deigned to ponder or penetrate, it is possible that you are in favor of [free] export for other reasons which have been either neglected or barely mentioned by the very people who defended it. Therefore, I would not be surprised if you combatted exportation with the same reasons that were used to recommend it, and then defended it with the opposite arguments. It would be quite a remarkable phenomenon, but I expect it.

The Marquis, to the President

The President is so kind as to ascribe to me intentions I do not have. I say and I persist in maintaining that the Knight claimed he was in favor of exportation solely to be like everybody else, or to exasperate us. Let him speak, and you will see whether I am right. Let us see why you have decided in favor of exportation.

The Knight

First, if the quantity of grain France produces is uncertain, there might be a real surplus that must be either exported or left to rot. Second, if the true purpose of government is population, and if that population is below what is possible in France, this gap will not be bridged for several generations. While waiting for this fortunate epoch, one must take the most sensible course of action for the moment. Legislation must always concern itself with the current situation, and never the future, because there is always time to modify the law when change occurs. Third, if the true wealth of a State must be expected from the progress of Manufactures,[5] there is a way to reconcile moderate, regulated exports with a low-paid labor force. Fourth, if grain is resistant to trade, as it were, because of its weight, delicacy, perishability, and difficulty of circulation in winter, it is, however, certain that a grain trade exists, and that it is the principal preoccupation of almost every poor and agrarian country. As far as France is concerned, it could be a source of profit which should not be neglected, even though one should not expect from it all the good it has been praised for. Fifth, if wholesale trade with foreign countries becomes a monopoly on its own, if retail trade evades the speculation of honest traders, if purchases are difficult and pressing, if the turnover is long, tedious, and full of hazards and waste, it is also true that art corrects Nature in almost everything, and that with time and care, it sometimes manages to completely conquer and tame her. Sixth, if the profits of trade and the value of grain remain almost entirely absorbed by hands that are less dear to the government than those of the Farmer, it is still more fitting that these profits should go into the hands of intermediaries rather than to nobody if the grain were left to rot in lofts. Seventh, finally, property and liberty are sacred rights of men; they are the first among our rights, they are part of us, they constitute our political essence as the body and soul constitute our physical one. Except for the links attaching us to society, nothing must disrupt them. Interests and harm done to third parties belong to the field of justice. The common interest and general harm belong to the field of politics. But when both powerful and demanding Goddesses were pacified, and when nothing hurt their feelings any more, when nothing concerned them, men then received their rights, they became free property owners again, and I know no other legitimate power on earth that could deprive them of these. Neither a Despot's whims on the one hand, nor a Metaphysician's speculations on the other, neither the demented screams of the crowd, nor the unfounded fears of a government that is unjust through weakness and arbitrary through timidity, have any legitimate right or valid excuse to meddle in our affairs.

5. [This had been the argument earlier in the work; see Dialogue Five, pp. 110–19.]

The Marquis

You see how right I was; the Knight agrees with everyone. I mean every true wit [*bel esprit*]. He says the same thing as all those wits, he speaks like them, and he has eventually come to use those high-flown words—property and liberty! This is the fundamental basis; this is what we must come to in the end!

The President

I beg your pardon, Marquis, but the Knight is far from agreeing with the Authors you have read. Do you see the exceptions he added to the rights to property and liberty?—The interest of a third party and the common interest. These exceptions are not as small as they seem to you. They can lead him very far. As for his reasons for adopting [free] export, I find him to be in no more agreement with anyone. He announces that exports will not produce those wonderful effects that were expected of them, but lesser ones. He claims that the profit will end up in other hands than those of the farmer. And finally, he wants art to correct everything that Nature opposes to the grain trade, and all the evil that manufactures would receive from an unlimited, ill-considered freedom of exportation. Nothing like that has been said, as far as I know. It was always firmly believed that all you needed was to pass an Edict for commerce, exports, and exchanges to run smoothly on their own, without complications or bad effects. It was even believed that no art, no rule, no precaution was necessary, and it was constantly maintained that agriculture was to be the foundation of national wealth, and that exportation was to be the basis of agriculture.

The Marquis

I was wrong, I concede. But by the way, my good Knight, how did the trial turn out for our Prelate?

The Knight

His misfortune was complete. All those who gave their verdicts after him agreed with his verdict, and disagreed with him. The will was quashed.

The Marquis

Ah, I am so glad for the sake of the Lawyer's honor. Now if I wanted to be mean, I would use your story to utter a prophecy concerning you, but I will not do it. I want to be kind and to keep still. I want to believe that you are genuinely convinced of the usefulness of free exportation as such. You will agree, however, that you cannot be greatly enthusiastic about this exportation, since you do not prefer the trade in foodstuffs over that of manufactures, and even in the grain trade, you maintained that the bulk of the profits will not end up in the farmer's hands.

35

"A Philosophical and Political History of the Settlements and Trade of the Europeans in the East and West Indies"

1770

GUILLAUME-THOMAS-FRANÇOIS, *abbé* Raynal, was born in 1713. After studying with and entering the Jesuit order, he became disaffected and left the order for Paris in 1747, becoming affiliated with St.-Sulpice parish. He was soon made editor of *Mercure de France*. His 1748 works on the Dutch Stadholderate and the English Parliament did much to make his reputation, and he was invited into the circles of government ministers and enlightened salon-goers, becoming a regular at the salons of Mme. Geoffrin, Helvétius, and Baron d'Holbach.

After writing numerous short works on history and European affairs, he finally brought out in 1770 his anonymous multivolume masterpiece *Histoire philosophique et politique, des établissements et du commerce des européens dans les deux Indes*. The work, said to have involved the collaboration of several other writers, including Diderot, caused a sensation and went through some thirty editions by 1789. It was put on the Index in 1774 and publicly burned. The book was found objectionable because of its treatment of religion and its advocacy of the popular right to consent to taxation and to revolt, among other things. Its sometimes incendiary treatment of the slave trade (Justamond ed., vol. 3, pp. 439–66) became canonical in the debate over abolition that it did much to spur. When an even more outspoken edition came out in 1781, the Parlement of Paris put out an *arrêt* against book and author, and Raynal was forced into exile. He traveled to Belgium, London, Germany, Prussia, and Switzerland, where he was mostly celebrated. Allowed to return to France but not to Paris in 1787, he was elected to the Third Estate for Marseilles in 1789, though he refused to serve because of his advanced age. In May of 1791, he made a famous written address to the National Assembly that was critical of revolutionary trends. Many angry pamphlets and caricatures followed, and he lost much of his property in 1793. He died in 1796.

The excerpt reprinted here, based on the second French edition of the *Histoire philosophique et politique,* is the author's general essay on commerce contained in book 19 of the English-language edition: *A Philosophical and political history of the settlements and trade of the Europeans in the East and West Indies,* translated by J. Justamond, 3rd ed. (London: Cadell, 1777), 5 vols., 5:492–511. Notes are by the present editor.

A Philosophical and Political History of the Settlements and Trade of the Europeans in the East and West Indies

If the art of navigation arose from fishing, as that of war did from the chace; the navy then owes its existence to commerce. The desire of gain first induced us to make voyages; and one world hath been conquered to enrich another. This object of conquest has been the foundation of commerce; in order to support commerce, naval forces have become necessary, which are themselves produced by the trading navigation. The Phenicians, situated on the borders of the sea at the confines of Asia and Africa, to receive and dispense all the riches of the ancient world, founded their colonies and built their cities, with no other view but that of commerce. At Tyre, they were the masters of the Mediterranean; at Carthage, they laid the foundations of a republic that traded by the ocean upon the richest of the European coasts.

The Greeks succeeded the Phenicians; as the Romans did the Carthaginians and the Greeks; they held the dominion of the sea as well as of the land; but they carried on no other kind of commerce, except that of conveying into Italy, for their own use, all the riches of Africa, Asia, and the conquered world. When Rome had invaded the whole world, and had lost all her acquisitions, commerce returned, as it were, to its original source towards the east. There it was established, while the Barbarians over-ran Europe. The empire was divided; the din of arms, and the art of war remained in the west; Italy however preserved its communication with the Levant, where all the treasures of India were circulated.

The Crusades exhausted in Asia all the rage of zeal and ambition, of war and fanaticism, with which the Europeans were possessed: but they were the cause of introducing into Europe a taste for Asiatic luxury; and redeemed by giving rise to some degree of traffic and industry, the blood and the lives they had cost. Three centuries taken up in wars and voyages to the east, gave to the restless spirit of Europe a recruit it stood in need of; that it might not perish by a kind of internal consumption: they prepared the way for that exertion of genius and activity, which since arose, and displayed itself in the conquest and trade of the West-Indies, and of America.

The Portuguese attempted by degrees to double the African coast. They successively seized upon all the points, and all the ports that must necessarily lead them to the Cape of Good Hope. They were engaged, for the space of fourscore years, in making themselves masters of all that western coast, where this great cape terminates. In 1497, Vasco de Gama surmounted this barrier; and returning by the eastern coast of Africa, arriving by a passage of twelve hundred leagues at the coast of Malabar, where all the treasures of the richest countries of Asia were to be circulated. This was the scene on which the Portuguese displayed all their conquests.

While this nation made itself master of the articles of trade, the Spaniards seized upon that which purchases them, the mines of gold and silver. These metals became not only a standard to regulate the value, but also the object of commerce. In this double use they soon engrossed all the rest. All nations were in want of them to facilitate the exchange of their commodities, and obtain the conveniencies they stood in need of. The luxury and the circulation of money in the south of Europe, changed the nature as well as the direction of commerce, at the same time that it extended its bounds.

But the two nations that had subdued the East and West Indies, neglected arts and agriculture. They imagined every thing was to be obtained by gold, without considering that it is labour alone that procures it: they were convinced, though late, and at their own expence, that the industry which they lost, was more valuable than the riches they acquired; and the Dutch taught them this severe instruction.

The Spaniards though possessed of all the gold in the world remained or became poor; the Dutch presently acquired riches, without either lands or mines. Holland is a nation at the service of all the rest, but who sells her services at a high price. As soon as she had taken refuge in the midst of the sea, with industry and freedom, which are her tutelary gods, she perceived that she had not a sufficient quantity of land to support the sixth part of her inhabitants. She then chose the whole world for her domain, and resolved to enjoy it by her navigation and commerce. She made all lands contribute to her subsistence; and all nations supply her with the conveniencies of life. Between the north and the south of Europe, she became what Flanders had been before, from which she had divided, in order to form an independent state entirely unconnected with it. Bruges and Antwerp had attracted Italy and Germany into their ports; Holland in her turn became the staple of all commercial powers, rich or poor. Not satisfied with inviting all other nations, she visited them herself, in order to procure from one what was wanted by another; to convey to the north, the merchandise of the south; to sell to the Spaniard ships for cargoes, and to exchange upon the Baltic wine for wood. She imitated the stewards and farmers of large estates, who by the immense profits they make in them, are enabled sooner or later to buy them up. Spain and Portugal have as it were been the cause that Holland has succeeded in taking from those powers part of their conquests in the East and West Indies, and almost the whole of the profit of their colonies. She availed herself of the indolence of these proud conquerors; and by her activity and vigilance, obtained the key of their treasures, leaving them nothing but the chest, which she took care to empty as fast as they replenished it. It is thus that a people of little refinement ruined two nations of polite and noble manners; but at the most honest and the most lawful game that can be met with in the several combinations of chance.

Every circumstance was favourable to the rise and progress of the commerce of this republic. Its position on the borders of the sea, at the mouths of several great rivers; its proximity to the most fertile or best cultivated lands of Europe; its natural connections with England and Germany, which defended it against France; the little extent and fertility of its own territory which obliged the inhabitants to become fishermen, sailors, brokers, bankers, carriers, and commissaries; in a word, to endeavour to live by industry for want of territory. Moral causes contributed with those of the climate and the soil, to establish and advance its prosperity. The liberty of its government, which opened an asylum to all strangers dissatisfied with their own; the freedom of its religion, which permitted a public and quiet profession of all other modes of worship; that is to say, the agreement of the voice of nature with that of conscience, of interests with duty; in a word, that toleration, that universal religion of all equitable and enlightened minds, friends to heaven and earth; to God, as to their father; to men, as to their brethren. In short, this commercial republic found out the secret of availing itself of all events, and of making even the calamities and vices of other nations concur in advancing its felicity. It turned to its own advantage the civil wars which fanaticism raised among people of a restless spirit, or which patriotism excited among a free people; it profited by the indolence and ignorance which bigotry supported among two nations who were under the influence of the imagination.

This spirit of industry in Holland, with which was intermixed a considerable share of that political art which sows the seeds of jealousy and discord among the nations, at length excited the attention of other powers. The English were the first to perceive that traffic might be carried on without the interposition of the Dutch. England, where the attempts of despotism had given birth to liberty, because they were antecedent to corruption and effeminacy, was desirous of obtaining riches by labour which alleviate the burden of it. The English first considered commerce as the proper science and support of an enlightened, powerful and even a virtuous people. They considered it rather as an improvement of industry than an acquisition of enjoyments; rather as an encouragement and a source of activity among the people, than a promoter of luxury and magnificence. Invited to trade by their situation, this became the spirit of their government, and the means of their ambition. All their schemes tended to this great object. In other monarchies, trade is carried on by the common people; in this happy constitution by the state or the whole nation: she carries it on indeed with a constant desire of dominion, which implies that of enslaving other people, but by means, at least, that constitute the happiness of the world before it is subdued. By war, the conqueror is little happier than the conquered; because injuries and massacres are their mutual object: but by commerce, the conquering people necessarily introduce industry into the country, which they would not have subdued if it had been already industrious, or which they would not maintain, if they had not brought industry in along with them. Upon these principles England had founded her commerce and her empire, and mutually and alternately extended one by the other.

The French, situated under as favourable a sky, and upon as happy a soil, have for a long time flattered themselves with the idea that they had much to give to other nations, without being under a necessity of asking scarce any return. But Colbert[1] was sensible that in the fermentation Europe was in at this time, there would be an evident advantage for the culture and productions of a country that should employ those of the whole world. He opened manufactures for all the arts. The woollens, silks, dyes, embroideries, the gold and silver stuffs, were brought to so great a degree of refinement in luxury and taste in the hands of the French, that they were in great request among those nobles who were in possession of the greatest landed property. To increase the produce of the arts, it was necessary to procure the first materials, and these could only be supplied by direct commerce. The chances of navigation had given France some possessions in the new world, as they had to all the plunderers that had frequented the sea. The ambition of some individuals had formed

1. [Jean-Baptiste Colbert, Controller-general of France, 1661–83.]

colonies there, which had been at first supported and even aggrandized by the trade of the Dutch and the English. A national navy must necessarily restore to the mother country this natural connection with its colonists. The government, therefore, established its naval forces upon the strength of its commercial navigation. The nation would then necessarily make a double profit upon the materials and the workmanship of the manufactures. The French pursued for a long time this precarious and temporary object of commerce, with an activity and spirit of emulation which must have made them greatly surpass their rivals; and they still enjoy that superiority over other nations, in all those arts of luxury and ornament which procure riches to industry.

The natural volatility of the national character and its propensity to trifling pursuits, hath brought treasures to the state, by the taste that has fortunately prevailed for its fashions. Like to that light and delicate sex, which teaches and inspires us with a taste for dress, the French reign in all courts, at least, by the toilet; and their art of pleasing is one of the mysterious sources of their fortune and power. Other nations have subdued the world by those simple and rustic manners, which constitute the virtues that are fit for war; to them it was given to reign over it by their vices. Their empire will continue, till they are degraded and enslaved by their masters by exertions of authority equally arbitrary and unlimited, when they will become contemptible in their own eyes. Then, they will lose, with their confidence in themselves, that industry, which is one of the sources of their opulence and of the springs of their activity. They will soon have neither manufactures, colonies nor trade.

This taste for luxury and ease hath given rise to a new principle of the moral world, which hath insinuated itself by degrees, till it is become, as it were, necessary to the existence of political bodies: it hath produced the love of labour, which at present constitutes the chief strength of a state. The sedentary occupations of the mechanic arts indeed, render men more liable to be affected by the injuries of the seasons, less fit to be exposed to the open air which is the first nutritive principle of life. But still, it is better that the human race should be enervated under the roofs of the workshops, than inured to hardships under tents; because war destroys, while commerce on the contrary gives new life to every thing. By this useful revolution in manners, the general maxims of politics have altered the face of Europe. It is no longer a people immersed in poverty that becomes formidable to a rich nation. Power is at present an attendant on riches, because they are no longer the fruit of conquest, but the produce of constant labour, and of a life spent in perpetual employment. Gold and silver corrupt only those indolent minds which indulge in the delights of luxury, upon that stage of intrigue and meanness, that is called greatness. But these metals employ the hands and arms of the people; they excite a spirit of agriculture in the fields; of navigation in the maritime cities; and in the center of the state they lead to the manufacturing of arms, cloathing, furniture, and the construction of buildings. A spirit of emulation exists between man and nature; they are perpetually improving each other. The people are formed and fashioned by the arts they profess. If there are some occupations which soften and degrade the human race, there are others by which it is hardened and repaired. If it be true that art renders them unnatural, they do not, at least, propagate in order to destroy themselves, as among the barbarous nations in heroic times. It is certainly an easy, as well as a captivating subject, to describe the Romans with the single art of war, subduing all the other arts, all other nations indolent or commercial, civilized or savage; breaking or despising the vases of Corinth, more happy with their gods made of clay, than with the golden statues of their worthless emperors. But it is a more pleasing, and perhaps, a nobler sight, to behold all Europe peopled with laborious nations, who are continually sailing round the globe, in order to cultivate and render it fit for mankind; to see them animate by the enlivening breath of industry, all the regenerating powers of nature; seek in the abyss of the ocean, and in the bowels of rocks, for new means of subsistence, or new enjoyments; stir and raise up the earth with all the mechanic powers invented by genius; establish between the two hemispheres by the happy improvements in the art of navigation, a communication of flying bridges, as it were, that re-unite one continent to the other; pursue all the tracks of the sun, overcome its annual barriers, and pass from the tropics to the poles upon the wings of the wind; in a word to see them open all the streams of population and pleasure, in order to pour them upon the face of the earth through a thousand channels. It is then, perhaps, that the divinity contemplates his work with satisfaction, and does not repent himself of having made man.

Such is the image of commerce; let us now admire the genius of the merchant. The same understanding that Newton had to calculate the motion of the stars, he exerts in tracing the progress of the commercial people that fertilize the earth. His problems are the more difficult to resolve, as the circumstances of them are not taken from the immutable laws of nature, as the systems of the geometrician are; but depend upon the caprices of men, and the uncertainty of a thousand events. That accurate spirit of combination that Cromwell and Richelieu[2] must have had, the one to destroy, the other, to establish despotic government, the merchant also possesses and carries it further: for he takes in both worlds at one view, and directs his operations upon an infinite variety of relative considerations, which it is seldom given to the statesman, or even to the philosopher, to comprehend and estimate. Nothing must escape him; he must foresee the influence of the seasons, upon the plenty, the scarcity, and the quality of provisions; upon the departure or return of his ships; the influence of political affairs upon those of commerce; the changes which war or peace must necessarily occasion in the prices and demands for merchandise, in the quantity and choice of provisions, in the state of the cities and ports of the whole world; he must know the consequences that an alliance of the two northern nations may have under the torrid zone; the progress, either towards aggrandizement or decay, of the several trading companies; the effect that the fall of any European power in India, may have over Africa and America; the stagnation that may be produced in certain countries, by the blocking up of some channels of industry; the reciprocal connection there is between most branches of trade, and the mutual assistances they lend by the temporary injuries they seem to inflict upon each other; he must know the proper time to begin, and when to stop in every new undertaking: in a word, he must be acquainted with the art of making all other nations tributary to his own, and of increasing his own fortune by increasing the prosperity of his country; or rather he must know how to enrich himself by extending the

2. [Oliver Cromwell (1599–1658), Lord Protector of the Commonwealth after the execution of Charles I in 1649. Armand Jean Du Plessis, Cardinal Richelieu (1585–1642), was chief minister (1624–42) in the government of Louis XIII.]

general prosperity of mankind. Such are the objects that the profession of the merchant engages him to attend to.

It is also the trader's peculiar business to search into the recesses of the human heart, and to treat with his equals apparently, as if they were honest, but, in reality, as if they were men of no probity. Commerce is a science that equally requires the knowledge of men and of things. Its difficulty arises undoubtedly less from the variety of objects about which it is conversant, than from the avidity of those who are engaged in it. If emulation increases the concurrence of efforts, jealousy prevents their success. If interest is the vice that destroys professions in general, what must be its effects upon that in particular to which it owes its existence? The avidity with which it is carried on is the cause of its destruction. The thirst of gain spreads over commerce a spirit of avarice that lays a restraint upon every thing, even the means of amassing.

Is that competition between different governments which induces them to restrain general industry by mutual prohibitions, to be ascribed to the merchant; or to that tyrannical exertion of authority, which in order to acquire riches without the assistance of commerce, lays a restraint on all branches of industry by subjecting them to corporations? Certainly on the latter; for all these societies[3] destroy the very spirit of commerce, which is liberty. To compel the indigent man to pay for the privilege of working, is to condemn him at once to idleness by the indigence he is reduced to, and to become indigent through idleness; it is to diminish the sum total of national labour; to impoverish the people by enriching the state; and to destroy them both.

The jealousy of trade between states is only a secret conspiracy to ruin each other, without any particular benefit to any one. Those who govern the people, exert the same skill in guarding against the industry of the nations, as in preserving themselves from the intrigues of the great. One individual alone, who is mean and destitute of every principle, is able to introduce a hundred restraints into Europe. New chains are contrived with as much expedition as destructive weapons. Prohibitions in

---

3. ["Corporations" and "societies" refer to the system of privileged guilds and merchant companies then prevalent in many parts of Europe.]

commerce, and extortions in the finance, have given rise to smugglers and galley slaves, to customs and monopolies, to pirates and excisemen. Centinels[4] and obstacles are placed in every part of the sea and of the land. The traveller enjoys no repose, the merchant no property; both are equally exposed to all the artifices of an insidious legislation, that gives rise to crimes by its prohibitions, and to penalties by crimes. They become culpable without knowing it, or without design: they are arrested, plundered and taxed, though innocent. The rights of the people are violated by their protectors; and those of the citizen by himself: the courtier is constantly endeavouring to disquiet the statesman; and the contractor oppresses the merchant. Such is the state of commerce in time of peace. But what shall we say of commercial wars?

It is natural enough, for a people pent up in the icy regions of the north, to dig out iron from the bowels of the earth that refuses them subsistence; and to reap the harvest of another nation by force of arms: hunger, which is restrained by no laws, cannot violate any, and seems to plead an excuse for these hostilities. Men must necessarily live by plunder, when they have no corn. But, when a nation enjoys the privilege of an extensive commerce, and can supply several other states from its superfluity; what motive can induce it to declare war against other industrious nations; to obstruct their navigation and their labours; in a word, to forbid them to live on pain of death? Why does it arrogate to itself an exclusive branch of trade, a right of fishing and sailing, as if it were a matter of property, and as if the sea were to be divided into acres as well as the land? The motives of such wars are easily discovered: we know that the jealousy of commerce is nothing more than a jealousy of power. But have any people a right to obstruct a work they cannot execute themselves, and to condemn another nation to indolence, because they themselves chuse to be entirely given up to it?

How unnatural and contradictory an expression is a war of commerce! Commerce is the source and means of subsistence; war of destruction. Commerce may, possibly, give rise to war, and continue it; but war puts a stop to every branch of commerce. Whatever advantage one nation may derive from another in trade, becomes a motive of industry and em-

---

4. [Sentinels.]

ulation to both: in war, on the contrary, the injury affects both; for plunder, fire and sword can neither improve lands, nor enrich mankind. The wars of commerce are so much the more fatal, as by the present superiority of the maritime powers over those of the continent, and of Europe over the three other parts of the world, the conflagration becomes general; and that the dissentions of two maritime powers excite the spirit of discord among all their allies, and occasion inactivity even among the neutral powers.

Coasts and seas stained with blood and covered with dead bodies; the horrors of war extending from pole to pole, between Africa, Asia and America, as well throughout the sea that separates us from the new world, as throughout the vast extent of the pacific ocean: such has been the spectacle exhibited in the two last wars, in which all the powers of Europe have been alternately shaken, or have distinguished themselves by some remarkable exertion.[5] The earth, however, was depopulated, and commerce did not supply the losses it had sustained; the lands were exhausted by taxes, and the channels of navigation did not assist the progress of agriculture. The loans of the state previously ruined the fortunes of the citizens by usurious profits, the forerunners of bankruptcy. Even those powers that were victorious oppressed by the conquests they had made, and having acquired a greater extent of land than they could keep or cultivate, were involved in the ruin of their enemies. The neutral powers who were desirous of enriching themselves in peace, in the midst of this commotion were exposed and tamely submitted to insults more disgraceful than the defeats of an open war.

How highly impolitic are those commercial wars, equally injurious to all the nations concerned, without being advantageous to such as are not engaged in them; those wars where the sailors become soldiers, and the merchant ships are turned into privateers; where the traffic between the mother countries and their colonies is interrupted, and the price of their reciprocal commodities is raised!

What a source of political abuses arises from those treaties of commerce which are productive of war! Those exclusive privileges which one

5. [Probably refers to the War of the Austrian Succession (1740–48) and the Seven Years War (1756–63).]

nation acquires from another, either for a traffic of luxury, or for the necessaries of life! A general freedom granted to industry and commerce is the only treaty which a maritime power should enforce at home, or negociate abroad. Such a conduct would make the people who pursued it be considered as the benefactors of the human race. The more labour was encouraged upon land, and the greater number of ships there were at sea, so much the more important to them would be the advantages they pursue and obtain by negociations and by war. For there will be no increase of riches in any country, if there be no industry among its neighbours, who can acquire nothing but by articles of exchange, or by the means of gold and silver. But without commerce and industry neither metals, nor manufactures of value can be obtained; nor can either of these sources of riches exist without liberty. The indolence of one nation is prejudicial to all the rest, either by increasing their labour, or by depriving them of what it ought to produce. The effect of the present system of commerce and industry is the total subversion of order.

The want of the fine fleeces of Spain is retrieved by the flocks of England, and the silk manufactures of Italy are carried on even in Germany; the wines of Portugal might be improved, were it not for the exclusive privileges granted to a particular company. The mountains of the north and south would be sufficient to supply Europe with wood and metals, and the vallies would produce a greater plenty of corn and fruits. Manufactures would be raised in barren countries, if these could be supplied with plenty of the necessaries of life by a free circulation. Whole provinces would not be left uncultivated in the heart of a country in order to fertilize some unwholesome morasses, where, while the people are supported by the productions of the land, the influence of the air and the water tends to their destruction. We should not see all the rich produce of commerce confined to particular cities of a large kingdom,[6] as the privileges and fortunes of the whole people are to particular families. Circulation would be quicker, and the consumption increased. Each province would cultivate its favourite production, and each family its own little field: and under every roof there would be one child to spare

---

6. [The reference is probably to France, which was frequently criticized by contemporaries for its uneven prosperity.]

for the purposes of navigation and the improvement of the arts. Europe, like China, would swarm with multitudes of industrious people.—Upon the whole, the freedom of trade would insensibly produce that universal peace which a brave but humane monarch once considered not as merely chimerical. The system of the happiness of nations arising from the improvement of reason would be founded on a turn for calculation and the spirit of oeconomy, which would prove a more effectual security of morals, than the visionary ideas of superstition. These presently disappear as soon as passions exert themselves, while reason gains strength and advances to maturity along with them.

36

On the Origin of the
Distinction of Ranks

1771

JOHN MILLAR of Glasgow, the son of a Scotch Presbyterian minister, was born in 1735. He grew up with his uncle on a small family estate near Glasgow after 1737. There, he studied with Adam Smith, among others, when Smith was teaching moral philosophy. Though intended for the ministry, he had doubts about the profession of faith and instead pursued the law. He served as tutor to the son of Lord Kames and came to know David Hume, whose metaphysical system he admired. He became an advocate in 1760 but abruptly changed course the next year by accepting for family reasons (he had just married) a less lucrative though more secure professorship of law at Glasgow, a post for which he was recommended by Smith and Kames. He soon had large followings of students in civil law and in jurisprudence. He also lectured on Scottish law, English law, and government. He and his wife, who had eleven children, also took in student boarders. He became a member of the Literary Society of Glasgow, where he defended Hume's theories against those of his friend and faculty colleague Thomas Reid. He outspokenly defended Whiggish causes such as parliamentary reform, abolitionism, and American independence, and was a member of the Society of the Friends of the People. He was sympathetic to the French Revolution and opposed war against France.

His main works, based on his lectures, were *On the Origin of the Dis-*

tinction of Ranks (1771), which was influenced by Montesquieu, Hume, and Smith, and was translated in his lifetime into French and German; and *Historical View of the English Government* (1787), a Whiggish history dedicated to Fox. He died in 1801.

The present excerpts are taken from the third edition (1779) of *On the Origin of the Distinction of Ranks* (originally published in 1771 as *Observations Concerning the Distinction of Ranks in Society*), in *John Millar of Glasgow (1735–1801)*, ed. William C. Lehmann (London: Cambridge University Press, 1960), chapter 1, section 6, "The effects of great opulence, and the culture of the elegant arts, upon the relative condition of the sexes," pp. 224–28, and chapter 2, section 2, "The influence of the improvement of arts upon the jurisdiction of the father," pp. 238–43, and are reprinted with the permission of Cambridge University Press. These excerpts were chosen because they apply a distinctively Scottish historical method to an understanding of the condition of women in commercial society. Unbracketed notes are by Millar; notes in brackets are by the Cambridge editor.

On the Origin of the Distinction of Ranks

The effects of great opulence, and the culture of the elegant arts, upon the relative condition of the sexes

The progressive improvements of a country are still attended with farther variations in the sentiments and manners of the inhabitants.

The first attention of a people is directed to the acquisition of the mere necessaries of life, and to the exercise of those occupations which are most immediately requisite for subsistence. According as they are successful in these pursuits, they feel a gradual increase of their wants, and are excited with fresh vigour and activity to search for the means of supplying them. The advancement of the more useful arts is followed by the cultivation of those which are subservient to pleasure and entertainment. Mankind, in proportion to the progress they have made in multiplying the conveniences of their situation, become more refined in their taste, and luxurious in their manner of living. Exempted from labour, and placed in great affluence, they endeavour to improve their enjoyments, and become addicted° to all those amusements and diversions which give an exercise to their minds, and relieve them from languor and weariness, the effects of idleness and dissipation. In such a state, the pleasures which nature has grafted upon the love between the sexes, become the source of an elegant correspondence, and are likely to have a general influence upon the commerce of society. Women of condition come to be more universally admired and courted upon account of the agreeable qualities which they possess, and upon account of the amusement which their conversation affords. They are encouraged to quit that retirement which was formerly esteemed so suitable to their character, to enlarge the sphere of their acquaintance, and to appear in mixed company, and in public meetings of pleasure. They lay aside the spindle and the distaff, and engage in other employments more agreeable to the fashion. As they are introduced more into public life, they are led to cultivate those talents which are adapted to the intercourse of the world, and to distinguish themselves by polite accomplishments that tend to heighten their personal attractions, and to excite those peculiar sentiments and passions of which they are the natural objects.

These improvements, in the state and accomplishments of the women, might be illustrated from a view of the manners in the different nations of Europe. They have been carried to the greatest height in France, and in some parts of Italy, where the fine arts have received the highest cultivation, and where a taste for refined and elegant amusement has been generally diffused. The same improvements have made their way into England and Germany; though the attention of the people to the more necessary and useful arts, and their slow advancement in those which are subservient to entertainment, has, in these countries, prevented the intercourse of the sexes from being equally extended. Even in Spain, where, from the defects of administration, or from whatever causes, the arts have for a long time been almost entirely neglected, the same effects of refinement are at length beginning to appear, by the admission of the women to that freedom which they have in the other countries of Europe.

Thus we may observe, that in refined and polished nations there is the same free communication between the sexes as in the ages of rudeness and barbarism. In the latter, women enjoy the most unbounded liberty, because it is thought of no consequence what use they shall make of it. In the former, they are entitled to the same freedom, upon account of those agreeable qualities which they possess, and the rank and dignity which they hold as members of society.

It should seem, however, that there are certain limits beyond which it is impossible to push the real improvements arising from wealth and opulence. In a simple age, the free intercourse of the sexes is attended with no bad consequences; but in opulent and luxurious nations, it gives rise to licentious and dissolute manners, inconsistent with good order, and with the general interest of society. The love of pleasure, when carried to excess, is apt to weaken and destroy those passions which it endeavours to gratify, and to pervert those appetites which nature has bestowed upon mankind for the most beneficial purposes. The natural tendency, therefore, of great luxury and dissipation is to diminish the rank and dignity of the women, by preventing all refinement in their connection with the other sex, and rendering them only subservient to the purposes of animal enjoyment.

> Prima peregrinos obscena pecunia mores
> Intulit; et turpi fregerunt secula luxû
> Divitiae molles. Quid enim Venus ebria curat?

The voluptuousness of the Eastern nations, arising from a degree of advancement in the arts joined, perhaps, to the effect of their climate, and the facility with which they are able to procure subsistence, has introduced the practice of polygamy; by which the women are reduced into a state of slavery and confinement, and a great proportion of the inhabitants are employed in such offices as render them incapable of contributing, either to the population, or to the useful improvements of the country.[1]

---

1. What is here said with respect to polygamy is only applicable to that institution as it takes place among opulent and luxurious nations; for in barbarous countries, where it is introduced in a great measure from motives of conveniency, and where it is accompanied with little or no jealousy, it cannot have the same consequences.

The excessive opulence of Rome, about the end of the common-wealth, and after the establishment of the despotism, gave rise to a de-gree of debauchery of which we have no example in any other European nation. This did not introduce polygamy, which was repugnant to the regular and well established police of a former period; though Julius Cae-sar is said to have prepared a law by which the *emperor* should be allowed to have as many wives as he thought fit. But the luxury of the people, be-ing restrained in this way, came to be the more indulged in every other; and the common prostitution of the women was carried to a height that must have been extremely unfavourable to the multiplication of the spe-cies; while the liberty of divorce was so much extended and abused, that, among persons of condition, marriage became a very slight and transient connection.[2]

The frequency of divorce, among the Romans, was attended with bad consequences, which were felt in every part of their domestic economy. As the husband and wife had a separation constantly in view, they could repose little confidence in each other, but were continually occupied by separate considerations of interest. In such a situation, they were not likely to form a strong attachment, or to bestow much attention to the joint concerns of their family. So far otherwise, the practice of stealing

---

2. By the Roman law, about this period, divorces were granted upon any pretence whatever, and might be procured at the desire of either party. At the same time, the man-ners, which produced this law, disposed the people very frequently to lay hold of the priv-ilege which it gave them; in so much that we read of few Romans of rank who had not been once divorced, if not oftener. To mention only persons of the gravest and most re-spectable character: M. Brutus repudiated his wife Claudia, though there was no stain upon her reputation. Cicero put away his wife Terentia, after she had lived with him thirty years, and also his second wife Publilia, whom he had married in his old age. His daughter Tullia was repudiated by Dolabella. Terentia, after she was divorced from Ci-cero, is said to have had three successive husbands, the first of whom was Cicero's enemy, Sallust the historian. It was formerly mentioned that M. Cato, after his wife Marcia had brought him three children, gave her away to his friend Hortensius. Many of those tri-fling causes which gave rise to divorce are taken notice of by Valerius Maximus. Seneca declares that some women of illustrious rank were accustomed to reckon their years, not by the number of consuls, but of husbands. [De beneficiis.] As a further proof of the profligacy of that age, it is observed that men were sometimes induced to marry from the prospect merely of enriching themselves by the forfeiture of the wife's dower, when she committed adultery. Valerius Maximus, lib. 6, c. 3.

from each other, in expectation of a divorce, became so general that it was not branded with the name of theft, but, like other fashionable vices, received a softening appellation.[3]

The bad agreement between married persons, together with the common infidelity of the wife, had a natural tendency to alienate the affections of a father from his children, and led him, in many cases, not only to neglect their education, but even to deprive them of their paternal inheritance. This appears to have been one great cause of that propensity, discovered by the people, to convey their estates by *will;* which, from the many statutes that were made, and the equitable decisions of judges that were given, in order to rectify the abuse, has rendered that branch of the Roman law, relating to testaments, more extensive and complicated than any other. The frequency of such deeds, to the prejudice of the heirs at law, created swarms of those legacy-hunters,[4] whose trade, as we learn from Horace, afforded the most infallible means of growing rich; and the same circumstance gave also great encouragement to the forgery or falsification of *wills*, a species of fraud which is much taken notice of by the writers of those times, and which has been improperly regarded as one of the general effects of opulence and luxury.[5]

In those voluptuous ages of Rome, it should seem that the inhabitants were too much dissipated by pleasure to feel any violent passion for an individual, and the correspondence of the sexes was too undistinguishing to be attended with much delicacy of sentiment. It may accordingly be remarked, that the writers of the Augustan age, who have afforded so many models of composition in other branches, have left no work of

---

3. The action for the recovery of such stolen goods was not called *conditio furtiva,* but *actio rerum amotarum.*

4. *Heredipetae.*

5. "Do thou, O prophet, tell me forthwith how I may amass riches, and heaps of money. In troth I have told you and tell you again. Use your craft to lie at catch for the last wills of old men: and do not, if one or two cunning chaps escape by biting the bait off the hook, either lay aside hope, or quit the art, though disappointed in your aim."

[See the whole of the 5th Satire, B. 2 of Horace.]

[Bracket note in original. Selection, 1, 21–26. Literal prose translation C. Smart, ed.]

The Volpone, of Johnson, is entirely founded upon this part of ancient manners; but the ridicule of that performance is in a great measure lost, as the original from which it is drawn, and of which it is a faithful copy, has no place in any modern country.

imagination, describing the manners of their own countrymen, in which love is supposed to be productive of any tragical, or very serious effects. Neither that part of the Eneid which relates to the death of Dido, nor the love-epistles of Ovid, both of which are founded upon events in a remote age, and in distant countries, can properly be considered as exceptions to what is here alleged. It also merits attention that when the Roman poets have occasion to represent their own sentiments in this particular, the subject of their description, not to mention more irregular appetites, is either the love of a concubine, or an intrigue with a married woman. This is not less apparent from the grave and tender elegies of Tibullus and Propertius, than from the gay and more licentious writings of Horace, of Ovid, and of Catullus. The style of those compositions, and the manners from which it was derived, while they degraded the women of virtue, contributed, no doubt, to exalt the character of a kept-mistress. The different situation of modern nations, in this respect, is perhaps the reason why they have no term corresponding to that of *amica* in Latin.

The acquisition of great wealth, and the improvement of the elegant arts, together with the free intercourse of the sexes, have, in some of the modern European nations, had similar consequences to what they produced in ancient Rome, by introducing a strong disposition to pleasure. This is most especially remarkable in France and Italy, the countries in which opulence was first acquired, and in which the improvements of society are supposed to have made the greatest advances. But in these countries, the authority obtained by the clergy after the establishment of the Christian religion, and the notions which they endeavoured to inculcate with regard to abstinence from every sensual gratification, have concurred with the influence of the former usage and laws, not only to exclude polygamy, but in a great measure to prevent the dissolution of marriage by voluntary divorce. Many disorders, therefore, which were felt in the luxurious ages of Rome, have thus been avoided; and in modern Europe, the chief effect of debauchery, beside the encouragement given to common prostitution, has been to turn the attention, from the pursuits of business or ambition, to the amusements of gallantry; or rather to convert these last into a serious occupation.

It is not intended, however, in this discourse, to consider those variations, in the state of women, which arise from the civil or religious government of a people, or from such other causes as are peculiar to the inhabitants of different countries. The revolutions that I have mentioned, in the condition and manners of the sexes, are chiefly derived from the progress of mankind in the common arts of life, and therefore make a part in the general history of society.

The influence of the improvement of arts upon the jurisdiction of the father

Such was the power, in early times, possessed by the head of a family. But the gradual advancement of a people in civilized manners, and their subjection to regular government, have a natural tendency to limit and restrain this primitive jurisdiction. When different families are united in a larger society, the several members of which have an intimate correspondence with each other, it may be expected that the exercise of domestic authority will begin to excite the attention of the public. The near relations of a family, who have a concern for the welfare of the children, and who have an opportunity of observing the manner in which they are treated, will naturally interpose by their good offices, and endeavour to screen them from injustice and oppression. The abuses which, on some occasions, are known and represented with all their aggravating circumstances, will excite indignation and resentment, and will at length give rise to such regulations as are necessary for preventing the like disorders for the future.

Those improvements in the state of society, which are the common effects of opulence and refinement, will at the same time dispose the father to use his power with greater moderation. By living in affluence and security, he is more at leisure to exert the social affections, and to cultivate those arts which tend to soften and humanize the temper. Being often engaged in the business and conversation of the world, and finding, in many cases, the necessity of conforming to the humours of those with whom he converses, he becomes less impatient of contradiction, and less apt to give way to the irregular sallies of passion. His parental affection, though not perhaps more violent, becomes at least more steady and uniform; and while it prompts him to undergo the labour that may be requisite in providing for his family, it is not incompatible with that discretion which leads him to bear with the frowardness, the folly and imprudence of his children, and in his behaviour towards them, to avoid equally the excess of severity and of indulgence.

On the other hand, the progress of arts and manufactures will contribute to undermine and weaken his power, and even to raise the members of his family to a state of freedom and independence.

In those rude and simple periods when men are chiefly employed in hunting and fishing, in pasturing cattle, or in cultivating the ground, the children are commonly brought up in the house of their father; and continuing in his family as long as he lives, they have no occasion to acquire any separate property, but depend entirely for subsistence upon that hereditary estate, of which he is the sole disposer and manager. Their situation, however, in this, as well as in many other respects, is greatly altered by the introduction of commerce and manufactures. In a commercial country, a great part of the inhabitants are employed in such a manner as tends to disperse the members of a family, and often requires that they should live at a distance from one another.

The children, at an early period of life, are obliged to leave their home, in order to be instructed in those trades and professions by which it is proposed they should earn a livelihood, and afterwards to settle in those parts of the country which they find convenient for prosecuting their several employments. By this alteration of circumstances they are emancipated from their father's authority. They are put in a condition to procure a maintainance without having recourse to his bounty, and by their own labour and industry are frequently possessed of opulent fortunes. As they live in separate families of their own, of which they have the entire direction, and are placed at such a distance from their father, that he has no longer an opportunity of observing and controlling their behaviour, it is natural to suppose that their former habits will be gradually laid aside and forgotten.

When we examine the laws and customs of polished nations, they appear to coincide with the foregoing remarks, and leave no room to doubt that, in most countries, the paternal jurisdiction has been reduced within narrower bounds, in proportion to the ordinary improvements of society. The Romans, who for several centuries were constantly employed in war, and for that reason gave little attention to the arts of peace, discovered more attachment to their barbarous usages than perhaps any other nation that arose to wealth and splendour; and their ancient practice, with respect to the power of the father, was therefore permitted to remain in the most flourishing periods of their government. The alterations in this particular, which were at length found expedient, having, for the most part, occurred in times of light and knowledge, are recorded with some degree of accuracy, and as they mark the progress of a great people in an important branch of policy, may deserve to be particularly considered.

We know nothing with certainty concerning the attempts which, in a very remote period, are supposed to have been made for restraining the exposition of infants. By a law of Romulus, parents are said to have been obliged to maintain their male children, and the eldest female, unless where a child was, by two of the neighbours called for the purpose, declared to be a monster. A regulation of the same nature is mentioned among the laws of the twelve tables; but there is ground to believe that little regard was paid to it; and even under the emperors, the exposing of new-born children, of either sex, appears to have been exceedingly common.

The first effectual regulations in favour of children were those which bestowed upon them a privilege of acquiring property independent of their father. During the free government of Rome, as war was the chief employment in which a Roman citizen thought proper to engage, and by which he had any opportunity of gaining a fortune, it appeared highly reasonable, that when he hazarded his person in the service of his country, he should be allowed to reap the fruit of his labour, and be entitled to the full enjoyment of whatever he had acquired. With this view, it was enacted by Julius and by Augustus Caesar, that whatever was gained by a son, in the military profession, should be considered as his own estate, and that he should be at liberty to dispose of it at pleasure.[6]

Some time after, when the practice of the law had also become a

6. It was called "peculium castrense."

lucrative profession, it was further established, that whatever a son acquired in the exercise of this employment, should in like manner become his own property, and should in no respect belong to the father.[7]

In a later age, when no employment was considered as too mean for the subjects of the Roman empire, the son became proprietor of what he could procure by the practice of the mechanical arts, and of whatever he obtained by donations, or by succession to his mother or maternal relations; though the *usufruct* of those acquisitions was, in ordinary cases, bestowed upon the father.[8]

It is uncertain at what time the Romans first began to limit the father in the power of selling his children for slaves. It appears, that before the reign of the emperor Dioclesian this privilege was entirely abolished, except in a singular case, in which it remained to the latest periods of the empire. To remove the temptation of abandoning new-born children, a permission was given to sell them, but with provision that they might, at any time after, be redeemed from the purchaser, by restoring the price which he had paid.

Exclusive of infants, the power over the life of children was first subjected to any limitation in the reign of Trajan, and of Hadrian his successor, who interposed, in some particular cases, to punish the wanton exercise of paternal authority. In the time of the emperor Severus, the father was not allowed to put his children to death in private, but when they committed a crime of an atrocious nature, was directed to accuse them before a magistrate, to whom he was impowered, in that case, to prescribe the particular punishment which he chose to have inflicted. At length this part of his jurisdiction was finally abolished by the emperor Constantine, who ordained that if a father took away the life of his child he should be deemed guilty of parricide.

These were the principal steps by which the Romans endeavoured to correct this remarkable part of their ancient law. It was natural to begin with the reformation of those particulars in which the greatest abuses

---

7. Peculium quasi castrense.

8. The subject so acquired was called *peculium adventitium.* Constantine made the first regulations concerning it, which were extended by his successors, especially by the emperor Justinian. Vid. Tit. Cod. de bon. matern.—Tit. de bon. quae lib.

were committed, and thence to proceed to others, which, however absurd in appearance, were less severely felt, and less productive of disorder and oppression. It seldom happened that a father, though permitted by law, was so hardened to the feelings of humanity and natural affection, as to be capable of imbruing his hands in the blood of a child whom he had brought up in his family; and accordingly no more than three or four instances of that nature are mentioned in the whole Roman history. He might oftener be tempted to neglect his children immediately after their birth, or be reconciled to the measure of reaping a certain profit at the expense of their freedom. But the part of his prerogative which he would probably exert in the most arbitrary manner, was that which related to the maintenance of his family, and the management of that property which had been procured by their industry and labour. Thus we find that, beside the early and ineffectual attempts to prevent the neglect of infants, the interpositions of the Roman legislature were directed first to secure the property, afterwards the liberty, and last of all the life and personal safety of the children.[9]

Upon comparing the manners of different countries, with regard to the subject of our present inquiry, it will be found that wherever polygamy is established, the authority enjoyed by the head of every family is usually carried to a greater height, and is more apt to remain in its full force, notwithstanding the improvements which, in other respects, the people may have attained. By the institution of polygamy, the children belonging to a person of opulent fortune, are commonly rendered so numerous as greatly to diminish the influence of paternal affection: not to mention that the confinement of his wives, and the jealousy, hatred, and dissension, which prevail among them, are productive of such intrigues to supplant or destroy one another, and to promote the interest of their respective children, that the husband, in order to repress these disorders, finds it necessary to preserve a strict discipline in his family, and to hold all its members in extreme subjection. This will suggest a reason for what is observed by Aristotle, that among the Persians, in his time, the power of a father over his children was no less absolute as that of a master over his slaves.

9. Aristot. Ethic: lib. 6. cap. 10.

In the empire of China, the same circumstance, together with that aversion which the people discover to every sort of innovation, has also enabled the father to maintain a great part of his original jurisdiction.[10] The father is said to have there the privilege of selling his children whenever he thinks proper; but if he intends to put them to death, it is necessary that he should bring them before a magistrate, and publicly accuse them. At the same time, whatever be the crime of which they are accused, they are held to be guilty, without any other proof but the bare assertion of the father.[11]

The custom of exposing infants was not restrained in China till very lately. Father Noel, in a relation presented to the general of the Jesuits in 1703, takes notice, that at Pekin a number of children were usually dropped or exposed every morning in the streets.

> As Pekin is excessively populous [continues that pious and Catholic father] and those who have more children than they can maintain do not scruple to drop them in places of public resort, where they either die miserably, or are devoured by beasts; one of our first cares is to send, every morning, catechists into the different parts of that great city, in order to baptize such of those children as are not dead. About twenty or thirty thousand children are exposed yearly, and of these our catechists baptize about three thousand; and had we twenty or thirty catechists, few of the children in question would die unbaptized.[12]

In those European nations which have made the greatest improvements in commerce and manufactures, great liberty is usually enjoyed by the members of every family; and the children are no farther subjected to the father than seems necessary for their own advantage. When they come to be of age, they have the full enjoyment and disposal of any separate property which they happen to acquire; and even during their fa-

---

10. Though in China a man is not allowed to have more wives than one, yet he may have any number of concubines; which, in the point under consideration, must have nearly the same effect. Le Compte's memoirs of China.

11. Ibid.

12. Travels of the Jesuits, compiled from their letters, translated by Lockman, vol. 1, p. 448.

ther's life, they are in some cases entitled to a fixed provision out of the family estate.

It can hardly be doubted that these regulations, which tend to moderate the excessive and arbitrary power assumed by the head of a family, are supported by every consideration of justice and utility. The opinion of Sir Robert Filmer, who founds the doctrine of passive obedience to a monarch, upon the unlimited submission which children owe to their father, seems, at this day, unworthy of the serious refutation which it has met with, and could only have gained reputation when men were just beginning to reflect upon the first principles of government. To say that a king ought to enjoy absolute power because a father has enjoyed it, is to defend one system of oppression by the example of another.

The interest of those who are governed is the chief circumstance which ought to regulate the powers committed to a father, as well as those committed to a civil magistrate; and whenever the prerogative of either is further extended than is requisite for this great end, it immediately degenerates into usurpation, and is to be regarded as a violation of the natural rights of mankind.

The tendency, however, of a commercial age is rather towards the opposite extreme, and may occasion some apprehension that the members of a family will be raised to greater independence than is consistent with good order, and with a proper domestic subordination. As, in every country, the laws enforced by the magistrate are in a great measure confined to the rules of justice, it is evident that further precautions are necessary to guard the morals of the inhabitants, and that, for this purpose, the authority of parents ought to be such as may enable them to direct the education of their children, to restrain the irregularities of youth, and to instil those principles which will render them useful members of society.

37

Commerce and Government Considered in Their Mutual Relationship 1776

ÉTIENNE BONNOT, *abbé* de Condillac, was born in Grenoble in 1714 into a family of local and royal officials. He had a brother who was also an important *philosophe*, Gabriel, *abbé* de Mably. Poor vision seems to have kept him from reading until at least the age of twelve, when he began to be educated by a local priest and at the Jesuit *collège*. He went to Paris and the Sorbonne, and became a priest in 1740, though he said only one Mass. He came instead to know the salon scene (especially Rousseau, Diderot, d'Holbach, Helvétius, and Voltaire) and take up English philosophy with enthusiasm. In 1746, he wrote a sensationalist work in the Lockean and Newtonian traditions (opposed to Descartes), *Essay on the origin of human knowledge,* which argued that all the higher mental powers derive from the senses. In 1749, his work *A Treatise on systems* argued for human limits to our knowledge, against the disordered imagination of philosophical systems. *A Treatise on the sensations* (1754) deepened this line of thinking. His *Course of Study* (*Cours d'étude*), based on his tutorial of the child Ferdinand, son of the Duke of Parma (1758–67), applied these ideas to education. He became a member of the Académie Française. Diderot was among the many Frenchmen influenced by Condillac's philosophy. In 1780, the Polish government invited him to write *Logic, or the first developments of the art of thinking.* That same year, he turned down an offer to tutor the dauphin's sons; he died in 1780.

The work excerpted here is his 1776 *Le Commerce et le gouvernement considérés relativement l'un à l'autre.* Notably, he makes subjective utility, not intrinsic quality, the touchstone of value and departs from the Physiocratic dogma that land alone is the source of all wealth, for which reason he was anathematized by that school. His ill-timed treatise was one of the most important general statements of market economics before Adam Smith, by whose work it was eclipsed. As such, it makes a fitting end to the present volume. The excerpts here, reprinted with permission, are from *Commerce and Government Considered in Their Mutual Relationship,* translated by Shelagh Eltis and edited by Shelagh Eltis and Walter Eltis (1776; reprint, Cheltenham: Elgar, 1997), chapters 1, 6, 7, and 8, pp. 81–89 and 99–107, which were chosen because they provide a useful introduction to his ideas on value and on the sources of wealth. Bracketed notes are by the present editor.

Commerce and Government Considered in Their Mutual Relationship

1. The basis of the value of things

Let us assume a small tribe which has just been established, which has brought in its first harvest, and which, since it is isolated, can only subsist on the product of the land it cultivates.

Let us also assume that after setting aside the necessary seed corn, they have a hundred muids[1] left; and that with this quantity, they can wait for a second crop without fear of scarcity.

1. [A dry measure of locally varying size.]

Carrying on with our assumption, for this amount to remove all fear of scarcity, it must be enough not only for their needs, but also to relieve their fears. Now, that can only be found in a certain degree of abundance. Indeed, when people judge in line with their apprehensions, what would suffice at a pinch is not enough; and they only believe they have enough in what is to a certain extent abundant.

The quantity which remains for our tribe, once the seed corn has been deducted, therefore makes, for this year, what we call abundance. Consequently if they have some muids more, they are in surplus and they would be in dearth if they had some less.

If a people could judge, exactly, the relationship between the quantity of corn it has, with the amount needed for its consumption, this known relationship would cause it always to know, with the same precision, whether it was in abundance, surplus, or dearth.

But it cannot judge this relationship precisely: because it has no way of informing itself exactly, either of the amount of corn it has, or of what it will consume. It is all the less able to do so, as it could not store the corn without waste, and the exact amount of this waste is by its nature unpredictable. If it estimates it then it is only roughly, and on the experience of several years.

However, in whatever way it judges the relationship, it is always true to say that the tribe believes that it is in abundance, when it thinks it has a sufficient amount of grain to set aside all fear of running out of it; that it believes it is in surplus, when it thinks it has more than enough to meet all its fears; and that it believes itself in dearth, when it thinks it only has a quantity which is inadequate to set aside its fears.

It is therefore in the opinion that is held of the quantities, rather than in the quantities themselves, that abundance, surplus or dearth are found: but they only rest on opinion because the amounts are assumed.

If, instead of a hundred muids, our tribe, after deducting seed corn, had two hundred, it would have a hundred which would be of no use for its consumption between one crop and another; and if it took no care over storing this surplus grain, the corn would ferment and go bad, and what was left of it would be useless for the following years.

Several consecutive years of a large harvest would do nothing but embarrass our tribe with a useless surplus, and it would soon happen that they sowed less land.

But harvests which are inadequate for the needs of the tribe will create awareness of the need to store the corn when there is a surplus. A way to do this will be sought, and when it is found, the corn that is useless in years of surplus will become useful in years of dearth. The hundred muids which the tribe has not consumed, and which it has known how to store, will make up the shortfall in several years when all that is left for its consumption, after seed corn has been deducted, is sixty or eighty muids.

Properly speaking there will no longer be a corn surplus, once it is known how to preserve it, because what is not consumed in one year can be consumed in another.

If our tribe was surrounded by other tribes, cultivators like itself, it would not have the same need to keep corn in granaries; because, by giving the surplus that it had in some other commodity, it could obtain for itself surplus corn from another tribe. But we have assumed it to be completely isolated.

We have two kinds of needs. One set follows from our makeup: we are created to need food, or to be unable to live without nourishment.

The other kind follows from our customs. Something which we could do without, because our constitution does not make it a need for us, becomes necessary by custom, and sometimes as necessary as if we had been constituted to need it.

I call *natural* the needs which follow from our constitution, and *artificial* those which we owe to habit formed by the use of things.

A wandering horde lives on the fruits which the land produces naturally: on the fish it catches, on the animals it kills hunting; and when the area it covers no longer provides its subsistence, it moves elsewhere. In this form of life we only see natural needs.

Our tribe can no longer wander. It has created for itself the need to live in its chosen place. It has made itself a need of the abundance which it finds in the fields it cultivates, and the bounty of the fruits it owes to its labour. It is not satisfied with hunting the animals which can provide its food and clothing, it raises them, and tries to increase their number to meet its consumption.

There you have a type of life in which we notice artificial needs, that is to say, needs which arise from the habit we have formed of satisfying natural needs by chosen methods.

You can see that these first artificial needs separate themselves as little as may be from natural ones. But you can also foresee that the tribe will form others which will move ever further from natural needs. That is what will happen when our tribe, having made progress in the arts, wants to satisfy its natural needs through more multifarious and refined ways. There will even come a time when the artificial needs, by dint of moving away from nature, will end up changing it completely and corrupting it.

The first needs which our tribe creates for itself are of the essence of the social order, and this would cease if these needs themselves ended. So one is thus justified in considering them as natural. Because if they are not so for the wandering savage, they become so for man in society, for whom they are absolutely necessary. That is why I shall from now on call *natural* not only the needs which follow from our makeup, but also those which are a consequence of the constitution of civil societies; and I shall understand by *artificial* those which are not essential to the social order, and without which, in consequence, civil societies could continue to exist.

We say that a thing is useful when it supplies some of our needs; and that it is useless when it meets none of them, or when we can do nothing with it. Its utility is therefore founded on the need we have for it.

Following this utility, we esteem it more or less, that is to say we judge whether it is more or less adapted to the uses to which we want to put it. Now this estimation is what we call *value*. To say that a thing has value is to say that it is, or that we think it is, good for some purpose.

The value of things is thus founded on their utility, or, which comes to the same, on the need we have of them, or, which again comes back to the same, on the use we can make of them.

As our tribe creates new needs for itself, it will learn to use for its tasks things of which it made nothing previously. It will therefore give in one time period value to things to which it gave none in another.

In abundance, need is felt less because people do not fear being without. For the opposite reason, people feel need more in scarcity and in dearth.

Now, because the value of things is based on need, it is natural that a more strongly felt need gives things a greater value, and that a less pressing need gives them less value. The value of things therefore grows with scarcity and decreases with abundance.

Value can even diminish in abundance to vanishing point. For instance, a surplus good will be without value every time one can do nothing with it, since then it would be completely useless.

Such would be a surplus in corn, if one considered it with reference to the year in which it does not contribute to the quantity needed for consumption. But if one considers it with reference to the following years, when the harvest may not be adequate, the surplus will have a value, because one judges that it could be part of the quantity required for the need one will have of it.

This need is distant. For that reason it does not give a good the same value as a present need. The latter makes one feel that the good is absolutely necessary now, and the other simply makes one judge that it could become so. One flatters oneself that it will not become necessary; and with that prejudice, as one is led not to foresee the need, one is also led to give less value to the good.

Greater or lesser value, the utility being the same, would be based simply on the degree of scarcity or of abundance, if this degree could always be known precisely; and then one would have the true value of each good.

But this degree can never be known. It is therefore chiefly on the estimation that we have of it that greater or lesser value is based.

If one assumes that a tenth of the corn needed for the tribe's consumption is lacking, nine-tenths would only have the value of ten if one estimated the scarcity accurately, and if one saw for certain that it really was only of a tenth.

That is just what one does not do. Just as people are complacent in abundance, so they are fearful in scarcity. In place of the tenth which is the shortfall, they judge that there are two-tenths, three-tenths or more deficient. They believe themselves to be at the point where corn will be completely unavailable; and the shortfall of a tenth will produce the same terror as if it were of a third or a half.

Once opinion has exaggerated the dearth, it is natural that those who have corn think to keep it for themselves; in fear of running out, they will set aside more of it than they need. It will therefore happen that the dearth will be really total, or near enough, for some of the tribe. In this state of affairs it is clear that the value of corn will grow in proportion to the exaggerated opinion of the dearth.

If the value of things is based on their utility, their greater or lesser value is thus based, the utility staying the same, on their scarcity or their abundance, or rather on the opinion we have of their scarcity and their abundance.

I say "the utility staying the same" because one has enough appreciation that, in supposing them equally rare or equally abundant, one judges them of more or less value, depending on whether one judges them more or less useful.

There are things which are so common that although they are very necessary, they seem to have no value. Such is water, it is found everywhere, people say, "It costs nothing to get it for oneself, and the value which it can gain through transport is not its value but only the value of the carriage costs."

It would be amazing if one paid carriage costs to get oneself something valueless.

A good does not have a value because it has a price, as people suppose, but it has a price because it has a value.

I say therefore that, even on the banks of a river, water has value, but the smallest possible, because there it is infinitely surplus to our needs. In an arid place by contrast it has a huge value, which one assesses according to how far away it is and the difficulty of getting hold of it. In such a case a thirsty traveller would give a hundred louis for a glass of water, and that glass of water would be worth a hundred louis. For value is not so much in the object as in how we esteem it, and this estimation is relative to our needs: it grows and diminishes, just as our need itself grows and diminishes.

As one judges that things have no value when one has assumed they cost nothing, one judges that they cost nothing when they cost no money. We have much difficulty in seeing the light. Let us try to put some precision in our ideas.

Even if one gives no money to obtain a thing it has a cost if it costs work. Now what is work?

It is an action, or series of actions, with the aim to gain from them. One can act without working: that is the case with idle men who act without making anything. To work is therefore to act to obtain a thing one needs. A day labourer whom I employ in my garden works to gain the wage I have promised him; and one must state that his work begins with the first blow of the spade: because if it did not begin with the first, one could not say where it began.

Following these preliminary reflections, I say that when I am far from the river, water costs me the action of going to get it; action which is work, since it is accomplished to get me something I need; and when I am at the river edge, water costs me the action of leaning over to get it; I agree that the action is very little work: it is even less than the first blow of the spade. But then again does not the water have only the smallest possible value at that time?

The water therefore has the value of the effort I make to get it. If I do not go to get it myself, I will pay for the work of the man who brings it to me; it is then valued at the wage I will give; and consequently the carriage costs give it a value. I give it this value myself, since I judge that it is worth these carriage costs.

You would be astounded if I said that air has a value; and yet I must say so, if I reason consistently. But what does it cost me? It costs me every effort I make to breathe it, to change it, to renew it. I open my window, I go out. Now each of these actions is work, very light work in truth, since the air, even more abundant than water, can only have a minute value.

I can say the same of light, of those rays which the sun spreads so profusely on the surface of the land: for it certainly costs us an effort or money to turn it to all our uses.

Those whom I contest consider it a great error to base value on utility, and they say that a thing cannot have value unless it has a certain degree of scarcity. *A certain degree of scarcity!* Now that I do not understand. I can conceive that a thing is scarce, when we *judge* that we do not have as much of it as we need for our use; that it is abundant, when we *judge* that we have all we need of it, and that it is in surplus, when we *judge* that we possess it beyond our needs. Finally I can conceive that a thing of which one makes nothing, and of which nothing can be made, has no value, and that on the other hand a thing has value when it has utility; and that if it did not have a value by its utility alone, it would not have a greater value in scarcity, and a lesser in abundance.

But one is led to regard value as an absolute quality, which is inherent in things independently of the judgements we bring to bear, and this confused notion is the source of bad reasoning. We must therefore remember that, although things only have a value because they have qualities which make them fitted to our use, they would have no value for us if we did not judge that they do indeed have these qualities. Their value therefore lies principally in the judgement we have of their utility; and they only have more or less value because we judge them more or less useful, or that, with the same utility, we judge them scarcer or more abundant. I have only rested so firmly on this point because it will provide the basis of this whole work.

[*In the 1798 edition, the final sentence of chapter 1 is omitted, and the following passage is added:*
Value being based on the opinion we hold of the utility of things, and the utility of things itself resting on the need we have of them, we must distinguish a natural value which only assumes natural needs, and an artificial value which only assumes artificial needs. Corn, for example, has a natural value among our tribe, because we assume that all the citizens have naturally the same need of it. But diamonds, if their use should be introduced among them, would only have an artificial value, since such a need, useless at least to society, could only be that of some individuals.

Natural value is directly the same for all, because it is the value of things absolutely essential to the support of society. On the other hand, artificial value, which is very great for some people, would not be in itself worthless for the others; but, because wealthy people will only get goods of an artificial value in so far as they give in exchange goods of natural value, it is a consequence that artificial value becomes, at least indirectly, a real value for everybody. So it is that things which are useless to the vast number of people end up being of general utility when they are considered the equivalent of something essential to all.

Value, of whatever kind, natural or artificial, thus exists principally in the opinions we hold of the utility of things; and one should not say with the *économiste*[2] writers, that it *consists in the exchange relationship of one thing and another:* that would be to suppose, with them, that the exchange preceded the value; this would reverse the order of ideas. Indeed, I should not

2. [I.e., the Physiocrats. See Du Pont de Nemours, chapter 33 in this volume.]

make any exchange with you, if I did not judge that the article you were handing over had a value; and you would make no exchange with me, if you did not judge likewise that what I was selling you has a value. The *économiste* writers have, if I may use a saying, thus put the cart before the horse.

This misconception seems a very small matter since it comes down to taking the second idea for the first. But it took no more to spread confusion. So the right value for an exchange relationship is a vague notion that people could not determine; and one may reckon that in dealing with economic science along these lines one will not be understood at all wherever value counts for something, that is, almost everywhere.

The object of a science is properly a problem which, like every problem to resolve, has as givens [*données*] knowns and unknowns. In Economic Science, the knowns are the means which we understand to be appropriate for obtaining abundance in certain forms, the unknowns are the means we still need to discover to obtain abundance in every way; and it is clear that, if the problem can be resolved, it is for the knowns to make the unknowns known to us.

This very complex problem comprises a large number of others each of which will give us new difficulties if we do not analyse them methodically; and we shall find ourselves, as has happened to all governments, falling into gross errors with each solution we think it right to proffer.

But the order that analysis prescribes is, firstly, to concern ourselves with the knowns, because, if we do not begin by determining them, it will be impossible to determine the value of the unknowns. Secondly, it requires us to look, among the knowns, for that which must be the principal one; because, if the principal known is not determined, one will not determine the others. Therefore let us look for it.

Among the means of obtaining abundance, I see first the cultivation of the land. But, if agriculture seems to begin before trade, it is certain that it cannot improve itself except in so far as trade establishes itself and spreads. Perfected agriculture, that is to say, agriculture which is bound to procure the greatest abundance, thus assumes trade. Trade assumes exchanges, or, as is basically the same thing, purchases and sales: the purchases and sales assume that things have a price and the price assumes that they have a value.

So there are the knowns; however confused they still are, I can at least see clearly in what order they initially present themselves; and that order, which I had to start by revealing, shows me the value of things as the first idea which needs to be determined and developed. From that point, the further forward I go, the more clearly I see my goal; because, from one chapter to the next, I shall always clear some unknowns, and one problem solved will bring forward the solution of a new problem. I may have carried out this plan badly: but it is none the less true that you will only deal properly with Economic Science in so far as you use my language, or correct it following my method, which is the only one.

This chapter will act as a basis for this work, which is why I have drawn it out perhaps to excess. However, I must allow myself another observation: it is essential.

In the current prejudice that definitions are the sole principles which can spread enlightenment, people think that they understand a word when they have seen what is called the definition; and, because they suppose that I myself am also making definitions, they will think they understand, for example, the word *value*, as soon as they have read what I say about it, at the very moment that I begin to analyse it. They will therefore rush to make objections which they would not have made if they had waited until the analysis was completed. That is what happened to those writers who thought they were refuting me, and who did not understand me at all.

If, in making definitions, one has the advantage of saying everything one wishes to say in just one proposition, it is that one is not saying everything necessary, and often one would be better to remain silent. Analysis does not pride itself on such brevity; as its aim is to develop an idea which must be grasped from different viewpoints, it can only succeed in so far as it has the word scrutinised in all the senses which show up all the concomitant ideas. We shall require several more chapters before we have finished analysing the word *value*, or at least before we have removed from it all the vague ideas that are attached to it, and which often make the language of Economic Science unintelligible.]

6. How trade increases the mass of wealth

We have seen that trade, which consists in the exchange of one article for another, is carried on chiefly by merchants, traders and dealers. Let us now try to understand the utility which society draws from all these men who have set up as agents between producers and consumers; and to that end, let us look at the source of wealth and the course it follows.

Wealth consists in an abundance of things which have a value, or, which comes to the same, in an abundance of things that are useful because we need them, or finally, which is again the same, in an abundance of things which are used for our food, for our clothing, for our housing, for our comforts, for our pleasures, for our enjoyment, in a word for our use.

Now, it is the earth alone which produces all these things. It is therefore the sole source of all wealth.

Naturally prolific, it produces by itself and without any work on our part. Savages, for instance, live off the fecundity of lands which they do not cultivate. But they need for their consumption a vast extent of land. Each savage can consume the product of a hundred arpents. Then again it is hard to imagine that he will always find plenty in that space.

It is that the earth, left to its own natural fecundity, produces everything indiscriminately. It is especially fecund in things which are useless to us and of which we can make no use.

If we make ourselves masters of her fecundity, and obstruct certain products to encourage other products, the land will become fertile. Because if we call land which produces plentifully and all at hazard *fecund*, we call land which produces plenty and to our wishes *fertile*.

It is only by observation and work that we will succeed in curtailing certain products and enabling other products to grow. We must discover how the land produces, if we want to multiply exclusively things for our use and eradicate all the rest.

The collection of observations to this end makes the theory of a science called *agriculture*, or cultivation of the fields; and the work of the settler who daily follows these observations constitutes the practice of this science. I shall call this practice *cultivation*.

The settler thus multiplies things which are for our use, which have a value, and the abundance of which makes what we call wealth. It is he who digs the ground, who opens the spring, who makes it spurt forth; it is to him that we owe abundance.

What then do we owe to merchants? If, as everyone supposes, one always exchanges a product of a uniform value against another product of the same value, one multiplies the exchanges in vain; it is clear that afterwards, as before, there will always be the same accumulation of values or of wealth.

But it is false that in exchanges one gives equal value for equal value. On the contrary, each of the contracting parties always gives a lesser value for a greater value. People would recognise that fact if they thought precisely, and you can already understand it from what I have said.

A woman whom I know, having bought a piece of land, counted out the money to pay for it, and said: "However, I am very happy to have a plot of land for that." There was very true reasoning in that artlessness. One can see that she attached little value to the money which she kept in her strongbox, and that, in consequence, she was giving a lesser value for a greater one. From another standpoint, the man who was selling the land was in the same position and he was saying: "I have sold it well." In fact he had sold it for thirty or thirty-five deniers. Thus he too reckoned on having given less for more. There is the position of all those who make exchanges.

Indeed, if one always exchanged equal value for equal value, there would be no gain to be made for either of the contracting parties. Now, both of them make a gain, or ought to make one. Why? The fact is that with things only having value in relation to our needs, what is greater for one person is less for another, and vice versa. [*Passage added here in 1798 is printed on page 651.*]

The error into which people fall on this subject comes [above all: 1798] from the way one talks of things which are traded, as though they had an absolute value; and that as a result people reckon that it is a matter of justice, that those who make exchanges give each other equal value for equal value. Far from noting that two contracting parties give each other less for more, people think, without much reflection, that that cannot be; and it seems that for one person always to give less, the other would have to be stupid enough always to give more, which one cannot suppose.

It is not the things necessary for our consumption that we are considered to put on sale: it is our surplus, as I have noted several times. We want to give up something which is useless to us to get ourselves something which we need: we want to give less for more.

The surplus of the settlers: there you have what supplies all the basis for commerce. The surplus is wealth, so long as they can find an outlet for it; because they procure for themselves something that has value for them, and they hand over something which has value for others.

If they were unable to make exchanges, their surplus would stay with them, and it would have no value for them. Indeed, surplus grain, which

I store in my barns without being able to exchange it, no more represents wealth to me than the grain which I have not yet pulled from the ground. So I will sow less next year, and I shall be none the poorer for having a smaller crop.

Now merchants are the channels of communication through which the surplus runs. From places where it has no value it passes into places where it gains value, and wherever it settles it becomes wealth.

The merchant therefore in a way makes something out of nothing. He does not till, but he brings about tillage. He induces the settler to draw an ever greater surplus from the land and he always makes new wealth from it. Through the meeting of the settler and the trader abundance spreads all the further, as consumption grows in proportion to the products, and reciprocally products increase with consumption.

A spring which disappears into rocks and sand is not wealth for me; but it becomes such, if I build an aqueduct to draw it to my meadows. This spring represents the surplus products for which we are indebted to the settlers, and the aqueduct represents the merchants.

[*Additional passage from 1798 edition referred to on page 650.*]

The advantage is reciprocal, and there you have no doubt what made them say that they gave each other equal value for equal value. But they have lacked consistency: since, precisely from the fact that the advantage is reciprocal, they should have concluded that each gives less for more.

People have said, you are confusing the value of things with the motive that leads to their exchange. Probably, and with reason, indeed value is the sole motive which can persuade me to act. What other could I have?

Value depends, they add, on the particular estimation each person makes of goods and consequently it will for ever vary. So it varies: is there anything which has an invariable value? I say therefore that in individual exchanges value is the particular estimation each person makes of goods; and I add that it is the general estimation that society itself makes of them, if we consider it in the markets where all end up agreeing on a measure to settle the respective value of goods, that is, the value they are given when they are considered against other goods.

But we must not confuse, as people are always doing, this measure of value with value itself. Properly speaking it is only the price which has been regulated in the markets by the rivalry of the sellers and buyers. For example, there will be general agreement that a barrel of wine is worth a muid of corn, which means that the one is the price of the other. So, if I want a muid of corn I must give a barrel of wine, and you will conclude, with reason, that it is not my particular judgement that fixes the price of corn; but it is none the less true that it fixes its value, and it alone fixes it. Because, once more, in such an exchange it is for me alone to judge the value the corn has for me; it only has one following my own estimation; and, although the market price sets the law for me, it is clear that I only give a barrel for a muid because I judge that the muid is worth more to me than the barrel. I should never end if I wanted to reply to all the objections of certain writers who, because one does not follow them, seem to want, from pique, not to understand what one is saying to them.]

7. How needs, in multiplying, give birth to the arts, and how the arts increase the mass of wealth

Just as I have distinguished natural needs and artificial needs, I shall also distinguish two kinds of necessary things; the first of primary need, which I shall refer back to natural needs; and the others of secondary need, which I shall refer back to artificial needs.

Such fruits as the land produces through fecundity alone are of prime necessity for a savage, because he needs them as a consequence of his makeup; and our wines, our brandies would be of secondary need for him, if, in trading with us, he acquired a taste for these drinks.

For our tribe, settled in the fields which it cultivates, corn is a thing of prime need, because it is necessary to it, as a result of the formation of a society which would not subsist without this aid. We must however place, among things of secondary need, all those which it could do without, while not ceasing to be a settled, agrarian society.

Observe the tribe while it is limited to things of prime need. This is the state where, without being poor, it has the least wealth. I say, *without being poor*, because there is only poverty where essential needs are not met, and it is not being poor to lack a type of wealth of which one has not acquired a need, and which one does not even know.

Therefore it is not in a state of poverty, it is rather in a state of *lacking*. Please allow me this word: that of *privation* would not convey my thought. For we deprive ourselves of those things which we have, or which we might have, and with which we are familiar; whereas we do not have those which we lack, often we do not even know of their existence.

In this state it is enough for our tribe not to be exposed to a lack of food, to shelter itself from the force of the elements, and to have the means of defence against its enemies. Its food, its clothing, its dwellings, its weapons are all rough and lack artistry. It only uses the commonest objects for its various tasks, and so it is sure not to lack them.

While lacking a host of things we appreciate, it is plentifully supplied with all those which it needs.

Nothing is expensive in the tribe. Just as in all the goods it uses there is nothing too choice, so there is also nothing too rare.

Currency would be useless to it, and it has none. Each person exchanges his surplus, and no one perceives a need to use metals, or anything else to that end.

Let us move to a time when it begins to enjoy goods of secondary need, and when these goods are none the less still of a kind to be able to be common to all. Then the tribe introduces higher quality into its food, its clothing, its dwellings, its weapons; it has more needs, more wealth.

However, there are no poor people among it; since I still only include in the goods of secondary need common goods which all can partake of more or less, and of which no one is entirely deprived.

In this position it is impossible for each person to provide by himself for all his needs. The farmer, busy in the fields, would not have the time free to make himself a coat, to build a house, to forge weapons, and he would not have the aptitude because these jobs require knowledge and a skill he does not possess.

Several groups will therefore form. Besides that of the farmers there will be tailors, architects, armourers. The three latter groups could not subsist on their own. It is the first group that will provide for their subsistence, and it will in addition provide the raw material for the arts.

When I distinguish four classes it is because we must choose a number. The tribe may and even must have many more. They will multiply in proportion as the arts come into being, and make progress.

All the groups, each busy with its own tasks, come together in competition to increase the mass of wealth, or the abundance of goods which have value. Because, if we have seen that primary wealth consists uniquely in the products of the land, we have also seen that these products only have value, and their abundance is only wealth, in so far as they are useful, or as they meet some of our needs.

It is the farmer who provides all the primary material. But such primary material, as would be useless and without value in his hands, becomes useful and obtains value when the artisan has found the way to make it serve the needs of society.

With each skill that begins, with each advance it makes, the farmer thus acquires new wealth, because he finds value in a product which previously had none.

This product, given value by the artisan, gives a fresh spur to commerce for which it is a new stock in trade; and it becomes a new source of wealth for the farmer because, as each product acquires value, he makes new consumption for himself.

Thus it is that all, farmers, merchants, artisans, come together to increase the mass of wealth.

If one compares the state of deprivation our tribe is in, when, without artisans, without merchants, it is confined to goods of prime need, with the state of plenty in which it finds itself, when, through the hard work of artisans and merchants, it enjoys goods of secondary need, that is, of a host of things that habit turns into needs for it; one will understand that the work of artisans and merchants is as much a source of wealth for it as the very work of the farmers.

Indeed, if on the one hand we have seen that the land is the source of products, and hence of wealth; we see on the other hand that industry gives value to a number of products, which otherwise would have none. It is therefore proved that in the final analysis industry is also a source of wealth. We shall expand on this matter some day soon. It has been much obscured by some writers.

8. Of wages

A merchant has made some advances. They consist in the price he gave for the things he wants to sell again, in carriage costs, in the costs of the warehouse, and in the day-to-day expenses of keeping the merchandise.

Now, not only does he have to be reimbursed for all these advances, but he also has to find a gain in carrying on his trade.

This gain is rightly what we call a wage [*salaire*]. One conceives that it must be made and portioned out turn by turn on all the goods he has for sale; and that it must be enough for his subsistence, that is to say to obtain for him the use of things of primary and secondary need.

But to what extent should the merchants enjoy these things? That is a matter which will regulate itself unaided, given that competition will force the merchants to live more or less economically; and since this competition will apply to all equally, we will know, in accordance with the general custom, the pleasures to which each of them can lay claim. They will calculate for themselves what wage they need for the pleasures which custom allows them, to obtain these for their families, to raise their children; and because they would have very little foresight if they were content with gaining the means to live from one day to the next, they will also calculate what they need to cope with accidents and, if possible, to improve their condition. They will try to bring all these gains into their wage. Those who would like to buy will try to beat down these gains; and they will beat them down all the more easily as an ever-increasing number of merchants will be eager to sell. The wage will be regulated on the one hand by the sellers' rivalry, and by the buyers' competition on the other.

The artisan's wage will be self-regulated in the same way. Suppose that there are only six tailors in the tribe and they cannot meet the demand for clothes, they will themselves fix their wage, or the price of their labour, and that price will be high.

That is a disadvantage, and they will fall into another when the lure of gain has multiplied the tailors beyond the tribe's needs. Then they will all find themselves reduced to lesser gains, those who have no custom will offer to work for the lowest price, and will force those who have custom to work also for a smaller wage. There will even be those who do not have enough to live on, and who will be forced to find another trade. The number of tailors will thus gradually come into line with the demand for them; and that is the moment when their wage will be regulated as it should be.

But there are trades which call for more intelligence, and trades which call for more skill; it takes more time to become skilful at them; one must bring more effort and more care to them. Therefore those who distinguish themselves at them will be authorised to demand better wages, and one will be forced to give these to them; because, as they will be few in number, they will have fewer competitors. People will get used to seeing them with a greater abundance of things of primary and secondary need; and in consequence custom will give them rights to this abundance. As they have greater and rarer talents, it is fair that they also make greater gains.

So it is that, when wages are regulated, they in their turn regulate consumption, to which everyone has a claim according to his status; and then one knows what are the primary and secondary needs which belong to each class. All the citizens do not share the same pleasures equally, but all have subsistence from their work; and though there are some richer people among them, no one is poor. There you have what happens in civil society, where order establishes itself freely, according to the particular and combined interests of all the citizens. Note that I say *freely*.

If I have only spoken, in this chapter, of the wage due to the artisan and the merchant, it is that by showing how prices regulate themselves in the market place, I have given a sufficient explanation of how the farmer's wage is regulated. It will do to note here that all the citizens [apart from those of the landowners who do nothing: *1798*] are given a wage with regard to each other. If the artisan and the merchant are paid by the farmer to whom they sell, the farmer is in his turn paid by the artisan and the merchant to whom he sells, and each of them gets paid for his work.

Glossary

Addict   To dedicate; to be "addicted" to something is to be dedicated to it in either a healthy or an unhealthy sense.

Commerçant   Someone who engages in the act of buying and selling; the term only came into general use in the eighteenth century; it does not appear in either the Furetière or the Académie Française dictionaries of the 1690s, nor in the ARTFL (American and French Research on the Treasury of the French Language) database for the seventeenth century.

Commerce   The act or process of buying and selling merchandise; figuratively, ordinary communication and correspondence with someone either for business reasons or for social ones, as in phrases such as "the commerce between the sexes," "a commerce of friendship," "a commerce of self-love." The figurative uses have been signalled in the text.

Contrat de constitution   An annuity; the creation of a pension, a charge, or some other legally binding instrument for conveying annual monetary return; the annual revenue (*rente*) is also sometimes called a constitution.

Cultivateur   Whoever actually works the land, not to be confused with its owner; usually connoting a relatively poor farmer. Became an important term only in the eighteenth century, especially with the Physiocrats. The term does not appear in the Académie Française dictionary and is described as "suspect" by Furetière.

Fermier   Whoever possesses the rights to harvest the fruits of a landed property (or, by extension, of a public office such as a tax jurisdiction), whether the owner or a tenant farmer.

Laboureur   Literally, the person whose occupation is to work the land, by moving it or turning it over, either for himself or for someone else, irrespective of ownership. An independent peasant, often of some means, sometimes with some social pretensions.

Lettre de cachet   Letter with a royal seal used for issuing an order of incarceration, without recourse to the courts.

Marchand   A merchant; someone whose principal occupation consists in buying and selling; alternatively, someone who has products manufactured for the purpose of selling them. Thus, often used in phrases containing the name of the product in question, such as "merchant drapers," "merchant-booksellers," "silk merchants."

Métayer   Farm worker who offers his labor to a landowner in exchange for a share in the produce. A widespread practice in many parts of France in the Old Regime.

Moeurs   Acquired or natural manners or morals, either for good or ill, for an individual or a people. The term can carry a descriptive or a prescriptive connotation.

Négociant   Merchant or banker who engages in trade either in currency or in merchandise; often connoting the wholesale or maritime trade.

Patrie   The place, area, or region where one is born; literally, fatherland. Acquires a national connotation only during and especially after the eighteenth century. Before then, the dictionaries sometimes specify that it can refer to the specific locale, province, state, or empire of birth.

Police   The general order observed and maintained by law and custom in a city or state. Especially concerns the conditions of sale of goods and merchandise by merchants and artisans, and the provisioning of the people, also the general cleanliness and security of a usually urban population. Sometimes the antonym is "barbarism."

Prerogative   An exclusive and special privilege, especially as it concerns the rights of monarchy.

Propriétaire   Legal owner of land or other property.

Rente The annual revenue from land or money; an agreed monetary return on the alienation of landed property; the annual return on a sum of money alienated by *contrat de constitution*.

Rentier Literally, the holder of an annuity or other source of regular income; figuratively, a person of independent means, a bourgeois who lives off his regular revenue without engaging in trade or industry.

Taille A direct tax levied mostly on land, calculated according to the status of either the individual (*taille personnelle*) or the property (*taille réelle*), depending on local law and custom.

Index

goods; luxuries; necessities; value;
wares
Gordon, Thomas, 193
Gournay, Vincent de, 371–73; biography,
450–53; ideas about commerce
and government, 456–64; ideas
about commerce and laws, 453–56;
legacy, 470–76, 569, 570; personal
characteristics, 464–65, 475; Turgot's
eulogy for, 448–49; writings of, and
influence on others, 465–70
government: arts of, 362–68; based on
checks and balances, 288; based on
natural law, 593–97; benefits from
trade, 82; drawbacks of powerful,
11–12; famine control by, 129–30; good,
10–11; Law's French system, 178–79;
legislative power, 577–78; main
objectives, 233, 486–87; national decline
due to, 487–94; protection of citizens,
456–64; separation of judicial powers,
578–81; where luxuries are controlled,
494–98. *See also* citizens; Constitution
of England; forms of government;
taxes
government expenditures, 581
greed. *See* avarice
guilds, 33–36, 389 n. 11, 454, 619 n. 3. *See
also* trading companies

handicraft trade. *See* manufacturing
Hanseatic league, 505, 515–16
happiness: human, 360; of a nation, 397,
404
Hazeland, William, 403
Heckscher, Eli, *Mercantilism*, 455 n. 11
hereditary monarchy, 590–93, 595
Hesiod, on emulation, 412 n. 7
high interest rates: advantage to trade,
112–13; disadvantages, 92, 95–99, 461
history: ancient, 84–89; commodities
traded in Europe, 511–13, 515, 516–17;

creation of the world, 63; European
commerce, 504–6, 507–9; European
trade with East and West Indies,
611–23; military, 364–65; of the naval
powers, 199–202; sumptuary laws, 258,
259–60. *See also* ancients; progress;
Rome
hoarding, 90, 189
Hobbes, Thomas, and Rousseau, 402 n. 18
Holland: commerce, politics, and
religion, 10–36; compared with
England, 429–32; compared with
France, 188; provisions for the poor, 133;
trade advances, 38–41; wealth, 613–14.
See also republics
honesty, 39; folly of, 217; opposed with
luxury, 234; relation to employment,
225; relation to national wealth, 226–27,
228–29; of sellers, 73
honor: effects of trade and wealth on,
432–33; importance, 445
hospitality among the ancients, 291, 508
hours of work, 321
house-building and trade, 91–92
human happiness, ingredients of, 360
human nature, 60–63; civilized versus
barbarous, 364; difference from beasts,
74; imperfect human knowledge, 105–
6; imperfection, 318; impossibility of
perfection, 210–11; Locke's view,
216 n. 11; Mandeville's view, 222; neither
perfect nor imperfect, 221. *See also* art
versus nature; morals; needs; progress;
self-interest; vice; virtue; wants
Hume, David, 358–59
hunting, societies based on, 632; versus
pastoral societies, 534, 641

idleness: effect on lower classes, 348–51;
effects of, 492–94; luxury as destroyer
of, 256; Rousseau's view, 402 n. 21;
wages of, 168

347–53; that affects trade, 90. *See also* avarice; corruption; crime; luxuries; passions; vanity; virtue

villains, 334, 335–36. *See also* servants; slaves

virtue: as cure for vice, 369–70; effect of practice of, on a people, 220–39; versus expediency, 220; in immoral nations, 195; men's oblique attacks upon, 223–24; relation to luxuries, 225; relation to national wealth, 204–18; relation to personal wealth, 323; relation to wealth, 486. *See also* morals; prudence; vice

Voltaire, 265–66; comments on Law's system of finance, 276–81; defense of his work, "The Worldling," 266–75

wages, 75; advances of money for, 538; effects of high, 249–50; necessary inequality of, 656; relation to advances of money, 654–55; relation to costs of production, 160; relation to foreign trade, 169; relation to prices, 169–70; taxes on, 588. *See also* labor; prices

Walwyn, William, 1–2

wants, 313; of the body, 73; divine necessity of, 216 n. 11; of the mind, 73. *See also* needs; passions

war: of Austrian Succession, 379, 453, 621; best government for, 86; compared with taxes, 279–80; Crusades, 504, 511, 612; English Civil War, 247; of the Grand Alliance, 363; impact of refined arts on, 363, 364–65; money supply needed, 126; national wealth and outcome of, 441–43; prosperity without, 247; relation to commerce, 56–57, 299, 615, 620–21; relation to foreign trade, 67–68; relation to luxuries, 257, 258; relation to trade, 82;

of the Roses, 247; Seven Years', 621; of Spanish Succession, 243, 256, 258, 279, 363, 498–99; superiority of commerce to, 615; traders' support of, 243. *See also* military; peace

wares: price, 75; quality, 72–73; quantity, 71–72; types traded, 69–70; value, 73

wealth: advantages, 172–77; definition, 426; desirability of equality, 406; distribution, 410–13; effect on character, 427; effect on honor, 432–33; effect on public spirit, 433–34; effect on religious principle, 429–32; ill-gotten, ill-used, 491; inequality, 489–91; necessity of inequality, 400–401; personal merit and, 322–23; redistribution, 501; *Reflections on the Formation and the Distribution of Wealth* (Turgot), 518; relation to arts, 653–54; relation to hard work, 253; relation to surplus, 650; relation to trade, 648–52; relation to virtue, 486; tendency to beget more wealth, 110; vice as an inconvenience of, 237; without work or land ownership, 519–20. *See also* luxuries; money; movable wealth; property

wealth of a nation: components of, 562–63; equal distribution, 411–12, 439–40; held by traders, 243; impact of luxuries on, 557; impact of population size on, 379; labor as, 384; reasons for Holland's wealth, 613–14; relation to honesty, 226–27, 228–29; relation to interest rates, 45–47; relation to labor, 169 n. 22; relation to luxuries, 485; relation to luxury, commerce, and arts, 393–402; relation to trade laws, 124, 127; similarity with individual wealth, 281; sources of, 184, 224–25, 372; vice as basis, 204–18; virtue as basis, 220–

This book is set in 11 on 14 Adobe Caslon, a 1990 interpretation by Carol Twombly of the classic face cut in the 1720s by the English typographer William Caslon (1692–1766). Caslon modelled the face after Dutch types of the late seventeenth century.

Printed on paper that is acid-free and meets the requirements of the American National Standard for Permanence of Paper for Printed Library Materials, Z39.48-1992.∞

Book design by Erin Kirk New,
   Athens, Georgia

Typography by Graphic Composition, Inc.,
   Athens, Georgia

Printed and bound by Worzalla Publishing Company,
   Stevens Point, Wisconsin